Virtuous Persons, Vicious Deeds

Virtuous Persons, Vicious Deeds
An Introduction to Ethics

ALEXANDER E. HOOKE

Villa Julie College

MAYFIELD PUBLISHING COMPANY

MOUNTAIN VIEW, CALIFORNIA

LONDON • TORONTO

Library of Congress Cataloging-in-Publication Data
Virtuous persons, vicious deeds : an introduction to ethics / [edited by] Alexander E. Hooke.
    p.   cm.
  ISBN 0-7674-0290-1
  1. Virtue. 2. Ethics. 3. Virtues. I. Hooke, Alexander E., 1952–   .
BJ1521.V59 1998
179′.9—dc21   98-30171
                                          CIP

Manufactured in the United States of America
10 9 8 7 6 5 4 3 2 1

Mayfield Publishing Company
1280 Villa Street
Mountain View, California 94041

Sponsoring editor, Ken King; production editor, Linda Ward; copy editor, Kay Mikel; design manager, Jean Mailander; text and cover designer, Ellen Pettengell; manufacturing manager, Randy Hurst. The text was set in 10/12 Sabon by G&S Typesetters and printed on 45# Chromatone Matte, by Banta Book Group.

Cover image: William Hogarth, Plate 3 from *A Rake's Progress*, 1735, etching and engraving. © British Museum.

Acknowledgments and copyrights continue at the back of the book on page 717, which constitutes an extension of the copyright page.

For Debbie, Erika, and Nicky

A man's maturity—consists in having found again the seriousness one had as a child, at play.

—Nietzsche

Preface

Virtue, then, as it seems, would be a kind of health and beauty and good condition of the soul, and vice would be disease, ugliness, and weakness.

—Plato, *The Republic*

I, Humility, queen of the Virtues, say: come to me, you Virtues, and I'll give you the skill to seek and find the drachma that is lost and to crown her who perseveres blissfully.

—Hildegard von Bingen, *Ordo Virtutum*

Since the time of Socrates and Plato, virtues and vices have dominated philosophical discussions of morality. Both religious and secular perspectives considered a correct understanding of virtue and its adversaries as central to an ethical life and a just community. What are the most important virtues? Which vices present the greatest danger? What is the value of virtue? How can we teach virtues and vices to children and students? These are the kinds of issues moral thinkers were expected to address. This emphasis, however, has shifted since roughly the eighteenth century. Virtue-based ethics was displaced by conduct-based ethics, and disputes about universal law, basic rights, intuitive goods, or utilitarian benefits became central to understanding and pursuing an ethical life or a just community.

Over the last twenty years, attention to the virtues and vices has been reenergized. Scholars and philosophers now address virtue ethics in professional journals and at conferences. Writers and essayists discuss virtues and vices in more popular forums. So it seems that many moral thinkers have detected weaknesses in a conduct-based approach to ethics, and reviving discussion about the virtues and vices represents an alternative to that approach.

Surprisingly, this revival has had little effect on moral pedagogy for undergraduate students. Introductory ethics students are generally either treated to a sundry list of virtues and vices or given a couple of selections about virtue ethics as a side issue to more central moral approaches. In either case students lose the opportunity to study virtue ethics as a significant and philosophically interesting approach to the good life.

This book gives students that opportunity. It first introduces them to some of the prominent approaches to ethics—relativism, egoism, utilitarianism, and deontology. In addition, it highlights several ongoing disputes in ethics, such as the biological influences on morality, the value of religion, and the nature of the self's relation to other selves. Then, with a mix of historical and contemporary writers from Western and non-Western perspectives, the text presents a range of specific virtues and vices. Many of the classic cardinal virtues (love, justice, hope, prudence, courage) and deadly vices (anger, envy, lust, pride, sloth) are discussed as central to moral character alongside other candidates, including loyalty, care, humility, and truthfulness.

In placing the discussion of virtues and vices within the context of other ethical approaches, students are encouraged to address the philosophical merits of specific virtues and vices. Is truthfulness always good? What is the nature of pride? Do dictums such as "love thy neighbor" mean we should care for only those we know or for strangers too? Is leisure time an opportunity to develop our human potential, or is it the devil's play time? Should happiness be strictly a personal matter, or should society have an interest in what individuals do in their free time? Does a spouse exchanging lustful words with a stranger on the Internet commit infidelity? What is the power of anger? Questions like these underscore the contrasting views of the contributors to this volume.

These disputes are not only philosophical in nature but involve everyday moral concerns. To understand ourselves and others as moral beings, we must examine the basis for our opinions on the right law or the justification for our actions in extraordinary situations. We must focus our attention on who we are and who we want ourselves and others to be. What is a true friend, a loyal colleague, an exemplary human being? At the same time, we must acknowledge that each of us is capable of vicious actions.

Virtuous Persons, Vicious Deeds offers students an approach to moral reflection that engages many philosophical and popular controversies surrounding everyday concerns. Whether used as a primary or secondary text in ethics, or even in a course on human nature, the tension and the complexity surrounding our judgments of virtues and vices come through in the readings.

Features of the text include:

- a variety of writers from different traditions in Western thought and non-Western thought, as well as those whose philosophical insights are developed from the social sciences and literary fields.

- insightful articles on a variety of virtues and vices.

- a sustained discussion of the relation of specific virtues to other virtues and vices.

- an introductory case study in each chapter that is a reflective or meditative invitation rather than a brief news report on the topic of the chapter.

- a discussion of the relation of virtue ethics to specific moral problems, such as abortion, assisted suicide, capital punishment, environmentalism, and family life.

- essays on the personal and social importance of specific virtues and vices such as sloth, vengeance, care, truthfulness, curiosity, gossip, and friendship.

- a comparison of virtue-based ethics to other modern approaches to morality, including utilitarianism, deontology, egoism, and relativism.
- an exploration of the relevance of virtue ethics to other recent philosophical issues, such as feminism and care, otherness, lust, free time, and virtual sex.

Acknowledgments

This project led me in directions I had neither expected nor knew existed. To navigate these changes, I found help from a variety of sources. Some of these influences occurred some time ago, and others might seem commonplace. Hence, those who have helped me may not realize it. Here is a word or two of gratitude.

Several institutions deserve thanks. The National Endowment for the Humanities granted me the opportunity to participate in two summer seminars, one led by William Connolly in political theory and the other led by J. B. Schneewind in early modern moral philosophy. Each taught me the interdisciplinary and historical importance of ethical thought. Professors in the philosophy departments at the University of Missouri (John Kultgen, Joseph Bien, Alexander von Schonborn, and Peter Markie) and Towson University (Walt Fuchs, John Murungi, Art Madden, and JoAnn Pilardi) offered memorable lessons from a variety of perspectives.

At Villa Julie College President Carolyn Manuszak, Dean Rose Dawson, and Liberal Arts Chair John Hoeprich have given me confidence and the freedom to pursue this and other projects. Three VJC individuals—Valerie Hollis, Carla Owens, and Bernie Cochran—have been invaluable, in part for trying to wean me away from my typewriter and into the electronic age. Their diligence and patience with the proposal, permissions, and manuscripts are greatly appreciated. My Fall 1997 Ethics class helped in the early stages.

Many at Mayfield have been very helpful. Linda Ward, Marty Granahan, and Josh Tepfer answered my numerous questions. Thanks to Steven Smith and Kay Mikel for their encouraging efforts in polishing the material. And special thanks to Ken King, who has been much more than an editor—he's been a mentor.

I would also like to acknowledge the reviewers, who gave of their time and provided thoughtful comments that have improved the final product. My thanks for their efforts go to Eric Kraemer, University of Wisconsin–La Crosse; Richard B. Miller, East Carolina University; James B. Sauer, St. Mary's University; Katherine Shamey, Santa Monica College; Steven Smith, Claremont McKenna College; W. Christopher Stewart, Houghton College; Edmund Tratebas, IUPU Columbus; and Jeffrey P. Whitman, Susquehanna University.

Whether virtue ethics should displace other theories is something for teachers and students to decide. But one advantage of the virtue ethics approach is its ability to draw out moral lessons from individuals and from experiences that elude resolution in public forums and docudramas. To the following individuals I also have much gratitude. The number next to their names refers to the reading I somehow associate with them. Some of the picks are tongue-in-cheek, others serious.

Joe Palmer (67) and Dick Monk (16, 28) have been substantive influences throughout, and I keep trying to learn their lessons. Christine Noya (61, 55), Gerald Majer and Kae Alessi (66, 69), and Debbie Blake (50) have always added a thoughtful voice or attentive ear to my speculations. Paul Ludger Evans (82), James Crews (79), and Brian Taylor (84) have illustrated different and valuable meanings of friendship. So have James Nowak (6), Wayne Hines (63), John Rose (56), Chris Dreisbach (52), Chris Buchar (7), and Peggy Zeller (53). The proprietors at Buckley's/Izzies (80)—Elaine, Evelyn, Lynn, Joan, and Mark—are always hospitable when I seek some solitude by their fireplace. Ricky Muth and the King's Court coalition (57) have also shown much kindness.

My mother Barbara Hooke (49, 50, 61) has always been a fundamental support, and I thank my brothers Jeff (81, 87) and Robert (34, 46) for what I have learned from them. The memory of my grandmother Magdalena Pfeiffer (68) still leaves an imprint on my interest in the ideas raised in many of the readings.

Contents

CHAPTER SEVEN

Self-Regarding Virtues   406

CHAPTER EIGHT

Morality and the Other   478

CHAPTER ONE

Why Be a Moral Person?

For I spend all my time going about trying to persuade you, young and old, to make your first and chief concern not for your bodies nor for your possessions, but for the highest welfare of your souls . . . wealth does not bring goodness, but goodness brings wealth and every other blessing, both to the individual and to the state.

—Socrates, *The Apology*

Anyone who now wishes to make a study of moral matters opens up for himself an immense field of study.

—Nietzsche, *The Gay Science*

When asking "why" of someone, we often have two meanings in mind. Sometimes we seek an explanation; other times we want a justification. An explanation gives an account of how something happens or what causes a certain event. "The car stopped because it ran out of gas" or "John got sick because he ate too much" are explanatory. A justification attempts to support or defend what someone does. "Jill lied to Jack because she did not want to hurt his feelings" and "Jack cheated because he saw others cheat and not get caught" illustrate justifications.

Distinguishing an explanation from a justification in ordinary usage is not always easy because they often overlap. To answer the "why" to a lie could involve both an explanation (the other's emotional state pushed one to lie) and a justification (it was the right thing to do under the circumstances). Depending on your perspective, an explanation or a justification can seem more of a rationalization or excuse making rather than a genuine effort to answer the "why." If I deceive another, I tend to accept my good reasons for my action. But if another deceives me, all the good reasons in the world appear as self-serving mental tricks in light of the feeling of betrayal or lesson of mistrust.

The explanation–justification distinction is especially important in moral education. In teaching one another central issues in ethics, do we emphasize the causes that make someone a moral person, or do we justify a particular vision of the good life? Should we survey the variety of moral systems developed by human beings or encourage the ability to judge or choose among the variety? Are convictions, values, or principles to be offered as a kind of intellectual smorgasbord, or should they be presented with the intent that the lives of students will be morally affected?

The readings in Chapter 1 address these questions from two different perspectives: explaining moral conduct or justifying the reasons for pursuing a moral life. Although they all agree that morality is a fundamental concern for humans, they disagree on related issues such as human nature, the purpose of being moral, and the universality of moral truths or values. More directly, they address whether we are moral because of cultural conditioning, genetic predisposition, religious upbringing, or simply out of the desire to be happy.

Harvard professor of psychiatry Robert Coles introduces a compelling dilemma raised by one of his undergraduate students. How is it, she asks him, that an "A" student in an ethics course can, as she ruefully discovers, be morally inept outside the course? Furthermore, can this student's behavior be justified, or is it only explainable by looking to external events?

William Sumner, a social scientist from Yale in the early 1900s, contends that morality is largely a matter of cultural traditions and institutions. His lucid descriptions of various rituals and customs are a classic statement of ethical relativism—the idea that moral beliefs are not universal but are valid only within the culture that espouses them.

Philosopher Richard Garrett illuminates the debate sparked by ethical relativism in a lively dialogue involving the characters Max, Homer, Dilemma, and Siddhartha. He concludes with a challenge to the ethical relativist.

A different take on the "why be moral" issue comes from the field of sociobiology. One of its leading proponents, zoology professor E. O. Wilson, believes that most behavior can be explained in terms of genetic makeup rather than ethical justifications. Being altruistic, in his view, is not a matter of high-mindedness but a selfish strategy for improving the species.

J. L. Mackie, a British philosopher, studies the case for sociobiology and finds a problem that can be addressed only by going beyond genetic accounts of moral behavior.

For many people thoughout the ages, religion has been the anchor to any substantive morality. Selections from the Old and New Testaments reflect an attitude that a moral person is guided by following the authority of God and sacred writings. A different perspective from Taoist thinker Chuang Tzu evokes a sense of freedom and humor to articulate the human concern for the good.

According to journalist and recent third-party presidential candidate Harry Browne, much of what passes for morality actually does more harm than good. He echoes a popular belief that any worthwhile morality has as its primary focus the happiness of the individual. Constraints such as guilt, sin, the golden rule, or social responsibility threaten a person's chances to enjoy life.

Nel Noddings, a philosopher of education, proposes a contrasting foundation for ethics. She suggests that it is not the individual self but the self-in-relation that initiates our ordinary experiences and our moral reflections.

1.

ROBERT COLES

Case Study: The Disparity between Intellect and Character

Robert Coles (b. 1929) is a professor of psychiatry and medical humanities at Harvard University and is well known for his study of children. Here Coles relates an episode in which one of his undergraduate students poses a dilemma involving many aspects of moral education. The student wants to know how it is possible that someone can get an excellent grade in an ethics course yet, outside the class, engage in morally suspicious conduct. For Coles this raises a question all moral thinkers need to address. That is, what is the relation between intelligence and moral character?

⊣ CRITICAL READING QUESTIONS ⊢

1. What evidence does the student offer to support the view that intelligent people are not always moral?
2. How can moral education lead to sterile discussion or cynicism?
3. Does Coles conclude that an ethics professor ought to grade a student in part based on the student's moral conduct or character?

Over 150 years ago, Ralph Waldo Emerson gave a lecture at Harvard University, which he ended with the terse assertion: "Character is higher than intellect." Even then, this prominent man of letters was worried (as many other writers and thinkers of succeeding generations would be) about the limits of knowledge and the nature of a college's mission. The intellect can grow and grow, he knew, in a person who is smug, ungenerous, even cruel. Institutions originally founded to teach their students how to become good and decent, as well as broadly and deeply literate, may abandon the first mission to concentrate on a driven, narrow book learning— a course of study in no way intent on making a connection between ideas and theories on one hand and, on the other, our lives as we actually live them.

Students have their own way of realizing and trying to come to terms with the split that Emerson addressed. A few years ago, a sophomore student of mine came

"The Disparity between Intellect and Character," *The Chronicle of Higher Education,* September 22, 1995, p. A68.

to see me in great anguish. She had arrived at Harvard from a Midwestern, working-class background. She was trying hard to work her way through college, and, in doing so, cleaned the rooms of some of her fellow students. Again and again, she encountered classmates who apparently had forgotten the meaning of *please,* of *thank you*—no matter how high their Scholastic Assessment Test scores—students who did not hesitate to be rude, even crude toward her.

One day she was not so subtly propositioned by a young man she knew to be a very bright, successful pre-med student and already an accomplished journalist. This was not the first time he had made such an overture, but now she had reached a breaking point. She had quit her job and was preparing to quit college in what she called "fancy, phony Cambridge."

The student had been part of a seminar I teach, which links Raymond Carver's fiction and poetry with Edward Hopper's paintings and drawings—the thematic convergence of literary and artistic sensibility in exploring American loneliness, both its social and its personal aspects. As she expressed her anxiety and anger to me, she soon was sobbing hard. After her sobs quieted, we began to remember the old days of that class. But she had some weightier matters on her mind and began to give me a detailed, sardonic account of college life, as viewed by someone vulnerable and hardpressed by it. At one point, she observed of the student who had propositioned her: "That guy gets all A's. He tells people he's in Group I [the top academic category]. I've taken two moral-reasoning courses with him, and I'm sure he's gotten A's in both of them—and look at how he behaves with me, and I'm sure with others."

She stopped for a moment to let me take that in. I happened to know the young man and could only acknowledge the irony of his behavior, even as I wasn't totally surprised by what she'd experienced. But I was at a loss to know what to say to her. A philosophy major, with a strong interest in literature, she had taken a course on the Holocaust and described for me the ironies she also saw in that tragedy— mass murder of unparalleled historical proportion in a nation hitherto known as one of the most civilized in the world, with a citizenry as well educated as that of any country at the time.

Drawing on her education, the student put before me names such as Martin Heidegger, Carl Jung, Paul De Man, Ezra Pound—brilliant and accomplished men (a philosopher, a psychoanalyst, a literary critic, a poet) who nonetheless had linked themselves with the hate that was Nazism and Fascism during the 1930s. She reminded me of the willingness of the leaders of German and Italian universities to embrace Nazi and Fascist ideas, of the countless doctors and lawyers and judges and journalists and schoolteachers, and, yes, even members of the clergy— who were able to accommodate themselves to murderous thugs because the thugs had political power. She pointedly mentioned, too, the Soviet Gulag, that expanse of prisons to which millions of honorable people were sent by Stalin and his brutish accomplices—prisons commonly staffed by psychiatrists quite eager to label those victims of a vicious totalitarian state with an assortment of psychiatric names, then shoot them up with drugs meant to reduce them to zombies.

I tried hard, toward the end of a conversation that lasted almost two hours, to salvage something for her, for myself, and, not least, for a university that I much respect, even as I know its failings. I suggested that if she had learned what she had just shared with me at Harvard—why, *that* was itself a valuable education acquired. She smiled, gave me credit for a "nice try," but remained unconvinced. Then she put this tough, pointed, unnerving question to me: "I've been taking all these philosophy courses, and we talk about what's true, what's important, what's *good*. Well, how do you teach people to *be* good?" And she added: "What's the point of *knowing* good, if you don't keep trying to *become* a good person?"

I suddenly found myself on the defensive, although all along I had been sympathetic to her, to the indignation she had been directing toward some of her fellow students, and to her critical examination of the limits of abstract knowledge. Schools are schools, colleges are colleges, I averred, a complaisant and smug accommodation in my voice. Thereby I meant to say that our schools and colleges these days don't take major responsibility for the moral values of their students, but, rather, assume that their students acquire those values at home. I topped off my surrender to the *status quo* with a shrug of my shoulders, to which she responded with an unspoken but barely concealed anger. This she expressed through a knowing look that announced that she'd taken the full moral measure of me.

Suddenly, she was on her feet preparing to leave. I realized that I'd stumbled badly. I wanted to pursue the discussion, applaud her for taking on a large subject in a forthright, incisive manner, and tell her she was right in understanding that moral reasoning is not to be equated with moral conduct. I wanted, really, to explain my shrug—point out that there is only so much that any of us can do to affect others' behavior, that institutional life has its own momentum. But she had no interest in that kind of self-justification—as she let me know in an unforgettable aside as she was departing my office: "I wonder whether Emerson was just being 'smart' in that lecture he gave here. I wonder if he ever had any ideas about what to *do* about what was worrying him—or did he think he'd done enough because he'd spelled the problem out to those Harvard professors?"

She was demonstrating that she understood two levels of irony: One was that the study of philosophy—even moral philosophy or moral reasoning—doesn't necessarily prompt in either the teacher or the student a determination to act in accordance with moral principles. And, further, a discussion of that very irony can prove equally sterile—again carrying no apparent consequences as far as one's everyday actions go.

When that student left my office (she would soon leave Harvard for good), I was exhausted and saddened—and brought up short. All too often those of us who read books or teach don't think to pose for ourselves the kind of ironic dilemma she had posed to me. How might we teachers encourage our students (encourage *ourselves*) to take that big step from thought to action, from moral analysis to fulfilled moral commitments? Rather obviously, community service offers us all a chance to put our money where our mouths are; and, of course, such service can enrich our understanding of the disciplines we study. A reading of *Invisible Man* (literature), *Tally's Corners* (sociology and anthropology), or *Childhood and Society* (psychology and psychoanalysis) takes on new meaning after some time spent in a ghetto school or a clinic. By the same token, such books can prompt us to think pragmatically about, say, how the wisdom that Ralph Ellison worked into his fiction might shape the way we get along with the children we're tutoring—affect our attitudes toward them, the things we say and do with them.

Yet I wonder whether classroom discussion, *per se,* can't also be of help, the skepticism of my student notwithstanding. She had pushed me hard, and I started referring again and again in my classes on moral introspection to what she had observed and learned, and my students more than got the message. Her moral righteousness, her shrewd eye and ear for hypocrisy hovered over us, made us uneasy, goaded us.

She challenged us to prove that what we think intellectually can be connected to our daily deeds. For some of us, the connection was established through community service. But that is not the only possible way. I asked students to write papers that told of particular efforts to honor through action the high thoughts we were discussing. Thus goaded to a certain self-consciousness, I suppose, students made various efforts. I felt that the best of them were small victories, brief epiphanies that might otherwise have been overlooked, but had great significance for the students in question.

"I thanked someone serving me food in the college cafeteria, and then we got to talking, the first time," one student wrote. For her, this was a decisive break with her former indifference to others she abstractly regarded as "the people who work on the serving line." She felt that she had learned something about another's life and had tried to show respect for that life.

The student who challenged me with her angry, melancholy story had pushed me to teach differently. Now, I make an explicit issue of the more than occasional disparity between thinking and doing, and I ask my students to consider how we all might bridge that disparity. To be sure, the task of connecting intellect to character is daunting, as Emerson and others well knew. And any of us can lapse into cynicism, turn the moral challenge of a seminar into yet another moment of opportunism: I'll get an A this time, by writing a paper cannily extolling myself as a doer of this or that "good deed"!

Still, I know that college administrators and faculty members everywhere are struggling with the same issues that I was faced with, and I can testify that many students will respond seriously, in at least small ways, if we make clear that we really believe that the link between moral reasoning and action is important to us. My experience has given me at least a measure of hope that moral reasoning and reflection can somehow be integrated into students'—and teachers'— lives as they actually live them.

QUESTIONS FOR ANALYSIS AND DISCUSSION

1. Is there any significant relation between intelligence and moral character? The case study presented by Coles gives several famous examples. Can you think of your own examples to support your answer?

2. The student is upset with the level of phoniness and hypocrisy she finds at the prestigious university. Do you think hypocrisy is always a sign of immorality? Is a person without hypocrisy therefore moral?

3. Does the case study support the view that morality is instinctive or learned? If instinctive (or innate), how can you account for the variety of moral beliefs people hold? If learned, who do you think are or should be our moral teachers?

2.

WILLIAM GRAHAM SUMNER

Folkways

A professor of social science at Yale, William Sumner (1840–1910) was at the forefront of the cultural relativism movement, which holds that moral good and bad are based solely on an individual society's sense of what would promote its own growth. Ethical relativism has always been a thorn in the side of moral philosophers who seek some universal truth to support an ethical value or principle. Sumner's distinct contribution is the empirical evidence and clear-cut reasoning he uses to articulate the case for relativism.

┤ CRITICAL READING QUESTIONS ├

1. What is a folkway? Find examples of folkways in Sumner's accounts.
2. Why does Sumner say that folkways are true in an essay that supports moral relativism?
3. Do folkways bring well-being to good people and harm to bad people in a particular society?
4. Are folkways logical? Are they rational?
5. In Sumner's view, why are people moral?
6. How do people learn folkways?

---

1. Definition and Mode of Origin of the Folkways

If we put together all that we have learned from anthropology and ethnography about primitive men and primitive society, we perceive that the first task of life is to live. Men begin with acts, not with thoughts. Every moment brings necessities

---

Selections from *Folkways* (Boston: Ginn & Co., 1907).

which must be satisfied at once. Need was the first experience, and it was followed at once by a blundering effort to satisfy it. It is generally taken for granted that men inherited some guiding instincts from their beast ancestry, and it may be true, although it has never been proved. If there were such inheritances, they controlled and aided the first efforts to satisfy needs. Analogy makes it easy to assume that the ways of beasts had produced channels of habit and predisposition along which dexterities and other psychophysical activities would run easily. Experiments with newborn animals show that in the absence of any experience of the relation of means to ends, efforts to satisfy needs are clumsy and blundering. The method is that of trial and failure, which produces repeated pain, loss, and disappointments. Nevertheless, it is a method of rude experiment and selection. The earliest efforts of men were of this kind. Need was the impelling force. Pleasure and pain, on the one side and the other, were the rude constraints which defined the line on which efforts must proceed. The ability to distinguish between pleasure and pain is the only psychical power which is to be assumed. Thus ways of doing things were selected, which were expedient. They answered the purpose better than other ways, or with less toil and pain. Along the course on which efforts were compelled to go, habit, routine, and skill were developed. The struggle to maintain existence was carried on, not individually, but in groups. Each profited by the other's experience; hence there was concurrence towards that which proved to be most expedient. All at last adopted the same way for the same purpose; hence the ways turned into customs and became mass phenomena. Instincts were developed in connection with them. In this way folkways arise. The young learn them by tradition, imitation, and authority. The folkways, at a time, provide for all the needs of life then and there. They are uniform, universal in the group, imperative, and invariable. As time goes on, the folkways become more and more arbitrary, positive, and imperative. If asked why they act in a certain way in certain cases, primitive people always answer that it is because they and their ancestors always have done so. A sanction also arises from ghost fear. The ghosts of ancestors would be angry if the living should change the ancient folkways.

2.   The Folkways Are a Societal Force

The operation by which folkways are produced consists in the frequent repetition of petty acts, often by great numbers acting in concert or, at least, acting in the same way when face to face with the same need. The immediate motive is interest. It produces habit in the individual and custom in the group. It is, therefore, in the highest degree original and primitive. By habit and custom it exerts a strain on every individual within its range; therefore it rises to a societal force to which great classes of societal phenomena are due. Its earliest stages, its course, and laws may be studied; also its influence on individuals and their reaction on it. It is our present purpose so to study it. We have to recognize it as one of the chief forces by which a society is made to be what it is. Out of the unconscious experiment which every repetition of the ways includes, there issues pleasure or pain, and then, so far as the men are capable of reflection, convictions that the ways are conducive to societal welfare. These two experiences are not the same. The most uncivilized men, both in the food quest and in war, do things which are painful, but which have been found to be expedient. Perhaps these cases teach the sense of social welfare better than those which are pleasurable and favorable to welfare. The former cases call for some intelligent reflection on experience. When this conviction as to the relation to welfare is added to the folkways they are converted into mores, and, by virtue of the philosophical and ethical element added to them, they win utility and importance and become the source of the science and the art of living.

28. Folkways Due to False Inference

Furthermore, folkways have been formed by accident, that is, by irrational and incongruous action, based on pseudo-knowledge. In Molembo a pestilence broke out soon after a Portuguese had died there. After that the natives took all possible measures not to allow any white man to die in their country. On the Nicobar islands some natives who had just begun to make pottery died. The art was given up and never again attempted. White men gave to one Bushman in a kraal a stick ornamented with buttons as a symbol of authority. The recipient died leaving the stick to his son. The son soon died. Then the Bushmen brought back the stick lest all should die. Until recently no building of incombustible materials could be built in any big town of the central province of Madagascar on account of some ancient prejudice. A party of Eskimos met with no game. One of them returned to their sledges and got the ham of a dog to eat. As he returned with the ham bone in his hand he met and killed a seal. Ever afterwards he carried a ham bone in his hand when hunting. The Belenda women (peninsula of Malacca) stay as near to the house as possible during the period. Many keep the door closed. They know no reason for this custom. "It must be due to some now forgotten superstition." Soon after the Yakuts saw a camel for the first time smallpox broke out amongst them. They thought the camel to be the agent of the disease. A woman amongst the same people contracted an endogamous marriage. She soon afterwards became blind. This was thought to be on account of the violation of ancient customs. A very great number of such cases could be collected. In fact they represent the current mode of reasoning of nature people. It is their custom to reason that, if one thing follows another, it is due to it. A great number of customs are traceable to the notion of the evil eye, many more to ritual notions of uncleanness. No scientific investigator could discover the origin of the folkways mentioned, if the origin had not chanced to become known to civilized men. We must believe that the known cases illustrate the irrational and incongruous origin of many folkways. In civilized history also we know that customs have owed their origin to "historical accident,"—the vanity of a princess, the deformity of a king, the whim of a democracy, the love intrigue of a statesman or prelate. By the institutions of another age it may be provided that no one of these things can affect decisions, acts, or interests, but then the power to decide the ways may have passed to clubs, trades unions, trust, commercial rivals, wire-pullers, politicians, and political fanatics. In these cases also the causes and origins may escape investigation.

29. Harmful Folkways

There are folkways which are positively harmful. Very often these are just the ones for which a definite reason can be given. The destruction of a man's goods at his death is a direct deduction for other-worldliness; the dead man is supposed to want in the other world just what he wanted here. The destruction of a man's goods at his death was a great waste of capital, and it must have had a disastrous effect on the interests of the living, and must have very seriously hindered the development of civilization. With this custom we must class all the expenditure of labor and capital on graves, temples, pyramids, rites, sacrifices, and support of priests, so far as these were supposed to benefit the dead. The faith in goblinism produced other-worldly interests which overruled ordinary worldly interests. Foods have often been forbidden which were plentiful, the prohibition of which injuriously lessened the food supply. There is a tribe of Bushmen who will eat no goat's flesh, although goats are the most numerous domestic animals in the district. Where totemism exists it is regularly accompanied by a taboo on eating the totem animal. Whatever may be the real principle in totemism, it overrules the interest in an abundant food supply. "The origin of the sacred regard paid to the cow must be sought in the primitive nomadic life of the Indo-European race," because it is common to Iranians and Indians of Hindostan. The Libyans ate oxen but not cows. The same was true of the Phœnicians and Egyptians. In some cases the sense of a food taboo is not to be learned. It may have been entirely capricious. Mohammed would not eat lizards, because he thought them the offspring of a metamorphosed clan of Israelites. On the other hand, the protective taboo which forbade killing crocodiles, pythons, cobras, and other animal enemies of man was harmful to his interests, whatever the motive. "It seems to be a fixed article of belief throughout southern India, that all who have willfully or accidentally killed a snake, especially a cobra, will certainly be punished, either in this life or the next, in one of three ways: either by childlessness, or by leprosy, or by ophthalmia." Where this faith exists man has a greater interest to spare a cobra than to kill it. India furnishes a great number of cases of harmful mores. "In India every tendency of humanity seems intensified and exaggerated. No country in the world is so conservative in its traditions, yet no country has undergone so many religious changes and vicissitudes." "Every year thousands perish of disease that might recover if they would take proper nourishment, and drink the medicine that science prescribes, but which they imagine that their religion forbids them to touch." "Men who can scarcely count beyond twenty, and know not the letters of the alphabet, would rather die than eat food which had been prepared by men of lower caste, unless it had been sanctified by being offered to an idol; and would kill their daughters rather than endure the disgrace of having unmarried girls at home beyond twelve or thirteen years of age." In the last case the rule of obligation and duty is set by the mores. The interest comes under vanity. The sanction of the caste rules is in a boycott by all members of the caste. The rules are often very harmful. "The authority of caste rests partly on written laws, partly on legendary fables or narratives, partly on the injunctions of instructors and priests, partly on custom and ussage, and partly on the caprice and convenience of its votaries." The harm of caste rules is so great that of late they have been broken in some cases, especially in regard to travel over sea, which is a great advantage to Hindoos. The Hindoo folkways in regard to widows and child marriages must also be recognized as socially harmful.

31. The Folkways Are "Right"; Rights, Morals

The folkways are the "right" ways to satisfy all interests, because they are traditional, and exist in fact. They extend over the whole of life. There is a right way to catch game, to win a wife, to make one's self appear, to cure disease, to honor ghosts, to treat comrades or strangers, to behave when a child is born, on the warpath, in council, and so on in all cases which can arise. The ways are defined on the negative side, that is, by taboos. The "right" way is the way which the ancestors used and which has been handed down. The tradition is its own warrant. It is not held subject to verification by experience. The notion of right is in the folkways. It is not outside of them, of independent origin, and brought to them to test them. In the folkways, whatever is, is right. This is because they are traditional, and therefore contain in themselves the authority of the ancestral ghosts. When we come to the folkways we are at the end of our analysis. The notion of right and ought is the same in regard to all the folkways, but the degree of it varies with the importance of the interest at stake. The obligation of conformable and cooperative action is far greater under ghost fear and war than in other matters, and the social sanctions are severer, because group interests are supposed to be at stake. Some usages contain only a slight element of right and ought. It may well be believed that notions of right and duty, and of social welfare, were first developed in connection with ghost fear and other-worldliness, and therefore that, in that field also, folkways were first raised to mores. "Rights" are the rules of mutual give and take in the competition of life which are imposed on comrades in the in-group, in order that the peace may prevail there which is essential to the group strength. Therefore rights can never be "natural" or "God-given," or absolute in any sense. The morality of a group at a time is the sum of the taboos and prescriptions in the folkways by which right conduct is defined. Therefore morals can never be intuitive. They are historical, institutional, and empirical.

World philosophy, life policy, right, rights, and morality are all products of the folkways. They are reflections on, and generalizations from, the experience of pleasure and pain which is won in efforts to carry on the struggle for existence under actual life conditions. The generalizations are very crude and vague in their germinal forms. They are all embodied in folklore, and all our philosophy and science have been developed out of them.

32. The Folkways Are "True"

The folkways are necessarily "true" with respect to some world philosophy. Pain forced men to think. The ills of life imposed reflection and taught forethought. Mental processes were irksome and were not undertaken until painful experience made them unavoidable. With great unanimity all over the globe primitive men followed the same line of thought. The dead were believed to live on as ghosts in another world just like this one. The ghosts had just the same needs, tastes, passions, etc., as the living men had had. These transcendental notions were the beginning of the mental outfit of mankind. They are articles of faith, not rational convictions. The living had duties to the ghosts, and the ghosts had rights; they also had power to enforce their rights. It behooved the living therefore to learn how to deal with ghosts. Here we have a complete world philosophy and a life policy deduced from it. When pain, loss, and ill were experienced and the question was provoked, Who did this to us? the world philosophy furnished the answer. When the painful experience forced the question, Why are the ghosts angry and what must we do to appease them? the "right" answer was the one which fitted into the philosophy of ghost fear. All acts were therefore constrained and trained into the forms of the world philosophy by ghost fear, ancestral authority, taboos, and habit. The habits and customs created a practical philosophy of welfare, and they confirmed and developed the religious theories of goblinism.

34. Definition of the Mores

When the elements of truth and right are developed into doctrines of welfare, the folkways are raised to another plane. They then become capable of producing inferences, developing into new forms, and extending their constructive influence over men and society. Then we call them the mores. The mores are the folkways, including the philosophical and ethical generalizations as to societal welfare which are suggested by them, and inherent in them, as they grow.

65. What Is Goodness or Badness of the Mores

It is most important to notice that, for the people of a time and place, their own mores are always good, or rather that for them there can be no question of the goodness or badness of their mores. The reason is because the standards of good and right are in the mores. If the life conditions change, the traditional folkways may produce pain and loss, or fail to produce the same good as formerly. Then the loss of comfort and ease brings doubt into the judgment of welfare (causing doubt of the pleasure of the gods, or of war power, or of health), and thus disturbs the unconscious philosophy of the mores. Then a later time will pass judgment on the mores. Another society may also pass judgment on the mores. In our literary and historical study of the mores we want to get from them their educational value, which consists in the stimulus or warning as to what is, in its effects, societally good or bad. This may lead us to reject or neglect a phenomenon like infanticide, slavery, or witchcraft, as an old "abuse" and "evil," or to pass by the crusades as a folly which cannot recur. Such a course would be a great error. Everything in the mores of a time and place must be regarded as justified with regard to that time and place. "Good" mores are those which are well adapted to the situation. "Bad" mores are those which are not so adapted. The mores are not so stereotyped and changeless as might appear, because they are forever moving towards more complete adaptation to conditions and interests, and also towards more complete adjustment to each other. . . . This indicates that the folkways are on their way to a new adjustment. The extreme of folly, wickedness, and absurdity in the mores is witch persecutions, but the best men of the seventeenth century had no doubt that witches existed, and that they ought to be burned. The religion, statecraft, jurisprudence, philosophy, and social system of that age all contributed to maintain that belief. It was rather a culmination than a contradiction of the current faiths and convictions, just as the dogma that all men are equal and that one ought to have as much political power in the state as another was the culmination of the political dogmatism and social philosophy of the nineteenth century. Hence our judgments of the good or evil consequences of folkways are to be kept separate from our study of the historical phenomena of them, and of their strength and the reasons for it. The judgments have their place in plans and doctrines for the future, not in a retrospect.

170. Social Selection by the Mores

The most important fact about the mores is their dominion over the individual. Arising he knows not whence or how, they meet his opening mind in earliest childhood, give him his outfit of ideas, faiths, and tastes, and lead him into prescribed mental processes. They bring to him codes of action, standards, and rules of ethics. They have a model of the man-as-he-should-be to which they mold him, in spite of himself and without his knowledge. If he submits and consents, he is taken up and may attain great social success. If he resists and dissents, he is thrown out and may be trodden under foot. The mores are therefore an engine of social selection. Their coercion of the individual is the mode in which they operate the selection, and the details of the process deserve study. Some folkways exercise an unknown and unintelligent selection. Infanticide does this. Slavery always exerts a very powerful selection, both physical and social.

439. Meaning of "Immoral"

When, therefore, the ethnographers apply condemnatory or depreciatory adjectives to the people whom they study, they beg the most important question which we want to investigate; that is, What are standards, codes, and ideas of chastity, decency, propriety, modesty, etc., and whence do they arise? The ethnographical facts contain the answer to this question, but in order to reach it we want a colorless report of the facts. We shall find proof that "immoral" never means anything but contrary to the mores of the time and place. Therefore the mores and the morality may move together, and there is no permanent or universal standard by which right and truth in regard to these matters can be established and different folkways compared and criticised. Only experience produces judgments of the expediency of some usages. For instance, ancient peoples thought pederasty was harmless and trivial. It has been well proved to be corrupting both to individual and social vigor, and harmful to interests, both individual and collective. Cannibalism, polygamy, incest, harlotry, and other primitive customs have been discarded by a very wide and, in the case of some of them, unanimous judgment that they are harmful. On the other hand, in the *Avesta* spermatorrhea is a crime punished by stripes. The most civilized peoples also maintain, by virtue of their superior position in the arts of life, that they have attained to higher and better judgments and that they may judge the customs of others from their own standpoint. For three or four centuries they have called their own customs "Christian," and have thus claimed for them a religious authority and sanction which they do not possess by any connection with the principles of Christianity. Now, however, the adjective seems to be losing its force. The Japanese regard nudity with indifference, but they use dress to conceal the contour of the human form while we use it to enhance, in many ways, the attraction. "Christian" mores have been enforced by the best breechloaders and ironclads, but the Japanese now seem ready to bring superiority in those matters to support their mores. It is now a known and recognized fact that our missionaries have unintentionally and unwittingly done great harm to nature people by inducing them to wear clothes as one of the first details of civilized influence. In the usages of nature peoples there is no correlation at all between dress and sentiments of chastity, modesty, decency, and propriety.

503. The Great Variety in the Codes

All the epics which have been treated in this chapter are branches or outreachings of the social code. They show how deep is the interest of human beings in the sex taboo, and in the self-perpetuation of society. Men have always tried, and are trying still, to solve the problem of well living in this respect. The men, the women, the children, and the society have joint and several interests, and the complication is great. At the present time population, race, marriage, childbirth, and the education of children present us our greatest problems and most unfathomable mysteries. All the contradictory usages of chastity, decency, propriety, etc., have their sense in some assumed relation to the welfare of society. To some extent they have come out of caprice, but chiefly they have issued from experience of good and ill, and are due to efforts to live well. Thus we may discern in them policies and philosophies, but they never proceed to form any such generalities as do rationally adopted motives. There is logic in the folkways, but never rationality. Given the premises, in a notion of kin, for instance, and the deductions are made directly and generally correctly, but the premises could never be verified, and they were oftener false than true. Each group took its own way, making its own assumptions, and following its own logic. So there was great variety and discord in their policies and philosophies, but within the area of a custom, during its dominion, its authority is absolute; and hence, although the usages are infinitely various, directly contradictory, and mutually abominable, they are, within their area of dominion, of equal value and force, and they are the standards of what is true and right. The groups have often tried to convert each other by argument and reason. They have never succeeded. Each one's reasons are the tradition which it has received from its ancestors. That does not admit of argument. Each tries to convince the other by going outside of the tradition to some philosophic standard of truth. Then the tradition is left in full force. Shocking as it must be to any group to be told that there is no rational ground for any one of them to convert another group to its mores (because this seems to imply, although it does not, that their folkways are not better than those of other groups), yet this must be said, for it is true. By experience and science the nations which by name are Christian have reached ways which are better fitted, on the whole, for well living than those of the Mohammedan nations, although this superiority is not by any means so complete and sweeping as current opinion in Christian countries believes. If Christians and Mohammedans come together and argue, they never make the slightest impression on each other. During the crusades, in Andalusia, and in cities of the near East where they live side by side, they have come to peace, mutual respect, and mutal influence. Syncretism begins. There is giving and taking. In Egypt at present the Moslems see the power of the English to carry on industry, commerce, and government, and this observation produces effect on the folkways. That is the chief way in which folkways are modified or borrowed. It was by this process that Greeks and Romans influenced the folkways of barbarians, and that white men have influenced those of Negroes, Indians, Polynesians, Japanese, etc.

QUESTIONS FOR ANALYSIS AND DISCUSSION

1. Looking through the lens of Sumner, what are some folkways in the United States today?

2. How do Americans learn folkways? If folkways or customs apply to all members of a society, how do you account for the disparity of moral attitudes and behavior of Americans?

3. From your readings, other course studies, or personal experiences, do you agree that common customs or cultural norms make for a better society? How do you think Sumner understands the social good?

4. Sumner lists many examples of moral behavior that may seem reprehensible to us. Can you think of conduct in the United States that is condoned or accepted by our moral rules but that might seem reprehensible to an outsider? Develop your own case and consider how you would respond to the outsider's view. Is it possible that the outsider can make the correct judgment?

5. In the case study by Coles, a student is bothered by the hypocrisy among even the best students and scholars. Suppose hypocrisy is a social custom; does this weaken the student's critique?

3.

RICHARD GARRETT

Dilemma's Case for Ethical Relativism

Richard Garrett is an American philosopher. His recent book on ethics consists of an extended dialogue on ethical relativism. In this excerpt Garrett arranges the discussion so that the case for relativism seems reasonable; he demands a thoughtful response rather than the potshots moralists often throw at relativists. A central issue here concerns the truth status of moral judgments.

CRITICAL READING QUESTIONS

1. Why does Siddhartha make an analogy between the shape of the earth and moral beliefs?
2. What is the point in raising medicine as a way of understanding or criticizing relativism?
3. Do the participants agree or disagree about why people try to be moral?
4. As the dialogue closes, which appeal forces Dilemma to reconsider his ideas: the appeal to a God? the appeal to the great evils perpetrated by humans? the appeal to reason? the appeal to the golden rule?

MAX: Homer, it is good to see you. You are just in time. Dilemma and I were just about to enter into another debate with our guest, Siddhartha, over the issue of relativism versus absolutism. Having seen Siddhartha in action the other night, I think we can use all the reinforcements we can get.

HOMER: What set you off this time?

MAX: Dilemma was telling Siddhartha about the Ikes who, when faced with extreme conditions of starvation, abandoned all of their normal patterns of interaction. He deliberately drew Siddhartha into the discussion by describing some of the horrible things that went on during the Ikes' last days.

HOMER: I must confess I don't know who the Ikes are.

"Dilemma's Case for Ethical Relativism," from *Dialogues Concerning the Foundations of Ethics* (Lanham, MD: Rowman & Littlefield, 1990), pp. 1–14.

MAX: "Were" would be putting it more accurately, Homer. The last of the Ikes died more than a decade ago.

HOMER: I see. Well, then, who were they?

MAX: They were an African tribe who, at one time, lived off the land by hunting. The African government forced them to abandon their hunting grounds and live in a much smaller area. The plan was that they would become farmers instead of hunters. But tragically, the Ikes could not adjust to the domestic rigors of farm life, and, eventually, they all died of starvation.

HOMER: And how did stories about the Ikes lead into a discussion of moral relativism and moral absolutism?

DILEMMA: I was telling Siddhartha about an anthropologist who was studying the Ikes during the later days of their civilization. The anthropologist mentioned numerous horrible incidents that took place.

HOMER: Such as what?

DILEMMA: In one case, a son stole food from his sick father until the old man finally died of starvation. In another case, two parents sent their three-year-old daughter out into the forest so that they would not have to feed her. When she kept returning after repeated attempts to get rid of her, the parents finally sealed her in a mud hut and left her there to die. At first the anthropologist was horrified by such incidents and condemned the Ikes for their callous actions. But as time went by, he had only sympathy for them. He concluded that he could not judge them by his standards, that, as other anthropologists before him had done after studying people of another culture, he could only judge them by their own standards, if at all. When I told Siddhartha I agreed with the anthropologist, Siddhartha took exception, as I anticipated he would.

SIDDHARTHA: Yes, I confess. I took Dilemma's bait. I said that although the anthropologist's sympathy for the Ikes was admirable and that I also agreed we should not judge them as human beings (for I believe we should leave that sort of thing to God), I could not entirely agree with the anthropologist's attitude.

HOMER: Where did you disagree?

SIDDHARTHA: I claimed that, although we can't stand in judgment of the moral worth of the Ikes, or anyone, we can morally evaluate their *actions* and ask ourselves: Did the various people in the stories do the right thing? More importantly I argued that it is not a question of their standards vs. ours, but of what is the right thing for *anyone* to do in such situations. I believe that what would be right for anyone would be right for everyone.

HOMER: I see. So, like a good moral relativist, Dilemma, you rejected the idea that there is a single, transcultural moral standard or norm by which all people's actions can be judged. Instead, you argued that we can only judge the Ikes by their own standards. Then you, Siddhartha, picked up the absolutist's banner and made the opposite claim, namely, that there is but one single morality by which the actions of the Ikes and everyone else can be judged. Is that the picture?

MAX: That is it exactly. At that point, I stepped in with the suggestion that since Siddhartha will be leaving us tomorrow, it would be valuable if each of us had an opportunity to state and defend his views and that Siddhartha should have the opportunity to question and comment upon each of us and also to have the last word, since he is our guest and the only absolutist amongst us.

HOMER: That sounds like a good plan to me.

MAX: Good, then please join us. You are just in time because Dilemma was just about to state his views on the matter.

HOMER: My pleasure. Please tell us your views, Dilemma.

DILEMMA: As I see it, the only way to approach the question of morality is in a scientific way. If you want to understand some phenomenon, you have to pay your dues with plenty of observation. Theories about morality—or anything else—are worthless unless they fit the data. If the Ikes were the only exception to our moral standards, Siddhartha, I would have to agree with you and say they had gone afoul. But the facts are otherwise. Anthropologists have found equally dramatic departures from our moral values in every part of the globe. The fact is, Siddhartha, that agreement in moral values is the exception, diversity is the rule. How, in face of such facts, dare we set up our values as the moral standards for all the world?

SIDDHARTHA: What do you mean by "our moral values," Dilemma?

DILEMMA: I mean our Western values, the values of middle America.

SIDDHARTHA: Then let me remind you that although I have spent half of my life in the West, I was raised in the East. As a transplanted Easterner on Western soil, I have been forced to think doubly about these questions, not simply as a professional philosopher, but more importantly as someone finding himself an adult confronted with very different moral values than I had known as a youngster. But speaking of facts, one of the facts that struck me when I came to America is how many Americas there really are. I do not find in your own country a single monolithic system of values, but a plurality of values. There are many different ethnic groups, religious groups, and classes in America, and they all have different moral values.

DILEMMA: Fine. I accept your point. But that only adds support to what I said, Siddhartha, by illustrating the tremendous variety of moral values that exist in the world. How, in the face of such overwhelming diversity of moral values, can you tell me there is only one morality?

SIDDHARTHA: There is no denying the facts, Dilemma. I wish to be as faithful to them as you do. It is not the facts that separate us. We both agree that there is an overwhelming variety of moral norms. What distinguishes us is our *interpretation* of the facts. You think it follows that because what-people-take-to-be-moral varies, what-really-is-moral varies. But that only follows if what-people-take-to-be-moral and what-really-is-moral amount to the same thing.

DILEMMA: And just what is the alternative to that?

SIDDHARTHA: I deny that what people take to be moral is necessarily the same as what really is moral. I explain the diversity of moral norms by assuming that the single universal morality is not known nor understood universally, that people are in various stages of understanding that single morality. That, after all, is an alternative.

DILEMMA: On what grounds?

SIDDHARTHA: Consider an analogy. Suppose we were to discover a tremendous diversity among cultures regarding the shape of the earth. Some thought it was flat, some that it was shaped like an egg, still others thought it to be like a pyramid. It would scarcely follow from the fact that various cultures have different conceptions of the earth's shape that the earth actually had many shapes. For you would not say that the real shape of the earth was necessarily the same thing as what people take it to be, would you?

DILEMMA: Heavens, no.

SIDDHARTHA: A better explanation of the diversity of opinions about the shape of the earth is to assume that the various cultures had incomplete and incorrect conceptions of the earth's real shape. Do you agree?

DILEMMA: Certainly.

SIDDHARTHA: Then with respect to the shape of the earth one can also be a relativist or an absolutist, and just now you told me you would remain an absolutist about the shape of the earth no matter how much diversity you found on the topic. That is exactly my stance on the matter of morality and the reason I remain unimpressed by all of the findings of the anthropologists.

DILEMMA: I can see why you consider my first argument inadequate, Siddhartha. By itself it proves nothing. But I think it, combined with a second consideration, constitutes a very powerful argument.

SIDDHARTHA: And what is that?

DILEMMA: Your reply to my first argument assumes that the analogy between the shape of the earth and morality holds, that they are the same sort of phenomenon. But I say they are not. The shape of the earth has to do with the earth and not with culture; but morality concerns culture, for morality is a part of a culture, and the shape of the earth is not. Hence, we have a right to expect a science such as anthropology, which studies cultures, to throw light upon morality, but not upon the shape of the earth.

SIDDHARTHA: Your point is well taken, Dilemma. So let me offer you a second analogy, one that is much closer to morality. Would you consider the practice of medicine a part of culture or not?

DILEMMA: I would certainly include medicine as part of a culture.

SIDDHARTHA: Well then, suppose that within the field of medicine itself, you discovered different approaches to treating cancer patients and various conceptions of what cancer was. Some people might conceive of cancer as a punishment by the gods, others might take it to be possession by evil spirits, and still others as the presence of viruses. Yet, suppose they are all dealing with the same thing; not all of these conceptions of cancer could be correct. Indeed, only one of these concepts could be the one that is completely adequate. Would you agree?

DILEMMA: I would.

SIDDHARTHA: So the picture we get is of a diversity of medicines with a variety of treatments for cancer—some of them quite inadequate, some helpful but crude, like removing the cancerous tissue by surgery, and some one or few, perhaps, maximally effective. Now tell me whose treatment of cancer is most likely to be effective—societies that have the best conception of what cancer is, or societies that have the most inadequate conception of what cancer is?

DILEMMA: It would be reasonable to suppose that the former had the best methods of treatment, of course.

SIDDHARTHA: Good. Then I want you to think of immorality as the cancer of society—the disorderly and destructive behavior of its members—and morality as the healthy state of society. The various mores or moral rules of the various societies correspond to their various treatment methods of that social cancer, of which each society has a more or less adequate conception. The more adequate a society's conception of the social cancer of immorality and of the state of social health or morality, the better its treatment of that disease is likely to be. My absolutist thesis is that all societies are struggling with essentially the same societal disease and are in need of attaining the same basic state of health—that morality or social health is essentially the same for all societies in spite of the diversity of treatment used to attain moral health.

DILEMMA: I can see a certain attractiveness in the model you offer, Siddhartha, but there is still one thing you are forgetting.

SIDDHARTHA: What is that?

DILEMMA: Modern medicine has made a certain progress over the years by demonstrating that medical practices and conceptions of illness can be firmly grounded in scientific research. Therefore, it is reasonable to speak of a more or less objective conception of illness and health in the field of medicine. That is, scientific medical research has demonstrated that some medical practices and some conceptions of health and illness are more adequate than others. But with respect to various moral practices and various conceptions of morality, things have turned out otherwise. Science has not been able to establish one set of moral practices or some one, or few, conceptions of morality to be superior to others. So here, I say, science points to a difference between medicine and morality.

SIDDHARTHA: I quite agree with you, Dilemma, that medicine and morality are not exactly analogous. For while medicine has to do with a mastery of our bodies, morality concerns the mastery of the whole self and of life as a whole and is not likely to be experimentally established in the same way that medicine has been. But that does not mean there is no rational way to decide which conception of morality is the more adequate or even the most adequate one. There are rational procedures other than experimentation for determining the truth of some propositions. No one has ever performed an experiment to demonstrate the Pythagorean theorem in geometry, yet no one who has seen the proof for it would deny that it is rationally grounded.

DILEMMA: I agree. But are you suggesting that morality is like mathematics? That an argument in ethics is like a proof in mathematics or geometry?

SIDDHARTHA: Not at all. I am simply suggesting that we must keep an open mind about what constitutes a rational demonstration or argument for some truth. We must take each argument, moral or otherwise, on its own merits and judge it accordingly. That is all I am saying. And so it is with respect to the absolutist's claim that there is only one true morality. We must look at the arguments presented on behalf of that claim and evaluate them on their own merit, without some preconception of what a good argument has to look like.

DILEMMA: I will accept your point for the time being, Siddhartha, just to see where you go from here, but there is something you are still overlooking.

SIDDHARTHA: What is that?

DILEMMA: There are good reasons to expect that morality cannot be established rationally. For if you look at the facts as I do, then you can't help but note that there is something very special about moral utterances that sets them off from ordinary statements.

SIDDHARTHA: What difference do you have in mind?

DILEMMA: Take first the ordinary statement, "It is raining out." In uttering such a statement, I am simply telling you what is the case. I am saying nothing about how you should act. In contrast, if I say "Murder is wrong," then I am really saying how you and others should behave. As far as I am concerned it is the same as having said "Thou shalt not kill." Moral pronouncements in general are like that. They are attempts to *command* people, to *direct* their behavior. If this is right, then moral pronouncements are best looked at as a special class of commands or as reports of commands.

SIDDHARTHA: "Commands" and "reports of commands"?

DILEMMA: Consider "Thou shalt not kill." Didn't Moses claim that this was a command from God?

SIDDHARTHA: He did.

DILEMMA: Well, then, I think it is safe to say that the early Jews looked upon moral norms as commands from God. Accordingly, "Killing is wrong" might be said to be a report of God's command for an ancient Jew, whereas "Thou shalt not kill" expresses the command itself. But looking at the matter from a scientific view, you can't explain what is really going on by looking at the command as issuing from God. The only alternative is to say that the command "Thou shalt not kill" really came from society itself. Society, not God, is the real authority behind the moral command. Society, not God, will punish those who break the moral command. Since different societies issue different moral commands, enforce different moral norms, what is moral is relative to the society in question. So if my theory that a moral pronouncement is simply a special sort of command from society is right, it is futile to look for the one single, right morality, since obviously these special sorts of commands we call morality really do vary from society to society, and that's that.

SIDDHARTHA: I believe your theory is quite mistaken, Dilemma. I don't deny that morality aims at guiding or directing people's behavior, nor that moral pronouncements such as "Thou shalt not kill" and "Murder is wrong" have a force comparable to a command. But none of this shows that they are commands issued by society. The real authority of moral statements to command the truly moral person derives from neither a fear of society nor from a fear of God, but rather out of a respect for doing what is right for the sake of doing what is right. Although it is true that some people do what they think is moral only because they fear that God or society will punish them, this is not the case with someone who is really moral, in my view. For in my view, if someone is really moral they do what is right simply because they believe it is the right thing to do and for no other reason. So for them all they care about is whether or not it is *true* that killing is morally wrong or not.

DILEMMA: And I say that truth has nothing to do with it. It is society's rewards and punishments alone that always make people do what their society calls right and avoid doing what their society calls wrong.

SIDDHARTHA: Are you saying that a society can't be mistaken in what norms it enforces, that a society can't have *false* beliefs about what moral norms it should have? Is that what you mean when you say truth has nothing to do with morality?

DILEMMA: That's it exactly.

SIDDHARTHA: But how can you explain social reform? Was slavery not morally and legally sanctioned here in America a little over a hundred years ago? And did Americans not come to say that slavery is wrong, that it is a mistake to believe that any human should live in bondage?

DILEMMA: What you are talking about is an inconsistency within the set of moral norms themselves. Americans came to see that slavery is wrong or mistaken only in the sense of realizing that it was inconsistent with their Christian and democratic moral norms, which hold that all men are free and equal. So I will admit that a society's moral norms can be mistaken in the sense that they are inconsistent with each other. But that is the only sense in which they can be wrong, and that is something that is compatible with moral relativity. For each society's moral norms have only to be consistent with themselves and not with the moral norms of other societies.

SIDDHARTHA: Nonetheless, we are making progress. For you are already admitting that a society can be mistaken about its moral norms, that it can have *false* beliefs about what norms it should or shouldn't have?

DILEMMA: I give you that much but no more, Siddhartha. In the matter of the internal consistency of its norms, a society can be mistaken. But that is all.

SIDDHARTHA: But can't the members of a society rationally examine its norms and find them wanting or defective in other ways?

DILEMMA: What has reason to do with it? Roughly, what a society calls good or right is what the members of that society find reinforcing or rewarding due to their genetic endowment and the natural and social conditions they live in. They can't stand outside their culture and evaluate it from a God-like perspective. Either you do or you don't find it reinforcing or rewarding to follow your society's moral norms. If it is reinforcing or rewarding to obey them, then you obey them. Otherwise you don't. It is not a matter of a rational decision. From a scientific point of view, your society shapes your moral behavior, not you. We are not free in the way required to make such a rational decision as you are suggesting.

SIDDHARTHA: Well then, let me ask you what we are all doing right now.

DILEMMA: What do you mean?

SIDDHARTHA: Consider the following description of what the four of us are doing right now: We are engaged in the process of making and listening to various assertions or conclusions for which we are giving reasons or premises. In short, we are formulating and considering various arguments, for an argument is nothing but a conclusion along with its premises. As we proceed with this process, we encounter arguments and counterarguments, arguments for and against some conclusion, and this enables us to see which arguments are the good ones and which are not as good or not good at all. So in doing this, we are assuming all along an ability on our part to discriminate, at least sometimes, between which arguments are the good ones and which the bad ones. Do you agree with me so far?

DILEMMA: I do.

SIDDHARTHA: Then note that as a consequence of this process, some of our beliefs or conclusions will change completely, some will be more or less changed, and still others will remain the same as when we began our discussion. More-over, as our beliefs change so will our behavior—what we say and do and even what we think to ourselves. Sometimes the changes that occur are trivial, but sometimes they are very important, and occasionally they are even critical. Finally, some of the changes in beliefs that can occur from discussions such as this are changes in beliefs about this or that moral norm. And such a change in belief can result in our willingness to act in accordance with that norm or in our refusal to do so. Can you deny any of this?

DILEMMA: I suppose I can't, no.

SIDDHARTHA: Well then, you can't deny that human beings have an ability to ra-tionally evaluate the moral norms of their society. For all I meant in saying this was that they have an ability to entertain arguments pro and con some moral norm of their society, to distinguish the good arguments from the bad, and to accept or reject that norm and act accordingly. You don't wish to deny that humans can do such a thing, do you?

DILEMMA: I suppose not.

SIDDHARTHA: That is a good supposition, for to suppose the opposite would put you in an embarrassing position.

DILEMMA: How is that?

SIDDHARTHA: Because, you would no sooner suppose the opposite, and I would ask you for an argument or reason for your opposite supposition. This would then place you in the embarrassing position of either not giving an argument because you want to remain consistent with your claim that people aren't rational, or of giving an argument and that would be inconsistent with that claim. For if people are not rational in my sense, then either they can't give or consider arguments at all, or they can't tell the difference between good and bad ones and act accordingly.

DILEMMA: I see your point. I see I have no choice but to agree with you or make a fool of myself.

SIDDHARTHA: Now that we can agree that humans are rational in the sense I have indicated, we can no longer say it is senseless to ask humans to rationally evalu-ate the norms of their society because such rationality is beyond them.

DILEMMA: I stand corrected on that account. But I still don't see on what grounds beyond internal inconsistency one can say that the norms of a society are wrong or that the people's beliefs about them are mistaken. It still seems to me that beyond internal consistency the only other thing people consider is their feelings, how they feel emotionally about this or that norm. And I don't see how you can argue about feelings. They are a product of conditioning, pure and simple.

SIDDHARTHA: Then you are overlooking people's interests. What I think or feel is in my interest and what really is in my interest may not be the same. I may feel or think it is not in my interest to go to the doctor. Yet I may go to the doctor and discover I have some very serious condition that was caught just in the nick of time. In that case, my feelings about not going to the doctor would have been contrary to my real interest. So when it comes to a person's true interests, reason is frequently a better guide than just feelings. I submit to you, Dilemma, that a second way that the members of a society may be mistaken about their moral norms is that they may believe those norms serve their interests when, in fact, they do not. If, for example, any society thought that murder, dishonesty, or thievery were norms that would serve their interests, they would soon discover that they were sadly mistaken.

DILEMMA: For the moment you have me cornered, Siddhartha.

SIDDHARTHA: I submit to you therefore that murder, dishonesty, and thievery are universally wrong, Dilemma, while respect for life, honesty, and respect for what belongs to another are universally right. They are morally right and wrong not just because society says they are, but for reasons quite apart from what society says. These things are right and wrong absolutely and not relative to some society.

DILEMMA: As I just admitted, you have stumped me for the moment. I think it is time to ask for reinforcements. I am certain there is something wrong with what you have concluded, but at the moment I can't put my finger on it.

MAX: Then I will take over for you, Dilemma, for I see how Siddhartha has trapped you.

DILEMMA: Good. Please proceed.

QUESTIONS FOR ANALYSIS AND DISCUSSION

1. Why does much of the discussion focus on true and false beliefs? What is the difference?

2. Sumner held that folkways are true. How do you think Siddhartha would respond to Sumner?

3. What is meant by "rational"? Siddhartha emphasizes that the way to challenge relativism relies on the belief that everyone has the capacity for being rational. Is this true? Are we rational in the same way?

4. Dilemma outlines several answers to the "why be moral" question, including the fear of punishment and the desire for reward. Do you think he has—despite the counterarguments of his friends—captured an insight about humanity? Explain your response.

4.

E. O. WILSON

The Morality of the Gene

Harvard zoologist E. O. Wilson (b. 1929) is one of the leading advocates for sociobiol-
ogy, a scientific approach that explains human social interaction largely as an expression
of biological rules that shape behavior. This selection begins one of his major statements
on sociobiology. Wilson believes that moral philosophers need to take account of recent
scientific evidence when forming their ethical theories. Specifically, he thinks the familiar
tension between self and other is misplaced. From an evolutionary perspective, an organ-
ism is mostly concerned with the well-being of the species. Hence, the concern of moralists
with egoism and altruism is largely a creation of ethics rather than a reflection of human
nature. A more accurate understanding of altruism, according to Wilson, comes from
scientists.

┤ CRITICAL READING QUESTIONS ├

1. Why does Wilson think Camus's claim—that suicide is the basic
   philosophical question—is wrong?
2. What is the importance of cooperation?
3. For Wilson, why do humans behave morally?

Camus said that the only serious philosophical question is suicide. That is wrong
even in the strict sense intended. The biologist, who is concerned with questions of
physiology and evolutionary history, realizes that self-knowledge is constrained
and shaped by the emotional control centers in the hypothalamus and limbic system of the brain. These centers flood our consciousness with all the emotions—
hate, love, guilt, fear, and others—that are consulted by ethical philosophers who
wish to intuit the standards of good and evil. What, we are then compelled to ask,
made the hypothalamus and limbic system? They evolved by natural selection.
That simple biological statement must be pursued to explain ethics and ethical
philosophers, if not epistemology and epistemologists, at all depths. Self-existence,

"The Morality of the Gene," from *Sociobiology: The New Synthesis* (Cambridge, MA: Harvard University Press, 1975), pp. 153–159. Notes have been omitted.

or the suicide that terminates it, is not the central question of philosophy. The hypothalamic-limbic complex automatically denies such logical reduction by countering it with feelings of guilt and altruism. In this one way the philosopher's own emotional control centers are wiser than his solipsist consciousness, "knowing" that in evolutionary time the individual organism counts for almost nothing. In a Darwinist sense the organism does not live for itself. Its primary function is not even to reproduce other organisms; it reproduces genes, and it serves as their temporary carrier. Each organism generated by sexual reproduction is a unique, accidental subset of all the genes constituting the species. Natural selection is the process whereby certain genes gain representation in the following generations superior to that of other genes located at the same chromosome positions. When new sex cells are manufactured in each generation, the winning genes are pulled apart and reassembled to manufacture new organisms that, on the average, contain a higher proportion of the same genes. But the individual organism is only their vehicle, part of an elaborate device to preserve and spread them with the least possible biochemical perturbation. Samuel Butler's famous aphorism, that the chicken is only an egg's way of making another egg, has been modernized: the organism is only DNA's way of making more DNA. More to the point, the hypothalamus and limbic system are engineered to perpetuate DNA.

In the process of natural selection, then, any device that can insert a higher proportion of certain genes into subsequent generations will come to characterize the species. One class of such devices promotes prolonged individual survival. Another promotes superior mating performance and care of the resulting offspring. As more complex social behavior by the organism is added to the genes' techniques for replicating themselves, altruism becomes increasingly prevalent and eventually appears in exaggerated forms. This brings us to the central theoretical problem of sociobiology: how can altruism, which by definition reduces personal fitness, possibly evolve by natural selection? The answer is kinship: if the genes causing the altruism are shared by two organisms because of common descent, and if the altruistic act by one organism increases the joint contribution of these genes to the next generation, the propensity to altruism will spread through the gene pool. This occurs even though the altruist makes less of a solitary contribution to the gene pool as the price of its altruistic act.

To his own question, "Does the Absurd dictate death?" Camus replied that the struggle toward the heights is itself enough to fill a man's heart. This arid judgment is probably correct, but it makes little sense except when closely examined in the light of evolutionary theory. The hypothalamic-limbic complex of a highly social species, such as man, "knows," or more precisely it has been programmed to perform as if it knows, that its underlying genes will be proliferated maximally only if it orchestrates behavioral responses that bring into play an efficient mixture of personal survival, reproduction, and altruism. Consequently, the centers of the complex tax the conscious mind with ambivalences whenever the organisms encounter stressful situations. Love joins hate; aggression, fear; expansiveness, withdrawal; and so on; in blends designed not to promote the happiness and survival of the individual, but to favor the maximum transmission of the controlling genes.

The ambivalences stem from counteracting pressures on the units of natural selection. . . . [W]hat is good for the individual can be destructive to the family; what preserves the family can be harsh on both the individual and the tribe to which its family belongs; what promotes the tribe can weaken the family and destroy the individual; and so on upward through the permutations of levels of organization. Counteracting selection on these different units will result in certain genes being multiplied and fixed, others lost, and combinations of still others held in static proportions. According to the present theory, some of the genes will produce emotional states that reflect the balance of counteracting selection forces at the different levels.

I have raised a problem in ethical philosophy in order to characterize the essential of sociobiology. Sociobiology is defined as the systematic study of the biological basis of all social behavior. For the present it focuses on animal societies, their population structure, castes, and communication, together with all of the physiology underlying the social adaptations. But the discipline is also concerned with the social behavior of early man and the adaptive features of organization in the more primitive contemporary human societies. Sociology *sensu stricto,* the study of human societies at all levels of complexity, still stands apart from sociobiology because of its largely structuralist and nongenetic approach. It attempts to explain human behavior primarily by empirical description of the outermost phenotypes and by unaided intuition, without reference to evolutionary explanations in the true genetic sense. It is most successful, in the way descriptive taxonomy and ecology have been most successful, when it provides a detailed description of particular phenomena and demonstrates first-order correlations with features of the environment. Taxonomy and ecology, however, have been reshaped entirely during the past forty years by integration into neo-Darwinist evolutionary theory—the "Modern Synthesis," as it is often called—in which each phenomenon is weighed for its adaptive significance and then related to the basic principles of population genetics. It may not be too much to say that sociology and the other social sciences, as well as the humanities, are the last branches of biology waiting to be included in the Modern Synthesis. One of the functions of sociobiology, then, is to reformulate the foundations of the social science in a way that draws these subjects into the Modern Synthesis. Whether the social sciences can be truly biologicized in this fashion remains to be seen.

. . . In the view presented here, the new sociobiology should be compounded of roughly equal parts of invertebrate zoology, vertebrate zoology, and population biology. . . . Biologists have always been intrigued by comparisons between societies of invertebrates, especially insect societies, and those of vertebrates. They have dreamed of identifying the common properties of such disparate units in a way that would provide insight into all aspects of social evaluation, including that of man. The goal can be expressed in modern terms as follows: when the same parameters and quantitative theory are used to analyze both termite colonies and troops of rhesus macaques, we will have a unified science of sociobiology. This may seem an impossibly difficult task. But as my own studies have advanced, I have been increasingly impressed with the functional similarities between invertebrate and vertebrate societies and less so with the structural differences that seem, at first glance, to constitute such an immense gulf between them. Consider for a moment termites and monkeys. Both are formed into cooperative groups that occupy territories. The group members communicate hunger, alarm, hostility, caste status or rank, and reproductive status among themselves by means of something on the order of 10 to 100 nonsyntactical signals. Individuals are intensely aware of the distinction between group mates and nonmembers. Kinship plays an important role in group structure and probably served as a chief generative force of sociality in the first place. In both kinds of society there is a well-marked division of labor, although in the insect society there is a much stronger reproductive component. The details of organization have been evolved by an evolutionary optimization process of unknown precision, during which some measure of added fitness was given to individuals with cooperative tendencies—at least toward relatives. The fruits of cooperativeness depend upon the particular conditions of the environment and are available to only a minority of animal species during the course of their evolution.

This comparison may seem facile, but it is out of such deliberate oversimplification that the beginnings of a general theory are made. The formulation of a theory of sociobiology constitutes, in my opinion, one of the great manageable problems of biology for the next twenty or thirty years. . . . Its central precept is that the evolution of social behavior can be fully comprehended only through an understanding, first, of demography, which yields the vital information concerning population growth and age structure, and, second, of the genetic structure of the populations, which tells us what we need to know about effective population size in the genetic sense, the coefficients of relationship within the societies, and the amounts of gene flow between them. The principal goal of a general theory of sociobiology should be an ability to predict features of social organization from a knowledge of these population parameters combined with information on the behavioral constraints imposed by the genetic constitution of the species. It will be a chief task of evolutionary ecology, in turn, to derive the population parameters from a knowledge of the evolutionary history of the species and of the environment in which the most recent segment of that history unfolded. The most important feature of the prolegomenon, then, is the sequential relation between evolutionary studies, ecology, population biology, and sociobiology.

In stressing the tightness of this sequence, however, I do not wish to underrate the filial relationship that sociobiology has had in the past with the remainder of behavioral biology. Although behavioral biology is traditionally spoken of as if it were a unified subject, it is now emerging as two distinct disciplines centered on neurophysiology and on sociobiology, respectively. The conventional wisdom also speaks of ethology, which is the naturalistic study of whole patterns of animal behavior, and its companion enterprise, comparative psychology, as the central, unifying fields of behavioral biology. They are not; both are destined to be cannibalized by neurophysiology and sensory physiology from one end and sociobiology and behavioral ecology from the other.

I hope not too many scholars in ethology and psychology will be offended by this vision of the future of behavioral biology. It seems to be indicated both by the extrapolation of current events and by consideration of the logical relationship behavioral biology holds with the remainder of science. The future, it seems clear, cannot be with the ad hoc terminology, crude models, and curve fitting that characterize most of contemporary ethology and comparative psychology. Whole patterns of animal behavior will inevitably be explained within the framework, first, of integrative neurophysiology, which classifies neurons and reconstructs their circuitry, and, second, of sensory physiology, which seeks to characterize the cellular transducers at the molecular level. Endocrinology will continue to play a peripheral role, since it is concerned with the cruder tuning devices of nervous activity. To pass from this level and reach the next really distinct discipline, we must travel all the way up to the society and the population. Not only are the phenomena best described by families of models different from those of cellular and molecular biology, but the explanations become largely evolutionary. There should be nothing surprising in this distinction. It is only a reflection of the larger division that separates the two greater domains of evolutionary biology and functional biology. As Lewontin has truly said: "Natural selection of the character states themselves is the essence of Darwinism. All else is molecular biology."

QUESTIONS FOR ANALYSIS AND DISCUSSION

1. Wilson suggests that moralists confuse their own key terms, such as altruism and egoism. How does Wilson define these terms? Do you agree with his definitions? Can you offer better definitions for these terms?

2. Though moral theories may be elegant, Wilson contends that they lack the ability to predict or explain human behavior. Consider your own example of a moral principle or value. Does it help you predict or explain how you or others will act? If not, is that a serious flaw in moral thinking?

3. Imagine an ethical relativist and a sociobiologist having a discussion about ethics. Do you think they would agree or disagree about the reasons people act morally? Be specific in your response and consider your own thoughts about their ideas.

4. Recent news stories have proposed a variety of genetic explanations for particular forms of human conduct, ranging from alcoholism to sexual orientation to eating habits to aggressiveness or passivity. Can you think of other examples? Do these examples support or weaken Wilson's argument? Clarify your answer.

5.

J. L. MACKIE

The Law of the Jungle: Moral Alternatives and Principles of Evolution

Can a nonscientist respond fairly to the sociobiologist? Philosopher J. L. Mackie (1917–1981) examines the central ideas and arguments of a genetic-based ethics to see if it holds up to logical analysis and common sense. In this selection he focuses on the ideas of Richard Dawkins, another scientist who believes we all have selfish genes that guide us in being social creatures. If Dawkins is correct, notes Mackie, we should be able to make sense of the old adage about the law of the jungle. If Dawkins cannot make sense of the adage, though, a genetic account of human morality may be inadequate.

CRITICAL READING QUESTIONS

1. What is meant by the law of the jungle?
2. How are memes and genes used to explain human behavior?
3. Why does Mackie use grudgers, cheaters, and suckers to illustrate his response to Dawkins?
4. What is the importance of distinguishing between long- and short-term behavior?

When people speak of "the law of the jungle," they usually mean unrestrained and ruthless competition, with everyone out solely for his own advantage. But the phrase was coined by Rudyard Kipling, in *The Second Jungle Book,* and he meant something very different. His law of the jungle is a law that wolves in a pack are supposed to obey. His poem says that "the strength of the Pack is the Wolf, and the strength of the Wolf is the Pack," and it states the basic principles of social co-operation. Its provisions are a judicious mixture of individualism and collectivism, prescribing graduated and qualified rights for fathers of families, mothers with cubs, and young wolves, which constitute an elementary system of welfare services. Of course, Kipling meant his poem to give moral instruction to human children,

---

"The Law of the Jungle: Moral Alternatives and Principles of Evolution," *Philosophy* (1978): 455–464.

but he probably thought it was at least roughly correct as a description of the social behaviour of wolves and other wild animals. Was he right, or is the natural world the scene of unrestrained competition, of an individualistic struggle for existence?

Views not unlike those of Kipling have been presented by some recent writers on ethology, notably Robert Ardrey and Konrad Lorenz. These writers connect their accounts with a view about the process of evolution that has brought this behaviour, as well as the animals themselves, into existence. They hold that the important thing in evolution is the good of the species, or the group, rather than the good of the individual. Natural selection favours those groups and species whose members tend, no doubt through some instinctive programming, to co-operate for a common good; this would, of course, explain why wolves, for example, behave cooperatively and generously towards members of their own pack, if indeed they do.

However, this recently popular view has been keenly attacked by Richard Dawkins in his admirable and fascinating book, *The Selfish Gene*.[1] He defends an up-to-date version of the orthodox Darwinian theory of evolution, with special reference to "the biology of selfishness and altruism." One of his main theses is that there is no such thing as group selection, and that Lorenz and others who have used this as an explanation are simply wrong. This is a question of some interest to moral philosophers, particularly those who have been inclined to see human morality itself as the product of some kind of natural evolution.[2]

It is well, however, to be clear about the issue. It is not whether animals ever behave for the good of the group in the sense that this is their conscious subjective goal, that they aim at the well-being or survival of the whole tribe or pack: the question of motives in this conscious sense does not arise. Nor is the issue whether animals ever behave in ways which do in fact promote the well-being of the group to which they belong, or which help the species of which they are members to survive: of course they do. The controversial issue is different from both of these: it is whether the good of the group or the species would ever figure in a correct evolutionary account. That is, would any correct evolutionary account take either of the following forms?

1. The members of this species tend to do these things which assist the survival of this species because their ancestors were members of a sub-species whose members had an inheritable tendency to do these things, and as a result that sub-species survived, whereas other sub-species of the ancestral species at that time had members who tended not to do these things and as a result their sub-species did not survive.

2. The members of this species tend to do these things which help the group of which they are members to flourish because some ancestral groups happened to have members who tended to do these things and these groups, as a result, survived better than related groups of the ancestral species whose members tended not to do these things.

In other words, the issue is this: is there natural selection by and for group survival or species survival as opposed to selection by and for individual survival (or, as we shall see, gene survival)? Is behaviour that helps the group or the species, rather than the individual animal, rewarded by the natural selection which determines the course of evolution?

However, when Dawkins denies that there is selection by and for group or species survival, it is not selection by and for individual survival that he puts in its place. Rather it is selection by and for the survival of each single gene—the genes being the unit factors of inheritance, the portions of chromosomes which replicate themselves, copy themselves as cells divide and multiply. Genes, he argues, came into existence right back at the beginning of life on earth, and all more complex organisms are to be seen as their products. We are, as he picturesquely puts it, gene-machines: our biological function is just to protect our genes, carry them around, and enable them to reproduce themselves. Hence the title of his book, *The Selfish Gene*. Of course what survives is not a token gene: each of these perishes with the cell of which it is a part. What survives is a gene-type, or rather what we might call a gene-clone, the members of a family of token genes related to one another by simple direct descent, by replication. The popularity of the notions of species selection and group selection may be due partly to confusion on this point. Since clearly it is only types united by descent, not individual organisms, that survive long enough to be of biological interest, it is easy to think that selection must be by and for species survival. But this is a mistake: genes, not species, are the types which primarily replicate themselves and are selected. Since Dawkins roughly defines the gene as "a genetic unit which is small enough to last for a number of generations and to be distributed around in the form of many copies," it is (as he admits) practically a tautology that the gene is the basic unit of natural selection and therefore, as he puts it, "the fundamental unit of self-interest," or, as we might put it less picturesquely, the primary beneficiary of natural selection. But behind this near-tautology is a synthetic truth, that this basic unit, this primary beneficiary, is a small bit of a chromosome. The reason why this is so, why what is differentially effective and therefore subject to selection is a small bit of a chromosome, lies in the mechanism of sexual reproduction by way of meiosis, with crossing over between chromosomes. When male and female cells each divide before uniting at fertilization, it is not chromosomes as a whole that are randomly distributed between the parts, but sections of chromosomes. So sections of chromosomes can be separately inherited, and therefore can be differentially selected by natural selection.

The issue between gene selection, individual selection, group selection, and species selection might seem to raise some stock questions in the philosophy of science. Many thinkers have favoured reductionism of several sorts, including methodological individualism. Wholes are made up of parts, and therefore in principle whatever happens in any larger thing depends upon and is explainable in terms of what happens in and between its smaller components. But though this metaphysical individualism is correct, methodological individualism does not follow from it. It does not follow that we must always conduct our investigations and construct our explanations in terms of component parts, such as the individual members of a group or society. Scientific accounts need not be indefinitely reductive. Some wholes are obviously more accessible to us than their components. We can understand what a human being does without analysing this in terms of how each single cell in his body or his brain behaves. Equally we can often understand what a human society does without analysing this in terms of the behaviour of each of its individual members. And the same holds quite generally: we can often understand complex wholes as units, without analysing them into their parts. So if, in the account of evolution, Dawkins's concentration upon genes were just a piece of methodological individualism or reductionism, it would be inadequately motivated. But it is not: there is a special reason for it. Dawkins's key argument is that species, populations, and groups, and individual organisms too, are as genetic units too temporary to qualify for natural selection. "They are not stable through evolutionary time. Populations are constantly blending with other populations and so losing their identity," and, what is vitally important, "are also subject to evolutionary change from within" (p. 36).

This abstract general proposition may seem obscure. But it is illustrated by a simple example which Dawkins gives (pp. 197–201).

A species of birds is parasitized by dangerous ticks. A bird can remove the ticks from most parts of its own body, but, having only a beak and no hands, it cannot get them out of the top of its own head. But one bird can remove ticks from another bird's head: there can be mutual grooming. Clearly if there were an inherited tendency for each bird to take the ticks out of any other bird's head, this would help the survival of any group in which that tendency happened to arise for the ticks are dangerous: they can cause death. Someone who believed in group selection would, therefore, expect this tendency to be favoured and to evolve and spread for this reason. But Dawkins shows that it would not. He gives appropriate names to the different "strategies," that is, the different inheritable behavioural tendencies. The strategy of grooming anyone who needs it he labels "Sucker." The strategy of accepting grooming from anyone, but never grooming anyone else, even someone who has previously groomed you, is called "Cheat." Now if in some population both these tendencies or strategies, and only these two, happen to arise, it is easy to see that the cheats will always do better than the suckers. They will be groomed when they need it, and since they will not waste their time pecking out other birds' ticks, they will have more time and energy to spare for finding food, attracting mates, building nests, and so on. Consequently the gene for the Sucker strategy will gradually die out. So the population will come to consist wholly of cheats, despite the fact that this is likely to lead to the population itself becoming extinct, if the parasites are common enough and dangerous enough, whereas a population consisting wholly of suckers would have survived. The fact that the group is open to evolutionary change from within, because of the way the internal competition between Cheat and Sucker genes works out, prevents the group from developing or even retaining a feature which would have helped the group as a whole.

This is just one illustration among many, and Dawkins's arguments on this point seem pretty conclusive. We need, as he shows, the concept of an *evolutionarily stable strategy* or ESS (p. 74 *et passim*). A strategy is evolutionarily stable, in relation to some alternative strategy or strategies, if it will survive indefinitely in a group in competition with those alternatives. We have just seen that where Cheat and Sucker alone are in competition, Cheat is an ESS but Sucker is not. We have also seen, from this example, that an ESS may not help a group, or the whole species, to survive and multiply. Of course, we must not leap to the conclusion that an ESS never helps a group or a species: if that were so we could not explain much of the behaviour that actually occurs. Parents sacrifice themselves for their children, occasionally siblings for their siblings, and with the social insects, bees and ants and termites, their whole life is a system of communal service. But the point is that these results are not to be explained in terms of group selection. They can and must be explained as consequences of the selfishness of genes, that is, of the fact that gene-clones are selected for whatever helps each gene-clone itself to survive and multiply.

But now we come to another remarkable fact. Although the gene is the hero of Dawkins's book, it is not unique either in principle or in fact. It is not the only possible subject of evolutionary natural selection, nor is it the only actual one. What is important about the gene is just that it has a certain combination of logical features. It is a replicator: in the right environment it is capable of producing multiple copies of itself; but in this process of copying some mistakes occur; and these mistaken copies—mutations—will also produce copies of themselves; and, finally, the copies produced may either survive or fail to survive. Anything that has these formal, logical, features is a possible subject of evolution by natural selection. As we have seen, individual organisms, groups, and species do not have the required formal features, though many thinkers have supposed that they do. They cannot reproduce themselves with sufficient constancy of characteristics. But Dawkins, in his last chapter, introduces another sort of replicators. These are what are often called cultural items or traits; Dawkins christens them *memes*—to make a term a bit like "genes"—because they replicate by memory and imitation (mimesis). Memes include tunes, ideas, fashions, and techniques. They require, as the environment in which they can replicate, a collection of minds, that is, brains that have the powers of imitation and memory. These brains (particularly though not exclusively human ones) are themselves the products of evolution by gene selection. But once the brains are there gene selection has done its work: given that environment, memes can themselves evolve and multiply in much the same way as genes do, in accordance with logically similar laws. But they can do so more quickly. Cultural evolution may be much faster than biological evolution. But the basic laws are the same. Memes are selfish in the same sense as genes. The explanation of the widespread flourishing of a certain meme, such as the idea of a god or the belief in hell fire, may be simply that it is an efficiently selfish meme. Something about it makes it well able to infect human minds, to take root and spread in and among them, in the same way that something about the smallpox virus makes it well able to take root and spread in human bodies. There is no need to explain the success of a meme in terms of any benefit it confers on individuals or groups; it is a replicator in its own right. Contrary to the optimistic view often taken of cultural evolution, this analogy shows that a cultural trait can evolve, not because it is advantageous to society, but simply because it is advantageous to itself. It is ironical that Kipling's phrase "the law of the jungle" has proved itself a more efficient meme than the doctrine he tried to use it to propagate.

So far I have been merely summarizing Dawkins's argument. We can now use it to answer the question from which I started. Who is right about the law of the jungle? Kipling, or those who have twisted his phrase to mean almost the opposite of what he intended? The answer is that neither party is right. The law by which nature works is not unrestrained and ruthless competition between individual organisms. But neither does it turn upon the advantages to a group, and its members, of group solidarity, mutual care and respect, and co-operation. It turns upon the self-preservation of gene-clones. This has a strong tendency to express itself in individually selfish behaviour, simply because each agent's genes are more certainly located in him than in anyone else. But it can and does express itself also in certain forms of what Broad called self-referential altruism, including special care for one's own children and perhaps one's siblings, and, as we shall see, reciprocal altruism, helping those (and only those) who help you.

But now I come to what seems to be an exception to Dawkins's main thesis, though it is generated by his own argument and illustrated by one of his own examples. We saw how, in the example of mutual grooming, if there are only suckers and cheats around, the strategy Cheat is evolutionarily stable, while the strategy Sucker is not. But Dawkins introduces a third strategy, Grudger. A grudger is rather like you and me. A grudger grooms anyone who has previously groomed him, and any stranger, but he remembers and bears a grudge against anyone who cheats him—who refuses to groom him in return for having been groomed—and the grudger refuses to groom the cheat ever again. Now when all three strategies are in play, both Cheat and Grudger are evolutionarily stable. In a population consisting largely of cheats, the cheats will do better than the others, and both suckers and grudgers will die out. But in a population that starts off with more than a certain critical proportion of grudgers, the cheats will first wipe out the suckers, but will then themselves become rare and eventually extinct: cheats can flourish only while they have suckers to take advantage of, and yet by doing so they tend to eliminate those suckers.

It is obvious, by the way, that a population containing only suckers and grudgers, in any proportions, but no cheats, would simply continue as it was. Suckers and grudgers behave exactly like one another as long as there are no cheats around, so there would be no tendency for either the Sucker or the Grudger gene to do better than the other. But if there is any risk of an invasion of Cheat genes, either through mutation or through immigration, such a pattern is not evolutionarily stable, and the higher the proportion of suckers, the more rapidly the cheats would multiply.

So we have two ESSs, Cheat and Grudger. But there is a difference between these two stable strategies. If the parasites are common enough and dangerous enough, the population of cheats will itself die out, having no defence against ticks in their heads; whereas a separate population of grudgers will flourish indefinitely. Dawkins says, "If a population arrives at an ESS which drives it extinct, then it goes extinct, and that is just too bad" (p. 200). True: *but is this not group selection after all?* Of course, this will operate only if the populations are somehow isolated. But if the birds in question were distributed in geographically isolated regions, and Sucker, Cheat and Grudger tendencies appeared (after the parasites became plentiful) in randomly different proportions in these different regions, then some populations would become pure grudger populations, and others would become pure cheat populations, but then the pure cheat populations would die out, so that eventually all surviving birds would be grudgers. And they would be able to re-colonize the areas where cheat populations had perished.

Another name for grudgers is "reciprocal altruists." They act as if on the maxim "Be done by as you did." One implication of this story is that this strategy is not only evolutionarily stable within a population, it is also viable for a population as a whole. The explanation of the final situation, where all birds of this species are grudgers, lies partly in the non-viability of a population of pure cheats. So this is, as I said, a bit of group selection after all.

It is worth noting how and why this case escapes Dawkins's key argument that a population is "not a discrete enough entity to be a unit of natural selection, not stable and unitary enough to be 'selected' in preference to another population" (p. 36). Populations can be made discrete by geographical (or other) isolation, and can be made stable and unitary precisely by the emergence of an ESS in each, but perhaps different ESSs in the different regional populations of the same species. This case of group selection is necessarily a second order phenomenon: it arises where gene selection has produced the ESSs which are then persisting selectable features of groups. In other words, an ESS may be a third variety of replicator, along with genes and memes; it is a self-reproducing feature *of groups*.

Someone might reply that this is not really group selection because it all rests ultimately on gene selection, and a full explanation can be given in terms of the long-run self-extinction of the Cheat gene, despite the fact that within a population it is evolutionarily stable in competition with the two rival genes. But this would be a weak reply. The monopoly of cheating *over a population* is an essential part of the causal story that explains the extinction. Also, an account at the group level, though admittedly incomplete, is here correct as far as it goes. The reason why all ultimately surviving birds of this species are grudgers is partly that *populations* of grudgers can survive whereas *populations* of cheats cannot, though it is also partly that although a population of suckers could survive—it would be favoured by group selection, if this possibility arose, just as much as a population of grudgers— internal changes due to gene selection after an invasion of Cheat genes would prevent there being a population of suckers. In special circumstances group selection (or population selection) can occur and could be observed and explained as such, without going down to the gene selection level. It would be unwarranted methodological individualism or reductionism to insist that we not merely can but must go down to the gene selection level here. We must not fall back on this weak general argument when Dawkins's key argument against group selection fails.

I conclude, then, that there can be genuine cases of group selection. But I admit that they are exceptional. They require rather special conditions, in particular geographical isolation, or some other kind of isolation, to keep the populations that are being differentially selected apart. For if genes from one could infiltrate another, the selection of populations might be interfered with. (Though in fact in our example *complete* isolation is not required: since what matters is whether there is more or less than a certain critical proportion of grudgers, small-scale infiltrations would only delay, not prevent, the establishing of pure populations.) And since special conditions are required, there is no valid general principle that features which would enable a group to flourish will be selected. And even these exceptional cases conform thoroughly to the general logic of Dawkins's doctrine.

Sometimes, but only sometimes, group characteristics have the formal features of replicators that are open to natural selection.

Commenting on an earlier version of this paper, Dawkins agreed that there could be group selection in the sort of case I suggested, but stressed the importance of the condition of geographical (or other) isolation. He also mentioned a possible example, that the prevalence of sexual reproduction itself may be a result of group selection. For if there were a mutation by which asexual females, producing offspring by parthenogenesis, occurred in a species, this clone of asexual females would be at once genetically isolated from the rest of the species, though still geographically mixed with them. Also, in most species males contribute little to the nourishment or care of their offspring; so from a genetic point of view males are wasters: resources would be more economically used if devoted only to females. So the genetically isolated population of asexual females would out-compete the normal sexually reproducing population with roughly equal numbers of males and females. So the species would in time consist only of asexual females. But then, precisely because all its members were genetically identical, it would not have the capacity for rapid adaptation by selection to changing conditions that an ordinary sexual population has. So when conditions changed, it would be unable to adapt, and would die out. Thus there would in time be species selection against any species that produced an asexual female mutation. Which would explain why nearly all existing species go in for what, in the short run, is the economically wasteful business of sexual reproduction.[3]

What implications for human morality have such biological facts about selfishness and altruism? One is that the possibility that morality is itself a product of natural selection is not ruled out, but care would be needed in formulating a plausible speculative account of how it might have been favoured. Another is that the notion of an ESS may be a useful one for discussing questions of practical morality. Moral philosophers have already found illumination in such simple items of game theory as the Prisoners' Dilemma; perhaps these rather more complicated evolutionary "games" will prove equally instructive. Of course there is no simple transition from "is" to "ought," no direct argument from what goes on in the natural world and among non-human animals to what human beings ought to do. Dawkins himself explicitly warns against any simple transfer of conclusions. At the very end of the book he suggests that conscious foresight may enable us to develop radically new kinds of behaviour. "We are built as gene machines and cultured as meme machines, but we have the power to turn against our creators. We, alone on earth, can rebel against the tyranny of the selfish replicators" (p. 215). This optimistic suggestion needs fuller investigation. It must be remembered that the human race as a whole cannot act as a unit with conscious foresight. Arrow's Theorem shows that even quite small groups of rational individuals may be unable to form coherent rational preferences, let alone to act rationally. Internal competition, which in general prevents a group from being a possible subject of natural selection, is even more of an obstacle to its being a rational agent. And while we can turn against some memes, it will be only with the help and under the guidance of other memes.

This is an enormous problematic area. For the moment I turn to a smaller point. In the mutual grooming model, we saw that the Grudger strategy was, of the three strategies considered, the only one that was healthy in the long run. Now something closely resembling this strategy, reciprocal altruism, is a well known and long established tendency in human life. It is expressed in such formulae as that justice consists in giving everyone his due, interpreted, as Polemarchus interprets it in the first book of Plato's *Republic,* as doing good to one's friends and harm to one's enemies, or repaying good with good and evil with evil. Morality itself has been seen, for example by Edward Westermarck, as an outgrowth from the retributive emotions. But some moralists, including Socrates and Jesus, have recommended something very different from this, turning the other cheek and repaying evil with good. They have tried to substitute "Do as you would be done by" for "Be done by as you did." Now this, which in human life we characterize as a Christian spirit or perhaps as saintliness, is roughly equivalent to the strategy Dawkins has unkindly labelled "Sucker." Suckers are saints, just as grudgers are reciprocal altruists, while cheats are a hundred per cent selfish. And as Dawkins points out, the presence of suckers endangers the healthy Grudger strategy. It allows cheats to prosper, and could make them multiply to the point where they would wipe out the grudgers, and ultimately bring about the extinction of the whole population. This seems to provide fresh support for Nietzsche's view of the deplorable influence of moralities of the Christian type. But in practice there may be little danger. After two thousand years of contrary moral teaching, reciprocal altruism is still dominant in all human societies; thoroughgoing cheats and thoroughgoing saints (or suckers) are distinctly rare. The sucker slogan is an efficient meme, but the sucker behaviour pattern far less so. Saintliness is an attractive topic for preaching, but with little practical persuasive force. Whether in the long run this is to be deplored or welcomed, and whether it is alterable or not, is a larger question. To answer it we should have carefully to examine our specifically human capacities and the structure of human societies, and also many further alternative strategies. We cannot simply apply to the human situation conclusions drawn from biological models. Nevertheless they are significant and challenging as models; it will need to be shown how and where human life diverges from them.

Notes

1. R. Dawkins, *The Selfish Gene* (Oxford, 1976).

2. I am among these: see p. 113 of my *Ethics: Inventing Right and Wrong* (Penguin, Harmondsworth, 1977).

3. This suggestion is made in a section entitled "The paradox of sex and the cost of paternal neglect" of the following article: R. Dawkins, "The value judgements of evolution," in M. A. H. Dempster and D. J. McFarland (eds.) *Animal Economics* (Academic Press, London and New York, forthcoming).

QUESTIONS FOR ANALYSIS AND DISCUSSION

1. What is your understanding of the law of the jungle? Social and political thinkers often distinguish the law of the jungle from the law of society. The

latter reflects our moral beliefs and principles of justice. From your reading of Mackie, are the two views incompatible?

2. In your opinion, does Mackie help us answer the "why be moral" question better than sociobiologists or cultural relativists?

3. Does the scenario involving cheaters, suckers, and grudgers adequately capture the behavioral options of humans? If so, does Mackie's depiction of the scenario support his conclusion? If not, what do you think is missing in this scenario?

6.

Selections from the *Holy Bible:* Ten Commandments, Beatitudes, and Parables

For many people ethical principles and values have substance only when backed by religion. This could involve belief in a deity, respect for a spiritual authority, or obedience to God or to a sacred text. Moreover, those who defend the religious framework of morality believe that secular (nonreligious) approaches ignore or trivialize the fundamental questions all humans raise, such as the relation between body and spirit, the difference between tangible and nontangible truths, or the need to reflect on our mortality. The selections that follow highlight some of the basic moral lessons of the Holy Bible.

CRITICAL READING QUESTIONS

1. Do the Ten Commandments offer an ethic that tells us what to do or what not to do?

2. What lesson is offered those considering the pursuit of pleasure or wealth?

3. Does "love thy neighbor" contain a specific direction for being moral?

"Selections from the *Holy Bible:* Ten Commandments, Beautitudes, and Parables," from the *Holy Bible* (New Revised Standard Version, 1989), Deuteronomy 5:1–22; Matthew 4:23–5:12, 19:16–26; Luke 17:19–31; Isaiah 55:1–13; John 8:2–11; Romans 7:1–25.

Deuteronomy 5:1–22

1 Moses convened all Israel, and said to them: Hear, O Israel, the statutes and ordinances that I am addressing to you today; you shall learn them and observe them diligently.

2 The LORD our God made a covenant with us at Horeb.

3 Not with our ancestors did the LORD make this covenant, but with us, who are all of us here alive today.

4 The LORD spoke with you face to face at the mountain, out of the fire.

5 (At that time I was standing between the LORD and you to declare to you the words of the LORD; for you were afraid because of the fire and did not go up the mountain.) And he said:

6 I am the LORD your God, who brought you out of the land of Egypt, out of the house of slavery;

7 you shall have no other gods before me.

8 You shall not make for yourself an idol, whether in the form of anything that is in heaven above, or that is on the earth beneath, or that is in the water under the earth.

9 You shall not bow down to them or worship them; for I the LORD your God am a jealous God, punishing children for the iniquity of parents, to the third and fourth generation of those who reject me,

10 but showing steadfast love to the thousandth generation of those who love me and keep my commandments.

11 You shall not make wrongful use of the name of the LORD your God, for the LORD will not acquit anyone who misuses his name.

12 Observe the sabbath day and keep it holy, as the LORD your God commanded you.

13 Six days you shall labor and do all your work.

14 But the seventh day is a sabbath to the LORD your God; you shall not do any work—you, or your son or your daughter, or your male or female slave, or your ox or your donkey, or any of your livestock, or the resident alien in your towns, so that your male and female slave may rest as well as you.

15 Remember that you were a slave in the land of Egypt, and the LORD your God brought you out from there with a mighty hand and an outstretched arm; therefore the LORD your God commanded you to keep the sabbath day.

16 Honor your father and your mother, as the LORD your God commanded you, so that your days may be long and that it may go well with you in the land that the LORD your God is giving you.

17 You shall not murder.

18 Neither shall you commit adultery.

19 Neither shall you steal.

20 Neither shall you bear false witness against your neighbor.

21 Neither shall you covet your neighbor's wife. Neither shall you desire your neighbor's house, or field, or male or female slave, or ox, or donkey, or anything that belongs to your neighbor.

22 These words the LORD spoke with a loud voice to your whole assembly at the mountain, out of the fire, the cloud, and the thick darkness, and he added no more. He wrote them on two stone tablets, and gave them to me.

Matthew 4:23–5:12

4:23 Jesus went throughout Galilee, teaching in their synagogues and proclaiming the good news of the kingdom and curing every disease and every sickness among the people.

24 So his fame spread throughout all Syria, and they brought to him all the sick, those who were afflicted with various diseases and pains, demoniacs, epileptics, and paralytics, and he cured them.

25 And great crowds followed him from Galilee, the Decapolis, Jerusalem, Judea, and from beyond the Jordan.

5:1 When Jesus saw the crowds, he went up the mountain; and after he sat down, his disciples came to him.

2 Then he began to speak, and taught them, saying:

3 "Blessed are the poor in spirit, for theirs is the kingdom of heaven.

4 "Blessed are those who mourn, for they will be comforted.

5 "Blessed are the meek, for they will inherit the earth.

6 "Blessed are those who hunger and thirst for righteousness, for they will be filled.

7 "Blessed are the merciful, for they will receive mercy.

8 "Blessed are the pure in heart, for they will see God.

9 "Blessed are the peacemakers, for they will be called children of God.

10 "Blessed are those who are persecuted for righteousness' sake, for theirs is the kingdom of heaven.

11 "Blessed are you when people revile you and persecute you and utter all kinds of evil against you falsely on my account.

12 "Rejoice and be glad, for your reward is great in heaven, for in the same way they persecuted the prophets who were before you."

Matthew 19:16–26

16 Then someone came to him and said, "Teacher, what good deed must I do to have eternal life?"

17 And he said to him, "Why do you ask me about what is good? There is only one who is good. If you wish to enter into life, keep the commandments."

18 He said to him, "Which ones?" And Jesus said, "You shall not murder; You shall not commit adultery; You shall not steal; You shall not bear false witness;

19 Honor your father and mother; also, You shall love your neighbor as yourself."

20 The young man said to him, "I have kept all these; what do I still lack?"

21 Jesus said to him, "If you wish to be perfect, go, sell your possessions, and give the money to the poor, and you will have treasure in heaven; then come, follow me."

22 When the young man heard this word, he went away grieving, for he had many possessions.

23 Then Jesus said to his disciples, "Truly I tell you, it will be hard for a rich person to enter the kingdom of heaven.

24 Again I tell you, it is easier for a camel to go through the eye of a needle than for someone who is rich to enter the kingdom of God."

25 When the disciples heard this, they were greatly astounded and said, "Then who can be saved?"

26 But Jesus looked at them and said, "For mortals it is impossible, but for God all things are possible."

Luke 17:19–31

19 "There was a rich man who was dressed in purple and fine linen and who feasted sumptuously every day.

20 And at his gate lay a poor man named Lazarus, covered with sores,

21 who longed to satisfy his hunger with what fell from the rich man's table; even the dogs would come and lick his sores.

22 The poor man died and was carried away by the angels to be with Abraham. The rich man also died and was buried.

23 In Hades, where he was being tormented, he looked up and saw Abraham far away with Lazarus by his side.

24 He called out, 'Father Abraham, have mercy on me, and send Lazarus to dip the tip of his finger in water and cool my tongue; for I am in agony in these flames.'

25 But Abraham said, 'Child, remember that during your lifetime you received your good things, and Lazarus in like manner evil things; but now he is comforted here, and you are in agony.

26 Besides all this, between you and us a great chasm has been fixed, so that those who might want to pass from here to you cannot do so, and no one can cross from there to us.'

27 He said, 'Then, father, I beg you to send him to my father's house—

28 for I have five brothers—that he may warn them, so that they will not also come into this place of torment.'

29 Abraham replied, 'They have Moses and the prophets; they should listen to them.'

30 He said, 'No, father Abraham; but if someone goes to them from the dead, they will repent.'

31 He said to him, 'If they do not listen to Moses and the prophets, neither will they be convinced even if someone rises from the dead.'"

Isaiah 55:1–13

1 Ho, everyone who thirsts, come to the waters; and you that have no money, come, buy and eat! Come, buy wine and milk without money and without price.

2 Why do you spend your money for that which is not bread, and your labor for that which does not satisfy? Listen carefully to me, and eat what is good, and delight yourselves in rich food.

3 Incline your ear, and come to me; listen, so that you may live. I will make with you an everlasting covenant, my steadfast, sure love for David.

4 See, I made him a witness to the peoples, a leader and commander for the peoples.

5 See, you shall call nations that you do not know, and nations that do not know you shall run to you, because of the LORD your God, the Holy One of Israel, for he has glorified you.

6 See the LORD while he may be found, call upon him while he is near;

7 let the wicked forsake their way, and the unrighteous their thoughts; let them return to the LORD, that he may have mercy on them, and to our God, for he will abundantly pardon.

8 For my thoughts are not your thoughts, nor are your ways my ways, says the LORD.

9 For as the heavens are higher than the earth, so are my ways higher than your ways and my thoughts than your thoughts.

10 For as the rain and the snow come down from heaven, and do not return there until they have watered the earth, making it bring forth and sprout, giving seed to the sower and bread to the eater,

11 so shall my word be that goes out from my mouth; it shall not return to me empty, but it shall accomplish that which I purpose, and succeed in the thing for which I sent it.

12 For you shall go out in joy, and be led back in peace; the mountains and the hills before you shall burst into song, and all the trees of the field shall clap their hands.

13 Instead of the thorn shall come up the cypress; instead of the brier shall come up the myrtle; and it shall be to the LORD for a memorial, for an everlasting sign that shall not be cut off.

John 8:2–11

2 Early in the morning he came again to the temple. All the people came to him and he sat down and began to teach them.

3 The scribes and the Pharisees brought a woman who had been caught in adultery; and making her stand before all of them,

4 they said to him, "Teacher, this woman was caught in the very act of committing adultery.

5 Now in the law Moses commanded us to stone such women. Now what do you say?"

6 They said this to test him, so that they might have some charge to bring against him. Jesus bent down and wrote with his finger on the ground.

7 When they kept on questioning him, he straightened up and said to them, "Let anyone among you who is without sin be the first to throw a stone at her."

8 And once again he bent down and wrote on the ground.

9 When they heard it, they went away, one by one, beginning with the elders; and Jesus was left alone with the woman standing before him.

10 Jesus straightened up and said to her, "Woman, where are they? Has no one condemned you?"

11 She said, "No one, sir." And Jesus said, "Neither do I condemn you. Go your way, and from now on do not sin again."

Romans 7:1–25

[1] Do you not know, brothers and sisters—for I am speaking to those who know the law—that the law is binding on a person only during that person's lifetime?

[2] Thus a married woman is bound by the law to her husband as long as he lives; but if her husband dies, she is discharged from the law concerning the husband.

[3] Accordingly, she will be called an adulteress if she lives with another man while her husband is alive. But if her husband dies, she is free from that law, and if she marries another man, she is not an adulteress.

[4] In the same way, my friends, you have died to the law through the body of Christ, so that you may belong to another, to him who has been raised from the dead in order that we may bear fruit for God.

[5] While we were living in the flesh, our sinful passions, aroused by the law, were at work in our members to bear fruit for death.

[6] But now we are discharged from the law, dead to that which held us captive, so that we are slaves not under the old written code but in the new life of the Spirit.

[7] What then should we say? That the law is sin? By no means! Yet, if it had not been for the law, I would not have known sin. I would not have known what it is to covet if the law had not said, "You shall not covet."

[8] But sin, seizing an opportunity in the commandment, produced in me all kinds of covetousness. Apart from the law sin lies dead.

[9] I was once alive apart from the law, but when the commandment came, sin revived

[10] and I died, and the very commandment that promised life proved to be death to me.

[11] For sin, seizing an opportunity in the commandment, deceived me and through it killed me.

[12] So the law is holy, and the commandment is holy and just and good.

[13] Did what is good, then, bring death to me? By no means! It was sin, working death in me through what is good, in order that sin might be shown to be sin, and through the commandment might become sinful beyond measure.

[14] For we know that the law is spiritual; but I am of the flesh, sold into slavery under sin.

[15] I do not understand my own actions. For I do not do what I want, but I do the very thing I hate.

[16] Now if I do what I do not want, I agree that the law is good.

[17] But in fact it is no longer I that do it, but sin that dwells within me.

¹⁸ For I know that nothing good dwells within me, that is, in my flesh. I can will what is right, but I cannot do it.

¹⁹ For I do not do the good I want, but the evil I do not want is what I do.

²⁰ Now if I do what I do not want, it is no longer I that do it, but sin that dwells within me.

²¹ So I find it to be a law that when I want to do what is good, evil lies close at hand.

²² For I delight in the law of God in my inmost self,

²³ but I see in my members another law at war with the law of my mind, making me captive to the law of sin that dwells in my members.

²⁴ Wretched man that I am! Who will rescue me from this body of death?

²⁵ Thanks be to God through Jesus Christ our Lord! So then, with my mind I am a slave to the law of God, but with my flesh I am a slave to the law of sin.

QUESTIONS FOR ANALYSIS AND DISCUSSION

1. Are the Ten Commandments a plausible framework for pursuing the good life? Is it possible to accept some Commandments while discarding others in order to outline a basic ethic?

2. Can any of the moral lessons in the Bible be the basis for a social morality without the general belief in the existence of God? Which arguments support an affirmative answer to this question? Could the believer in God offer a rejoinder about the futility of an ethics without God? Develop your response.

3. Briefly consider the "why be moral" question from a Biblical perspective. To what extent does it contrast with the sociobiologist or cultural relativist approach? Be specific.

4. Suppose someone says that morality is largely a matter of respecting an authority that tells us what to do. Further, the authority has goals in mind that are too great for individuals to understand; hence, part of being a moral person is to obey without expecting to understand. From these assumptions, is it reasonable to propose that God, genes, and culture are different names for the same kind of moral authority? That is, we follow the authority's rules even though we do not fully understand them.

5. A political movement is emerging in California to place the Ten Commandments in the halls and rooms of public schools. Proponents say that this does not violate the separation of church and state specified in the Constitution. Moreover, reminding people of the Commandments will contribute to moral education and increase moral conduct. Imagine the Ten Commandments being placed in your high school or on the front door of your college classroom. Do you think this would improve moral conduct? Explain your response.

7.

CHUANG TZU

Let It Be: Meditations on Tao and Freedom

Little is known of the personal life of Chuang Tzu (c. 350 B.C.). He was a voluminous and widely respected writer who was more than a disciple of Taoism; he was a philosopher in his own manner. He wrote using a variety of resources, including parables and humor. As some of the following selections indicate, Chuang Tzu's view of the good life takes a different twist on human suffering and injustice. To catch the subtleties of his writing, a careful reading is recommended.

CRITICAL READING QUESTIONS

1. What is the context for Chuang Tzu's phrase, "Let it be! Let it be!"?
2. Why does the Invocator of the Ancestors ask himself, "I wonder why I look at things differently from a pig"?
3. In the story about Yen Ho, who is tutoring the unvirtuous prince? Why are animals such as a praying mantis, tiger, and horse introduced?
4. What is the relation between action and happiness?

Master Tung-kuo asked Chuang Tzu, "This thing called the Way—where does it exist?"

Chuang Tzu said, "There's no place it doesn't exist."

"Come," said Master Tung-kuo, "you must be more specific!"

"It is in the ant."

"As low a thing as that?"

"It is in the panic grass."

"But that's lower still!"

"It is in the tiles and shards."

"How can it be so low?"

"It is in the piss and dung."

"Let It Be: Meditations on Tao and Freedom," from *Chuang Tzu: Basic Writings*, translated by Burton Watson (New York: Columbia University Press, 1969), pp. 16, 31–38, 58–61, 111–114. Some notes have been omitted.

The Invocator of the Ancestors, dressed in his black, square-cut robes, peered into the pigpen and said, "Why should you object to dying? I'm going to fatten you for three months, practice austerities for ten days, fast for three days, spread the white rushes, and lay your shoulders and rump on the carved sacrificial stand—you'll go along with that, won't you? True, if I were planning things from the point of view of a pig, I'd say it would be better to eat chaff and bran and stay right there in the pen. But if I were planning for myself, I'd say that if I could be honored as a high official while I lived, and get to ride in a fine hearse and lie among the feathers and trappings when I died, I'd go along with that. Speaking for the pig, I'd give such a life a flat refusal, but speaking for myself, I'd certainly accept. I wonder why I look at things differently from a pig."

Discussion on Making All Things Equal
(Section 2)

Tzu-ch'i of South Wall sat leaning on his armrest, staring up at the sky and breathing—vacant and far away, as though he'd lost his companion.[1] Yen Ch'eng Tzu-yu, who was standing by his side in attendance, said, "What is this? Can you really make the body like a withered tree and the mind like dead ashes? The man leaning on the armrest now is not the one who leaned on it before!"

Tzu-ch'i said, "You do well to ask the question, Yen. Now I have lost myself. Do you understand that? You hear the piping of men, but you haven't heard the piping of earth. Or if you've heard the piping of earth, you haven't heard the piping of Heaven!"

Tzu-yu said, "May I venture to ask what this means?"

Tzu-ch'i said, "The Great Clod belches out breath and its name is wind. So long as it doesn't come forth, nothing happens. But when it does, then ten thousand hollows begin crying wildly. Can't you hear them, long drawn out? In the mountain forests that lash and sway, there are huge trees a hundred spans around with hollows and openings like noses, like mouths, like ears, like jugs, like cups, like mortars, like rifts, like ruts. They roar like waves, whistle like arrows, screech, gasp, cry, wail, moan, and howl, those in the lead calling out *yeee!*, those behind calling out *yuuu!* In a gentle breeze they answer faintly, but in a full gale the chorus is gigantic. And when the fierce wind has passed on, then all the hollows are empty again. Have you never seen the tossing and trembling that goes on?"

Tzu-yu said, "By the piping of earth, then, you mean simply [the sound of] these hollows, and by the piping of man [the sound of] flutes and whistles. But may I ask about the piping of Heaven?"

---

[1] The word "companion" is interpreted variously to mean his associates, his wife, or his own body.

Tzu-ch'i said, "Blowing on the ten thousand things in a different way, so that each can be itself—all take what they want for themselves, but who does the sounding?"[2]

Great understanding is broad and unhurried; little understanding is cramped and busy. Great words are clear and limpid; little words are shrill and quarrelsome. In sleep, men's spirits go visiting; in waking hours, their bodies hustle. With everything they meet they become entangled. Day after day they use their minds in strife, sometimes grandiose, sometimes sly, sometimes petty. Their little fears are mean and trembly; their great fears are stunned and overwhelming. They bound off like an arrow or a crossbow pellet, certain that they are the arbiters of right and wrong. They cling to their position as though they had sworn before the gods, sure that they are holding on to victory. They fade like fall and winter—such is the way they dwindle day by day. They drown in what they do—you cannot make them turn back. They grow dark, as though sealed with seals—such are the excesses of their old age. And when their minds draw near to death, nothing can restore them to the light.

Joy, anger, grief, delight, worry, regret, fickleness, inflexibility, modesty, willfulness, candor, insolence—music from empty holes, mushrooms springing up in dampness, day and night replacing each other before us, and no one knows where they sprout from. Let it be! Let it be! [It is enough that] morning and evening we have them, and they are the means by which we live. Without them we would not exist; without us they would have nothing to take hold of. This comes close to the matter. But I do not know what makes them the way they are. It would seem as though they have some True Master, and yet I find no trace of him. He can act—that is certain. Yet I cannot see his form. He has identity but no form.

The hundred joints, the nine openings, the six organs, all come together and exist here [as my body]. But which part should I feel closest to? I should delight in all parts, you say? But there must be one I ought to favor more. If not, are they all of them mere servants? But if they are all servants, then how can they keep order among themselves? Or do they take turns being lord and servant? It would seem as though there must be some True Lord among them. But whether I succeed in discovering his identity or not, it neither adds to nor detracts from his Truth.

Once a man receives this fixed bodily form, he holds on to it, waiting for the end. Sometimes clashing with things, sometimes bending before them, he runs his course like a galloping steed, and nothing can stop him. Is he not pathetic? Sweating and laboring to the end of his days and never seeing his accomplishment, utterly exhausting himself and never knowing where to look for rest—can you help pitying him? I'm not dead yet! he says, but what good is that? His body decays, his mind follows it—can you deny that this is a great sorrow? Man's life has always been a muddle like this. How could I be the only muddled one, and other men not muddled?

If a man follows the mind given him and makes it his teacher, then who can be without a teacher? Why must you comprehend the process of change and form

---

[2] Heaven is not something distinct from earth and man, but a name applied to the natural and spontaneous functioning of the two.

your mind on that basis before you can have a teacher? Even an idiot has his teacher. But to fail to abide by this mind and still insist upon your rights and wrongs—this is like saying that you set off for Yüeh today and got there yesterday. This is to claim that what doesn't exist exists. If you claim that what doesn't exist exists, then even the holy sage Yü couldn't understand you, much less a person like me!

Words are not just wind. Words have something to say. But if what they have to say is not fixed, then do they really say something? Or do they say nothing? People suppose that words are different from the peeps of baby birds, but is there any difference, or isn't there? What does the Way rely upon,[3] that we have true and false? What do words rely upon, that we have right and wrong? How can the Way go away and not exist? How can words exist and not be acceptable? When the Way relies on little accomplishments and words rely on vain show, then we have the rights and wrongs of the Confucians and the Mo-ists. What one calls right the other calls wrong; what one calls wrong the other calls right. But if we want to right their wrongs and wrong their rights, then the best thing to use is clarity.

Everything has its "that," everything has its "this." From the point of view of "that" you cannot see it, but through understanding you can know it. So I say, "that" comes out of "this" and "this" depends on "that"—which is to say that "this" and "that" give birth to each other. But where there is birth there must be death; where there is death there must be birth. Where there is acceptability there must be unacceptability; where there is unacceptability there must be acceptability. Where there is recognition of right there must be recognition of wrong; where there is recognition of wrong there must be recognition of right. Therefore the sage does not proceed in such a way, but illuminates all in the light of Heaven.[4] He too recognizes a "this," but a "this" which is also "that," a "that" which is also "this." His "that" has both a right and a wrong in it; his "this" too has both a right and a wrong in it. So, in fact, does he still have a "this" and "that"? Or does he in fact no longer have a "this" and "that"? A state in which "this" and "that" no longer find their opposites is called the hinge of the Way. When the hinge is fitted into the socket, it can respond endlessly. Its right then is a single endlessness and its wrong too is a single endlessness. So I say, the best thing to use is clarity.

To use an attribute to show that attributes are not attributes is not as good as using a nonattribute to show that attributes are not attributes. To use a horse to show that a horse is not a horse is not as good as using a non-horse to show that a horse is not a horse, Heaven and earth are one attribute; the ten thousand things are one horse.

What is acceptable we call acceptable; what is unacceptable we call unacceptable. A road is made by people walking on it; things are so because they are called so. What makes them so? Making them so makes them so. What makes them not so? Making them not so makes them not so. Things all must have that which is so;

---

[3] Following the interpretation of Chang Ping-lin. The older interpretation of *yin* here and in the following sentences is, "What is the Way hidden by," etc.

[4] *T'ien,* which for Chuang Tzu means Nature or the Way.

things all must have that which is acceptable. There is nothing that is not so, nothing that is not acceptable.

For this reason, whether you point to a little stalk or a great pillar, a leper or the beautiful Hsi-shih, things ribald and shady or things grotesque and strange, the Way makes them all into one. Their dividedness is their completeness; their completeness is their impairment. No thing is either complete or impaired, but all are made into one again. Only the man of far-reaching vision knows how to make them into one. So he has no use [for categories], but relegates all to the constant. The constant is the useful; the useful is the passable; the passable is the successful; and with success, all is accomplished. He relies upon this alone, relies upon it and does not know he is doing so. This is called the Way.

But to wear out your brain trying to make things into one without realizing that they are all the same—this is called "three in the morning." What do I mean by "three in the morning"? When the monkey trainer was handing out acorns, he said, "You get three in the morning and four at night." This made all the monkeys furious. "Well, then," he said, "you get four in the morning and three at night." The monkeys were all delighted. There was no change in the reality behind the words, and yet the monkeys responded with joy and anger. Let them, if they want to. So the sage harmonizes with both right and wrong and rests in Heaven the Equalizer. This is called walking two roads. . . .

Supreme Happiness
(Section 18)

Is there such a thing as supreme happiness in the world or isn't there? Is there some way to keep yourself alive or isn't there? What to do, what to rely on, what to avoid, what to stick by, what to follow, what to leave alone, what to find happiness in, what to hate?

This is what the world honors: wealth, eminence, long life, a good name. This is what the world finds happiness in: a life of ease, rich food, fine clothes, beautiful sights, sweet sounds. This is what it looks down on: poverty, meanness, early death, a bad name. This is what it finds bitter: a life that knows no rest, a mouth that gets no rich food, no fine clothes for the body, no beautiful sights for the eye, no sweet sounds for the ear.

People who can't get these things fret a great deal and are afraid—this is a stupid way to treat the body. People who are rich wear themselves out rushing around on business, piling up more wealth than they could ever use—this is a superficial way to treat the body. People who are eminent spend night and day scheming and wondering if they are doing right—this is a shoddy way to treat the body. Man lives his life in company with worry, and if he lives a long while, till he's dull and doddering, then he has spent that much time worrying instead of dying, a bitter lot indeed! This is a callous way to treat the body.

Men of ardor are regarded by the world as good, but their goodness doesn't succeed in keeping them alive. So I don't know whether their goodness is really good or not. Perhaps I think it's good—but not good enough to save their lives. Perhaps I think it's no good—but still good enough to save the lives of others. So I say, if your loyal advice isn't heeded, give way and do not wrangle. Tzu-hsü wrangled and lost his body.[1] But if he hadn't wrangled, he wouldn't have made a name. Is there really such a thing as goodness or isn't there?

What ordinary people do and what they find happiness in—I don't know whether such happiness is in the end really happiness or not. I look at what ordinary people find happiness in, what they all make a mad dash for, racing around as though they couldn't stop—they all say they're happy with it. I'm not happy with it and I'm not unhappy with it. In the end is there really happiness or isn't there?

I take inaction to be true happiness, but ordinary people think it is a bitter thing. I say: the highest happiness has no happiness, the highest praise has no praise. The world can't decide what is right and what is wrong. And yet inaction can decide this. The highest happiness, keeping alive—only inaction gets you close to this!

Let me try putting it this way. The inaction of Heaven is its purity, the inaction of earth is its peace. So the two inactions combine and all things are transformed and brought to birth. Wonderfully, mysteriously, there is no place they come out of. Mysteriously, wonderfully, they have no sign. Each thing minds its business and all grow up out of inaction. So I say, Heaven and earth do nothing and there is nothing that is not done. Among men, who can get hold of this inaction?

Yen Ho, who had been appointed tutor to the crown prince, son of Duke Ling of Wei, went to consult Chü Po-yü.[2] "Here is this man who by nature is lacking in virtue. If I let him go on with his unruliness I will endanger the state. If I try to impose some rule on him, I will endanger myself. He knows enough to recognize the faults of others, but he doesn't know his own faults. What can I do with a man like this?"

"A very good question," said Chü Po-yü. "Be careful, be on your guard, and make sure that you yourself are in the right! In your actions it is best to follow along with him, and in your mind it is best to harmonize with him. However, these two courses involve certain dangers. Though you follow along, you don't want to be pulled into his doings, and though you harmonize, you don't want to be drawn out too far. If in your actions you follow along to the extent of being pulled in with him, then you will be overthrown, destroyed, wiped out, and brought to your knees. If in your mind you harmonize to the extent of being drawn out, then you will be talked about, named, blamed, and condemned. If he wants to be a child, be a child with him. If he wants to follow erratic ways, follow erratic ways with him.

[1] Wu Tzu-hsü, minister to the king of Wu, repeatedly warned the king of the danger of attack from the state of Yüeh. He finally aroused the king's ire and suspicion and was forced to commit suicide in 484 B.C.

[2] Yen Ho was a scholar of Lu, Chü Po-yü a minister of Wei. The crown prince is the notorious K'uai-k'uei, who was forced to flee from Wei because he plotted to kill his mother. He reentered the state and seized the throne from his son in 481 B.C.

If he wants to be reckless, be reckless with him. Understand him thoroughly, and lead him to the point where he is without fault.

"Don't you know about the praying mantis that waved its arms angrily in front of an approaching carriage, unaware that they were incapable of stopping it? Such was the high opinion it had of its talents. Be careful, be on your guard! If you offend him by parading your store of talents, you will be in danger!

"Don't you know how the tiger trainer goes about it? He doesn't dare give the tiger any living thing to eat for fear it will learn the taste of fury by killing it. He doesn't dare give it any whole thing to eat for fear it will learn the taste of fury by tearing it apart. He gauges the state of the tiger's appetite and thoroughly understands its fierce disposition. Tigers are a different breed from men, and yet you can train them to be gentle with their keepers by following along with them. The men who get killed are the ones who go against them.

"The horse lover will use a fine box to catch the dung and a giant clam shell to catch the stale. But if a mosquito or a fly lights on the horse and he slaps it at the wrong time, then the horse will break the bit, hurt its head, and bang its chest. The horse lover tries to think of everything, but his affection leads him into error. Can you afford to be careless?"

⚜ ⚜ ⚜

"The fish trap exists because of the fish; once you've gotten the fish, you can forget the trap. The rabbit snare exists because of the rabbit; once you've gotten the rabbit, you can forget the snare. Words exist because of meaning; once you've gotten the meaning, you can forget the words. Where can I find a man who has forgotten words so I can have a word with him?"

QUESTIONS FOR ANALYSIS AND DISCUSSION

1. Chuang Tzu emphasizes the importance of clarity, even though many of his points are made through riddles. Do you find this inconsistent? Do you think the riddles express their points clearly? Identify a passage that supports your view.

2. Does the belief about changing one's attitude toward suffering rather than changing the causes of suffering indicate a passive or indifferent ethic? Or does it call for a radical and dynamic shift in one's understanding of the world and oneself? Cite passages that highlight your viewpoint.

3. Chuang Tzu avoids giving a list of rules or laws to govern conduct. In light of the discussion about cultural folkways, laws of genetic behavior, or religious commandments, does his approach offer stronger or weaker reasons for trying to be moral?

8.

HARRY BROWNE

The Unselfishness Trap

A popular journalist and third-party presidential candidate in 1996, Harry Browne
(b. 1933) is widely known for his incisive critiques of the do-gooders of the world. For
him they appear in numerous forms, from religious networks to Good Samaritans to over-
bearing governments. Although do-gooders seem to have decent motives in helping other
people, Browne suggests that they actually threaten—and even do—much harm. Tradi-
tional moralists want everyone to be good for altruistic reasons. When we are not altruis-
tic, we are accused of being selfish, sinful, or unjust. In a word, the moralists set up a
guilt trap. Browne rebuts conventional moralists by charging them with an insincere and
impractical sense of helping people be happy. The best way to ensure worldly happiness is
to let individuals do what they think is in their own self-interest. Ethical egoism is both a
more honest and a more productive ethic.

CRITICAL READING QUESTIONS

1. What is Browne's point in raising the red ball analogy?
2. Why does Browne express suspicion rather than gratitude when a neighbor offers some fresh baked goodies to her new neighbor?
3. How does Browne relate self-knowledge to self-interest?
4. What is meant by egoism?

The Unselfishness Trap is the belief that you must put the happiness of others ahead of your own.

Unselfishness is a very popular ideal, one that's been honored throughout recorded history. Wherever you turn, you find encouragement to put the happiness of others ahead of your own—to do what's best for the world, not for yourself.

If the ideal is sound, there must be something unworthy in seeking to live your life as you want to live it.

"The Unselfishness Trap," from *How I Found Freedom in an Unfree World* (New York: Macmillan, 1973), pp. 451–457.

So perhaps we should look more closely at the subject—to see if the ideal *is* sound. For if you attempt to be free, we can assume that someone's going to consider that to be selfish.

. . .[E]ach person always acts in ways he believes will make him feel good or will remove discomfort from his life. Because everyone is different from everyone else, each individual goes about it in his own way.

One man devotes his life to helping the poor. Another one lies and steals. Still another person tries to create better products and services for which he hopes to be paid handsomely. One woman devotes herself to her husband and children. Another one seeks a career as a singer.

In every case, the ultimate motivation has been the same. Each person is doing what *he* believes will assure his happiness. What varies between them is the *means* each has chosen to gain his happiness.

We could divide them into two groups labeled "selfish" and "unselfish," but I don't think that would prove anything. For the thief and the humanitarian each have the same motive—to do what he believes will make him feel good.

In fact, we can't avoid a very significant conclusion: *Everyone is selfish.* Selfishness isn't really an issue, because everyone selfishly seeks his own happiness.

What we need to examine, however, are the means various people choose to achieve their happiness. Unfortunately, some people oversimplify the matter by assuming that there are only two basic means; sacrifice yourself for others or make them sacrifice for you. Happily, there's a third way that can produce better consequences than either of those two.

A Better World?

Let's look first at the ideal of living for the benefit of others. It's often said that it would be a better world if everyone were unselfish. But would it be?

If it were somehow possible for everyone to give up his own happiness, what would be the result? Let's carry it to its logical conclusion and see what we find.

To visualize it, let's imagine that happiness is symbolized by a big red rubber ball. I have the ball in my hands—meaning that I hold the ability to be happy. But since I'm not going to be selfish, I quickly pass the ball to you. I've given up my happiness for you.

What will you do? Since you're not selfish either, you won't keep the ball; you'll quickly pass it on to your next-door neighbor. But he doesn't want to be selfish either, so he passes it to his wife, who likewise gives it to her children.

The children have been taught the virtue of unselfishness, so they pass it to playmates, who pass it to parents, who pass it to neighbors, and on and on and on.

I think we can stop the analogy at this point and ask what's been accomplished by all this effort. Who's better off for these demonstrations of pure unselfishness?

How would it be a better world if everyone acted that way? Whom would we be unselfish for? There would have to be a selfish person who would receive, accept, and enjoy the benefits of our unselfishness for there to be any purpose to it. But that selfish person (the object of our generosity) would be living by lower standards than we do.

For a more practical example, what is achieved by the parent who "sacrifices" himself for his children, who in turn are expected to sacrifice themselves for *their* children, etc.? The unselfishness concept is a merry-go-round that has no ultimate purpose. No one's self-interest is enhanced by the continual relaying of gifts from one person to another to another.

Perhaps most people have never carried the concept of unselfishness to this logical conclusion. If they did, they might reconsider their pleas for an unselfish world.

Negative Choices

But, unfortunately, the pleas continue, and they're a very real part of your life. In seeking your own freedom and happiness, you have to deal with those who tell you that you shouldn't put yourself first. That creates a situation in which you're pressured to act negatively—to put aside your plans and desires in order to avoid the condemnation of others.

As I've said before, one of the characteristics of a free man is that he's usually choosing positively—deciding which of several alternatives would make him the happiest; while the average person, most of the time, is choosing which of two or three alternatives will cause him the least discomfort.

When the reason for your actions is to avoid being called "selfish" you're making a negative decision and thereby restricting the possibilities for your own happiness.

You're in the Unselfishness Trap if you regretfully pay for your aunt's surgery with the money you'd saved for a new car, or if you sadly give up the vacation you'd looked forward to in order to help a sick neighbor.

You're in the trap if you feel you're *required* to give part of your income to the poor, or if you think that your country, community, or family has first claim on your time, energy, or money.

You're in the Unselfishness Trap any time you make negative choices that are designed to avoid being called "selfish."

It isn't that no one else is important. You might have a self-interest in someone's well-being, and giving a gift can be a gratifying expression of the affection you feel for him. But you're in the trap if you do such things in order to appear unselfish.

Helping Others

There *is* an understandable urge to give to those who are important and close to you. However, that leads many people to think that indiscriminate giving is the key to one's own happiness. They say that the way to be happy is to make others happy; get your glow by basking in the glow you've created for someone else.

It's important to identify that as a personal opinion. If someone says that giving is the key to happiness, isn't he saying that's the key to *his* happiness?

I think we can carry the question further, however, and determine how efficient such a policy might be. The suggestion to be a giver presupposes that you're able to judge what will make someone else happy. And experience has taught me to be a bit humble about assuming what makes others happy.

My landlady once brought me a piece of her freshly baked cake because she wanted to do me a favor. Unfortunately, it happened to be a kind of cake that was distasteful to me. I won't try to describe the various ways I tried to get the cake plate back to her without being confronted with a request for my judgment of her cake. It's sufficient to say that her well-intentioned favor interfered with my own plans.

And now, whenever I'm sure I know what someone else "needs," I remember that incident and back off a little. There's no way that one person can read the mind of another to know all his plans, goals, and tastes.

You may know a great deal about the desires of your intimate friends. But *indiscriminate* gift-giving and favor-doing is usually a waste of resources—or, worse, it can upset the well-laid plans of the receiver.

When you give to someone else, you might provide something he values—but probably not the thing he considers most important. If you expend those resources for *yourself,* you automatically devote them to what you consider to be most important. The time or money you've spent will most likely create more happiness that way.

If your purpose is to make someone happy, you're most apt to succeed if you make yourself the object. You'll never know another person more than a fraction as well as you can know yourself.

Do you want to make someone happy? Go to it—use your talents and your insight and benevolence to bestow riches of happiness upon the one person you understand well enough to do it efficiently—yourself. I guarantee that you'll get more genuine appreciation from yourself than from anyone else.

Give to you.

Support your local self.

Alternatives

. . .[I]t's too often assumed that there are only two alternatives: (1) sacrifice your interests for the benefit of others; or (2) make others sacrifice their interests for you. If nothing else were possible, it would indeed be a grim world.

Fortunately, there's more to the world than that. Because desires vary from person to person, it's possible to create exchanges between individuals in which both parties benefit.

For example, if you buy a house, you do so because you'd rather have the house than the money involved. But the seller's desire is different—he'd rather have the money than the house. When the sale is completed, each of you has received something of greater value than what you gave up—otherwise you wouldn't have entered the exchange. Who, then, has had to sacrifice for the other?

In the same way, your daily life is made up of dozens of such exchanges—small and large transactions in which each party gets something he values more than what he gives up. The exchange doesn't have to involve money; you may be spending time, attention, or effort in exchange for something you value.

Mutually beneficial relationships are possible when desires are compatible. Sometimes the desires are the same—like going to a movie together. Sometimes the desires are different—like trading your money for someone's house. In either case, it's the *compatibility* of the desires that makes the exchange possible.

No sacrifice is necessary when desires are compatible. So it makes sense to seek out people with whom you can have mutually beneficial relationships.

Often the "unselfishness" issue arises only because two people with nothing in common are trying to get along together—such as a man who likes bowling and hates opera married to a woman whose tastes are the opposite. If they're to do things together, one must "sacrifice" his pleasure for the other. So each might try to encourage the other to be "unselfish."

If they were compatible, the issue wouldn't arise because each would be pleasing the other by doing what was in his own self-interest.

An efficiently selfish person *is* sensitive to the needs and desires of others. But he doesn't consider those desires to be demands upon him. Rather, he sees them as *opportunities*—potential exchanges that might be beneficial to him. He identifies desires in others so that he can decide if exchanges with them will help him get what he wants.

He doesn't sacrifice himself for others, nor does he expect others to be sacrificed for him. He takes the third alternative—he finds relationships that are mutually beneficial so that no sacrifice is required.

Please Yourself

Everyone is selfish; everyone is doing what he believes will make himself happier. The recognition of that can take most of the sting out of accusations that you're being "selfish." Why should you feel guilty for seeking your own happiness when that's what everyone else is doing, too?

The demand that you be unselfish can be motivated by any number of reasons: that you'd help create a better world, that you have a moral obligation to be unselfish, that you give up your happiness to the selfishness of someone else, or that the person demanding it has just never thought it out.

Whatever the reason, you're not likely to convince such a person to stop his demands. But it will create much less pressure on you if you realize that it's *his* selfish reason. And you can eliminate the problem entirely by looking for more compatible companions.

To find constant, profound happiness requires that you be free to seek the gratification of your own desires. It means making positive choices.

If you slip into the Unselfishness Trap, you'll spend a good part of your time making negative choices—trying to avoid the censure of those who tell you not to think of yourself. You won't have time to be free.

If someone finds happiness by doing "good works" for others, let him. That doesn't mean that's the best way for you to find happiness.

And when someone accuses you of being selfish, just remember that he's only upset because you aren't doing what *he* selfishly wants you to do.

QUESTIONS FOR ANALYSIS AND DISCUSSION

1. Analogies are often used to clarify or justify an uncertain idea. Do you think Browne's analogy about playing with a ball accomplishes his purpose? Why, or why not?

2. Browne's emphasis on self-interest and the sociobiology theory of the selfish gene seem to have much in common at first glance. Do you think they are in fundamental agreement about why we should be moral? Explain your response.

3. Browne claims that he is largely admitting an obvious fact: Everyone is selfish. From this a corollary is acknowledged: Altruistic conduct is actually self-interest in a less obvious form. Do you agree? Can you think of examples of persons or deeds that have only the well-being of others in mind? Would these examples be enough to refute Browne's position? Why, or why not?

9.

NEL NODDINGS

Relational Virtues

Nel Noddings (b. 1929), a theorist on education and author of numerous works on moral pedagogy, is one of the early and best-known proponents of the care ethic (see her selection in Chapter 8). Here she outlines a rejoinder to ethical egoists. Their first mistake, according to Noddings, is to conceive of human life as primarily a self-or-other proposition. In fact, our original experiences do not arise out of isolated self-interest but out of relationships. An ethic that recognizes this will focus on values and principles much differently from an ethic that assumes the primary experience to be individualistic.

CRITICAL READING QUESTIONS

1. How does Noddings define "relational ontology"?
2. What is the relation between a relational virtue and a relational task?
3. Who does Noddings nominate for weak or strong moral role models, and why?

"Relational Virtues," from *Women and Evil* (Berkeley: University of California Press, 1989), pp. 236–241. Notes have been omitted.

Now I want to say more about the transformation of relation that can be accomplished through the two kinds of changes that seem feasible, and I want to show how this transformation can lead in the direction of revolutionary change. Again there are tasks for both philosophers and educators.

. . .Women have for centuries been defined in relation—Dan's wife, Johnny's mother, Bill's daughter—and the health and stability of relations have been matters of survival for us. As this old pattern changes and women begin to define themselves in the public world, there is a real danger that we will lose the strengths of relational thinking. This is why educators must provide the kinds of experience that may promote relational thinking and philosophers must explore the underpinnings of relational thinking in relational ontologies.

An ethic of caring is based on a relational ontology; that is, it takes as a basic assumption that all human beings—not just women—are defined in relation. It is not just that *I* as a preformed continuous individual enter *into* relations; rather, the *I* of which we speak *so* easily is itself a relational entity. *I* really am defined by the set of relations into which my physical self has been thrown. This is not to adopt a total determinism, because *relation* involves affective response in each of the emerging entities, and this response is at least partly under the control of the present occupants of the relation. We cannot escape our relational condition, but we can reflect on it, evaluate it, move it in a direction we find good. We are neither totally free and separate in our affective and volitional lives, as many existentialists would have us believe, nor totally determined by the physical conditions of our past.

Caring is not an individual virtue, although certain virtues may help sustain it. Rather, caring is a relational state or quality, and it requires distinctive contributions from carer and cared for. A relation may deteriorate either because no one takes *care*—that is, attends to the messages and needs of the other—or because there is no response from the cared for. When either party rivets attention on himself or herself, for example, as the self-sacrificial and virtuous carer, a pathological condition arises. A child may be smothered, for example, by a woman who "lives" for her children; such a woman sees only her contribution to the relation. In general, pathologies of caring, whether public or private, manifest themselves in actual helplessness or feelings of helplessness in those "cared for."

Relational virtues are of two kinds: virtues that belong to the relation itself and individual virtues that enhance relations. Caring, friendship, companionship, and empathy are of the first kind, although they are not discrete. The task of philosophers with respect to this class of relational virtues is to describe the contributions of each member of the relation, the conditions under which the relation develops positively or negatively, and the place of such virtues with respect to individual virtues and vices. The task of educators is to encourage the actual growth of relational virtues, to explore relational themes in literature and history, and to establish learning conditions that permit people to contribute to their own relational growth.

Closely related to relational virtues are relational tasks. Teaching, parenting, advising, mediating, and helping are all relational tasks. Their success depends not only on the goodwill, sensitivity, and skills of the more powerful member of the relation, but also on the goodwill, skills, and responsiveness of the less powerful member. It is ridiculous to study any of these relational tasks by focusing only on the teacher, parent, adviser, mediator, or helper. Research that radically separates teacher and student into treatments and outcomes inadvertently ratifies the evils of separation and helplessness. It supposes that something the teacher-as-treatment does causes a particular effect in a class of students.Even in studies that acknowledge an interaction between what the teacher does and what particular students are capable of doing, we find the same defect. There is no way to account for the obvious fact that teaching-learning is relational, not just interactive. A student may do better, achieve more, out of love for his or her teacher (or out of hate), out of rivalry with another student (or as a result of helping another student), or out of understanding a concept (or catching on to the awful truth that understanding is irrelevant). Clearly, achieving a slightly higher grade on some test may be something to rejoice over, something to deplore, or something to safely ignore. It tells us nothing about the student's likely contribution to good or evil in the world.

The second class of relational virtues is the set of individual virtues that contributes to the quality of relations. Schools have always attended to the so-called virtues of character. Early in this century the Character Development League published *Character Lessons in American Biography,* a guide to character education for use in "public schools and home instruction." It extolled, grade by grade, the traits of obedience, honesty, truthfulness, unselfishness, sympathy, consecration to duty, usefulness, industry, perseverance, patience, self-respect, purity, self-control, fortitude, courage, heroism, contentment, ambition, temperance, courtesy, comradeship, amiability, kindness to animals, justice, habits, fidelity, determination, imagination, hopefulness, patriotism, and character—the last established by the practice of the preceding "principles of morality." I have taken the trouble to reproduce the entire list because it illustrates vividly the task we need to undertake. Almost every trait on the list needs analysis from the relational perspective. *Character Lessons* introduces fidelity, for example, as "an essential in crystallizing habits"—as a virtue students should cultivate in connection to principles, not in connection to persons and relations. These meanings are not, of course, entirely separate. One may cultivate a habit faithfully out of genuine concern for others, but the focus of such fidelity is still oneself and one's status with respect to a principle. The point is that almost every virtue has a dark side that we must examine in the context of relation.

Not only should schools teach the relational nature of virtue thematically and directly, but they should also approach conflicts and disputes relationally. In studying past and present conflicts, such as those between the Israelis and the Palestinians, the Sandinistas and the contras, and Iran and Iraq, a relational perspective should be enlightening. Students need not take sides or decide who is right. Their task should be to study the problem with questions of reconciliation as a guide. How can these people come together to live in peace? Students are not, of course, in a position to effect the policies they might create in response to such a question, but both their present learning and their future attitudes may be deeply affected as a result.

Some may object that a study plan of this sort induces a lack of commitment. After all, is not one side usually more right than the other? Should we not commit ourselves to standing by those nations and groups that share our principles? The answer to this objection is to stop thinking in terms of a zero-sum game, in terms of either/or. We should stand by both parties. We should stand sympathetically between the apparently evil and the apparently good and work toward reconciliation. The naive temptation, as we have seen, is to attribute good qualities to our allies and monstrous ones to our opponents. We see this inclination regularly even at the highest levels of government. But an opposite danger also arises. During the Vietnam War many intellectuals rejected the naive temptation. They saw clearly that the United States was supporting a repressive regime and that their own government was committing shameful deeds. This realization led some to suppose that the other side must be right. (Someone must be right, and if our side is wrong, then . . .)

Thinking in oppositional terms supports partisanship and reduces the likelihood of reconciliation. Further, it makes the development of beneficent patriotism very difficult. Intelligent students are often disillusioned and make the mistake noted above, namely, that their own government is totally wrong. Those exposed to little inquiry and critical thinking embrace a simplistic version of chauvinistic patriotism. Careful study from a relational perspective should reveal both strengths and weaknesses in the nation's past activities and present policies. There are things of which American citizens can be proud. That more people want to enter the United States than to leave it is something to be proud of. We can be proud also of our unfortified borders. The economic hegemony that reduces the need for border fortification should be a matter of far less pride. The point is that identifying and analyzing faults in ourselves or in our friends should not lead to abandonment and betrayal but to a deeper appreciation of how hard it is to avoid evil and a greater sense of affiliation with those we might otherwise label enemies.

In the relational study of conflict the parties should be allowed as nearly as possible to speak in their own voices. Textbooks generally reduce the discussion of conflict to an abstract recital of "facts." Sometimes they attempt to present a balanced picture, but the passion of genuine conflict dissolves in the bland language of an impartial recorder. The relational perspective demands restoration of the aggrieved voices. We should hear the hate, fear, terror, cruelty, and all the excesses that accompany conflict in their most eloquent expressions. When we *live* with warring parties, we often find it hard to take sides. What we want to do is to stop the suffering, to explain each side to the other, to mediate. For women "to mediate" does not mean to decide who is right and what the loser should pay to the winner; it means to bring together, to reconcile. We do not expect all the good deeds to be on one side and all the monstrous ones on the other.

Adopting a relational approach is in itself a form of deep commitment. It signifies that we care enough about each other to learn more about human relations. Clearly it will also identify new models of relations and individual behavior for special attention and emulation. Moderation in the pursuit of wealth would, for example, become an admirable trait. Some time ago the nightly news reported a survey of the "heroes" teachers selected to present to their students. Several teachers selected Lee Iacocca. Why? Because, they said, his success proves that a person can make it in this country by striving. A far better model from the relational perspective would be Atticus Finch, the small-town lawyer and wonderful father in *To Kill a Mockingbird*. In Atticus (so addressed even by his children) we find a model of steady integrity, of fidelity to persons—both to his children and to the innocent black man he was assigned to defend—of reasonable contentment with ordinary life and its achievable dignity. Atticus did not admire great wealth. Great personal wealth can no longer be a criterion of health and success; pursuing it must be seen as a sign of sickness in the individual and in the society that encourages such pursuit.

Educational efforts to encourage moderation are essential. States can redistribute wealth by force and adopt ideologies to justify the redistribution. But unless people understand and admire moderation as a relational virtue, their longing to contend, surpass, and prove themselves superior to others will result in behavior very like the pursuit of wealth. Power or fame may substitute for wealth. Before people can safely emerge from oppression they must have models of moderation, and so the education of such models must be part of the pedagogy of both oppressors and oppressed.

Moderation as I have described it does not entail mediocrity. Just as Finny in *A Separate Peace* found joy in surpassing his own previous performances, so most of us can strive for higher levels of performance in many things we do so long as the effort does not destroy others or lead to a debilitating neglect of relation. We must understand and choose moderation. We might then experience a tremendous sense of freedom, well-being, and renewed interest in the wonders of everyday life.

A relational approach suggests the careful study of relational virtues—both those that belong to relations and those individual virtues that contribute to positive relations. It also suggests the meticulous analysis of virtues, traits, and ways of life such as *striving*. We should pick apart each item of the long list in *Character Lessons* to locate the evil that so often accompanies individual virtue. Educators should commit themselves to this analysis and to the study of themes and counterthemes that arise as a result. Instructional arrangements should reflect this commitment by establishing conditions in which positive relations may flourish.

QUESTIONS FOR ANALYSIS AND DISCUSSION

1. Many consider the care ethic to have emerged from recent developments in feminist scholarship. Do you think Noddings believes the care ethic is essentially a morality of or for women?

2. Though she doesn't specify names, Harry Browne's version of egoism seems a likely target for Noddings's critique of the illusion of individualism. How might Browne be defended?

3. As Noddings describes them, relational virtues are universal. That is, they arise from experiences all humans have, namely, the experience of being with someone else. In addition, she believes that moral education should emphasize the relational ethic rather than offer odd-ball counterexamples that have little to do with everyday life. But doesn't her approach diminish or harness the

freedom many individuals seek when defining their own lives? Although our early experiences may be rooted in relationships, why should a morality insist that we maintain or enrich relationships if an individualistic ethic brings greater happiness? Consider your answer in light of your reading of other selections in this chapter.

CHAPTER TWO

How Can I Judge Moral Conduct?

Judge not and you will not be judged; condemn not, and you will not be condemned; forgive, and you will be forgiven.

—*Holy Bible,* Luke 6:37

The power of moral judgment is, in fact, not a luxury, not a perverse indulgence of the self-righteous. It is a necessity.

—Mary Midgely, *Heart and Mind*

People are ambivalent when it comes to making judgments. Frequently a judgment is construed as impinging on individuality or freedom. We are warned about "passing judgment" or "judging a book by its cover." Some individuals respond to judgments as if they were a personal affront, as in "how dare you judge me."

Yet people must make judgments every day. In deciding what to eat for lunch, you make a judgment about the taste or nutritional value of the food. When you are taking a test, your instructor is judging your ability to recall or analyze assigned material. When the course is over, you are given an opportunity to judge the teacher by completing an evaluation form. In choosing whether to go to a party with friends, stay home and finish your school work, or ignore both and instead sneak over to your lover's place for a late night break, you are making a judgment about the pleasures and pains in your life.

As the epigraph from Mary Midgely suggests, making judgments is part of the human condition. In many fields of study these judgments are relatively straightforward. Disputes in mathematics, history, or medicine can be resolved through a careful review of calculations, facts, or diagnoses. If you and a classmate disagree about a historical point, you can check a book or a journal or ask a history professor. But if you and a classmate disagree about what is right or wrong, good or bad, on what basis can you reach some resolution? In ethics the basis for the validity or significance of moral judgments is problematic.

It is tempting to conclude that there is no such basis. One view is that moral judgments are expressions of personal preferences. Unless your choices involve breaking a law or violating another's rights, there are no grounds for saying they are true or false, right or wrong. Some have named this view moral subjectivism, and others espouse a view called ethical skepticism. Subjectivism refers to the personal meaning of a judgment, and skepticism denotes that we cannot know the meaning or truth of a judgment. In either case, when moral conduct is viewed in these ways, judgment is fairly minimal.

One rejoinder to this minimalist approach stresses the dynamic and dramatic context of moral judgments. Moral judgments are more than personal preferences or common opinions; they are value statements. They say something about how we view the world not only as it is but as it should be. In praising or censuring the morality of another person, or in appreciating or condemning another's action, we are saying something about how the rest of us might change, how our laws or institutions can be improved. From this viewpoint, moral judgments reflect a vision of the good that any moral person should consider as a way of improving our everyday world.

The readings in Chapter 2 address two issues in light of these observations. First, what is the status of moral judgments? And second, on what basis should we make moral judgments?

The case study by American philosopher Alphonso Lingis clarifies the seriousness of the issues involved when philosophy speaks for others. He then cites a report of two women in South America who were tortured and lived to tell their stories.

Thomas Nagel, a philosophy professor at New York University, argues for the objective basis of morality by challenging the moral subjectivist and the skeptic. Nagel concludes that as long as humans expect a justification for their actions, morality is part of rational discussion.

What is this objective basis? Jeremy Bentham, one of the founders of modern utilitarianism, claims pleasure and pain are the universal bases of any rational and social ethic. His calculus is offered as a guide to help us make better moral judgments and improve our chances for happiness.

Philosopher James Rachels reviews the case for utilitarianism. He raises some standard objections to it and explains how the utilitarian can deflect them. However, Rachels concludes with a challenge to the completeness of utilitarianism as an ethical system.

Immanuel Kant, one of the most important thinkers in modern philosophy, believes that moral judgment should focus on intentions and duties rather than on results. According to Kant, the universality of ethics is rooted in the ability to reason and conceive of moral law.

Kant's ideas are captured in a dialogue penned by Bonnie Stelmach, a philosopher from Canada. Imagining a dialogue between a granddaughter and her grandfather, Stelmach clarifies some difficult concepts of Kant's moral perspective while highlighting an important weakness.

Simone de Beauvoir, a prominent French existentialist, believes that abstract theories can help us with moral dilemmas but only to a point. Concrete situations are so unique and complex that an attitude of ambiguity must be respected as part of moral thought and action.

Finally, ancient Chinese thinker Lao Tzu questions the efforts of humans to develop artificial codes of conduct. These codes often derail rather than guide us toward the harmonious relation with nature, or what Lao Tzu calls "the way."

10.

ALPHONSO LINGIS

Case Study: A Doctor in Havana

A professor at Pennsylvania State University, Alphonso Lingis (b. 1933) is known both as a translator (of Maurice Merleau-Ponty and Emmanuel Levinas) and as a writer. Many of his writings interweave his thoughts on major philosophers with his personal encounters during his travels in remote places (see his selection in Chapter 10). In this selection Lingis describes some of the tasks of philosophy, particularly in relation to matters of truth, speech, and the body. These brief descriptions serve as an introduction to a report about torture where the victims survived and were able to talk about their harrowing experience.

⊣ CRITICAL READING QUESTIONS ⊢

1. Which kinds of speech does Lingis discuss? What is meant by serious speech?
2. Is torture the work of barbarians or civilized individuals?
3. What purpose do the torturers seem to have in mind in their treatment of the two women prisoners?

Speech can be impulsive, ideolectic, capricious, inconsequential. What we call speech that is serious claims to speak the truth. The truth concerns the community. Statements can be true only in the discourse of an established community which determines what could count as observations, what standards of accuracy in

---

"A Doctor in Havana," from *Abuses* (Berkeley: University of California Press, 1994), pp. 33–42. Some notes have been omitted.

determining observations are possible, how the words of common language are restricted and defined for use in different scientific disciplines, practical or technological enterprises, ritual practices, and entertainment with others.

Every community excludes certain statements as incompatible with the body of statements established as true. Every community excludes certain kinds of statements as not being able to be true. Every community excludes certain individuals, whose basic antisocial act consists in not making sense, identifying them as fanatics, as subversives, mystics, savages, infantile, insane. One does not answer what they say seriously; one meets what they say with silence, one employs force—the force of pedagogy, psychiatry, and the police—to make them speak in the ways of truth.

Torture is not simply the persistence of animal savagery in institutionalized forms of society. Would the solitary monster be produced not by an atavist regression to the instincts of beasts of prey but by a condensation in him or her of violent methods elaborated in institutions? It seems clear that confirmed rapists act not out of the raw sex drive stripped of social control but out of the contraction in them of the institutional imagos and practices of the millennial patriarchal society. The one who gouges out the eyes of his victim has not regressed to the presocialized instincts of apes but has ascended to the ranks of the Ottoman Janissaries and the Roman Inquisition. The one who gouges out his own eyes, who devises dungeons and gibbets for himself, has made occult pacts with the dark powers of the social order.

The torturer works to tear away at the victim's body and prove to him that he is a terrorist or psychotic and that what he believed in is delusions. The victim himself must supply the proof, by his confession. He is not being asked to declare to be true what he knows to be false. The torturer demands of the antisocial one that he confess that he is incapable of the truth, that his bestial body is incapable of lucidity and discernment, that it is nothing but corruption and filth.

Torturers are armed with the implements supplied by ancient practice and modern psychotechnology. They are agents working in the Intelligence Division. The instruments and techniques of torture do have the power to render a body impotent and brutish, tearing away at its integrity, proving it is spineless and gutless. Modern pharmacology each week provides new methods to neutralize the organic chemistry that crystallizes visions and that excludes convictions.

The confession uttered will be integrated into the common discourse that circulates in the community, and which each one joins whenever he speaks seriously. The cries and bestial moans out of which it came will be lost in the night and the fog.

⁂

To speak seriously is not simply to establish and communicate what is true. To speak is to respond to someone who has presented himself or herself. One catches up the tone of his address, her question, his voice resounds in one's own, one answers in the words and forms of speech which are hers. To respond is to present oneself, with one's past, one's resources, and the lines one has cast ahead of one—offering them to the one that faces, whose voice is an appeal and a contestation.

As one speaks to the one present, one responds to him with the voice of the child one was, of one's parents, one's teachers, responds to the words of persons who have passed on, who have passed away. And one offers a response not just to close the question in the now; one's response already invokes her assent or her contestation. When, on the Himalayan path, someone asks one the way, one's response addresses the hour ahead of him, or the days, or the lifetime, and undertakes already to answer for it. One always speaks to the departed, and for those who will be there after one departs. One's words answer for one's death and for the time after one's death.

Speech can be carefree, nonchalant, and frivolous, its patterns forming only to decorate the now of our encounter. But when it is serious, it speaks for the silent and silenced.

⚜ ⚜ ⚜

A relay for the circulation of the established discourse, the I arises in the effort to speak on one's own. To do so is to silence the circulation of the established truths in oneself. One's silence is tortured by the spasms and pain of silenced bodies with which those truths were established. One's silence tortures them: AIDS victims identified by established means of research as homosexuals and drug addicts cast out into the streets, Africans not heard by jetliners roaring overhead without dropping tons of the surplus grains heaped up in American granaries, Quechua peasants delivered over to military operations programmed in Pentagon computers, forty thousand children dying each day in the fetid slums of Third World cities, an Auschwitz every three months.

One has to speak for the silenced. But does not one's own speech silence their outcries? One gathers up the words of defiance and faith uttered by those shot before mass graves, one gathers up the words they left with their comrades, their children. One publishes the diaries of Ché. The established discourse, having consolidated its forces to determine things and situations by their death, easily proves they are the economic plans of the unemployable, the political hallucinations of the unsocializable, the utopian programs of fanatics, Maoists in a Peru which is 60 percent urbanized. The documentation of their agonies neutralizes itself.

Responding to those who approach and speak, one captures their voices in one's own, and one's voice animates only the words and forms of speech and the truth of those who have passed away. In the formulations of one's significant speech the cries of the tortured are muffled. Screams in the night are translated into images that circulate in electronic transmitters. They merge into the din of machines and the collisions of nature.

The words and the images relayed die away into a silence heavy with muffled sobs and screams. One's own words choke one's voice; they postpone the day when one would lay down with the tortured, to wash their wounds, weep with them. Even then, one must speak on one's own. The words that are one's own are not certifications but responses that are questions and pledges, answering now for one's silence and one's death and for the time after one's death.

⚜ ⚜ ⚜

"Luis is a plastic surgeon and burn specialist. Luis was visited by a government official who told him that two young women, one Brazilian and the other Uruguayan, would soon be brought to his office for evaluation and treatment. He was urged to provide them with extra-special attention, for their problems were of an unusual nature and required utmost sensitivity.

"It turned out that the two were participants in the urban guerrilla movement in Brazil, whose then military regime had gained a worldwide reputation for brutal and 'inventive' torture of political prisoners. The two women, whose names Luis never learned, visited him in his office, separately, that day.

"It was not physical pain that Luis's two new patients displayed, for their wounds or afflictions were not very recent. As soon as they walked into his office, Luis understood the magnitude of barbarism that had been visited upon these two otherwise normal and attractive women.

"They had been captured in Brazil and taken to the infamous DOPS, an acronym for the regime's special counterinsurgency police. There, they expected, they would be tortured and interrogated for days on end, as so many of their comrades had been—many dying in the process, others surviving as half-vegetables, and a handful freed as a result of successful guerrilla actions. The women knew that 'special treatment' was reserved for members of their sex—the sexual depravity of Brazil's torturers, especially one named Fleury (who led the Death Squad in his spare time), had become well known. So terrible and sophisticated had torture become, as documented by Amnesty International, the Bertrand Russell Tribunal, and other human rights agencies, that the opposition movement had instructed its members to resist or try to resist for at least 48 hours—to give the organizational structures and comrades with whom the captured members had contact time to change addresses, codes, meeting places, etc. It was assumed that the prisoner would be made to talk. It was only the rarest of cases that could totally resist, maintaining absolute silence in the face of such devastating methods.

"Their expectations and fears turned out to be wrong, strangely enough. After several hours of being made to wait in a locked, bare room, they were taken, blindfolded, for a ride to what turned out to be a modern, well-appointed hospital or private clinic some distance from São Paulo. They were locked into rooms without windows, given hospital gowns, and told they would be given the 'best of treatment' and would 'get better soon.' Doctors and nurses, courteous but closed-mouthed when asked what was going to happen, took the women's vital signs and medical histories—the normal routine before surgery. Fresh flowers were brought into the rooms daily. A maddening sort of terror began to set in amidst all this antiseptic civility and preparations for treatment for a malady the women knew they did not have.

"As it turned out, the women themselves were the 'malady.' In their very flesh they would have to pay for having dared to resist. The 'treatment' was different in the two cases, although identical in purpose. One of the women had her mouth taken away from her. The other lost half her nose. And they were released after several days with the gentle suggestion that they be sure to visit their comrades to show off their 'cures.' They had been turned into walking advertisements of terror, agents of demoralization and intimidation.

"It seems that, in the case of the woman whose mouth had been shut, the most sophisticated techniques of plastic surgery had been employed. Great care had been taken by her medical torturers to obliterate her lips forever, using cuts and stitches and folds that would frustrate even the best reconstructive techniques. . . . A small hole had been left in the face to allow the woman to take liquids through a straw and survive.

"During her initial interview with Luis, she had written on a piece of paper that 'they also did something to my teeth.' But when Luis and the medical team reopened the hole where her mouth had been, the sight was far more sickening than they had expected: All the teeth had been removed and two dog fangs—incisors— had been inserted in their place.

"'We did the best we could and gave her a hole resembling a mouth,' Luis said a few weeks later, 'and dentists will give her a set of teeth. But "ugly" is too kind a word to describe the way her mouth still looks.' Luis's face was tight, the color of a tightly clenched fist. Suddenly, he softened: 'But you know, that woman is extraordinarily beautiful. Do you know what she said after coming out of the anesthesia, her first words since undergoing her loss of speech? 'I will return. No one will ever silence me.'

"The other woman had had half her nose removed, skin, cartilage, and all. A draining, raw, and frightening wound was her 'treatment,' the sign she was to carry around with her to warn people that rebellion was a 'disease' and torture the 'cure.' Luis spoke little about her case, other than to say that a combination of skin grafts and silicone implants would restore a modicum of normalcy to her appearance."[1]

QUESTIONS FOR ANALYSIS AND DISCUSSION

1. A good portion of the selection is devoted to a lengthy report on the torture. Why do you think Lingis omits his own commentary following the report?

2. Can torture be rational? Can it be moral? Consider your response in light of the experiences of the women, or other accounts of torture.

3. Can you suggest a way to either explain or justify torture? Can you offer a genetic account of torture? If so, does this minimize the moral condemnation of torture?

---

[1] Robert Cohen, "In Brazil the Women Boast About Their Plastic Surgery," Covert Action Information Bulletin, Winter, 1986.

11.

THOMAS NAGEL

The Objective Basis of Morality

Thomas Nagel (b. 1937) is a philosophy professor at New York University. He has written extensively on morality and social justice. Here he challenges the concept of cultural relativism of the ethical subjectivist by asking the reader to consider an ordinary event when someone injures another. Isn't the first response not only physical but also mental? That is, while reacting to the pain are we not also demanding "why" of the person doing the harm? According to Nagel, this demand calls for a justification on the part of the person inflicting the suffering. Insofar as the justification involves communication and reason, it involves an objective basis of morality.

CRITICAL READING QUESTIONS

1. What are the chief points Nagel uses in developing his position on objectivity in moral thought?
2. How does Nagel respond to several conventional guides for moral judgment and conduct?
3. Why does Nagel introduce consistency as central to moral reasoning?

Suppose you work in a library, checking people's books as they leave, and a friend asks you to let him smuggle out a hard-to-find reference work that he wants to own.

You might hesitate to agree for various reasons. You might be afraid that he'll be caught, and that both you and he will then get into trouble. You might want the book to stay in the library so that you can consult it yourself.

But you may also think that what he proposes is wrong—that he shouldn't do it and you shouldn't help him. If you think that, what does it mean, and what, if anything, makes it true?

To say it's wrong is not just to say it's against the rules. There can be bad rules which prohibit what isn't wrong—like a law against criticizing the government. A rule can also be bad because it requires something that *is* wrong—like a law that requires racial segregation in hotels and restaurants. The ideas of wrong and right

---

"The Objective Basis of Morality," from *What Does It All Mean?* (New York: Oxford University Press, 1987), pp. 59–67, 71–75.

are different from the ideas of what is and is not against the rules. Otherwise they couldn't be used in the evaluation of rules as well as of actions.

If you think it would be wrong to help your friend steal the book, then you will feel uncomfortable about doing it: in some way you won't want to do it, even if you are also reluctant to refuse help to a friend. Where does the desire not to do it come from; what is its motive, the reason behind it?

There are various ways in which something can be wrong, but in this case, if you had to explain it, you'd probably say that it would be unfair to other users of the library who may be just as interested in the book as your friend is, but who consult it in the reference room, where anyone who needs it can find it. You may also feel that to let him take it would betray your employers, who are paying you precisely to keep this sort of thing from happening.

These thoughts have to do with effects on others—not necessarily effects on their feelings, since they may never find out about it, but some kind of damage nevertheless. In general, the thought that something is wrong depends on its impact not just on the person who does it but on other people. They wouldn't like it, and they'd object if they found out.

But suppose you try to explain all this to your friend, and he says, "I know the head librarian wouldn't like it if he found out, and probably some of the other users of the library would be unhappy to find the book gone, but who cares? I want the book; why should I care about them?"

The argument that it would be wrong is supposed to give him a reason not to do it. But if someone just doesn't care about other people, what reason does he have to refrain from doing any of the things usually thought to be wrong, if he can get away with it: what reason does he have not to kill, steal, lie, or hurt others? If he can get what he wants by doing such things, why shouldn't he? And if there's no reason why he shouldn't, in what sense is it wrong?

Of course most people do care about others to some extent. But if someone doesn't care, most of us wouldn't conclude that he's exempt from morality. A person who kills someone just to steal his wallet, without caring about the victim, is not automatically excused. The fact that he doesn't care doesn't make it all right: He *should* care. But *why* should he care?

There have been many attempts to answer this question. One type of answer tries to identify something else that the person already cares about, and then connect morality to it.

For example, some people believe that even if you can get away with awful crimes on this earth, and are not punished by the law or your fellow men, such acts are forbidden by God, who will punish you after death (and reward you if you didn't do wrong when you were tempted to). So even when it seems to be in your interest to do such a thing, it really isn't. Some people have even believed that if there is no God to back up moral requirements with the threat of punishment and the promise of reward, morality is an illusion: "If God does not exist, everything is permitted."

This is a rather crude version of the religious foundation for morality. A more appealing version might be that the motive for obeying God's commands is not fear but love. He loves you, and you should love Him, and should wish to obey His commands in order not to offend Him.

But however we interpret the religious motivation, there are three objections to this type of answer. First, plenty of people who don't believe in God still make judgments of right and wrong, and think no one should kill another for his wallet even if he can be sure to get away with it. Second, if God exists, and forbids what's wrong, that still isn't what *makes* it wrong. Murder is wrong in itself, and that's *why* God forbids it (if He does.) God couldn't make just any old thing wrong— like putting on your left sock before your right—simply by prohibiting it. If God would punish you for doing that it would be inadvisable to do it, but it wouldn't be wrong. Third, fear of punishment and hope of reward, and even love of God, seem not to be the right motives for morality. If you think it's wrong to kill, cheat, or steal, you should want to avoid doing such things because they are bad things to do to the victims, not just because you fear the consequences for yourself, or because you don't want to offend your Creator.

This third objection also applies to other explanations of the force of morality which appeal to the interests of the person who must act. For example, it may be said that you should treat others with consideration so that they'll do the same for you. This may be sound advice, but it is valid only so far as you think what you do will affect how others treat you. It's not a reason for doing the right thing if others won't find out about it, or against doing the wrong thing if you can get away with it (like being a hit and run driver).

There is no substitute for a direct concern for other people as the basis of morality. But morality is supposed to apply to everyone: and can we assume that everyone has such a concern for others? Obviously not: some people are very selfish, and even those who are not selfish may care only about the people they know, and not about everyone. So where will we find a reason that everyone has not to hurt other people, even those they don't know?

Well, there's one general argument against hurting other people which can be given to anybody who understands English (or any other language), and which seems to show that he has *some* reason to care about others, even if in the end his selfish motives are so strong that he persists in treating other people badly anyway. It's an argument that I'm sure you've heard, and it goes like this: "How would you like it if someone did that to you?"

It's not easy to explain how this argument is supposed to work. Suppose you're about to steal someone else's umbrella as you leave a restaurant in a rainstorm, and a bystander says, "How would you like it if someone did that to you?" Why is it supposed to make you hesitate, or feel guilty?

Obviously the direct answer to the question is supposed to be, "I wouldn't like it at all!" But what's the next step? Suppose you were to say, "I wouldn't like it if someone did that to me. But luckily no one *is* doing it to me. I'm doing it to someone else, and I don't mind that at all!"

This answer misses the point of the question. When you are asked how you would like it if someone did that to you, you are supposed to think about all the feelings you would have if someone stole your umbrella. And that includes more than just "not liking it"—as you wouldn't "like it" if you stubbed your toe on a rock. If someone stole your umbrella you'd *resent* it. You'd have feelings about the umbrella thief, not just about the loss of the umbrella. You'd think, "Where does he get off, taking my umbrella that I bought with my hard-earned money and that

I had the foresight to bring after reading the weather report? Why didn't he bring his own umbrella?" and so forth.

When our own interests are threatened by the inconsiderate behavior of others, most of us find it easy to appreciate that those others have a reason to be more considerate. When you are hurt, you probably feel that other people should care about it: you don't think it's no concern of theirs, and that they have no reason to avoid hurting you. That is the feeling that the "How would you like it?" argument is supposed to arouse.

Because if you admit that you would *resent* it if someone else did to you what you are now doing to him, you are admitting that you think he would have a reason not to do it to you. And if you admit that, you have to consider what that reason is. It couldn't be just that it's *you* that he's hurting, of all the people in the world. There's no special reason for him not to steal *your* umbrella, as opposed to anyone else's. There's nothing so special about you. Whatever the reason is, it's a reason he would have against hurting anyone else in the same way. And it's a reason anyone else would have too, in a similar situation, against hurting you or anyone else.

But if it's a reason anyone would have not to hurt anyone else in this way, then it's a reason *you* have not to hurt someone else in this way (since *anyone* means *everyone*). Therefore it's a reason not to steal the other person's umbrella now.

This is a matter of simple consistency. Once you admit that another person would have a reason not to harm you in similar circumstances, and once you admit that the reason he would have is very general and doesn't apply only to you, or to him, then to be consistent you have to admit that the same reason applies to you now. You shouldn't steal the umbrella, and you ought to feel guilty if you do.

Someone could escape from this argument if, when he was asked, "How would you like it if someone did that to you?" he answered, "I wouldn't resent it at all. I wouldn't *like* it if someone stole my umbrella in a rainstorm, but I wouldn't think there was any reason for him to consider my feelings about it." But how many people could honestly give that answer? I think most people, unless they're crazy, would think that their own interests and harms matter, not only to themselves, but in a way that gives other people a reason to care about them too. We all think that when we suffer it is not just bad *for us,* but *bad, period.*

The basis of morality is a belief that good and harm to particular people (or animals) is good or bad not just from their point of view, but from a more general point of view, which every thinking person can understand. That means that each person has a reason to consider not only his own interests but the interests of others in deciding what to do. And it isn't enough if he is considerate only of some others—his family and friends, those he specially cares about. Of course he will care more about certain people, and also about himself. But he has some reason to consider the effect of what he does on the good or harm of everyone. If he's like most of us, that is what he thinks others should do with regard to him, even if they aren't friends of his.

. . .

The question whether moral requirements are universal comes up not only when we compare the motives of different individuals, but also when we compare the moral standards that are accepted in different societies and at different times. Many things that you probably think are wrong have been accepted as morally correct by large groups of people in the past: slavery, serfdom, human sacrifice, racial segregation, denial of religious and political freedom, hereditary caste systems. And probably some things you now think are right will be thought wrong by future societies. Is it reasonable to believe that there is some single truth about all this, even though we can't be sure what it is? Or is it more reasonable to believe that right and wrong are relative to a particular time and place and social background?

There is one way in which right and wrong are obviously relative to circumstances. It is usually right to return a knife you have borrowed to its owner if he asks for it back. But if he has gone crazy in the meantime, and wants the knife to murder someone with, then you shouldn't return it. This isn't the kind of relativity I am talking about, because it doesn't mean morality is relative at the basic level. It means only that the same basic moral principles will require different actions in different circumstances.

The deeper kind of relativity, which some people believe in, would mean that the most basic standards of right and wrong—like when it is and is not all right to kill, or what sacrifices you're required to make for others—depend entirely on what standards are generally accepted in the society in which you live.

This I find very hard to believe, mainly because it always seems possible to criticize the accepted standards of your own society and say that they are morally mistaken. But if you do that, you must be appealing to some more objective standard, an idea of what is *really* right and wrong, as opposed to what most people think. It is hard to say what this is, but it is an idea most of us understand, unless we are slavish followers of what the community says.

There are many philosophical problems about the content of morality—how a moral concern or respect for others should express itself; whether we should help them get what they want or mainly refrain from harming and hindering them; how impartial we should be, and in what ways. I have left most of these questions aside because my concern here is with the foundation of morality in general—how universal and objective it is.

I should answer one possible objection to the whole idea of morality. You've probably heard it said that the only reason anybody ever does anything is that it makes him feel good, or that not doing it will make him feel bad. If we are really motivated only by our own comfort, it is hopeless for morality to try to appeal to a concern for others. On this view, even apparently moral conduct in which one person seems to sacrifice his own interests for the sake of others is really motivated by his concern for himself: he wants to avoid the guilt he'll feel if he doesn't do the "right" thing, or to experience the warm glow of self-congratulation he'll get if he does. But those who don't have these feelings have no motive to be "moral."

Now it's true that when people do what they think they ought to do, they often feel good about it: similarly if they do what they think is wrong, they often feel bad. But that doesn't mean that these feelings are their motives for acting. In many cases the feelings result from motives which also produce the action. You wouldn't feel good about doing the right thing unless you thought there was some other reason to do it, besides the fact that it would make you feel good. And you wouldn't feel guilty about doing the wrong thing unless you thought that there was some other reason not to do it, besides the fact that it made you feel guilty: something which made it *right* to feel guilty. At least that's how things should be. It's true that some people feel irrational guilt about things they don't have any independent reason to think are wrong—but that's not the way morality is supposed to work.

In a sense, people do what they want to do. But their reasons and motives for wanting to do things vary enormously. I may "want" to give someone my wallet only because he has a gun pointed at my head and threatens to kill me if I don't. And I may want to jump into an icy river to save a drowning stranger not because it will make me feel good, but because I recognize that his life is important, just as mine is, and I recognize that I have a reason to save his life just as he would have a reason to save mine if our positions were reversed.

Moral argument tries to appeal to a capacity for impartial motivation which is supposed to be present in all of us. Unfortunately it may be deeply buried, and in some cases it may not be present at all. In any case it has to compete with powerful selfish motives, and other personal motives that may not be so selfish, in its bid for control of our behavior. The difficulty of justifying morality is not that there is only one human motive, but that there are so many.

QUESTIONS FOR ANALYSIS AND DISCUSSION

1. Why does Nagel distinguish between the harm of someone stealing from you and the harm of stubbing your toe? If no one likes pain, does it make a difference whether its source is an accident or another person?

2. Imagine you are making a moral judgment about a person or an action. How often do you rely on the approaches Nagel discusses but rejects? Do you think his criticisms of a specific approach deserve a response? Choose one of the approaches and defend it.

3. If you generally agree with Nagel's criticisms of other approaches, do you think his conclusion leaves us with a reasonable alternative? Use Nagel's example of the library episode or your own example to develop your answer.

4. In late 1997 Pennsylvania judge Lisa Richette cleared a man of murder charges because she was convinced that the victim, his common-law wife of twenty years, was casting a voodoo spell. A high priestess from the Africa-based religion Santeria testified that the "ju-ju" spell can cause the target to suffer panic attacks. The murder suspect tried to free himself of the terror first by buying special candles at an occult store. When this did not work, he proceeded to get a pistol and shoot his wife. He drew a conviction of involuntary manslaughter rather than first degree murder. Would this be an example of objective moral reasoning? Explain your response.

12.

JEREMY BENTHAM

Hedonic Calculus

One of the most influential figures in modern utilitarianism, Jeremy Bentham (1748–1832) was a firm believer that ethics is an integral part of everyday life. He was quite active in the political life of England during much of his life and designed the Panopticon, a circular prison that would be cost-effective, efficient, and helpful in reforming England's growing criminal population. Penal colonies at that time were considered an uneven but costly experiment. Bentham's political ventures were consistent with his utilitarian axiom that the primary ethical concern was producing the "greatest good for the greatest number." The good, in his view, was an objective matter, consisting of an evaluation of pleasure versus pain. It is objective too, insofar as Bentham's version of hedonism is not limited to the subjective views of ethical egoism. Moreover, an ethic geared toward producing more pleasure than pain was preferable to other ethical theories.

┤ CRITICAL READING QUESTIONS ├

1. What are four traditional sanctions of pleasure and pain?
2. Is Bentham's primary emphasis on the pleasure of the self or the pleasure of the community?
3. Who does Bentham consider an authority on one's pleasures and pains?
4. How do the seven criteria of the hedonic calculus work?

Of the Four Sanctions or Sources of Pain and Pleasure

I. It has been shown that the happiness of the individuals, of whom a community is composed, that is their pleasures and their security, is the end and the sole end which the legislator ought to have in view: the sole standard, in

---

"Hedonic Calculus," from *The Principles of Morals and Legislation* (Buffalo, NY: Prometheus, 1988), Chapters 1 and 2. Notes have been omitted.

conformity to which each individual ought, as far as depends upon the legislator, to be *made* to fashion his behaviour. But whether it be this or any thing else that is to be *done,* there is nothing by which a man can ultimately be *made* to do it, but either pain or pleasure. Having taken a general view of these two grand objects (*viz.* pleasure, and what comes to the same thing, immunity from pain) in the character of *final* clauses; it will be necessary to take a view of pleasure and pain itself, in the character of *efficient* causes or means.

II. There are four distinguishable sources from which pleasure and pain are in use to flow: considered separately, they may be termed the *physical,* the *political,* the *moral,* and the *religious:* and inasmuch as the pleasures and pains belonging to each of them are capable of giving a binding force to any law or rule of conduct, they may all of them be termed *sanctions.*

III. If it be in the present life, and from the ordinary course of nature, not purposely modified by the interposition of the will of any human being, nor by any extraordinary interposition of any superior invisible being, that the pleasure or the pain takes place or is expected, it may be said to issue from or to belong to the *physical sanction.*

IV. If at the hands of a *particular* person or set of persons in the community, who under names correspondent to that of *judge,* are chosen for the particular purpose of dispensing it, according to the will of the sovereign or supreme ruling power in the state, it may be said to issue from the *political sanction.*

V. If at the hands of such *chance* persons in the community, as the party in question may happen in the course of his life to have concerns with, according to each man's spontaneous disposition, and not according to any settled or concerted rule, it may be said to issue from the *moral* or *popular sanction.*

VI. If from the immediate hand of a superior invisible being, either in the present life, or in a future, it may be said to issue from the *religious sanction.*

VII. Pleasures or pains which may be expected to issue from the *physical, political,* or *moral* sanctions, must all of them be expected to be experienced, if ever, in the *present* life: those which may be expected to issue from the *religious* sanction, may be expected to be experienced either in the *present* life or in a *future.*

VIII. Those which can be experienced in the present life, can of course be no others than such as human nature in the course of the present life is susceptible of: and from each of these sources may flow all the pleasures or pains of which, in the course of the present life, human nature is susceptible. With regard to these then (with which alone we have in this place any concern) those of them which belong to any one of those sanctions, differ not ultimately in kind from those which belong to any one of the other three: the only difference there is among them lies in the circumstances that accompany their production. A suffering which befalls a man in the natural and spontaneous course of things, shall be styled, for instance, a *calamity;* in which case, if it be supposed to befall him through any imprudence of his, it may be styled a punishment issuing from the physical sanction. Now this same suffering, if inflicted by the law, will be what is commonly called a *punishment;* if incurred for want of any friendly assistance, which the misconduct, or

supposed misconduct, of the sufferer has occasioned to be withholden, a punishment issuing from the *moral* sanction; if through the immediate interposition of a
particular providence, a punishment issuing from the religious sanction.

IX. A man's goods, or his person, are consumed by fire. If this happened to
him by what is called an accident, it was a calamity: if by reason of his own imprudence (for instance, from his neglecting to put his candle out) it may be styled a
punishment of the physical sanction: if it happened to him by the sentence of the
political magistrate, a punishment belonging to the political sanction; that is, what
is commonly called a punishment: if for want of any assistance which his *neighbour* withheld from him out of some dislike to his *moral* character, a punishment
of the *moral* sanction: if by an immediate act of *God's* displeasure, manifested on
account of some *sin* committed by him, or through any distraction of mind, occasioned by the dread of such displeasure, a punishment of the *religious* sanction.

X. As to such of the pleasures and pains belonging to the religious sanction,
as regard a future life, of what kind these may be we cannot know. These lie not
open to our observation. During the present life they are matter only of expectation: and, whether that expectation be derived from natural or revealed religion,
the particular kind of pleasure or pain, if it be different from all those which lie
open to our observation, is what we can have no idea of. The best ideas we can
obtain of such pains and pleasures are altogether unliquidated in point of quality.
In what other respects our ideas of them *may* be liquidated will be considered in
another place.

XI. Of these four sanctions the physical is altogether, we may observe, the
ground-work of the political and the moral: so is it also of the religious, in as far
as the latter bears relation to the present life. It is included in each of those other
three. This may operate in any case, (that is, any of the pains or pleasures belonging
to it may operate) independently of *them*: none of *them* can operate but by means
of this. In a word, the powers of nature may operate of themselves; but neither the
magistrate, nor men at large, *can* operate, nor is God in the case in question *supposed* to operate, but through the powers of nature.

XII. For these four objects, which in their nature have so much in common, it
seemed of use to find a common name. It seemed of use, in the first place, for the
convenience of giving a name to certain pleasures and pains, for which a name
equally characteristic could hardly otherwise have been found: in the second place,
for the sake of holding up the efficacy of certain moral forces, the influence of
which is apt not to be sufficiently attended to. Does the political sanction exert an
influence over the conduct of mankind? The moral, the religious sanctions do so
too. In every inch of his career are the operations of the political magistrate liable
to be aided or impeded by these two foreign powers: who, one or other of them,
or both, are sure to be either his rivals or his allies. Does it happen to him to leave
them out in his calculations? he will be sure almost to find himself mistaken in the
result. Of all this we shall find abundant proofs in the sequel of this work. It be-
hoves him, therefore, to have them continually before his eyes; and that under such
a name as exhibits the relation they bear to his own purposes and designs.

Value of a Lot of Pleasure or Pain, How to Be Measured

I. Pleasures then, and the avoidance of pains, are the *ends* which the legislator has in view: it behooves him therefore to understand their *value*. Pleasures and pains are the *instruments* he has to work with: it behooves him therefore to understand their force, which is again, in other words, their value.

II. To a person considered *by himself,* the value of a pleasure or pain considered *by itself,* will be greater or less, according to the four following circumstances:

1. Its *intensity.*
2. Its *duration.*
3. Its *certainty* or *uncertainty.*
4. Its *propinquity* or *remoteness.*

III. These are the circumstances which are to be considered in estimating a pleasure or a pain considered each of them by itself. But when the value of any pleasure or pain is considered for the purpose of estimating the tendency of any *act* by which it is produced, there are two other circumstances to be taken into the account; these are,

5. Its *fecundity,* or the chance it has of being followed by sensations of the *same* kind: that is, pleasures, if it be a pleasure: pains, if it be a pain.
6. Its *purity,* or the chance it has of *not* being followed by sensations of the *opposite* kind: that is, pains, if it be a pleasure: pleasures, if it be a pain.

These two last, however, are in strictness scarcely to be deemed properties of the pleasure or the pain itself; they are not, therefore, in strictness to be taken into the account of the value of that pleasure or that pain. They are in strictness to be deemed properties only of the act, or other event, by which such pleasure or pain has been produced; and accordingly are only to be taken into the account of the tendency of such act or such event.

IV. To a *number* of persons, with reference to each of whom the value of a pleasure or a pain is considered, it will be greater or less, according to seven circumstances: to wit, the six preceding ones; *viz.*

1. Its *intensity.*
2. Its *duration.*
3. Its *certainty* or *uncertainty.*
4. Its *propinquity* or *remoteness.*
5. Its *fecundity.*
6. Its *purity.*

And one other; to wit:

7. Its *extent;* that is, the number of persons to whom it *extends;* or (in other words) who are affected by it.

V. To take an exact account then of the general tendency of any act, by which the interests of a community are affected, proceed as follows. Begin with any one person of those whose interests seem most immediately to be affected by it: and take an account,

1. Of the value of each distinguishable *pleasure* which appears to be produced by it in the *first* instance.

2. Of the value of each *pain* which appears to be produced by it in the *first* instance.

3. Of the value of each pleasure which appears to be produced by it *after* the first. This constitutes the *fecundity* of the first *pleasure* and the *impurity* of the first *pain*.

4. Of the value of each *pain* which appears to be produced by it after the first. This constitutes the *fecundity* of the first *pain,* and the *impurity* of the first pleasure.

5. Sum up all the values of all the *pleasures* on the one side, and those of all the pains on the other. The balance, if it be on the side of pleasure, will give the *good* tendency of the act upon the whole, with respect to the interests of that *individual* person; if on the side of pain, the *bad* tendency of it upon the whole.

6. Take an account of the *number* of persons whose interests appear to be concerned; and repeat the above process with respect to each. *Sum up* the numbers expressive of the degrees of *good* tendency, which the act has, with respect to each individual, in regard to whom the tendency of it is *good* upon the whole: do this again with respect to each individual, in regard to whom the tendency of it is *good* upon the whole: do this again with respect to each individual, in regard to whom the tendency of it is *bad* upon the whole. Take the *balance;* which, if on the side of *pleasure,* will give the general *good tendency* of the act, with respect to the total number or community of individuals concerned; if on the side of pain, the general *evil tendency,* with respect to the same community.

VI. It is not to be expected that this process should be strictly pursued previously to every moral judgment, or to every legislative or judicial operation. It may, however, be always kept in view: and as near as the process actually pursued on these occasions approaches to it, so near will such process approach to the character of an exact one.

VII. The same process is alike applicable to pleasure and pain, in whatever shape they appear: and by whatever denomination they are distinguished: to pleasure, whether it be called *good* (which is properly the cause or instrument of pleasure) or *profit* (which is distant pleasure, or the cause or instrument of distant pleasure,) or *convenience,* or *advantage, benefit, emolument, happiness,* and so forth: to pain, whether it be called *evil,* (which corresponds to *good*) or *mischief,* or *inconvenience,* or *disadvantage,* or *loss,* or *unhappiness,* and so forth.

VIII. Nor is this a novel and unwarranted, any more than it is a useless theory. In all this there is nothing but what the practice of mankind, wheresoever they have a clear view of their own interest, is perfectly conformable to. An article of property, an estate in land, for instance, is valuable, on what account? On account of the pleasures of all kinds which it enables a man to produce, and what comes to the same thing the pains of all kinds which it enables him to avert. But the value of such an article of property is universally understood to rise or fall according to the length or shortness of the time which a man has in it: the certainty or uncertainty of its coming into possession: and the nearness or remoteness of the time at which, if at all, it is to come into possession. As to the *intensity* of the pleasures which a man may derive from it, this is never thought of, because it depends upon the use which each particular person may come to make of it; which cannot be estimated till the particular pleasures he may come to derive from it, or the particular pains he may come to exclude by means of it, are brought to view. For the same reason, neither does he think of the *fecundity* or *purity* of those pleasures.

Thus much for pleasure and pain, happiness and unhappiness, in *general*. We come now to consider the several particular kinds of pain and pleasure.

QUESTIONS FOR ANALYSIS AND DISCUSSION

1. Given that happiness is found by seeking pleasure and avoiding pain, does Bentham satisfy Nagel's quest for an objective basis for morality? Explain.

2. What do you think can be accomplished by using the hedonic calculus? Devise your own example of a dilemma involving rules, laws, or values and apply Bentham's calculus to reach a moral resolution of the dilemma. Be specific in your example and application.

3. Bentham is straightforward in his depiction of human nature. Do you agree or disagree with his belief that humans are primarily devoted to seeking pleasure and avoiding pain? What might be a counterexample or counterargument to his view?

13.

JAMES RACHELS

The Debate over Utilitarianism

James Rachels (b. 1941) is a professor at the University of Alabama, Birmingham. In addition to his many publications on ethics, justice, and euthanasia, Rachels has written about chess and movies. This selection reviews the case for utilitarianism, clarifying some

"The Debate over Utilitarianism," from *The Elements of Moral Philosophy* (New York: McGraw Hill, 1986), pp. 90–103.

central tenets and misconceptions. In Rachels's view critics often offer distorted views of the moral ideas raised by Bentham, John Stuart Mill, and other utilitarian proponents. These distorted views do not help students advance in moral reasoning nor do they do justice to a worthy and widely held ethical theory. Nevertheless, Rachels concludes his lucid and sympathetic account with a serious challenge to utilitarianism, one that evokes a moral intuition held by many but that apparently lies outside the framework of utilitarian thought.

CRITICAL READING QUESTIONS

1. Which three components does Rachels see as defining the utilitarian outlook?
2. How does Rachels distinguish hedonism from happiness?
3. What is the difference between act and rule utilitarianism?
4. Why does Rachels raise the issue of desert in concluding his essay?

The utilitarian doctrine is that happiness is desirable, and the only thing desirable, as an end; all other things being desirable as means to that end.

—John Stuart Mill, *Utilitarianism*

Man does not strive after happiness; only the Englishman does that.

—Friedrich Nietzsche, *Twilight of the Idols*

The Resilience of the Theory

Classical Utilitarianism—the theory defended by Bentham and Mill—can be summarized in three propositions:

First, actions are to be judged right or wrong solely in virtue of their consequences. Nothing else matters. Right actions are, simply, those that have the best consequences.

Second, in assessing consequences, the only thing that matters is the amount of happiness or unhappiness that is caused. Everything else is irrelevant. Thus right actions are those that produce the greatest balance of happiness over unhappiness.

Third, in calculating the happiness or unhappiness that will be caused, no one's happiness is to be counted as more important than anyone else's. Each person's welfare is equally important. As Mill put it in his *Utilitarianism,*

> the happiness which forms the utilitarian standard of what is right in conduct, is not the agent's own happiness, but that of all concerned. As between his own happiness and that of others, utilitarianism requires him to be as strictly impartial as a disinterested and benevolent spectator.

Thus right actions are those that produce the greatest possible balance of happiness over unhappiness, with each person's happiness counted as equally important.

The appeal of this theory to philosophers, economists, and others who theorize about human decision making has been enormous. The theory continues to be widely accepted, even though it has been challenged by a number of apparently devastating arguments. These antiutilitarian arguments are so numerous, and so persuasive, that many have concluded the theory must be abandoned. But the remarkable thing is that so many have *not* abandoned it. Despite the arguments, a great many thinkers refuse to let the theory go. According to these contemporary utilitarians, the antiutilitarian arguments show only that the classical theory needs to be *modified;* they say the basic idea is correct and should be preserved, but recast into a more satisfactory form.

In what follows, we will examine some of these arguments against Utilitarianism, and consider whether the classical version of the theory may be revised satisfactorily to meet them. These arguments are of interest not only for the assessment of Utilitarianism but for their own sakes, as they raise some additional fundamental issues of moral philosophy.

Is Happiness the Only Thing That Matters?

The question *What things are good?* is different from the question *What actions are right?* and Utilitarianism answered the second question by referring back to the first one. Right actions, it says, are the ones that produce the most good. But what is good? The classical utilitarian reply is: one thing, and one thing only, namely happiness. As Mill put it, "The utilitarian doctrine is that happiness is desirable, and the only thing desirable, as an end; all other things being desirable as means to that end."

The idea that happiness is the one ultimate good (and unhappiness the one ultimate evil) is known as *Hedonism.* Hedonism is a perennially popular theory that goes back at least as far as the ancient Greeks. It has always been an attractive theory because of its beautiful simplicity, and because it expresses the intuitively plausible notion that things are good or bad only on account of the way they make us *feel.* Yet a little reflection reveals serious flaws in the theory. The flaws stand out when we consider examples like these:

1. A promising young pianist's hands are injured in an automobile accident so that she can no longer play. Why is this a bad thing for her? Hedonism would say it is bad because it causes her unhappiness. She will feel frustrated and upset whenever she thinks of what might have been, and *that* is her misfortune. But this way of explaining the misfortune seems to get things the wrong way around. It is not as though, by feeling unhappy, she has made an otherwise neutral situation into a bad one. On the contrary, her unhappiness is a rational response to a situation that *is* unfortunate. She could have had a career as a concert pianist, and now she cannot. *That* is the tragedy. We could not eliminate the tragedy just by getting her to cheer up.

2. You think someone is your friend, but really he ridicules you behind your back. No one ever tells you, so you never know. Is this situation unfortunate for you? Hedonism would have to say no, because you are never caused any unhappiness by the situation. Yet we do feel that there is something bad going on here. You *think* he is your friend, and you are "being made a fool," even though you are not aware of it and so suffer no unhappiness.

Both these examples make the same basic point. We value all sorts of things, including artistic creativity and friendship, for their own sakes. It makes us happy to have them, but only because we *already* think them good. (We do not think them good *because* they make us happy—this is what I meant when I said that Hedonism "gets things the wrong way around.") Therefore we think it a misfortune to lose them, independently of whether or not the loss is accompanied by unhappiness.

In this way, Hedonism misunderstands the nature of happiness. Happiness is not something that is recognized as good and sought for its own sake, with other things appreciated only as means of bringing it about. Instead, happiness is a response we have to the attainment of things that we recognize *as* goods, independently and in their own right. We think that friendship is a good thing, and so having friends makes us happy. That is very different from first setting out after happiness, then deciding that having friends might make us happy, and then seeking friends as a means to this end.

Today, most philosophers recognize the truth of this. There are not many contemporary hedonists. Those sympathetic to Utilitarianism have therefore sought a way to formulate their view without assuming a hedonistic account of good and evil. Some, such as the English philosopher G. E. Moore (1873–1958), have tried to compile short lists of things to be regarded as good in themselves. Moore suggested that there are three obvious intrinsic goods—pleasure, friendship, and aesthetic enjoyment—and that right actions are those that increase the world's supply of such things. Other utilitarians have tried to bypass the question of how many things are good in themselves, leaving it an open question and saying only that right actions are the ones that have the best results, *however* goodness is measured. (This is sometimes called *Ideal Utilitarianism*.) Still others try to bypass the question in another way, holding only that we should act so as to maximize the satisfaction of people's *preferences*. (This is called *Preference Utilitarianism*.) . . . [A]lthough the hedonistic assumption of the classical utilitarians has largely been rejected, contemporary utilitarians have not found it difficult to carry on. They do so by urging that Hedonism was never a necessary part of the theory in the first place.

Are Consequences All That Matter?

The claim that only consequences matter *is*, however, a necessary part of Utilitarianism. The most fundamental idea underlying the theory is that in order to determine whether an action would be right, we should look at *what will happen as a result of doing it.* If it were to turn out that some *other* matter is also important in determining rightness, then Utilitarianism would be undermined at its very foundation.

The most serious antiutilitarian arguments attack the theory at just this point: they urge that various other considerations, in addition to utility, are important in determining whether actions are right. We will look briefly at three such arguments.

1. *Justice.* Writing in the academic journal *Inquiry* in 1965, H. J. McCloskey asks us to consider the following case:

> Suppose a utilitarian were visiting an area in which there was racial strife, and that, during his visit, a Negro rapes a white woman, and that race riots occur as a result of the crime, white mobs, with the connivance of the police, bashing and killing Negroes, etc. Suppose too that our utilitarian is in the area of the crime when it is committed such that his testimony would bring about the conviction of a particular Negro. If he knows that a quick arrest will stop the riots and lynchings, surely, as a utilitarian, he must conclude that he has a duty to bear false witness in order to bring about the punishment of an innocent person.

This is a fictitious example, but that makes no difference. The argument is only that *if* someone were in this position, then on utilitarian grounds he should bear false witness against the innocent person. This might have some bad consequences—the innocent man might be executed—but there would be enough good consequences to outweigh them: the riots and lynchings would be stopped. The best consequences would be achieved by lying; therefore, according to Utilitarianism, lying is the thing to do. But, the argument continues, it would be wrong to bring about the execution of the innocent man. Therefore, Utilitarianism, which implies it would be right, must be incorrect.

According to the critics of Utilitarianism, this argument illustrates one of the theory's most serious shortcomings: namely, that it is incompatible with the ideal of justice. Justice requires that we treat people fairly, according to their individual needs and merits. The innocent man has done nothing wrong; he did not commit the rape and so he does not deserve to be punished for it. Therefore, punishing him would be unjust. The example illustrates how the demands of justice and the demands of utility can come into conflict, and so a theory that says utility is the *whole* story cannot be right.

2. *Rights.* Here is a case that is *not* fictitious; it is from the records of the U.S. Court of Appeals, Ninth Circuit (Southern District of California), 1963, in the case of *York* v. *Story:*

> In October, 1958, appellant [Ms. Angelynn York] went to the police department of Chino for the purpose of filing charges in connection with an assault upon her. Appellee Ron Story, an officer of that police department, then acting under color of his authority as such, advised appellant that it was necessary to take photographs of her.

Story then took appellant to a room in the police station, locked the door, and directed her to undress, which she did. Story then directed appellant to assume various indecent positions, and photographed her in those positions. These photographs were not made for any lawful purpose.

Appellant objected to undressing. She stated to Story that there was no need to take photographs of her in the nude, or in the positions she was directed to take, because the bruises would not show in any photograph. . . .

Later that month, Story advised appellant that the pictures did not come out and that he had destroyed them. Instead, Story circulated these photographs among the personnel of the Chino police department. In April, 1960, two other officers of that police department, appellee Louis Moreno and defendant Henry Grote, acting under color of their authority as such, and using police photographic equipment located at the police station made additional prints of the photographs taken by Story. Moreno and Grote then circulated these prints among the personnel of the Chino police department. . . .

Ms. York brought suit against these officers and won. Her *legal* rights had clearly been violated. But what of the *morality* of the officers' behavior?

Utilitarianism says that actions are defensible if they produce a favorable balance of happiness over unhappiness. This suggests that we consider the amount of unhappiness caused to Ms. York and compare it with the amount of pleasure taken in the photographs by Officer Story and his cohorts. It is at least possible that more happiness than unhappiness was caused. In that case, the utilitarian conclusion apparently would be that their actions were morally all right. But this seems to be a perverse way to approach the case. Why should the pleasure afforded Story and his cohorts matter at all? Why should it even count? They had no right to treat Ms. York in that way, and the fact that they enjoyed doing so hardly seems a relevant defense.

To make the point even clearer, consider an (imaginary) related case. Suppose a Peeping Tom spied on Ms. York by peering through her bedroom window, and secretly took pictures of her undressed. Further suppose that he did this without ever being detected and that he used the photographs entirely for his own amusement, without showing them to anyone. Now under these circumstances, it seems clear that the *only* consequence of his action is an increase in his own happiness. No one else, including Ms. York, is caused any unhappiness at all. How, then, could Utilitarianism deny that the Peeping Tom's actions are right? But it is evident to moral common sense that they are not right. Thus, Utilitarianism appears to be an incorrect moral view.

The moral to be drawn from this argument is that Utilitarianism is at odds with the idea that people have *rights* that may not be trampled on merely because one anticipates good results. This is an extremely important notion, which explains why a great many philosophers have rejected Utilitarianism. In the above cases, it is Ms. York's right to privacy that is violated; but it would not be difficult to think of similar cases in which other rights are at issue—the right to freedom of religion, to free speech, or even the right to life itself. It may happen that good purposes are served, from time to time, by ignoring these rights. But we do not think that our rights *should* be set aside so easily. The notion of a personal right is not a utilitarian notion. Quite the reverse: it is a notion that places limits on how an individual may be treated, regardless of the good purposes that might be accomplished.

3. *Backward-Looking Reasons.* Suppose you have promised someone you will do something—say, you promised to meet him downtown this afternoon. But when the time comes to go, you don't want to do it—you need to do some work and would rather stay home. What should you do? Suppose you judge that the utility of getting your work accomplished slightly outweighs the inconvenience your friend would be caused. Appealing to the utilitarian standard, you might then conclude that it is right to stay home. However, this does not seem correct. The fact that *you promised* imposes an obligation on you that you cannot escape so easily. Of course, if the consequences of not breaking the promise were *great*—if, for example, your mother had just been stricken with a heart attack and you had to rush her to the hospital—you would be justified in breaking it. But a *small* gain in utility cannot overcome the obligation imposed by the fact that you promised. Thus Utilitarianism, which says that consequences are the only things that matter, seems mistaken.

There is an important general lesson to be learned from this argument. Why is Utilitarianism vulnerable to this sort of criticism? It is because the only kinds of considerations that the theory holds relevant to determining the rightness of actions are considerations having to do with the *future*. Because of its exclusive concern with consequences, Utilitarianism has us confine our attention to what *will happen* as a result of our actions. However, we normally think that considerations about the *past* also have some importance. The fact that you promised your friend to meet him is a fact about the past, not the future. Therefore, the general point to be made about Utilitarianism is that it seems to be an inadequate moral theory because it excludes what we might call backward-looking considerations.

Once we understand this point, other examples of backward-looking considerations come easily to mind. The fact that someone did not commit a crime is a good reason why he should not be punished. The fact that someone once did you a favor may be a good reason why you should now do him a favor. The fact that you did something to hurt someone may be a reason why you should now make it up to her. These are all facts about the past that are relevant to determining our obligations. But Utilitarianism makes the past irrelevant, and so it seems deficient for just that reason.

The Defense of Utilitarianism

Taken together, the above arguments form an impressive indictment of Utilitarianism. The theory, which at first seemed so progressive and commonsensical, now seems indefensible: it is at odds with such fundamental moral notions as justice and individual rights, and seems unable to account for the place of backward-looking reasons in justifying conduct. The combined weight of these arguments has prompted many philosophers to abandon the theory altogether.

Many thinkers, however, continue to believe that Utilitarianism, in some form, is true. In reply to the arguments, three general defenses have been offered.

The First Line of Defense

The first line of defense is to point out that the examples used in the antiutilitarian arguments are unrealistic and do not describe situations that come up in the real world. Since Utilitarianism is designed as a guide for decision making in the situations we actually face, the fanciful examples are dismissed as irrelevant.

The three antiutilitarian arguments share a common strategy. First a case is described, and then it is noted that from a utilitarian point of view a certain action seems to be required—that is, a certain action would have the best consequences. It is then said that this action is not right. Therefore, it is concluded, the utilitarian conception of rightness cannot be correct.

This strategy succeeds only if we admit that the actions described *really would* have the best consequences. But the utilitarian need not admit this. He can object that, in the real world, bearing false witness does *not* have good consequences. Suppose, in the case described by McCloskey, the "utilitarian" tried to incriminate the innocent man in order to stop the riots. His effort might not succeed; his lie might be found out, and then the situation would be even worse than before. Even if the lie did succeed, the real culprit would remain at large, to commit additional crimes. Moreover, if the guilty party were caught later on, which is always a possibility, the liar would be in deep trouble, and confidence in the criminal justice system would be undermined. The moral is that although one might *think* that one can bring about the best consequences by such behavior, one can by no means be certain of it. In fact, experience teaches the contrary: utility is not served by framing innocent people. Thus the utilitarian position is *not* at odds with commonsense notions of justice in such cases.

The same goes for the other cases cited in the antiutilitarian arguments. Violating people's rights, breaking one's promises, and lying all have bad consequences. Only in philosophers' imaginations is it otherwise. In the real world, Peeping Toms are caught, just as Officer Story and his cohorts were caught; and their victims suffer. In the real world, when people lie, others are hurt and their own reputations are damaged; and when people break their promises, they lose their friends.

Therefore, far from being incompatible with the idea that we should not violate people's rights or lie or break our promises, Utilitarianism explains *why* we should not do those things. Moreover, apart from the utilitarian explanation, these duties would remain mysterious and unintelligible. What could be more mysterious than the notion that some actions are right "in themselves," severed from any notion of a good to be produced by them? Or what could be more unintelligible than the idea that people have "rights" unconnected with any benefits derived from the acknowledgment of those rights? Utilitarianism is not incompatible with common sense; on the contrary, Utilitarianism *is* commonsensical.

The Second Line of Defense

The first line of defense contains more bluster than substance. While it can plausibly be maintained that *most* acts of false witness and the like have bad consequences in the real world, it cannot reasonably be asserted that *all* such acts have bad consequences. Surely, in at least some real-life cases, one can bring about good results by doing things that moral common sense condemns. Therefore, in at least some real-life cases Utilitarianism will come into conflict with common sense. Moreover, even if the antiutilitarian arguments had to rely exclusively on fictitious examples, those arguments would nevertheless retain their power; for showing that Utilitarianism has unacceptable consequences in hypothetical cases is a perfectly valid way of pointing up its theoretical defects. The first line of defense, then, is weak.

The second line of defense admits all this and proposes to save Utilitarianism by giving it a new formulation. In revising a theory to meet criticism, the trick is to identify precisely the feature of the theory that is causing the trouble and to change *that,* leaving the rest of the theory undisturbed as much as possible.

The troublesome aspect of the theory was this: the classical version of Utilitarianism implied that *each individual action* is to be evaluated by reference to its own particular consequences. If on a certain occasion you are tempted to lie, whether it would be wrong is determined by the consequences of *that particular lie.* This, the theory's defenders said, is the point that causes all the trouble; even though we know that *in general* lying has bad consequences, it is obvious that sometimes particular acts of lying can have good consequences.

Therefore, the new version of Utilitarianism modifies the theory so that individual actions will no longer be judged by the Principle of Utility. Instead, *rules* will be established by reference to the principle, and individual acts will then be judged right or wrong by reference to the rules. This new version of the theory is called *Rule-Utilitarianism,* to contrast it with the original theory, now commonly called *Act-Utilitarianism.*

Rule-Utilitarianism has no difficulty coping with the three antiutilitarian arguments. An act-utilitarian, faced with the situation described by McCloskey, would be tempted to bear false witness against the innocent man because the consequences of *that particular act* would be good. But the rule-utilitarian would not reason in that way. He would first ask, "What *general rules of conduct* tend to promote the greatest happiness?" Suppose we imagine two societies, one in which the rule "Don't bear false witness against the innocent" is faithfully adhered to, and one in which this rule is not followed. In which society are people likely to be better off? Clearly, from the point of view of utility, the first society is preferable. Therefore, the rule against incriminating the innocent should be accepted, and *by appealing to this rule,* the rule-utilitarian concludes that the person in McCloskey's example should not testify against the innocent man.

Analogous arguments can be used to establish rules against violating people's rights, breaking promises, lying, and so on. We should accept such rules because following them, as a regular practice, promotes the general welfare. But once having appealed to the Principle of Utility to establish the rules, we do not have to invoke the principle again to determine the rightness of particular actions. Individual actions are justified simply by appeal to the already-established rules.

Thus Rule-Utilitarianism cannot be convicted of violating our moral common sense, or of conflicting with ordinary ideas of justice, personal rights, and the rest. In shifting emphasis from the justification of acts to the justification of rules, the theory has been brought into line with our intuitive judgments to a remarkable degree.

The Third Line of Defense

Finally, a small group of contemporary utilitarians has had a very different response to the antiutilitarian arguments. Those arguments point out that the classical theory is at odds with ordinary notions of justice, individual rights, and so on; to this, their response is, essentially, "So what?" In 1961 the Australian philosopher J. J. C. Smart published a monograph entitled *An Outline of a System of Utilitarian Ethics;* reflecting on his position in that book, Smart said:

> Admittedly, utilitarianism does have consequences which are incompatible with the common moral consciousness, but I tended to take the view "so much the worse for the common moral consciousness." That is, I was inclined to reject the common methodology of testing general ethical principles by seeing how they square with our feelings in particular instances.

Our moral common sense is, after all, not necessarily reliable. It may incorporate various irrational elements, including prejudices absorbed from our parents, our religion, and the general culture. Why should we simply assume that our feelings are always correct? And why should we reject a plausible, rational theory of ethics such as Utilitarianism simply because it conflicts with those feelings? Perhaps it is the feelings, not the theory, that should be discarded.

In light of this, consider again McCloskey's example of the person tempted to bear false witness. McCloskey argues that it would be wrong to have a man convicted of a crime he did not commit, because it would be unjust. But wait: such a judgment serves *that man's* interests well enough, but what of the *other* innocent people who will be hurt if the rioting and lynchings are allowed to continue? What of them? Surely we might hope that we never have to face a situation like this, for the options are all extremely distasteful. But if we *must* choose between (a) securing the conviction of one innocent person and (b) allowing the deaths of several innocent people, is it so unreasonable to think that the first option, bad as it is, is preferable to the second?

On this way of thinking, Act-Utilitarianism is a perfectly defensible doctrine and does not need to be modified. Rule-Utilitarianism, by contrast, is an unnecessarily watered-down version of the theory, which gives rules a greater importance than they merit. Act-Utilitarianism is, however, recognized to be a radical doctrine which implies that many of our ordinary moral feelings may be mistaken. In this respect, it does what good philosophy always does—it challenges us to rethink matters that we have heretofore taken for granted.

What Is Correct and What Is Incorrect in Utilitarianism

There is a sense in which no moral philosopher can completely reject Utilitarianism. The consequences of one's actions—whether they promote happiness, or cause misery—must be admitted by all to be extremely important. John Stuart Mill once remarked that, insofar as we are benevolent, we must accept the utilitarian standard; and he was surely right. Moreover, the utilitarian emphasis on impartiality must also be a part of any defensible moral theory. The question is whether these are the *only* kinds of considerations an adequate theory must acknowledge. Aren't there *other* considerations that are also important?

If we consult what Smart calls our "common moral consciousness," it seems that there are *many* other considerations that are morally important. But I believe the radical act-utilitarians are right to warn us that "common sense" cannot be trusted. Many people once felt that there is an important difference between whites and blacks, so that the interests of whites are somehow more important. Trusting the "common sense" of their day, they might have insisted that an adequate moral theory should accommodate this "fact." Today, no one worth listening to would say such a thing. But who knows how many *other* irrational prejudices are still a part of our moral common sense? At the end of his classic study of race relations, *An American Dilemma* (1944), the Swedish sociologist Gunnar Myrdal reminds us:

> There must be still other countless errors of the same sort that no living man can yet detect, because of the fog within which our type of Western culture envelops us. Cultural influences have set up the assumptions about the mind, the body, and the universe with which we begin; pose the questions we ask; influence the facts we seek; determine the interpretation we give these facts; and direct our reaction to these interpretations and conclusions.

The strength of Utilitarianism is that it firmly resists "corruption" by possibly irrational elements. By sticking to the Principle of Utility as the *only* standard for judging right and wrong, it avoids all danger of incorporating into moral theory prejudices, feelings, and "intuitions" that have no rational basis.

The warning should be heeded. "Common sense" can, indeed, mislead us. At the same time, however, there might be at least some nonutilitarian considerations that an adequate theory *should* accept, because there *is* a rational basis for them. Consider, for example, the matter of what people deserve. A person who has worked hard in her job may deserve a promotion more than someone who has loafed, and it would be unjust for the loafer to be promoted first. This is a point that we would expect any fair-minded employer to acknowledge; we would all be indignant if we were passed over for promotion in favor of someone who had not worked as hard or as well as we. Now utilitarians might agree with this, and say that it can be explained by their theory—they might argue that it promotes the general welfare to encourage hard work by rewarding it. But this does not seem to be an adequate explanation of the importance of desert. The woman who worked harder has a superior claim to the promotion, *not* because it promotes the general welfare for her to get it, but *because she has earned it*. The reason she should be promoted has to do with *her* merits. This does not appear to be the kind of consideration a utilitarian could admit.

Does this way of thinking express a mere prejudice, or does it have a rational basis? I believe it has a rational basis, although it is not one that utilitarians could accept. We ought to recognize individual desert as a reason for treating people in certain ways—for example, as a reason for promoting the woman who has worked harder—because that is the principal way we have of treating individuals as autonomous, responsible beings. If in fact people have the power to choose their own actions, in such a way that they are *responsible* for those actions and what results from them, then acknowledging their deserts is just a way of acknowledging their standing as autonomous individuals. In treating them as they deserve to be treated, we are responding to the way they have freely chosen to behave. Thus in some instances we will not treat everyone alike, because people are not just members of an undifferentiated crowd. Instead, they are individuals who, by their own choices, show themselves to deserve different kinds of responses.

. . . I will draw only this conclusion about Utilitarianism: although it emphasizes points that any adequate moral theory must acknowledge, Utilitarianism is not itself a fully adequate theory because there is at least one important matter—individual desert—that escapes its net.

QUESTIONS FOR ANALYSIS AND DISCUSSION

1. One of the strengths of utilitarianism, in Rachels's account, is how well it accords with commonsense morality. What do you think common sense is? Can common sense be a helpful gauge for appreciating a moral theory such as utilitarianism?

2. Many critics of utilitarianism contend that it lacks an adequate sense of justice or fairness. For example, a group of people may have produced a great amount of happiness, but the distribution may be unequal. A small minority may enjoy an abundance of goods, whereas the majority enjoy a minimum of goods. Do you think Rachels has a satisfactory response to this? Explain your answer.

3. Rachels begins his essay with two epigraphs. The second one suggests that humans do not always seek happiness, implying that other motives may drive human action. What is your view of this dispute? Is happiness too subjective or too vague to be used as a basis for understanding human aspirations? Develop your opinion in light of Rachels's discussion.

14.

IMMANUEL KANT

Good Will and Duty

The German philosopher Immanuel Kant (1724–1804) is generally ranked as one of the most influential thinkers in the history of Western thought. He was familiar with all the intellectual and scientific trends of his time and incorporated them into his philosophical works. One of the most important changes in ethics during Kant's time involved the role of God in defining the good. Simply put, the role of God was diminishing. No longer were moralists debating how the moral good is anchored by the word of God or the truths of sacred literature. Instead, the anchor of moral truths was to be found in law, nature, happiness, or human reason. This secular ethic—that is, an ethic formulated or under-stood outside the framework of religion—was gaining in popularity. Yet philosophers were unwilling to give up on a universal basis for morality. In Kant's case this basis was not happiness but good will, as developed into respect for duty and moral law.

CRITICAL READING QUESTIONS

1. For Kant, why are goods such as health, wealth, and intelligence not unconditional goods?
2. What is the relation between a maxim and a moral law?
3. Why does Kant think that a moral person could not make a promise with the intention of breaking it?
4. Why is suicide considered wrong?

Nothing can possibly be conceived in the world, or even out of it, which can be called good without qualification, except a Good Will. Intelligence, wit, judgment, and the other *talents* of the mind, however they may be named, or courage, reso-lution, perseverance, as qualities of temperament, are undoubtedly good and desir-able in many respects; but these gifts of nature may also become extremely bad and mischievous if the will which is to make use of them, and which, therefore, consti-

---

"Good Will and Duty," from *Fundamental Principles of the Metaphysic of Ethics,* translated by T. K. Abbott (London: Longmans, Green and Co., Ltd., 1873), pp. 30–39, 44–59, 71. Some notes have been omitted.

tutes what is called *character,* is not good. It is the same with the *gifts of fortune.* Power, riches, honour, even health, and the general well-being and contentment with one's condition which is called *happiness,* inspire pride, and often presumption, if there is not a good will to correct the influence of these on the mind, and with this also to rectify the whole principle of acting, and adapt it to its end.
. . .

A good will is good not because of what it performs or effects, not by its aptness for the attainment of some proposed end, but simply by virtue of the volition, that is, it is good in itself, and considered by itself is to be esteemed much higher than all that can be brought about by it in favour of any inclination, nay, even of the sum total of all inclinations. Even if it should happen that, owing to special disfavour of fortune, or the niggardly provision of a step-motherly nature, this will should wholly lack power to accomplish its purpose, if with its greatest efforts it should yet achieve nothing, and there should remain only the good will (not, to be sure, a mere wish, but the summoning of all means in our power), then, like a jewel, it would still shine by its own light, as a thing which has its whole value in itself. Its usefulness or fruitlessness can neither add to nor take away anything from this value. . . .

To be beneficent when we can is a duty; and besides this, there are many minds so sympathetically constituted that, without any other motive of vanity or self-interest, they find a pleasure in spreading joy around them, and can take delight in the satisfaction of others so far as it is their own work. But I maintain that in such a case an action of this kind, however proper, however amiable it may be, has nevertheless no true moral worth, but is on a level with other inclinations, *e.g.* the inclination to honour, which, if it is happily directed to that which is in fact of public utility and accordant with duty, and consequently honourable, deserves praise and encouragement, but not esteem. For the maxim lacks the moral import, namely, that such actions be done *from duty,* not from inclination. Put the case that the mind of that philanthropist were clouded by sorrow of his own extinguishing all sympathy with the lot of others, and that while he still has the power to benefit others in distress, he is not touched by their trouble because he is absorbed with his own; and now suppose that he tears himself out of this dead insensibility, and performs the action without any inclination to it, but simply from duty, then first has his action its genuine moral worth. Further still; if nature has put little sympathy in the heart of this or that man; if he, supposed to be an upright man, is by temperament cold and indifferent to the sufferings of others, perhaps because in respect of his own he is provided with the special gift of patience and fortitude, and supposes, or even requires, that others should have the same—and such a man would certainly not be the meanest product of nature—but if nature had not specially framed him for a philanthropist, would he not still find in himself a source from whence to give himself a far higher worth than that of a good-natured temperament could be? Unquestionably. It is just in this that the moral worth of the character is brought out which is incomparably the highest of all, namely, that he is beneficent, not from inclination, but from duty.

To secure one's own happiness is a duty, at least indirectly; for discontent with one's condition, under a pressure of many anxieties and amidst unsatisfied wants, might easily become a great *temptation to transgression of duty*. But here again, without looking to duty, all men have already the strongest and most intimate inclination to happiness, because it is just in this idea that all inclinations are combined in one total. But the precept of happiness is often of such a sort that it greatly interferes with some inclinations, and yet a man cannot form any definite and certain conception of the sum of satisfaction of all of them which is called happiness. It is not then to be wondered at that a single inclination, definite both as to what it promises and as to the time within which it can be gratified, is often able to overcome such a fluctuating idea, and that a gouty patient, for instance, can choose to enjoy what he likes, and to suffer what he may, since, according to his calculation, on this occasion at least, he has [only] not sacrificed the enjoyment of the present moment to a possibly mistaken expectation of a happiness which is supposed to be found in health. But even in this case, if the general desire for happiness did not influence his will, and supposing that in his particular case health was not a necessary element in this calculation, there yet remains in this, as in all other cases, this law, namely, that he should promote his happiness not from inclination but from duty, and by this would his conduct first acquire true moral worth.

It is in this manner, undoubtedly, that we are to understand those passages of Scripture also in which we are commanded to love our neighbour, even our enemy. For love, as an affection, cannot be commanded, but beneficence for duty's sake may; even though we are not impelled to it by any inclination—nay, are even repelled by a natural and unconquerable aversion. This is *practical* love, and not *pathological*—a love which is seated in the will, and not in the propensions of sense—in principles of action and not of tender sympathy; and it is this love alone which can be commanded.

The second * proposition is. That an action done from duty derives its moral worth, *not from the purpose* which is to be attained by it, but from the maxim by which it is determined, and therefore does not depend on the realization of the object of the action, but merely on the *principle of volition* by which the action has taken place, without regard to any object of desire. It is clear from what precedes that the purposes which we may have in view in our actions, or their effects regarded as ends and springs of the will, cannot give to actions any unconditional or moral worth. In what, then, can their worth lie, if it is not to consist in the will and in reference to its expected effect? It cannot lie anywhere but in the *principle of the will* without regard to the ends which can be attained by the action. For the will stands between its *à priori* principle, which is formal, and its *à posteriori* spring, which is material, as between two roads, and as it must be determined by something, it follows that it must be determined by the formal principle of volition when an action is done from duty, in which case every material principle has been withdrawn from it.

The third proposition, which is a consequence of the two preceding, I would express thus: *Duty is the necessity of acting from respect for the law.* I may have

---

* [The first proposition was that, to have moral worth, an action must be done from duty.]

inclination for an object as the effect of my proposed action, but I cannot have *respect* for it, just for this reason, that it is an effect and not an energy of will. . . .

Thus the moral worth of an action does not lie in the effect expected from it, nor in any principle of action which requires to borrow its motive from this expected effect. For all these effects—agreeableness of one's condition, and even the promotion of the happiness of others—could have been also brought about by other causes, so that for this there would have been no need of the will of a rational being; whereas it is in this alone that the supreme and unconditional good can be found. The pre-eminent good which we call moral can therefore consist in nothing else than *the conception of law* in itself, *which certainly is only possible in a rational being*, in so far as this conception, and not the expected effect, determines the will. This is a good which is already present in the person who acts accordingly, and we have not to wait for it to appear first in the result.

But what sort of law can that be, the conception of which must determine the will, even without paying any regard to the effect expected from it, in order that this will may be called good absolutely and without qualification? As I have deprived the will of every impulse which could arise to it from obedience to any law, there remains nothing but the universal conformity of its actions to law in general, which alone is to serve the will as a principle, *i.e.* I am never to act otherwise than so *that I could also will that my maxim should become a universal law.* Here now, it is the simple conformity to law in general, without assuming any particular law applicable to certain actions, that serves the will as its principle, and must so serve it, if duty is not to be a vain delusion and a chimerical notion. The common reason of men in its practical judgments perfectly coincides with this, and always has in view the principle here suggested. Let the question be, for example: May I when in distress make a promise with the intention not to keep it? I readily distinguish here between the two significations which the question may have: Whether it is prudent, or whether it is right, to make a false promise. The former may undoubtedly often be the case. I see clearly indeed that it is not enough to extricate myself from a present difficulty by means of this subterfuge, but it must be well considered whether there may not hereafter spring from this lie much greater inconvenience than that from which I now free myself, and as, with all my supposed *cunning,* the consequences cannot be so easily foreseen but that credit once lost may be much more injurious to me than any mischief which I seek to avoid at present, it should be considered whether it would not be more *prudent* to act herein according to a universal maxim, and to make it a habit to promise nothing except with the intention of keeping it. But it is soon clear to me that such a maxim will still only be based on the fear of consequences. Now it is a wholly different thing to be truthful from duty, and to be so from apprehension of injurious consequences. In the first case, the very notion of the action already implies a law for me; in the second case, I must first look about elsewhere to see what results may be combined with it which would affect myself. For to deviate from the principle of duty is beyond all doubt wicked; but to be unfaithful to my maxim of prudence may often be very advantageous to me, although to abide by it is certainly safer. The shortest way, however, and an unerring one, to discover the answer to this question whether a lying promise is consistent with duty, is to ask myself, Should I be content that my maxim (to extricate myself from difficulty by a false promise) should hold good as a universal law, for myself as well as for others? and should I be able to say to myself, "Every one may make a deceitful promise when he finds himself in a difficulty from which he cannot otherwise extricate himself"? Then I presently become aware that while I can will the lie, I can by no means will that lying should be a universal law. For with such a law there would be no promises at all, since it would be in vain to allege my intention in regard to my future actions to those who would not believe this allegation, or if they over-hastily did so would pay me back in my own coin. Hence my maxim, as soon as it should be made a universal law, would necessarily destroy itself.

I do not, therefore, need any far-reaching penetration to discern what I have to do in order that my will may be morally good. Inexperienced in the course of the world, incapable of being prepared for all its contingencies, I only ask myself: Canst thou also will that thy maxim should be a universal law? If not, then it must be rejected, and that not because of a disadvantage accruing from it to myself or even to others, but because it cannot enter as a principle into a possible universal legislation, and reason extorts from me immediate respect for such legislation. I do not indeed as yet *discern* on what this respect is based (this the philosopher may inquire), but at least I understand this, that it is an estimation of the worth which far outweighs all worth of what is recommended by inclination, and that the necessity of acting from *pure* respect for the practical law is what constitutes duty, to which every other motive must give place, because it is the condition of a will being good *in itself,* and the worth of such a will is above everything.

. . .

From what has been said, it is clear that all moral conceptions have their seat and origin completely *à priori* in the reason, and that, moreover, in the commonest reason just as truly as in that which is in the highest degree speculative; that they cannot be obtained by abstraction from any empirical, and therefore merely contingent knowledge; that it is just this purity of their origin that makes them worthy to serve as our supreme practical principle, and that just in proportion as we add anything empirical, we detract from their genuine influence, and from the absolute value of actions; that it is not only of the greatest necessity, in a purely speculative point of view, but is also of the greatest practical importance to derive these notions and laws from pure reason, to present them pure and unmixed, and even to determine the compass of this practical or pure rational knowledge, *i.e.* to determine the whole faculty of pure practical reason; and, in doing so, we must not make its principles dependent on the particular nature of human reason, though in speculative philosophy this may be permitted, or may even at times be necessary; but since moral laws ought to hold good for every rational creature, we must derive them from the general concept of a rational being. In this way, although for its *application* to man morality has need of anthropology, yet, in the first instance, we must treat it independently as pure philosophy, *i.e.* as metaphysic, complete in itself (a thing which in such distinct branches of science is easily done); knowing well that unless we are in possession of this, it would not only be vain to determine the moral element of duty in right actions for purposes of speculative criticism, but it would be impossible to base morals on their genuine principles, even for common practical purposes, especially of moral instruction, so as to produce pure moral dispositions, and to engraft them on men's minds to the promotion of the greatest possible good in the world.

. . .

Everything in nature works according to laws. Rational beings alone have the faculty of acting according *to the conception* of laws, that is according to principles, *i.e.* have a *will*. Since the deduction of actions from principles requires *reason,* the will is nothing but practical reason. If reason infallibly determines the will, then the actions of such a being which are recognised as objectively necessary are subjectively necessary also, *i.e.* the will is a faculty to choose *that only* which reason independent on inclination recognises as practically necessary, *i.e.* as good. But if reason of itself does not sufficiently determine the will, if the latter is subject also to subjective conditions (particular impulses) which do not always coincide with the objective conditions; in a word, if the will does not *in itself* completely accord with reason (which is actually the case with men), then the actions which objectively are recognised as necessary are subjectively contingent, and the determination of such a will according to objective laws is *obligation,* that is to say, the relation of the objective laws to a will that is not thoroughly good is conceived as the determination of the will of a rational being by principles of reason, but which the will from its nature does not of necessity follow.

The conception of an objective principle, in so far as it is obligatory for a will, is called a command (of reason), and the formula of the command is called an Imperative.

All imperatives are expressed by the word *ought* [or *shall*], and thereby indicate the relation of an objective law of reason to a will, which from its subjective constitution is not necessarily determined by it (an obligation). They say that something would be good to do or to forbear, but they say it to a will which does not always do a thing because it is conceived to be good to do it. . . .

Now all *imperatives* command either *hypothetically* or *categorically.* The former represent the practical necessity of a possible action as means to something else that is willed (or at least which one might possibly will). The categorical imperative would be that which represented an action as necessary of itself without reference to another end, *i.e.* as objectively necessary.

Since every practical law represents a possible action as good, and on this account, for a subject who is practically determinable by reason, necessary, all imperatives are formulæ determining an action which is necessary according to the principle of a will good in some respects. If now the action is good only as a means *to something else,* then the imperative is *hypothetical;* if it is conceived as good *in itself* and consequently as being necessarily the principle of a will which of itself conforms to reason, then it is *categorical.*

Thus the imperative declares what action possible by me would be good, and presents the practical rule in relation to a will which does not forthwith perform an action simply because it is good, whether because the subject does not always know that it is good, or because, even if it know this, yet its maxims might be opposed to the objective principles of practical reason.

Accordingly the hypothetical imperative only says that the action is good for some purpose, *possible* or *actual*. In the first case it is a Problematical, in the second an Assertorial practical principle. The categorical imperative which declares an action to be objectively necessary in itself without reference to any purpose, *i.e.* without any other end, is valid as a (practical) Apodictic principle.

. . .

Finally, there is an imperative which commands a certain conduct immediately, without having as its condition any other purpose to be attained by it. This imperative is Categorical. It concerns not the matter of the action, or its intended result, but its form and the principle of which it is itself a result; and what is essentially good in it consists in the mental disposition, let the consequence be what it may. This imperative may be called that of Morality.

. . .

We shall therefore have to investigate *à priori* the possibility of a categorical imperative, as we have not in this case the advantage of its reality being given in experience, so that [the elucidation of] its possibility should be requisite only for its explanation, not for its establishment. In the meantime it may be discerned beforehand that the categorical imperative alone has the purport of a practical law: all the rest may indeed be called *principles* of the will but not laws, since whatever is only necessary for the attainment of some arbitrary purpose may be considered as in itself contingent, and we can at any time be free from the precept if we give up the purpose: on the contrary, the unconditional command leaves the will no liberty to choose the opposite; consequently it alone carries with it that necessity which we require in a law.

Secondly, in the case of this categorical imperative or law of morality, the difficulty (of discerning its possibility) is a very profound one. It is an *à priori* synthetical practical proposition; and as there is so much difficulty in discerning the possibility of speculative propositions of this kind, it may readily be supposed that the difficulty will be no less with the practical.

In this problem we will first inquire whether the mere conception of a categorical imperative may not perhaps supply us also with the formula of it, containing the proposition which alone can be a categorical imperative; for even if we know the tenor of such an absolute command, yet how it is possible will require further special and laborious study, which we postpone to the last section.

When I conceive a hypothetical imperative in general I do not know beforehand what it will contain until I am given the condition. But when I conceive a categorical imperative I know at once what it contains. For as the imperative contains besides the law only the necessity that the maxims* shall conform to this law, while the law contains no conditions restricting it, there remains nothing but the general

---

* A maxim is a subjective principle of action, and must be distinguished from the *objective principle,* namely, practical law. The former contains the practical rule set by reason according to the conditions of the subject (often its ignorance or its inclinations), so that it is the principle on which the subject *acts;* but the law is the objective principle valid for every rational being, and is the principle on which it *ought to act,* that is, an imperative.

statement that the maxim of the action should conform to a universal law, and it is this conformity alone that the imperative properly represents as necessary.

There is therefore but one categorical imperative, namely this: *Act only on that maxim whereby thou canst at the same time will that it should become a universal law.*

Now if all imperatives of duty can be deduced from this one imperative as from their principle, then, although it should remain undecided whether what is called duty is not merely a vain notion, yet at least we shall be able to show what we understand by it and what this notion means.

Since the universality of the law according to which effects are produced constitutes what is properly called *nature* in the most general sense (as to form), that is, the existence of things so far as it is determined by general laws, the imperative of duty may be expressed thus: *Act as if the maxim of thy action were to become by thy will a Universal Law of Nature.* . . .

1. A man reduced to despair by a series of misfortunes feels wearied of life, but is still so far in possession of his reason that he can ask himself whether it would not be contrary to his duty to himself to take his own life. Now he inquires whether the maxim of his action could become a universal law of nature. His maxim is: From self-love I adopt it as a principle to shorten my life when its longer duration is likely to bring more evil than satisfaction. It is asked then simply whether this principle founded on self-love can become a universal law of nature. Now we see at once that a system of nature of which it should be a law to destroy life by means of the very feeling whose special nature it is to impel to the improvement of life would contradict itself, and therefore could not exist as a system of nature; hence that maxim cannot possibly exist as a universal law of nature, and consequently would be wholly inconsistent with the supreme principle of all duty.

2. Another finds himself forced by necessity to borrow money. He knows that he will not be able to repay it, but sees also that nothing will be lent to him, unless he promises stoutly to repay it in a definite time. He desires to make this promise, but he has still so much conscience as to ask himself: Is it not unlawful and inconsistent with duty to get out of a difficulty in this way? Suppose however that he resolves to do so, then the maxim of his action would be expressed thus: When I think myself in want of money, I will borrow money and promise to repay it, although I know that I never can do so. Now this principle of self-love or of one's own advantage may perhaps be consistent with my whole future welfare; but the question now is, is it right? I change then the suggestion of self-love into a universal law, and state the question thus: How would it be if my maxim were a universal law? Then I see at once that it could never hold as a universal law of nature but would necessarily contradict itself. For supposing it to be a universal law that everyone when he thinks himself in a difficulty should be able to promise whatever he pleases, with the purpose of not keeping his promise, the promise itself would become impossible, as well as the end that one might have in view in it, since no one would consider that anything was promised to him, but would ridicule all such statements as vain pretences.

3. A third finds in himself a talent which with the help of some culture might make him a useful man in many respects. But he finds himself in comfortable circumstances, and prefers to indulge in pleasure rather than to take pains in enlarging and improving his happy natural capacities. He asks, however, whether his maxim of neglect of his natural gifts, besides agreeing with his inclination to indulgence, agrees also with what is called duty. He sees then that a system of nature could indeed subsist with such a universal law although men (like the South Sea islanders) should let their talents rust, and resolve to devote their lives merely to idleness, amusement, and propagation of their species—in a word, to enjoyment; but he cannot possibly *will* that this should be a universal law of nature, or be implanted in us as such by a natural instinct. For, as a rational being, he necessarily wills that his faculties be developed, since they serve him, and have been given him, for all sorts of possible purposes.

. . .

We have thus established at least this much, that if duty is a conception which is to have any import and real legislative authority for our actions, it can only be expressed in categorical, and not at all in hypothetical imperatives. We have also, which is of great importance, exhibited clearly and definitely for every practical application the content of the categorical imperative, which must contain the principle of all duty if there is such a thing at all. We have not yet, however, advanced so far as to prove *à priori* that there actually is such an imperative, that there is a practical law which commands absolutely of itself, and without any other impulse, and that the following of this law is duty.

. . .

If then there is a supreme practical principle or, in respect of the human will, a categorical imperative, it must be one which, being drawn from the conception of that which is necessarily an end for every one because it is *an end in itself*, constitutes an *objective* principle of will, and can therefore serve as a universal practical law. The foundation of this principle is: *rational nature exists as an end in itself.* Man necessarily conceives his own existence as being so: so far then this is a *subjective* principle of human actions. But every other rational being regards its existence similarly, just on the same rational principle that holds for me: so that it is at the same time an objective principle, from which as a supreme practical law all laws of the will must be capable of being deduced. Accordingly the practical imperative will be as follows: *So act as to treat humanity, whether in thine own person or in that of any other, in every case as an end withal, never as means only.* We will now inquire whether this can be practically carried out.

To abide by the previous examples:

Firstly, under the head of necessary duty to oneself: He who contemplates suicide should ask himself whether his action can be consistent with the idea of humanity *as an end in itself.* If he destroys himself in order to escape from painful circumstances, he uses a person merely as a *mean* to maintain a tolerable condition up to the end of life. But a man is not a thing, that is to say, something which can be used merely as means, but must in all his actions be always considered as an end in himself. I cannot, therefore, dispose in any way of a man in my own person so as to mutilate him, to damage or kill him. . . .

Secondly, as regards necessary duties, or those of strict obligation, towards others; he who is thinking of making a lying promise to others will see at once that he would be using another man *merely as a mean,* without the latter containing at the same time the end in himself. For he whom I propose by such a promise to use for my own purposes cannot possibly assent to my mode of acting towards him, and therefore cannot himself contain the end of this action. This violation of the principle of humanity in other men is more obvious if we take in examples of attacks on the freedom and property of others. For then it is clear that he who transgresses the rights of men, intends to use the person of others merely as means, without considering that as rational beings they ought always to be esteemed also as ends, that is, as beings who must be capable of containing in themselves the end of the very same action. . . .

. . . Hence follows the third practical principle of the will, which is the ultimate condition of its harmony with the universal practical reason, viz.: the idea of *the will of every rational being as a universally legislative will.*

On this principle all maxims are rejected which are inconsistent with the will being itself universal legislator. Thus the will is not subject simply to the law, but so subject that it must be regarded *as itself giving the law,* and on this ground only, subject to the law (of which it can regard itself as the author). . . .

QUESTIONS FOR ANALYSIS AND DISCUSSION

1. Some observers say that Kant actually captures a commonsense view of morality that stresses fairness and consistency. His categorical imperative has been called a secular golden rule. Do you see evidence for this observation in the reading? Do you see evidence to reject the commonsense view?

2. Kant writes that humans can conceive of moral law because they have reason. What do you think this means? Does it imply that nonrational people cannot be moral?

3. Utilitarians criticize Kant for neglecting the importance of consequences and happiness in moral deliberations. Can you find evidence from the selection to support or challenge this criticism?

4. Does every maxim have moral significance? That is, does Kant help us to know when to universalize a maxim and when we needn't do so? Discuss an example not given by Kant.

15.

BONNIE STELMACH

A Dialogue between Generations for the "Soul" Purpose of Understanding Immanuel Kant's Categorical Imperative

A recent graduate student in the philosophy of education at Simon Fraser University in Canada, Bonnie Stelmach illustrates a conversation between a student struggling with the moral ideas of Kant and her grandfather. The story begins when the student, Sophy, needs to finish a paper in ethics and is asked by grandfather Phil why she is so troubled. As Stelmach presents it, Sophy is troubled by two things. First, like any student, she is worried about completing a decent paper for her instructor. Second, and more important, she is perplexed about all the ideas that arise in studying Kant's moral position. Like a patient Socrates, grandfather Phil elicits from his granddaughter an already impressive and lucid review of Kant's key terms, including free will, intention, law, conflicting duties, and the nature of the conscious self. The dialogue closes with an account of a possibly serious weakness in Kant's position.

CRITICAL READING QUESTIONS

1. Phil and Sophy at first compare the categorical imperative with the golden rule. But seeing Kant's morality in this sense is not conclusive. Why isn't the golden rule that simple?

2. According to Stelmach, are acting from inclination and acting from duty morally equivalent?

3. What are the two components of the self? How are they related to Kant's moral views?

4. How does Stelmach distinguish between universal and absolute?

Let no one when young delay to study philosophy, nor when he is old grow weary of his study. For no one can come too early or too late to secure the health of his soul.

—Epicurus

"A Dialogue between Generations for the 'Soul' Purpose of Understanding Immanuel Kant's Categorical Imperative," *Cogito*, July 1996: 142–151. Notes have been omitted.

Sophy, donning a look of contemplation and frustration, is approached by her Grandfather, Phil . . .

GRANDFATHER PHIL: Sophy, you look like you're very bothered about something.

SOPHY: Oh, hi Grampa Phil. Ya, I'm trying to write a paper for my moral philosophy course, and I'm just not sure if I understand the theory that I want to write about.

PHIL: Maybe I can help.

SOPHY: No offence, Grampa, but I doubt you've even heard of the stuff I'm studying.

PHIL: Try me.

SOPHY: The categorical imperative?

PHIL: Ah, yes, Immanuel Kant.

SOPHY: Uh, ya, that's right. I'm impressed.

PHIL: You shouldn't be, Sophy. Just because I'm not a *university* student doesn't mean I can't be a student of philosophy, especially since philosophy helps one gain understanding of his world. Why, philosophy is the most sophisticated form of self-awareness. I would have expected your professor to have told you that.

SOPHY: Oh of course. I just didn't expect someone of your age to be interested in philosophy.

PHIL: And I wouldn't expect someone of *your* age to be so narrow-minded! But let's get on with helping you understand Kant's categorical imperative. Why don't you explain the theory to me.

SOPHY: Okay, I'll try. Well, Kant believes that the solution to a moral dilemma is arrived at by subscribing to an absolute moral principle.

PHIL: And what is that principle?

SOPHY: Kant puts it this way: "Act only according to that maxim by which you can at the same time will that it should become a universal law." He calls this the categorical imperative.

PHIL: Sounds like the Golden Rule.

SOPHY: Actually, it's not the same. The Golden Rule would mean I should treat you the way I would like to be treated. The idea of reciprocity between parties is paramount for the Golden Rule to succeed. But it doesn't necessarily prescribe moral action.

PHIL: It doesn't? But it's what they teach in Sunday school.

SOPHY: Oh boy, that's a whole other can of worms! But consider this example: suppose I were a masochist. If physical pain brought gratification for me,

I would enjoy having others inflict pain on me. The Golden Rule would then allow me to inflict pain on others. Does that sound moral to you, Grampa Phil?

PHIL: No, but how does the categorical imperative prevent this? It seems to me that one could make masochism universal.

SOPHY: Well, I think Kant would disagree. You see, we can't just follow our desires and make them universal moral laws. Masochism is an inclination—one, oddly enough, may derive pleasure from it. The categorical imperative is based on reason, which is divorced from inclination, feeling, or desire. According to Kant, pure practical reason requires us to act morally.

PHIL: So in other words, one will always be moved to act morally because his reasoning tells him to abide by the absolute moral principle—the categorical imperative. That sounds rather simple. But is it really? I seem to recall poring over Kant's philosophy for weeks.

SOPHY: You're absolutely right. It's not so elementary.

PHIL: Absolutely, eh?

SOPHY: Very cute, Grampa Phil. Seriously though, Kant presents a rather convoluted theory. As I've been trying to flesh it out, I've come across some ideas that seem arguable.

PHIL: Great! I love a good argument.

SOPHY: Yes, well, a *good* argument is also what my professor expects. Wrestling with a philosophical giant such as Kant, however, is an arduous task!

PHIL: But remember, Sophy, that you are on your way to Ithaca, and you should not hurry your journey, for it is better that it take you many years so that you can reap the benefits of your journey.

SOPHY: Years?! This paper is due in one week.

PHIL: Take the theory apart piece by piece is what I mean, my Dear.

SOPHY: Right. Well, as I said, paramount to Kant's moral philosophy is the idea that there is an objective moral law which man must follow. My question is, why does man follow it?

PHIL: Let me see what I remember about Kant. Ah, yes. First of all, one of the conditions of the moral law is that it must be universalizable. A second condition is that it treat people as ends, and never as means. And also, the law is self-legislated.

SOPHY: So then I will follow the law because it's what I'd expect everyone else to do in the same situation.

PHIL: Right.

SOPHY: The "people as ends" part is unclear.

PHIL: Remember that a counterpart of the universalizability principle is that moral action always treats people as ends in themselves. He clarifies this by distinguishing between the categorical imperative and a hypothetical imperative. We already know the content of the former; let's consider the latter.

SOPHY: I remember! A hypothetical imperative is based on the idea that one decides his action in accordance with the desired end. So let's say I want to go out with this really great guy, but he has a cousin in town whom he can't leave. The only way I can go out with this guy is if his cousin can have a date too. Suppose I tell my room-mate that there's someone who's really interested in meeting her—the cousin—and this encourages her to go out with me and my guy. In this case, I've decided my action according to what end result I was after, and I used my room-mate as a means to this end.

PHIL: Right, so your decision is binding on the end result you're after.

SOPHY: The categorical imperative does not look for the desired end though, right? By following the principle, people are treated as ends in themselves. But even following the categorical imperative seems to result in a trade-off.

PHIL: How so?

SOPHY: Well, take Kant's own Case of the Inquiring Murderer. If a man fleeing from a murderer runs past you, and the murderer follows him shortly thereafter and asks if you know where his victim fled to, Kant says that you should never lie because telling the truth is an absolute moral principle. It seems to me, though, that you would be jeopardizing someone's life.

PHIL: Kant claims that consequences are not to be considered. We cannot always predict the right consequences.

SOPHY: He seems to denigrate people's knowledge of potential consequences.

PHIL: For Kant the point is really not whether consequences can be accurately predicted. To him, such utilitarian calculations use people as means to an end, whereas, the categorical imperative values all people equally. Following the law makes it so because it is universal, which means all others would choose to do the same.

SOPHY: All others could choose someone to be a victim of a murderer. That doesn't seem right.

PHIL: It seems too rigorous, doesn't it? How do you think Kant would justify it?

SOPHY: Well, I suppose he may accept that there could be exceptions, as long as the exceptions are universalizable. So, for example, the rule could be to tell the truth unless it will result in someone's life being endangered. But there are an infinite number of moral situations. How can I know every rule to cover every situation?

PHIL: Think about it.

SOPHY: The way to make moral decisions is to always refer to the categorical imperative?

PHIL: Exactly. And if you can universalize your action, it's the right one.

SOPHY: There's only one principle then. I guess it's like math. One doesn't need to know the products for the multiplication of every possible combination of numbers. One only needs to understand the basic function of multiplication.

PHIL: That analogy seems to work.

SOPHY: Still, I am uncomfortable with this idea of principled behavior. It seems to legislate a kind of inflexible principle. Isn't there a point where this moral law becomes inhuman? Take for instance the inquiring murderer. Telling the truth requires one to completely ignore the fact that his honesty could result in another person's death. I don't think any ordinary, thinking person could refrain from considering this. Kant seems to be flirting with a rather inhumane mentality.

PHIL: I concur.

SOPHY: Now let's go back to this point about the categorical imperative being self-legislated. I thought it was an objective principle.

PHIL: Well, it's objective, but it's subjective in a way too. In his *Lectures on Ethics* Kant says that "no being, even the divine being, is an author of moral laws, since they do not originate from choice but are practically necessary." We could say that they are objectively necessary—based on reason, not inclination, remember?

SOPHY: Okay, so "the person whose reason completely rules his life will always choose to perform these objectively necessary actions."

PHIL: Right, and "they become *subjectively* necessary by becoming the objects of his personal policy; and they become such on *a priori* grounds, not from inclination." Hey, it's all coming back to me!

SOPHY: So that's why the categorical imperative is self-legislated. And the crucial point for Kant is that it is *a priori* and not chosen because of one's inclination. Now let's see if I can articulate this idea of *a priori*. I did some reading on it.

PHIL: Good. It's an important part of the thesis.

SOPHY: By *a priori* Kant means that it is "necessarily valid always and for everyone."

PHIL: So then that means that the categorical imperative exists independently of circumstance or inclination, and that it is necessary for all rational agents to follow?

SOPHY: Yes. This is a problematic area for me. Kant says it is not personal inclination which makes one follow the categorical imperative, but what he calls pure practical reason. But I'm not sure I can accept Kant's notion of reason.

PHIL: His idea of rationality does seem to be central to the theory.

SOPHY: Unequivocally. Kant says that people have both reason and desire, but that moral action is determined by the overriding force of reason. Desire, then, is constrained. I'm not sure about that.

PHIL: Do you think moral action is tainted by inclination or desire?

SOPHY: I wouldn't say *tainted*. Kant claims that moral acts are performed for the sake of duty. In other words, it is one's duty to follow the categorical imperative. Moreover, Kant draws a distinction between acts that are done out of duty, and those that are done out of inclination. I would think, however, that inclination would have to be involved in order for duty to have force. For instance, David Hume argued that morality required judgment, but without sense, we would not be moved to perform moral acts.

PHIL: Remember, for Kant, reason is the dictator. So this means reason dictates that one has a duty to abide by the moral law. And reason is the master of emotion, impulse, etcetera, not the slave of passions as Hume maintained.

SOPHY: I understand the *function* of reason in Kant's theory; however, I do not agree with the *nature* of reason which he postulates.

PHIL: Ah, I see. Kant argues that "to exercise practical reason is to distance oneself from one's circumstances." And you want to contest this.

SOPHY: Indeed. The mere act of practical reasoning suggests completely divorcing oneself from inclination. I find this questionable.

PHIL: Well, Kant does not suggest that inclination is not present during a moral moment, so to speak. In fact, duty and inclination can both be present at the time of moral action, but one must be motivated by duty—in other words pure practical reason—to label his action as moral.

SOPHY: So his main point is that duty must also be present at the time of inclination in order for an action to be considered good.

PHIL: Yes.

SOPHY: But one may feel a duty to act, plus a positive inclination to do so. Who's to say duty is the motivating reason?

PHIL: I think Kant may reply by saying "it is the reasons which are present when the time comes to act which must be taken account of when the causal relevance of reasons is being assessed." In other words, Kant wouldn't discount duty sharing with inclination in a moral act, but the reason we call an act moral is by virtue of one's response to duty, not desire.

SOPHY: Yes, but dispassionate choice can only be cool, it cannot be cold. Can we remove ourselves completely from our desires?

PHIL: Maybe not, but Kant wouldn't advocate the making of moral judgments according to one's desires or inclinations.

SOPHY: Like I said, one could have a positive inclination to do good.

PHIL: Possibly. However, Kant believed the emotions to be too capricious to be reliable in moral judgment. This is why moral action must be performed on principle.

SOPHY: This seems to be a rather crude view of emotions. It suggests that we have no way of adjusting them, and I would disagree with that. For example, we often learn to control our temper, or refrain from crying.

PHIL: Yes, you have a point, but have you not also experienced times when you couldn't control your anger or your tears? You see, Kant was also of the opinion that emotions are passively experienced. Even though certain events, people, or objects may arouse anger, sadness, or joy, you have no real control over it. If receiving flowers brings you joy, it would be rather difficult to change that joy to anger, wouldn't it?

SOPHY: Your point is well-taken, Grampa. It just seems counter intuitive for a "creature for whom acting on self-interest is reasonable [to] act contrary to his own interests." Let's reconsider the Case of the Inquiring Murderer. Suppose the victim that the murderer was chasing happened to be your own child. It doesn't seem likely that one would be able to ignore this fact; one would have to be moved by his desire to protect his child. Yet, Kant would have the morally responsible agent tell the truth.

PHIL: This relates to what you said about Kant flirting with an inhumane mentality.

SOPHY: Right.

PHIL: It does appear that Kant is portraying a rather dichotomized view of human nature.

SOPHY: Yes, and I think you've just suggested a crucial point.

PHIL: What is that?

SOPHY: Kant's view of human nature. Perhaps his views about rationality need to be understood within the framework of his conceptualization of human nature.

PHIL: Well, obviously he believes human nature is dominated by reason.

SOPHY: Correct. But how does he justify that? What I mean is, how can desire and emotion be discounted, when you and I both know that our feelings are operative in our decisions?

PHIL: They're only discounted in moral decisions.

SOPHY: Yes, I understand that. But I wonder how. Now be patient, Grampa, for I need to sort out Kant's explanations for how it is that reason is divorced from inclination and, furthermore, how it is that reason comes about when one is placed in a moral situation.

PHIL: Go on, Sophy. I'm interested.

SOPHY: According to Kant's philosophy, human nature is made up of two selves: the phenomenal and the noumenal. The phenomenal part of our nature involves our sense perception and ordered experience. This would be what you might refer to as the empirical world because it encompasses the idea of man as affected by space, time and natural causality. The phenomenal sense of self is passive because it is subject to the natural laws, as well as the passions. The phenomenal self is causally determined.

PHIL: The phenomenal self, I take it, is not where moral agency originates.

SOPHY: No, it isn't. The moral self is in the realm of noumena. This is what is completely unknown and unknowable, according to Kant.

PHIL: Is it like the conscience or sub-conscience?

SOPHY: Not really, because we do have access to our conscience. Noumena is a metaphysical concept. It translates into "things-in-themselves." It has nothing to do with how one perceives things, but rather, the way things really are. Whereas the phenomenal self is affected by emotion and experience, the noumenal self is understood as the intelligible world, remote from such experiences.

PHIL: But I thought the noumenal was unknown to us. How, then, can it be intelligible?

SOPHY: What Kant means by this, I think, is that this is where pure practical reason comes from. It's unknowable in the terms we typically understand; that is, we do not perceive it as such, it is just *there*.

PHIL: Wow, this seems odd. How does this relate to morality?

SOPHY: The "noumenal . . . [is] the metaphysical condition of our moral agency." "When we assume the role of moral agents, we 'transpose ourselves into members of the intelligible world,' regard our existence as not subject to the empirical conditions of space, time, or natural causality, and think ourselves free."

PHIL: Kant's theory seems to lose coherence at this point. At least for me. On one hand, our lives are at the mercy of desire and causality, but on the other hand, we are supposedly free from this by virtue of also living in an "intelligible" world where reason reigns supreme.

SOPHY: I concur. This is precisely the confusion I feel over Kant's claim that reason is removed from feeling. I feel there needs to be some sort of reconciliation between phenomena and noumena. Furthermore, if rationality is embodied by the noumenal self, this implies that reason is automatic. And if reason is automatic, then we are all perfectly rational.

PHIL: Hm, I see. Surely we're not all perfectly rational. If we were to assume that good reasons for a particular course of action are objective, and that the course of reasoning is the same for all people, then by virtue of their rationality, all people should arrive at the same conclusions about moral decisions.

SOPHY: Ya, why are some people more rational than others?

PHIL: Perhaps we are to consider rationality as a condition that human beings are *capable* of, but not one which they are necessarily always in.

SOPHY: Well, the moral law is always valid and always applicable to everyone, regardless even if everyone were selfish and maleficent. This establishes the *a priori* nature of the moral law. And I think we can deduce that any act which is performed out of inclination, even if it were a good act, could not be considered moral in Kant's terms. It is following the moral law which makes an act good. But neither of these considerations explains that reason automatically directs us to the moral law. In fact, I'm not confident about the noumenal sense of self.

PHIL: Let's look at this issue of reconciliation between the phenomenal and noumenal selves . . . Noumena govern phenomena. This is how Kant explains pure practical reasoning. Your frustration seems to stem from the fact that Kant claims that there are these two selves existing in human nature, and it is the noumenal self—a seemingly rather abstract concept of self—which is summoned for moral action. How does this occur?

SOPHY: Kant claims that the will is the governor. Just as Kant distinguishes between two selves, he differentiates between two types of will. What he calls *Willkur* is the part of the will which refers to an empirical dimension, involving feeling, passion, desire, and so forth. The *Wille* is the practical reason independent of inclination. Although they differ, they are not meant to be thought of as two separate wills, but merely two aspects of the same. The *Wille* possesses the capacity to comprehend empirical desires, and exerts pressure on *Willkur* for what ought to be.

PHIL: *Wille* is free from desire then?

SOPHY: Exactly. And speaking of free . . . Freedom is a *sine qua non* of morality.

PHIL: A what?

SOPHY: *Sine qua non*—an indispensable condition.

PHIL: Oh.

SOPHY: Kant's idea of freedom is fashioned around a "concept of reason as a free causality capable of asserting itself in the face of the laws of causation."

PHIL: This means that our consciousness of the moral law "necessitates a free causality of pure practical reason, i.e. a capacity of the will to act from purely rational motives." Hm. But if freedom of the will triggers our capacity for pure practical reason, this really only means a capacity for morality, not morality itself.

SOPHY: I suppose that is a good point; however, there is a more significant weakness. To recapitulate, the free will gives us "the power to act from a wholly nonsensuous or *a priori* motive, to conform our will to a moral law self-given by our own reason." Reason is noumenal, ergo reason is in the abstract. This would seem to imply that there is no human agency involved in moral action; moral judgment is a function of a faculty which is metaphysical in nature, and thus, beyond our comprehension, perception, or control.

PHIL: You're right, Sophy, this does make Kant's theory dubious.

SOPHY: I have a related question. If we were to accept that moral actions are the product of pure practical reasoning—abstract reasoning in other words—what would this imply about our inclinations? Specifically, "are we in no way morally accountable for our inclinations themselves?" Kant seems to be concerned only that reason overrides inclination, but doesn't moral character also depend on the desire to do moral acts? Kant assigns the noumenal self the role of moral agency but is our empirical character considered morally neutral?

PHIL: Good question! Recall, however, that Kant admits the existence of inclinations that run contrary to the categorical imperative. Such inclinations are beyond one's control, he claims. What is significant for Kant, then, is not the inclination itself, but the consenting to it.

SOPHY: Maybe an example would clarify what you mean.

PHIL: Alright. Let's refer again to the Case of the Inquiring Murderer. When the murderer asks you about the whereabouts of his victim, you may be tempted to lie in order to save the victim. Kant would say the temptation to lie is not morally blameworthy. BUT if you actually DO lie, then you have committed an immoral act.

SOPHY: It appears that I was right then. The theory excuses one from being morally responsible because it is assumed that pure practical reason will take command. Even though the will must choose the moral act, the will is abstract, and not something one perceives. If the will doesn't choose to act morally, it seems to be a matter of an underdeveloped rationality. The question that follows from this is how does one develop morally? It seems to be a rather untenable task when the agent of morality—pure practical reason—is beyond one's ordinary perception.

PHIL: Are you satisfied with these implications?

SOPHY: No, not at all. Kant makes a distinction between man's empirical dispositions and the moral use he makes of them. If someone is base, therefore, it's okay, just as long as he obeys his moral obligations.

PHIL: What do you see as the problem with that?

SOPHY: It seems pathological, doesn't it? I mean, if someone were notoriously tempted to be immoral, yet always did the right thing, wouldn't you label this as an example of schizophrenia or something?

PHIL: Why don't we leave that for the psychologists to ponder? What is the issue for philosophers?

SOPHY: As I see it, a morality which would allow for inclinations which oppose the moral maxim epitomizes insincerity. This is an insecure moral theory. To follow a law is one thing, but to be committed to it is another. Commitment to morality seems to be more socially desirable.

PHIL: Agreed.

SOPHY: Furthermore, I detect a contradiction in Kant's theory. Kant argues that the nature of man is such that he cannot be held morally responsible for natural tendencies which are contrary to morality. It logically follows that he should not be given credit for moral deeds because the vehicle for moral judgment is reason, which Kant describes as dispositional, rather than consciously cultivated.

PHIL: Yes, and this relates back to the incoherency problem that I expressed before.

SOPHY: You seemed to be accurate about that, for Kant does create a sharp dichotomy between man's empirical nature and his ability to reason. More significantly though, his view of rationality is incomprehensible and, in fact, removes moral responsibility from the individual.

PHIL: But how about the idea of the absolute moral principle? Surely that is solid.

SOPHY: I don't think one exists. Kant says a principle is absolute because it is universalizable. However, universalizability does not translate into absolutism. It means you can generalize, but it doesn't imply that you can deem it absolute. And surely, even absolute principles could conflict.

PHIL: Well, this has been an exhausting discussion, Sophy!

SOPHY: I know. Unfortunately, it has not been exhaustive.

PHIL: I suppose we could discuss freedom in more depth.

SOPHY: Yes, we could also delve into Kant's idea of transcendental apperception.

PHIL: What?

SOPHY: Well, you get my point. I think we've identified a *key* flaw in Kant's theory, however. Perhaps now I have some material to deal with for this paper I have to write. This dialogue has helped me sort the ideas out. Ironically though, the more I think I know about Kant's theory, the more I realize I know nothing at all!

PHIL: Ah, yes, Sophy. That is the nature of this philosophical beast, isn't it?

. . . *and on that thought, Sophy sat down to begin writing her term paper on Kant's categorical imperative.*

QUESTIONS FOR ANALYSIS AND DISCUSSION

1. Sophy and Phil agree that Kant does not take consequences into consideration. Why do they believe that? Do you think that is a fair conclusion? Explain.

2. How is self-interest understood in Kant's moral scheme? Do you believe that his categorical imperative relies on the idea that we should always be altruistic?

3. Philosophers often try to develop a moral theory that reflects common moral intuitions. Recall how utilitarians felt the emphasis on consequences and happiness accords with the commonsense view that people want an ethics to produce some good. Many suggest that Kant makes a similar appeal, except that his duty ethics echoes the commonsense view that the golden rule is the basis for morality. In light of Phil and Sophy's discussion about the golden rule, has Kant developed a theory that reflects common sense? If yes, then is his theory opposed to a utilitarian effort to combine common sense and the desire for happiness? If Kant does not reflect a common sense of morality, is that a problem for his or any theory that seems to ignore common sense? Develop your response in light of your understanding of a commonsense morality.

16.

SIMONE DE BEAUVOIR

The Ethics of Ambiguity

*A prominent existentialist, Simone de Beauvoir (1908–1986) was adept in numerous
fields. Novelist, political critic, social historian, as well as philosopher, de Beauvoir is
generally recognized as one of the founders of modern feminism with her landmark book,*
The Second Sex. *The fame of this work overshadows her other tome,* The Coming
of the Aged, *a social critique of the attitudes and treatment of the elderly in Western
culture. In this selection de Beauvoir outlines some central themes of existentialism to show
how certainty in ethics is often an elusive goal. Given the complexity of human predicaments, one needs to appreciate an ambiguous attitude while making moral decisions. This
ambiguity, according to de Beauvoir, does not entail moral skepticism or egoism.*

CRITICAL READING QUESTIONS

1. Cite an example given by de Beauvoir and describe how it is understood from an existential perspective.
2. Which of the following best expresses de Beauvoir's sense of ambiguity: happiness, freedom, laws, or love?
3. How does an existential ethic help in judging moral conduct?
4. What is the difference between ambiguity and absurdity?

Ambiguity

The notion of ambiguity must not be confused with that of absurdity. To declare
that existence is absurd is to deny that it can ever be given a meaning; to say that it
is ambiguous is to assert that its meaning is never fixed, that it must be constantly
won. Absurdity challenges every ethics; but also the finished rationalization of the
real would leave no room for ethics; it is because man's condition is ambiguous
that he seeks, through failure and outrageousness, to save his existence. Thus, to
say that action has to be lived in its truth, that is, in the consciousness of the an-

---

"Ambiguity," from *Ethics of Ambiguity,* translated by Bernard Frechtman (New York: Citadel Press, 1976), pp. 129–130, 134–137, 142–144, 155–159.

tinomies which it involves, does not mean that one has to renounce it. In *Plutarch Lied* Pierrefeu rightly says that in war there is no victory which can not be regarded as unsuccessful, for the objective which one aims at is the total annihilation of the enemy and this result is never attained; yet there are wars which are won and wars which are lost. So is it with any activity; failure and success are two aspects of reality which at the start are not perceptible. That is what makes criticism so easy and art so difficult: the critic is always in a good position to show the limits that every artist gives himself in choosing himself; painting is not given completely either in Giotto or Titian or Cezanne; it is sought through the centuries and is never finished; a painting in which all pictorial problems are resolved is really inconceivable; painting itself is this movement toward its own reality; it is not the vain displacement of a millstone turning in the void; it concretizes itself on each canvas as an absolute existence. Art and science do not establish themselves despite failure but through it; which does not prevent there being truths and errors, masterpieces and lemons, depending upon whether the discovery or the painting has or has not known how to win the adherence of human consciousness; this amounts to saying that failure, always ineluctable, is in certain cases spared and in others not.

. . .

It will be said that these considerations remain quite abstract. What must be done, practically? Which action is good? Which is bad? To ask such a question is also to fall into a naive abstraction. We don't ask the physicist, "Which hypotheses are true?" Nor the artist, "By what procedures does one produce a work whose beauty is guaranteed?" Ethics does not furnish recipes any more than do science and art. One can merely propose methods. Thus, in science the fundamental problem is to make the idea adequate to its content and the law adequate to the facts; the logician finds that in the case where the pressure of the given fact bursts the concept which serves to comprehend it, one is obliged to invent another concept; but he can not define *a priori* the moment of invention, still less foresee it. Analogously, one may say that in the case where the content of the action falsifies its meaning, one must modify not the meaning, which is here willed absolutely, but the content itself; however, it is impossible to determine this relationship between meaning and content abstractly and universally: there must be a trial and decision in each case. But likewise just as the physicist finds it profitable to reflect on the conditions of scientific invention and the artist on those of artistic creation without expecting any ready-made solutions to come from these reflections, it is useful for the man of action to find out under what conditions his undertakings are valid. We are going to see that on this basis new perspectives are disclosed.

In the first place, it seems to us that the individual as such is one of the ends at which our action must aim. Here we are at one with the point of view of Christian charity, the Epicurean cult of friendship, and Kantian moralism which treats each man as an end. He interests us not merely as a member of a class, a nation, or a collectivity, but as an individual man. This distinguishes us from the systematic politician who cares only about collective destinies; and probably a tramp enjoying his bottle of wine, or a child playing with a balloon, or a Neapolitan lazzarone loafing in the sun in no way helps in the liberation of man; that is why the abstract will of the revolutionary scorns the concrete benevolence which occupies itself in satisfying desires which have no morrow. However, it must not be forgotten that there is a concrete bond between freedom and existence; to will man free is to will there to *be* being, it is to will the disclosure of being in the joy of existence; in order for the idea of liberation to have a concrete meaning, the joy of existence must be asserted in each one, at every instant; the movement toward freedom assumes its real, flesh and blood figure in the world by thickening into pleasure, into happiness. If the satisfaction of an old man drinking a glass of wine counts for nothing, then production and wealth are only hollow myths; they have meaning only if they are capable of being retrieved in individual and living joy. The saving of time and the conquest of leisure have no meaning if we are not moved by the laugh of a child at play. If we do not love life on our own account and through others, it is futile to seek to justify it in any way.

However, politics is right in rejecting benevolence to the extent that the latter thoughtlessly sacrifices the future to the present. The ambiguity of freedom, which very often is occupied only in fleeing from itself, introduces a difficult equivocation into relationships with each individual taken one by one. Just what is meant by the expression "to love others"? What is meant by taking them as ends? In any event, it is evident that we are not going to decide to fulfill the will of every man. There are cases where a man positively wants evil, that is, the enslavement of other men, and he must then be fought. It also happens that, without harming anyone, he flees from his own freedom, seeking passionately and alone to attain the being which constantly eludes him. If he asks for our help, are we to give it to him? We blame a man who helps a drug addict intoxicate himself or a desperate man commit suicide, for we think that rash behavior of this sort is an attempt of the individual against his own freedom; he must be made aware of his error and put in the presence of the real demands of his freedom. Well and good. But what if he persists? Must we then use violence? There again the serious man busies himself dodging the problem; the values of life, of health, and of moral conformism being set up, one does not hesitate to impose them on others. But we know that this pharisaism can cause the worst disasters: lacking drugs, the addict may kill himself. It is no more necessary to serve an abstract ethics obstinately than to yield without due consideration to impulses of pity or generosity; violence is justified only if it opens concrete possibilities to the freedom which I am trying to save; by practising it I am willy-nilly assuming an engagement in relation to others and to myself; a man whom I snatch from the death which he had chosen has the right to come and ask me for means and reasons for living; the tyranny practised against an invalid can be justified only by his getting better; whatever the purity of the intention which animates me, any dictatorship is a fault for which I have to get myself pardoned. Besides, I am in no position to make decisions of this sort indiscriminately; the example of the unknown person who throws himself in to the Seine and whom I hesitate whether or not to fish out is quite abstract; in the absence of a concrete bond with this desperate person my choice will never be anything but a contingent facticity. If I find myself in a position to do violence to a child, or to a melancholic, sick, or distraught person the reason is that I also find myself charged with his upbringing, his happiness, and his health: I am a parent, a teacher, a nurse, a doctor, or a friend. . . . So, by a tacit agreement, by the very fact that I am solicited, the strictness of my decision is accepted or even desired; the more seriously I accept my responsibilities, the more justified it is. That is why love authorizes severities which are not granted to indifference. . . .

Thus, we can set up point number one: the good of an individual or a group of individuals requires that it be taken as an absolute end of our action; but we are not authorized to decide upon this end *a priori*. The fact is that no behavior is ever authorized to begin with, and one of the concrete consequences of existentialist ethics is the rejection of all the previous justifications which might be drawn from the civilization, the age, and the culture; it is the rejection of every principle of authority. To put it positively, the precept will be to treat the other (to the extent that he is the only one concerned, which is the moment that we are considering at present) as a freedom so that his end may be freedom; in using this conducting-wire one will have to incur the risk, in each case, of inventing an original solution. Out of disappointment in love a young girl takes an overdose of pheno-barbital; in the morning friends find her dying, they call a doctor, she is saved; later on she becomes a happy mother of a family; her friends were right in considering her suicide as a hasty and heedless act and in putting her into a position to reject it or return to it freely. But in asylums one sees melancholic patients who have tried to commit suicide twenty times, who devote their freedom to seeking the means of escaping their jailers and of putting an end to their intolerable anguish; the doctor who gives them a friendly pat on the shoulder is their tyrant and their torturer. A friend who is intoxicated by alcohol or drugs asks me for money so that he can go and buy the poison that is necessary to him; I urge him to get cured, I take him to a doctor, I try to help him live; insofar as there is a chance of my being successful, I am acting correctly in refusing him the sum he asks for. But if circumstances prohibit me from doing anything to change the situation in which he is struggling, all I can do is give in; a deprivation of a few hours will do nothing but exasperate his torments uselessly; and he may have recourse to extreme means to get what I do not give him. That is also the problem touched on by Ibsen in *The Wild Duck*. An individual lives in a situation of falsehood; the falsehood is violence, tyranny: shall I tell the truth in order to free the victim? It would first be necessary to create a situation of such a kind that the truth might be bearable and that, though losing his illusions, the deluded individual might again find about him reasons for hoping. What makes the problem more complex is that the freedom of one man almost always concerns that of other individuals. Here is a married couple who persist in living in a hovel; if one does not succeed in giving them the desire to live in a more healthful dwelling, they must be allowed to follow their preferences; but the situation changes if they have children; the freedom of the parents would be the ruin of their sons, and as freedom and the future are on the side of the latter, these are the ones who must first be taken into account. The Other is multiple, and on the basis of this new questions arise.

One might first wonder for whom we are seeking freedom and happiness. When raised in this way, the problem is abstract; the answer will, therefore, be arbitrary, and the arbitrary always involves outrage. It is not entirely the fault of the district social-worker if she is apt to be odious; because, her money and time being limited, she hesitates before distributing it to this one or that one, she appears to others as a pure externality, a blind facticity. Contrary to the formal strictness of Kantianism for whom the more abstract the act is the more virtuous it is, generosity seems to us to be better grounded and therefore more valid the less distinction there is between the other and ourself and the more we fulfill ourself in taking the other as an end. That is what happens if I am engaged in relation to others. The Stoics impugned the ties of family, friendship, and nationality so that they recognized only the universal form of man. But man is man only through situations whose particularity is precisely a universal fact. There are men who expect help from certain men and not from others, and these expectations define privileged lines of action. It is fitting that the negro fight for the negro, the Jew for the Jew, the proletarian for the proletarian, and the Spaniard in Spain. But the assertion of these particular solidarities must not contradict the will for universal solidarity and each finite undertaking must also be open on the totality of men.

    . . . Indeed, on the one hand, it would be absurd to oppose a liberating action with the pretext that it implies crime and tyranny; for without crime and tyranny there could be no liberation of man; one can not escape that dialectic which goes from freedom to freedom through dictatorship and oppression. But, on the other hand, he would be guilty of allowing the liberating movement to harden into a moment which is acceptable only if it passes into its opposite; tyranny and crime must be kept from triumphantly establishing themselves in the world; the conquest of freedom is their only justification, and the assertion of freedom against them must therefore be kept alive.

Conclusion

Is this kind of ethics individualistic or not? Yes, if one means by that that it accords to the individual an absolute value and that it recognizes in him alone the power of laying the foundations of his own existence. It is individualism in the sense in which the wisdom of the ancients, the Christian ethics of salvation, and the Kantian ideal of virtue also merit this name; it is opposed to the totalitarian doctrines which raise up beyond man the mirage of Mankind. But it is not solipsistic, since the individual is defined only by his relationship to the world and to other individuals; he exists only by transcending himself, and his freedom can be achieved only through the freedom of others. He justifies his existence by a movement which, like freedom, springs from his heart but which leads outside of him.

    This individualism does not lead to the anarchy of personal whim. Man is free; but he finds his law in his very freedom. First, he must assume his freedom and not flee it; he assumes it by a constructive movement: one does not exist without doing something; and also by a negative movement which rejects oppression for oneself and others. In construction, as in rejection, it is a matter of reconquering freedom on the contingent facticity of existence, that is, of taking the given, which, at the start, *is there* without any reason, as something willed by man. A conquest of this kind is never finished; the contingency remains, and, so that he may assert his will, man is even obliged to stir up in the world the outrage he does not want. But this element of failure is a very condition of his life; one can never dream of eliminating it without immediately dreaming of death. This does not mean that one should consent to failure, but rather one must consent to struggle against it without respite.

Yet, isn't this battle without victory pure gullibility? . . .

We have already attempted to answer this objection. One can formulate it only by placing himself on the grounds of an inhuman and consequently false objectivity; within Mankind men may be fooled; the word "lie" has a meaning by opposition to the truth established by men themselves, but Mankind can not fool itself completely since it is precisely Mankind which creates the criteria of true and false. In Plato, art is mystification because there is the heaven of Ideas; but in the earthly domain all glorification of the earth is true as soon as it is realized. Let men attach value to words, forms, colors, mathematical theorems, physical laws, and athletic prowess; let them accord value to one another in love and friendship, and the objects, the events, and the men immediately *have* this value; they have it absolutely. It is possible that a man may refuse to love anything on earth; he will prove this refusal and he will carry it out by suicide. If he lives, the reason is that, whatever he may say, there still remains in him some attachment to existence; his life will be commensurate with this attachment; it will justify itself to the extent that it genuinely justifies the world.

This justification, though open upon the entire universe through time and space, will always be finite. Whatever one may do, one never realizes anything but a limited work, like existence itself which tries to establish itself through that work and which death also limits. It is the assertion of our finiteness which doubtless gives the doctrine which we have just evoked its austerity and, in some eyes, its sadness. As soon as one considers a system abstractly and theoretically, one puts himself, in effect, on the plane of the universal, thus, of the infinite. That is why reading the Hegelian system is so comforting. I remember having experienced a great feeling of calm on reading Hegel in the impersonal framework of the Bibliotheque Nationale in August 1940. But once I got into the street again, into my life, out of the system, beneath a real sky, the system was no longer of any use to me: what it had offered me, under a show of the infinite, was the consolations of death; and I again wanted to live in the midst of living men. I think that, inversely, existentialism does not offer to the reader the consolations of an abstract evasion: existentialism proposes no evasion. On the contrary, its ethics is experienced in the truth of life, and it then appears as the only proposition of salvation which one can address to men. Taking on its own account Descartes' revolt against the evil genius, the pride of the thinking reed in the face of the universe which crushes him, it asserts that, despite his limits, through them, it is up to each one to fulfill his existence as an absolute. Regardless of the staggering dimensions of the world about us, the density of our ignorance, the risks of catastrophes to come, and our individual weakness within the immense collectivity, the fact remains that we are absolutely free today if we choose to will our existence in its finiteness, a finiteness which is open on the infinite. And in fact, any man who has known real loves, real revolts, real desires, and real will knows quite well that he has no need of any outside guarantee to be sure of his goals; their certitude comes from his own drive. There is a very old saying which goes: "Do what you must, come what may." That amounts to saying in a different way that the result is not external to the good will which fulfills itself in aiming at it. If it came to be that each man did what he must, existence would be saved in each one without there being any need of dreaming of a paradise where all would be reconciled in death.

QUESTIONS FOR ANALYSIS AND DISCUSSION

1. A standard criticism of existentialism is its emphasis on the individual's own role in establishing meaning for events and goals. Despite her efforts to counter this criticism, de Beauvoir still emphasizes the individual's active response when making a genuine moral decision. Do you think she has succeeded? Why, or why not?

2. Consider a moral controversy today. How would an existentialist analyze it? Do you believe that an existentialist ethic could contribute to our efforts in judging moral conduct?

3. De Beauvoir rejects a calculation of pleasures and pains as a method for making moral decisions. Why does she say this? How might a utilitarian counter her argument? Where do you stand in this dispute?

4. In Chapter 1 several writers proposed that moral conduct is largely a result of either cultural influence or genetic makeup. How does de Beauvoir's focus on freedom relate to the moral views of sociobiology, cultural relativism, or egoism? Clarify your response.

17.

LAO TZU

Wisdom and Artificial Codes

According to the founder of Taoism, Lao Tzu (c. 570 B.C.), many human efforts toward developing a moral system may be futile. The title of his best-known work, Tao Te Ching, *has been translated numerous ways. "Tao" itself has been rendered as "the Way" or "the One." "Te" is generally translated as "power," "character," or "virtue." Hence, a*

"Wisdom and Artificial Codes," from *Tao Teh King*, interpreted by Archie J. Bahm (New York: Frederick Ungar, 1958), sections VIII–XXIV.

literal meaning of the title could be "Way-Virtue-Classic." Taoism contrasts with Confucianism in several important ways, most notably in the attitude toward social rules and public leadership. Whereas for Confucious a moral person tried to obey specific commands or rules of government, Lao Tzu often talks about the difficulty of articulating the proper guides to moral conduct and the value of noncomformity. If anything, the moral authority for humans is found not in social or political institutions but in nature. Taoism, then, is not easily persuaded by the complicated analyses and reasons that comprise much of moral reflection.

CRITICAL READING QUESTIONS

1. Why does Lao Tzu compare human conduct with the behavior of water?
2. What is the view of self-sufficiency?
3. For Lao Tzu, do the positive aspects of life exclude the negative?
4. What is meant by "artificial codes"?

VIII

The best way to conduct oneself may be observed in the behavior of water.
Water is useful to every living thing, yet it does not demand pay in return for its services; it does not even require that it be recognized, esteemed, or appreciated for its benefits.
This illustrates how intelligent behavior so closely approximates the behavior of Nature itself.
If experience teaches that houses should be built close to the ground,
That friendship should be based upon sympathy and good will,
That good government employs peaceful means of regulation,
That business is more successful if it employs efficient methods,
That wise behavior adapts itself appropriately to the particular circumstances,
All this is because these are the easiest ways.
If one proceeds naturally, without ambition or envy, everything works out for the best.

IX

Going to extremes is never best.
For if you make a blade too sharp, it will become dull too quickly.

And if you hoard all the wealth, you are bound to be attacked.

If you become proud and arrogant regarding your good fortune, you will naturally beget enemies who jealously despise you.

The way to success is this: having achieved your goal, be satisfied not to go further.

For this is the way Nature operates.

X

If you would retain a wholesome personality, must you not restrain your lower interests from dominating over your higher interests?

If you wish to live healthily, should you not breathe naturally, like a child, and not hold your breath until your vitality is nearly exhausted?

If you desire to realize the potentialities of your indescribable original nature, how can you insist that some selected aspect of your personality is really superior to that original nature?

If you are required to govern others, ought you not be able to guide them by example, rather than by forcing your will upon them?

If Nature's way is a joint process of initiation and completion, sowing and reaping, producing and consuming, can you lightly demand that you deserve always to play the role of the consumer?

If you desire to know the natures of the various kinds of things, must you meddle with them, experiment with them, try to change them, in order to find out?

Nature procreates all things and then devotes itself to caring for them,

Just as parents give birth to children without keeping them as slaves.

It willingly gives life, without first asking whether the creatures will repay for its services.

It provides a pattern to follow, without requiring anyone to follow it.

This is the secret of intelligent activity.

XI

Every positive factor involves its negative or opposing factor; for example:

In order to turn a wheel, although thirty spokes must revolve, the axle must remain motionless; so both the moving and the non-moving are needed to produce revolution.

In order to mold a vase, although one must use clay, he must also provide a hollow space empty of clay; so both clay and the absence of clay are required to produce a vessel.

In order to build a house, although we must establish solid walls, we must also provide doors and windows; so both the impenetrable and penetrable are essential to a useful building.

Therefore, we profit equally by the positive and the negative ingredients in each situation.

XII

Interest in the varieties of color diverts the eye from regarding the thing which is colored.

Attention to the differences between sounds distracts the ear from consideration for the source of the sounds.

Desire for enjoyment of the various flavors misdirects the appetite from seeking foods which are truly nourishing.

Excessive devotion to chasing about and pursuing things agitates the mind with insane excitement.

Greed for riches ensnares one's efforts to pursue his healthier motives.

The intelligent man is concerned about his genuine needs and avoids being confused by dazzling appearances.

He wisely distinguishes the one from the other.

XIII

Pride and shame cause us much fearful anxiety.

But our inner peace and distress should be our primary concerns.

Why do pride and shame cause us so much fearful anxiety?

Because:

Pride attaches undue importance to the superiority of one's status in the eyes of others;

And shame is fear of humiliation at one's inferior status in the estimation of others.

When one sets his heart on being highly esteemed, and achieves such rating, then he is automatically involved in fear of losing his status.

Then protection of his status appears to be his most important need. And humiliation seems the worst of all evils.

This is the reason why pride and shame cause us so much fearful anxiety.

Why should our inner peace and distress be our primary concerns?

Because:

The inner self is our true self; so in order to realize our true self, we must be willing to live without being dependent upon the opinions of others. When we are completely self-sufficient, then we can have no fear of disesteem.

He who wisely devotes himself to being self-sufficient, and therefore does not depend for his happiness upon external ratings by others, is the one best able to set an example for, and to teach and govern, others.

XIV

Since what is ultimate in Nature cannot be seen with one's eyes, it is spoken of as invisible.

Since it cannot be heard with one's ears, it is called inaudible.

Since it cannot be grasped in one's hands, it is thought of as intangible.

But not even all three of these together can adequately describe it.

Nature did not originate in beginnings, and will not reach its goal in endings.

Rather it acts unceasingly, without either absolute beginnings or final endings.

If we cannot describe it intelligibly, this is because it is beyond our understanding.

Nature is the formless source of all forms, and yet it remains unaffected by its forms.

Thus it appears to us as if mysterious.

No matter how closely we scrutinize its coming toward us, we cannot discover a beginning.

No matter how long we pursue it, we never find its end.

One must comprehend the way in which the original Nature itself operates, if he wishes to control present conditions.

That is, he should study the ultimate source itself.

This is the way to understand how Nature behaves.

XV

In primitive times, intelligent men had an intuitively penetrating grasp of reality which could not be stated in words.

Since their instinctive beliefs have not been recorded for us, we can only infer them from old sayings which have come down to us.

Regarding caution when crossing a stream in winter: the more nervous you are, the more likely you are to slip and fall.

Regarding suspicion of enemies: the more you fear others, the more they will be afraid of you.

Regarding courtesy as a guest: the longer you stay, the more you become indebted to your host.

Regarding melting ice: the more you do to prevent it from melting, the quicker it melts.

Regarding making furniture: the more you carve the wood, the weaker it gets.

Regarding digging ditches: the steeper you slope their sides, the sooner they will wash down.

Regarding muddy water: the more you try to stir the dirt out of it, the murkier it gets.

What, then, should we do in order to clear the muddy water? Leave it alone and the dirt will settle out by itself.

What, then, must we do in order to achieve contentment? Let each thing act according to its own nature, and it will eventually come to rest in its own way.

Those who fully comprehend the true nature of existence do not try to push things to excess.

And because they do not try to push things to excess, they are able to satisfy their needs repeatedly without exhausting themselves.

XVI

In order to arrive at complete contentment, restrain your ambitions.

For everything which comes into being eventually returns again to the source from which it came.

Each thing which grows and develops to the fullness of its own nature completes its course by declining again in a manner inherently determined by its own nature.

Completing its life is as inevitable as that each thing shall have its own goal.

Each thing having its own goal is necessary to the nature of things.

He who knows that this is the ultimate nature of things is intelligent; he who does not is not.

Being intelligent, he knows that each has a nature which is able to take care of itself. Knowing this, he is willing that each thing follow its own course.

Being willing to let each thing follow its own course, he is gracious. Being gracious, he is like the source which graciously gives life to all.

Being like the gracious source of all, he embodies Nature's way within his own being. And in thus embodying Nature's way within himself, he embodies its perpetually recurrent principles within himself.

And so, regardless of what happens to his body, there is something about him which goes on forever.

XVII

The most intelligent leaders bring about results without making those controlled realize that they are being influenced.

The less intelligent seek to motivate others by appeals to loyalty, honor, self-interest, and flattery.

Those still less intelligent employ fear by making their followers think they will not receive their rewards.

The worst try to force others to improve by condemning their conduct.

But since, if leaders do not trust their followers then their followers will not trust the leaders,

The intelligent leader will be careful not to speak as if he doubted or distrusted his follower's ability to do the job suitably.

When the work is done, and as he wanted it done, he will be happy if the followers say: "This is just the way we wanted it."

XVIII

When people try to improve upon, and thus deviate from, the way Nature itself naturally functions, they develop artificial codes of right and wrong.

When knowledge becomes highly abstract, men are deceived by mistaking abstractions for realities.

When instinctive family sympathies are replaced by rules for proper conduct, then parents become "responsible" and children become "dutiful."

When corruption replaces genuine benevolence in government, then loyalty oaths are demanded of officials.

XIX

Therefore—

If we ignore intricate learning and knowledge of petty distinctions, we shall be many times better off.

If we neglect to insist upon the formal proprieties of etiquette, our intuitive sympathies will return.

If we abolish opportunities for profiteering "within the law," incentive for political corruption will disappear.

If the foregoing three principles are unclear, then at least the following are understandable:

Simply be yourself.

Act naturally.

Refrain from self-assertiveness.

Avoid covetousness.

XX

If we stop fussing about grammatical trivialities, we will get along much better.

The difference between "Yes" and "Ya" is insignificant as compared with a genuine distinction like "Good" and "Bad."

Yet some people are as fearful of making a grammatical mistake as of committing a vital error.

How stupid to waste our lives in infinite details!

While others enjoy devoting themselves to ceremonious holiday celebrations, such as the spring festivals, I stay at home as unperturbed as a helpless babe.

So while others are feasting, I appear neglected.

Am I the one who is a misguided fool?

When every one else is exuberant, I continue to be disinterested.

When everyone else is alert to the niceties of etiquette, I persist in being indifferent.

I am as unconcerned as the rolling ocean, without a care to bother me.

While others behave like busybodies, I alone remain placid and resist arousement.

How can I withstand the pressure of public opinion? Because I am succored by Mother Nature herself.

XXI

Intelligence consists in acting according to Nature.

Nature is something which can be neither seen nor touched.

Yet all of the forms which can possibly be seen or touched are latent within it.

And all of the things that will actually be seen or touched are embedded as potentialities within it.

Deep in its depths are activating forces.

No matter how unplumbable the depths, these forces unfailingly sustain the world as it appears to us.

From the beginning until now, they have never ceased to express themselves in appearances.

How do I know all this to be so? It is intuitively self-evident, for every existing thing testifies to it, including what appears right here and now.

XXII

Submit to Nature if you would reach your goal.

For, whoever deviates from Nature's way, Nature forces back again.

Whoever gives up his desire to improve upon Nature will find Nature satisfying all his needs.

Whoever finds his desires extinguished will find more desires arising of their own accord.

Whoever desires little is easily satisfied.

Whoever desires much suffers frustration.

Therefore, the intelligent person is at one with Nature, and so serves as a model for others.

By not showing off, he is exemplary.

By not asserting that he is right, he does the right thing.

By not boasting of what he will do, he succeeds in doing more than he promises.

By not gloating over his successes, his achievements are acclaimed by others.

By not competing with others, he achieves without opposition.

Therefore the old saying is not idle talk:

"Submit to Nature if you would reach your goal."

For this is the only genuine way.

XXIII

Things which act naturally do not need to be told how to act.

The wind and rain begin without being ordered, and quit without being commanded.

This is the way with all natural beginnings and endings.

If Nature does not have to instruct the wind and rain, how much less should man try to direct them?

Whoever acts naturally is Nature itself acting.

So whoever acts intelligently is intelligence acting.

And whoever acts unintelligently is unintelligence in action.

By acting naturally, one reaps Nature's rewards.

So by acting intelligently, one achieves intelligent goals,

Whereas by acting unintelligently, one comes to an unintelligent end.

Those who do not trust Nature as a model cannot be trusted as guides.

XXIV

One who tries to stand on tiptoe cannot stand still.

One who stretches his legs too far cannot walk.

One who advertises himself too much is ignored.

One who is too insistent on his own views finds few to agree with him.

One who claims too much credit does not get even what he deserves.

One who is too proud is soon humiliated.

These, when judged by the standards of Nature, are condemned as "Extremes of greediness and self-destructive activity."

Therefore, one who acts naturally avoids such extremes.

QUESTIONS FOR ANALYSIS AND DISCUSSION

1. Throughout the selection Lao Tzu tells us that our conduct should resemble the workings of nature. How do you understand the workings of nature? Is this a guide for our own morality?

2. Inner peace is one value emphasized by Lao Tzu. What does this mean? Do you think it implies an ethic that is primary concerned with self and neglects the well-being of others?

3. Many of the passages remind us that leading the moral life involves simplicity. If so, why do so many of us have difficulty being good?

4. From other readings you have covered so far, which ones might best exemplify the notion of "artificial codes"? Do you think characterizing a morality as artificial is a criticism? Could you defend any one of the moral perspectives as artificial because nature does not reveal to us a guide for moral conduct? That is, even though a moral theory as outlined by a utilitarian or an egoist or a relativist has flaws, is it still preferable to a moral attitude that looks to nature as a guide? Develop your thoughts on this dispute.

CHAPTER THREE

What Is Virtue Ethics?

VIRTUES, n. pl. Certain Abstentions

—Ambrose Bierce, *The Devil's Dictionary*

There are youthful mathematical geniuses, but rarely, if ever, youthful moral geniuses, and this shows us something significant about the sort of knowledge that moral knowledge is. Virtue ethics builds this in . . . by couching its rules in terms whose applications may indeed call for the most delicate and sensitive judgment.

—Rosalind Hursthouse, *"Virtue Theory and Abortion"*

You may recall a recent court case in which a jury awarded more than $1 million to a woman who was burned by a spilled cup of hot coffee sold by a well-known fast food restaurant. When the news hit the airwaves, moral observers had a grand time—yet another sign that our culture is morally corrupt, they bemoaned. The greed of the plaintiff and her lawyers, the dubious suffering resulting from a spilled cup of coffee, and the inequities of our system of justice were all topics for discussion. Indeed, the vices so apparent in the plaintiff's case were fodder for public discussion about the moral decay of the average citizen.

Consider another scenario. Suppose the plaintiff first sought to avoid pursuing legal action. Suppose she had tried to contact management, asking for an apology and reimbursement for her medical costs, which were not easy to recover given her age, income, and the severity of the burns—as anyone could attest. Suppose that the fast food chain's representatives continued to ignore or dismiss the injured woman's requests until she finally heeded friends' advice and consulted an attorney. And finally, suppose that instead of settling out of court to cover her medical and now growing legal expenses, the fast food chain put up a big fight to avoid acknowledging its responsibility for the injured woman's plight. In fact, this is what did happen. Yet moral critics have devoted little attention to this version of the plaintiff's moral character. Here she showed forgiveness, temperance, and patience—even hope—by expecting the restaurant to deal with her as a human being in good faith.

In either case it is hard to begrudge the plaintiff her award. She did not break any law and won by judgment from the courts. And let's be honest—who among us would mind making an easy million simply by suffering from hot coffee spilled on a leg or arm? Many have suffered a lot more and received a lot less.

Yet who would you rather have as a friend, a neighbor, a spouse, or a colleague? The individual portrayed in the first scenario or in the second?

For many approaches to ethics, these questions are of secondary importance. Approaches that focus on rights, greatest happiness principles, duties, or self-interest (as discussed in Chapters 1 and 2) regard actions, rules, or results as the center of moral thought. But the cornerstone of virtue-based ethics involves questions about the kind of moral character we expect of others and of ourselves.

A virtue ethics approach to morality emphasizes the value of becoming a certain kind of person—one who has both learned and wants to do the good deed. A virtuous person uses his or her strengths and positive values to overcome the tendencies or temptations opposed to virtues—namely, the vices. This tension provides a dramatic element in virtue ethics. All our efforts to become moral persons can be quickly erased by the potential harm rendered in committing a vicious deed. For example, how often have you seen the trust shared by friends destroyed by a single act of dishonesty? Virtue ethics emphasizes the kind of persons we should strive to become rather than focusing on the sorts of things we should do.

For moral philosophers, if virtue ethics is to contend with or displace utilitarianism or deontology (the study of moral obligation), it must address three points. First, does virtue ethics have a universal basis? Second, does it contain a personal as well as a social sense of well-being? And third, can virtue ethics help us resolve specific moral conflicts?

If the history of moral thought were the deciding criterion, this would be, in common parlance, a "no-brainer." Moral thought has been dominated by discussion of virtues and vices. However, in the last two or three centuries this discussion has yielded to an increased focus on rights, social justice, duties, and personal happiness. The recent revival of virtue ethics has been labeled a conservative backlash to more progressive moral attitudes. And indeed, some of the more notable figures entering the public discussion of the virtues are officials in politically conservative organizations. From a historical perspective this is somewhat ironic. The two most famous proponents of the virtues, Socrates and Jesus—both executed for their moral teachings—were challengers of the status quo.

History and politics aside, there are philosophical reasons for questioning the centrality of the virtues for a moral life. First, are the virtues universal? Some defenders of virtue ethics have trouble accounting for the fact that not everyone is subject to the same vices. Neither does everyone enjoy the same virtues. Moreover, critics of virtue ethics point out that it is not clear how virtuous persons contribute to a unified sense of the common good or social happiness. Second, does the emphasis on developing moral character undercut the importance of establishing policies or institutions that give a social basis for realizing the good life? Skeptics wonder if a virtuous life can fully replace civil rights or principles of justice as the guide to moral culture. Third, are the key ideas of virtue ethics too vague to help us resolve moral controversies? Many of us want help in understanding and answering current moral questions involving abortion, assisted suicide, sexual conduct, family life, or lying and deception. Can the study of virtues and vices assist us in answering these questions?

The selections in this chapter introduce some basic moral issues centered around virtues and vices. The case study by literature professor Lore Segal highlights a touching and tragic episode involving two widely respected virtues, truthfulness and hope.

Indian philosopher M. Hiriyanna reviews four classes of values and distinguishes two related types of virtues, self-regarding and other-regarding. Both are essential to moral purification or *moksha.*

Why are the virtues so difficult to live by? Paul Jordan-Smith, a folklorist, concisely describes the power of the vices, or sins. Though the popular tradition features seven deadly sins, there has been a lively debate about both the variety of vices and the deadliest of vices.

Benjamin Franklin, an early American statesman and inventor, prescribes a diligent pursuit of a virtuous life. Given the difficulty of the task, he outlines a day-to-day schedule for embracing one virtue at a time. Some, he admits, are more difficult than others.

Aristotle is widely considered Western philosophy's first systematic thinker about the virtues. A student of Plato, Aristotle refines his teacher's ideas on virtues, interweaving political, pedagogical, and intellectual factors into a coherent whole. He emphasizes development of moral character through a rational development of moral habits.

David Carr, a British philosopher, reviews current criticisms of virtue ethics. Carr contends that the critics fail to see how virtue ethics is the basis for both a personal and a communitarian morality.

18.

LORE SEGAL

Case Study: My Grandfather's Walking Stick, or The Pink Lie

Many problems in ethics are introduced as conflicts among duties, rights, or principles. English professor Lore Segal (b. 1928) recounts the lives of her grandparents, beginning with their painful experiences in World War II, highlighting a conflict between two perennial virtues, hope and truthfulness. Segal presents several persuasive reasons to support

"My Grandfather's Walking Stick, or The Pink Lie," *Social Research,* Fall 1996, 63(3): 931–941.

either virtue in moments of emotional and moral crisis. She closes with her slant on the
conflict and asks the reader to evaluate his or her own response to the story.

┤ **CRITICAL READING QUESTIONS** ├

1. What are two differences between the dictionary definition of a lie and Segal's notion of a pink lie?
2. Does hope involve or reject falsehood? Why?
3. How does the walking stick reflect an appeal to hope or truthfulness?

Human Kind
  cannot bear very much reality.
         —T. S. Eliot

When Pandora had upended her box of calamities over the earth, there fell out, so says the story, a last straggler: hope.

Hope pities us and lies. It pities our terrors and invites us to tell ourselves that the things we fear happen to other people. We are a special case. When it comes to us, says hope, calamity will turn aside, may yet turn to our advantage.

Hope pities our dowdiness. It promises that we will find the treasure, marry the prince, and inherit the kingdom. Hope says that it is our birthright to win the lottery[1] and write a classic. If we are American it will be a best seller. We will make the NBA, be the next Michael Jackson, become president.

And hope pities our disappointment with the world. It tells us to look forward to the time of the messiah to come, or backward to the paradise that must surely have been. The heart rebels at the truth that what is is it. Somewhere, says hope, in our past or in our future there has just got to be a golden age.

Friends to whom I argue my contention that hoping contains an inherent lie disagree violently. The Oxford English Dictionary (OED) explains their reaction: it defines the lie as "a false statement made with intent to deceive; a criminal falsehood," and goes on to say, "In mod. use, the word is normally a violent expression of moral disapprobation, which in polite conversation tends to be avoided, the synonym *falsehood* or *un-truth* being often substituted as relatively euphemistic."

The OED lists only one other category, our old friend the white lie, and defines it as "a consciously untrue statement which is not considered criminal; a falsehood rendered venial or praiseworthy by its motive."

---

[1] In a recent television interview, a professional sweepstakes organizer explained the statistical improbability of winning. Asked why he thought the public continued to enter sweepstakes he replied that all considered themselves "special cases." The only realists, he said, are depressed people.

I wish to advance the pink or rose-colored lie and define it as an unconsciously untrue statement never considered blameworthy because it is not considered to be a falsehood.

I want to look at the pink lie in terms of the three aspects of the OED's definition of the lie and the white lie: function, intentionality, and moral reputation.

To take the last first. Hope has a universally favorable press. The 23rd Psalm ranks it with faith, hope, and charity, which is to say, with love.

And it is true that hope's gentle falsehoods are essential to our progress. It is the dream of an improbably prosperous outcome that initiates, and lets us persevere in, our best and worst ambitions. We need hope to power any action not of the instinctive kind. What personal, civic, or criminal act would we undertake—who would marry, run for office, plan a heist or an essay, start a polar expedition or a war—without the hope of better success than we have reason and experience to believe to be plausible?

Doctors tell us that hope assists the process of healing. Perhaps our very instincts lose courage where we stop hoping: I remember the evening, at supper, when my grandmother stopped lifting her fork up to her mouth.

Hope's necessary falsehoods are the tools in our survival kit and blessedly preserve us from intellectual despair, the sin accounted as the seventh and deadliest because it demonstrates an absence of Faith.

Hope's rose-colored falsehoods function to deceive ourselves and to participate in the deceptions practiced by our community. Hope ignores the evidence of history and experience; it lies in face of its better knowledge in order to con us out of knowing what we know and into thinking what we wish.

In the Sixties we held hands and sang "We shall overcome," adding "some day," which used to make my eyes itch. "Some day" means "obviously not today nor probably tomorrow either, but surely on some future day," where the word "surely" gives the lie to its definition. "Surely" means to mean "I am certain this is so" but functions to put certainty in question. If I say, "I will surely finish writing this essay today," you understand me to mean that I *wish* that I would finish it, as well as my *un*certainty as to my ability to do so. I do not say, "I will surely die," for that would mean I think my death admits of a question requiring denial.

When we sang of "some day" on which the world would have overcome our mutual prejudice and hatreds, we were singing of the day the messiah is going to come, and he is always going to come if you are a Jew, or come for the second time if you are Christian, on "some day" for which we want to weep with desire.

But some day, before he comes, alternately returns, we are going [to] die, and that is something we lie about privately, to ourselves, and holding hands, communally.

My late husband used to tell the story of a Martian chief who summons his head astronaut and orders an expedition to the earth. The chief is puzzled by an anomaly he has been observing over the eons: Earthlings appear to be born to live for a period of time after which they die. Now a race, he argues, that knows it is going to die would be incapable of doing what Earthlings can be observed to do day in and day out: get out of bed, dress, go to their jobs, come home, eat their suppers, drink, laugh; on occasion they clap their hands.

Had the expedition in David's story taken place, the head astronaut would have brought the explanation home: the human race knows it is mortal but does not believe it. It believes what the serpent spoke to our mother Eve: "You are not going to die," he told her, which she understood to mean that Adam and the children would surely die but not she, Eve; she was a special case, and so she took the apple and bit it.

Curious, the difference to our feelings when the doctor has numbered the years we will live: the difference is not the limited number; the number was always limited. It is the number made actual that disables the lie of the "special case" and forces us to believe what we know: we will die.

Community systematizes the private lie, and the language backs it. We say "a life has been saved" when we mean a death has been postponed. Usage promises that we merely pass away or, more hopefully, on.

There is a wonderful variety of beliefs by means of which we Earthlings disbelieve our ceasing:[2] Christianity says our behavior determines whether we live our deaths in bliss or punishment, or circling in limbo while the question continues in abeyance.

Gehenna, the place of Jewish afterlife, does not abandon us: we may get to come back out. It does not say to where. The Jewish mind, though unwilling to imagine its own annihilation, refuses to settle the question or to obsess about it.

The Greek hero could, with special dispensation, cross Acheron and visit his dead fathers in Hades where he would live out his own death.

The Pharaohs spent the national treasury on furnishing themselves a location and supplying it with their worldly toys—pets, dishes, ornaments—so that their preserved selves would continue in luxury.

I have a friend who believes in the transmigration of his soul for another round of life which must, surely, make up to him for the unfairness meted out to his industry and talent in this one. And, he argues, that life would not punish babies with illness, abuse, or the sufferings of the Holocaust unless they deserved it for what they must have perpetrated in some previous existence. His proof is his heart's certainty that life *could not,* in both these instances, be as unfair as he knows, from his own observation, that it is. The trick is to locate hope's proof in that bourn from which no traveler returns to explode the story.

Give me an ounce of civet, good apothecary, to sweeten my imagination.

—William Shakespeare

We must, finally, settle the question of intentionality: how, if we believe our lie, can we be said to intend to deceive? Is a statement false when the liar is persuaded of its truth as a matter of faith, for instance, or the result of a successful act of self deception? Or can we ask ourselves the extent to which we choose—to which we give ourselves permission—to not know what we know?

I have a friend who advocates denial as a serviceable method for dealing with truths she would not know how to handle or how to bear. When I offered to join

---

[2] Ignore, reader, the belief to which you subscribe yourself and join me in wondering at the other ones.

her in grieving over a piece of mortal news affecting a mutual friend she proposed instead that we disbelieve it together.

This is the honest lie. It is more common not to acknowledge up front what it is that we are up to.

In a late essay entitled "The Memory of the Offense" (1989), Primo Levi discusses the revisionism of a too painful past by both victim and perpetrator of that monumental offense we call Holocaust. "A person who has been wounded tends to block out the memory so as not to renew the pain; the person who has inflicted the wound pushes the memory deep down to be rid of it, to alleviate the feeling of guilt" (p. 24).

Primo Levi sketches the incremental stages by which the perpetrator provides himself this alleviation:

> There are, it is true, those who lie consciously, coldly falsifying reality itself, but more numerous are those who weigh anchor, move off, momentarily or forever, from genuine memories and fabricate for themselves a convenient reality . . . they feel repugnance for things done or suffered and tend to replace them with others. The substitution may be in full awareness, with an invented scenario, mendacious, restored, but less painful than the real one; they repeat the description to others, but also to themselves, and the distinction between true and false progressively loses its contours, and man ends up fully believing the story he has told so many times and continues to tell, polishing and retouching here and there the details which are least credible or incongruous or incompatible with the acquired picture of historically accepted events (p. 27).

What was remembered and stated in "initial bad faith has become good faith." The liar no longer knows what he knows. He believes that his lie is the truth.

To illustrate the sufferer's use of false hope to help him bear an extreme situation, Primo Levi recalls Alberto D., a "fraternal friend" of his time in Auschwitz. Alberto was

> a robust, courageous young man, more clearsighted than the average and therefore very critical of the many who fabricated for themselves, and reciprocally administered to each other, consolatory illusions ("The war will be over in two weeks," "There will be no more selections," "The English have landed in Greece.". . . rumors heard nearly every day and punctually given the lie by reality) (p. 33).

Reality presently brought the selection that chose Alberto's father for the gas chamber.

> In the space of a few hours Alberto changed. He had heard rumors that seemed to him worthy of belief: The Russians are close by, the selection [that had taken his father] was not a selection like the others, it was not for the gas chamber. It had chosen prisoners who were tired but not ill. Alberto even knew where they would be sent, to Jaworzno, not far away to a special camp for convalescents, only for light labor.
>
> Naturally his father was never seen again and Alberto himself vanished during the evacuation march from the camp, in January 1945 (pp. 33–34).

After the war, Primo Levi went to visit Alberto's village, and Alberto's family was doing what Alberto had done, rejecting the unendurable truth and constructing an alternative that continued hopeful: Alberto "had hidden in the forest and was safe in Russian hands; he had not yet been able to send word, but would do so soon." A year later "the truth was slightly changed: Alberto was in a Soviet clinic, he was fine; but he had lost his memory, he no longer remembered his name; he was improving though. [His mother] had this from a reliable source" (p. 34).

It troubles us, as it troubled Primo Levi, that the perpetrator and his victim belong to the same species and operate according to instincts common to both: "Here, as with other phenomena, we are dealing with a paradoxical analogy between victim and oppressor, and we are anxious to be clear: both are in the same trap, but it is the oppressor, and he alone, who has prepared it and activated it, and if he suffers from this, it is right that he should suffer" (p. 25).

And our justice judges the identical psychological operations differently: the criminal, wanting to lessen the pain of guilt, revises—re-sees—the past and restores himself in his own eyes to the condition of innocence—of not knowing he has committed a crime. His intention, acknowledged or not, is to exonerate himself from the need for contrition or amendment in order to avoid deserved punishment. It is not the lie told to others—it is the lie *he has given himself permission to tell himself* that is his second crime.

When the sufferers revise their past or present of undeserved pain, they grab on to falsehoods that are venial, that is to say "easily excused or forgiven; pardonable." We wish them godspeed.

❧ ❧ ❧

Here, finally, are two rose-colored memories in which the liar is my mother; it is she who caught herself at it, she who tells that story on herself.

The story requires reiteration of the history I keep hoping to have finished telling: Hitler annexed Austria in March 1938. In December my father got me included in a transport of 500 Jewish children leaving for safety in England. My mother and father were lucky to obtain the visas to follow in March 1939.

My mother used to embarrass me. She never met an English person without asking for the visa to get *her* parents out of Hitler's Vienna. I have come across a 25 word Red Cross letter dated "18.11.40." On one side my mother has printed (I translate) "WE ARE ALL THREE TOGETHER AND VERY HAPPY. PAUL AND EDITH LIVE VERY NEAR AND WE SEE THEM OFTEN, FRANZI." On the verso my grandmother's handwriting replies, "We are glad that you are well. We are well too. Why do Paul and Edith not write. We worry. Father, Mother."

In her refugee English my mother explained to every English person how Vienna's Aryanized shops were off limits to Jews. Since her brother Paul and his bride, Edith, had also emigrated to England, my mother's parents would starve were it not for Frau Resi. Frau Resi was my mother's cleaning woman. She had taken my grandmother's gold jewelry, broken it up, and was selling it piecemeal and, at great risk to herself, brought my grandparents food to eat.

I remember Frau Resi's raisin eyes. She was a tiny woman. Frau Resi's husband, a cobbler, was a communist and dangerously outspoken anti-Nazi. She used to bring her little boy, Erich, to play with me, sitting underneath my mother's baby grand piano. I liked Erich, who let me boss him. I have what must be a false memory of an event I can know only from my mother's telling for it goes back to a time when she was an inexperienced young housewife. My mother had demanded some chore that Frau Resi considered silly for she had responded memorably: "*Da hat sich die gnä' Frau einen Schass eingetretan.*" The sadly insufficient translation will have to be: "There's where madam has put her foot in a fart." My mother says that as she opened her mouth to voice an offended reprimand, she began instead helplessly to laugh. Frau Resi joined her. It was the beginning of a mutually devoted friendship between the two women and lasted until the Nazi edict forbade Aryans to work in Jewish households.

Then my father was fired from the bank, and our apartment, including the piano under which Erich and I had sat, was also Aryanized. We moved into the living quarters over my grandparents' dry goods store on the main square of Fischamend, a village close to the Czechoslovak border. Today, Fischamend is ten minutes by car from the Vienna airport.

The local Nazis were the boys and girls with whom my mother and my uncle Paul had gone to school. They wrote "*Kauft nicht beim Juden*" (Do not buy from the Jew) in blood-colored paint on the walls and lobbed stones into my bedroom. They leaned ladders against the upstairs windows, climbed in and out, and took things away with them, including the radio on which we had been surreptitiously listening to Radio Free Europe. They backed a truck to the door and emptied out the store. They returned at night, knocked about the three men—my grandfather, my father, and Paul—and gave us till day break to get out of the village. My grandfather and my mother were made to stay behind and close up house and store.

We fast forward to the nineteen-forties. Paul and Edith emigrated to the Dominican Republic, where the pregnant twenty-one-year-old died. My Uncle Paul obtained the visa that got my grandparents out of Europe.

My grandfather died in the Dominican Republic. My father had died in England a week before the end of the European war. In the early Fifties, our family's remnant—my grandmother, Paul, my mother, and I—arrived in America, one by one, in the order in which our immigration quotas came due. My grandmother died in New York in 1958.

It is the Nineties. My uncle Paul has a bad back and asks my mother for my grandfather's walking stick. My mother says the Nazis had not permitted my grandfather to take his stick out of the Fischamend house. She remembers asking the fellow, Herrmann, and remembers Herrmann not answering her. He had pointed them out the door.

My mother remembers how she and my grandfather crossed the village square on foot, passed under the archway of Fischamend's medieval clock tower, which had a weather vane in the shape of a fish on its end. As they approached the iron bridge that spans the River Fischer, a bus coming from the direction of the Czech border stopped for them. It brought my mother and my grandfather to Vienna.

My mother looks in the closet of her Manhattan apartment, and here is my grandfather's walking stick. My grandfather's stick has a very small hole in the underside of the handle. The hole is too small—the way the neck of the bottle is too small to have admitted the fully rigged sailing ship that can be clearly seen on the inside—to have admitted the pebble or marble that can be clearly heard rattling inside the hollow handle.

Now if my grandfather's walking stick had had to be left in the Fischamend house, it stands to reason that it could never have got to my grandmother's sister Frieda's Vienna apartment in which my grandparents lived until Tante Frieda and her husband were taken away to Buchenwald, where they were killed. The stick could not, consequently, have moved with my grandparents into the apartment in the Rotenturmstrasse where they lived until Paul sent the visa, could not have come on the boat with them to the Dominican Republic, nor have been flown with my grandmother from the Dominican Republic to New York City. And yet here, leaning in the corner of my mother's Riverside Drive closet, is grandfather's walking stick.

My mother watches her memory unravel: if the walking stick had not been left behind in Fischamend on that morning in August 1938, had my mother and my grandfather walked across the square, passed under the arch and been picked up by the bus which brought them to Vienna? "There never was a bus route between the Czech border and Vienna," says my mother. How did my mother and my grandfather get to Vienna? My mother cannot remember. What she remembers is the non-existent bus stopping for them on the iron bridge, and the bus driver getting out and helping my grandfather up the steps.

"And I've been thinking and thinking about Frau Resi breaking up mother's gold," says my mother. "What does that mean to 'break' it? I have never understood how you could 'break' gold up. *What* gold? Omama didn't have jewelry except for a gold watch, which she had sold years before to pay for Tante Frieda's stomach operation."

My mother concludes that she had *hoped* someone was bringing my grandparents food to eat because she could not have lived if she imagined them hungering.

And what of the bus on the iron bridge? I believe it is the work of the straggler, Hope, operating backward to redeem an intolerable history. I think that a blessed, rose-colored falsehood introduced into that vicious era two righteous gentiles of my mother's imagining—a kind bus-driver, the heroic cleaning woman—to make the past thinkable, the world livable.

QUESTIONS FOR ANALYSIS AND DISCUSSION

1. People often distinguish between malicious lies and white lies. Does Segal's proposal for a third kind of lie give us a more reasonable option that holds lying to be benevolent?

2. Why is hope so important in Segal's account of her family's history? Given the experiences of her parents and grandparents, do you think some other emotional or moral drive—anger, revenge, forgiveness, or some other possibility—might be better than hope? Explain your response.

3. What is the point of the epigraph that introduces the essay?

4. If virtue ethics is primarily concerned with the character of persons, how do you understand the characters presented by Segal? Do they offer a variety or uniformity of moral views?

19.

M. HIRIYANNA

Philosophy of Values

In the history of moral thought, a variety of lists have been developed that either rank or explain the importance of virtues. Indian philosopher M. Hiriyanna (1871–1950) be-lieves that values belong to one of the two functions of knowledge. Specifically, values have to do with practical knowledge. Moral values also have different functions and need to be understood in light of the major ideas of Indian thought, such as dharma and karma. Central to this outlook are the virtues of the soul.

CRITICAL READING QUESTIONS
---

1. For Hiriyanna, what is the difference between matters of fact and matters of value?
2. While *moksha* seems to be the highest goal, why does Hiriyanna delay his discussion of it?
3. Nine virtues are listed. Which ones seem self-regarding? Which are other-regarding?
4. What is the difference between instrumental values and intrinsic values?

Indian thinkers commonly speak of two functions of knowledge—one which is theoretical, viz. revealing the existence of some object (artha-paricchitti), and the other which is practical, viz. affording help in the attainment of some purpose in

"Philosophy of Values," from *The Spirit of Modern India*, edited by Robert A. McDermott and Y. S. Naravane (New York, NY: Thomas Crowell, 1974), pp. 66–81. Notes have been omitted.

life (phala-prapti). The results of these two functions of knowledge are respectively what we mean by "fact" and "value." A thirsty traveller, who happens to come upon a sheet of fresh water, discovers a fact; and, when later he quenches his thirst by drinking the water, he realizes a value. These functions are regarded as closely connected with each other, since the knowledge of a fact usually leads to the pursuit of some value. The number of facts that may be known, it is clear, are innumerable; and the values that may be realized through their knowledge are equally so. It is with the latter that we are concerned here. The Sanskrit word used for "value" means "the object of desire" (ishta), and the term may therefore be generally defined as "that which is desired." The opposite of value or "disvalue" may be taken as "that which is shunned or avoided" (dvishta). For the sake of brevity, we shall speak only of values; but what is said of them will, with appropriate changes, apply to disvalues also.

Four Classes of Values

One of the distinguishing features of Indian philosophy is that, as a consequence of the pragmatic view it takes of knowledge, it has, throughout its history, given the foremost place to values. Indeed, they form its central theme; and questions like those of "being" and of "knowing" come in only as a matter of course. It may, on this account, be described as essentially a philosophy of values. There are various problems connected with value. For instance, it may be asked whether we desire things because they are of value, or whether they are of value because we desire them. For want of space, we cannot consider such general questions here, however important and interesting they may be. We shall confine our attention to the values included in the well-known group of four, viz. dharma (virtue), artha (wealth), kāma (pleasure), and moksha (self-realization). We shall only observe, in passing, that values may be either instrumental or intrinsic. Thus in the example given above, water is an instrumental value; and the quenching of thirst by means of it is an intrinsic value. That is, though the term "value" is primarily used for the ends that are sought, often the means to their attainment are also, by courtesy, called so.

Though all the above four are ordinarily reckoned as values of life, a distinction is sometimes made within them, according to which only the first three are regarded so, excluding the last one of moksha. Early works like the Rāmāyana and the Mahābhārata, for example, often refer to them alone. But it would be wrong to conclude therefrom that the fourth value of moksha was not known at the time, for these epics and other early works themselves refer to it also. In fact, the ideal of moksha is at least as old as the Upanishads. The restriction of the name of "value" to "the aggregate of three" or the tri-varga, as this group is designated, probably only means that the writers of the works in question address themselves chiefly to the common people, for whom the final ideal of moksha is of little immediate interest. Whatever the reason for this inner distinction may be, it is a convenient one; and we shall adopt it in our treatment of the subject here.

Instrumental and Psychological Values—Artha and Kāma

To take up the tri-varga for consideration first: In this group of three, artha may be said to stand for economic value; kāma, for psychological value; and dharma, for moral value. To speak in the main, artha is an instrumental value, for it is helpful in satisfying one or other of the diverse needs of life. Their satisfaction is kāma, which is an intrinsic value, since it does not admit of the question "why?" We may, for example, ask why we seek food; but we cannot similarly ask for what we seek, the satisfaction arising from the partaking of it. We describe it as a "psychological value," not in its usual sense of subjective value in general, but in that of an end which satisfies the natural impulses of an individual as such. These two values of artha and kāma are sought not only by man, but by all sentient creatures. The only difference is that, while man can seek them knowingly, the other creatures do so instinctively. In this distinction, we find the characteristic feature of purushārthas or "human values," viz. that they represent ends that are *consciously* pursued by man. When they are sought otherwise by him, as they sometimes are, they may remain values but cease to be purushārthas. The possibility of his seeking them unconsciously is due to the fact that man combines in himself the character of an animal and that of a self-conscious agent—that he is not merely a spiritual but also a natural being. The wants which are common to man and the lower animals and whose urge is natural, rather than spiritual, are self-preservation and the propagation of offspring, or, as it may otherwise be stated, race-preservation.

Moral Value—Dharma

The case is quite different as regards dharma, for its appeal is restricted to man. While it is virtually unknown to the lower animals, man may be said to be innately aware of it. In this consists its uniqueness as compared with the other two values of artha and kāma, and we shall presently see in what respect it is superior to them. We have rendered it as "moral value"; and some forms of Indian thought, like early Buddhism, will bear us out completely. But in others, especially the so-called orthodox systems, the connotation of the term is much wider, for they include under it not only moral but also religious values, such as are detailed in the ritualistic portions of the Vedas. But, in accordance with a principle recognized from very early times, viz. that ceremonial is of little avail to those who are morally impure, the practice of virtue becomes a necessary condition of ritualistic life. We also find it stated in some ancient works of this tradition that, as between ritual and virtue, the latter is certainly to be preferred. The Mahābhārata, in a familiar verse, declares that "speaking the truth is far better than celebrating many horse-sacrifices." Gautama, one of the oldest among the law-givers, places what he terms the "virtues of the soul" (ātma-guna), like kindness and purity, above mere ceremonial. These are the reasons why we have rendered the term as "moral value," and we shall confine our attention in what follows solely to that aspect of dharma.

The notion of dharma, thus restricted, is so familiar that it is hardly necessary to refer to examples of virtues whose cultivation it signifies. Yet to give a general idea of them, we shall refer to one of the several lists of them found in old works.

Yājnavalkya, in the Smriti which goes by his name, reckons them as nine—non-injury, sincerity, honesty, cleanliness, control of the senses, charity, self-restraint, love, and forbearance. It will be seen that some of these, like non-injury and charity, have a reference to the good of others or are altruistic, while others, like sincerity and self-restraint, serve to develop one's own character and will. It should not, however, be thought that this division into self-regarding and other-regarding virtues is a hard and fast one; for, as an individual has no life of his own independently of society, the former has a bearing on the latter, as surely as the latter has on the former.

Relation of Dharma to Kāma

What is the relation of dharma to artha and kāma? Or, as artha is ordinarily but a means to kāma, we may narrow the scope of our question and ask, "What is the relation of dharma to kāma?" If kāma stands for pleasure, as stated above, we may say that it is desired by all, for pleasure is always welcome to everyone. Indeed, we cannot help desiring our own felicity. But not everything desired is necessarily *desirable*. A sick person may long for a certain kind of food, but it may not at all be advisable for him to partake of it from the standpoint of his physical well-being. That is, kāma, while it may be an object of desire, may not always be desirable; and, though appearing to be a true value of life, it may not really be so or may even prove to be a disvalue. How then can we distinguish these two kinds of kāma? To speak with reference only to the tri-varga which we are now considering, dharma furnishes the necessary criterion. That variety of kāma is a true value, which is in accord with the requirements of dharma, but not any other. In thus helping us to discriminate between good and bad kāma or in rationalizing life, as we might put it, consists the superiority of dharma, which is thus reckoned as the highest of the three values. This conception of dharma as a regulative principle is so important in the philosophy of conduct that all the Shastras and all the higher literature of India (the latter, though only impliedly) emphasize it. That is, for example, what Sri Krishna means when he says in the Gītā, "Dharmāviruddhah . . . kāmo'smi" (I am kāma, not at strife with dharma).

Dharma As a Means and an End

Having considered the general nature of dharma and its relation to kāma, and therefore also to artha, which commonly is but a means to it, we may ask whether its function is limited to regulating the pursuit of these two values or whether it has any purpose of its own. There are two answers to be given to this question.

(1) The popular view, and probably also the older of the two, is that it has a purpose of its own. In this view, then, dharma is conceived as an instrumental value. A steadfast pursuit of it, in its double aspect of self-regarding and other-regarding virtues, results in one's good here as well as elsewhere; and this good—whether it stands for worldly happiness or heavenly bliss—is, as a whole, designated abhyudaya or "prosperity." Further, it is believed that dharma not only leads to the good, but that it does so invariably. Here is another reason for its

superiority over the other two values, whose pursuit may or may not be successful. But it should be added that, for the attainment of the fruit of dharma, one may have to wait for long. The important point, however, is that it is sure to yield its fruit at some time, even though it be after many vicissitudes. It is the possible post-ponement of the result to an indefinite future that explains the common indiffer-ence of men towards dharma, notwithstanding their awareness of its excellence. It is this human shortsightedness that Vyasa, for example, has in his mind when, in concluding the Mahābhārata, he says, "Here I am, crying out with uplifted arms that dharma brings with it both artha and kāma; but no one listens to me." The same feeling of sad astonishment at human folly is echoed in a common saying that "People want the fruits of dharma, but not dharma itself."

(2) The other view is that dharma is an intrinsic value, and therefore an end in and for itself. It is maintained by some Mimamsakas, viz. those of the Prabhakara school. They ridicule the idea that virtue should appeal to man's interest for being practised. That would be to look upon man as a creature of inclination and forget that he is a moral agent, who has the power to do what he ought and to abstain from doing what he ought not. Further, they allege that such a view makes dharma not only a means, but also a means to the admittedly inferior value of kāma, by making it minister to the doer's felicity. However unexceptionable the kāma pur-sued may be in its nature, and whatever altruistic activity it may incidentally in-volve, it finally stands for a subjective end or, in plainer terms, for self-love. If there is a moral principle, it must be absolute in the sense that it has nothing to do with our likes and dislikes and that it should be followed solely out of respect for it. It is the nature of dharma, they say, to be thus ultimate. Here we have the well-known principle of practising virtue *for its own sake;* and the student of Western philoso-phy will see in it a general kinship with Kant's teaching of the "categorical impera-tive," that is, a command about which there is nothing contingent or conditional.

This will, no doubt, appear at first as a very exalted view of dharma or "duty," if we may use that term instead, worthy to evoke our admiration. But it is really untenable, because it is based upon unsound psychology. It assumes that voluntary activity is possible without any end in view or, to put the same in another way, that it forms its own end (svayam-prayojana-bhūta). But how can anything be its own consequence? To accept such a view, as Shankara observes, changes what is put forward as a gospel of duty into a "gospel of drudgery." For, in that case, devotion to duty would mean present toil; and dereliction of it, future evil, so that whether a person does his duty or leaves it undone, he has only trouble as his lot in life. Hence this view of dharma has not come to prevail. It was once for all given up in India when Mandana, a contemporary of Shankara, enunciated the principle that "nothing prompts a man to acts of will, but what is a means to some desired end."

Dharma Subserves Moksha

So much about the tri-varga. When we shift our standpoint from the system of the three values to that of the four (catur-varga) including moksha, we find the concep-tion of dharma undergoing a profound change, which makes it superior to that in either of the above views. It continues here to be regarded as an instrumental value, as in the first of them, but the end which it is taken to serve is not the agent's "prosperity." It is rather the purification of one's character or, as the term used for it in Sanskirt means, "the cleansing of one's mind" (sattva-shuddhi) by purging it of all lower or selfish impulses. This cleansing is effected through the performance of the duties for which dharma stands in the manner taught in the Gītā, that is, without any thought whatsoever of their fruit. Thus, if the former view commends partial abnegation of kāma and thereby rationalizes life's activities, as we have said, the present one commends its total abnegation and thus spiritualizes them. Its true character of a higher value is restored to dharma here, for, in contrast with the other view, it wholly ceases to be subservient to kāma. The weakness of that view, then, is not in its conception of dharma as a means to an end, but only in its insistence that the end is some form of happiness for the doer. In this rejection of "prosperity" or personal benefit as the aim, the present view resembles that of the Prabhakara school; but, at the same time, it differs vitally from that view in holding that dharma has an end, and thus denying that there can be any voluntary activity without an appropriate motive. It is this changed conception of dharma that has come to prevail in Indian philosophy, and not either of the above.

Aids to Moksha—Morality and Knowledge

But it may be said that moral purification or the conquest of the lower self is too negative in its nature to prompt voluntary activity. So it is necessary to add that actually, in this view, self-conquest is only the immediate end of dharma, while its final aim is moksha or self-realization. This is the ultimate value; and its conception is quite positive, since it consists not merely in subjugating the lower self, but also in growing into the higher one; it implies also the transcending of the narrow, grooved life and the gaining of a larger, ampler life. This change in the older view of dharma or its transvaluation, viz. that it is a means to moksha, is already made in the Upanishads. But it is not the only means and requires, as indicated by our characterization of the final goal, to be supported by a knowledge of what the higher or true self is. And it cannot be known fully and well, unless it is known in its relation to the rest of reality. This knowledge of the self in relation to its environment, social and physical, represents philosophic truth. Like the good, then, the true also is here conceived as an instrumental value, both alike being means to moksha. The several systems differ in the place they assign to these two means in the scheme of life's discipline. But it will suffice for our purpose to say, following Shankara, that a successful pursuit of the good is required as a condition indispensable for the pursuit of the true.

We have seen that seeking the good is essentially for the purification of character. The search after the true is for removing our ignorance (avidyā) about the ultimate reality, which is the necessary implication of all our efforts to philosophize. But for such ignorance, man's desire to know the nature of reality, which is so natural to him, would be wholly unintelligible. This desire, so far as it is theoretical, is satisfied when we learn the final truth and are intellectually convinced of it. But intellectual conviction is not all that is needed for reaching the goal, since the actual effects of the ignorance are directly experienced by us in daily life and require, if they are to be removed, an equally direct experience of the truth about reality. For example, most of us feel the empirical self to be the true Self, while the fact, according to many of the systems, is that it is not so. But a mere intellectual conviction, which is what is commonly meant by philosophic truth, is scarcely of use in dismissing such beliefs. A perceptual illusion, for instance, is dispelled only by a perceptual experience of the fact underlying the illusion and not, say, by a hearsay knowledge of it. Seeing, as they say, is believing. Hence all the Indian schools prescribe a proper course of practical discipline to bring about this consummation, viz. transforming a mere intellectual conviction into direct experience. The chief element in it is dhyāna or yoga which means learning to steady the mind and, thereafter, constantly dwelling upon the truth, of which one has been intellectually convinced, until it culminates in direct experience. It is then that the aspirant realizes himself and becomes spiritually free.

Nature of Moksha

What is the exact nature of this ultimate ideal called moksha? It is held by some to be a state of absolute bliss; and by others, as one merely of absence of all pain and suffering. The distinction depends upon a difference in the conception of the self in the various systems. Bliss or joy is intrinsic to it, according to some, and it therefore naturally reveals itself when the self is released from bondage. According to others, neither bliss nor its opposite belongs to the self, and it is therefore without either in the condition of moksha when its true nature is restored to it. Before describing this condition further, it is necessary to refer briefly to an objection that is sure to occur to the reader at the above characterization of moksha in terms of pleasure and absence of pain, viz. that the ideal is hedonistic—a view which is now regarded as psychologically quite faulty. This is an objection which, on a superficial view, applies to the whole of the Indian theory of value; but whatever the answer to that general objection may be, the charge of hedonism does not, in the least, affect the conception of the ultimate value with which we are now concerned. For the pleasure for which it stands should be unmixed, and there should be no lapse from it when it is once attained—conditions which the kind of pleasure the hedonist has in view does not, and is not meant to, satisfy. In fact, moksha means absolute or unconditioned bliss (or, alternatively, absence of suffering), which is vastly different from the pleasure that hedonism holds to be the supreme end of life.

Now to revert to the consideration of the nature of moksha. Shankara has remarked that attaining the goal of life signifies nothing more than perfecting the means to it. That is to say, the end here is not external to the means, but is only the means stabilized. This gives us a clue as regards the kind of life which a knower leads, and enables us thereby to grasp the exact meaning of moksha. We have mentioned two aids to the attainment of the goal, pursuing the good and acquiring a knowledge of the true self. Corresponding to these, the life of the knower, broadly speaking, will be characterized by two features. In the first place, it will be entirely free from the tyranny of the egoistic self, and therefore also free from the feverish activity for gratifying personal desires, which can never be completely gratified. In the second place, it will be marked by an unshakable conviction in the unity of all, and consequently by love for others—love for them, not as equals but as essentially one with oneself. Such love will necessarily prompt the freed man to work for their good, for while there is nothing that he wants for himself, he sees them immersed in so much ignorance and suffering. No doubt, he was doing unselfish work even before he became free; but that was, more or less, the result of conscious strife. Now it becomes quite spontaneous. . . . There is in this regard the magnanimous example of Buddha who, we may remark by the way, is only one instance among several that have appeared in the spiritual history of India. Hence, though the final aim of life or the ultimate value is here stated to be self-realization, it is really very much more, for it also signifies doing one's utmost to secure universal good.

We have described the state of moksha from the standpoint of what is called jīvanmukti or "liberation while one is still alive," for it is sure to make a better appeal to the modern mind. This ideal, however, is not accepted in all the systems, but only in some like the Advaita, Sānkhya-yoga, and Buddhism. The others insist that spiritual freedom will not actually be attained until after physical death. It is known as videhamukti. But even these systems may be said to admit jīvanmukti in fact, though not in name, for they postulate final release in the case of an enlightened person as soon as he leaves his physical body, implying thereby that there is nothing more to be done by him for attaining moksha. The distinction between the two views reduces itself finally to whether or not the discipline prescribed for the spiritual aspirant should as such (that is, under a sense of constraint) continue in the interval between the dawn of true knowledge and the moment of physical death. According to those who do not accept the ideal of jīvanmukti, it should continue, while according to the rest, it need not.

QUESTIONS FOR ANALYSIS AND DISCUSSION

1. Hiriyanna defines value as "the object of desire" or "that which is desired." Moreover, he calls this a function of knowledge. Critics of moral thinking claim that values do not deal with knowledge but with some other issue, such as opinion, conviction, or principle. How do you understand this dispute? Can you defend Hiriyanna from the critics?

2. The good, according to Hiriyanna, is seen as the purification of character. Does that imply an egoist approach to morality? Cite passages from the selection to support or reject this inference.

3. Consider the meaning of the nine virtues introduced by Hiriyanna. Do any of the virtues help shed light on the case study by Lore Segal?

4. What is the relation between self-conquest and self-realization? Many of the writers in Chapters 1 and 2 addressed the universality of moral truths. Much of what Hiriyanna says about the virtues is in the context of a specific way of thinking that relies on fundamental ideas peculiar to a religious outlook. Does this weaken the case that virtues can be universal? Can you make a case for a universal ethic emerging from the key points raised in the essay? Be specific in your response.

20.

PAUL JORDAN-SMITH

Seven (and more) Deadly Sins

Why are the virtues so difficult to live by? Folklorist and essayist Paul Jordan-Smith reviews the list of vices (or sins) and describes how temptations have dragged humans away from the good life. The classic position articulated by Christian tradition is that there are seven capital (or deadly) vices. Yet other temptations and evils are also worthy candidates for vices because they, too, have been widely recognized for their powers in leading humans to immorality. It is tempting to disregard the seven (or more) sins as little more than historical intrigue. But, as Jordan-Smith insightfully notes, a trip to the shopping mall, a couple of hours watching TV, or a flip through the pages of the daily newspaper quickly reminds us that the ancient vices are still with us. We just give them new names today.

⊣ CRITICAL READING QUESTIONS ⊢

1. What is the "saligia"? Why was the acronym taught to moral persons?
2. Which of the seven sins or vices is expressed in the Ten Commandments?
3. Are the seven vices listed in any particular order, or is the "saligia" chosen because it is easy to recite?
4. Why are they often called deadly sins? Which is the deadliest?
5. Why is pride considered the queen of sins?

A joke recently going the rounds says that humankind is divided into two groups: those that divide humankind into two groups, and those that don't. One might extend this witticism philosophically and say that there are those who create formal expressions of order and those who do not, perhaps because they do not perceive order, or maybe because they pay it no mind. Many such formal expressions have entered our thought without our knowing quite how they got there. Early

---

"Seven (and more) Deadly Sins," *Parabola,* Winter 1985: 34–45.

and medieval Christianity expressed the sevenfold division of vicious human inherencies as the Seven Deadly Sins, or the Seven Capital (or Cardinal, or Principal)
Vices. How did the formulation come about? Why, and in what sense, were these
seven sins (or vices) considered "deadly"? How are they regarded today, their formulation having become an artifact of a bygone day?

The earliest formal expression in the Western traditions of the sinful nature of
man is the Decalogue (cf. *Exodus* 20:1–17; *Deuteronomy* 5:6–21), which de-
lineates areas in which human beings are prone to weakness. The number *seven*
makes its appearance briefly in *Proverbs* 6:16–19: "These six things doth the Lord
hate: yea, seven are an abomination unto him: a proud look, a lying tongue, and
hands that shed innocent blood, an heart that deviseth wicked imaginations, feet
that be swift in running to mischief, a false witness that speaketh lies, and he that
soweth discord among brethren." The sacred number seven makes an early appearance here; however, these aren't the seven we are looking for, although three
of these—lasciviousness (Lust), wrath (Anger), and Envy—appear in *Galatians*,
5:19–21.

The next listing we come across is in one of the most interesting of early
Christian pseudo-revelatory writings, the *Shepherd of Hermas,* composed around
148 A.D. The third section of the book contains several parables; of interest is the
ninth, in which is described the building of a tower by twelve maidens in white
raiment. Hermas is represented in the work as a particularly dense specimen with
whom his various angelic guides become repeatedly exasperated, all but stamping
their etheric feet at his persistent thickheadedness. In the fifteenth section of the
parable, he asks about the tower, which is built on a rock rising in the middle of a
plain surrounded by twelve mountains. The tower is the Church, it is explained to
him, and the rock is the Son of God (not Peter, curiously). The twelve maidens in
white raiment stand for various virtues, as explained by Hermas's angelic guide.
There were also twelve maidens in black, whose office had been to cause various
building stones of the tower to be rejected:

> "Hear also," said [the angel], "the names of the women who have black raiment. Of
> these also four are more powerful. The first is Unbelief, the second Impurity, the third
> Disobedience, and the fourth Deceit; and those who follow them are called Grief,
> Wickedness, Licentiousness, Bitterness, Lying, Foolishness, Evil-speaking, Hate."

This is one of the earliest attempts to delineate vicious inherencies in any formal
or orderly fashion. Of the twelve vices enumerated (any of which, the angel tells
Hermas, is sufficient to prevent the Beatific Vision), none of the traditional seven
is specifically given, although *Licentiousness* is akin to Lust. The inclusion of *Grief,*
however, demands some explanation. This word in the Greek of Hermas is *Lype,*
which in classical Greek means *grief, distress,* or *painful sadness.* Among the early
desert fathers, however, the word is taken to include *envy,* and as such it indicates
not the pain of spiritual suffering but an exaggerated indulgence in wishing that
things were other than the way they are.

We next come to the *Confessions* of St. Augustine (A.D. 354–430). Following
the well-known passage in Book II about stealing pears when he was sixteen,
Augustine gives a list of fifteen sins, citing six of the classic Seven Deadly Sins:

superbia (Pride), *ignavia* (Sloth; the later term is *acedia* or *accidie*), *luxuria* ("Expensiveness" in Watt's seventeenth-century English; later translated as Lust), *avaritia* (Covetousness, Greed), *invidia* (Watt's "Emulation," later Envy, here distinguished from *tristitia*, the usual Latin for the Greek *Lype*), and *ira* (Anger); the missing seventh sin is Gluttony, which is subsumed with Lust under "Expensiveness." Augustine is not being systematic here, however. His fifteen sins (or fourteen, counting *ignorantia* and *stultitia* as one, since the verb used is singular) is largely a literary formulation, not part of systematic theology.

In the first epistle of the Augustan writer Horace, dated around 20 B.C., there appears a list of vices which must be guarded against: *avaritia* (covetousness), *laudis amor* (love of praise, vainglory), *invidus* (envy), *iracundus* (wrath), *iners* (sloth), *vinosus* (literally, love of wine, by extension, gluttony), and *amator* (love of love, that is, lust). Although the Latin terms differ from the standard formulation, it is with this list that all of the Seven Deadly Sins make their first appearance together, though outside a religious doctrine *per se*. Horace was an Epicurean, however, and if one understands that philosophy aright, these excesses detract from the serenity (*ataraxia*) which Epicurus had established as the most desirable end for man.

Perhaps the earliest Christian formulation of sins is that of Augustine's contemporary, the desert father Evagrios of Pontus. Evagrios made his way from Asia Minor into Egypt, where to the dismay of the Coptic church he established a Rule of desert asceticism. He was a follower of Origen, so his theology was condemned by the Fifth Ecumenical Council (A.D. 553) along with Origenism in general, but as that council was patently manipulated by the emperor Justinian to exclude most Western theologians, it seems to have had little effect on Evagrios's reputation. Indeed, his *Praktikos* and other writings influenced St. Benedict in establishing his monastic Rule. Evagrios was famous for his dictum that women and bishops constituted the greatest temptations to monks, and that both should be avoided as much as possible.

The *Praktikos* is a collection of very brief, pithy chapters on aspects of the ascetic life. It was conceived as part of a larger work, but was also written to stand as an independent treatise. Early on in the work, Evagrios lists the "Eight Kinds of Evil Thoughts":

> There are eight general and basic categories of thoughts in which are included every thought. First is that of gluttony, then impurity, avarice, sadness, anger, *acedia*, vainglory, and last of all pride.

It is with St. Gregory the Great (A.D. 540–604) that we first find the sevenfold division in Christian literature. In his *Morals on the Book of Job* (xxxi, 87) we find the first formulation of the seven *principia vitia* (principle vices) or *peccata capitalia* (capital sins):

> For the tempting vices, which fight against us in invisible contest in behalf of pride which reigns over them, some of them go first, like captains, others follow, after the manner of an army. For all faults do not occupy the heart with equal access. But while the greater and the few surprise a neglected mind, the smaller and the numberless pour

themselves upon it in a whole body. For when pride, the queen of sins, has fully possessed a conquered heart, she surrenders it immediately to seven principal sins, as if to
some of her generals, to lay it waste. . . . For pride is the root of all evil, of which it is
said, as Scripture bears witness; *Pride is the beginning of all sin.* But seven principal
vices, as its first progeny, spring doubtless from this poisonous root, namely vain glory,
envy, anger, melancholy, avarice, gluttony, lust.

Gregory goes on (xxxi, 88) to give the names of some of the foot soldiers of the
vicious captaincies:

From vainglory there arise disobedience, boasting, hypocrisy, contentions, obstinacies,
discords, and the presumption of novelties. From envy there spring hatred, whispering,
detraction, exultation at the misfortunes of a neighbor, and affliction at his prosperity.
From anger are produced strifes, swelling of mind, insults, clamor, indignation, blas-
phemies. From melancholy there arise malice, rancor, cowardice, despair, slothfulness
in fulfilling the commands, and a wandering of the mind on unlawful objects. From
avarice there spring treachery, fraud, deceit, perjury, restlessness, violence, and hard-
ness of heart against compassion. From gluttony are propagated foolish mirth, scurril-
ity, uncleanness, babbling, dullness of sense in understanding. From lust are generated
blindness of mind, inconsiderateness, inconstancy, precipitation, self-love, hatred of
God, affection for this present world, but dread or despair of that which is to come.

For any systematic treatment after Gregory it is necessary to leap over the next
seven centuries to St. Thomas Aquinas, and examine his treatment of the various
sins from several points of view (see the *Summa Theologica,* Qq. 72–73). By this
time, the formulation of Seven Deadly Sins had become an established expression
in Christian theology. Distinctions such as those between *mortal* and *venial* sins
took pre-eminence in any discourse on the nature of human behavior, and from
this time on, we see a shift towards the development of a pastoral doctrine of sin
rather than a theological one. From the next seven centuries, the teachings of
the Angelic Doctor were to dictate the limits of doctrinal development within the
Roman communion.

As a systematic theology of sin began to develop, Gregory, Aquinas, and other
writers divided the seven sins into two categories, namely *spiritual* sins (pride,
anger, envy, covetousness, sloth) and *carnal* sins (lust, gluttony). While each of the
sins may be regarded as having both carnal and spiritual manifestations, their centers of gravity, as it were, are determined by this twofold distinction. Eventually,
they came to be given in a specific order and denoted by the acronym *saligia,* which
is composed of the initial letters of each of the sins in their Latin denomination:
Superbia (Pride), *Avaritia* (Greed, Covetousness), *Luxuria* (Lust), *Invidia* (Envy),
Gula (Gluttony), *Ira* (Anger), and *Acedia* or *Accidie* (Sloth).

The principal use of the word *saligia* is to remember the sins, not only by name
and number, but also by the *order* in which they are given. They are seen to constitute a progression, from the least to the most deadly. Thus *Pride,* in the theology
of Gregory and Aquinas, is the "queen of all sins," but while both consider it distinct from *vainglory,* Aquinas holds vainglory to be a daughter of pride, derived
from it but not itself among the seven. Although it heads the list, Pride is con-

sidered the most escapable, since humility, its contrary, can be brought about by human action. The state of pride, then, is a vulnerable state (one even speaks of "wounded pride"), one in which the penetration of suffering can still save the soul. The soul in its descent becomes less and less vulnerable as it approaches the utter passivity of sloth at the bottom-most place in the order. As Aquinas has it: "We might say that all the sins which are due to ignorance can be reduced to sloth, to which pertains the negligence by which a man refuses to acquire spiritual goods because of the attendant labor; for the ignorance that can cause sin is due to negligence. . . ." (Q. 84, Art. 4, Rep. Obj. 5). Perhaps one should say that the progression is from the least toward the most *deathly,* the utter inactivity of sloth being most like death.

The formulations of a time we have commonly come to regard as "repressed" and steeped in ignorance seem unlikely today to touch our sensibilities. In 1912, the *Catholic Encyclopedia* presented a theology of sin which to a very great extent reflected the predominantly Thomistic thinking of the Church through the preceding eighteen centuries. The current edition treats the subject in psychological terms, almost as if sins were little more than quirks of the personality, to be treated by the modern pastor by psychotherapeutic methods. A more prevalent attitude regards the topic as outmoded, possibly dangerous, as if it were a sin to talk about sin. . . .

Are we not subject to sin in our enlightened days? Or have the Seven Deadly Sins no longer the force or significance they had in former times? Perhaps the fact that they all have various human inherencies as their centers of gravity has led to the notion that since sin is an inevitable aspect of human behavior, it ought to be treated much more tolerantly. To this, Evagrios replies:

> It is not in our power to determine whether we are disturbed by these thoughts, but it is up to us to decide if they are to linger within us or not and whether or not they are to stir up our passions.

Today, of course, the stirring up of passions gets mixed reviews. It is a virtue to feel passionate about some things—provided that they are the right things. But what are the right things? It was never a sin to be passionate about God, for example; yet religious passion today raises suspicions of mental illness. Doubtless much of what passes for religious fervor is just exactly that, but perhaps the baby goes out with the bath water rather often. A passion for the acquisition of material goods, on the other hand, is one widespread contemporary form of covetousness. While not universally considered praiseworthy, it often leads one to indulging in excesses which would have raised the eyebrows of the most liberal Epicurean. A case could be made that each of the Seven Deadly Sins has come to be looked on almost as a virtue largely because in our mistrust of systematic religion we have lost the knowledge of distinctions. We can no longer discriminate when one of our appetites, carnal or spiritual, has become an end in itself, has passed from the disturbance of our thoughts to the stirring up of our passions. Still, each of the old catechetical sins is well known to us, only now we pay the inherent dangers little heed; since each sin has its virtuous counterpart, we are apt to mistake one for the other.

By *Proverbs* 16:18 we are informed that "Pride goeth before destruction, and an haughty spirit before a fall." The "haughty spirit" in the King James (and the Jerusalem) Bible is rendered as "arrogance" in the New English Bible. The *Septuagint* has it as *kakaphrosyne*, which means "evil thinking," but the generally accepted meaning is similar to the common understanding of *vainglory*. The distinction may be purely literary, arising out of the kind of parallel construction that characterizes *Proverbs*. In any case, it was taken as a distinction of kind by later scholars, resulting in theological discrimination.

The *Catholic Encyclopedia* defines Pride as "the excessive love of one's own excellence," noting that in Aquinas, "vainglory, ambition, and presumption are commonly enumerated as the offspring vices of pride, because they are well adapted to serve its inordinate aims." Evagrios says that "it induces the monk to deny that God is his helper and to consider that he himself is the cause of virtuous actions. Further, he gets a big head in regard to the brethren, considering them stupid because they do not all have this same opinion of him." Of vainglory, he writes:

> It leads them to desire to make their struggles known publicly, to hunt after the praise of men. This in turn leads to their illusory healing of women, or to their hearing fancied sounds as the cries of demons—crowds of people who touch their clothes. This demon predicts besides that they will attain to the priesthood. . . . It is only with considerable difficulty that one can escape the thought of vainglory. For what you do to destroy it becomes the principle of some other form of vainglory. . . . I have observed the demon of vainglory being chased by nearly all the other demons, and when his pursuers fell, shamelessly he drew near and unfolded a long list of his virtues.

Among the virtues of the demon of pride, as Aquinas pointed out, is ambition, highly praised in our day in self-help books on how to get on in the business world; "Looking out for Number One" is the operative phrase. But there are other demonic virtues as well, some of them attributable to the ethics of the so-called "me generation," but they apply in less obvious form to the rest of us as well. Self-esteem and self-respect masquerade as virtues, and advertising appeals to these aspects of pride by presenting beautiful egoists who praise products because "I'm worth it," or "'cause I believe in me." We buttress our insecurity in the face of a society that threatens extinction of individuality by affirming "black pride" and "gay pride." These we hold to be unassailable by all but the most oppressive and repressive elements, considering such people "stupid because they do not all have this same opinion." Pride here asserts its true name, complete with its list of virtues, and we fear to face it critically because we no longer know how to distinguish the true from the false among the forces that move us.

The *Catholic Encyclopedia* says that covetousness "differs from concupiscence only in the implied notion of nonpossession, and thus may cover all things which are sought after inordinately." By 1912, covetousness was regarded as an "inclination to sin," and like several of the other sins, forms of it were regarded as "positively commendable" by the clergy under Pius X. This innocent phrase appears in a number of articles, the general tenor of which seems to indicate that *sin,* at least considered in the pastoral sense, was already not such a burning issue as it once had been.

The various words used to translate *avaritia*—covetousness, greed, avarice— appear to connote a hunger after things which one does not possess, and this is the sense in which it is understood above. Evagrios however sheds some interesting light on the subject by examining not the sin's most superficial and obvious forms, but what in the contemplative life were its insidious temptations:

> Avarice suggests to the mind a lengthy old age, inability to perform manual labor (at some future date), famines that are sure to come, sickness that will visit us, the pinch of poverty, the great shame that comes from accepting the necessities of life from others.

Evagrios goes right to the heart of the matter: avarice is not defined by pure material greed, but by the principle of *thinking about what does not yet exist,* a kind of preoccupation with imaginary or future things such as hopes and fears. That one could be greedy about what one fears is a subtlety that escapes our ordinary thinking. The distinctive feature here is that the future enters into the sin. This differentiates it from *sadness* (*tristitia,* often related with envy and sloth), in which the future is replaced by the past and present, and which has to do with more immediate deprivations.

Covetousness appears, of course, in the Decalogue, specifically in the Tenth Commandment. It is like Lust, in that there is a craving to possess, but things rather than people. Greed is also similar to Envy, from which it is separated in the *saligia* order by Lust. One might say that greed is envy without the personal dimension: "I want. . . ." without regard to the fact that "you have."

So much has been written about contemporary materialism that it would hardly seem necessary to say anything further about our modern view of greed. As with the other sins, the obvious becomes a cloak for the subtler manifestations. Our daydreams, beloved to us for their therapeutic resolution of our hopes and fears, are also a splendid field of action for this demon. Since our indulgence in daydreaming has such a positive value, we often hear it praised as "creative." In this we are probably not far wrong, and the scholastics would be shocked by the arrogance of our attempts to imitate the Creator by spinning dreams in which our enemies are dispatched and our ambitions fulfilled to the nth degree.

Lust is "the inordinate craving for, or indulgence of, the carnal pleasure which is experienced in the human organs of generation" (*Catholic Encyclopedia*). Aquinas, in his chapter on concupiscence (*Summa Theologica,* II–I, Q. 30), makes the distinction between taking pleasure in things that are suitable to the nature of the animal and in things that are only apprehended as suitable—in other words "beyond that which nature requires." He is not speaking here of lust *per se,* but of desire, which manifests itself in a number of sins, lust being one of them.

In a time of sexual "liberation," we find it difficult to regard lust as a sin, as well perhaps as the other six. Like greed, the essence of the sin is imagination, which we take to be creative when it is not overtly destructive. Lust adds the personal element lacking in greed, but it does so in an impersonal way, treating the person lusted after as a thing, the "object of desire." It seems only too obvious to point out how advertising exploits our weakness in this area. It has been found, for instance, that men's pupils dilate when they are given a glimpse of female flesh, and that with careful timing an image of the product can replace the "object of desire" in a television commercial. Thus we are led from Lust to Greed, both sins upon which the advertising industry thrives.

Inasmuch as the ancient writers such as Evagrios used the word "sadness" to denote what the Latin doctors called envy, it seems appropriate that Aquinas should lead off his discussion of envy (*Summa Theologica,* II–II, Q. 36) by explaining why envy is a kind of sorrow: "Now the object both of charity and of envy is our neighbor's good, but by contrary movements, since charity rejoices in our neighbor's good, while envy grieves over it. . . ." It is also a capital vice because, "just as acedia is grief for a Divine spiritual good, so envy is grief for our neighbor's good." There is also a kind of envy which is accounted as a sin against the Holy Ghost (and therefore unforgivable), "namely envy of another's spiritual good, which envy is a sorrow for the increase of God's grace, and not merely for our neighbor's good."

Evagrios gives a more subtle definition of envy, focusing not so much on the sorrow for another's good (which does not seem very much different from covetousness) as upon the chimeras of present and past times, or of places other than here. In this regard, envy is similar to gluttony and lust, in being built on imagination. Another critical feature for Evagrios is *attachment:*

> For sadness is a deprivation of sensible pleasure, whether actually present or only
> hoped for. And so if we continue to cherish some affection for anything in this world it
> is impossible to repel this enemy, for he lays his snares and produces sadness precisely
> where he sees we are particularly inclined.

Envy can also be seen as a marriage of Greed and Lust, which immediately precede it in the *saligian* order. Whereas satiety appeases momentarily, though does not completely assuage those two, insatiability is the very essence of Envy. Satiety is anathema to its operation, and in this respect it paves the way for Gluttony. Advertising, a rich field for examples of the appeal to our baser nature, again and again exploits our inclinations to envy, usually through the dynamic of *comparison.* When we compare ourselves to our neighbors, we indulge in a moment of envy or of pride, for either we are better off than they or they than we. When it is the former, it is pride, and when the latter, envy. But since this gives rise to such virtues as ambition and avarice (and sometimes lust), we are assured that all is well with our troubled souls.

In the thought of Aquinas, the center of gravity of gluttony is the word "too": "too soon, too expensively, too much, too eagerly, too daintily." The word "self-concern" is germinal also.

The cure, in Evagrios's Rule, was a bread-and-water diet, since "satiety desires a variety of dishes but hunger thinks itself happy to get its fill of nothing more than bread." In other words, he prescribes a return to a normal definition of the necessity of food.

The word "gluttony" has a strong visual imagery: we see an inordinately fat man or woman stuffing food down until he or she bursts. But is quantity the whole issue? C. S. Lewis provides the following from *The Screwtape Letters:*

> But what do quantities matter, provided we can use a human belly and palate to produce querulousness, impatience, uncharitableness and self-concern? Glubose has this old woman well in hand. She is a positive terror to hostesses and servants. She is always turning from what has been offered her to say with a demure little sigh and a smile, "Oh please, please . . . *all* I want is a cup of tea, weak but not too weak, and the teeniest weeniest bit of really crisp toast." You see? Because what she wants is smaller and less costly than what has been set before her, she never recognizes as gluttony her determination to get what she wants, however troublesome it may be to others. At the very moment of indulging her appetite she believes that she is practicing temperance.

The *Catholic Encyclopedia* defines anger as "the desire of vengeance" and goes on to say that the sinfulness depends on "the quality of the vengeance and the quantity of the passion. When these are in conformity with the prescriptions of balanced reason, anger is not a sin." It can, according to the article's author, even be "positively commendable," under certain circumstances. It depends on the circumstances, of course.

Evagrios appears somewhat less flexible, taking anger in the sense of "a boiling and stirring up of wrath against one who has given injury—or is thought to have done so." He links it with indignation, which he sees as its long-lasting effect, giving rise to "alarming experiences by night," followed by other evils, including a form of paranoia.

Aquinas holds that:

> the movement of anger has a twofold tendency: namely, to vengeance itself, which it desires and hopes for as being a good, and in which consequently it takes pleasure; and to the person on whom it seeks vengeance, as to something contrary and hurtful, which bears the character of evil.

In this argument, he is following the thought of his principle guide, Aristotle, in stating that men do not seek evil *as evil,* but always seek what they apprehend as good and avoid what they apprehend as evil. He goes on (quoting from the *Ethics*):

> ". . . anger listens somewhat to reason" in so far as reason denounces the injury inflicted, "but listens not perfectly," because it does not observe the rule of reason as to the measure of vengeance. Anger, therefore, requires an act of reason, and yet proves a hindrance to reason.

In a similar vein, but addressing himself more to the practical aspects of the contemplative life, Evagrios notes that:

> Anger is given to us so that we might fight against the demons and strive against every pleasure. Now it happens that the angels suggest spiritual pleasure to us and the beatitude that is consequent upon it so as to encourage us to turn our anger against the

demons. But these, for their part, draw our anger to wordly desires and constrain us—contrary to our nature—to fight against our fellow men to the end that, blinded in mind and falling away from knowledge, our spirit should become a traitor to virtue.

This note of Evagrios's indicates that the propensities which lead us into temptation have a positive aspect as well, and may become virtues if we allow ourselves to be delivered from evil. It is in this sense that any propensity can be regarded as "commendable." The problem of righteous anger lies not in the anger *per se* but in the contamination of the self, so that it becomes *self-righteous,* and it is seldom that we see a truly righteous anger.

The critical words of Aquinas regarding sloth as spiritual negligence have been quoted already. Its manifestations in the contemplative life, as documented by Evagrios, bring other aspects into consideration most vividly. He speaks of *acedia* as "the noonday demon" (the main meal was at 3:00 P.M., during the monastic ninth hour):

The demon of *acedia*—also called the noonday demon—is the one that causes the most serious trouble of all. He presses his attack upon the monk about the fourth hour and besieges the soul until the eighth hour. First of all he makes it seem that the sun barely moves, if at all, and that the day is fifty hours long. Then he constrains the monk to look constantly out the windows, to walk outside the cell, to gaze carefully at the sun to determine how far it stands from the ninth hour, to look now this way and now that to see if perhaps. . . . Then too he instills in the heart of the monk a hatred for the place, a hatred for his very life itself, a hatred for manual labor. He leads him to reflect that charity has departed from among the brethren, that there is no one to give encouragement. Should there be someone at this period who happens to offend him in some way or other, this too the demon uses to contribute further to his hatred. This demon drives him along to desire other sites where he can more easily procure life's necessities, more readily find work and make a real success of himself. He goes on to suggest that, after all, it is not the place that is the basis of pleasing the Lord. God is to be adored everywhere. He joins to these reflections the memory of his dear ones and of his former way of life. He depicts life stretching out for a long period of time, and brings before the mind's eye the toil of the ascetic struggle and, as the saying has it, leaves no leaf unturned to induce the monk to forsake his cell and drop out of the fight.

Simple "laziness," which contemporary usage attributes to sloth, does not fully characterize this sin, which has borne several names, from Horace's *iners* ("inertia") to Evagrios's *acedia* to the *tristitia* of Augustine and Gregory. A term like *self-pity,* on the other hand, conveys both utter self-centeredness and the sadness spoken of by earlier writers ("sorrow" is misleading, as one can feel righteous sorrow, i.e., remorse, for one's sins). One can be deceived by appearances here as well. Someone who spends leisure time dozing in a hammock or on a beach may seem lazy, but such a form of inertia probably would have been thought trivial by the scholastics, whereas the mindless industry of the "workaholic" might be seen as true spiritual negligence.

What purpose did such formulations serve in their day? Are they of any use now? By regarding these products of a systematic, if dated, theology as archeological specimens of a bygone day, and by resorting to stereotypical imagery (most of it carnal and material) instead of pondering the elements of the formulation, we trivialize these ancestral ideas and dismiss them from our consideration. If once they served as a form by which one might examine one's personal motivations and the movements of the soul, they now are little more than artifacts. Shy of religion, we discard the forms and the knowledge which they contain along with the enfeebled institutions which engendered them. We take the form to *be* the knowledge, rather than the container of a wisdom to be released to our understanding through active contemplation.

Which delighteth the devil no end.

QUESTIONS FOR ANALYSIS AND DISCUSSION

1. If the sins or vices are so powerful, how can we battle them? Jordan-Smith indicates that for traditional moralists one of the functions of religion was to give a framework for understanding the virtues and vices. This framework also assisted moral persons in battling the temptations that lead to vicious deeds and their evil consequences. Do we need a religious framework? If not, can another framework suffice, such as a political or scientific one? Does overcoming the vices require a framework?

2. Many of the vices appeal to physical pleasures. Could a hedonist (one who believes that the primary goods are based on pleasures) or a utilitarian (one who believes pleasure for the greatest number is the moral goal) argue that the vices are really misnamed? For example, the delight in food is gluttony only when carried to the extreme. Envy, by itself, amounts to little more than comparing ourselves to others. In other words, vices generally describe those who are too weak or ignorant to handle the variety of pleasures life makes available to us. Hence, vices are not really immoral in any general sense. In light of Jordan-Smith's account, how do you respond to the view of the hedonist or utilitarian?

3. Jordan-Smith clarifies how some of the early Christian thinkers believed there was a special order of the vices. From your readings, observations, or experiences outside an ethics course, describe how succumbing to one vice leads to other vices. Does your example support the traditional order or propose a different dynamic?

4. Some believe that virtues rather than laws or rights or commandments are the best antidotes to the vices. Using the list of nine virtues of M. Hiriyanna, do you think that a life of virtue can overcome the temptations that highlight the dangers of the vices? Explain your answer by juxtaposing specific virtues and vices.

21.

BENJAMIN FRANKLIN

Thirteen Virtues and Seeking Moral Perfection

Only nine virtues? Only seven vices? American statesman, writer, and inventor Benjamin Franklin (1706–1790) believed a moral person must strive to embrace thirteen virtues. In this selection from his Autobiography, *Franklin outlines a method for improving oneself ethically. Given the difficulty of the task, he cautions the reader against trying to become virtuous all at once. Instead, he recommends a rigorous daily schedule by which the individual develops one virtue at a time. This moral development, according to Franklin, requires careful vigilance over one's daily habits and common inclinations so that vicious deeds are less likely to be committed.*

CRITICAL READING QUESTIONS

1. Which virtues does Franklin see as relatively easy and which difficult to master? Why?
2. How many virtues did Franklin originally plan to pursue? Which did he add, and why?
3. For Franklin, what is the purpose of leading a virtuous life?
4. Does Franklin's schedule contain a certain order for moral development? Or is it arbitrary, for example, that silence precedes frugality or that tranquility precedes chastity?

. . . I conceived the bold and arduous project of arriving at moral perfection. I wished to live without committing any fault at any time; I would conquer all that either natural inclination, custom, or company might lead me into. As I knew, or thought I knew, what was right and wrong, I did not see why I might not always do the one and avoid the other. But I soon found I had undertaken a task of more difficulty than I had imagined. While my care was employed in guarding against one fault, I was often surprised by another; habit took the advantage of inattention; inclination was sometimes too strong for reason. I concluded, at length, that the mere speculative conviction that it was our interest to be completely virtuous,

---

"Thirteen Virtues and Seeking Moral Perfection," from *Autobiography* (NY: Cignet, 1961), pp. 93–104. Notes have been omitted.

was not sufficient to prevent our slipping; and that the contrary habits must be broken, and good ones acquired and established, before we can have any dependence on a steady, uniform rectitude of conduct. For this purpose I therefore contrived the following method.

In the various enumerations of the moral virtues I had met with in my reading, I found the catalogue more or less numerous, as different writers included more or fewer ideas under the same name. Temperance, for example, was by some confined to eating and drinking, while by others it was extended to mean the moderating every other pleasure, appetite, inclination, or passion, bodily or mental, even to our avarice and ambition. I proposed to myself, for the sake of clearness, to use rather more names, with fewer ideas annexed to each, than a few names with more ideas; and I included under thirteen names of virtues all that at that time occurred to me as necessary or desirable, and annexed to each a short precept, which fully expressed the extent I gave to its meaning.

These names of virtues, with their precepts, were:

1. Temperance

Eat not to dullness; drink not to elevation.

2. Silence

Speak not but what may benefit others or yourself; avoid trifling conversation.

3. Order

Let all your things have their places; let each part of your business have its time.

4. Resolution

Resolve to perform what you ought; perform without fail what you resolve.

5. Frugality

Make no expense but to do good to others or yourself; *i.e.*, waste nothing.

6. Industry

Lose no time; be always employed in something useful; cut off all unnecessary actions.

7. Sincerity

Use no hurtful deceit; think innocently and justly; and, if you speak, speak accordingly.

8. Justice

Wrong none by doing injuries, or omitting the benefits that are your duty.

9. Moderation

Avoid extremes; forbear resenting injuries so much as you think they deserve.

10. Cleanliness

Tolerate no uncleanliness in body, clothes, or habitation.

11. Tranquillity

Be not disturbed at trifles, or at accidents common or unavoidable.

12. Chastity

Rarely use venery but for health or offspring, never to dullness, weakness, or the injury of your own or another's peace or reputation.

13. Humility

Imitate Jesus and Socrates.

My intention being to acquire the habitude of all these virtues, I judged it would be well not to distract my attention by attempting the whole at once, but to fix it on one of them at a time; and, when I should be master of that, then proceed to another, and so on till I had gone through the thirteen; and, as the previous acquisition of some might facilitate the acquisition of certain others, I arranged them with that view, as they stand above. Temperance first, as it tends to procure that coolness and clearness of head, which is so necessary where constant vigilance was to be kept up, and guard maintained against the unremitting attraction of ancient habits, and the force of perpetual temptations. This being acquired and established, Silence would be more easy; and my desire being to gain knowledge at the same time that I improved in virtue, and considering that in conversation it was obtained rather by the use of the ears than of the tongue, and therefore wishing to break a habit I was getting into of prattling, punning, and joking, which only made me acceptable to trifling company, I gave Silence the second place. This and the next, Order, I expected would allow me more time for attending to my project and my studies. Resolution, once become habitual, would keep me firm in my endeavors to obtain all the subsequent virtues; Frugality and Industry freeing me from my remaining debt, and producing affluence and independence, would make more easy the practice of Sincerity and Justice, etc. Conceiving, then, that, agreeably to

the advice of Pythagoras in his *Golden Verses,* daily examination would be necessary, I contrived the following method for conducting that examination.

I made a little book in which I allotted a page for each of the virtues. I ruled
each page with red ink, so as to have seven columns, one for each day of the week,
marking each column with a letter for the day. I crossed these columns with thirteen red lines, marking the beginning of each line with the first letter of one of the
virtues; on which line, and in its proper column, I might mark, by a little black
spot, every fault I found upon examination to have been committed respecting that
virtue upon that day.

I determined to give a week's strict attention to each of the virtues successively.
Thus, in the first week, my great guard was to avoid every the least offense against
Temperance, leaving the other virtues to their ordinary chance, only marking every
evening the faults of the day. Thus, if in the first week I could keep my first line,
marked T, clear of spots, I supposed the habit of that virtue so much strengthened,
and its opposite weakened, that I might venture extending my attention to include
the next, and for the following week keep both lines clear of spots. Proceeding thus
to the last, I could go through a course complete in thirteen weeks, and four
courses in a year. And like him who, having a garden to weed, does not attempt to
eradicate all the bad herbs at once, which would exceed his reach and his strength,
but works on one of the beds at a time, and, having accomplished the first, proceeds to a second, so I should have, I hoped, the encouraging pleasure of seeing on
my pages the progress I made in virtue, by clearing successively my lines of their
spots, till in the end, by a number of courses, I should be happy in viewing a clean
book, after a thirteen weeks' daily examination.

This my little book had for its motto these lines from Addison's *Cato:*

Here will I hold. If there's a power above us
(And that there is, all nature cries aloud
Thro' all her works), He must delight in virtue;
And that which He delights in must be happy.

Another from Cicero:

O vitæ Philosophia dux! O virtutum indagatrix expultrixque vitiorum! Unus dies, bene
et ex præceptis tuis actus, peccanti immortalitati est anteponendus.

Another from the Proverbs of Solomon, speaking of wisdom or virtue:

Length of days is in her right hand, and in her left hand riches and honor. Her ways are
ways of pleasantness, and all her paths are peace.–iii. 16, 17.

And conceiving God to be the fountain of wisdom, I thought it right and necessary to solicit his assistance for obtaining it; to this end I formed the following
little prayer, which was prefixed to my tables of examination, for daily use.

O powerful Goodness! bountiful Father! merciful Guide! Increase in me that wisdom
which discovers my truest interest. Strengthen my resolutions to perform what that wisdom dictates. Accept my kind offices to thy other children as the only return in my
power for thy continual favors to me.

I used also sometimes a little prayer which I took from Thomson's *Poems*, viz.:

Father of light and life, thou Good Supreme!
O teach me what is good; teach me Thyself!
Save me from folly, vanity, and vice,
From every low pursuit; and fill my soul
With knowledge, conscious peace, and virtue pure;
Sacred, substantial, never-fading bliss!

The precept of Order requiring that every part of my business should have its allotted time, one page in my little book contained the following scheme of employment for the twenty-four hours of a natural day.

I entered upon the execution of this plan for self-examination, and continued it with occasional intermissions for some time. I was surprised to find myself so much fuller of faults than I had imagined; but I had the satisfaction of seeing them diminish. To avoid the trouble of renewing now and then my little book, which, by scraping out the marks on the paper of old faults to make room for new ones in a new course, became full of holes, I transferred my tables and precepts to the ivory leaves of a memorandum book, on which the lines were drawn with red ink, that made a durable stain, and on those lines I marked my faults with a black-lead pencil, which marks I could easily wipe out with a wet sponge. After a while I went through one course only in a year, and afterward only one in several years, till at length I omitted them entirely, being employed in voyages and business abroad, with a multiplicity of affairs that interfered; but I always carried my little book with me.

My scheme of Order gave me the most trouble; and I found that, though it might be practicable where a man's business was such as to leave him the disposition of his time, that of a journeyman printer, for instance, it was not possible to be exactly observed by a master who must mix with the world and often receive people of business at their own hours. Order, too, with regard to places for things, papers, etc., I found extremely difficult to acquire. I had not been early accustomed to it, and, having an exceeding good memory, I was not so sensible of the inconvenience attending want of method. This article, therefore cost me so much painful attention and my faults in it vexed me so much, and I made so little progress in amendment, and had such frequent relapses that I was almost ready to give up the attempt, and content myself with a faulty character in that respect, like the man who, in buying an ax of a smith, my neighbor, desired to have the whole of its surface as bright as the edge. The smith consented to grind it bright for him if he would turn the wheel; he turned while the smith pressed the broad face of the ax hard and heavily on the stone which made the turning of it very fatiguing. The man came every now and then from the wheel to see how the work went on and at length would take his ax as it was, without farther grinding. "No," said the smith, "turn on, turn on; we shall have it bright by and by; as yet, it is only speckled." "Yes," says the man, "*but I think I like a speckled ax best.*" And I believe this may have been the case with many who, having, for want of some such means as I employed, found the difficulty of obtaining good and breaking bad habits in other points of vice and virtue, have given up the struggle, and concluded that "a speckled ax was best"; for something, that pretended to be reason, was every now and then suggesting to me that such extreme nicety as I exacted of myself might be a kind of foppery in morals, which, if it were known, would make me ridiculous; that a perfect character might be attended with the inconvenience of being envied and hated; and that a benevolent man should allow a few faults in himself, to keep his friends in countenance.

In truth, I found myself incorrigible with respect to Order; and now I am grown old and my memory bad, I feel very sensibly the want of it. But, on the whole, though I never arrived at the perfection I had been so ambitious of obtaining, but fell far short of it, yet I was, by the endeavor, a better and a happier man than I otherwise should have been if I had not attempted it; as those who aim at perfect writing by imitating the engraved copies, though they never reach the wished-for excellence of those copies, their hand is mended by the endeavor, and is tolerable while it continues fair and legible.

It may be well my posterity should be informed that to this little artifice, with the blessing of God, their ancestor owed the constant felicity of his life, down to his seventy-ninth year, in which this is written. What reverses may attend the remainder is in the hand of Providence; but, if they arrive, the reflection on past happiness enjoyed ought to help his bearing them with more resignation. To Temperance he ascribes his long-continued health, and what is still left to him of a good constitution; to Industry and Frugality, the early easiness of his circumstances and acquisition of his fortune, with all that knowledge that enabled him to be a useful citizen, and obtained for him some degree of reputation among the learned; to Sincerity and Justice, the confidence of his country, and the honorable employs it conferred upon him; and to the joint influence of the whole mass of virtues, even in the imperfect state he was able to acquire them, all that evenness of temper, and that cheerfulness in conversation, which makes his company still sought for and agreeable even to his younger acquaintances. I hope, therefore, that some of my descendants may follow the example and reap the benefit.

It will be remarked that, though my scheme was not wholly without religion, there was in it no mark of any of the distinguishing tenets of any particular sect. I had purposely avoided them; for, being fully persuaded of the utility and excellence of my method, and that it might be serviceable to people in all religions, and intending sometime or other to publish it, I would not have anything in it that should prejudice anyone, of any sect, against it. I purposed writing a little comment on each virtue, in which I would have shown the advantages of possessing it, and the mischiefs attending its opposite vice; and I should have called my book *The Act of Virtue,* because it would have shown the means and manner of obtaining virtue, which would have distinguished it from the mere exhortation to be good, that does not instruct and indicate the means, but is like the apostle's man of verbal charity, who only, without showing to the naked and hungry how or where they might get clothes or victuals, exhorted them to be fed and clothed.—James ii. 15, 16.

But it so happened that my intention of writing and publishing this comment was never fulfilled. I did, indeed, from time to time, put down short hints of the sentiments, reasonings, etc., to be made use of in it, some of which I have still by me; but the necessary close attention to private business in the earlier part of my

life, and public business since, have occasioned my postponing it; for, it being connected in my mind with a great and extensive project that required the whole man
to execute, and which an unforeseen succession of employs prevented my attending
to, it has hitherto remained unfinished.

In this piece, it was my design to explain and enforce this doctrine, that vicious
actions are not hurtful because they are forbidden, but forbidden because they are
hurtful, the nature of man alone considered; that it was, therefore, everyone's interest to be virtuous who wished to be happy even in this world; and I should, from
this circumstance (there being always in the world a number of rich merchants,
nobility, states, and princes, who have need of honest instruments for the management of their affairs, and such being rare), have endeavored to convince young
persons that no qualities were so likely to make a poor man's fortune as those of
probity and integrity.

My list of virtues contained at first but twelve; but a Quaker friend having
kindly informed me that I was generally thought proud; that my pride showed itself
frequently in conversation; that I was not content with being in the right when
discussing any point, but was overbearing, and rather insolent, of which he convinced me by mentioning several instances; I determined endeavoring to cure myself, if I could, of this vice or folly among the rest, and I added Humility to my list,
giving an extensive meaning to the word.

I cannot boast of much success in acquiring the reality of this virtue, but I had a
good deal with regard to the appearance of it. I made it a rule to forbear all direct
contradiction to the sentiments of others, and all positive assertion of my own. I
even forbid myself, agreeably to the old laws of our Junto, the use of every word
or expression in the language that imported a fixed opinion, such as *certainly,
undoubtedly,* etc., and I adopted, instead of them, *I conceive, I apprehend,* or *I
imagine* a thing to be so or so; or it *so appears to me at present.* When another
asserted something that I thought an error, I denied myself the pleasure of contradicting him abruptly, and of showing immediately some absurdity in his proposition; and in answering I began by observing that in certain cases or circumstances
his opinion would be right, but in the present case there *appeared* or *seemed* to me
some difference, etc. I soon found the advantage of this change in my manner; the
conversations I engaged in went on more pleasantly. The modest way in which I
proposed my opinions procured them a readier reception and less contradiction;
I had less mortification when I was found to be in the wrong, and I more easily
prevailed with others to give up their mistakes and join with me when I happened
to be in the right.

And this mode, which I at first put on with some violence to natural inclination,
became at length so easy, and so habitual to me, that perhaps for these fifty years
past no one has ever heard a dogmatical expression escape me. And to this habit
(after my character of integrity) I think it principally owing that I had early so
much weight with my fellow citizens when I proposed new institutions, or alter-
ations in the old, and so much influence in public councils when I became a member, for I was but a bad speaker, never eloquent, subject to much hesitation in my
choice of words, hardly correct in language, and yet I generally carried my points.

In reality, there is, perhaps, no one of our natural passions so hard to subdue as
pride. Disguise it, struggle with it, beat it down, stifle it, mortify it as much as one

pleases, it is still alive, and will every now and then peep out and show itself; you will see it, perhaps, often in this history; for, even if I could conceive that I had completely overcome it, I should probably be proud of my humility. . . .

QUESTIONS FOR ANALYSIS AND DISCUSSION

1. Franklin claims that while he was working on temperance he would leave "the other virtues to their ordinary chance." Do you think this approach is plausible? Are the virtues independent of one another?

2. Franklin's exercise involves a "plan for self-examination." Indeed, except for a brief note about a Quaker friend, Franklin mentions no other influences in his seeking moral perfection. What conclusions can be drawn about his attitudes toward moral pedagogy, happiness, or sociability?

3. Franklin admits that he had much trouble with the virtue of Order. Which of the virtues he enumerates would give you the most or least trouble to perfect? Which ones do you think other people—friends, coworkers, fellow students—have the most trouble with?

22.

ARISTOTLE

Virtue and Moral Character

A student of Plato, Aristotle (384–322 B.C.) is widely considered to be the first systematic thinker of a virtue-based ethics. He developed a coherent view of moral conduct that integrated his ideas on politics, education, social classes, and human well-being. His influence on the history of ethics in Western philosophy is profound. Aristotle thought that reason is the primary guide to developing the good and happy life. But reason itself is not enough. Leading a virtuous life is an ongoing effort, beginning in childhood and continuing throughout life as we practice right habits and nurture good character. This selection highlights Aristotle's understanding of virtues in relation to other arts and to the development of good character.

"Virtue and Moral Character," from *Nicomachean Ethics*, Book II, Chapters 1–9, translated by W. D. Ross (Oxford, England: Oxford University Press, 1925). Notes have been omitted.

| CRITICAL READING QUESTIONS |

1. How does Aristotle distinguish passions, faculties, and states of character?
2. What are the similarities and differences between virtues and arts?
3. What is meant by liberality? Why is its excess or defect immoral?
4. Is virtue a compromise between two extremes, in Aristotle's view?
5. Are the passions rational?

Book II

1. Virtue, then, being of two kinds, intellectual and moral, intellectual virtue in the main owes both its birth and its growth to teaching (for which reason it requires experience and time), while moral virtue comes about as a result of habit, whence also its name *ethike* is one that is formed by a slight variation from the word *ethos* (habit). From this it is also plain that none of the moral virtues arises in us by nature; for nothing that exists by nature can form a habit contrary to its nature. For instance the stone which by nature moves downwards cannot be habituated to move upwards, not even if one tries to train it by throwing it up ten thousand times; nor can fire be habituated to move downwards, nor can anything else that by nature behaves in one way be trained to behave in another. Neither by nature, then, nor contrary to nature do the virtues arise in us; rather we are adapted by nature to receive them, and are made perfect by habit.

Again, of all the things that come to us by nature we first acquire the potentiality and later exhibit the activity (this is plain in the case of the senses; for it was not by often seeing or often hearing that we got these senses, but on the contrary we had them before we used them, and did not come to have them by using them); but the virtues we get by first exercising them, as also happens in the case of the arts as well. For the things we have to learn before we can do them, we learn by doing them, e.g. men become builders by building and lyre-players by playing the lyre; so too we become just by doing just acts, temperate by doing temperate acts, brave by doing brave acts.

This is confirmed by what happens in states; for legislators make the citizens good by forming habits in them, and this is the wish of every legislator, and those who do not effect it miss their mark, and it is in this that a good constitution differs from a bad one.

Again, it is from the same causes and by the same means that every virtue is both produced and destroyed, and similarly every art; for it is from playing the lyre that both good and bad lyre-players are produced. And the corresponding statement is true of builders and of all the rest; men will be good or bad builders as a result of building well or badly. For if this were not so, there would have been no need of a teacher, but all men would have been born good or bad at their craft. This, then, is the case with the virtues also; by doing the acts that we do in our transactions with other men we become just or unjust, and by doing the acts that we do in the presence of danger, and being habituated to feel fear or confidence, we become brave or cowardly. The same is true of appetites and feelings of anger; some men become temperate and good-tempered, others self-indulgent and irascible, by behaving in one way or the other in the appropriate circumstances. Thus, in one word, states of character arise out of like activities. This is why the activities we exhibit must be of a certain kind; it is because the states of character correspond to the differences between these. It makes no small difference, then, whether we form habits of one kind or of another from our very youth; it makes a very great difference, or rather *all* the difference.

2. Since, then, the present inquiry does not aim at theoretical knowledge like the others (for we are inquiring not in order to know what virtue is, but in order to become good, since otherwise our inquiry would have been of no use), we must examine the nature of actions, namely how we ought to do them; for these determine also the nature of the states of character that are produced, as we have said. Now, that we must act according to the right rule is a common principle and must be assumed—it will be discussed later, i.e. both what the right rule is, and how it is related to the other virtues. But this must be agreed upon beforehand, that the whole account of matters of conduct must be given in outline and not precisely, as we said at the very beginning that the accounts we demand must be in accordance with the subject-matter; matters concerned with conduct and questions of what is good for us have no fixity, any more than matters of health. The general account being of this nature, the account of particular cases is yet more lacking in exactness; for they do not fall under any art or precept but the agents themselves must in each case consider what is appropriate to the occasion, as happens also in the art of medicine or of navigation.

But though our present account is of this nature we must give what help we can. First, then, let us consider this, that it is the nature of such things to be destroyed by defect and excess, as we see in the case of strength and of health (for to gain light on things imperceptible we must use the evidence of sensible things); both excessive and defective exercise destroys the strength, and similarly drink or food which is above or below a certain amount destroys the health, while that which is proportionate both produces and increases and preserves it. So too is it, then, in the case of temperance and courage and the other virtues. For the man who flies from and fears everything and does not stand his ground against anything becomes a coward, and the man who fears nothing at all but goes to meet every danger becomes rash; and similarly the man who indulges in every pleasure and abstains from none becomes self-indulgent, while the man who shuns every pleasure, as boors do, becomes in a way insensible; temperance and courage, then, are destroyed by excess and defect, and preserved by the mean.

But not only are the sources and causes of their origination and growth the same as those of their destruction, but also the sphere of their actualization will be the same; for this is also true of the things which are more evident to sense, e.g. of strength; it is produced by taking much food and undergoing much exertion, and it is the strong man that will be most able to do these things. So too is it with the virtues; by abstaining from pleasures we become temperate, and it is when we have become so that we are most able to abstain from them; and similarly too in the case of courage; for by being habituated to despise things that are terrible and to stand our ground against them we become brave, and it is when we have become so that we shall be most able to stand our ground against them.

3. We must take as a sign of states of character the pleasure or pain that ensues on acts; for the man who abstains from bodily pleasures and delights in this very fact is temperate, while the man who is annoyed at it is self-indulgent, and he who stands his ground against things that are terrible and delights in this or at least is not pained is brave, while the man who is pained is a coward. For moral excellence is concerned with pleasures and pains; it is on account of the pleasure that we do bad things, and on account of the pain that we abstain from noble ones. Hence we ought to have been brought up in a particular way from our very youth, as Plato says, so as both to delight in and to be pained by the things that we ought; for this is the right education.

Again, if the virtues are concerned with actions and passions, and every passion and every action is accompanied by pleasure and pain, for this reason also virtue will be concerned with pleasures and pains. This is indicated also by the fact that punishment is inflicted by these means; for it is a kind of cure, and it is the nature of cures to be effected by contraries.

Again, as we said but lately, every state of soul has a nature relative to and concerned with the kind of things by which it tends to be made worse or better; but it is by reason of pleasures and pains that men become bad, by pursuing and avoiding these—either the pleasures and pains they ought not or when they ought not or as they ought not, or by going wrong in one of the other similar ways that may be distinguished. Hence men even define the virtues as certain states of impassivity and rest; not well, however, because they speak absolutely, and do not say "as one ought" and "as one ought not" and "when one ought or ought not," and the other things that may be added. We assume, then, that this kind of excellence tends to do what is best with regard to pleasures and pains, and vice does the contrary.

The following facts also may show us that virtue and vice are concerned with these same things. There being three objects of choice and three of avoidance, the noble, the advantageous, the pleasant, and their contraries, the base, the injurious, the painful, about all of these the good man tends to go right and the bad man to go wrong, and especially about pleasure; for this is common to the animals, and also it accompanies all objects of choice; for even the noble and the advantageous appear pleasant.

Again, it has grown up with us all from our infancy; this is why it is difficult to rub off this passion, engrained as it is in our life. And we measure even our actions, some of us more and others less, by the rule of pleasure and pain. For this reason, then, our whole inquiry must be about these; for to feel delight and pain rightly or wrongly has no small effect on our actions.

Again, it is harder to fight with pleasure than with anger, to use Heraclitus' phrase, but both art and virtue are always concerned with what is harder; for even the good is better when it is harder. Therefore for this reason also the whole concern both of virtue and of political science is with pleasures and pains; for the man who uses these well will be good, he who uses them badly bad.

That virtue, then, is concerned with pleasures and pains, and that by the acts from which it arises it is both increased and, if they are done differently, destroyed, and that the acts from which it arose are those in which it actualizes itself—let this be taken as said.

4. The question might be asked, what we mean by saying that we must become just by doing just acts, and temperate by doing temperate acts; for if men do just and temperate acts, they are already just and temperate, exactly as, if they do what is in accordance with the laws of grammar and of music, they are grammarians and musicians.

Or is this not true even of the arts? It is possible to do something that is in accordance with the laws of grammar, either by chance or at the suggestion of another. A man will be a grammarian, then, only when he has both done something grammatical and done it grammatically; and this means doing it in accordance with the grammatical knowledge in himself.

Again, the case of the arts and that of the virtues are not similar; for the products of the arts have their goodness in themselves, so that it is enough that they should have a certain character, but if the acts that are in accordance with the virtues have themselves a certain character it does not follow that they are done justly or temperately. The agent also must be in a certain condition when he does them; in the first place he must have knowledge, secondly he must choose the acts, and choose them for their own sakes, and thirdly his action must proceed from a firm and unchangeable character. These are not reckoned in as conditions of the possession of the arts, except the bare knowledge; but as a condition of the possession of the virtues knowledge has little or no weight, while the other conditions count not for a little but for everything, i.e. the very conditions which result from often doing just and temperate acts.

Actions, then, are called just and temperate when they are such as the just or the temperate man would do; but it is not the man who does these that is just and temperate, but the man who also does them *as* just and temperate men do them. It is well said, then, that it is by doing just acts that the just man is produced, and by doing temperate acts the temperate man; without doing these no one would have even a prospect of becoming good.

But most people do not do these, but take refuge in theory and think they are being philosophers and will become good in this way, behaving somewhat like patients who listen attentively to their doctors, but do none of the things they are ordered to do. As the latter will not be made well in body by such a course of treatment, the former will not be made well in soul by such a course of philosophy.

5. Next we must consider what virtue is. Since things that are found in the soul are of three kinds—passions, faculties, states of character, virtue must be one of these. By passions I mean appetite, anger, fear, confidence, envy, joy, friendly feeling, hatred, longing, emulation, pity, and in general the feelings that are accompanied by pleasure or pain; by faculties the things in virtue of which we are said to be capable of feeling these, e.g. of becoming angry or being pained or feeling pity;

by states of character the things in virtue of which we stand well or badly with reference to the passions, e.g. with reference to anger we stand badly if we feel it violently or too weakly, and well if we feel it moderately; and similarly with reference to the other passions.

Now neither the virtues nor the vices are *passions,* because we are not called good or bad on the ground of our passions, but are so called on the ground of our virtues and our vices, and because we are neither praised nor blamed for our passions (for the man who feels fear or anger is not praised, nor is the man who simply feels anger blamed, but the man who feels it in a certain way), but for our virtues and our vices we *are* praised or blamed.

Again, we feel anger and fear without choice, but the virtues are modes of choice or involve choice. Further, in respect of the passions we are said to be moved, but in respect of the virtues and the vices we are said not to be moved but to be disposed in a particular way.

For these reasons also they are not *faculties;* for we are neither called good nor bad, nor praised nor blamed, for the simple capacity of feeling the passions; again, we have the faculties by nature, but we are not made good or bad by nature; we have spoken of this before.

If, then, the virtues are neither passions nor faculties, all that remains is that they should be *states of character.*

Thus we have stated what virtue is in respect of its genus.

6. We must, however, not only describe virtue as a state of character, but also say what sort of state it is. We may remark, then, that every virtue or excellence both brings into good condition the thing of which it is the excellence and makes the work of that thing be done well; e.g. the excellence of the eye makes both the eye and its work good; for it is by the excellence of the eye that we see well. Similarly the excellence of the horse makes a horse both good in itself and good at running and at carrying its rider and at awaiting the attack of the enemy. Therefore, if this is true in every case, the virtue of man also will be the state of character which makes a man good and which makes him do his own work well.

How this is to happen we have stated already, but it will be made plain also by the following consideration of the specific nature of virtue. In everything that is continuous and divisible it is possible to take more, less, or an equal amount, and that either in terms of the thing itself or relatively to us; and the equal is an intermediate between excess and defect. By the intermediate in the object I mean that which is equidistant from each of the extremes, which is one and the same for all men; by the intermediate relatively to us that which is neither too much nor too little—and this is not one, nor the same for all. For instance, if ten is many and two is few, six is the intermediate, taken in terms of the object; for it exceeds and is exceeded by an equal amount; this is intermediate according to arithmetical proportion. But the intermediate relatively to us is not to be taken so; if ten pounds are too much for a particular person to eat and two too little, it does not follow that the trainer will order six pounds; for this also is perhaps too much for the person who is to take it, or too little—too little for Milo, too much for the beginner in athletic exercises. The same is true of running and wrestling. Thus a master of any art avoids excess and defect, but seeks the intermediate and chooses this— the intermediate not in the object but relatively to us.

. . .

Again, it is possible to fail in many ways (for evil belongs to the class of the unlimited, as the Pythagoreans conjectured, and good to that of the limited), while to succeed is possible only in one way (for which reason also one is easy and the other difficult—to miss the mark easy, to hit it difficult); for these reasons also, then, excess and defect are characteristic of vice, and the mean of virtue;

> For men are good in but one way, but bad in many.

Virtue, then, is a state of character concerned with choice, lying in a mean, i.e. the mean relative to us, this being determined by a rational principle, and by that principle by which the man of practical wisdom would determine it. Now it is a mean between two vices, that which depends on excess and that which depends on defect; and again it is a mean because the vices respectively fall short of or exceed what is right in both passions and actions, while virtue both finds and chooses that which is intermediate. Hence in respect of its substance and the definition which states its essence virtue is a mean, with regard to what is best and right an extreme.

But not every action nor every passion admits of a mean; for some have names that already imply badness, e.g. spite, shamelessness, envy, and in the case of actions adultery, theft, murder; for all of these and suchlike things imply by their names that they are themselves bad, and not the excesses or deficiencies of them. It is not possible, then, ever to be right with regard to them; one must always be wrong. Nor does goodness or badness with regard to such things depend on committing adultery with the right woman, at the right time, and in the right way, but simply to do any of them is to go wrong. It would be equally absurd, then, to expect that in unjust, cowardly, and voluptuous action there should be a mean, an excess, and a deficiency; for at that rate there would be a mean of excess and of deficiency, an excess of excess, and a deficiency of deficiency. But as there is no excess and deficiency of temperance and courage because what is intermediate is in a sense an extreme, so too of the actions we have mentioned there is no mean nor any excess and deficiency, but however they are done they are wrong; for in general there is neither a mean of excess and deficiency, nor excess and deficiency of a mean.

7. We must, however, not only make this general statement, but also apply it to the individual facts. For among statements about conduct those which are general apply more widely, but those which are particular are more genuine, since conduct has to do with individual cases, and our statements must harmonize with the facts in these cases. We may take these cases from our table. With regard to feelings of fear and confidence courage is the mean; of the people who exceed, he who exceeds in fearlessness has no name (many of the states have no name), while the man who exceeds in confidence is rash, and he who exceeds in fear and falls short in confidence is a coward. With regard to pleasures and pains—not all of them, and not so much with regard to the pains—the mean is temperance, the excess self-indulgence. Persons deficient with regard to the pleasures are not

often found; hence such persons also have received no name. But let us call them "insensible."

With regard to giving and taking of money the mean is liberality, the excess and the defect prodigality and meanness. In these actions people exceed and fall short in contrary ways; the prodigal exceeds in spending and falls short in taking, while the mean man exceeds in taking and falls short in spending. (At present we are giving a mere outline or summary, and are satisfied with this; later these states will be more exactly determined.) With regard to money there are also other dispositions—a mean, magnificence (for the magnificent man differs from the liberal man; the former deals with large sums, the latter with small ones), an excess, tastelessness and vulgarity, and a deficiency, niggardliness; these differ from the states opposed to liberality, and the mode of their difference will be stated later.

With regard to honour and dishonour the mean is proper pride, the excess is known as a sort of "empty vanity," and the deficiency is undue humility; and as we said liberality was related to magnificence, differing from it by dealing with small sums, so there is a state similarly related to proper pride, being concerned with small honours while that is concerned with great. For it is possible to desire honour as one ought, and more than one ought, and less, and the man who exceeds in his desires is called ambitious, the man who falls short unambitious, while the intermediate person has no name. The dispositions also are nameless, except that that of the ambitious man is called ambition. Hence the people who are at the extremes lay claim to the middle place; and we ourselves sometimes call the intermediate person ambitious and sometimes unambitious, and sometimes praise the ambitious man and sometimes the unambitious. The reason of our doing this will be stated in what follows; but now let us speak of the remaining states according to the method which has been indicated.

With regard to anger also there is an excess, a deficiency, and a mean. Although they can scarcely be said to have names, yet since we call the intermediate person good-tempered let us call the mean good temper; of the persons at the extremes let the one who exceeds be called irascible, and his vice irascibility, and the man who falls short an inirascible sort of person, and the deficiency inirascibility.

There are also three other means, which have a certain likeness to one another, but differ from one another: for they are all concerned with intercourse in words and actions, but differ in that one is concerned with truth in this sphere, the other two with pleasantness; and of this one kind is exhibited in giving amusement, the other in all the circumstances of life. We must therefore speak of these too, that we may the better see that in all things the mean is praiseworthy, and the extremes neither praiseworthy nor right, but worthy of blame. Now most of these states also have no names, but we must try, as in the other cases, to invent names ourselves so that we may be clear and easy to follow. With regard to truth, then, the intermediate is a truthful sort of person and the mean may be called truthfulness, while the pretence which exaggerates is boastfulness and the person characterized by it a boaster, and that which understates is mock modesty and the person characterized by it mock-modest. With regard to pleasantness in the giving of amusement the intermediate person is ready-witted and the disposition ready wit, the excess is buffoonery and the person characterized by it a buffoon, while the man who falls short is a sort of boor and his state is boorishness. With regard to the remaining kind of pleasantness, that which is exhibited in life in general, the man who is pleasant in the right way is friendly and the mean is friendliness, while the man who exceeds is an obsequious person if he has no end in view, a flatterer if he is aiming at his own advantage, and the man who falls short and is unpleasant in all circumstances is a quarrelsome and surly sort of person.

There are also means in the passions and concerned with the passions; since shame is not a virtue, and yet praise is extended to the modest man. For even in these matters one man is said to be intermediate, and another to exceed, as for instance the bashful man who is ashamed of everything; while he who falls short or is not ashamed of anything at all is shameless, and the intermediate person is modest. Righteous indignation is a mean between envy and spite, and these states are concerned with the pain and pleasures that are felt at the fortunes of our neighbours; the man who is characterized by righteous indignation is pained at undeserved good fortune, the envious man, going beyond him, is pained at all good fortune, and the spiteful man falls so far short of being pained that he even rejoices. But these states there will be an opportunity of describing elsewhere; with regard to justice, since it has not one simple meaning, we shall, after describing the other states, distinguish its two kinds and say how each of them is a mean; and similarly we shall treat also of the rational virtues.

. . .

9. That moral virtue is a mean, then, and in what sense it is so, and that it is a mean between two vices, the one involving excess, the other deficiency, and that it is such because its character is to aim at what is intermediate in passions and in actions, has been sufficiently stated. Hence also it is no easy task to be good. For in everything it is no easy task to find the middle, e.g. to find the middle of a circle is not for every one but for him who knows; so, too, any one can get angry—that is easy—or give or spend money; but to do this to the right person, to the right extent, at the right time, with the right motive, and in the right way, *that* is not for every one, nor is it easy; wherefore goodness is both rare and laudable and noble.

Hence he who aims at the intermediate must first depart from what is the more contrary to it, as Calypso advises—

Hold the ship out beyond that surf and spray.

For of the extremes one is more erroneous, one less so; therefore, since to hit the mean is hard in the extreme, we must as a second best, as people say, take the least of the evils; and this will be done best in the way we describe.

But we must consider the things towards which we ourselves also are easily carried away; for some of us tend to one thing, some to another; and this will be recognizable from the pleasure and the pain we feel. We must drag ourselves away to the contrary extreme; for we shall get into the intermediate state by drawing well away from error, as people do in straightening sticks that are bent.

Now in everything the pleasant or pleasure is most to be guarded against; for we do not judge it impartially. We ought, then, to feel towards pleasure as the elders of the people felt towards Helen, and in all circumstances repeat their saying; for if we dismiss pleasure thus we are less likely to go astray. It is by doing this, then, (to sum the matter up) that we shall best be able to hit the mean. . . .

Book III

1. Since virtue is concerned with passions and actions, and on voluntary passions and actions praise and blame are bestowed, on those that are involuntary pardon, and sometimes also pity, to distinguish the voluntary and the involuntary is presumably necessary for those who are studying the nature of virtue, and useful also for legislators with a view to the assigning both of honours and of punishments.

Those things, then, are thought involuntary, which take place under compulsion or owing to ignorance; and that is compulsory of which the moving principle is outside, being a principle in which nothing is contributed by the person who is acting or is feeling the passion, e.g. if he were to be carried somewhere by a wind, or by men who had him in their power.

QUESTIONS FOR ANALYSIS AND DISCUSSION

1. Aristotle offers several examples of the means between extremes. Devise your own example and use Aristotle's criteria to weigh the moral aspects of your example.

2. How does Aristotle discuss the virtuous life in relation to pleasure and pain? Do you think his ideas complement the utilitarian who emphasizes pleasure and pain as the basis of the moral life? If not, which passages indicate that Aristotle is not a utilitarian?

3. How can moral character be developed? Aristotle describes several ways of detecting moral persons or actions as indicators of good character. Can moral character be shaped without confronting ethical dilemmas in everyday life?

23.

DAVID CARR

The Primacy of Virtues in Ethical Theory: Part II

One frequent criticism of virtue ethics concerns its apparent lack of a social morality. According to British philosopher David Carr, this criticism is unfounded. Carr argues that a central component of virtue ethics is a communitarian perspective, which offers a richer understanding of social life than other approaches in ethics.

CRITICAL READING QUESTIONS

1. What is meant by a teleological theory?
2. Why does Carr distinguish between an internal and external view of the good?
3. Does Carr think the "spectatorial" view describes virtue ethics?

---

1. Moral Value and the Virtues

The quite serious criticisms to which we subjected realism and non-cognitivism in the first part of this article would appear to point us in the direction of a *teleological* theory of value in general and of moral value in particular. Moreover a teleological ethics would, of course, seek to construe moral goodness or value on precisely the same sort of model of fitness for a purpose by which we generally judge objects of common or garden utility to be of value; indeed, undoubtedly the best known of teleological ethical theories is that which goes by the name of *utilitarianism*. To a large degree, of course, it is just this sort of purported analogy between functional and moral goodness which neo-Kantian non-cognitivist views wish to repudiate by separating, as far as possible, moral motivation from natural human interests. Thus, it is well known that whilst prescriptivists are willing to concede the possibility of a descriptive sense of goodness or value in the non-moral realm they nevertheless insist that these terms must have a non-descriptive "evaluative" sense in the moral sphere. However, many reasons have been offered by critics of non-cognitivism for regarding this as a rather unlikely story—not least

---

"The Primacy of Virtues in Ethical Theory: Part II," *Cogito*, Spring 1996: 34–40. Notes have been omitted.

that this alleged double life of moral terms would appear to implicate much standard prescriptive inference in quite hopeless fallacies of equivocation.

But if it is proper to construe goodness and value in teleological terms in moral as in other spheres of human life, what sorts of things could be said to exhibit moral goodness or value and what sort of function or purpose might we reasonably take them to be serving with regard to human interests? With regard to the main goal which anything rightly describable as morally good or valuable would have to serve, the broad answer which has been returned in the teleological tradition deriving from Aristotle is that it is *eudaemonia* or wellbeing—understood as general success or prosperity in our projects and endeavours but with particular regard to the distinctively rational and social dimensions of human life. Thus, to flourish in human terms is to exhibit a measure of excellence in one's intellectual and interpersonal as well as material or practical affairs; precisely, it is to have made progress regarding the acquisition of a range or repertoire of principled dispositions ordinarily referred to as intellectual and moral virtues. Just as effective cutting is best served by sharpness of the knife, then, so human flourishing is best promoted by the widespread development of certain objective qualities of character and conduct conducive to positive personal projects and interpersonal association; in short, human happiness is generally better served in circumstances in which people are *actually* wise, just, kind, charitable, compassionate, courageous, self-controlled, tolerant, courteous and forgiving than in those in which they are ignorant, unfair, mean, spiteful, bigoted, envious, inhospitable, vain, self-indulgent and cruel.

One should beware, however, of a very common objectivist and reductionist interpretation of teleological ethics (to which we have already alluded in speaking of utilitarianism) associated with so-called *consequentialism*. In fact, although it is not obviously consistent with his overall scepticism about the objectivity of moral values, it is nevertheless a clearly discernible line of thought in the philosophy of Hume that certain types of conduct ought to be morally encouraged precisely because they may lead to a greater level of social harmony and cooperation. Whilst Hume was both sceptical and disparaging concerning the value of what he referred to as the "monkish" virtues of much traditional religious morality, then, he clearly did regard certain dispositions as objectively valuable for the realization of certain social outcomes which he also construed as constitutive of general human happiness. There can also be little doubt that these consequentialist aspects of his views had considerable influence on the later attempts of such early utilitarians as Bentham and James Mill to define actions as morally right or wrong by reference to their measurable potential for the production of happiness construed, as its most basic, in terms of simple pleasure.

Despite the fact that they have occasionally been run together as simply two different varieties of teleological ethics, however, it is important to distinguish an ethics of virtue from utilitarianism precisely in so far as the second is, but the first is not, a form of consequentialism—and, indeed, virtue theorists have been among the most trenchant critics of utilitarianism. From a virtue-theoretical perspective it would appear the main problem of utilitarian and other consequentialist views is that they fail to distinguish significantly, if at all, between the different ways in which means are related to ends in the practical realm of moral as distinct from technical or instrumental reasoning. Whilst it is true that Aristotle, in his writings on virtue, himself leans heavily in one place on an analogy between the development of virtues and the acquisition of skills, he is elsewhere quite clear how the two differ and about the *internal* rather than *external* nature of the relationship of means to ends which distinguishes moral from productive reasoning. The point, of course, is that whereas a skill, such as sawing wood, is causally separable from the outcome it produces (a pile of logs) a virtue such as honesty or fairness cannot likewise be conceived as separate from the ends of truth and justice. Since truth and justice are part of what we *mean* by that human flourishing which honesty and fairness serve to promote, they are better regarded as *constitutive* of those ends rather than causally productive of them—and this is precisely, of course, what many philosophers have meant by speaking of the virtues as ends in themselves or as "their own reward."

It is for this reason, however, that in the context of moral or evaluative enquiry means are not readily intersubstitutable as is the case with instrumental means; one means is not as good as another for a given moral end. Notoriously, of course, consequentialists are given to painting themselves into some awkward ethical corners in this respect; if the torture and murder of one innocent man may be envisaged as a means to the prevention of large-scale human misery and suffering, then whatever our ordinary moral intuitions might lead us to regard as corrupt or wicked conduct may well reappear, by some bizarre process of ethical laundering, as defensible—even praiseworthy. Indeed, any individual with the temerity to insist that such an act of unjust scapegoating would be quite beyond the moral pale is liable to be branded as the kind of morally squeamish pharisee who selfishly exalts his own conscience or integrity above the common good.

However, having missed the principal point behind the virtue theorists' distinction of moral and evaluative reasoning from productive reasoning—that the former, unlike the latter, is concerned with the discernment and achievement of goods and goals which are of intrinsic rather than instrumental value in human affairs— consequentialism proceeds to confound confusion by failing to separate the issue of what might constitute the least worst practical option in certain intolerable moral circumstances from that of what, in the light of anything construable as an intelligible *moral* conception, we might count as a *good* or right action. For, of course, whereas there is plain contradiction in admitting (as a consequentialist surely must) that X is a type of action which is objectively conducive to human suffering, but we must regard it as right or good here; there is not the least hint of contradiction involved in recognising that X is actually and objectively a *wrong* action, but we have here no option but to perform it to avoid some worse consequence—although saying as much may not in the least absolve us from the responsibility, blame or guilt which follows from doing X.

2. Problems Concerning the Identity of Virtues

According to a non-consequentialist teleological ethics, then, ideas of virtue are central to the understanding of human moral life, and virtues are essentially principled dispositions susceptible of objective appraisal as morally good or bad in the

light of normative standards acknowledging the ethical significance of both motives and consequences. From this point of view the trouble with other ethical theories such as moral realism, non-cognitivism and consequentialism is that they are
reductive and thereby inclined to emphasize only one aspect of virtue at the expense of others; in view of this it may well be nearer the mark to credit virtues with
the same sort of status in ethical theory as some have attributed to persons in philosophical psychology—as irreducible "basic particulars."

This is not to deny, however, that serious problems concerning the identity of
virtues remain. Indeed, following our observations in the last section concerning
the internal or conceptual rather than external or causal nature of the relationship
between particular virtues, and those goals of human flourishing to which they
conduce, it might now be objected that our account begins to look circular in precisely the way that we earlier accused prescriptivism of being circular in defining
values in terms of general commitments. For in the light of our denial that the
relationship between virtues and ends is a productive one, are we not now entitled
to stipulate what we like as goals of human flourishing and then define as virtues
whatever dispositions conduce to them? We should remember, however, that identification of a principled human preference or form of conduct as a virtue is not, as
in the case of non-cognitivism, merely to express approval of or commitment to it.
Indeed, the claim on the part of virtue theorists that values and virtues are to be
regarded as objective features of mundane states of affairs or events does not
shorten the gap between how things are and how we ought to act any more than
any other ethical claim does. Thus, two agents may entirely agree concerning objective facts but still beg to differ concerning what should be done because they
regard as significant different value implications of a given state of affairs. This
point applies to virtues as much as to other values, of course, since recognising a
trait of character as a virtue does not entail a commitment to the pursuit of the
associated course of action, unless someone shares the goals of that virtue and
regards the action as appropriate in the circumstances. So the precise point of lo-
cating the idea of a virtue at the heart of our reflections on the nature of morality
is specifically to identify an objective basis for such reflections which lies *beyond*
individual commitment or personal determination to regard as right or good only
what fits in with our plans.

However, since values are features of things regarded as significant for a purpose, it can be expected that, even if recognizing such values does not commit
agents to their pursuit, it must nevertheless strongly incline them in that direction
if they have those purposes; and since moral virtues are regarded as *ex hypothesi*
conducive to *human* flourishing, how can it be doubted that any rational human
agent would have at least some of the purposes inherent in virtues? Thus, as Hume
himself recognised, since the common personal and interpersonal virtues of self-
control, justice, tolerance and benevolence have evidently greater potential for the
promotion of human flourishing over profligacy, injustice, prejudice and spite it is
reasonable to expect that rational agents would aspire to promote these positive
qualities on their own part as well as that of others.

But it may well now be said that rather than eliminating the boot-straps circularity of virtue theory, this observation simply throws it into greater relief. For,

even if we dismiss the "alternative" value preferences of sadists, masochists and misanthropists as abnormally perverse, deviant or even irrational, it cannot be seriously denied that human beings do differ significantly in their precise estimates of what is virtuous and what is not and in the priorities which they accord to different virtues. Thus, in practically the same breath in which he extolled the social virtues, Hume also condemned the "monkish" ones. In short, the problem of the objectivity of virtues seems to persist even when we have separated the issue of what is of value from that of personal commitment—precisely because the value which human agents discern in particular dispositions, unlike that which they discern in a sharp knife, can only be expected to reflect the interests which they do *actually* have as human agents in the light of a particular conception of the good life.

It should be clear from what has been said so far, however, that much scepticism concerning the possibility of objective rational evaluation of human interests, or the conceptions of good life in which such interests are implicated, is in itself question-begging and arises from a certain misconception of the operations of human intellect in relation to experience—a misconception which is deeply entrenched in classical empiricism.

3. The Social Character of Virtues

Actually, the empiricist "passive spectator" view of human reason would appear to underlie both modern non-cognitivist and moral realist misconceptions of the role of evaluative deliberation in human affairs; essentially, the former locates values in non-cognitive subjective states rather than in the world and the latter locates values in a reality conceived as independent of human interests primarily because *neither* is able to make much sense of the idea of distinctively evaluative reasoning. Moreover, because the "spectatorial" view of the relationship between reason and experience is also a fundamentally individualist conception of the role of intellect and deliberation, both views fail to appreciate the extent to which values are matters less of individual intuition or personal choice and more of the human inheritance of ideals and aspirations enshrined in complex, essentially social, forms of life. The mainstream tradition in which by and large virtue theorists stand, however, is also a *communitarian* tradition which emphasizes the deep cultural roots and social circumstances of evaluative enquiry and which furthermore construes culture as a web of established practices enmeshed in forms of evaluative discourse precisely concerned to identify what has been characterized as a "best moral picture." Thus, far from it being proper to regard values as the deliverences of personal or subjective decision they are better conceived as products of long traditions of public and interpersonal reflection upon what is best worth striving for in human life.

However, it may now appear that this transposition of the problem of the source of evaluation from the private and personal to the public and social key simply relocates the philosophical difficulties relating to the ethical centrality of virtues, in so far as this fresh stress on the social and cultural roots of values—especially in

the light of emphases by virtue theorists from Aristotle to present-day communi-
tarians on the "internal" character of evaluative deliberation—might well seem to
represent a leap from the subjectivist frying pan into the fires of vicious relativism.
For, although I may be entitled to claim even a high measure of objectivity on
behalf of my character assessments within the standards set by a given culture or
community—this woman just does count as loyal here and that man as courageous there—we can all too readily recognize the dangers of generalizing across
different human social and cultural contexts. Indeed, is not the most important
lesson that the modern human sciences of sociology and anthropology have had to
teach us that normative standards and ideals do differ radically from one culture
to another and that conduct regarded as expressive of a given virtue in one place
may not so count in another?

It is arguable, however, that this generalized relativist critique of the objectivity
of virtues rests upon a tangle of confusions at least one of which—the confusion
of what counts as a virtue with its particular cultural instantiations—should be
apparent in the very statement of the above objection. For, from the fact that it is
wrong to drive on the right hand side of the road in the United Kingdom but on
the left hand side in Canada it hardly follows that there is anything relative about
the rules of good driving as such; on the contrary, it only shows that it is generally
right to drive on the appropriate side of the road (even though, of course, there is
no such conduct as driving *as such* which is not driving on one side of the road or
the other) and this is for readily intelligible reasons which are about as objective as
they come. The same point surely applies, however, to thinking about the importance of moral virtues in human life; that patient endurance of one's sufferings may
count as a virtue in one context but not in another does not show that virtues are
relative—only, to the contrary, that it may be appropriate to express courage in
different ways in different circumstances—a point which is central to Aristotle's
own account of virtue.

Indeed, it is likely that what speaks above all for the idea that the virtues should
be accorded primacy in our reflections about the objective basis of human moral
conduct is precisely the fact that certain fundamental human qualities or dispositions of compassion, courage, self-control, honesty, justice, tolerance and so on are
celebrated well-nigh universally in the best moral pictures, traditions and narratives of an otherwise bewildering diversity of human cultures and that such also
familiar and dreary human shortcomings as malice, envy, lust, greed and so on are
equally regarded as *vices*. The terminology of virtues and vices is arguably the common cross-cultural currency of human moral life by which men of good will from
diverse cultures are able to recognize their moral kinship precisely in view of their
mutual access to this primitive conceptual apparatus of ethical evaluation.

Of course, this is not to deny that there are or have been human societies and
cultures which have endorsed all kinds of vice and cruelty in the pursuit of one
social or cultural goal or another. Again, however, I do not think that this observation presents a serious difficulty for the main argument of this paper. It is just
another relativist mistake to maintain that a particular ideal or aspiration is apt
for moral legitimation merely on the grounds that it is entertained by large numbers of people, on the contrary, it is clear that social ideals and aspirations them-

selves attract moral evaluation in the terminology of virtues and vices—according to whether they are just, honest, charitable, tolerant, vengeful or cruel and so on. A rather more serious problem in the wake of a "rival traditions" view of the place of the virtues in moral life, I suspect, arises not from the fact that people have sometimes sought to pursue what is vicious under cover of what is virtuous, but from different cultures and systems of belief according rather different *priorities* to what have been, all the same, widely regarded as different virtues. The controversies which can arise from the fact that whereas one culture is inclined to regard love as the highest of the virtues, for another it is courage or justice, however, may only be resolvable—if indeed they are resolvable at all—at the very deepest levels of metaphysical enquiry into the ultimate meaning and destiny of human nature and endeavour.

QUESTIONS FOR ANALYSIS AND DISCUSSION

1. Throughout much of the early part of the essay, Carr is careful to separate his notion of the good from utilitarianism. Which ideas help Carr make this separation? Do you think it works?

2. For Carr the major problem for supporters of virtue ethics is not justifying it but determining the right order or ranking of the virtues. In light of Jordan-Smith's essay on the vices, or Hiriyanna's or Franklin's essays on virtues, can you rank the virtues to fit Carr's vision of a communitarian morality? If so, specify the key virtues and explain your choices. If not, clarify your reasons.

3. Many thinkers believe that the virtues rather than other moral values are the key to helping humans lead happy lives. Do you think morality is or should be directly connected to human happiness? If so, do the theories from Chapter 1 or 2 introduce directions for happiness that are favorable over the directions outlined by the defenders of virtue? Choose one or two selections from the earlier readings to explain your reasons.

CHAPTER FOUR

The Whole Truth and Nothing But the Truth

Human life is thus only a perpetual illusion; men deceive and flatter each other. . . . [A man] does not wish anyone to tell him the truth; he avoids telling it to others, and all these dispositions so removed from justice and reason, have a natural root in his heart.

—Pascal, *Pensees*

The task of speaking the truth is an infinite labor: to respect it in its complexity is an obligation that no power can afford to shortchange, unless it would impose the silence of slavery.

—Michel Foucault, "The Masked Philosopher"

The expectation that humans tell each other the truth is so widespread that various moral reminders are taken for granted. Every witness in the court of justice takes an oath to tell "nothing but the truth." The trust we have in one another is unimaginable without mutual respect for truthfulness. The Ninth Commandment forbids telling a lie. In Chapter 3 M. Hiriyanna lists sincerity and honesty as two of the nine moral virtues. For Plato, the lover of knowledge is one who seeks and speaks truth; it is this love that guides the just and happy life.

Do these praises of truth indicate a universal ethic? Or do they reflect an uneasy fact?—living by and for the truth is difficult.

Ordinary dealings with deception and lying are so common that we give them little thought. Indeed, as the Pascal epigraph suggests, deceit may be essential to human life. According to some social scientists, when a baby cries, the infant is not expressing pain but feigning pain to manipulate the responses of the parent. On a first date, do you compliment your date's parents because you like the decor of their living room or because you want them to think well of you long enough to let you whisk their child into the darkness of the night? Upon graduation, as you nervously prepare for that big job interview, do you plan to tell the company that it is merely a stepping-stone for your ambitious career, or will you indicate that working for this company until you retire is the realization of all your dreams?

Despite the mundane evidence, many philosophers are reluctant to assume a cavalier attitude toward deception and lying. Why? First, there is a general assumption that humans value truth and knowledge as distinct goods. Science, curiosity, understanding, and wisdom are worthy enterprises on their own terms. Second, an essential component of moral consideration is self-knowledge. Sincerity, responsibility, and credibility involve the belief that a person has some sense of self. As Thomas Nagel reminds us in Chapter 2, morality relies in part on our ability to give an account of why we did this rather than that. And third, social interaction seems impossible to value or achieve unless some recognition of truthfulness is present. If you consult a doctor or a lawyer, you expect that he or she will do their best to apprise you of the situation. When a stranger asks directions to a campus building, it is assumed that you will be sincere in your guidance.

The tension between the love of truth—in terms of both truthfulness and the value of seeking knowledge—and our everyday conduct, which involves deception or lying, is addressed in the selections in this chapter.

Historian Wendy Doniger's case study illuminates this tension in the erotic dimension of human life. Deceptions, masquerades, frauds, feigned emotions, and words of betrayal rank high among the ploys humans use with one another to satisfy their carnal or sexual desires. Memorable pop songs, such as "Will You Still Love Me Tomorrow?" or Alanis Morrisette's "You Oughta Know," also focus on this theme.

Philosopher Sissela Bok argues that lying cannot be justified so easily, regardless of human conduct. The frequency and uneven acceptability of an action does not count as moral approval. Moreover, she concludes, truth-telling is morally superior to deception in nearly all cases, including erotic ones.

In his rejoinder, philosopher David Nyberg claims that Bok overrates the value of truth-telling. There is good reason for deceiving one another—it works. It works not only for the liar but also for the listener. Many of us are unprepared to speak the truth or to hear the truth, particularly about those things we care about, such as ourselves, friends or family, or even our ideals.

In philosopher Mary Mothersill's view, public controversies reinforce the importance of valuing the relation between trust and honesty. Justification for a lie, she notes, must be undertaken in a public forum.

Raymond Smullyan, philosopher and professional magician, engages us with a lively and witty dialogue about possible motives for telling the truth. The more this issue is analyzed, speculate some of the dialogue's participants, the clearer it becomes that one can tell the truth (as Simplicus does) and not know why.

Philosopher Gilbert Meilaender shifts the focus to the love of knowledge and examines human curiosity. Mindful of the disputes between Augustine (who thought curiosity a dangerous vice) and Bertrand Russell (who believed even idle curiosity to be a good), Meilaender sketches a middle ground.

A different version of the love for knowledge is found in gossip. Though it can be an enjoyable love—one experienced on a daily basis—gossip also can inflict injury and pain. Sissela Bok again has much to contribute to our understanding of the value of truth, in this case exploring the intriguing role of gossip.

24.

WENDY DONIGER

Case Study: Sex, Lies, and Tall Tales

Truth—speaking it and seeking it—is an essential value in human life. Truthfulness underlies trust in social interaction and in the search for knowledge. It sparks serious scholarship, trivial pursuits, intimate conversation, and local gossip. Despite this universal respect for truth, philosophers continue to debate the nature of truth as well as the moral goodness of truth. Perhaps nowhere is the value of truth more complicated than in the area of human sexuality and love.

Historian of religions Wendy Doniger (b. 1940) articulates these complications by reviewing some famous masquerades and deceptions. Does this mean that human sexual behavior requires the lie? Doniger offers several perspectives and invites the reader to consider the extent to which humans deceive one another in areas that, for many people, involve their inner or true selves.

CRITICAL READING QUESTIONS

1. What is meant by the phrase "veritas in coitu"?
2. More often than not, according to Doniger's survey, what is the difference between men's and women's sexual lies? What examples are given to illustrate these differences?
3. What is meant by sexual fraud? How is it related to seduction?

Sexual Truth

People all over the world tell this story about sexual lying: you go to bed with someone you think you know, and when you wake up you discover that it was someone else—another man, or another woman, or a man instead of a woman, or a woman instead of a man, or a god, or a snake, or a complete stranger, or your own wife or husband, or your mother. Why were you not able to tell the difference

"Sex, Lies, and Tall Tales," *Social Research*, Fall 1996, 63(3): 663–672, 692–696. Some notes have been omitted.

in the dark? The plot seems to have fascinated people of many cultures and should make it onto anyone's list of the Ten Greatest Hits of World Mythology. It is at the heart of what Shakespearean scholars call "the bed trick" and Freud called the Family Romance. In the Western tradition alone, there are Rachel and Leah, Tamar and Judah, and (I think) Ruth and Naomi in the Hebrew Bible; Amphitryon in the Greek and Roman traditions; the begetting of King Arthur by a masquerading father, and Elaine masquerading as Guenever with Launcelot. There are the sexual masquerades in Boccaccio and in so many of Shakespeare's plays, especially *All's Well That Ends Well* and *Measure for Measure,* and in opera: Mozart's *The Marriage of Figaro* and *Cosi fan Tutte,* Richard Strauss's *Rosenkavalier* and *Arabella,* Johann Strauss's *Fledermaus.* There are the trans-sexual masquerades in the contemporary theater (*M. Butterfly, Prelude to a Kiss*) and cinema (*Some Like It Hot, Tootsie, The Crying Game*), to say nothing of the infinite variety of sexual masquerades in the *Arabian Nights.* Though scholars of high culture (particularly opera and Shakespeare) have tended to regard the bed trick as a cheap trick, a stupid plot, it never seems to lose its audience appeal. One Biblical scholar has noted that despite the fact that bedside lights and pillow-talk made the bed trick harder and harder to take seriously after the seventeenth century, "the irony of physical closeness and mental distance which underlies it persists in the modern understanding of sex."

Many of these stories argue that sex tells the truth: if there is *veritas in vino,* there is surely *veritas in coitu.* The brutal form of the paradigm states that truth inheres in the physical act of sex; the more romantic form of the same paradigm seeks the truth in the more spiritual act of falling in love, which is, of course, not at all the same thing as falling into bed. These latter stories argue that love, sexual love, is the most reliable criterion of personal identity: the one you love is the one you know, and the one you know is the real one. That the sexual act is the ultimate key to concealed identity is a Freudian assumption, which Michel Foucault sums up very well indeed:

> [W]e also admit that it is in the area of sex that we must search for the most secret and profound truths about the individual, that it is there that we can best discover what he is and what determines him. And if it was believed for centuries that it was necessary to hide sexual matters because they were shameful, we now know that it is sex itself which hides the most secret parts of the individual: the structure of his fantasies, the roots of his ego, the forms of his relationship to reality. At the bottom of sex, there is truth (Foucault, 1980, pp. x–xi).

But Freud did not invent the belief that sex is where we find the truth about an individual's often masquerading identity; he borrowed it from the texts of stories from other times and other cultures. In this view, the body tells the truth: the real person is the person glimpsed in bed, while the person whom we see at other times is a veneer, a superficial double. As John Hubner recently remarked of pornography, "Sex strips away identities it takes a lifetime to build. A naked aroused man is not a brain surgeon or a university president or a Methodist bishop. He is an animal with an erection" (Hubner, 1993, p. xx).

Sexual Lies

It could be argued that *all* forms of love are deluding, including love of one's children (as in the Scottish joke about the mother of one of a band of bagpipers: "Everyone's out of step but our wee Geordie"), love of country (easily transformed into murderous and often suicidal fanaticism), even love of animals ("The owner's eye maketh the horse fat," say the English). But sexual love is arguably (and I will argue it) the most deluding form of love. Does sex tell the truth or lie? Can you recognize your lover in the dark? These questions are clearly related: if sex lies, you cannot tell who you are in bed with. The word "false" thus has both a weak and a strong meaning: in its weak form, its normal form, a woman is "false" to her lover if she makes love with someone else; in its stronger, mythological form, she is "false" to him if she *is* someone else. In the first case, the oath of love is a false copy of the true oath; in the second, the person is a false copy of the true lover.

When Isolde played her bed trick, she "devised the best ruse that she could at this juncture, namely that they should simply ask [her maid] Brangane to lie at [her husband] Mark's side during the first night." And the author remarks, "Thus love instructs honest minds to practice perfidy." It is only partly an accident of the English language that we lie *to* the people we lie *with*. As Shakespeare puns, in Sonnet 138: "Therefore I lie with her, and she with me,/ And in our faults by lies we flattered be." Nor is this idea limited to English literature: Manu, the great Hindu lawmaker, remarks that "there is no crime in a (false) oath about women whom one desires, or about marriages." Even in contemporary legal debates about sexual fraud, it is often assumed that "lying is integral to the 'dance' of sexual initiation and negotiation. . . . To lie to a sexual partner is to share a leap of fancy—all very harmless and justifiable" (Larson, 1993, p. 449). This leads the feminist legal scholar Jane E. Larson to ask, "[I]s it ever reasonable to believe a lover? Were our grandmothers right in telling us that men always lie for sex, and the woman who listens is a fool? This counsel rests on the presumption that lying for sex is in 'the rules of the game.'" (Larson, 1993, p. 465). Larson argues that the courts must change the game, but the myths reveal how very deeply entrenched a game it is. As Judge Richard Posner points out, "The problems of proof of seduction by false pretenses . . . are exquisitely difficult" (Posner, 1992, p. 393).

The ancient wisdom of the grandmothers persists in the cynicism with which we regard sociological surveys of sexual behavior. Anthony Lane, reviewing such a survey, put the matter with his characteristic wry humor:

> These books are not about sex. They are not even about dancing. They are about lying. They are constructed with admirable clarity, but they represent the one plus ultra of fuzziness—the unalterable fuzz of our duplicity, the need to hide the truth from other people in the hope that we will cease to recognize it ourselves. Read a sentence such as, "Men report that they experience fellatio at a far greater rate than women report providing it," and you find yourself glancing down a long, shady vista of self-delusion. This is not a question of inefficient research, or of culpable hypocrisy, or even of that much loved villain of the piece, the male boast; it is simply what T. S. Eliot called bovarysme, "the

human will to see things as they are not," and throughout *The Social Organization of Sexuality* it never once failed to give me a good laugh.

Self-delusion is indeed the key, for we lie to others in order to lie to ourselves. We lie to ourselves in bed when we lie about who our partners are and about who we are. Though we may think we are "our real selves" in sex, we may actually be least so. As Lord Henry remarks, in Oscar Wilde's *The Picture of Dorian Gray,* "When one is in love, one always begins by deceiving one's self, and one always ends by deceiving others. That is what the world calls romance" (Wilde, 1890, p. 200). John Donne argued a similar point (in "A Lecture Upon the Shadow"):

> So whilst our infant love did grow,
> Disguises did, and shadowes, flow,
> From us, and our cares; but, now 'tis not so.
> . . . . .
> Except our loves at this noone stay,
> We shall new shadowes make the other way.
>> As the first were made to blinde
>> Others; these which come behinde
> Will worke upon our selves, and blind our eyes.

Men lie in sexual situation: Pinocchios all, their noses stretch in resonance with (a Freudian might say upward displacement from) their lower noses. Men lie more easily than women culturally in cultures, such as ours, where they have tradition- ally had more freedom than women to move about. And men are also more in- clined to lie in cultures, such as ours, where with one hand (the right hand of the superego) they impose monogamous constraints that, with the other hand (the left hand of the id), they evade. Tyrants make liars, they say; monogamous soci- eties make sexual liars. Ours is by no means the only such society, of course; in the medieval Japanese novel, *The Changelings,* when the wife of the transsexual masquerader Chunagon quite naturally fails to recognize him, he shamelessly accuses her of failing to recognize him because she has slept with another man.

Where men's sexual lies, by and large, are cultural, involving social disguises and Byzantine plots, women's sexual lies, by and large, are physical, involving darkness and distortions of the body—faking large breasts and small feet and red lips. It is easier for women than for men to lie physically in some ways, faking orgasms, for example, a widely attested skill. But it is more difficult (though by no means impossible) for women to lie about other physical aspects of sex, such as maidenheads, and getting pregnant, the big truth teller. Pregnancy may be a proof and therefore a problem, proof that adultery has taken place: hence, the accusation against Tamar (*Genesis* 38), Mary (*Matthew* 1.18–25), and many other women. But sometimes pregnancy is the solution, proof that the woman is fertile—when barrenness, rather than fertility, is the problem—or that her husband enjoys sleep- ing with her after all—when rejection, that is, *his* barrenness, is the problem. This, too, is true of Tamar and also of Shakespeare's Helena in *All's Well That Ends Well.*

Men, on the other hand, have more difficulty in lying about other physical as- pects of sex, such as desire: it is hard to fake—and sometimes hard to conceal—

an erection. (Even chimpanzees have this problem; when a chimp woos a female in heat, he displays his erection, but if a more powerful male should happen to come by at this time, the first chimp quickly puts his hands over his crotch). Pinocchio's nose, after all, declared to the world that he was lying. And there is a dissymmetry in the timing of the physical lying and truth-telling of men and women: men's physical truth-test comes earlier, with desire, while for women, the truth test comes later, with pregnancy. This dissymmetry suggests one reason why the stories about sexual lies are not symmetrical, or interchangeable: that is, you cannot take the stories about men and tell them about women, or the reverse; different details give them different shapes.

But sexual lies, however common, are not cheap; we pay dearly for them. For sexual love is not just a way of knowing who your lover is; it may also be a way of knowing who you are, through the mirror of those whom you love and who love you. As Shakespeare puts it, it is "ourselves we see in ladies' eyes" (*Love's Labour's Lost* 4.3); or, again, John Donne (in "The Good Morrow"): "My face in thine eye, thine in mine appears." When we deceive others about our sexual identity, therefore, or are deceived by them, we lose one of the main anchors of our own sense of identity, especially since we are lying to ourselves when we are lying to them. As one of the inadvertently masquerading brothers in Shakespeare's *Comedy of Errors* remarks, "Am I . . . Known unto these, and to myself disguised?" (2.2) A remark echoed by the bridegroom who says to himself, when he finds his beautiful young bride apparently changed into a hideous old woman: "Am I myself, or not myself?" And Kleist's Alcmena remarks, when she cannot tell if the man she has slept with is her husband Amphitryon or Zeus, "Is my reflection in the mirror mine? Would he be stranger to me than myself?" The ease with which most sexual liars fool their victims seems to suggest a paradox: we like to believe that the one we love is unique and makes us unique, but many sexual partners look alike in the dark. The shadow side of this concept reveals another tragic paradox of the sexual masquerade: masqueraders usually believe that they will only be loved if they cease being who they really are. Thus, when Cyrano de Bergerac supplies the words with which his soldier friend woos Roxanne, both men lose, for each feels that Roxanne truly loves the other.

. . .

Sexual Lying in Real Life

On hearing stories about sexual masquerades, contemporary listeners often protest, "But of course, such a thing could not really happen." How could it be possible that someone could sleep with two different people on several occasions and never tell the difference? Or, in the case of one person masquerading as two different people, how could the partner *not* tell the sameness? This is the problem of realistic recognition—or unrealistic non-recognition. How realistically do stories about sexual lying deal with the problems that might be involved in bringing it off? What realistic explanations can we construct to believe in? What excuses have people made to explain how they could get away with it? What ways are there of, on the one hand, detecting the deception, telling one person from another in bed, or, on the other hand, of perpetrating the deception, fooling someone in bed?

Though it has been argued that in Renaissance England, "There is little indication that bed-tricks were of social practise," there is evidence that the wife of "the last great *Earle of Oxford* . . . was brought to his bed under the notion of his *Mistris.*" And in the thirteenth century the wife of the false Count Baldwin of Flanders "lived with him familiarly for over three years 'without ever perceiving or even suspecting the fraud,'" despite the doubts constantly expressed by the count's daughter Jeanne.

Successful transsexual masqueraders seem to cause the most shock; the notorious case of M. Boursicot, the French diplomat who lived for twenty years with a Chinese man whom he mistook for a woman, inspired David Henry Hwang's play *M. Butterfly* (1988). Such masqueraders are sometimes quickly unmasked; people do notice the difference. But sometimes they do not.

. . .

Sexual Fraud: "Loopholes in the Penal Code"

Let us return now to real life for one final group of bed tricks: those that end up in law courts.

In legal terms, a sexual masquerade is one subdivision of sexual fraud, which includes not only other sorts of lies (such as saying that you are using contraception when you are not, or that you do not have AIDS when you do), but two senses of "impersonating a spouse," one of which is our sexual masquerade while the other simply involves pretending that you have married your victim when you have not. The Model Penal Code paragraph 213.1(2)(c) contains a provision criminalizing the seduction of a woman by impersonating her husband. Such laws were popular in many states at one time and are still on the books in a few states today.

Some of these multiple men fool multiple women, as in this newspaper report:

Nashville, Tenn. The phone rings late at night. In a sexy whisper, a man persuades a woman to unlock her door, undress, put on a blindfold and wait for him in bed. At least three women did so, thinking he was their boyfriend, and had sex with the so-called Fantasy Man. One woman had sex with him twice a week for two months. Now they want police to charge Raymond Mitchell III with rape. The 45-year-old businessman says he was just fulfilling the women's fantasies and the sex was consensual. Police are not sure what to do. Investigators are looking at whether Mitchell claimed to be someone else, which could constitute rape by fraud. . . . Connie Vaupel, who got Mitchell, a co-worker, charged with attempted rape in 1989, defended the alleged victims. "These are not stupid women," she said. "They were convinced of something that was not true. He had enough information beforehand to convince them. Believe me, this guy is slick.". . . The Tennessee Sentencing Commission . . . in 1989 updated an 1870 criminal statute on "fictitious husband rape" and came up with Tennessee's current rape-by-fraud statute. About 40 states have similar laws, and prosecutors have won rape-by-fraud cases across the country. . . .

And more information is given in the "Box":

Raymond Mitchell's accusers are: a 26 year-old woman who realized that Fantasy Man was not her boyfriend as soon as he touched her. She feared that he would hurt her if she resisted. A woman in her mid-30s who thought Fantasy Man was a man from Texas she had met a week before. She had sex with Fantasy Man twice before calling the Texan and realizing the truth. A woman in her early 20s who said she had sex with Fantasy Man twice a week for two months because she believed he was her boy-friend. She realized the truth when her blindfold slipped (*San Francisco Chronicle*, February 3, 1995).

One woman *did* see through the trick but was virtually raped. The others, however, saw and heard just what they hoped to see and hear, just like the people in myths.

A legal case involved identical male twins in 1994:

A twin accused of deceiving his brother's girlfriend into having sexual intercourse won dismissal of a sexual misconduct charge this week after a Nassau County judge decided there was not statutory basis for prosecution. The judge ruled that what amounted to loopholes in the Penal Law mandated dismissal tied to facts in a case he described as "truly novel." The key elements missing in the statutory framework, District Court Judge John Michael Gallaso explained in People v. Lamont Hough, was the Legislature's exclusion of *fraud, deception or impersonation* in defining sexual misconduct where there was lack of consent. . . . The charge against Lamont Hough alleged he made an early morning visit to the home of the girlfriend of his twin brother, Lenny. The woman, in her complaint, said she consented to intercourse in her darkened apartment believing the man was her boyfriend. Only afterwards, when the man asked, "Are you going to tell Lenny?" did she realize the deception. . . . The judge wrote . . . "The lack of consent results from the complainant's mistaken belief, resulting from defendant's alleged fraud, that the body she made love with was that of her boyfriend" (People v. Hough, *New York Law Journal*, January 18, 1994, emphasis added).

The "loopholes in the Penal Law" are the driving force behind the enormous body of folklore dealing with this theme, and if the judge in this case had read those stories he would not have found it "truly novel." The belief that the woman made love with a body, rather than a person, is a masterpiece of the legal mind at work.

The court transcript notes several inconsistencies: "It is interesting to note that complainant states that she left the door unlocked for her boyfriend, yet she stated that she had just given him a key. . . . Complainant got out of bed and, curiously enough, turned off the light located near the door rather than turn it on. . . . Complainant began talking to the male as if it were her boyfriend Lenny but was looking away from him while they were in the bed."

Both by insisting on darkness ("curiously enough") and by looking away, the victim (if indeed she is the victim) stymies sight. But are there no other ways of telling who you are in bed with? The other bases of the woman's non-recognition of the man in her bed are quite traditional:

> Complainant believed the male was her boyfriend because it sounded like him. . . . Complainant opened the door and thought it was Lenny who entered the apartment, as it was dark and she couldn't see. The male, who smelt of alcohol, got into bed next to the complainant. . . . The male began to touch the complainant's breasts and complainant responded "Oh boy, your [*sic*] drunk and horny." He then asked her to have sex with him and she told him to make it quick because she had to work in the morning. . . . Complainant wasn't looking at the male's face.

Darkness, inattention, time ("make it quick"), and self-deception (as well as the resembling voice)—they are all there. Case dismissed.

In yet another case of this type, in Arizona, a woman was at first fooled by the man's silence but then came to recognize her husband, not by his behavior in bed, but by other, more trivial factors. The defendant testified: "When I got in bed with her, she thought I was her husband and kept calling me 'CHARLIE.' I didn't want to talk, because she would know I wasn't her husband and I took her pajama bottoms off. She didn't know that I wasn't her husband until we had had intercourse." Again the clue of the voice is deflected. But, then how did she know? She told the judge: "Well, at that time something came to my mind that it couldn't be my husband because the defendant had his, just recent, a haircut, I could feel it, and my husband hadn't had a haircut, and the smell of tobacco on his breath. My husband doesn't smoke." That is how.

Judge Richard Posner discusses a specific instance of sex by fraud in addition to the cases we have just noted (a man who has sex with a woman by impersonating her husband): a medical practitioner who inserts his penis into a patient's body under the guise of administering "medical treatment" (Posner, 1992, pp. 392–393). A gynecologist who repeatedly had intercourse with a young and, apparently, very inexperienced patient in the guise of treating her menstrual cramps was convicted of rape. In other cases, too, the woman apparently believed that the "instrument" used to perform the examination was a speculum or other medical instrument, when in fact it was the physician's penis. One physician used his penis in place of a medical instrument during an examination to discover the source of a patient's vision problem. Unless we resort to Freudian ideas of upward displacement, and despite the belief which pervades our stories that vision is an essential criterion of identity (you cannot tell them apart in the dark), it is difficult to imagine how this misunderstanding came to pass.

Posner distinguishes between the sorts of lies that people tell in bed and the sorts of lies that they tell in other circumstances:

> [G]enerally it is not a crime to use false pretenses to entice a person into a sexual relationship. Seduction, even when honeycombed with lies that would convict the man of fraud if he were merely trying to obtain money, is not rape. . . . It is otherwise if the man is impersonating the woman's husband or claims to be administering medical treatment to the woman rather than to be inserting his penis in her. In both cases the

act itself, were the true facts known to the woman, would be disgusting as well as humiliating, rather than merely humiliating as in the case of the common misrepresentation of dating and courtship (Posner, 1992).

Apparently it is humiliating but not a crime to trick a woman into bed using "the common misrepresentations of dating and courtship" and "false pretenses," though it is a crime to trick her out of money using the same sorts of lies. But Posner assumes that it becomes disgusting as well as humiliating if the man pretends to be her husband (or a speculum), and exciting a woman's disgust is, apparently, a criminal act. By this account, we must ask whether Martin Guerre's wife was at the end disgusted (having been really fooled by the sexual lie) or "merely" humiliated (having been fooled at first by the small lies but then having seen through the big lie). The mind, at least the non-legal mind, boggles.

References

Foucault, Michel, *Introduction to Hercule Barbin: Being the Recently Discovered Memoirs of a Nineteenth-Century French Hermaphrodite*, Richard McDougall, trans. (New York: Pantheon Books, 1980).

Hubner, John, *Bottom Feeders: From Free Love to Hard Core—The Rise and Fall of Counterculture Heroes Jim and Artie Mitchell* (Garden City, NJ: Doubleday, 1993).

Larson, Jane E., "'Women Understand So Little, They Call My Good Nature "Deceit"': A Feminist Rethinking of Seduction," *Columbia Law Review* 93 (1993): 374–472.

Posner, Richard A., *Sex and Reason* (Cambridge, MA: Harvard University Press, 1992).

Wilde, Oscar, *The Picture of Dorian Gray* (London, 1890; 1891), Donald L. Lawler, ed. (New York: Norton, 1988).

QUESTIONS FOR ANALYSIS AND DISCUSSION

1. Doniger introduces an ambiguity about the truth in human sex. On one hand it seems to be fraught with deception, but on the other hand it reveals some inner truths about the self. Do you think this is an accurate portrayal of humans in sexual settings? in nonsexual settings?

2. Suppose someone believes there is no core or inner self. That is, the self is a pliable or multiple entity that changes situationally. Would accepting this entail a belief that deception is not a serious moral issue?

3. Doniger cites Judge Posner's explanation that false pretenses in sex are often legal whereas false pretenses in financial matters are generally criminal. Do you accept Posner's distinction? Would this distinction apply in other areas of life, such as job interviews, advertising, or seeking professional advice?

25.

On Truth-Telling

*The ability to tell the truth and valuing that ability are essential to the good life. Phi-
losopher Sissela Bok (b. 1934) states that this is the reason lying and deception are moral
wrongs. And they are wrong in nearly all areas of human life, from drastic and tragic
situations to ordinary and well-intentioned settings. With clear and thoughtful reflections
on a variety of thinkers, Bok carves out her position that only a rare and reasoned lie is
morally justifiable. In three sections from her seminal book,* On Lying, *Bok outlines the
central features of her view.*

CRITICAL READING QUESTIONS

1. For Bok, what is the value of truth-telling?
2. How does she distinguish between deception and lying?
3. On what basis does Bok acknowledge the moral possibility of lying?

Introduction

*When regard for truth has been broken down or even slightly weakened, all things will
remain doubtful.*

> —St. Augustine, "On Lying"

*Doth any man doubt, that if there were taken out of men's minds vain opinions, flatter-
ing hopes, false valuations, imaginations as one would, and the like, but it would leave
the minds of a number of men poor shrunken things, full of melancholy and indisposi-
tion, and unpleasing to themselves?*

> —Bacon, "Of Truth"

*After prolonged research on myself, I brought out the fundamental duplicity of the hu-
man being. Then I realized that modesty helped me to shine, humility to conquer, and
virtue to oppress.*

> —Camus, *The Fall*

"On Truth-Telling," from *Lying: Moral Choice in Public and Private Life* (New York: Pantheon,
1978), pp. xv–xviii, 17–28. Notes have been omitted.

Should physicians lie to dying patients so as to delay the fear and anxiety which the truth might bring them? Should professors exaggerate the excellence of their students on recommendations in order to give them a better chance in a tight job market? Should parents conceal from children the fact that they were adopted? Should social scientists send investigators masquerading as patients to physicians in order to learn about racial and sexual biases in diagnosis and treatment? Should government lawyers lie to Congressmen who might otherwise oppose a much-needed welfare bill? And should journalists lie to those from whom they seek information in order to expose corruption?

We sense differences among such choices; but whether to lie, equivocate, be silent, or tell the truth in any given situation is often a hard decision. Hard because duplicity can take so many forms, be present to such different degrees, and have such different purposes and results. Hard also because we know how questions of truth and lying inevitably pervade all that is said or left unspoken within our families, our communities, our working relationships. Lines seem most difficult to draw, and a consistent policy out of reach.

I have grappled with these problems in my personal life as everyone must. But I have also seen them at close hand in my professional experience in teaching applied ethics. I have had the chance to explore particular moral quandaries encountered at work, with nurses, doctors, lawyers, civil servants, and many others. I first came to look closely at problems of professional truth-telling and deception in preparing to write about the giving of placebos. And I grew more and more puzzled by a discrepancy in perspectives: many physicians talk about such deception in a cavalier, often condescending and joking way, whereas patients often have an acute sense of injury and of loss of trust at learning that they have been duped.

I learned that this discrepancy is reflected in an odd state of affairs in medicine more generally. Honesty from health professionals matters more to patients than almost everything else that they experience when ill. Yet the requirement to be honest with patients has been left out altogether from medical oaths and codes of ethics, and is often ignored, if not actually disparaged, in the teaching of medicine.

As I widened my search, I came to realize that the same discrepancy was present in many other professional contexts as well. In law and in journalism, in government and in the social sciences, deception is taken for granted when it is felt to be excusable by those who tell the lies and who tend also to make the rules. Government officials and those who run for elections often deceive when they can get away with it and when they assume that the true state of affairs is beyond the comprehension of citizens. Social scientists condone deceptive experimentation on the ground that the knowledge gained will be worth having. Lawyers manipulate the truth in court on behalf of their clients. Those in selling, advertising, or any form of advocacy may mislead the public and their competitors in order to achieve their goals. Psychiatrists may distort information about their former patients to preserve confidentiality or to keep them out of military service. And journalists, police investigators, and so-called intelligence operators often have little compunction in using falsehoods to gain the knowledge they seek.

Yet the casual approach of professionals is wholly out of joint with the view taken by those who have to cope with the consequences of deception. For them, to be given false information about important choices in their lives is to be rendered powerless. For them, their very autonomy may be at stake.

There is little help to be found in the codes and writings on professional ethics. A number of professions and fields, such as economics, have no code of ethics in the first place. And the existing codes say little about when deception is and is not justified.

The fact is that reasons to lie occur to most people quite often. Not many stop to examine the choices confronting them; existing deceptive practices and competitive stresses can make it difficult not to conform. Guidance is hard to come by, and few are encouraged to consider such choices in schools and colleges or in their working life.

As I thought about the many opportunities for deception and about the absence of a real debate on the subject, I came to associate these with the striking recent decline in public confidence not only in the American government, but in lawyers, bankers, businessmen, and doctors. In 1960, many Americans were genuinely astonished to learn that President Eisenhower had lied when asked about the U-2 incident, in which an American spy plane and pilot had been forced down in the Soviet Union. But only fifteen years later, battered by revelations about Vietnam and Watergate, 69 percent of the respondents to a national poll agreed that "over the last ten years, this country's leaders have consistently lied to the people."

The loss of confidence reaches far beyond government leadership. From 1966 to 1976, the proportion of the public answering yes to whether they had a great deal of confidence in people in charge of running major institutions dropped from 73 percent to 42 percent for medicine; for major companies from 55 percent to 16 percent; for law firms from 24 percent (1973) to 12 percent; and for advertising agencies from 21 percent to 7 percent.

Suspicions of widespread professional duplicity cannot alone account for the loss of trust. But surely they aggravate it. We have a great deal at stake, I believe, in becoming more clear about matters of truth-telling, both for our personal choices and for the social decisions which foster or discourage deceptive practices. And when we think about these matters, it is the reasons given for deceiving which must be examined. Sometimes there *may* be sufficient reason to lie—but when? Most often there is not—and why? Describing how things are is not enough.

II. Truthfulness, Deceit, and Trust

Suppose men imagined there was no obligation to veracity, and acted accordingly; speaking as often against their own opinion as according to it; would not all pleasure of conversation be destroyed, and all confidence in narration? Men would only speak in bargaining, and in this too would soon lose all mutual confidence.

—Francis Hutcheson, *A System of Moral Philosophy*

A great man—what is he?. . . He rather lies than tells the truth; it requires more spirit and will. There is a solitude within him that is inaccessible to praise or blame, his own justice that is beyond appeal.

—Friedrich Nietzsche, *The Will to Power*

Lying, after all, is suggestive of game theory. It involves at least two people, a liar and someone who is lied to; it transmits information, the credibility and veracity of which are important; it influences some choice another is to make that the liar anticipates; the choice to lie or not to lie is part of the liar's choice of strategy; and the possibility of a lie presumably occurs to the second party, and may be judged against some a priori expectations; and the payoff configurations are rich in their possibilities . . .

—Thomas Schelling, "Game Theory and the Study of Ethical Systems"

Deceit and violence—these are the two forms of deliberate assault on human beings. Both can coerce people into acting against their will. Most harm that can befall victims through violence can come to them also through deceit. But deceit controls more subtly, for it works on belief as well as action. Even Othello, whom few would have dared to try to subdue by force, could be brought to destroy himself and Desdemona through falsehood.

The knowledge of this coercive element in deception, and of our vulnerability to it, underlies our sense of the *centrality* of truthfulness. Of course, deception—again like violence—can be used also in self-defense, even for sheer survival. Its use can also be quite trivial, as in white lies. Yet its potential for coercion and for destruction is such that society could scarcely function without some degree of truthfulness in speech and action.*

Imagine a society, no matter how ideal in other respects, where word and gesture could never be counted upon. Questions asked, answers given, information exchanged—all would be worthless. Were all statements randomly truthful or deceptive, action and choice would be undermined from the outset. There must be a minimal degree of trust in communication for language and action to be more than stabs in the dark. This is why some level of truthfulness has always been seen as essential to human society, no matter how deficient the observance of other moral principles. Even the devils themselves, as Samuel Johnson said, do not lie to one another, since the society of Hell could not subsist without truth any more than others.

A society, then, whose members were unable to distinguish truthful messages from deceptive ones, would collapse. But even before such a general collapse, individual choice and survival would be imperiled. The search for food and shelter could depend on no expectations from others. A warning that a well was poisoned or a plea for help in an accident would come to be ignored unless independent confirmation could be found.

All our choices depend on our estimates of what is the case; these estimates must

---

* But truthful statements, though they are not meant to deceive, can, of course, themselves be coercive and destructive; they can be used as weapons, to wound and do violence.

in turn often rely on information from others. Lies distort this information and therefore our situation as we perceive it, as well as our choices. A lie, in Hartmann's words, "injures the deceived person in his life; it leads him astray."

To the extent that knowledge gives power, to that extent do lies affect the distribution of power; they add to that of the liar, and diminish that of the deceived, altering his choices at different levels. A lie, first, may misinform, so as to obscure some *objective,* something the deceived person wanted to do or obtain. It may make the objective seem unattainable or no longer desirable. It may even create a new one, as when Iago deceived Othello into wanting to kill Desdemona.

Lies may also eliminate or obscure relevant *alternatives,* as when a traveler is falsely told a bridge has collapsed. At times, lies foster the belief that there are more alternatives than is really the case; at other times, a lie may lead to the unnecessary loss of confidence in the best alternative. Similarly, the estimates of *costs and benefits* of any action can be endlessly varied through successful deception. The immense toll of life and human welfare from the United States' intervention in Vietnam came at least in part from the deception (mingled with self-deception) by those who channeled overly optimistic information to the decision-makers.

Finally, the degree of *uncertainty* in how we look at our choices can be manipulated through deception. Deception can make a situation falsely uncertain as well as falsely certain. It can affect the objectives seen, the alternatives believed possible, the estimates made of risks and benefits. Such a manipulation of the dimension of certainty is one of the main ways to gain power over the choices of those deceived. And just as deception can initiate actions a person would otherwise never have chosen, so it can prevent action by obscuring the necessity for choice. This is the essence of camouflage and of the cover-up—the creation of apparent normality to avert suspicion.

Everyone depends on deception to get out of a scrape, to save face, to avoid hurting the feelings of others. Some use it much more consciously to manipulate and gain ascendancy. Yet all are intimately aware of the threat lies can pose, the suffering they can bring. This two-sided experience which we all share makes the singleness with which either side is advocated in action all the more puzzling. Why are such radically different evaluations given to the effects of deception, depending on whether the point of view is that of the liar or the one lied to?

The Perspective of the Deceived

Those who learn that they have been lied to in an important matter—say, the identity of their parents, the affection of their spouse, or the integrity of their government—are resentful, disappointed, and suspicious. They feel wronged; they are wary of new overtures. And they look back on their past beliefs and actions in the new light of the discovered lies. They see that they were manipulated, that the deceit made them unable to make choices for themselves according to the most adequate information available, unable to act as they would have wanted to act had they known all along.

It is true, of course, that personal, informed choice is not the only kind available to them. They may *decide* to abandon choosing for themselves and let others decide for them—as guardians, financial advisors, or political representatives. They may even decide to abandon choice based upon information of a conventional nature altogether and trust instead to the stars or to throws of the dice or to soothsayers.

But such alternatives ought to be personally chosen and not surreptitiously imposed by lies or other forms of manipulation. Most of us would resist loss of control over which choices we want to delegate to others and which ones we want to make ourselves, aided by the best information we can obtain. We resist because experience has taught us the consequences when others choose to deceive us, even "for our own good." Of course, we know that many lies are trivial. But since we, when lied to, have no way to judge which lies are the trivial ones, and since we have no confidence that liars will restrict themselves to just such trivial lies, the perspective of the deceived leads us to be wary of *all* deception.

Nor is this perspective restricted to those who are actually deceived in any given situation. Though only a single person may be deceived, many others may be harmed as a result. If a mayor is deceived about the need for new taxes, the entire city will bear the consequences. Accordingly, the perspective of the deceived is shared by all those who feel the consequences of a lie, whether or not they are themselves lied to. When, for instance, the American public and world opinion were falsely led to believe that bombing in Cambodia had not begun, the Cambodians themselves bore the heaviest consequences, though they can hardly be said to have been deceived about the bombing itself.

An interesting parallel between skepticism and determinism exists here. Just as skepticism denies the possibility of *knowledge,* so determinism denies the possibility of *freedom.* Yet both knowledge and freedom to act on it are required for reasonable choice. Such choice would be denied to someone genuinely convinced—to the very core of his being—of both skepticism and determinism. He would be cast about like a dry leaf in the wind. Few go so far. But more may adopt such views selectively, as when they need convenient excuses for lying. Lies, they may then claim, do not add to or subtract from the general misinformation or "unfreedom" of those lied to. Yet were they to adopt the perspective of the deceived, such excuses for lying to them would seem hollow indeed. Both skepticism and determinism have to be bracketed—set aside—if moral choice is to retain the significance for liars that we, as deceived, know it has in our lives.

Deception, then, can be coercive. When it succeeds, it can give power to the deceiver—power that all who suffer the consequences of lies would not wish to abdicate. From this perspective, it is clearly unreasonable to assert that people should be able to lie with impunity whenever they want to do so. It would be unreasonable, as well, to assert such a right even in the more restricted circumstances where the liars claim a good reason for lying. This is especially true because lying so often accompanies every *other* form of wrongdoing, from murder and bribery to tax fraud and theft. In refusing to condone such a right to decide when to lie and when not to, we are therefore trying to protect ourselves against lies which help to execute or cover up all other wrongful acts.

For this reason, the perspective of the deceived supports the statement by Aristotle:

> Falsehood is in itself mean and culpable, and truth noble and full of praise.

There is an initial imbalance in the evaluation of truth-telling and lying. Lying requires a *reason*, while truth-telling does not. It must be excused; reasons must be produced, in any one case, to show why a particular lie is not "mean and culpable."

The Perspective of the Liar

Those who adopt the perspective of would-be liars, on the other hand, have different concerns. For them, the choice is often a difficult one. They may believe, with Machiavelli, that "great things" have been done by those who have "little regard for good faith." They may trust that they can make wise use of the power that lies bring. And they may have confidence in their own ability to distinguish the times when good reasons support their decision to lie.

Liars share with those they deceive the desire not to *be* deceived. As a result, their choice to lie is one which they would like to reserve for themselves while insisting that others be honest. They would prefer, in other words, a "free-rider" status, giving them the benefits of lying without the risks of being lied to. Some think of this free-rider status as for them alone. Others extend it to their friends, social group, or profession. This category of persons can be narrow or broad; but it does require as a necessary backdrop the ordinary assumptions about the honesty of most persons. The free rider trades upon being an exception, and could not exist in a world where everybody chose to exercise the same prerogatives.

At times, liars operate as if they believed that such a free-rider status is theirs and that it excuses them. At other times, on the contrary, it is the very fact that others *do* lie that excuses their deceptive stance in their own eyes. It is crucial to see the distinction between the free-loading liar and the liar whose deception is a strategy for survival in a corrupt society.

All want to avoid being deceived by *others* as much as possible. But many would like to be able to weigh the advantages and disadvantages in a more nuanced way whenever they are themselves in the position of choosing whether or not to deceive. They may invoke special reasons to lie—such as the need to protect confidentiality or to spare someone's feelings. They are then much more willing, in particular, to exonerate a well-intentioned lie on their own part; dupes tend to be less sanguine about the good intentions of those who deceive them.

But in this benevolent self-evaluation by the liar of the lies he might tell, certain kinds of disadvantage and harm are almost always overlooked. Liars usually weigh only the immediate harm to others from the lie against the benefits they want to achieve. The flaw in such an outlook is that it ignores or underestimates two additional kinds of harm—the harm that lying does to the liars themselves and the harm done to the general level of trust and social cooperation. Both are cumulative; both are hard to reverse.

How is the liar affected by his own lies? The very fact that he *knows* he has lied, first of all, affects him. He may regard the lie as an inroad on his integrity; he certainly looks at those he has lied to with a new caution. And if they find out that he has lied, he knows that his credibility and the respect for his word have been damaged. When Adlai Stevenson had to go before the United Nations in 1961 to tell falsehoods about the United States' role in the Bay of Pigs invasion, he changed the course of his life. He may not have known beforehand that the message he was asked to convey was untrue; but merely to carry the burden of being the means of such deceit must have been difficult. To lose the confidence of his peers in such a public way was harder still.

Granted that a public lie on an important matter, once revealed, hurts the speaker, must we therefore conclude that *every* lie has this effect? What of those who tell a few white lies once in a while? Does lying hurt them in the same way? It is hard to defend such a notion. No one trivial lie undermines the liar's integrity. But the problem for liars is that they tend to see *most* of their lies in this benevolent light and thus vastly underestimate the risks they run. While no one lie always carries harm for the liar, then, there is *risk* of such harm in most.

These risks are increased by the fact that so few lies are solitary ones. It is easy, a wit observed, to tell a lie, but hard to tell only one. The first lie "must be thatched with another or it will rain through." More and more lies may come to be needed; the liar always has more mending to do. And the strains on him become greater each time—many have noted that it takes an excellent memory to keep one's un-truths in good repair and disentangled. The sheer energy the liar has to devote to shoring them up is energy the honest man can dispose of freely.

After the first lies, moreover, others can come more easily. Psychological barri-ers wear down; lies seem more necessary, less reprehensible; the ability to make moral distinctions can coarsen; the liar's perception of his chances of being caught may warp. These changes can affect his behavior in subtle ways; even if he is not found out he will then be less trusted than those of unquestioned honesty. And it is inevitable that more frequent lies *do* increase the chance that some will be dis-covered. At that time, even if the liar has no personal sense of loss of integrity from his deceitful practices, he will surely regret the damage to his credibility which their discovery brings about. Paradoxically, once his word is no longer trusted, he will be left with greatly *decreased* power—even though a lie often does bring at least a short-term gain in power over those deceived.

Even if the liar cares little about the risks to others from his deception, therefore, all these risks to himself argue in favor of at least weighing any decision to lie quite seriously. Yet such risks rarely enter his calculations. Bias skews all judgment, but never more so than in the search for good reasons to deceive. Not only does it combine with ignorance and uncertainty so that liars are apt to overestimate their own good will, high motives, and chances to escape detection; it leads also to over-confidence in their own imperviousness to the personal entanglements, worries, and loss of integrity which might so easily beset them.

The liar's self-bestowed free-rider status, then, can be as corrupting as all other unchecked exercises of power. There are, in fact, very few "free rides" to be had through lying. I hope to examine, in this book, those exceptional circumstances where harm to self and others from lying is less likely, and procedures which can isolate and contain them. But the chance of harm to liars can rarely be ruled out altogether.

Bias causes liars often to ignore the second type of harm as well. For even if they make the effort to estimate the consequences to *individuals*—themselves and others—of their lies, they often fail to consider the many ways in which deception can spread and give rise to practices very damaging to human communities. These practices clearly do not affect only isolated individuals. The veneer of social trust is often thin. As lies spread—by imitation, or in retaliation, or to forestall suspected deception—trust is damaged. Yet trust is a social good to be protected just as much as the air we breathe or the water we drink. When it is damaged, the community as a whole suffers; and when it is destroyed, societies falter and collapse.

We live at a time when the harm done to trust can be seen first-hand. Confidence in public officials and in professionals has been seriously eroded. This, in turn, is a most natural response to the uncovering of practices of deceit for high-sounding aims such as "national security" or the "adversary system of justice." It will take time to rebuild confidence in government pronouncements that the CIA did not participate in a Latin American coup, or that new figures show an economic upturn around the corner. The practices engendering such distrust were entered upon, not just by the officials now so familiar to us, but by countless others, high and low, in the government and outside it, each time for a reason that seemed overriding.

Take the example of a government official hoping to see Congress enact a crucial piece of antipoverty legislation. Should he lie to a Congressman he believes unable to understand the importance and urgency of the legislation, yet powerful enough to block its passage? Should he tell him that, unless the proposed bill is enacted, the government will push for a much more extensive measure?

In answering, shift the focus from this case taken in isolation to the vast practices of which it forms a part. What is the effect on colleagues and subordinates who witness the deception so often resulting from such a choice? What is the effect on the members of Congress as they inevitably learn of a proportion of these lies? And what is the effect on the electorate as it learns of these and similar practices? Then shift back to the narrower world of the official troubled about the legislation he believes in, and hoping by a small deception to change a crucial vote.

It is the fear of the harm lies bring that explains statements such as the following from Revelations (22.15), which might otherwise seem strangely out of proportion:

> These others must stay outside [the Heavenly City]: dogs, medicine-men, and fornicators, and murderers, and idolaters, and everyone of false life and false speech.

It is the deep-seated concern of the multitude which speaks here; there could be few contrasts greater than that between this statement and the self-confident, individualistic view by Machiavelli:

Men are so simple and so ready to obey present necessities, that one who deceives will always find those who allow themselves to be deceived.

. . .

QUESTIONS FOR ANALYSIS AND DISCUSSION

1. Philosophers often test a theory by means of counterexample. They construct a scenario in which the moral solution seems intuitively sensible but is rejected by the theory in question. Can you devise a counterexample to test Bok's moral theory about truthfulness? How might Bok respond to your scenario?

2. Do you agree with Bok's position on the social important of truth-telling? Is the only alternative to valuing truth a cavalier attitude that encourages individuals to decide on their own when to be truthful or deceitful?

3. Bok highlights her analysis with several epigraphs. How do they set up Bok's major points? Do you find them fitting? In what ways do the epigraphs fail to capture the insight about truthfulness Bok suggests they have? Select two or three of the epigraphs and discuss their meaning.

26.

DAVID NYBERG

Truth Telling Is Morally Overrated

Contrary to Bok's high regard for truthfulness, philosopher David Nyberg (b. 1943) believes moralists exaggerate the viciousness of lying. Telling lies, deceiving one another, and offering partial truths are integral to the decency of everyday life. Moreover, argues Nyberg, the moral weight in deception lies in worrying not only over whether I should tell a lie but also in whether I want to hear the truth. In realistic images, Nyberg portrays most moral persons as reaching an unstated agreement that there are certain truths,

"Truth Telling Is Morally Overrated," from *The Varnished Truth: Truth Telling and Deceiving in Ordinary Life* (Chicago: University of Chicago Press, 1993), chapter 1. Notes have been omitted.

*particularly about ourselves, that we prefer not to have. This excerpt is from the opening
of his recent book on the value of truthfulness. (See reading 47 in Chapter 6 for more of
Nyberg's thoughts on truth.)*

CRITICAL READING QUESTIONS

1. Does Nyberg think all forms of deception are acceptable?
2. What is meant by practical intelligence?
3. Why is the story about Richard titled "The High IQ Half-Wit"?
4. What distinction is made between deception from the "top down"
   and from the "bottom up"?

Charm is a way of getting the answer yes without asking a clear question.

—Albert Camus

A little inaccuracy sometimes saves tons of explanation.

—H. H. Munro (Saki)

A man who tells the truth should keep his horse saddled.

—Caucasus Proverb

With an ever weakening resistance, I have come to admit that the need for misrepresenting some aspects of truth and reality in my own life is nearly an everyday
occurrence; in times of crisis it can be compelling.

This book is about the moral complexity of truth telling and deception. It attempts to understand the complementary roles of truth telling and deceiving in
ordinary human communication. It records a struggle to see why, when deceiving
is publicly condemned, it is privately practiced by almost everybody. Perhaps the
reason for this seeming hypocrisy is that both the public condemnation of deception and its private practice are indispensable to the smooth running of our social
lives. It is even possible that deception could be an important aspect of moral decency, since most people who are morally decent do in fact practice deception
while earnestly maintaining to others, and sometimes to themselves, that they do
not, or that they always feel guilty when they do. Deception is not easy to talk
about frankly. Many people tend to see it as either odious and therefore an unfit
topic for conversation, or completely obvious as "the lubricant" that keeps society
going and therefore unworthy of discussion. I think our difficulty in talking frankly
about it stems partly from our tacit understanding that to do so would often place
us at a practical disadvantage; after all, in what cases would it be wise to tell the
truth about the role of deception in *your* life?

Some Foolish Questions

Imagine what you would answer if someone posed these questions to you:

Is there anything you have done that you would very much like to forget so there would be no danger of having to tell the truth about it if somebody asked?

After seven years of marriage and two children, Lisa is no longer sexually aroused by her husband, Larry. She blames herself for being frigid and does her best to depreciate the importance of sex in their relationship. On sudden notice, Lisa's job takes her to France for a week; two days before she returns home she has a heart-swelling, soul-stirring, sensational fling with a man she'll never see again. Her sexuality is vivacious once more. She knows confessing to the affair would deeply threaten Larry, whom she loves. How should she handle her eventful insight and renewed sensuality?

If Lisa told you about her affair, would you cover for her?

When you tell your friends and family about your experiences on a trip, do you strive for scrupulous accuracy or do you hope to arouse interest, which may require embellishment and exaggeration and possibly the deletion of facts?

The doctors have said they are certain you have but six months to live. One effect of this news is that you become completely unconcerned about what others think of you. Would you say or do anything differently—that is, more spontaneously or honestly?

Your two closest friends offer to tell you, with unchecked candor and without regard for your feelings, everything they think about you. Would you want them to do it?

These two friends ask you to do the same for them. Would you?

What else besides honesty do you value most in friendship?

Have you ever disliked and disrespected someone you worked for, and told them so—while you still needed the job?

Have you ever taken sick days from work when you were well enough to go in?

The insolent checkout clerk at the supermarket in the mall mistakenly gives you $10 extra change. Would you keep it? Would anything change if the clerk had been helpful and polite? If you had known the clerk personally?

The same thing happens two days later at the mom and pop corner store where you go several times a week. Would you make a fuss over giving the $10 back to signal and underscore your honesty?

How much taxable income would you feel justified in omitting from your tax return? Less than $100? $500? $1,000 or more?

Have you ever said that you never lie? Was that a lie?

For most people at least some of these questions have no obvious and unequivocal answers. We live in a labyrinthine world of puzzling objects, enigmatical events, and partially unintelligible (sometimes even mystical) relationships that we cannot hope ever to comprehend entirely. Things happen; we witness some aspects of an event from a particular vantage point; we interpret what we have taken in with our senses; we discover or compose an acceptable meaning from that subjectively limited rendering of "fact"; we express an edited, personalized version of the result, to a selected audience, at a chosen time, if we want to. There is a vast psychological distance between the "things that happen" and what we are later able to say about them, no matter how sincerely we try to be objective and to get it right. Lifelong uncertainty about the "truth" is an attribute of human sensibility; it is a product of the interplay of memory and imagination, history and choice.

I am interested here in the moral value of truth, such as we think we can know it. Some of the questions that need to be addressed are: What exactly are we required to *do* with the truth once we know it, have it, feel it, or whatever? Is there a moral command that implies a duty to dish it out without garnish to everyone who passes by? Or does the obligation not arise until we are asked to tell the truth? Does it matter who asks? Does it matter what exactly is asked in the way of truth telling? Does it matter how we feel about the situation? Must we will ourselves always to make our words and actions conform to our thoughts and feelings, regardless of all other considerations? If we wish to act morally, have we no choice but to be ardently consistent truth tellers?

We tend to assume that truthfulness and morality go together in a clear and simple way. What happens to this assumption when we ask a few more probing questions such as: Is truthfulness a moral value of a special kind? If so, what kind, and how does it fit in with other moral values such as compassion, charity, discretion, friendship? Does truth telling really have intrinsic moral value, or is it better understood as an instrumental value—should we serve it, or should it serve us? How does the answer to that question affect the injunction always to tell the truth? Do we have a right to the truth from others? If we did have such a right, would we actually use it all the time? Do we really have any idea what a world of truth tellers would be like? Is such a world what we want?

In an ordinary community of morally decent people there is a need for trust and community standards for truth telling, but an ordinary community, unlike the ideal scientific community, must continually face the ambiguous problem of when to tell how much of what truth to whom. Telling the whole truth about everything to everybody all the time is an impossibility, but even if it were possible, it probably wouldn't be desirable. The question is: of all the things we *could* say, what *should* we say?

Deception is a touchy subject. Before serious misunderstandings begin to form, it would be a good idea to state clearly that I repudiate all harmfully exploitative deceptions such as consumer fraud, insider trading, the misuse of public office and public trust for personal self-interest, kids hiding their dope and alcohol and pregnancies from their parents, husbands and wives cheating on each other, large-scale tax evasion, used car dealers painting over rust and turning back odometers, the false and vicious reasoning of racism and sexism, televangelists preying on vulnerable, semiliterate audiences, cigarette advertising, and so on. The list of reprehensible exploitations is enormous and grows longer daily. I do despise and reject all this corruption. However, it is a mistake to despise and reject all the other forms of deception, too, just because we have had experience with these contemptible ones. It would be the same kind of mistake as rejecting all politics just because we have been burned by some corrupt politicians; or disapproving of all scientific research involving humans and animals because some of it is carried out inhumanely on noncrucial questions; or discounting the value of all religious leaders just because some of them are fools and fanatical egomaniacs. We need to sort out what is and what is not morally justifiable deception, just as we must sort out moral from immoral behavior in politics, science, and religion.

. . .

As children we are taught to revere the principle of truth telling before we have achieved a clear understanding of what truth is. For a child, how is the truth different from a captivating story that takes us off into other vivid realities? From saying things that make people feel good? From whatever saves us when we are in danger? Truth, fantasy, goodness, happiness, excitement are not automatically separated in the thoughts of young children. They have to be taught to isolate truth and truth telling for special treatment. As our experiences widen, however, we also learn through wonderfully indirect and subtle means that truth telling, like every other moral principle, has its drawbacks in practice, and sometimes we have to pass over it in our calculations for getting on as decent and successful human beings.

Deception is found in every culture (only attitudes toward it differ), probably because it provides advantage in carrying out one's intentions, and because it offers a chance to escape confrontations without having to fight. We humans are active, creative mammals who can represent what exists as if it did not, and what doesn't exist as if it did. And we do this easily and routinely. Concealment, obliqueness, silence, outright lying—all help to hold Nemesis at bay; all help us abide too large helpings of reality. T. S. Eliot was right when he reminded us that "Humankind/ Cannot bear very much reality." In civilization no less than in the wilderness, survival at the water hole does not favor the fully exposed and unguarded self. Deception, it seems, is a vital part of practical intelligence.

Practical Intelligence

Much of human interaction is taken up with the giving and getting of impressions, which are composed of some plain truth and some fancy, some display and some concealment, something said and something suggesting, something focused and something blurred. All this for the purpose of getting done what you want to do.

The Cagey Veterinarian

Dr. Gregory, a very thoughtful veterinarian who at first bridled at the suggestion that deception was a part of his practical intelligence, later gave me this example as a sort of humorous confession.

Veterinary Deception: Always rub the pet's skin with alcohol before giving the injection. The owner has been taught for decades that this is proper procedure. Reality of Veterinary Deception: Rubbing the skin with alcohol before giving an injection does no good at all. It's pure show (it takes about five minutes for alcohol to kill a significant amount of bacteria on the skin, and that is too long to wait with an anxious animal on the table and many more in the waiting room). For me the habit is so deep that I really feel strange when I fail to do it, regardless of the farce of doing it. It took me about fifteen years to realize that the only thing it does is cause me more pain when I prick myself rather than the dog (usually because of a sudden movement of the pet). Then I figured the alcohol probably increased the dog's pain as much as it did mine.

At first I handled the situation by injecting near but not actually at the spot I placed the alcohol, but I knew someday some sharp client who asks questions would pick up on the sham. Now I use the antiseptic chlorhexadine, which does no more real good than alcohol but does not cause the stinging.

In this case, Dr. Gregory's willingness to deceive serves as a welcome reassurance for the owner. He has combined his scientific knowledge with practical intelligence. His clients keep coming back (for excellent care); business is good; no harm done. The situation is much the same for physicians.

Acting Like a Doctor

Dr. Stephen Hoffman has written about his need for a modern medical equivalent of chanting and playing drums in coping with many patients' wish to believe and to be healed. His experiences with patients in a hospital emergency ward have helped him realize that an important part of being a doctor is being a dramatist. On his way to meet a patient, he prepares himself:

> I must lead off with the right persona. Each type of patient—the adolescent with a drug overdose, the middle-aged man with chest pain or the depressed elderly woman—calls for a certain demeanor. A doctor tries to assume it from the outset, adjusting it as he goes on, as he would the fit of his white coat.

Confronting a twenty-seven-year-old woman who has been on the Pill for five days and is worried about a stroke because she has developed a "weak foot," he adopts a calming manner, performs an examination, and delivers the good news that her strength and sensation are normal, and that it takes much longer for the risk of stroke to be affected by the Pill.

> "It's not in my head, if that's what you mean," she snaps.
>
> When I try to persuade her that nothing seems amiss, she balks. "Well, something is definitely wrong!"
>
> I stall for a second, realizing that I've failed. I haven't responded to the need that brought her to the hospital late on a Sunday night. Even though I've done what was medically called for, I never like it when a patient leaves feeling angry or dissatisfied; I tend to take such reactions personally. What's more, the threat of malpractice is seldom far from my mind. While I believe I've exercised proper judgment, I know that in the charged atmosphere of the courtroom, good judgment alone doesn't always suffice. It's time, then, to improvise. Like Prospero in *The Tempest,* only through "some vanity of mine art" can I make "my project gather to a head."

Dr. Hoffmann goes on to do what he has learned many people expect of doctors: he performs the artful ritual of the medicine man, calculated to make the patient feel better. He resorts to theater:

> I stage a dazzlingly detailed neurologic exam. There are props: a reflex hammer and an ophthalmoscope, each of which I move about in carefully choreographed patterns. There are dramatic asides—thoughtful "hmmm's"—and flourishes, too, like the motions I put my patient through to test for rare, abnormal reflexes. I even bring in special effects, such as a black and white striped tape which I move back and forth hypnotically before the woman's eyes, testing for subtle changes in her vision. Throughout it all, I'm careful to concentrate on my delivery, timing my words, smiles and gestures for best effect. My last act is to order an X-ray of the neck to make absolutely sure that impingement of a nerve root isn't the cause of her problems.

The doctor's final act is to talk with his patient once again. He states that the thorough workup has revealed nothing wrong but acknowledges the fact that her symptoms are surely bothering her and encourages her to come back for more tests if they persist. She is pleased and grateful. "For sheer healing power," he writes, "nothing can match the theater."

This kind of dissembling is common among doctors, but motives vary. When is it done for the sake of the patient, and when for the doctor's own self-interest, whether for the further cultivation of his image as God's chosen helper or for the prudent reason of protecting himself against potential litigation? Doctors do slant the truth sometimes to avoid making patients feel angry or unimportant. That's what medical jargon is for: you come in feeling a pain in your back and leave with knowledge that your problem is lumbosacral sprain. The pain is still there but you feel better about it because it has been professionally recognized and identified.

Dr. Hoffman acknowledges that his kind of theater is expensive, and that health care costs rise because of it. Patients pay the bills for all the props and flourishes. Is the cost worth the show?

> What should I have done, then? Stop short of any drama and allow her to leave unhappy? Dispense the unembellished truth and let her walk away with serious questions about her health—and my competence? Before I can give the matter more thought, though, the charge nurse tells me that I have another patient. I clear my voice and straighten my white coat. Curtain time is never far away.

The High IQ Half-Wit

Now let's consider someone unwilling to deceive, and the price of his "sincerity."

Richard had just been accepted as a doctoral candidate in a psychology department which is generally acknowledged to have one of the best programs in the country. His undergraduate grades were nearly perfect, his GRE scores were in the highest percentile, he had an IQ score (whatever that means) of 160, and his application file contained recommendations chock-full of praise for his academic achievements along with predictions of great future success. The faculty members of the department were unanimous in ranking him their number one candidate.

As expected, Richard performed brilliantly in his course work and research. He was successful in attaining a large grant to support his dissertation, which won an award for being the best in its field that year. In light of his sparkling record as a superior student with superior intelligence it is no wonder that he came to think very highly of himself. But Richard's self-esteem grew along with his achievements to such an extent that he became unselfconsciously arrogant, intolerant of others whose minds were not as quick and nimble as his own, and a boastfully self-promoting advocate of his theory of intelligence, which he argued was original and perhaps even revolutionary. He was so consumed with himself, with laying the foundations for the distinguished career he envisioned, that he earned a reputation as an arrogant SOB. When his advisor and other concerned faculty confronted him with this fact, Richard showed no inclination to alter his behavior. He believed some people had a right to be arrogant; his record and his obvious intelligence justified his attitude, he thought, and he was not about to be pressured into playing games of pretending differently.

Surprise, surprise. All of Richard's classmates were offered good positions upon their graduation, but he was turned down after every interview. He was first in the class, but he did not receive a single job offer. Why? He was too dumb to hide the fact in his interviews that he was an arrogant SOB, and nobody wanted to have him as a colleague, no matter how high his test scores, no matter how distinguished his dissertation. He failed to see the value in pretending to be less arrogant than he sincerely felt he had a right to be. He also failed to realize that his future professional success depended in some degree upon meeting the social requirements of the place where he did his work as well as upon that work itself. While he had achieved a high score on an abstract IQ test, he had a relatively undeveloped practical intelligence to go with it. His classmates' practical, or contextual, intelligence included the knowledge that sometimes *seeming* can be more important than stubborn, no-nonsense veraciousness. They clearly fared better than Richard. They knew something he didn't—they knew how to act appropriately in an interview context. No doubt they had accepted the wisdom of such advice as was recently offered to college graduates:

> *During the Interview:*
> Don't act as if you're squeezing the recruiter into your busy schedule. Even if you're the kind of student who is in demand, you'll increase the number of offers you receive if you appear enthusiastic. Come across as a soon-to-be-professional. Dress comfortably but appropriately, and in most cases, conservatively. Practice your handshake so that your grip is firm and friendly. Be yourself. Experienced recruiters can spot students who say things they think the interviewer wants to hear.

. . .

Interviewing is for impressing the interviewer (who has already read all about you), if you want the job. Sometimes that means seeming to be more or less of something than you really feel. Refusing to acknowledge this, and sticking instead to the ideal of If-I-feel-it-then-I'll-say-it-because-it's-true, may have the virtue of being purely sincere, but it is not always the practically intelligent course to take. It is a great distortion to believe you are speaking the truth simply because you say what you think. It is possible to be sincere and wrong. It is also possible to be sincere, right, and dumb. Could it be that to employ this form of deception discreetly is an important part of what it means to be contextually, or practically, intelligent?

Maybe this question ought to be incorporated into Richard's theory, and into his thinking about his next job interview. It is even likely that consideration of the question will lead Richard to a more realistic view of his own strengths and limitations, a view that will have the effect of further enabling him by broadening his intelligence, and at the same time teaching him the cost of arrogant veracity.

Deception from the Bottom Up and Top Down

Dr. Gregory and Dr. Hoffmann learned that pretending was part of their jobs as healers, a lesson Richard had not yet come to grips with as an academic psychologist. It is not always clear what motivates a desire to pretend—it is sometimes self-interest and sometimes the interests of others. Nor is it always clear whether pretending will benefit or damage a particular relationship. Dr. Hoffmann's next patient may react in an altogether less appreciative way to his performance. Perhaps Richard's ineptitude at pretending worked out for the best—if not from his own, then at least from his would-be colleagues' point of view.

A basic philosophical question is raised here that bears on the course this book will take: should we evaluate the inclination to deceive in each instance and determine its moral status in the particular circumstances given? This is the view from the bottom up. Or should we think about it more abstractly, as an exception that always needs justifying against a background of truth telling, and determine its moral status in principle, once and for all? This is to look at deception from the top down, in the way such philosophers as Sissela Bok look at lying.

Since I disagree with some important aspects of Bok's approach and with some of her most important general conclusions, it would be useful (at least to those readers who have not read Bok), and fair to her, if I outline here what I take her to be saying, so our differences can be clearly seen. Before doing that, however, I want to state that I am not interested in lining up all my authoritative ducks in a row to do battle with hers, nor am I interested in building a comprehensive, systematic refutation of her work. Rather, I want to use her book to illustrate the top-down approach, which is representative of some widely held beliefs about truth telling, and then, in the following chapters, I want to display as best I can the bottom-up approach, to raise doubts and questions, to encourage people to reconsider, to think again about what they take for granted on the subject of deception.

What is Bok's book about? She appears to be chiefly motivated in her writings by two concerns. The first is for what she sees as the casual attitude so many professionals take to the practice of deception in their work (business, government, law, medicine, etc.), compared with her own troubling experience in facing hard choices about truth telling. Her second concern is about the "striking recent decline in public confidence not only in the American government, but in lawyers, bankers, businessmen, and doctors." Bok suspects there is a causal relationship between the casual attitude of professionals toward deception and the decline in public confidence, although we don't really know whether this perceived "decline" in public confidence is actually the result of improved methods in the polling of public opinion, or of better investigative reporting that brings more information to the public eye about what has long been going on behind the scenes, or—as Bok implies—whether it reflects a palpable increase in the practice of deception. Whatever the correct explanation may be, her concerns are sincere and serve as strong motivation to become more clear about matters of truth telling.

On the assumption that this casual attitude about truth telling is both morally wrong and destructive of public confidence, Bok formulates the central question she hopes to answer: "Is there, then, a theory of moral choice which can help in quandaries of truthtelling and lying?" The way she states her question gives us a clue as to what she assumes at the outset, and determines at least partially the route she will take in answering it. First of all, she wants to develop a *theory,* which is a statement of the general laws or principles of something; in this case that something is the rational activity of deciding whether to lie. She intends to propose a theory that can tell us when a decision to lie is morally justified or at least excusable, a theory that will, if put into general practice, help to reverse the decline in public trust, thereby improving the moral character of society. Her approach is deliberately abstract in its focus on theory, principles, and rational decision making, although the tone of her arguments is often quite personal. Unlike most philosophers who take this top-down approach to the study of lying, she does not trouble herself for long with questions about the nature of truth, or of truth telling, which can easily end up frustrating the entire enterprise. Nor does she confront the immense complexity of deception broadly conceived. Instead, she chooses to look primarily at clear-cut lies. She defines a lie as "any intentionally deceptive message which is *stated.*" This definition is meant to separate lying from the larger category of deception which includes, but is not limited to, such statements.

Her search for a theory of choice is initiated on a strong presumption against any lie's being excusable or justifiable, but with an awareness that "sometimes there *may* be sufficient reason to lie." She presumes further that "lying requires a reason, while truth telling does not." By this she means that every lie is a suspect deviation from an orthodox norm of truth telling and as such, each decision to lie requires a rational exoneration. So the value of her theory will be to provide the principles that can be used to judge the reasons given to defend any decision to lie.

Her conception of the problem emphasizes the long-term general effects of the "practice" of lying on whole societies. In her view, the major reason why lies are morally wrong is not simply that they cause "immediate harm to others." It is rather that they harm the liars themselves and harm the "general level of trust and social cooperation. Both [harms] are cumulative; both are hard to reverse." This image of generalized harm is central to Bok's position and deserves a fuller description:

> . . . even if [liars] make the effort to estimate the consequences to *individuals*—
> themselves and others—of their lies, they often fail to consider the many ways in which
> deception can spread and give rise to practices very damaging to human communities.

These practices clearly do not affect only isolated individuals. The veneer of social trust is often thin. As lies spread—by imitation, or in retaliation, or to forestall suspected deception—trust is damaged. Yet trust is a social good to be protected just as much as the air we breathe or the water we drink. When it is damaged, the community as a whole suffers; and when it is destroyed, societies falter and collapse.

This vision of how lies may lead to social collapse is a slightly modified version of Kant's absolutist position on why truthfulness should be considered an unconditional duty:

Truthfulness in statements which cannot be avoided is the formal duty of an individual to everyone, however great may be the disadvantage accruing to himself or to another. Thus the definition of a lie as merely an intentional untruthful declaration to another person does not require the additional condition that it must harm another. . . . For a lie always harms another; if not some other particular man, still it harms mankind generally, for it vitiates the source of law itself.

Hesitantly, Bok rejects the absolutist prohibition of all lies, even though she maintains allegiance to the justification for it:

In the absence of some vast terror associated with lying, which goes far beyond the presumption against lying stated [earlier], I have to agree that there are at least *some* circumstances which warrant a lie. And foremost among them are those where innocent lives are at stake, and where only a lie can deflect the danger.

But, in taking such a position, it would be wrong to lose the profound concern which the absolutist theologians and philosophers express—the concern for the harm to trust and to oneself from lying, quite apart from any immediate effects from any one lie.

On the subject of warranted lies, Bok's language remains extremely reluctant: "Only where a lie is a *last resort* can one even begin to consider whether or not it is morally justified."

Bok explains that the reasons one may offer as an excuse for having told a lie usually appeal to one or more of these four principles: "that of avoiding harm, that of producing benefits, that of fairness, and that of veracity." Her analysis of these principles leads her to say that "inevitably, most of these excuses will fail to persuade." Furthermore, no reason offered as an excuse need even be evaluated "if the liar knew of a truthful alternative to secure the benefit, avoid the harm, or protect fairness. Even if a lie saves a life, it is unwarranted if the liar was aware that a truthful statement could have done the same." But then she softens this a little by saying that "because the reasons themselves are present to larger and smaller degrees, one cannot always say that a lie seems or does not seem excusable."

Accepting reasons as *excuse* is essentially forgiving a wrong; forgiving does not mean that the wrong was not wrong, only that it is forgivable. Accepting reasons as *justification* is another matter. To justify a lie is very different than to excuse one. It is here, on the question of justifying lies, that Bok makes her most significant contribution to the theory she has set out to develop. First, she sets down the conditions of justification:

> To justify is to defend as just, right, or proper, by providing adequate reasons. It means to hold up to some standard, such as a religious or legal or moral standard. Such justification requires an audience: it may be directed to God, or a court of law, or one's peers, or one's own conscience; but in ethics it is most appropriately aimed, not at all one individual or audience, but rather at "reasonable persons" in general.

In this statement we can see again the abstract character of her top-down approach. In Bok's view, justification is a matter of scrutinizing concrete instances of individual behavior in the light of religious, legal, or moral standards (principles) before an audience of fictional characters (reasonable persons in general, or the idealized "moral agent") who are taken implicitly to represent more principles (about right and wrong, rational and irrational, etc.). While acknowledging a difficulty in assuring the "reasonableness" of any available public, she adheres to the approach nonetheless.

After a detailed discussion of publicity—the willingness to make a public statement and defense—which Bok believes is a crucial constraint in justifying any moral choice, she thus summarizes her findings on the theory of choice with regard to lying:

> Such, then, are the general principles which I believe govern the justification of lies. As we consider different kinds of lies, we must ask, first, whether there are alternative forms of action which will resolve the difficulty without the use of a lie [lying can be an option only as a last resort when no truth telling alternative is possible]; second, what might be the moral reasons brought forward to excuse the lie [the best are self-defense and life-saving, or extreme triviality], and what reasons can be raised as counter-arguments [for example, no one should be subject to deception without informed, voluntary consent]. Third, as a test of these two steps, we must ask what a public of reasonable persons might say about such lies. Most lies will clearly fail to satisfy these questions of justification.

The publicity test is the key: what should other (reasonable) people say about the decision to lie, or the particular lie itself (Bok is not entirely clear on which she means). In the remainder of her book, Bok takes up some kinds of lies that might conceivably pass the three-part test. Lying to enemies, for example, may be justified, but only when: there is *no* truth telling alternative; there is a *crisis;* and there are openly (lawfully) declared hostilities. The overall conclusion yielded by Bok's discussion of many challenging examples (placebos, letters of recommendation, private lives of public figures, the timing of crucial economic policy changes, perjury, and many more) is neatly summarized in her own words:

> Some lies—notably minor white lies and emergency lies rapidly acknowledged—may be more *excusable* than others, but only those deceptive practices which can be openly debated and consented to in advance are *justifiable* in a democracy.

Bok warns that both the spread and abuse of lies can be expected if we don't have, and use,

> clear-cut standards as to what is acceptable. In the absence of such standards, instances of deception can and will increase, bringing distrust and thus more deception, loss of

personal standards on the part of liars and so yet more deception, imitation by those who witness deception and the rewards it can bring, and once again more deception.

She then invokes the authority of Augustine to make her point even more dramatically: "... little by little and bit by bit this will grow and by gradual accessions will slowly increase until it becomes such a mass of wicked lies that it will be utterly impossible to find any means of resisting such a plague grown to huge proportions through small additions."

Both in her own words and in her citation of Augustine, Bok relies on what logicians and lawyers call the slippery slope argument to set up what I call the domino theory of lying. The slippery slope argument goes like this: If I'm allowed to lie once about this subject, then I will lie about it again, and then I'll lie about other things as well. Furthermore, if I'm allowed to lie, then you'll want to lie, and soon you will lie about everything, and then everybody will want to lie about everything, too. This progression will damage and eventually destroy public trust. The way to prevent this from happening is to adopt a policy that makes lying so difficult to get away with that no one will even want to try. This is the concept of deterrence. (The same concept is used to justify capital punishment for some crimes. However, there is no evidence to support the hopeful assumption that such a policy works to deter the crimes in question.)

My view, on the other hand, is that trust in others is a cooperative, life-preserving relationship that often depends upon the adroit management of deception, sometimes even lying, for its very subsistence.

We can always get a philosopher to translate personal troubles into ethics, but there is often a cost for this service. Paradoxical as it sounds at first, we may achieve simplicity at the cost of clarity. If I want to know whether I should deceive *you,* about *this, now,* the philosopher is likely to rephrase my question into something like: "When should one tell the truth, or something less?" Replacing the particularity of "I" with the generality of "one" tends to simplify the problem right from the start by abstracting from the details of personal involvement. That could be a mistake, and I think it often is a mistake in the top-down perspective on moral questions, because by achieving distance (abstraction, generality) on the subject, we lose the ability to perceive its telling details. I am interested in particular cases and the boundaries of contrast in discrete relationships more than I am interested in abstractions and universal principles. The impersonal generality of top-down moral theory comes from the expectation, or the wish, that the truth about morality will turn out to be simple. That wish for simplicity entices the philosopher to search for the fewest possible principles to cover the greatest number of cases. In contrast, the personal particularity characteristic of bottom-up moral theory reflects an appreciation for the details required for achieving clarity.

Like other domino theorists Bok is stricken by the question, "What if everybody deceived everybody else!?" The answer is, of course: everybody already does. We all value the truth and yet we are *all* ordinary human deceivers; we neither want to know all the truth nor tell it all. Deception is not so much a plague as it is part of the atmosphere that sustains life. The dreaded domino was toppled thousands of years ago ("I said in my haste, All men are liars"—Psalm 116:11), and deception has been part of the status quo ever since. Social life without deception to keep it going is a fantasy. Bok's top-down view does not allow her to see this, or to agree with it, because the oversimple principle of truth telling is in the way. We'll look more closely at these two perspectives on moral judgment [later]. For now, it can be said that both views agree on at least one part of the problem, namely, that people should not deceive simply whenever they feel like it.

Truth Telling Is Morally Overrated

As I said, this book is about the moral complexity of deception. The central problem is this: even though we have come to know that life without deception is not possible, we have not diligently trained ourselves to deceive thoughtfully and judiciously, charitably, humanely, and with discretion. As George Steiner has argued, "the human capacity to utter falsehood, to lie, to negate what is the case, stands at the heart of speech . . . and culture." A sympathetic account of deception is absolutely necessary to an adequate reckoning of human conduct, and therefore to an understanding of useful moral principles and moral education.

The truth telling injunction is deceptively simple. It sounds not merely possible but positively easy: Give plain and frank expression to what is in your mind; don't misrepresent your thoughts or feelings. But should we really refrain from lying to a violent criminal simply because there may be a truthful alternative? Should we answer a child's every question about sex, divorce, death, and disease regardless of any probably disturbing, even destructive consequences of doing so? Should we give frank expression to every strong feeling of contempt, envy, lust, and self-pity? Should we tell our friends the truth when we believe it will shatter their self-confidence? The list of possible "exceptions" is endless, and many of them are justifiable even if they fail to pass Bok's three-principle test.

What in the world is so awfully good about telling the truth all the time? Why should we feel obligated to excuse or justify every exception? Haven't we got the value of truth telling just a little out of focus? Can it be that truth telling is morally overrated?

. . .

Deception is very much with us, but that should be no cause for despair. On the contrary, there are many reasons why we ought to be thankful for the inventive craft, and for all those agreeable and useful things it enables us to do.

> And, after all, what is a lie? 'Tis but
>   The truth in masquerade; and I defy
> Historians, heroes, lawyers, priests, to put
>   A fact without some leaven of a lie.
> The very shadow of true Truth would shut
>   Up annals, revelations, poesy,
> And prophecy—except it should be dated
> Some years before the incidents related.

QUESTIONS FOR ANALYSIS AND DISCUSSION

1. Nyberg readily admits that sometimes lying is wrong. Does Nyberg make an adequate case for the distinction between acceptable and unacceptable deception or lying?

2. In childhood we learn various ways to justify getting around the truth. The principle about never telling a lie, then, is an exaggerated and often harmful guide to conduct, says Nyberg. How, then, does Nyberg explain a child's disappointment when being lied to?

3. Three epigraphs introduce this selection. Choose one and discuss how it illustrates Nyberg's position.

4. Although Nyberg respects the thoughtfulness of Bok's arguments, he believes that her argument lacks a commonsense account of practical life. In everyday life we not only find it convenient to hedge the truth but are often expected to deceive or lie. Can you defend Bok from Nyberg's criticisms? Is there a third position on truthfulness that would avoid the idealism of Bok and the practicality of Nyberg? Develop your response to their debate.

5. Occasionally a television show, fairy tale, movie, or play will dramatize the attempt to go a certain period of time without telling a lie. The character playing this part tries to be as candid as possible. The result is, by turns, comical or tragic, suggesting that truthfulness is not an absolute good. Do such presentations support Nyberg or Bok, or a third position? Offer your own examples to illustrate your view.

27.

MARY MOTHERSILL

Some Questions about Truthfulness and Lying

Do current events shed new light on moral attitudes of truthfulness? Philosophy professor emeritus at Barnard College and senior scholar at Columbia University Mary Mothersill (b. 1923) assumes that truthfulness is an important value but observes that many public figures offer a poor moral education for citizens with their flagrant use of deception. There

"Some Questions about Truthfulness and Lying," *Social Research*, Fall 1996, 63(3): 913–929. Notes have been omitted.

may be times when a responsible leader has to engage in an act of deception. Yet, according to Mothersill, many individuals take advantage of the notion of "common good" to deceive for ultimately self-serving interests. She reflects on the meaning of these recent lessons and asks the reader to consider whether truthfulness exists as an independent virtue or whether it makes sense only when embraced by a person who practices the other virtues.

CRITICAL READING QUESTIONS

1. Why does Mothersill distinguish between pretending to believe and genuinely believing in truthfulness as a virtue?
2. How does the Pentagon's strategy of lying or the recent novel *Primary Colors* (written by an anonymous author since revealed to be former *Newsweek* writer Joe Klein) illustrate Mothersill's concerns about public truthfulness?
3. Do consequentialists and Kantians agree or disagree on the morality of lying?

Is truthfulness a moral virtue? Does it belong up there on the marquee with wisdom, courage, and temperance? Most of us would say that it does, or that was my first thought anyway. I want to be open with my friends and expect the same from them; I want children who speak their minds without subterfuge; I want to vote for candidates who are honest and honorable. Tradition sanctions this view. Moral codes, sacred as well as secular, prohibit lying. In legal proceedings, those who testify bind themselves to tell the truth. How can there be a question? But there is something puzzling: while we say that truthfulness is good and lying is bad, the way we act suggests that that is not what we really believe. We think of utterly truthful persons as a hazard, and as for lying, we all lie all the time. That there is a gulf between what we think we ought to do and what we do in fact is hardly a novel observation; the world is a wicked place. Still there is an oddity here: a person shows that she is committed to a moral rule—"Tell the truth. Do not lie"—in a variety of different ways. She follows the rule herself and encourages others to do so. She blames and perhaps tries to punish those who violate the rule. If she herself suffers a lapse, she feels guilt and remorse and sometimes a need to confess and make restitution. One can see the pattern in other elementary rules—"Keep your promises." "Help those who are in distress." "Do no harm."—but truth-telling is different. Some lies are egregious; we wince when we recollect them. But by and large we lie our ways through life with a relatively clear conscience; and we expect other people to lie, and so we make our plans accordingly. It's not just that we do not act in accord with our principles, but that we do not *feel* the way someone who really believed that lying is wrong would feel. If this is a fact, what explains it? It seems to me that there are two possibilities: it may be that in saying that truthfulness is a virtue we are not ourselves being truthful. Saying something is a virtue when you do not believe that it is [is] not exactly a lie—when I get around to a definition, I will show why not—but it is disingenuous and counter-truthful. Hypocrisy, according to La Rochefoucauld, is "the homage that vice pays to virtue," and I believe that there is quite a bit of hypocrisy going around. But this complicates matters, since if I go to the trouble of *pretending* to value truthfulness, must it not be because I think that the genuine article really does have value? But perhaps—the second possibility—it is less hypocrisy than confusion about what belief in truthfulness really commits us to, in which case some progress may be possible.

Notice that, "Do not lie," like "Do no harm," is a command that has substance. It is not definitional and empty like, "Justice means giving every man his due," or "You ought not to do what is morally wrong." There may be hard, borderline situations, but there are plenty of clear cases. We know what it means to obey and to disobey the commandment, "Do not lie." How is it that we can be relaxed and tolerant about some lies (and not just our own) and yet greatly exercised by the iniquity of others? Is it being found out that matters? When columnist William Safire said in print that Hillary Clinton was a "congenital liar" readers who were by no means Clinton fans were genuinely shocked. "You lie!" is a strong insult.

Our conflicted views about truth-telling emerge in the mixed messages we send our children. A necessary step in learning a first language is grasping the difference between a true sentence and a false one. A child who gets it right, who can identity and classify an individual, object, or person in his immediate environment, is applauded; if he gets it wrong, he is corrected. It is no great leap for him, then, to the thought that there are sentences which one would like to be true but which are false. He who utters such a sentence with the intention of inducing his hearer to believe it tells his first lie. If it is detected, retribution is swift and apt to be severe. Childish mistakes are innocent; childish lies are not. The one is *getting* something wrong, the other doing something wrong. I have known parents, otherwise mild-mannered and reasonable folk, who are enraged by the discovery of a lie on the part of their offspring.

The first lesson children learn is categorical: "Do not lie." That the obligation to truthfulness is unconditional is something that most adults, including most philosophers, do not believe. But there are two notable exceptions: Augustine holds that all lies are forbidden because every lie in whatever circumstances is hateful to God. Kant's view is that truthfulness is always and everywhere a duty, and that every lie violates the fundamental principle of morality and negates the self-respect and dignity of the liar as well as of his victim. Preschool children are not theologians or philosophers, but they are Kantians in spirit; they understand absolute prohibitions and often become skilled at detecting and denouncing the lies of others. This becomes a source of social embarrassment, and the child, having learned not to lie, has to learn that lying is a part of life and a requisite of good manners. Kant would say that if you do not like your relatives or the sandwich you are offered for lunch, keep quiet about it, but some parents demand more: aversion must be concealed, interest and affection simulated. This is a first lesson in hypocrisy.

What about lying in public life? Nobody claims to be in favor of it, but it is hard to predict what cases will evoke righteous indignation and which will be dismissed with a shrug. It seems not to depend on how consequential the issue is. Ordinary people do not appear to be greatly incensed by allegations raised in the Whitewater inquiry. No doubt, they think, there was corruption, shady deals, and cover-ups, but only what is normal in small town, old boy politics and, besides, it happened a long time ago. But then ordinary people were not greatly concerned by the uncovering of high-level lies in the Savings and Loans scandals—where huge amounts of taxpayers' money were squandered. Candidates for public office in this election year carry on as if their first priority is to establish their moral credentials a[s] truth-tellers. Not just Clinton and Dole but ambitious outsiders—Ross Perot, Pat Buchanan—are equally earnest. Everyone has an Honest Abe outfit. How much is pretense? If the candidates were really on the level, would they allow, even encourage their campaign managers, public relations staffs, and other "handlers" to talk so casually about putting a "spin" on stories or about "perception management"? Candidates use their self-ascribed truthfulness as a launching pad for accusing their rivals of mendacity. Interesting paradoxes arise. Two candidates, A and B. A says, "I am a truthful person so you can take my word for it: B is a liar." B says, "I am a truthful person so you can take my word for it: A is a liar." Two possibilities. Both A and B are truthful persons but both are, as it happens, mistaken about the facts. Alternatively, neither is truthful but both are, as it happens, right about the facts. My impression is that given the choice, most voters would favor the second interpretation. I also think that they would prefer either A or B to a third candidate C, who professed himself to be a truthful person and assured us that both A and B were also truthful persons. If so, how so? Is it that we believe that no politician is truthful so that anyone who claims to be is lying? Or do we believe that any politician, truthful or not, who believes that his rivals are truthful is bound to be incompetent in virtue of his stupidity? Do we believe that no one can achieve anything of significance in public life without lying, that anyone worthy of office will have dirty hands? If so, is such a belief cynical, or is it rather an honest acknowledgment of the demands of *Realpolitik?* Difficult questions, and here is another puzzle: if we believe that the practice of lying is a necessary evil, something that must be countenanced if we want to elect those who will govern well and if we want our children to prosper in society, then why think of lying as an evil at all? Why not be candid about what, as it appears, we really believe: in some circumstances lying does harm and is wrong; in some circumstances it does good and is okay; and often it is totally inconsequential and it does not matter whether we lie or not?

As a reminder of the apparently arbitrary way in which blame is allocated, consider and try to explain the difference in public response to two recent cases where lies were exposed. Rumors about the not-so-perfect record of American weapons have circulated since the end of the 1991 Persian Gulf war. In early July, the program evaluation division of the General Accounting Office issued a report based on the examination of over a million pieces of Pentagon data and interviews with more than one hundred pilots, commanders, and war planners. According to Tim Weiner of *The New York Times:*

Well after the war that devastated Iraq was done, the Pentagon lied about the performance of many of its most advanced weapons systems, particularly the F-117 Stealth fighter, the Tomahawk land-attack missile and laser-guided "smart" bombs the General Accounting Office reported last week. . . . What military officers and arms makers said about their weapons was "over-stated, misleading, inconsistent with the best available data, or unverifiable" the report said. For example, the Air Force told Congress that the Stealth fighter had an 80 percent success rate on its bombing runs. In fact, the rate was more like 40 percent. Why? The accounting office found that commanders defined "success" as launching a bomb or missile, not hitting a target (*The New York Times,* July 9, 1996, p. 1).

As far as I know, there has been no official Pentagon response, but one author of the report found grounds for noting that the lies in question were "part of a strategy to justify future weapons spending."

"The better the F117 looks, the better the B-2 looks," (an author of the report) said, referring respectively to the Stealth fighter ($100 million a plane in 1990) and the Stealth bomber ($2.2 billion a plane in 1996, though it has yet to be tested in combat). The tens of billions of dollars spent in these smart systems were well spent, the argument goes, and much more money should be spent in the future on newer, better, smarter weapons (*The New York Times,* July 9, 1996, p. 1).

Apart from one or two letters to the editor, both supportive of the Pentagon's procedure, there has been very little public response. Since over the next decade several hundred billion dollars are at stake, one would think that Congress at least should be interested. As Tim Weiner notes, however, the only possibly relevant news is that the division of program evaluation is being dismantled and as a result of budgetary cuts imposed by Congress will disappear in a few weeks.

The second case, though comparatively inconsequential, has excited much controversy. *Primary Colors,* a reputedly sensational *roman á clef* about the 1992 Clinton campaign was published by Random House with the author listed as "Anonymous." It became a best seller, and much time and attention was devoted to trying to figure out who the author could be. On Wednesday, July 17, 1996, Joe Klein, a political columnist for *Newsweek* and a commentator for CBS News, called a news conference to announce that he was the author. His announcement prompted some harsh comments. Journalists in particular felt that he had behaved badly—Tom Brokaw (NBC News) called him a liar—not because of his having published anonymously, but because as one frequently mentioned suspects, he had made a point of denying authorship. "For God's sake, definitely I didn't write it," he was quoted as saying to *The New York Times.* Maynard Parker, editor of *Newsweek,* knew of Klein's authorship but concealed his knowledge from his own reporters. CBS executives, who were not informed, expressed themselves as "disturbed by Klein's lack of forthcomingness," and the journalistic community as a whole took a grave view of Klein's conduct.

What was the objection? If it was that journalists are bound by a professional code of honor that demands truthfulness (particularly in addressing one's peers), Klein's explanation was that he signed on as "anonymous" because he wanted the book to be judged on its merits. As for his denials of authorship, he is quoted as saying, "It wasn't easy but I felt that there are times when I've had to lie to protect a source and I put this in that category." Asked for opinions, non-journalists tended to be indulgent. Stephen Hess of the Brookings Institute is quoted: "Look, people lie to reporters every day. What annoys journalists is that this was a member of their community, a friend of theirs. Since I am not a journalist and Mr. Klein is not a friend of mine, I am no more offended by his lying than I would be if the president of the Widget Corporation lied to protect his patent." Hess' assumption that what is wrong among journalists (and friends) is all right for businessmen, or at least for heads of corporations, is echoed by Klein himself who is quoted as saying, "I think I have an obligation to be truthful in all matters that related to my role as a columnist for *Newsweek* or as a commentator for CBS and I think I have been. I also had an obligation to Random House and to myself and to the integrity of this project."

Many people found the incident merely amusing, a sort of practical joke, and Klein, photographed with a broad smile at his news conference initially adopted a jaunty stance. Now, having been urged by *Newsweek* to have man-to-man discussions with his colleagues and having resigned from (or been dropped by) CBS, he speaks as a penitent and regrets his errors in print.

Putting the two examples together suggests a use for the familiar distinction between an excuse ("It was too bad, but I had to do it") and justification ("I suddenly thought how to save the day by lying; thank God I thought of it in time"). Of course, without more information on the Pentagon case, we cannot have a firm opinion, but from what we can gather from the GAO report, the argument would be an attempted justification. It might run as follows:

> In war time we are duty bound to use every technical resource that will save American lives, and in attacking the enemy we are bound to do whatever is possible to minimize civilian casualties. The F-117 fighter and the laser-guided smart bombs were used in the Gulf War with a view to saving American lives and minimizing civilian casualties. No one can prove that this plan did not work; there might well have been more deaths on both sides if conventional weapons had been used. The data and the statistics derived from them admit to various interpretations. Since the President and Congress rely on statistics in deciding what to allocate to the military, since the state-of-the-art weapons are expensive, since we may confront another Sadaam Hussein (or the very same one) at any moment, it is our patriotic duty and in accord with our humanitarian commitments to do whatever we can to persuade the government to earmark whatever funds our experts say that they require to keep us in the forefront of weapons systems research and development.

Klein's defense, by contrast, is an excuse rather than a justification. Even at the stage where he viewed his deception as amusing, he did not claim that he had acted for the best or that his lie was sanctified by a noble end. He described himself as someone caught up in a moral dilemma, torn between competing obligations, who follows the course of what seems to him the lesser of two evils.

Both justifying and excusing presuppose that what was done was in some way questionable. Under what assumptions was the lie open to criticism? In the Klein case, it is clear enough: by a tacit gentleman's agreement, journalists do not lie to one another although how they conduct themselves with those outside the club is their own business. In the Pentagon case, the idea is that since Congress is responsible for making budget decisions, it is important that recommendations from the armed services be based on data that are true to the facts and not skewed or distorted. In both cases, the defense appeals to values that are presented as being higher than those that govern ordinary practice and sufficient to outweigh the negative value of the lie. Leaving aside differences of magnitude of the two cases, how plausible in each case is the proffered defense? Both strike me as weak. First, it is hard to make out what the alleged overriding values are supposed to be. What is to be put in the balance against costs to the tax payer is not saving American lives and minimizing civilian casualties, but rather the assurance (which turns out to have little factual warrant) that future developments in weapons systems research will eventually *lead* to saving American lives, and so forth. As for Klein and his conflict of loyalties, what exactly was his "obligation" to Random House (beyond delivering a manuscript)? How was his lying to his colleagues necessary to preserving "the integrity of his project"? Given the presumption that lying is wrong, the reasons offered as over-riding do not convince.

A further point: how do we know that Klein or the (conjectural) Pentagon apologists are telling the truth about their reasons for lying? In both cases, the lies served the interests of the liars. In Washington, as elsewhere, power and prestige go with budgetary increases, so Pentagon ambition and strategy would explain Pentagon lies without pious gestures toward the saving of lives. Keep the public guessing was a shared marketing device on the part of Random House. Klein is reputed to have made six million dollars on *Primary Colors,* and, hence, he too had strong prudential reasons to lie.

Does it follow that both defenses are based on second-order lies, lies about reasons for first order lying? Not necessarily: we may have our suspicions, but we may be wrong. Here is a technical point that is relevant: any individual, person, object, speech-act can be the topic of a very large number of true descriptions. The assertion ". . . definitely I did not write it" constituted a lie on Klein's part, but this is consistent with that particular speech act's being many other things as well. It might, for example, be something he planned in advance; it might have been the keeping of a promise; it might have been an act about which he told himself that he was speaking not as a journalist but as an entrepreneur; it might have been an act designed to please his publisher and to enhance the volume of sales. Some such descriptions we may know to have been true; about others we can only speculate. . . . The lingo of political correctness abounds in euphemisms as does campaign rhetoric. They are meant to be not exactly transparent, but more like a code that can be deciphered without too much labor. If you say that you believe in family values, then the *cognoscenti* will recognize that you do not approve of homosexual marriages, and the non-*cognoscenti* will suppose you to be saying something nice about motherhood and apple-pie. No lie is involved, and while something deceptive and bad is going on, it is not easy to see who is deceived and about what.

What do philosophers have to tell us about the ethics of lying? Two kinds of theory dominate the field: one is consequentialism, which has it that an action or type of action is right or wrong depending on its consequences (or anticipated consequences) for human welfare. The second is Kantian theory, either as conceived by Kant or as presented by one of the several philosophers who have built on Kantian foundations. On this second view, moral principles are not arrived at by seeing what happens when people act in certain ways—when they keep their promises, for example, or when they lie. A moral principle cannot be either supported or undercut by the facts; it is arrived at by an exercise of practical reasoning, and it is absolute. Both consequentialists and Kantians think that lying is bad and ought to be discouraged, but their reasons differ.

Consequentialists depend on "slippery slope" arguments: lying is addictive; one lie may do no harm, but one leads to another and eventually deception becomes a way of life. Then they say, "And what if this happened to *everybody?*" and claim that disastrous consequences would be sure to follow. No one would know what or whom to believe. Science, business, commerce, communication itself would be in jeopardy. So better not to take even the first step. The Kantian view, mentioned in passing above, is to the effect that lying is wrong in itself and independent of its consequences and its motives. It is wrong because it constitutes a denial of human dignity and, thus, of the whole idea of morality as different from mere prudence.

The consequentialist doctrine appears to me to have serious flaws. No evidence is offered for the claim that lying is an addiction, and if, as is reported, there are people who get along for years on maintenance doses of heroin, it would seem odd if there are not those who lie regularly but are not swept away by a passion for lying. Similarly for the what-would-happen-if-question, which seems not to have been thought out. If lying as a common habit leads to the breakdown of communication, you would expect the results to be linear: the more lies, the greater and more widespread the misunderstanding. But if my impressionistic view of the current scene is correct, if lying is prevalent in every department of private and public life, then we ought to be speaking increasingly at cross purposes. I do not see this happening. The skills required by diplomats, negotiators, and businessmen depend on an ability to anticipate, counter, and put to good use the lies they encounter. It may make for complications, keeping track, for example, of double and triple bluffing, but there are few signs of impending chaos. As for the Kantian view, although it has considerable intuitive force, it encounters the difficulties I mentioned in talking about the socialization of children. If, as many believe, it is morally permissible to injure and even to kill someone in self-defense, then it is hard not to admit that at least some lies are allowable.

. . .

Perhaps the merits of truthfulness have been oversold because it is imagined that the truthful person is one who says only what is true. If that were so, and if we could count on him not to babble and to address just those questions which interest us, then he would indeed be an invaluable resource. Everyone could use a prophet and seer who is infallible. To be truthful, however, requires no such gifts. The truthful person may be ignorant, stupid, irrational, and (I suppose) mad. He is an expert on one thing at most, his own beliefs, feelings, and attitudes, which he is happy to share with others. "At most": we can be mistaken or confused or self-deceived about our own opinions. If Freud is right, the most powerful fantasies and emotions are no more accessible to the truthful than to the rest of us. Sincerity is no guarantee of insight.

It becomes increasingly difficult to envisage truthfulness as in itself a virtue. When does it come into play? In choosing a surgeon, a wilderness guide, or an auto-mechanic one would look for someone who knew what she was doing rather than one who was candid about what she thought. Perhaps it is in personal relations that truthfulness counts. I suppose that were I assured of the affection, respect, and sympathetic understanding of a friend, I would like him to be truthful, but is there anything to be gained by my learning of the myriad ways, some petty and some not so petty, in which I irritate or enrage my fellow human beings? Apart from what concerns me, how interested am I in the inner life of other people? Suppose the truthful person is a coward; do I want to hear about his fears and sinking spells? Suppose he is intemperate; do I want to know about his hangovers and about every time he feels that he needs a drink?

A topic discussed by classical and mediaeval philosophers is the unity of the virtues. Plato believed that you could not have one without having them all. Is that plausible? Common sense would suggest the contrary and would hold that strength and weakness can go together; a woman may be brave but not wise, magnanimous but not prudent, for example. Truthfulness does not fit easily into such a trade-off. "He is a bully and a selfish brute, but at least he is truthful." Can one say such things? Perhaps. What does seem clear is that someone whose truthfulness we admire is someone who has all the other virtues. Even that is not enough since one can exemplify every morally good quality and still be a terrific bore.

I do not know how to answer the question with which I began, nor do I see my way through the tangled ethics of lying. The issues here are real and not merely verbal, and they do not seem to me insoluble. I hope to get back to them and in the meantime commend them to your attention.

QUESTIONS FOR ANALYSIS AND DISCUSSION

1. Mothersill highlights moral hypocrisy—people claiming to believe in truthfulness while they practice deception. Do you think a person can be virtuous yet still commit acts of deception without being hypocritical? Explain your position.

2. In light of her discussion of the Pentagon and the anonymous novel *Primary Colors*, do you believe there is a defense for military deception or literary disguise? Give your reasons.

3. The case study by Wendy Doniger emphasizes the relation between deceit and sexual conduct. How do you think Mothersill—or Bok or Nyberg—would respond to Doniger's discussion? Select specific passages from the readings to show their moral views regarding possible deceit in matters of love.

4. With philosophical frankness, Mothersill concludes on a note of self-doubt regarding her own convictions on the moral status of truthfulness. She asks the reader to continue reflecting on these matters, particularly on whether the vir-

tue of truthfulness can stand alone or must be part of other virtues. Consider your own observations and experiences. Under what conditions do you take truthfulness and deceit seriously or lightly? At what point do you consider a lie unacceptable? Does it matter whether you are telling the lie or are the recipient of one?

28.

RAYMOND SMULLYAN

Why Are You Truthful?

Many thinkers distinguish between motive, action, and consequences when assessing a moral person. To identify the reasons for telling the truth seems simple enough, particularly if one claims law, duty, good results, or virtue as a moral guideline. For Raymond Smullyan (b. 1919), philosopher and master of logic puzzles, finding the reasons for telling the truth is fraught with subtle complications. Constructing an imaginary dialogue among representatives of various philosophical perspectives, Smullyan delights the reader with an insightful search for both the correct and the good reason for telling the truth.

⊣ CRITICAL READING QUESTIONS ⊢

1. What is the difference between a religious and a nonreligious reason for truth telling? Can you find examples for each from the dialogue?
2. Why does a hedonist or a mystical hedonist tell the truth?
3. What is the point in talking about the nature of "tree" in the dialogue?
4. Why do Frank and George defend truthfulness in light of the self?

MORALIST: I have gathered you good people together on this occasion because I know that you are among the most truthful people on earth, and so I propose that we hold a symposium on truthfulness. I wish to learn from each of

---

"Why Are You Truthful?" from *5,000 B.C. and Other Philosophical Fantasies* (New York: St. Martin's Press, 1984), pp. 3–13.

you your reasons for being truthful. Adrian, what is your reason for being truthful?

ADRIAN: My reason is quite simple. It says in the Bible that one should be truthful, and I take the Bible seriously. Since my greatest duty on earth is obedience to the will of God and God commands me to be truthful, my reason for being truthful is obvious.

MORALIST: Very good! And you, Bernard, why are you truthful?

BERNARD: I also take the Bible very seriously. The one thing in the Bible that impresses me most is the Golden Rule: Do unto others as you would have others do unto you. Since I wish others to be truthful with me, I am accordingly truthful with them.

MORALIST: Excellent! And you, Carey, what are your reasons for being truthful?

CAREY: My reasons have nothing to do with religion. I am truthful on purely ethical grounds. I desire to be virtuous, and since truthfulness is one of the virtues and lying is one of the vices, then to be virtuous it is necessary for me to be truthful.

EPISTEMOLOGIST (who is, strangely enough, in this group though he wasn't invited): I find this reason peculiar! Carey evidently doesn't value truthfulness in its own right but only because it belongs to the more general category of virtue, and it is this more general category that he values. Indeed, his very way of putting it: "To be virtuous it is necessary for me to be truthful," his very use of the word *necessary* suggests that he is reluctant to be truthful but is nevertheless truthful only as a *means* to another end, that end being virtue itself. This is what I find so strange! Furthermore, I think—

MORALIST: Sorry to interrupt you, old man, but it was not my intention that we criticize the speakers as they go along. I prefer on this occasion to let the speakers simply state their views; we can reserve critical analysis for another time. And so, Daniel, why are you truthful?

DANIEL: My reasons are also nonreligious—or at least nontheistic. I am a great admirer of the ethics of Immanuel Kant. I realize that his ethical attitudes were, at least psychologically, tied up with his religious ones, but many people who reject Kant's theistic views nevertheless accept his moral ones. I am one such person. I am truthful out of obedience to Kant's categorical imperative, which states that one should never perform any act unless one wills that act to be universal law. Since it is obvious that if everybody lied there would be utter chaos, I clearly cannot will it to be universal law that everybody lies. The categorical imperative hence implies that I, too, should not lie.

MORALIST: Very good! And you, Edward, what are your reasons for being truthful?

EDWARD: My reasons are purely humanistic and utilitarian. It is obvious that truthfulness is beneficial to society, and since my main interest in life is to benefit society, then accordingly I am truthful.

MORALIST: Splendid! And you, Frank, why are you truthful?

FRANK: In order to live up to my name. Since my name is Frank, then it behooves me to be frank with people.

MORALIST: Stop being facetious! This is a serious symposium! What about you, George, why are you truthful?

GEORGE: Because I am a selfish bastard!

MORALIST: What!

GEORGE: Exactly! The few times I have lied, I have ended up getting it in the neck! It's not other people I care about; I care about myself. I don't want any trouble! I have simply learned from hard and bitter experience that honesty is the best policy.

MORALIST: What about you, Harry?

HARRY: My ethical orientation is rather similar to that of George. But instead of using the rather harsh phrase *selfish bastard,* I would prefer to classify myself as a hedonist; I perform only those acts calculated to maximize my pleasure in life. I am not as fanatical as George; I place *some* value on other people's happiness but not as much as on my own. And I have much rational evidence that in the long run I will be happiest if I am always truthful.

MORALIST: So you are a hedonist! In other words, you are truthful because it gives you *pleasure* to be truthful, and you avoid lying because you find lying painful. Is that it?

HARRY: Not quite. I do not necessarily derive *immediate* pleasure from being truthful. Indeed, sometimes it is immediately painful. But I am a thoughtful and rational person; I am always willing to sacrifice my immediate pleasures for the sake of my ultimate good. I always plan ahead. Therefore, I am truthful since as I told you I have rational evidence that my being truthful is best for me in the long run.

MORALIST: What is this evidence?

HARRY: That is too long a story for us to go into now. I think we should instead hear the views of the other speakers.

MORALIST: Very good. What about you, Irving?

IRVING: I am also a hedonist.

MORALIST: That so far makes three of you! George, Harry, and you.

IRVING: Yes, but I am not like the others.

MORALIST: How so?

IRVING: You mean how not! By temperament, I feel very different from George, and unlike Harry I am not the rational type of hedonist. Rather, I am a mystical hedonist.

MORALIST: A mystical hedonist? That's a strange combination! I have never heard that one before. What on earth do you mean by a *mystical* hedonist?

IRVING *(sadly):* I don't know!

MORALIST: You don't know? How come you don't know?

IRVING: Well, you see, since I am a mystical hedonist, I am also a hedonist. I feel that if I knew what I meant by a mystical hedonist, I would be less happy than I am not knowing what I mean. Therefore, on hedonistic grounds it is better that I do not know what I mean by a mystical hedonist.

MORALIST: But if you don't even know what you *mean* by a mystical hedonist, how can you possibly know that you are one?

IRVING: Good question! As you say, since I am unable to define a *mystical hedonist,* I couldn't possibly have rational grounds for knowing that I am one. Yet, in fact, I *do* know that I am one. This is precisely where my mysticism comes in.

MORALIST: Oh, my God! This is too complicated for *me!*

IRVING: Me, too.

MORALIST: At any rate, what is your reason for being truthful? The same as Harry's?

IRVING: The reason is the same, but my *justification* of the reason is totally different.

MORALIST: I don't understand. Can you explain this?

IRVING: Why, yes. Like Harry, I believe that my telling the truth is best for me in the long run. But unlike Harry, I have no rational evidence for this. Indeed, all the rational evidence I have is quite to the contrary. Therefore, the *rational* thing for me to do is to lie. But I have a strange intuition that I had best tell the truth. And being a mystic, I trust my intuition more than my reason. Hence, I tell the truth.

MORALIST: Most extraordinary! And what about you, Jacob?

JACOB: My truthfulness is a matter of contingency, not choice.

MORALIST: I don't understand you!

JACOB: I have simply never had the opportunity to lie.

MORALIST: I understand you even less!

JACOB: My attitude is as follows: Obviously, no one in his right mind would ever think of lying to his friends; it only makes sense to lie to one's enemies. If any enemy ever threatened to harm me, I would not for a moment hesitate to lie to divert his attack. But since I have no enemies and never have had any enemies, the opportunity for me to lie has never presented itself.

MORALIST: How singular! And what about you, Kurt; what are your reasons for being truthful?

KURT: I have only one reason. I am truthful simply because I *feel* like being truthful; I have no other reason than that.

MORALIST: But that is no reason!

KURT: Of course it is a reason! As I just told you, it's my *only* reason.

MORALIST: But your reason is no good!

KURT: Whoever said that I had a *good* reason? I said that it's my reason; I didn't say it was a *good* one.

MORALIST: Oh, but just because you feel like being truthful, it does not follow that you *should* be truthful. Of course, I believe that you should be truthful but not merely because you *feel* like it. There are many things I feel like doing, but I don't do them because I know that I shouldn't do them. Not everything that one feels like doing is necessarily right! So why is your feeling like being truthful an adequate justification of your being truthful?

EPISTEMOLOGIST: I thought we weren't supposed to argue with the speakers.

MORALIST: I shall ignore that remark. I repeat my question: Just because you feel like being truthful, why does it follow that you should be truthful?

KURT: *Should* be truthful? Who the hell ever said that I *should* be truthful?

MORALIST: Don't tell me now that you believe that you *shouldn't* be truthful!

KURT: Of course not! I don't give a damn what I should or shouldn't do!

MORALIST: Oh, come now; surely you want to do what you believe you ought to do!

KURT: What I *ought* to do! I couldn't care less! Look, man, I don't give one hoot for all your ethics, morality, religion, rights and wrongs, oughts and shoulds! As I told you, I feel like being truthful and that is my only reason.

MORALIST: But I am trying to explain to you that that reason is inadequate!

KURT: I don't give a damn whether it is adequate or not! It so happens I *feel* like being truthful! Do you mind?

MORALIST: No, I don't mind. I don't mind at all. Only you needn't be so belligerent about it! Now what about you, Larry? Why are you truthful?

LARRY: Why does a tree grow?

MORALIST: Look now, we are not here to play mystical games with each other. I asked you a serious question.

LARRY: And I gave you a serious answer.

MORALIST: Oh, come now, what does a tree growing have to do with your being truthful?

LARRY: More perhaps than you realize.

MORALIST: I wish that you would stop giving these cryptic responses! What are you, one of these Zen Buddhists or something?

LARRY: Yes.

MORALIST: Oh, no wonder you talk in this strange manner! But you can't tell me why you are truthful?

LARRY: Can you tell me why a tree grows?

MORALIST: I still don't see what the growth of a tree has to do with your being truthful.

LARRY: More perhaps than you realize.

MORALIST: So we are back to that again! You Zen men are the most frustrating creatures to talk to!

LARRY: In that case, why do you talk to us? But I'm glad you called me a *creature*. That at least shows that you have *some* insight into the true relationship between me and a tree.

MORALIST: Oh, really now, in what significant way are you like a tree?

LARRY: In what significant way am I different?

MORALIST: Oh, surely now, you regard yourself as a *little* more significant than a tree, don't you?

LARRY: Not at all.

MORALIST: But do you not realize that a tree is at a lower stage of life than a man?

LARRY: I find your use of the word *lower* ill advised. It is psychologically misleading and sets an emotional tone that is tantamount to begging the question. I would prefer to say that a tree is at an *earlier* stage of life.

MORALIST: Let's not be pedantic and quibble about words! In this context, *lower* and *earlier* mean exactly the same thing.

LARRY: Oh no they don't! *Objectively* they may have the same meaning in this context but *subjectively* they certainly do not. One would say that a child is at an earlier stage of life than an adult but surely not at a lower stage. This latter mode of speech gives the impression that an adult is superior to a child, which I don't believe many would wish to do.

MORALIST: All right, have it your way; so you're *not* superior to a tree. But why are you truthful? And please don't answer my question again with the question, "Why does a tree grow?"

LARRY: If you tell me why a tree grows, then perhaps I can tell you why I am truthful.

MORALIST: I still don't see the connection between the two! Why must I first tell you why a tree grows?

LARRY: Because I have great difficulty understanding your use of the word *why*. I was hoping that if you told me why a tree grows then I could gather enough data on your use of this word to help me answer your question more satisfactorily.

MORALIST: Oh, so our difficulty is semantical! In that case, I'll use a different word. What is your *reason* for being truthful?

LARRY: Does everything have to have a reason?

MORALIST: Well of course!

LARRY: Really now! Does a tree have a reason for growing?

MORALIST: Of course not. At least, I don't think so.

LARRY: Then why should I have a reason for being truthful?

MORALIST: Because you are not a tree!

LARRY: So because I am not a tree, it follows that I should have a reason for being truthful?

MORALIST: Oh heavens, you are only confusing matters! Look, a tree is not a conscious being; it has no free will and makes no choices. So one would hardly expect a tree to have a reason for growing, but one would expect *you* to have a reason for what you do!

LARRY: I grant you that if I were not conscious then I would not possibly have a reason for *anything* I do. But it does not therefore follow that because I *am* conscious I must have a reason for *everything* I do. In particular, I have absolutely no reason for being truthful.

MORALIST: No reason? None at all?

LARRY: None whatsoever!

MORALIST: Fantastic! In other words, you are in the same category as Kurt. You feel like being truthful and that is the only reason you are.

LARRY: No, no, not at all! You totally miss my point! As Kurt told you, his feeling like being truthful is, for him, his *reason* for being truthful. But I have *no* reason at all!

MORALIST: You mean that you don't even feel like being truthful?

LARRY: What a strange non sequitur! Of course I feel like being truthful; otherwise I wouldn't be truthful.

MORALIST: So I was right! That *is* your reason for being truthful.

LARRY: I am sorry, but you are still confused. I both feel like being truthful and am truthful but there is no evidence that either of these two phenomena is the reason of the other.

MORALIST: Look, I just can't believe that you have *no reason at all* for being truthful! You *must* have a reason; you just don't know what it is!

LARRY: At this point, I am not sure just which of several possible meanings of the word *reason* you have in mind. When you ask the reason for my being truthful, are you asking for my *motive* or *purpose* in being truthful, or are you seeking the *cause* of my truthfulness? Or are you perhaps asking whether I am truthful out of some *principle* like virtue or duty or obedience to God or the desire to serve humanity or to be personally well off? Which of these meanings do you have in mind?

MORALIST: Take your choice!

LARRY: I would rather you choose.

MORALIST: Very well then. Which of these principles you mentioned is relevant to your case?

LARRY: None of them.

MORALIST: Then what *is* the principle you follow?

LARRY: None whatsoever. I am not truthful on principle.

MORALIST: All right then, let's go over to another of your suggested meanings, cause. What is the cause of your being truthful?

LARRY: I have no idea.

MORALIST: Aren't you helpful!

LARRY: I am trying to be.

MORALIST: You certainly don't *seem* to be trying! At any rate, let's go on to the next possibility. What is your motive or purpose in being truthful?

LARRY: I am not aware of any motive, and I certainly have no purpose in being truthful. Does a tree have any motive or purpose in growing?

MORALIST: Why must you keep picking on that poor tree?

LARRY: Why do you keep picking on *me?*

MORALIST: I'm not picking on you! I'm trying to *help* you. I'm trying to help you know yourself better.

LARRY: Why on earth should I want to know myself better?

MORALIST: Well, don't you want to?

LARRY: Of course not. Why should I want to do such a foolish thing?

MORALIST: What's so foolish about it? Recall Shakespeare's saying, "Know thyself."

LARRY: I guess it's all right for those who like that sort of thing.

MORALIST: And did not Socrates say that the unexamined life is not worth living?

LARRY: Isn't that a bit on the arrogant side? Who is Socrates to decide which lives are worth living and which not? Does a tree examine its life?

MORALIST: Socrates was talking about human beings, not trees!

LARRY: What is the difference?

MORALIST: Oh, so we're back to that again! Look, I don't have the time to spend with you playing these useless word games! Since you stubbornly deny that your truthfulness is to any purpose, then I think further conversation is futile.

LARRY: Good grief, how you have misunderstood me! I never said that my being truthful is to no purpose!

MORALIST: Of course you did! A short while back you distinctly said that you had no purpose in being truthful.

LARRY: That is true. Indeed, *I* have no purpose in being truthful. But that does not mean that there *is* no purpose in my being truthful. Of course there is a purpose—I feel a very important one—but this purpose is not mine.

MORALIST: Now I don't understand you at all!

LARRY: Isn't that amazing; you understand the matter perfectly with a tree but not with a human! That so beautifully reveals how differently you think of the two. You grant that a tree has no reason or purpose in growing since you say that a tree is not a conscious entity. Yet that does not mean that the growing of a tree *serves* no purpose. Now you will say that since I, unlike a tree, am a conscious entity, I not only *serve* purposes but have my *own* purposes, and indeed I often do. When I came here tonight, I had the definite purpose of speaking with you all. But that does not mean that everything I do I necessarily do for a purpose. In particular, my being truthful serves absolutely no purpose of *mine*. But I do not doubt that it serves a very important purpose. You see now why I compare my being truthful to the growing of a tree?

MORALIST: Yes, now for the first time I begin to get an inkling of what you are saying. I don't think I would agree with your point of view, but I do find it of interest, and I wish we had more time to go into details, but the evening is getting well on, and we should not neglect our final speaker, Simplicus. Actually, I planned this occasion primarily in Simplicus's honor as a tribute to a great and truthful man, one who is probably more truthful than all of us. All of us here tell nothing but the truth, but Simplicus also always tells the *whole* truth. Therefore, he should be most competent to analyze the real purpose of truthfulness. And so we ask you, Simplicus, what is *your* reason for being truthful?

SIMPLICUS: Me? Truthful? I had no idea that I was.

QUESTIONS FOR ANALYSIS AND DISCUSSION

1. How is the Moralist portrayed in this dialogue? Does he have any similarities with thinkers from earlier selections that you have covered?

2. Is the term "reason" used throughout the dialogue with the same meaning? If so, what is the meaning? If not, what are the different meanings of "reason," and which speakers represent them?

3. Near the end of the dialogue we learn that the speakers were meeting to honor Simplicus. What is the point of the conclusion where Simplicus utters one line?

29.

GILBERT MEILAENDER

It Killed the Cat: The Vice of Curiosity

A related dispute in philosophy centers on the value of knowledge itself. Should we always seek knowledge? Are there limits to our love of knowledge that, when transgressed, bring irreparable harm? How can any serious moralist tell college students that not all knowledge is worth having? Gilbert Meilaender (b. 1946), a philosopher at the University of Notre Dame, addresses these questions by reviewing the nature of curiosity. He first recounts a couple of classic stories involving curiosity. Then he clarifies Augustine's argument on the vice of curiosity. Finally, Meilaender sets out the difference between curiosity as a virtue and as a vice.

| CRITICAL READING QUESTIONS |

1. In *The Magician's Nephew*, what is the power of curiosity? Is it a dangerous or benevolent power for all the characters?

2. How does the "mangled corpse" illustrate the perennial temptation of the lust of the eyes?

3. What is the difference between useful and useless knowledge?

"It Killed the Cat: The Vice of Curiosity," from *The Theory and Practice of Virtue* (Notre Dame, IN: University of Notre Dame Press, 1984), pp. 127–151. Notes have been omitted.

Long ago there was a man of great intellect and great courage. He was a remarkable man, a giant, able to answer questions that no other human being could answer, willing boldly to face any challenge or problem. He was a confident man, a masterful man. He saved his city from disaster and ruled it as a father rules his children, revered by all. But something was wrong in his city. A plague had fallen on generation; infertility afflicted plants, animals, and human beings. The man confidently promised to uncover the cause of the plague and to cure the infertility. Resolutely, dauntlessly, he put his sharp mind to work to solve the problem, to bring the dark things to light. No secrets, no reticences, a full public inquiry. He raged against the representatives of caution, moderation, prudence, and piety, who urged him to curtail his inquiry; he accused them of trying to usurp his rightfully earned power, of trying to replace human and masterful control with submissive reverence. The story ends in tragedy: He solved the problem but, in making visible and public the dark and intimate details of his origins, he ruined his life, and that of his family. In the end, too late, he learns about the price of presumption, of overconfidence, of the overweening desire to master and control one's fate. In symbolic rejection of his desire to look into everything, he punishes his eyes with self-inflicted blindness.

Sophocles seems to suggest that such a man is always in principle—albeit unwillingly—a patricide, a regicide, and a practitioner of incest. We men of modern science may have something to learn from our forebear, Oedipus. It appears that Oedipus, being the kind of man an Oedipus is (the chorus calls him a paradigm of man), had no choice but to learn through suffering. Is it really true that we too have no other choice?

Stop an average set of parents on the street, ask them whether they think it good to stimulate their children's curiosity, and an affirmative answer is almost a certainty. Curiosity in the young child is, we are assured, one of the signs of high intelligence. Our schools initiate special programs for "gifted children" (who turn out to be rather large in number) designed, among other things, to stimulate the curiosity of such children. The bits and pieces of psychology we all pick up suggest that human beings have a natural curiosity, that to inhibit it is to prevent our full development as persons, and even that much psychological illness comes from the attempt *not* to know certain truths about ourselves. Not to be curious turns out to be a sign of limited intelligence, moral weakness which fears responsibility, even illness.

One of the books I read to my children—not in an attempt to stimulate their curiosity but simply because I believe in sharing with them things I care about—has caused me to wonder whether curiosity is so unambiguously a good. In *The Magician's Nephew* C. S. Lewis helps the child—and the adult—see that there may be something excessive, something morally troublesome, in a certain kind of curiosity.

Polly and Digory are curious children, curious about the empty house a little down the street. As a result they end up, not in that empty house, but in the study of Digory's Uncle Andrew. For years Uncle Andrew has been dabbling in magic, trying to discover the secret of the box of dust left him by his godmother, Mrs. Lefay. Just before her death, Uncle Andrew had promised that he would burn the box without opening it. That promise he did not keep for a reason he makes clear to Digory. "Men like me who possess hidden wisdom, are freed from common rules just as we are cut off from common pleasures. Ours, my boy, is a high and lonely destiny" (p. 16). After many years of study and much experimenting on guinea pigs—some of whom died, some of whom exploded, at least one of whom disappeared—Uncle Andrew succeeded in fashioning the dust into rings: yellow rings which would cause anyone touching them to vanish into another world; green rings to bring them back (or so Uncle Andrew hoped). Having tricked Polly into taking a yellow ring—and vanishing—Uncle Andrew then persuades Digory that it is his duty to go after her, carrying along a green ring by which they can both return.

Clearly, something has gone wrong with Uncle Andrew's curiosity. Indeed, later when he himself gets into the newly created world of Narnia, he is unable to marvel at the wonder of the world coming into existence. He becomes interested only when he discovers that a piece of scrap iron tossed into the fertile soil of Narnia might grow into a battleship. He sees nothing in Narnia except commercial possibilities (pp. 98f.).

Uncle Andrew's entire life has been dominated by a vice of curiosity, but others are also curious. Polly and Digory were curious about the empty house—and ended up in Uncle Andrew's study. Polly is curious about the yellow ring—and finds herself in another world. Digory, having followed her, is curious about other worlds and wants to explore rather than return immediately—and, as a result, they end up in the seemingly dead world of Charn. In the palace of Charn, where Digory and Polly see figures of former kings and queens now dead, they find "a little golden arch from which there hung a little golden bell; and beside this there lay a little golden hammer to hit the bell with" (p. 44). On the pillar holding arch and bell a short poetic stanza is cut in stone.

> Make your choice, adventurous Stranger;
> Strike the bell and bide the danger,
> Or wonder, till it drives you mad,
> What would have followed if you had. (p. 44)

Polly is at once ready to leave, but Digory cannot. Driven by the belief that he must know what he can know, he responds.

> "Oh but don't you see it's no good!" said Digory. "We can't get out of it now. We shall always be wondering what would have happened if we had struck the bell. I'm not going home to be driven mad by always thinking of that. No fear!" (pp. 44f.)

This time the consequences of Digory's curiosity are more momentous. He strikes the bell, the world of Charn begins to crumble at the tone, and Jadis, last of the queens of Charn, comes to life. As they hurry with her to escape the falling ruins, Jadis tells Digory and Polly of Charn's last days. She and her sister had struggled over the kingdom. Both sides had promised not to use magic in the struggle. First Jadis's sister broke her promise—foolishly, since only Jadis knew "the secret of the Deplorable Word" (p. 54). Other rulers of Charn, while knowing that there was such a word which "if spoken with the proper ceremonies, would destroy all living things except the one who spoke it," had taken oaths not even to seek to know the word (p. 54). Jadis, however, had "learned it in a secret place and paid a terrible price to learn it" (p. 54). And having learned it, she used it. In the moment of her sister's seeming victory, she spoke the Deplorable Word—and Charn was no more.

The vice of curiosity—in Uncle Andrew, Digory and Polly, Jadis—exacts its price. Jadis—and with her evil—is brought to the new world of Narnia in the very moment of its creation. The toll falls heaviest, at least for a time, on Digory. When he realizes that Narnia is like a land of youth, Digory begins to hope for a chance to take back some of the fruit of Narnia to his mother, who is dying. Aslan, however, sends him on a journey. Digory is to go beyond the borders of Narnia, into the Western Wild, till he finds "a green valley with a blue lake in it, walled round by mountains of ice. At the end of the lake there is a steep, green hill. On the top of that hill there is a garden. In the centre of that garden is a tree. Pluck an apple from that tree and bring it back to me" (p. 128). From that apple will grow the Tree of Protection which will keep Narnia safe from Jadis for many a year.

Digory reaches the garden. Written on its gate is this stanza:

> Come in by the gold gates or not at all,
> Take of my fruit for others or forbear,
> For those who steal or those who climb my wall
> Shall find their heart's desire and find despair. (p. 141)

Digory enters (through the gates), picks an apple from the tree, and puts it in his pocket. Before putting it away, though, he cannot resist smelling it.

> It would have been better if he had not. A terrible thirst and hunger came over him and a longing to taste that fruit. He put it hastily into his pocket; but there were plenty of others. Could it be wrong to taste one? (p. 142)

Digory is saved from the temptation to take for himself—saved partly because he notices in the tree above a bird watching him, partly because the precept "Do Not Steal" had been hammered into his head as a boy.

He must yet face, however, a far more powerful temptation. Having resisted the desire to take for himself, he will now be tempted to take for others. Jadis has come to the garden ahead of Digory. He sees her now and turns to flee, but she stops him.

> "Foolish boy," said the Witch. "Why do you run from me? I mean you no harm. If you do not stop and listen to me now you will miss some knowledge that would have made you happy all your life." (p. 144)

Why, she asks, take back the apple of youth to the Lion Aslan? Why not eat it himself and live forever with her? But that temptation—the appeal to Digory's curiosity and his desire for mastery—has already been overcome. Digory will not take for himself. Then Jadis cuts deeper. Why not take the apple for his mother?

> "Use your Magic and go back to your own world. A minute later you can be at your Mother's bedside, giving her the fruit. Five minutes later you will see the colour coming back to her face. She will tell you the pain is gone. Soon she will tell you she feels

stronger. Then she will fall asleep—think of that; hours of sweet natural sleep, without pain, without drugs. Next day everyone will be saying how wonderfully she has recovered. Soon she will be quite well again. All will be well again. Your home will be happy again. You will be like other boys." (p. 145)

Why not indeed? The poem on the gates had, after all, said, "Take of my fruit for others or forbear." At the witch's suggestion, Digory gasps, realizing that "the most terrible choice lay before him" (p. 145). Aslan's instructions had been clear: to take one apple from the tree and return with it. Digory must now choose. He can obey those instructions or he can disobey in order to help his mother. He is strengthened to some extent in the face of this temptation by remembering once again the limits which the moral code imposes. He has made a promise to the Lion.

> "Mother herself," said Digory, getting the words out with difficulty, "wouldn't like it— awfully strict about keeping promises—and not stealing—and all that sort of thing. *She'd* tell me not to do it—quick as anything—if she was here." (p. 146)

Jadis suggests that no one need ever know what Digory has done, since he can leave Polly behind in Narnia. And suddenly Digory realizes that Jadis cares for him and his mother no more than she cares for Polly. She cares only that he join her in vice, that as her own curiosity has impelled her to eat the fruit of that tree, so should he. Realizing that, Digory returns at once and hears Aslan's "Well Done."

Later, when the apple has been planted and the Tree of Protection grown at once into a towering tree, Aslan gives Digory an apple from it to take to his mother. And Aslan explains that the tree will keep Jadis away from Narnia, since, having eaten its fruit in the wrong way and at the wrong time, she will forever loathe the fruit. Yet, the magic in the fruit will work. She has, as the poem on the gate of the garden warned, found her heart's desire and found despair.

> "She has won her heart's desire; she has unwearying strength and endless days like a goddess. But length of days with an evil heart is only length of misery and already she begins to know it. All get what they want: they do not always like it." (p. 157)

Aslan also explains that had Digory stolen an apple it would have healed his mother, but it would not have brought joy. "The day would have come when both you and she would have looked back and said it would have been better to die in that illness" (p. 158).

An adult reading *The Magician's Nephew* can hardly fail to note that curiosity is, in this story, a vice. And we may hope that children also absorb this insight as they absorb so much else from the stories they hear and read. Nevertheless, it is just as clear that we do not learn from *The Magician's Nephew* that the pursuit of knowledge is itself bad. Readers of this story, and of *The Lion, The Witch, and the Wardrobe*, will know that Digory grew up to become Professor Kirke—a man not only learned but wise. If curiosity is a vice, therefore, it cannot be equated simply with the desire to know. The story sometimes suggests that curiosity is vicious when it involves the pursuit of useless knowledge—but more often that the vice of curiosity involves a search for power and control, a thirst that *must* be filled, a pursuit not limited by the claims of morality.

. . .

Augustine: The Lust of the Eyes

In Book X of his *Confessions* Augustine, having charted the course by which he was drawn to faith, takes stock of his present condition. He considers that he must confess not only his past but also his present; for the journey toward virtue never ends in this life, and only God can see us whole and entire. To that end he discusses some of the temptations to which a Christian is subject, considering the degree to which he is successful in his own struggle against them. Many of these temptations he includes within the threefold biblical rubric, "the lust of the flesh and the lust of the eyes and the pride of life" (I John 2:16).

He discusses first the lusts of the flesh, considering the pleasures made possible by our bodily senses. Thus, he discusses the proper use of food and music, hewing always to the line that the pleasures themselves are good, but we are not when we fail to refer them back to the God who gives them. The same is true, it turns out, of the desire for knowledge; for Augustine then turns in X, 35 to the "lust of the eyes," which here means not one of the temptations given in bodily sensation but the temptation which comes from the desire to see, to know.

The lust of the eyes is, Augustine writes, "in many ways more dangerous" than the lust of the flesh. This vice, "dignified by the names of learning and science" is "a kind of empty longing and curiosity which aims not at taking pleasure in the flesh but at acquiring experience through the flesh." We note that Augustine does *not* write that all learning and science are merely vice; he says that sometimes we practice vice and dignify it with the honorable names of learning and science. This vice of curiosity, which Augustine terms the lust of eyes, is quite different from our more ordinary search for pleasures through the lust of the flesh. Augustine notes perceptively that curiosity, our desire to *see,* may lead us to seek what is not in the ordinary sense pleasurable at all. Like Uncle Andrew studying the secret of the magic dust, or Jadis trying to learn the Deplorable Word, we may expend life and energy, we may suffer greatly, "simply because of the lust to find out and know." Curiosity may move us to seek, not what is beautiful, sweet, or harmonious, but the opposite of these. We may, Augustine writes, chancing upon a strikingly contemporary example, rush to see a "mangled corpse," though there is certainly no pleasure in the sight. It arouses in us horror; yet we desire to see.

Some of Augustine's other examples may strike us as trivial. Can it be vice if, while walking through the country, Augustine finds himself stopping out of curiosity to watch a dog coursing a hare? Or catches himself idly observing a spider entangling flies in its web? Or even, can it be serious vice when we listen to gossip out of curiosity and are drawn to take a serious interest in it? We may have difficulty imagining that any of these can involve serious vice. But, of course, a temptation immediately seen as temptation is no temptation at all. Hence, Screwtape's advice to Wormwood:

> You will say that these are very small sins; and doubtless, like all young tempters, you are anxious to be able to report spectacular wickedness. But do remember, the only thing that matters is the extent to which you separate the man from the Enemy. It does not matter how small the sins are, provided that their cumulative effect is to edge the man away from the Light and out into the Nothing. Murder is no better than cards if cards can do the trick. Indeed, the safest road to Hell is the gradual one—the gentle slope, soft underfoot, without sudden turnings, without milestones, without signposts.

When we focus on that aspect of morality which evaluates our deeds and their effects for good or ill upon our neighbors, we are certainly entitled to view with relative equanimity that curiosity which stops to watch the hounds chasing hares. But when we consider traits of character and the development in us of both virtue and vice, what is for the moment insignificant from the point of view of the neighbor may nevertheless be all-important. It is, therefore, worth taking Augustine seriously and asking what he thinks is vice in curiosity.

Some of his examples suggest that curiosity might simply be a desire to know what is useless. He writes: "From the same motive [curiosity] men proceed to investigate the workings of nature which is beyond our ken—things which it does no good to know and which men only want to know for the sake of knowing." An antiquated view, we are likely to respond, which had it triumphed would have left us without the benefits of modern science. But there is a little more than this to Augustine's understanding of curiosity. The same Augustine who can write here in his *Confessions*, "I am not interested in knowing about the courses of the stars," could also years later write the following striking paragraph in his *City of God*:

> Who can adequately describe, or even imagine, the work of the Almighty? . . . There are all the important arts discovered and developed by human genius, some for necessary uses, others simply for pleasure. Man shows remarkable powers of mind and reason in the satisfaction of his aims, even though they may be unnecessary, or even dangerous and harmful; and those powers are evidence of the blessings he enjoys in his natural powers which enable him to discover, to learn, and to practise those arts. Think of the wonderful inventions of clothing and building, the astounding achievements of human industry! Think of man's progress in agriculture and navigation; of the variety, in conception and accomplishment, man has shown in pottery, in sculpture, in painting; the marvels in theatrical spectacles, in which man's contrivances in design and production have excited wonder in the spectators and incredulity in the minds of those who heard of them; all his ingenious devices for the capturing, killing, or taming of wild animals. Then there are all the weapons against his fellow-man in the shape of prisons, arms, and engines of war; all the medical resources for preserving or restoring health; all the seasonings or spices to gratify his palate or to tickle his appetite. Consider the multitudinous variety of the means of information and persuasion, among which the spoken and written word has the first place; the enjoyment afforded to the mind by the trappings of eloquence and the rich diversity of poetry; the delight given to the ears by the instruments of music and the melodies of all kinds that man has discovered. Con-

sider man's skill in geometry and arithmetic, his intelligence shown in plotting the positions and courses of the stars. How abundant is man's stock of knowledge of natural phenomena! It is beyond description, especially if one should choose to dwell upon particulars, instead of heaping all together in a general mass. Finally, the brilliant wit shown by philosophers and heretics in defending their very own errors and falsehoods is something which beggars imagination!

The man who could write these lines and marvel at the discoveries of the human mind—"some for necessary uses, others simply for pleasure"—appreciated the dangers involved in our desire to know but was not likely to rest content in a characterization of curiosity as a search for useless knowledge. It is important to note that in the sentences which follow immediately his criticism of our desire to know "things which it does no good to know" Augustine mentions magic and the desire even of religious believers to have signs and portents from God, "simply for the experience of seeing them."

We come closer to Augustine's central concern when we note that he describes curiosity as "the empty desire to possess." What is crucial is not so much what is known as how and why we seek to know. Robert Meagher has pointed to a central Augustinian distinction between what Meagher calls the "life of wisdom" and the "life of power." For a human being to achieve happiness, Augustine believed, two things were necessary: (1) the wisdom to will what is good, and (2) the power to possess what one wills. The misery of human life, for Augustine, was that we are forced to choose between these two requirements; we cannot have both. We must either (1) will what is good, but not possess it, or (2) possess what we will, but not will what is good.

> What clearly follows from these two alternatives is an altogether Augustinian distinction between two fundamental possibilities available to human being; we may call them the life of wisdom and the life of power. . . . It seems that one may either strive to want the right thing, or strive to have what one wants. The search for wisdom somehow involves the renunciation of power, the renunciation of possession, while the search for power somehow involves the renunciation of wisdom, since it presupposes the appropriateness of what it is striving to attain. . . . Each of these two lives has its own peculiar threat or risk. The life of wisdom is threatened by final resourcelessness, by the possibility that in the end one will possess no more than one does in the course of one's life. The life of power, on the other hand, is threatened by final foolishness, by the possibility that in the end one will find one's attainment futile or even bitter.

This context helps us to understand Augustine's characterization of that curiosity which is vice as "the empty desire to possess." He means, I think, that sometimes our desire to know is only a greedy longing for a new kind of experience: We seek not simply increased understanding of the creation; we want the thrill of seeing, the experience of knowing. This empty desire to possess is vice. And it is, we can now see, something quite different from a desire for "useless" knowledge. We may want to know what seems useless but want thereby simply increased understanding of the creation *given* us, a creation we neither possess nor control. We may, on the other hand, seek to know something of benefit to many others; yet we may be moved not by thought of their benefit but by our desire to *see*. The "empty desire to possess" which Augustine regards as vice cannot coexist with an appreciation of the world as given us, as placed into our care. If our world has been given us, even our quest to know is limited by the Giver—it is a search for understanding, not for power or esoteric experience. Hence, what is crucial for Augustine is not the substance of the knowledge we seek but the motive which stirs the intellect. There are substantive limits, of course, but only because a desire to know certain things is incompatible with the receptive spirit which accepts the world from God and finds its limit in God. Hard as it may be to state the limits precisely, it is the part of virtue to recognize those times when we must not gratify our desire to know.

Many possibilities may pique my curiosity—I may wonder how my neighbor's wife performs in bed; how human beings respond to experiments harmful to their bodies, or even to suffering; how the development of a fertilized egg could be stimulated to produce a monster rather than a normal human being; how to preserve a human being alive forever. I may wonder, but it would be wrong to seek to know. Not, in every case, because I cannot know, but because I cannot possess such knowledge while willing what is good. To accept such limits is, of course, to face what Meagher terms the threat of "final resourcelessness," but that is the risk Augustine would have us run. To love the good and to possess what we love are, in his life, not always compatible. Hence, to seek always to love the good is to commit ourselves to a life that seeks to receive, not to possess.

Although Augustine does not outline for us any general principle by which we can always distinguish a proper desire for knowledge from the vice of curiosity, we can learn from him the attitude which may at least make virtue possible—an attitude characterized by a reverent desire to understand creation rather than a longing to possess the experience of knowing. Such a life may be threatened by final resourcelessness. That should be no surprise; for those who have pondered the meaning of virtue and vice have always returned to the question, "Can a good man be harmed?" Virtue itself can offer no guarantees that all endings will be as happy as Digory's. But this much must be certain for anyone who has been instructed by Augustine: Curiosity, indulged without a sense of limits, must be vice in us and must lead to that final foolishness in which we possess what we love—and find that it does not satisfy.

The Vice of Curiosity

To be curious is not simply to hanker after useless knowledge, but it is true that curiosity may often lead us into explorations and investigations which appear unlikely to benefit anyone in particular. . . .

Sometimes, of course, our investigations and explorations are motivated not so much by curiosity as by the need to help someone. The researcher who is moved by curiosity to see what happens when sperm fertilizes ovum in a laboratory is not in precisely the same position as the researcher who investigates the same process because he hopes to help an infertile couple have children of "their own." Often of course—perhaps almost always—such research will be driven by both motivations. And each requires moral evaluation. Neither is, in itself and apart from further argument, sufficient justification. That we seek knowledge which will benefit others does not mean our search should recognize no limits. In such a case the end—benefit to others—is certainly worthy and justifies some means, but it will not justify *any* means. But I have not here been concerned with that kind of desire for knowledge. Instead, I have tried to pay attention to the appetite for knowledge which we often term curiosity and which seeks no end beyond the knowledge itself. The search is its own warrant, a search natural, compelling, and fulfilling for human beings; yet here also the appetite is not, in itself and without further argument, always sufficient justification. Such curiosity, when it becomes "the empty desire to possess" rather than to receive, when it seeks simply the enjoyment of seeing rather than understanding of created reality, has been thought by Christians to be vice. To be curious about the *creation* is to desire knowledge about a world which comes from One whose being and will limit us. An appetite for knowledge which lacks that vision of the world as creation is in peril of becoming the vice of curiosity. We cannot specify in detail the limits which must always circumscribe our urge to know. Perhaps we should not even attempt such specification; the path of virtue is not laid out in advance. But when the desire to know becomes a desire to control more than to receive, a thirst which must be satisfied, when it tempts us to transgress the limits and demands of ordinary morality—then we may be sure that the vice of curiosity lies near at hand.

To remember that curiosity killed the cat is to remember that the appetite for knowledge is not virtue but the raw material out of which we make either virtue or vice—and that vice is always destructive. If nothing else, it leads to that blindness which is self-inflicted; for if we do not see the world as the creation given to us, we do not, finally, see. This is simply one more instance of a fundamental truth of the moral life: to seek to master and to possess as our own whatever we love, even so certain a good as knowledge, is a sure sign that we do not love rightly. The end must be that having eyes, we do not see. Such blindness can perhaps be controlled by the disciplined cultivation of moral virtue, but its cure may require a remedy greater than virtue itself can offer.

QUESTIONS FOR ANALYSIS AND DISCUSSION

1. Meilaender's discussion is derived from children's stories and religious thinkers. Do you think his depiction of the vicious aspects of curiosity could apply to other domains such as medical research, space exploration, or genetic analysis?

2. The First Amendment in the Bill of Rights guarantees a free press. Many interpret this as allowing any information to flow freely from one citizen to another without external intervention. In addition, this right permits the press to investigate any suspicions about a person based on the public's right to know.

How does Meilaender's view of curiosity fit with this interpretation of the First Amendment? Is another interpretation of the First Amendment more accommodating to the dangers of curiosity?

3. One ongoing concern in ethics is the universality of a theory's core tenets or values. People everywhere seem to respect honesty, or at least make judgments regarding the ability to know when to deceive. Is curiosity a vice in the universal sense? Neither Meilaender nor Augustine show that curiosity could be a matter of individual variations. Some of us can handle the fruits from a lust for knowledge, and some of us cannot, a skeptic of Meilaender must contend. What could Meilaender say in defense of the status of curiosity as a situational vice?

4. Have you ever wanted to ask someone about an issue that bothers or intrigues you but did not because you were afraid of learning something you would regret knowing? Has someone asked you such a question? Did you consider lying because you did not want to reveal a secret about yourself, or because you believed the other person could not handle the truth you would be giving?

30.

SISSELA BOK

Gossip

One commonplace experience of curiosity is gossip. Whether during lunch break, hanging out with friends at the local bar, or waking to the day's hot media items, gossip is part of daily life. But philosophers mostly dismiss it. Idle chatter, empty talk, and a string of meaningless clichés are among the ways serious thinkers discount the value of gossip. We are reluctant to praise gossiping, even as we participate in it. You might want to be recognized as a good person, a good worker, maybe even a good lover, but few confess a desire to be known as a good gossip. Most would interpret such a label an insult rather than a compliment. Sissela Bok examines the moral significance of gossiping for those who value speaking and seeking truth. Pay special attention to the surprising conclusion, wherein Bok challenges the conventional attitudes philosophers have held on gossip.

"Gossip," from *Secrets: On the Ethics of Concealment and Revelation* (New York: Vintage, 1984), chapter 7. Notes have been omitted.

┤ CRITICAL READING QUESTIONS ├

1. Can you recognize at least three different meanings of gossip in Bok's essay?
2. What have anthropologists learned about gossip that's been over-looked by conventional thinkers?
3. What is the difference between rumor and gossip, according to Bok?
4. Which four elements comprise Bok's meaning of gossip?
5. Can you name the three categories of reprehensible gossip? Are they always immoral?

Definitions

> Round the samovar and the hostess the conversation had been meanwhile vacillat-ing . . . between three inevitable topics: the latest piece of public news, the theater, and scandal. It, too, came finally to rest on the last topic, that is, ill-natured gossip. . . . and the conversation crackled merrily like a burning fagot-stick.

Tolstoy's group portrait from *Anna Karenina* brings to mind many a cluster of malicious gossips, delighting in every new morsel of intimate information about others, the more scandalous the better. So well do we recognize this temptation, and so often do we see it indulged, that it is easy to think of all gossip as petty, ill-willed, too often unfounded—as either trivial and thus demeaning to those whose lives it rakes over, or else as outright malicious. In either case, gossip seems inher-ently questionable from a moral point of view.

Dictionary definitions reinforce the view of gossip as trivial. Thus the *American Heritage Dictionary* defines it as "trifling, often groundless rumor, usually of a personal, sensational, or intimate nature; idle talk."

Thinkers who adopt a normative point of view often stress the more negative evaluation of gossip. Aristotle wrote of that tantalizing and yet strangely limited "great-souled man," who "claims much and deserves much," that he is no gossip [*anthropologos*],

> for he will not talk either about himself or about another, as he neither wants to receive compliments nor to hear other people run down . . . ; and so he is not given to speaking evil himself, even of his enemies, except when he deliberately intends to give offense.

Thomas Aquinas distinguished "talebearers" from "backbiters": both speak evil of their neighbors, but a talebearer differs from a backbiter "since he intends, not to speak ill as such, but to say anything that may stir one man against an-other," in order to sever friendship.

Kierkegaard abhorred gossip. He spoke out against its superficiality and its false fellow-feeling. Gossip and chatter, he wrote, "obliterate the vital distinction be-tween what is private and what is public" and thereby trivialize all that is inward and inherently inexpressible. He castigated his own age as one in which the expanding press offered snide and leveling gossip to a garrulous, news-hungry public. Heidegger likewise, in pages echoing those of Kierkegaard, deplored idle talk as "something which anyone can rake up." He held that it perverts genuine efforts at understanding by making people think they already know everything. And in their 1890 article on the right to privacy, Samuel Warren and Louis Brandeis spoke of gossip with similar distaste, assailing in particular its spread in the expanding yellow press: "Gossip is no longer the resource of the idle and vicious but has become a trade which is pursued with industry as well as effrontery."

Cheap, superficial, intrusive, unfounded, even vicious: surely gossip can be all that. Yet to define it in these ways is to overlook the whole network of human exchanges of information, the need to inquire and to learn from the experience of others, and the importance of not taking everything at face value. The desire for such knowledge leads people to go beneath the surface of what is said and shown, and to try to unravel conflicting clues and seemingly false leads. In order to do so, information has to be shared with others, obtained from them, stored in memory for future use, tested and evaluated in discussion, and used at times to encourage, to entertain, or to warn.

Everyone has a special interest in personal information about others. If we knew about people only what they wished to reveal, we would be subjected to ceaseless manipulation; and we would be deprived of the pleasure and suspense that comes from trying to understand them. Gossip helps to absorb and to evaluate intimations about other lives, as do letters, novels, biography, and chronicles of all kinds. In order to live in both the inner and the shared worlds, the exchange of views about each—in spite of all the difficulties of perception and communication—is indispensable.

Thanks to the illuminating studies of gossip by anthropologists and others—in villages around the world as in offices, working teams, schools, or conventions—we now have a livelier and clearer documentation of the role it actually plays. These studies have disproved the traditional stereotype of women as more garrulous and prone to gossip than men, and have shown how such forms of communication spring up in every group, regardless of sex. By tracing the intricate variations of gossip, these writings have led to a subtler understanding of how it channels, tests, and often reinforces judgments about human nature.

Before considering the moral problems that some forms of gossip clearly raise, we must therefore define it in a less dismissive way than those mentioned at the beginning of this chapter. We shall then be able to ask what makes it more or less problematic from a moral point of view, and weigh more carefully the dangers that Kierkegaard, Heidegger, and others have signaled.

I shall define gossip as informal personal communication about other people who are absent or treated as absent. It is informal, first of all, unlike communication in court proceedings or lectures or hospital records or biographies, in that it lacks formal rules setting forth who may speak and in what manner, and with what limitations from the point of view of accuracy and reliability. It is informal, too, in that it takes place more spontaneously and relies more on humor and guesswork, and in that it is casual with respect to who ends up receiving the information, in spite of the frequent promises not to repeat it that are ritualistically exacted along its path. (In each of these respects, gossip nevertheless has standards as well, though usually unspoken, as all who have tried to take part in gossip and been rebuffed have learned.) And the formal modes of discourse may themselves slip into more or less gossipy variations.

Secrecy is one of the factors that make gossip take the place of more formal communication about persons. Gossip increases whenever information is both scarce and desirable—whenever people want to find out more about others than they are able to. It is rampant, for instance, in speculations about the selection of prize-winners, or the marriage plans of celebrities, or the favors of a capricious boss. Gossip is more likely, too, when formal modes of discourse, though possible, have drawbacks for the participants. Thus hospital and school personnel gossip about their charges rather than entering the information on institutional records. And those who have the power to retaliate should they learn that their personal affairs are discussed are criticized in gossip rather than to their faces.

. . .

The second element in my definition of gossip is personal communication. The original source of what is said may be hidden or forgotten, but each time, gossip is communicated by one or more persons to others, most often in personal encounters, but also by telephone, by letter, or, in the last few centuries, in the mass media. This personal element, combined with the third—that the information is also *about* persons—makes gossip a prime vehicle for moral evaluation. Part of the universal attraction of gossip is the occasion it affords for comparing oneself with others, usually silently, while seeming to be speaking strictly about someone else. Few activities tempt so much to moralizing, through stereotyped judgments and the head-shaking, seemingly all-knowing distancing of those speaking from those spoken about. The result is hypocrisy—judging the lives of others as one would hardly wish one's own judged. As one student of the anthropology of gossip has said:

> If I suggest that gossip and scandal are socially virtuous and valuable, this does not mean that I always approve of them. Indeed, in practice I find that when I am gossiping about my friends as well as my enemies I am deeply conscious of performing a social duty; but that when I hear they gossip viciously about me, I am rightfully filled with righteous indignation.

Because gossip is primarily about persons, it is not identical with the larger category of rumor; there can be rumors of war or rumors of an imminent stock-market collapse, but hardly gossip. And there can be stories, but not gossip, about the foibles and escapades of animals, so long as humans are not part of the plot, or the animals taken to represent individual persons or endowed with human characteristics.

Gossip, finally, is not only about persons but about persons absent, isolated, or excluded, rather than about the participants themselves. The subjects of gossip, while usually physically absent, can also be treated as if they were absent should they be part of the group engaging in gossip. While the conversation is directed past them and around them, they are then its targets, and are meant to overhear it.

Least of all can people gossip about themselves, unless they manage to treat themselves as if they were absent, and as subjects of scandal or concern. Though it is hard to gossip about oneself, one can lay oneself open to gossip, or talk about one's doings that include others in such a way as to arouse gossip. Compare, from this point of view, the rumored divorce and the announced one, or the gossip about a young girl's pregnancy and her acknowledgment of it.

These four elements of gossip—that it is (1) informal (2) personal communication (3) about persons who (4) are absent or excluded—are clearly not morally problematic in their own right. Consider the many harmless or supportive uses of gossip: the talk about who might marry, have a baby, move to another town, be in need of work or too ill to ask for help, and the speculations about underlying reasons, possible new developments, and opportunities for advice or help. Some may find such talk uninteresting, even tedious, or too time-consuming, but they can hardly condemn it on moral grounds.

On the other hand, it is equally easy to conceive of occasions when the four elements do present moral problems. The informality and the speculative nature of what is said may be inappropriate, as it would be if gossip were the basis for firing people from their jobs. The communication about other persons may be of a degrading or invasive nature that renders it inappropriate, whether in gossip or in other discourse. And the talk about persons in their absence—behind their backs—is sometimes of such a nature as to require that it either be spoken to their faces or not spoken at all. Pirandello's play *Right You Are! (If You Think So)* shows how irresistibly such gossip can build up among men and women in a small town, and the havoc it can wreak.

For an example of gossip that is offensive on all such grounds, and as a contrast to the many forms of harmless gossip mentioned earlier, consider the alleged leak by an FBI official to a Hollywood columnist about the private life of the actress Jean Seberg. The leak indicated that she had engaged in extramarital relations with a member of the Black Panther Party, who was said to have fathered her unborn child. It was meant to cast suspicion on her support of black nationalist causes. Reprinted by *Newsweek*, it was disseminated, as intended, throughout the world. Such uses of gossip have not been rare. They injure most directly the person whose reputation they are meant to call in question. But they debilitate as well those who take part in manufacturing and spreading the rumor, and their superiors who are responsible for permitting such a scheme to go ahead; and thus they endanger still others who may be the targets of similar attacks. Such acts, with all their ramifications, overstep all bounds of discretion and of respect for persons. They are especially reprehensible and dangerous when undertaken in secrecy by a government agency in the name of the public's best interest.

In between these extremes of innocuousness and harm lie most forms of gossip: the savoring of salacious rumors, the passing on of unverified suspicions, the churning over seemingly self-inflicted burdens in the lives of acquaintances, and the consequent self-righteousness and frequent hypocrisy of those passing judgment in gossip. No testing ground for the exercise of discretion and indiscretion is more common than such everyday probing and trading of personal matters. Just as all of us play the roles of host and guest at different times, so all of us gossip and are gossiped about. Gossip brings into play intuitive responses to the tensions of insider and outsider, and forces us to choose between concealing and revealing, between inquisitiveness and restraint. Each of us develops some standards, however inarticulate, however often honored in the breach, for amounts and kinds of gossip we relish, tolerate, or reject. Can these standards be made more explicit? If so, how might we weigh them?

Reprehensible Gossip

Why is gossip like a three-pronged tongue? Because it destroys three people: the person who says it, the person who listens to it, and the person about whom it is told.

—The Babylonian Talmud

Not all gossip, as I have defined it, is injurious or otherwise to be avoided. But when it is, it can harm all who take part in it, as the Babylonian Talmud warned. Out of respect for oneself as much as for others, therefore, it matters to discern such cases. Three categories of gossip should be singled out as especially reprehensible: gossip in breach of confidence, gossip the speaker knows to be false, and unduly invasive gossip.

It is wrong, first of all, to reveal in gossip what one has promised to keep secret. This is why the gossip of doctors at staff meetings and cocktail parties about the intimate revelations of their patients is so inexcusable. True, pledges of confidentiality must at times be broken—to save the life of an adolescent who confides plans of suicide, for example. But such legitimate breaches could hardly be carried out through gossip, because of its lack of discrimination with respect to who ends up hearing it. Such information should, rather, be disclosed only to those who have a particular need to know, and with the utmost respect for the privacy of the individual concerned.

Must we then bar all gossip conveyed in spite of a pledge of silence? And would we then not exclude *most* gossip? After all, few pieces of information are more rapidly disseminated than those preceded by a "promise not to tell." At times such a promise is worthless, a mere empty gesture, and both parties know it; one can hardly call the subsequent repeating of the "secret" a breach of confidence. Sometimes the person who asks for the promise before sharing his bits of gossip may believe it to be more binding than it turns out to be. But, as La Rochefoucauld asked, why should we imagine that others will keep the secret we have ourselves been unable to keep? At still other times, a promise may have been sincere, but should never have been made to begin with. Many promises of secrecy are exacted with the aggressive intent of burdening someone, or of creating a gulf between that individual and others. The best policy is to be quite sparing in one's promises of secrecy about any information, but scrupulous, once having given such a promise, in respecting it.

Second, gossip is unjustifiable whenever those who convey it know that it is false and intend to deceive their listeners (unlike someone who makes it clear that he exaggerates or speaks in jest). Whether they spread false gossip just to tell a good story, or to influence reputations, perhaps even as a weapon—as when newly separated spouses sometimes overstate each other's misdeeds and weaknesses in speaking to friends—they are exceeding the bounds of what they owe to their listeners and to those whose doings they misrepresent. The same is true of the false gossip that can spring up in the competition for favor, as in office politics or in academic backbiting, and of collective strategies for deceit. Thus in the re-election campaign of President Nixon in 1972, some individuals had been assigned the task of spreading false rumors about his opponents. Conspiratorial groups and secret police have employed such methods through the ages. Whatever the reason, there can be no excuse for such dissemination of false gossip.

Might there not be exceptional circumstances that render false gossip excusable?* I argued, in *Lying,* that certain lies might be excusable, such as those that offer the only way to deflect someone bent on violence. But whatever lies one might tell such an assailant, false gossip about third parties would hardly provide the requisite help at such a time of crisis; and if by any chance the assailant could be stalled simply by talking about other persons, there would be no need to use falsehood in so doing.

Are there forms of false gossip that correspond to innocent white lies? Gossip to please someone on his deathbed, for instance, who has always enjoyed hearing about the seedy and salacious doings of his friends, by a wife who can think of nothing truthful that is sufficiently titillating? Should she then invent stories about neighbors or friends, thinking that no harm could come thereof, since her husband would not live to spread the stories further? Such a way out would be demeaning for both, even if it injured no one else: demeaning to the dying man in the unspoken judgment about what would most please him, and in the supposition that lying to him would therefore be acceptable; and demeaning to his wife, as she reflected back on her inability to muster alternative modes of silence and speech at such a time. No matter how well meant, falsehoods about the lives of others bear little resemblance to harmless white lies.

Much of the time, of course, those who convey false gossip do not know it to be false. It may rest on hearsay, or be unverified, or be pure speculation. Often the facts cannot easily *be* verified, or not without serious intrusion. Thus to spread rumors that a person is a secret alcoholic is made more serious because of the difficulty that listeners have in ascertaining the basis of the allegation. At times such gossip cannot be known to be true by the speakers, nor credibly denied by the subjects. This was one reason why the dissemination of the rumor about Jean Seberg's unborn baby was so insidious. She had no way before the baby's birth to demonstrate the falsity of the rumor.

---

* One could imagine a club dedicated to false gossip, in which members vied with one another for who could tell the most outrageous stories about fellow human beings. So long as all knew the tales were false, and the stories went no farther, the practice would not be a deceptive one, and more allied to storytelling and fiction than to the intentional misleading about the lives of others that is what renders false gossip inexcusable. Such a club, however, would be likely to have but few members; for gossip loses its interest when it is *known* to be false.

In the third place, gossip may be reprehensible, even if one has given no pledge of silence and believes one's information correct, simply because it is unduly invasive. On this ground, too, planting the rumor about Jean Seberg's sexual life and the identity of the father of her unborn child was unjustifiable, regardless of whether the FBI thought the story accurate or not.

Is any gossip, then, unduly invasive whenever it concerns what is private, perhaps stigmatizing, often secret? If so, much of the gossip about the personal lives of neighbors, co-workers, and public figures would have to be judged inexcusable. But such a judgment seems unreasonable. It would dismiss many harmless or unavoidable exchanges about human foibles. To such strictures, the perspective of Mr. Bennett in Jane Austen's *Price and Prejudice* should give pause: "For what do we live," he asked, "but to make sport for our neighbors and to laugh at them in turn?"

How then might we sort out what is unduly invasive from all the gossip about private and secret lives? To begin with, there is reason to stop to consider whether gossip is thus invasive whenever those whose doings are being discussed claim to feel intruded upon. But these claims must obviously not be taken at face value: they are often claims to ownership of information about oneself. While such claims should give gossipers pause, they are not always legitimate. People cannot be said, for instance, to own aspects of their lives that are clearly evident to others and thus in fact public, such as a nasty temper or a manipulative manner, nor can they reasonably argue that others have no right to discuss them. Least of all can they suppress references to what may be an "open secret," known to all, and half-suspected even by themselves—a topic treated in innumerable comedies about marital infidelity. Similarly, more concealed aspects of their lives may be of legitimate interest to others—their mistreatment of their children, for example, or their past employment record. And the information that government leaders often try to withhold through claims to executive privilege is often such that the public has every right to acquire it. At such times, gossip may be an indispensable channel for public information.

Merely to *say* that gossip about oneself is unduly invasive, therefore, does not make it so. I would argue that additional factors must be present to render gossip unduly invasive: the information must be about matters legitimately considered private; and it must hurt the individuals talked about.* They may be aware of the spreading or of the harm; or else they may be injured by invasive gossip without

---

*For this reason, gossip should give pause whenever the speaker believes it may reach someone in a position to injure the person spoken of. If the listener is a judge, for instance, or an executive having the power to make decisions over someone's employment, the gossiper must weigh his words with care. Even when the listener is not in an official position, gossip directed to him is problematic if he is given to injurious responses: if he is malicious, slanderous, indiscreet, profiteering, or in any way likely to put the information to inappropriate use. Gossip is problematic, too, if the listener is a poor intermediary: perhaps one who exaggerates gossip in conveying it further, or who is likely to misunderstand it and spread it in false garb, or is unable to discriminate in turn between listeners, so that he conveys the gossip to one who is incompetent or dangerous.

ever knowing why—fail to keep their jobs, perhaps, because of rumors about their unspoken political dissent. But the speculations in bars or sewing circles concerning even the most intimate aspects of the married life of public figures is not intrusive so long as it does not reach them or affect their lives in any way. Such talk may diminish the speakers, but does not intrude on the persons spoken about.

While the three categories of reprehensible gossip—gossip in breach of confidence, gossip that is known to be false, and gossip that is clearly invasive—should be avoided, each one has somewhat uncertain boundaries and borderline regions. One cannot always be sure whether one owes someone silence, whether one is conveying false gossip, or whether what is said of an intimate nature about people will find its way back to them or otherwise hurt them. In weighing such questions, discretion is required; and, given the capacity of gossip to spread, it is best to resolve doubts in favor of silence.

Extra caution is needed under certain circumstances, when the temptation to indulge in any of the three forms may be heightened. At such times, the borderline cases carry an even stronger presumption against taking part in gossip. Discretion is then needed more than ever to prevent gossip from blending with one or more of the kinds earlier ruled out. The desire to have an effect, first of all, to impress people, perhaps to deal a blow, easily leads to greater pressure to breach secrecy or exaggerate in gossip or to speak intrusively about others. As soon as a speaker gains in any way from passing on gossip, these pressures arise. Prestige, power, affection, intimacy, even income (as for gossip columnists): such are the gains that gossipers envisage. It cannot be wrong to gain from gossip in its own right, since in one sense most gossip aims at a gain of some sort—if nothing else, in closeness to the listener, or in the status of someone who seems to be "in the know." But the prospect of such gain increases the likelihood that promises will be broken, unverified rumors passed on, privacy invaded. The misfortunes of another may then be used in such a way as to traffic in them. This is in part why the inside gossip of the former employee or the divorced spouse is more troubling when it is published for financial gain or as revenge.

A desire for gain of a different kind motivates those who take special pleasure in passing on discreditable gossip. Maimonides, like Aquinas and many others, distinguished the talebearer from the person who speaks to denigrate: the scandalmonger, or, as Maimonides expressed it, "the evil tongue." He spoke, too, of "the dust of the evil tongue": the insinuations that sow suspicion without shedding light either on the implied offense or on the evidence concerning it. Before scandalmongers and insinuators are known as such, they can destroy trust among friends or in entire communities; in consequence they have been more distasteful to commentators than all others. And yet, all disparaging or discreditable personal information cannot be avoided. On the contrary, it must sometimes be conveyed, as when the deceitful or the aggressive or, indeed, the indiscreet are pointed out to put newcomers on their guard. Consider, as an illustration of such cautioning remarks, the following exchange in a Mexican village:

> Down the path someone spotted a young man named Xun, whose reputation as a drunkard made everyone anxious to be on his way.

"If you meet him drunk on the path, he has no mercy. He won't listen to what you say, that Xun."

"He doesn't understand what you say; you're right. If he's just a bit tight when you meet him on the path—puta, 'Let's go, let's go,' he'll say. You will be forced to drink."

"But doesn't he get angry?"

"No, no. He'll just say, 'Let's go have a little soft drink.'"

"He's good-natured."

"But he doesn't bother to ask if you're in a hurry to get someplace . . ."

"No, he's good-hearted . . ."

"If you find yourself in a hurry to get somewhere and you see him coming the best thing to do is hide . . ."

". . . or run away."

And with that, the various men went on about their business.

Trivializing Gossip

Beyond such questions of avoiding reprehensible and harmful gossip lies a larger one: that of the tone gossip can lend to discourse about human lives. It is this tone that Kierkegaard and Heidegger aimed at, in arguing that gossip streamlines and demeans what is spoken. What is utterly private and inward, Kierkegaard held, cannot be expressed; as a result, talking about it must necessarily distort and trivialize. Gossip therefore has a leveling effect, in conveying as shallow and ordinary what is unfathomable. It levels, moreover, by talking of all persons in the same terms, so that even the exceptionally gifted, the dissident, and the artist are brought down to the lowest common denominator. Finally, it erases and levels the differences between the different modes of talking, so that all is glossed over in the same superficial and informal chatter.

According to such a view, the informality with which we talk about the weather or the latest price rises can only trivialize what we say about human beings. And this informality of gossip can combine with the special liberties taken in the absence of those spoken about so as to permit the speaker to indulge in a familiarity disrespectful of their humanity and in turn of his own. It was this reflection that gossip casts on so many who convey it that made George Eliot compare it to smoke from dirty tobacco pipes: "it proves nothing but the bad taste of the smoker."

Gossip can also trivialize and demean when it substitutes personal anecdote for a careful exploration of ideas. Someone incapable of taking up political or literary questions without dwelling endlessly on personalities can do justice neither to the ideas nor to the persons under debate.

Such gossip can be an intoxicating surrogate for genuine efforts to understand. It can be the vehicle for stereotypes—of class, for instance, or race or sex. It turns easily into a habit, and for some a necessity. They may then become unable to think of other human beings in other than trivial ways. If they cannot attribute scope and depth and complexity to others, moreover, it is unlikely that they will perceive these dimensions in themselves. All news may strike them as reducible to certain trite formulas about human behavior; all riddles seem transparent.

Many do not merely gossip but are known *as* gossips. They may serve an important group function; but such a role should cause concern to the individuals thus labeled. It is far more likely to tempt to breaches of confidence, to falsehoods, to invasive gossiping—and thus to a general loss of discernment about reasons to avoid gossip and persons to shield from it. At the extreme of this spectrum is the pathological gossip, whose life revolves around prying into the personal affairs of others and talking about them.

Plutarch wrote of the garrulous that they deny themselves the greatest benefits of silence: hearing and being heard. In their haste to speak, they listen but poorly; others, in turn, pay little heed to their words. And Heidegger expounded on the strange way in which gossip and all facile discourse, so seemingly open and free-ranging, turns out instead to inhibit understanding: "by its very nature, idle talk is a closing-off, since to go back to the ground of what is talked about is something which it *leaves undone.*" Those whose casual talk stops at no boundaries, leaves no secret untouched, may thereby shut themselves off from the understanding they seem to seek. Gossip can be the means whereby they distance themselves from all those about whom they speak with such seeming familiarity, and they may achieve but spurious intimacy with those *with whom* they speak. In this way gossip can deny full meaning and depth to human beings, much like some forms of confession: gossip, through such trivializing and distancing; confession, through molding those who confess and overcoming their independence.

These warnings go to the heart of the meaning of discernment concerning human beings, including oneself, and of its links with the capacity to deal with openness and secrecy. Quite apart from the obvious problems with false or invasive gossip discussed earlier, all gossip can become trivializing in tone, or turn into garrulity.

Yet gossip need not deny meaning and debilitate thus. Those who warn against it often fail to consider its extraordinary variety. They ignore the attention it can bring to human complexity, and are unaware of its role in conveying information without which neither groups nor societies could function. The view of all gossip as trivializing human lives is itself belittling if applied indiscriminately. When Kierkegaard and Heidegger speak out against idle talk, gossip, and chatter, and against "the public" and the "average understanding" taken in by such discourse, they erase differences and deny meaning in their own way. One cannot read their strictures without sensing their need to stand aloof, to maintain distance, to hold common practices vulgar. In these passages, they stereotype social intercourse and deny it depth and diversity, just as much as gossip can deny those of individuals. When moral judgment takes such stereotyped form, it turns into moralizing: one more way in which moral language can be used to avoid a fuller understanding of human beings and of their efforts to make sense of their lives.

QUESTIONS FOR ANALYSIS AND DISCUSSION

1. Of the meanings of gossip addressed by Bok, which do you find the most accurate? Can you think of another definition that better captures the meaning of gossip?

2. Sociologists and anthropologists believe that gossip has a functional purpose and is an important part of communication. Sociability often requires the looseness and suggestiveness of gossip. Does this view contribute to the moral acceptability of gossip? If not, what is your counterargument? If you agree, explain why we are hesitant to identify good gossips.

3. What practical advice does Bok offer to avoid or resist reprehensible gossip? Do you think a more aggressive challenge to reprehensible gossip should be made? Clarify your response.

4. Consider some ordinary examples of gossip in your life. Do you and your friends talk about the friend who didn't make it to the party? Do you and your classmates exchange tidbits about the teacher? How often do your co-workers spark some gossipy news during a lunch break? After reading Bok's essay, how would you assess the kinds of gossip you read, hear, or engage in?

CHAPTER FIVE

Struggling with Anger, Envy, and the Virtues

So the angry person is at once two creatures: gross and bestial in the fulfillment of his appetites, desiccated, fleshless, nearly skeletal with the effort to keep active the tiny coal that fuels his passion.

—Mary Gordon, "Anger"

"I don't like him."—Why?—"I am not equal to him."—Has any human being ever answered that way?

—Friedrich Nietzsche, *Beyond Good and Evil*

Anger is the vice most closely identified with our animal nature. We often resort to bestial descriptions to portray angry deeds. "Mad dog," "raging bull," or "spewing venom" are some of the epithets used to illustrate the animality of the enraged person. However, cynics would say these descriptions are unfair to animals. No animal is so ingenious in expressing anger as diversely and intensely as the human.

Throughout the ages, public torture and executions were considered legitimate exercises of political or religious authority. These exercises were not arbitrary or wanton. Punishments were often calculated to inflict the maximum pain without the victim losing consciousness. It was not uncommon for punishment to be turned into an awesome public spectacle, the intent being to dissuade others from criminal pursuits. It is tempting to conclude that, by comparison, modern civilization has progressed from the barbaric ways of our ancestors. Yet today's critics might disagree. Capital punishment is steadily increasing. Moreover, relatives of murder victims are claiming their right to witness executions. Members of the press claim a similar right. Are televised executions next?

In recent years the media has reported a new cultural phenomenon—"road rage." Across America drivers of all ages are engaging in retribution against perceived threats on the roadways. Giving another driver the finger, tailgating, edging a driver off the road, or simply reaching for a gun to settle a score are becoming commonplace responses across the country. A recent cover story by the weekly *U.S. News & World Report* cited a range of examples, including a 75-year-old

Utah driver who first threw his prescription bottle, and then aimed his car at the knees of an offending driver. Two Virginia commuters disputed control of the fast lane so intently that they both crossed the center line and were killed. Additional evidence of our fascination with anger can be seen on television talk shows featuring ordinary citizens so upset by what a friend, family member, or lover is doing that shouting matches and fisticuffs are standard repertoire.

If anger is a near universal trait, how can it be wrong? Is anger ever good? Many moral thinkers believe a distinction must be made between righteous or just anger and irrational or unjust anger. Just anger is both understandable and proper if you believe that wrongful injuries and social transgressions must be addressed by punishing wrongdoers. But those same people would claim that unjust anger is wrong because it does not satisfy revenge with proper proportion. The personal and social disputes about what counts as proper proportion are central to understanding the moral value of anger.

A related but more insidious vice identified by some moralists is envy. Like anger, envy is a direct threat to both personal and social well-being. As with anger, the envious person must lash out at someone else to be satisfied. The dynamic of envy differs from that of anger in that the envious person has not been noticeably or intentionally harmed by another. Rather, the envious person feels that he or she is not content or happy because of what another has or does. Worse, the envious person is only momentarily satisfied should the target of the envy experience misfortune or failure. At least the angry person gains a sense of completeness in knowing that the other person suffered. There is no satisfaction for the envious person. Someone, somewhere, always does or has something that reminds the envious person of what he or she lacks. It is not easy for moral thinkers to decide whether anger or envy is the more dangerous characteristic. For those interested in virtue ethics, it is essential to consider which virtues, if any, can best counter the forces of anger or envy.

The readings in this chapter are chosen for their ability to draw out the nature of both anger and envy and their respective moral features. The case study by historian William Burrows is an excerpt from his book on American vigilantism. Here he focuses on the peculiar force of an angry mob whose acts of aggression and violence are more than the sum of the individuals making up the mob. An angry individual may be a coward, but in a group that person can suddenly take on a strange form of boldness.

Poet and essayist W. H. Auden discusses the relation of anger to other vices. He points out that anger is often an expression of vanity because the angry person believes his existence—and suffering—is more important than anyone else's.

St. Thomas Aquinas, probably the most systematic Christian philosopher, distinguishes types of vengeance. In many cases it is contrary to God's command to act on one's anger. However, he argues that severe punishment is legitimate in certain circumstances.

Essayist and novelist Mary Gordon is not convinced that anger can ever be morally justified. Gordon is not so much bothered by whether the wrongdoer deserves to be punished but by what anger does to the angry person. Anger transforms.

Gordon provides an insightful depiction of the force of anger, including a personal anecdote in which her son did not even recognize his enraged mother. Gordon ends with an observation about silence and forgiveness.

Understanding the nature of anger takes on a level of social urgency in the debates on capital punishment. As the United States and other countries throughout the world increase their use of executions, moral thinkers continue to debate the merits of this extreme form of punishment. Included here are three positions. Law professor Jack Greenberg argues that capital punishment is wrong on several counts; he pays particular attention to the unfair method used in deciding which criminals get executed. Public policy professor Ernest van den Haag counters Greenberg's views by noting the logic and justice in ensuring that those who have committed great and irreparable harm will be given the greatest punishment society can administer. But even if Greenberg is correct and the death penalty is applied in a biased manner, van den Haag argues that this is not sufficient reason to reject the morality of retribution. A third position involves the virtue of clemency or mercy. According to ancient Stoic philosopher Seneca, the danger of executions is that they allow anger and cruelty to overcome the other virtues humans respect. Though in his own time public bloodbaths from the torture of criminals were not uncommon, Seneca appeals to political leaders to show mercy on behalf of the general good. Seneca's voice echoes down the years as people continue to appeal to state or national leaders to halt executions.

In his now classic work, *A Theory of Justice,* philosopher John Rawls gives little attention to the role of the virtues in ethical theory. Establishing and articulating the principles of justice as conceived by rational persons is his primary concern. However, he devotes two sections of the last chapter to a single vice—envy. Left unchecked, envy can undermine all our efforts in pursuing a just society.

Friedrich Nietzsche, the nineteenth-century German philosopher, offers a view of humans in which envy occupies a central place. Despite the efforts of moral thinkers who denounce envy, Nietzsche suggests that the plight of most humans is such that seeing—or at least wishing for—the downfall of others is an unalterable part of gaining satisfaction in life. On a more positive note, Nietzsche expands on the idea of a bestowing virtue, which is found in a kind of selfishness that is not based on greed or envy.

31.

WILLIAM E. BURROWS

Case Study: Vigilante!

What does anger look like in the flesh? Historian William Burrows (b. 1937) offers a variety of illustrations that have at least one feature in common: people are out of control. Indeed, anger has a contagious quality to it. Anger erupts spontaneously, without any coherent plan, and has noticeable and usually destructive results. In the United States, as Burrows notes, vigilantes and lynch mobs are notable examples of how anger affects otherwise decent individuals. Moreover, under the guise of self-protection or loss of confidence in law enforcement agencies (such as police or the court system), vigilantes often find justification for their anger.

CRITICAL READING QUESTIONS

1. What two reasons does Burrows give for distinguishing an angry mob of twenty-five individuals from twenty-five angry individuals?
2. Burrows cites five characteristics of vigilantism. Which involve moral issues?
3. Which emotions of the ordinary citizen are likely to bring a tolerance of or a desire for vigilantes?

"One of the most terrifying of all sights, according to [Jacques] Cousteau, is the 'dance of death' by sharks when they surround a passive victim. After a dozen or so killer sharks circled an injured baby whale for several hours with no sign of attack, suddenly one bit into its flesh. Within moments pandemonium broke loose; the sharks tore and ripped flesh, leaped over each other, attacked again and again until soon only blood and bones remained." A Johns Hopkins University psychologist reported the same thing, according to [psychologist Phillip G.] Zimbardo, after watching hungry snakes in a cage with live mice. Regardless of how hungry the snakes were, they did not attack for a long time. As soon as the first mouse had been struck, however, more strikes followed in rapid succession, until five or six mice had been killed. "The attack itself appears to provide a

---

"Vigilante!" from *Vigilante!* (New York: Harcourt Brace Jovanovich, 1976), pp. 276–281. Notes have been omitted.

self-excitation feedback which stimulates more attack." Finally, Zimbardo cites an art critic's review of an act by Yoko Ono called "Cut Piece." "She sat in her best dress and invited the audience to cut it up with a pair of scissors. At first, there was an awful silence. Then—well—it was terrible. Once they started, they couldn't stop. They went wild. She was left naked, of course." Precisely the same thing has happened at sporting events when two or three angry spectators have turned an entire stadium into a scene of frenzy (as happened when more than 300 people were killed and about 500 others were injured in a riot at a soccer match between Argentina and Peru in May 1964).

What does all this mean? It means, basically, that twenty-five people working together against a target are more dangerous than twenty-five of them acting individually: first, because they are more likely to express their aggression freely when they are anonymous and share responsibility for the outcome, and, second, because the actions of each individual have a stimulating effect on the others— each feels freer and is, indeed, motivated to exceed the actions of the others. That hackneyed scene in which the mob remains docile until one member throws a rock, and then everyone is throwing rocks, is an obvious example. Zimbardo has split students into two groups, one taking the part of themselves—students—and the other of the police on a bust. He observed that those acting out the police role got so carried away that they actually roughed up and brutalized the student group; they fell into their roles and acted with the kind of fervor they expected of the police.

It is difficult to tell whether Americans are more violent and insensitive to violence now than they were a century ago. It is tempting to say that they are, but that may be due in part to the fact that we live today, not yesterday, and therefore have no perfect means of comparison. The media explosion puts Charles Whitman, who killed fourteen people and injured thirty-three from his sniping position in the University of Texas tower, right in our living rooms and in full color. Similarly, we have seen the atrocities in Vietnam and Cambodia performed as nightly rituals and therefore assume that we are more violent and insensitive than ever. Yet General Winfield Scott had this to say about the Texas volunteers who invaded Mexico in 1846 and '47: they "committed atrocities to make Heaven weep and every American of Christian morals blush for his country. Murder, robbery and rape of mothers and daughters in the presence of tied-up males of the families have been common all along the Rio Grande." Mexican newspaper editors called them "vandals and monsters," who had been vomited from hell and were "thirsty with desire to appropriate our riches and our beautiful damsels." There may in fact, then, have been as many sadistic lunatics running around in the eighteenth and nineteenth centuries as there are today, if not more, but many of their escapades simply either went unreported or didn't circulate widely.

Now, however, I can sit in a theater and listen to an ethnically mixed audience applaud while Paul Kersey calmly shoots muggers and watches their blood spill out. I can watch Clint Eastwood and his likes "drop" six men in almost as many seconds, some falling into horse troughs with a satisfying splash, others rolling delightfully off roofs, and note that the people around me are giggling. I hear audiences snicker and laugh during scenes of rape, murder, and torture, and it makes me wonder whether the threshold isn't actually rising steadily.

On September 23, 1967, then, 200 students at the University of Oklahoma chanted "Jump, jump" to a mentally disturbed fellow student perched on a tower there. He did. On April 13, 1964, in Albany, New York, many in a crowd estimated at about 4,000 also shouted "Jump! Jump! Jump!" to a man contemplating a similar suicide leap. His seven-year-old nephew was trying to talk him out of it, while adults screamed, "C'mon, you're chicken" and "You're yellow." Some were placing bets that he would leap to his death (they lost), and one well-dressed man was quoted by the *New York Times* as having said, "I hope he jumps on this side. We couldn't see him if he jumped over there."

Zimbardo quotes a letter written to the *San Francisco Chronicle* of February 29, 1969, by some University of California Admissions Office clerks, who accused the police of the bloody beating of students, staff, and reporters without provocation. The letter said that one of the students, being beaten as he was dragged down the stairs, screamed, "Please don't hit me anymore! Won't someone help me?" *The more he begged, the more they hit.* And an American sergeant who took part in the interrogation and torturing of Vietcong prisoners recalled that "first you strike to get mad, then you strike because you are mad, and in the end you strike because of the sheer pleasure of it."

We have seen that the vigilante reaction is very much with us, though sometimes in altered form, and that the potential for violence and brutality still exists, perhaps more so on today's frontier than yesterday's. It remains to speculate, then, on whether vigilantism has a future, and, if so, why.

We have learned several hard lessons about vigilantism while examining its course during the past 200 or so years. It is useful to recapitulate five of the most salient characteristics of vigilantism right here and then apply them to a little projection.

1. The *right* of Americans to become vigilantes stems directly from three postulates that existed in 1776 and that exist, undiminished, today: the sovereignty of the people, the right to rebel, and the law of survival. Americans, in other words, assume that they have the inalienable ultimate right and duty to do whatever they feel is necessary to safeguard what they perceive as their interests, and that includes taking the law into their own hands.

2. Under the right combination of circumstances, Americans are prone to use violence in order to safeguard their perceived interests. They see violence as a legitimate means of protection and will not hesitate to use it when they think that there is little or no alternative. In addition, their threshold for violence and brutality, if it has not increased, certainly is extremely high and is likely to remain so.

3. Americans understand now, as they have always understood, that concerted group action is likely to accomplish what individual action often cannot, particularly in confrontation situations (as between gangs of thugs and groups of armed citizens). They are, in other words, fully prepared at any given time to form into groups for collective defense—some passive, like the Maccabees, others active, as the current Montana group says it is. For all of their pronouncements about rugged individualism, Americans are addicted to joining garden clubs, parent-teacher associations, Masonic lodges, veterans' organizations, antidefamation leagues, street gangs and clubs, tenant groups, and vigilance committees.

4. By the very nature of the diversity of people in America, coupled with its riches and free-enterprise system, confrontation situations have been and continue to be incessant. The ultimate arbiter of these confrontations, or so it is believed, is the law-enforcement system. It follows, then, that a lack of confidence in that system—in its presence when needed and in its impartiality—is very likely to result in panic and then in thoughts about citizen self-defense.

5. Vigilance committees form only when the upper segment of society feels threatened by the lower segment, when those with something become afraid that those without want to steal it from them. This polarization, actual or imagined, comes only during hard times—such as existed throughout the American frontier experience and during the Great Depression of the 1930s—or during times of racial and religious strife, when the dominant groups think they are socially or economically threatened by their inferiors.

In order to be able to make an educated guess on the prospects for continued or increased vigilantism in the United States, it is necessary to find out, I think, whether the elements just listed are likely to become confluent (if, indeed, they can be said to exist). Going to the police or to the Justice Department is next to useless, and so is poll taking; officials often don't know a vigilante reaction when they see one, and citizens under extreme pressure can be expected to see things quite differently than they do while answering theoretical questions at their front doors. The homicide and robbery rates could jump 100 per cent with no citizen backlash, for example, or they could stay the same and finally provoke a violent reaction. The nucleus of the problem is that there is absolutely no way to tell the precise point at which a given community will have had it and will decide to strike back with a vengeance. Who can ascertain the emotional point at which the fans in a soccer stadium will run riot or predict the moment at which one of the circling sharks will make that first attack? No one knows how far people have to be pushed before they become fit to kill, because people and circumstances vary so much.

The first four elements necessary for vigilante activity—acceptance of the right to engage in it, belief in the alternative of violence, propensity to organize for the common good, and lack of confidence in the system's ability to protect the individual—all exist right now. The first three of these have, I think, been well established. The fourth, too, is very much in evidence: lack of confidence in the system's ability to protect the individual from predators.

There is a definite trend in this country, in rural as well as urban and suburban regions, to view law-enforcement officials and the judiciary as being increasingly incapable of coping with criminals. Stories told by those in the cities who have come home to burglarized apartments only to hear policemen all but dismiss the crimes as inconsequential, compared with what might have happened, are becoming folklore. The burglary victims are being told that they were actually lucky— that it could have been worse. They are being told by the policemen who routinely arrive to make reports that the theft of jewelry, works of art collected over the years, hard-earned television sets, tape recorders, and radios is relatively unimportant. "If you'd been home," the police often assure the stunned victims, "you'd probably be dead right now. Those dope fiends are killers." Having been cleaned out of perhaps $10,000 worth of possessions, the burglary victim is supposed to feel relief; so, too, should the mugging victim who escapes with only bruises; so, too, should the residents of an apartment house in which someone else was robbed and murdered. The relief, if there is any, is very short-lived and is closely followed by an abiding frustration, fear, and bitterness. Those emotions are being followed, in turn, by the purchase of large dogs and guns and, in every city in the country, by the formation of block watchers and street patrols or by the hiring of guards to perform the same functions for which an increasing amount of tax money is being collected.

QUESTIONS FOR ANALYSIS AND DISCUSSION

1. Burrows introduces this selection with three examples of group aggression. Do you agree that they depict a kind of anger in which the participants are out of control?

2. Many of the examples Burrows offers are well known, and many of us have been part of large groups whose emotions were intense—a sporting event, a rock concert, or a political rally, for example. Yet we do not always get caught up in these emotions, nor do we let the anger of others influence us. Do these examples refute Burrows's case? Why, or why not?

3. The phenomenon called road rage is increasingly common on our highways. Given Burrows's analysis of vigilantes, do you think those engaging in road rage acts are minor vigilantes? Be specific in your answer.

32.

W. H. AUDEN

Anger

Is all anger the same? According to poet and essayist W. H. Auden (1907–1973), there is a rich variety in anger. It is spoken about in great myths and literature; there is often a mix of pain and pleasure in the feeling of anger. It is both an ally and an enemy of other vices. Anger is mostly futile or unneeded for human happiness, but no human society can get rid of it. For Auden this makes reflection on anger an intriguing reflection on oneself.

"Anger," from *The Seven Deadly Sins* (New York: William Morrow, 1970), pp. 79–87.

Interweaving personal remarks with general observations, Auden's wit helps clarify the stakes in moral disputes about the value of anger.

┤ **CRITICAL READING QUESTIONS** ├

1. What is the difference between natural and voluntary anger? Can you find your own example for each?
2. What is the relation of anger to sloth? to pride?
3. How does Auden describe the relation between voluntary and righteous anger?
4. Why does Auden note the possibility that an anti-Nazi would be disappointed if Hitler is destroyed?

Like all the sins except pride, anger is a perversion, caused by pride, of something in our nature which in itself is innocent, necessary to our existence and good. Thus, while everyone is proud in the same way, each of us is angry or lustful or envious in his own way.

Natural, or innocent, anger is the necessary reaction of a creature when its survival is threatened by the attack of another creature and it cannot save itself (or its offspring) by flight. Such anger, accompanied by physiological changes, like increased secretion of adrenalin, inhibits fear so that the attacked creature is able to resist the threat to its extinction. In the case of young creatures that are not yet capable of looking after themselves, anger is a necessary emotion when their needs are neglected; a hungry baby does right to scream. Natural anger is a reflex reaction, not a voluntary one; it is a response to a real situation of threat and danger, and as soon as the threat is removed, the anger subsides. No animal lets the sun go down upon its wrath. Moreover, [Konrad] Lorentz has shown that, in fights between the social animals, when, by adopting a submissive posture, the weaker puts itself at the mercy of the stronger, this inhibits further aggression by the latter.

Anger, even when it is sinful, has one virtue; it overcomes sloth. Anybody, like a schoolmaster, a stage director or an orchestral conductor, whose business it is to teach others to do something, knows that, on occasions, the quickest—perhaps the only—way to get those under him to do their best is to make them angry.

Anger as a sin is either futile (the situation in which one finds oneself cannot or should not be changed, but must be accepted) or unnecessary (the situation could be mastered as well or better without it). Man is potentially capable of the sin of anger because he is endowed with memory—the experience of an event persists—and with the faculty of symbolization (to him, no object or event is simply itself). He becomes actually guilty of anger because he is first of all guilty of the sin of pride, of which anger is one of many possible manifestations.

Because every human being sees the world from a unique perspective, he can, and does, choose to regard himself as its centre. The sin of anger is one of our reactions to any threat, not to our existence, but to our fancy that our existence is more important than the existence of anybody or anything else. None of us wishes to be omnipotent, because the desires of each are limited. We are glad that other things and people exist with their own ways of behaving—life would be very dull if they didn't—so long as they do not thwart our own. Similarly, we do not want others to conform with our wishes because they must—life would be very lonely if they did—but because they choose to; we want DEVOTED slaves.

The British middle-class culture in which I grew up strongly discouraged overt physical expression of anger; it was far more permissive, for example, towards gluttony, lust and avarice. In consequence, I cannot now remember "losing" my temper so that I was beside myself and hardly knew what I was doing. Since childhood, at least, I have never physically assaulted anyone, thrown things or chewed the carpet. (I do, now and again, slam doors.) Nor have I often seen other people do these things. In considering anger, therefore, most of my facts are derived from introspection and may not be valid for others, or from literature, in which truth has to be subordinated to dramatic effect. No fits of temper in real life are quite as interesting as those of Lear, Coriolanus or Timon.

In my own case—I must leave the psychological explanation to professionals—my anger is more easily aroused by things and impersonal events than by other people. I don't, I believe, really expect others to do what I wish and am seldom angry when they don't; on the other hand I do expect God or Fate to oblige me. I do not mind losing at cards if the other players are more skilful than I, but, if I cannot help losing because I have been dealt a poor hand, I get furious. If traffic lights fail to change obligingly to red when I wish to cross the road, I am angry; if I enter a restaurant and it is crowded, I am angry. My anger, that is to say, is most easily aroused by a situation which is (a) not to my liking, (b) one I know I cannot change, and (c) one for which I can hold no human individual responsible.

Change of Nature

This last condition is the most decisive. I like others to be on time and hate to be kept waiting, but if someone deliberately keeps me waiting because, say, he is annoyed with me or wishes to impress me with his importance, I am far less angry than I am if I know him to be unpunctual by nature. In the first case, I feel I must be partly responsible—if I had behaved otherwise in the past, he would not have kept me waiting; and I feel hopeful—perhaps I can act in the future in such a way that our relationship will change and he will be punctual next time. In the second case, I know that it is in his nature to be late for others, irrespective of their relationship, so that, in order to be on time, he would have to become another person.

My fantastic expectation that fate will do as I wish goes so far that my immediate reaction to an unexpected event, even a pleasant surprise, is anger.

Among the British middle class, repressed physical violence found its permitted substitute in verbal aggression, and the more physically pacific the cultural subgroup (academic and clerical circles, for instance), the more savage the tongue—

one thinks of the families in Miss Compton-Burnett's novels, or of Professor Housman jotting down deadly remarks for future use.

Compared with physical aggression, verbal aggression has one virtue; it does not require the presence of its victim. To say nasty things about someone behind his back is at least preferable to saying them to his face. On the other hand, for intelligent and talented persons, it has two great moral dangers. First, verbal malice, if witty, wins the speaker social approval. (Why is it that kind remarks are very seldom as funny as unkind?) Secondly, since, in verbal malice, the ill-will of the heart is associated with the innocent play of the imagination, a malicious person can forget that he feels ill-will in a way that a physically aggressive person cannot. His audience, however, is not so easily deceived. Two people may make almost the same remark; one, we feel immediately, is being only playful, the other has a compulsive wish to denigrate others.

Self-Importance

Simone Weil has described how, when she was suffering from acute migraine, she felt a desire to strike others on the same spot where she felt the pain herself. Most acts of cruelty, surely, are of this kind. We wish to make others suffer because we are impotent to relieve our own sufferings (which need not, of course, be physical). Any threat to our self-importance is enough to create a lifelong resentment, and most of us, probably, cherish a great deal more resentment than we are normally aware of. I like to fancy myself as a kindhearted person who hates cruelty. And why shouldn't I be kind? I was loved as a child, I have never suffered a serious injury either from another individual or from society, and I enjoy good health. Yet, now and again, I meet a man or a woman who arouses in me the desire to ill-treat them. They are always perfectly harmless people, physically unattractive (I can detect no element of sexual sadism in my feelings) and helpless. It is, I realize with shame, their helplessness which excites my ill-will. Here is someone who, whatever I did to him or her, would not fight back, an ideal victim, therefore, upon whom to vent all my resentments, real or imagined, against life.

If it were really possible for suffering to be transferred like a coin from one person to another, there might be circumstances in which it was morally permissible; and if, however mistakenly, we believed that it was possible, acts of cruelty might occasionally be excusable. The proof that we do not believe such a transfer to be possible is that, when we attempt it, we are unsatisfied unless the suffering we inflict upon others is at least a little greater than the suffering that has been inflicted upon ourselves.

The transferability-of-suffering fallacy underlies the doctrine of retributive punishment, and there is so little evidence that the threat of punishment—the threat of public exposure is another matter—is an effective deterrent to crime, or that its infliction—self-inflicted penance is again another matter—has a reformatory effect, that it is impossible to take any other theory of punishment seriously. By punishment, I mean, of course, the deliberate infliction of physical or mental suffering beyond what the safety of others requires. There will probably always be persons who, whether they like it or not, have to be quarantined, some, perhaps, for the rest of their lives.

"Righteous Anger"

The anger felt by the authorities which makes them eager to punish is of the same discreditable kind which one can sometimes observe among parents and dog-owners, an anger at the lack of respect for his betters which the criminal has shown by daring to commit his crime. His real offence in the eyes of the authorities is not that he has done something wrong but that he has done something which THEY have forbidden.

"Righteous anger" is a dubious term. Does it mean anything more than that there are occasions when the sin of anger is a lesser evil than cowardice or sloth? I know that a certain state of affairs or the behaviour of a certain person is morally evil and I know what should be done to put an end to it; but, without getting angry, I cannot summon up the energy and the courage to take action.

Righteous anger can effectively resist and destroy evil, but the more one relies upon it as a source of energy, the less energy and attention one can give to the good which is to replace the evil once it has been removed. That is why, though there may have been some just wars, there has been no just peace. Nor is it only the vanquished who suffer; I have known more than one passionate anti-Nazi who went to pieces once Hitler had been destroyed. Without Hitler to hate, their lives had no *raison d'être*.

"One should hate the sin and love the sinner." Is this possible? The evil actions which I might be said to hate are those which I cannot imagine myself committing. When I read of the deeds of a Hoess or an Eichmann, from whom I have not personally suffered, though I certainly do not love them, their minds are too unintelligible to hate. On the other hand, when I do something of which I am ashamed, I hate myself, not what I have done; if I had hated it, I should not have done it.

I wish the clergy today—I am thinking of the Anglican Church because She is the one I know best—would not avoid, as they seem to, explaining to us what the Church means by Hell and the Wrath of God. The public is left with the impression, either that She no longer believes in them or that She holds a doctrine which is a moral monstrosity no decent person could believe.

Theological definitions are necessarily analogical, but it is singularly unfortunate that the analogies for Hell which the Church has used in the past should have been drawn from Criminal Law. Criminal laws are imposed laws—they come into being because some people are not what they should be, and the purpose of the law is to compel them by force and fear to behave. A law can always be broken and it is ineffective unless the authorities have the power to detect and punish, and the resolution to act at once.

To think of God's laws as imposed leads to absurdities. Thus, the popular conception of what the Church means by Hell could not unfairly be described as follows. God is an omniscient policeman who is not only aware of every sin we have committed but also of every sin we are going to commit. But for seventy years or so He does nothing, but lets every human being commit any sin he chooses. Then, suddenly, He makes an arrest and, in the majority of cases, the sinner is sentenced to eternal torture.

Souls in Hell

Such a picture is not without its appeal; none of us likes to see his enemies, righteous or unrighteous, flourishing on earth like a green bay tree. But it cannot be called Christian. Some tender-minded souls have accepted the analogy but tried to give eternity a time limit: in the end, they say, the Devil and damned will be converted. But this is really no better. God created the world; He was not brought in later to make it a good one. If His love could ever be coercive and affect the human will without its co-operation, then a failure to exercise it from the first moment would make Him directly responsible for all the evil and suffering in the world.

If God created the world, then the laws of the spiritual life are as much laws of our nature as the laws of physics and physiology, which we can defy but not break. If I jump out of the window or drink too much I cannot be said to break the law of gravity or a biochemical law, nor can I speak of my broken leg or my hangover as a punishment inflicted by an angry Nature. As Wittgenstein said: "Ethics does not treat of the world. Ethics must be a condition of the world like logic." To speak of the Wrath of God cannot mean that God is Himself angry. It is the unpleasant experience of a creature, created to love and be happy, when he defies the laws of his spiritual nature. To believe in Hell as a possibility is to believe that God cannot or will not ever compel us to love and be happy. The analogy which occurs to me is with neurosis. (This, of course, is misleading too because, in these days, many people imagine that, if they can call their behaviour neurotic, they have no moral responsibility for it). A neurotic, an alcoholic, let us say, is not happy; on the contrary, he suffers terribly, yet no one can relieve his suffering without his consent and this he so often withholds. He insists on suffering because his ego cannot bear the pain of facing reality and the diminution of self-importance which a cure would involve.

If there are any souls in Hell, it is not because they have been sent there, but because Hell is where they insist upon being.

QUESTIONS FOR ANALYSIS AND DISCUSSION

1. Auden believes categorizing anger as a sin is either futile or unnecessary. If so, why do you think anger is so widespread? Do you think Auden believes we are born sinful, irrational, or free? Pick one—sinful, irrational, or free—and develop a discussion of Auden's central point around it.

2. Could a Christian, or moral believer of any religion, want there to be a horrible place awaiting those who are targets of our wrath?

3. Why does Auden question the familiar axiom, "One should hate the sin and love the sinner"? How does his approach involve a question about oneself? Do you agree with the sense of shame described by Auden?

4. How do you understand Auden's conclusion about the possible explanation of those souls who would be candidates for a Hell? Do you agree with his distinction between "being sent to" and "insist on being in" Hell? What is your response to Auden's conclusion that Hell is reserved only for those who insist on being angry? Is the target of anger or the angry person central to your explanation?

33.

ST. THOMAS AQUINAS

On Vengeance

If all humans feel anger at one time or another, can they ever act on it? For medieval Christian philosopher St. Thomas Aquinas (1225–1274) the desire for vengeance is a difficult moral problem. Under the influence of Aristotle, Aquinas realizes that the angry person often loses a sense of reason and proportion. Worse, adds Aquinas, the tendency to carry out acts of vengeance mistakenly gives the angry person a sense of authority that belongs only to God. Does that mean humans are never justified in punishing wrong-doers? No, answers Aquinas, for society does have a legitimate responsibility to protect its members and to keep a careful eye on immoral persons. Punishment is part of this responsibility.

┤ CRITICAL READING QUESTIONS ├

1. How does Aquinas distinguish the wrath of God from human anger?
2. What are the main differences between righteous and unrighteous anger?
3. What reasons does Aquinas give to justify society's right to punish wrongdoers?

"On Vengeance," from *The Summa Theologica*, Vol. II, translated by the Fathers of the English Dominican Province (Westminster, MD: Christian Classic, 1911), Q. 108. Notes have been omitted.

Question 108
Vengeance

Next, we must discuss vengeance; there are four points of inquiry:

1. whether vengeance is lawful;
2. a special virtue;
3. the way in which it is carried out;
4. those against whom it is to be directed.

Article 1. Whether Vengeance Is Permissible

THE FIRST POINT: 1. Vengeance seems to be unlawful. He sins who takes on himself what belongs to God. Vengeance, however, belongs to God, for in *Deuteronomy*, according to one reading, it is written, *Revenge is mine and I will repay.* All vengeance, therefore, is unlawful.

2. Further, we do not bear with a person against whom we take vengeance. We must, however, bear with the wicked; on the verse, *As the lily among the thorns,* the *Gloss* comments, *The one who could not put up with the wicked was not good himself.* Therefore not even with regard to the wicked is vengeance to be taken.

3. Further, vengeance is achieved through punishment, which in turn is a cause of slavish fear. Since Augustine asserts that the New Law is a law not of fear but of love, at least under the New Testament there should be no vengeance.

4. Further, to avenge oneself is to retaliate for wrongs to oneself. Yet apparently not even a judge is allowed to punish those wronging himself; thus Chrysostom, *From Christ's example let us learn to bear injuries to ourselves with greatness of soul, but not to suffer wrongs against God even by giving ear to them.* Vengeance, then, would seem to be unlawful.

5. Further, the sin of the many is more injurious than the sin of one person; *Of three things my heart has been afraid, the accusations of a city and the gathering together of the people.* Yet vengeance may not be taken on the sin of a whole group, since the *Gloss* on the words in *Matthew, Lest perhaps . . . you root up the wheat . . . suffer both to grow,* comments, *Neither a whole people nor its ruler should be excommunicated.* Neither, then, is any other kind of vengeance lawful.

On the other hand we should expect from God only what is good and lawful. But vengeance upon enemies is to be expected from God; in *Luke* there is the rhetorical question, *And will not God revenge his elect who cry to him day and night?* Therefore vengeance is not in itself evil and unlawful.

REPLY: Vengeance is accomplished by some punishment being inflicted upon one who has given offence. In vengeance, therefore, the attitude of the avenger must be considered. Should his intention be centered chiefly upon the evil done to the recipient and is satisfied with that, then the act is entirely unlawful. Taking delight in evil done to another is in fact a type of hatred, the opposite of that charity with which we are bound to love all. Nor is there any excuse just because the evil is intended towards one who has himself unjustly inflicted injury, even as there is no excuse for hating someone who already hates us. A person has no right to sin against another because the other first sinned against him; this is to be overcome by evil, which St Paul forbids, *Be not overcome by evil, but overcome evil by good.*

Vengeance, however, can be lawful—so long as all proper conditions are safeguarded—if the intention of the avenger is aimed chiefly at a good to be achieved by punishing a wrongdoer; thus, for example, at the correction of the wrongdoer, or at least at restraining him and relieving others; at safeguarding the right and doing honour to God.

Hence: 1. One who exacts vengeance of the wicked in keeping with his own station does not arrogate to himself what is God's; rather he simply exercises a God-given power. St Paul says of the earthly ruler, *He is God's minister, an avenger to execute wrath upon him that doeth evil.* However, if in wreaking vengeance someone exceeds the divinely established order, he usurps what is God's and sins.

2. The good bear with the wicked by patience in sustaining the wrongs done them personally to the extent required; they do not bear with them to the point of allowing wrongs against God or neighbour. Chrysostom notes, *It is commendable when someone is patient about injury to himself; it is wicked to take no notice of wrongs against God.*

3. The law of the Gospel is indeed the law of love. This is why there is no need to instil fear through punishment in those who live rightly out of love (and these alone belong in truth to the New Testament), but in those who are not drawn to the good out of love and who belong to the Church in name but not in life.

4. A personal wrong can sometimes rebound upon God or the Church; then the individual should himself seek redress for the injury done him. These are examples: Elias made fire come down upon those who had come to seize him; Eliseus cursed the youths who made fun of him; Pope Sylvester excommunicated those who exiled him. When an injury is in fact strictly personal, one should bear with it patiently, but only if this can be done sensibly; the precepts of patience cited here are to be understood as referring to one's inner willingness, as Augustine states.

5. When an entire community sins, vengeance should be taken on the whole group or on a notable segment; examples of the first are the Egyptians pursuing the children of Israel and being drowned in the Red Sea, and the utter destruction of the Sodomites; of the second, the punishment of those who adored the golden calf. When, however, there is some hope for the correction of the group, severe vengeance should be limited to a few principal figures, so that through their punishment the rest may be made fearful; an example, the Lord ordering the leaders of the people to be hanged for the sins of all.

When the community as a whole has not sinned, but only a part of it, then it is possible to separate the wicked from the good and make them the object of vengeance. This is true, however, only if it can be done without scandal to the rest; otherwise the whole community is to be spared and severity mitigated. The same reasoning applies to a leader whom a community has followed. His sin has to be tolerated if it cannot be punished without scandal to the many, unless the sin were so heinous that it did more spiritual or temporal damage to the group than any scandal from his being punished could do.

Article 2. Whether Vengeance Is One Specific Virtue

THE SECOND POINT: 1. Vengeance does not seem to be a special virtue distinct from others. As the good are rewarded for good deeds, so the wicked are punished for acting evilly. Now rewarding the good does not involve some new specific virtue, but is simply an act of commutative justice. For a like reason vengeance should not be proposed as a special virtue.

2. Further, there is no call for a special virtue in regard to an act towards which man is already sufficiently disposed through other virtues. As to seeking redress for injuries, a person is well enough prepared by the virtue of courage and by zeal. Vengeance, then, ought not to be accounted a special virtue.

3. Further, whereas there is a specific vice against every specific virtue, opposed to vengeance there seems to be no specific vice. Vengeance, then, is not a specific virtue.

⚜ ⚜ ⚜

On the other hand, Cicero counts it as a part of justice.

⚜ ⚜ ⚜

REPLY: As Aristotle teaches in the *Ethics*, while completeness in virtue comes about by habituation or some other cause, the predisposition for virtue is innate. Hence it is clear that virtues bring about a proper development of tendencies that are innate and that are included in natural law. Accordingly, to every distinct bent of nature, there corresponds some specific virtue.

There is a specific innate tendency to get rid of what is harmful; a sign of this in brute animals is that there is a contending power distinct from the impulse power. A human being repels what is harmful by self-defence, either warding off injuries, or, if they have already been inflicted, avenging them, not with the intention of doing harm but of repelling a wrong. This is what vengeance is about; Cicero says, *By vengeance we resist force or wrong and in general anything sinister* (i.e. hostile) *either by self-defence or by retaliating.* Vengeance, therefore, is a specific virtue.

Hence: 1. To acquit a legal debt is the concern of commutative justice; a moral debt, arising from personal favours, the concern of gratitude. In a like way, the punishment of offences where public order is at stake, is the concern of commutative justice; vengeance has place where the issue is the right to personal safety of the individual from whom an evil is repulsed.

2. Courage opens the way for vengeance by removing an obstacle, the fear namely of a pressing danger. For its part, zeal, as it means the fervour of love,

functions as a first root of vengeance in the sense that one seeks to right wrongs against God or neighbour because charity causes him to see these wrongs as done to himself. In any case, the acts of all virtues stem from charity as their root; in one of his homilies Gregory says, *The branch, a good work, is withered unless it grows out of its root, charity.*

3. There are in fact two vices against vengeance. By excess there is the sin of cruelty or ferocity, going beyond measure in punishing. The other is a vice by way of defect, as when someone fails to inflict punishment at all—*He that spares the rod spoils the child.* For its part, the virtue of vengeance means that in redressing wrongs a person keep to a right measure with proper regard for all circumstances.

Article 3. Whether Vengeance Should Be Carried Out by Means of Conventional Forms of Punishment

THE THIRD POINT: 1. Vengeance, it seems, should not be exercised through the usual forms of human punishment. Obviously, to put a person to death is to uproot him, and to uproot the cockle, symbol of the *children of the wicked one,* is against our Lord's command in *Matt.* Offenders, therefore, are not to be put to death.

2. Further, it seems that all who sin mortally merit the same punishment, so that if some of these receive capital punishment, all should. This is obviously false.

3. Further, public punishment publicizes a crime. This would seem to have a harmful effect on the community, namely that the example of sin would become the occasion for more sin. Therefore it seems that for no sin should capital punishment be inflicted.

❧ ❧ ❧

On the other hand, there are prescriptions of divine law with regard to these penalties, as shown above.

❧ ❧ ❧

REPLY: Vengeance is lawful and virtuous to the extent that its purpose is to check evil. Some people, having no liking for virtue, are kept from sinning solely through fear of losing things dearer to them than what they would get out of sinning; only in this way may fear curb sin. Reprisal for sin, consequently, should consist in depriving a person of the things dearest to him.

Such things are these: life, soundness of body, personal liberty and outward advantages like wealth, homeland and reputation. Thus according to Augustine, *Cicero writes that there are eight types of penalty in law,* namely *death* (this deprives a man of his life); *flogging* and *retaliation, i.e. an eye for an eye* (these mean loss of bodily integrity); *bondage* and *chains* (these take away personal liberty); *exile* (the loss of homeland); *damages* (these cost a man his wealth); *disgrace* (the ruin of his reputation).

Hence: 1. Our Lord forbade the cockle to be uprooted when there was any fear that the wheat would be torn up with it. Sometimes, however, it is possible to get rid of the wicked by death, not only without peril to good people, but even to their great advantage. In such an instance capital punishment can be inflicted upon the wicked.

2. All who sin mortally are deserving of eternal death, speaking of the retribution in the after-life that comes under the infallibility of God's judgment. Since in this life, however, punishments have more of a medicinal purpose, the death penalty is to be exacted only for crimes which involve dire injury to others.

3. When along with the sin its punishment is made plain, namely death or other things terrifying to men, then any leaning towards the sin is checked. The punishment terrifies more than sin attracts.

QUESTIONS FOR ANALYSIS AND DISCUSSION

1. Aquinas discusses anger in terms of reason and religious belief. Do you think these approaches are compatible with one another? Explain your response.

2. Aquinas is careful to distinguish the authority of God from that of humans, particularly when it comes to gaining vengeance. Yet anger often involves an intensity and rage in which one forgets everything except the object of one's passion. Is the respect for God the best way to prevent this forgetfulness? Can you think of a better source of prevention?

3. Auden implies that a sincere Christian should not wish great suffering for another. Yet Aquinas contends that even capital punishment is morally legitimate if the crime warrants it. Do you think these positions are irreconcilable? Clarify your reasons.

34.

MARY GORDON

Anger

In addition to being the most bestial, anger is a candidate for the sin that can actually be good. According to essayist and novelist Mary Gordon (b. 1949), it is one of the most complex vices. The experience of anger can be exhilarating, and in being angry, we gain a feeling of strength unmatched by other passions or vices. For Gordon this makes it especially tricky. The power of anger is such that it transforms the angry per-

---

"Anger," from *Deadly Sins* (New York: William Morrow, 1993), pp. 27–39.

son. Gordon introduces two virtues to withstand the potential harms brought on by an-
gry deeds.

CRITICAL READING QUESTIONS

1. Gordon describes the bodily sensations of the angry person. Which part of the body is the center of anger? Why?
2. What is Gordon's main point in relating a personal anecdote about becoming enraged over an apparently ordinary event?
3. How does Gordon think the temptation to act on anger can be overcome?

There would be no point to sin if it were not the corridor to pleasure, but the corridor of anger has a particularly seductive, self-deceiving twist. More than any of the other sins, anger can be seen to be good, can perhaps even begin by being good. Jesus himself was angry, brandishing his whip and thrillingly overturning tables: coins, doves flying, the villainous sharpsters on their knees to save their spoils. It would seem to run in the family; by far the angriest character in the Old Testament is God.

Of all the sins, only anger is connected in the common tongue to its twinned, entwined virtue: justice. "Just anger," we say. Impossible even to begin to imagine such a phrase made with the others: try as you will, you can't get your mouth around the words "just sloth," or "just covetousness," to say nothing of the deadly breakfast cereal that sticks to the ribs for all eternity, "just lust."

Anger is electric, exhilarating. The angry person knows without a doubt he is alive. And the state of unaliveness, of partial aliveness, is so frequent and so frightening, the condition of inertia common, almost, as dirt, that there's no wonder anger feels like treasure. It goes through the body like a jet of freezing water; it fills the veins with purpose; it alerts the lazy eye and ear; the sluggish limbs cry out for movement; the torpid lungs grow rich with easy breath. Anger flows through the entire body, stem to stern, but its source and center is the mouth.

Its taste draws from those flavors that appeal to the mature and refined palate: the mix of sour, bitter, sweet, and salt, and something else, something slightly frightening, something chemical or at least inorganic, something unhealthful, something we suspect should not be there, a taste that challenges us because it might be poison—but if not, think what we have been able to withstand, then crave. Gin and Campari, the vinegary mint sauce alongside the Easter lamb, a grapefruit ice to cleanse the palate between heavy courses, a salad of arugula and cress, the salt around the margarita glass, all of them seeming to promise wisdom and a harsh, ascetic health.

The joy of anger is the joy—unforgettable from childhood—of biting down on a loose tooth. The little thorn (our own!) pressing into the tender pinkness of the gum, the labial exploration, the roughness we could impose on the thick and foolish tongue (a punishment for the times it failed us by refusing to produce the proper word?), and the delicious wince when we had gone too far. The mouth as self-contained, containing oracle. The truth: pain is possible. The freedom: I can both inflict and endure. The harsh athletic contest, ultimately satisfying because of the alarming and yet deeply reassuring taste of blood.

Even the ancillary words, the names of anger's sidekicks, are a pleasure on the tongue. Spite, vengeance, rage. Just listen to the snaky "s," the acidic, arrowlike soft "g," the lucid, plosive "t" preceded by the chilled long "i," then dropped. The onomatopoeia of drawn swords. Nothing muffled, muffling, nothing concealing, nothing to protect the weak. To live in anger is to forget that one was ever weak, to believe that what others call weakness is a sham, a feint that one exposes and removes, like the sanitizing immolation of a plague-ridden house. The cruelty essential for the nation's greater health, because, after all, the weak pull down the strong. The angry one is radiant in strength, and, blazing like the angel with the flaming sword, banishes the transgressors from the garden they would only now defile.

Deadly anger is a hunger, an appetite that can grow like a glutton's or a lion's, seeking whom it may devour. Once fed, the creature grows hypnotized by itself. The brilliant Ford Madox Ford created an unforgettable character almost entirely moved by anger, Sylvia Tietjens, the beautiful, sadistic wife of the hero of his tetralogy, *Parade's End*. Sylvia's mother explains her daughter's rage by using herself as an example: "I tell you I've walked behind a man's back and nearly screamed because of the desire to put my nails into the veins of his neck. It was a fascination."

This fascination begins in the mouth, then travels to the blood, thence to the mind, where it creates a connoisseur. One begins to note the intricate workmanship of one's own anger and soon to worship it, to devote oneself to its preservation, like any great work of art. Simple anger, the shallow, unaddictive kind, starts with a single action, and calls forth a single and finite response. You have done this to me, I will do that to you. An eye for an eye and a tooth for a tooth. In this bargain, there is hope for an end: eventually there will be no more eyes or teeth. But deadly anger is infinite; its whorls, emanating from themselves, grow ever smaller, but there is no end to the possibility of inward turning, inward fecundation.

Deadly anger is fanatic of embellishment. The angry person, like a Renaissance prince with endless coffers, travels the world in search of the right gem, the most exquisitely tinted snatch of silk, the perfect quarter-inch of ivory, the most incandescent golden thread, the feathers of the rara avis. The original cause of anger, like the base metal below the ornament, may long have been obscured by the fantastic encrustation. Even the plain desire to hurt may be lost in the detail of the justification for the hurting or the elaborations of the punishment. Anger takes on a life of its own, or it divorces itself from life in the service of death dealing, or life denying, or the compulsion to make someone's life unendurable simply for the sake of doing it, simply because it has become the shape of the angry one's life to punish.

The habit of punishment is quickly acquired and self-supporting. It has one food, plentiful and easily obtained: the need for blame. In this, it is a really very comprehensible attempt to render a senseless universe sensible. Everything that is, particularly everything that one wishes were otherwise, must have its cause, and so its causer. Perhaps the person taken over by deadly anger is for this reason, at bottom, pitiable, like Dostoyevsky's Grand Inquisitor, who demanded death on a large scale so that suffering could be reduced. We destroyed the village in order to save it. I destroy you because all that is wrong must be your fault. Accident is a concept of the weak-minded: what is wrong is someone's fault. Yours. And I must punish you. Furthermore, I demand that you see the rightness of your punishment.

This is the difference between the good, the necessary anger, the enlivening anger, and the deadly kind. The first is tied to justice, the death-dealing kind to punishment. This is the reason that the Greeks, who assumed their gods to be irrational, killing men like flies for their sport, wrote about anger so differently from the writers of the Old Testament, who assumed God to be a partner in their covenant. Saul's irrational and jealous rage, prompting him to seek David's death, is punished by the Lord. Moses' higher rage, causing the Levites to murder thousands of the children of Israel who had worshiped the golden calf, was prompted by their violation of the law. But Achilles, dragging the corpse of Hector around the walls of Troy, was acting from no impulse of justice or law. Only from an insistence upon mastery, upon a display of power, which makes a defiled thing of its object. Thinking it is fixed on its object, deadly anger actually forgets him, and is carried up in the black cloud of its own dominion. The country of deadly anger, with its own cultures, its own laws. A country ruled by a tyrant so obsessed with the fulfillment of his desire that all else is lost.

I am reminded of a story the Polish writer Ryszard Kapuscinski told me once about Idi Amin. Amin ordered, as he often did, one of his ministers to be summarily executed. The man was hanged. The next day, Amin said: "And where is my friend the minister, who is so amusing? Bring him here, I wish to see him." When he was told the man had been executed, he ordered the execution of those who had complied with his original orders.

Anger, in feeding on itself, creates around itself the overfed flesh of limitless indulgence. At the same time it emanates a styptic breath that withers hope and youth and beauty. So the angry person is at once two creatures: gross and bestial in the fulfillment of his appetites, desiccated, fleshless, nearly skeletal with the effort to keep active the tiny coal that fuels his passion.

If the word "sin" has any useful meaning at all in a time when there is no possibility of redemption, it must speak about a distortion so severe that the recognizable self is blotted out or lost. Many current thinkers wish to abandon the idea of a continuous self; novelists have always known that selves are fleeting, malleable, porous. Nevertheless some recognizable thing, something constant enough to have a name sensibly fixed to it, seems to endure from birth to death. Sin makes the sinner unrecognizable.

I experienced this once myself, and I remember it because it frightened me. I became an animal. This sinful experience occurred—as so many do—around the occasion of a dinner party. It was a hot August afternoon. I was having ten people for dinner that evening. No one was giving me a bit of help. I was, of course, feeling like a victim, as everyone does in a hot kitchen on an August day. (It is important to remember that the angry person's habit of self-justification is often connected to his habit of seeing himself as a victim.) I had been chopping, stirring, bending over a low flame, and all alone, alone! The oven's heat was my purgatory, my crucible.

My mother and my children thought this was a good time for civil disobedience. They positioned themselves in the car and refused to move until I took them swimming. Now my children were at tender ages at that time, seven and four. My mother was seventy-eight and, except for her daily habit of verbal iron-pumping, properly described as infirm. They leaned on the horn and shouted my name out the window, well within hearing of the neighbors, reminding me of my promise to take them to the pond.

There are certain times when a popular cliché disgorges itself from the dulled setting of overuse and comes to life, and this was one of them. I lost it. I lost myself. I jumped on the hood of the car. I pounded on the windshield. I told my mother and my children that I was never, ever going to take any of them anywhere and none of them were ever going to have one friend in any house of mine until the hour of their death, which, I said, I hoped was soon. I couldn't stop pounding on the windshield. Then the frightening thing happened. I became a huge bird. A carrion crow. My legs became hard stalks; my eyes were sharp and vicious. I developed a murderous beak. Greasy black feathers took the place of arms. I flapped and flapped. I blotted out the sun's light with my flapping. Each time my beak landed near my victims (it seemed to be my fists on the windshield, but it was really my beak on their necks) I went back for more. The taste of blood entranced me. I wanted to peck and peck forever. I wanted to carry them all off in my bloody beak and drop them on a rock where I would feed on their battered corpses till my bird stomach swelled.

I don't mean this figuratively: I became that bird. I had to be forced to get off the car and stop pounding the windshield. Even then I didn't come back to myself. When I did, I was appalled. I realized I had genuinely frightened my children. Mostly because they could no longer recognize me. My son said to me: "I was scared because I didn't know who you were."

I understand that this is not a sin of a serious nature. I know this to be true because it has its comic aspects, and deadly sin is characterized by the absence of humor, which always brings life. But because of that experience and others I won't tell you about, I understand the deadly sin of anger. I was unrecognizable to myself and, for a time, to my son, but I think I still would have been recognizable to most of the rest of the world as human. Deadly sin causes the rest of the human community to say: "How can this person do this thing and still be human?"

The events in the former Yugoslavia seem to me to characterize perfectly the results of deadly anger. We outsiders are tormented and bedeviled by unimaginable behavior from people who seemed so very like ourselves. They didn't look like our standard idea of the other: they read the same philosophers as we, and we vacationed among them, enjoying their food, their music, their ordinary pleasantries. And yet, a kind of incomprehensible horror has grown up precisely because of an anger that has gone out of control and has fed on itself until all human eyes are blinded by the bloated flesh of overgorged anger. People who five years ago ate together, studied together, even married, have sworn to exterminate one another in the most bloody and horrifying ways. Hundreds of years of mutual injustices, treasured like sacred texts, have been gone over, resurrected, nurtured, so that a wholly new creature has been brought to life, a creature bred on anger to the exclusion of vision. Hypnotic, addictive vengeance, action without reflection has taken over like a disease. Thousands upon thousands of women have been raped; impregnation has become a curse, a punishment. The old are starved, beautiful ancient cities destroyed. The original cause of the anger is less important now than the momentum that has built up.

This is the deadly power of anger: it rolls and rolls like a flaming boulder down a hill, gathering mass and speed until any thought of cessation is so far beside the point as to seem hopeless. It is not that there is no cause for the anger; the heavy topsoil of repressed injustice breeds anger better than any other medium. But the causes are lost in the momentum of the anger itself, and in the insatiable compulsion to destroy everything so that the open maw of rage may be fed.

The only way to stop this kind of irrational anger is by an act of equally irrational forgiveness. This is difficult to achieve because anger is exciting and enlivening, and forgiveness is quiet and, like small agriculture or the domestic arts, labor-intensive and yielding of modest fruit. Anger has the glamour of illicit sex, forgiveness the endlessly flexible requirements of a long marriage. Anger feeds a sense of power; forgiveness reminds us of our humbleness—that unpopular commodity, so misunderstood (Uriah Heep is not humble; Félicité in Flaubert's "Simple Heart" is). To forgive is to give up the exhilaration of one's own unassailable rightness. "No cause, no cause," says Cordelia at the end of *King Lear,* enabling the broken father to become a "foolish fond old man." "The great rage . . . is kill'd in him," says the doctor. But Cordelia's words turn a dead place into a garden where they can sit, "God's spies," and wait for what we all wait for, the death that we cannot keep back.

Only the silence and emptiness following a moment of forgiveness can stop the monster of deadly anger, the grotesque creature fed and fattened on innocent blood (and what blood is not, in itself, innocent?). The end of anger requires a darkness, the living darkness at the center of the "nothing" that Lear learns about, the black of Mark Rothko's last panels, a black that contains in itself, invisible, the germs from which life can reknit itself and spring. Its music is the silence beyond even justice, the peace that passes understanding, rare in a lifetime or an age, always a miracle past our deserving, greater than our words.

QUESTIONS FOR ANALYSIS AND DISCUSSION

1. Gordon suggests that anger is the only vice that could have the adjective "just" in front of it. Consider the list of vices described by Jordan-Smith in Chapter 3. Do you think other vices could, under the right conditions, be considered just? Explain your answer.

2. Many moral thinkers are worried about pain and pleasure because each has the capacity to transform the self. Do you agree with Gordon's contention that anger is unique in its transforming powers?

3. The experience of anger is often affected by understanding its cause. Somehow, our suffering is lessened when we have a better sense of its source. A fatal plane crash brings great sorrow to the friends and relatives of the victims. Sometimes anger comes along with the sorrow, particularly when no one can explain what went wrong. Yet senseless acts of terror, such as the Oklahoma City bombing, generate much greater anger among the victims' friends and families. How does Gordon's essay help us understand these different responses to sorrow? Do you think Aquinas or Auden offer a different understanding? Support your response with specific passages.

4. Is Gordon's call for silence and mercy practical? Are these responses morally valuable? Clarify your position on the moral status of anger in light of her conclusion using your own examples.

35.

JACK GREENBERG

Against the American System
of Capital Punishment

If anger is irrational and wild, how is it that anger is often carefully directed? One argument for society's right to punish is that it alleviates individuals of the uneasy burden of seeking proportionate punishment on their own. In ongoing controversies about capital punishment, almost no one denies that some crimes are so heinous that only execution can be a fitting penalty. According to law professor Jack Greenberg (b. 1924), however, society's rage at the criminal is infrequently strictly a matter of vengeance. Statistics show that a disproportionate number of black males are either on death row or have been executed. In Greenberg's view this is clear evidence that capital punishment is not about vengeance per se but rather is an expression of unjust vengeance.

"Against the American System of Capital Punishment," *Harvard Law Review* 99 (1986): 1670–1680. Some notes have been omitted.

CRITICAL READING QUESTIONS

1. Why does Greenberg see the case of John Spenkelink as symptomatic of the weaknesses of capital punishment in America?
2. What is the difference between deterrence and retribution?
3. Which appeal does Greenberg favor in his argument: the rights of the criminal, the compassion of religious believers, or the decency of American civilization?
4. Why does Greenberg think the deterrence factor has little influence in preventing premeditated murders?

Over and over, proponents of the death penalty insist that it is right and useful. In reply, abolitionists argue that it is morally flawed and cite studies to demonstrate its failure to deter. Were the subject not so grim and compelling, the exchanges would, by now, be tiresome.

Yet all too frequently, the debate has been off the mark. Death penalty proponents have assumed a system of capital punishment that simply does not exist: a system in which the penalty is inflicted on the most reprehensible criminals and meted out frequently enough both to deter and to perform the moral and utilitarian functions ascribed to retribution. Explicitly or implicitly, they assume a system in which certainly the worst criminals, Charles Manson or a putative killer of one's parent or child, for example, are executed in an evenhanded manner. But this idealized system is *not* the American system of capital punishment. Because of the goals that our criminal justice system must satisfy—deterring crime, punishing the guilty, acquitting the innocent, avoiding needless cruelty, treating citizens equally, and prohibiting oppression by the state—America simply does not have the kind of capital punishment system contemplated by death penalty partisans.

Indeed, the reality of American capital punishment is quite to the contrary. Since at least 1967, the death penalty has been inflicted only rarely, erratically, and often upon the least odious killers, while many of the most heinous criminals have escaped execution. Moreover, it has been employed almost exclusively in a few formerly slave-holding states, and there it has been used almost exclusively against killers of whites, not blacks, and never against white killers of blacks. This is the American system of capital punishment. It is this system, not some idealized one, that must be defended in any national debate on the death penalty. I submit that this system is deeply incompatible with the proclaimed objectives of death penalty proponents.

I. The American System of Capital Punishment

Here is how America's system of capital punishment really works today. Since 1967, the year in which the courts first began to grapple in earnest with death penalty issues, the death penalty has been frequently imposed but rarely enforced.

Between 1967 and 1980, death sentences or convictions were reversed for 1899 of the 2402 people on death row, a reversal rate of nearly eighty percent. These reversals reflected, among other factors, a 1968 Supreme Court decision dealing with how juries should be chosen in capital cases, a 1972 decision declaring capital sentences unconstitutional partly because they were imposed arbitrarily and "freakishly," and a 1976 decision holding mandatory death sentences unconstitutional. Many death sentences were also invalidated on a wide variety of commonplace state-law grounds, such as hearsay rule violations or improper prosecutorial argument.

This judicial tendency to invalidate death penalties proved resistant to change. After 1972, in response to Supreme Court decisions, many states adopted new death penalty laws, and judges developed a clearer idea of the requirements that the Court had begun to enunciate a few years earlier. By 1979, the efforts of state legislatures finally paid off when John Spenkelink became the first person involuntarily[1] executed since 1967. Nevertheless, from 1972 to 1980, the death penalty invalidation rate declined to "only" sixty percent. In contrast, ordinary noncapital convictions and sentences were almost invariably upheld.

Today, the death row population has grown to more than 1600 convicts. About 300 prisoners per year join this group, while about 100 per year leave death row, mainly by reason of judicial invalidations but also by execution and by death from other causes. Following Spenkelink's execution, some states began to put some of these convicted murderers to death. Five persons were executed involuntarily in 1983, twenty-one in 1984, and fourteen in 1985. Nevertheless, the number of actual executions seems to have reached a plateau. The average number of executions in the United States hovers at about twenty per year; as of March 1, only one person has been executed in 1986. Yet even if this number doubled, or increased fivefold, executions would not be numerous either in proportion to the nation's homicides (approximately 19,000 per year) or to its death row population (over 1600).

One reason for the small number of executions is that the courts continue to upset capital convictions at an extraordinarily high rate, albeit not so high as earlier. Between January 1, 1982 and October 1, 1985, state supreme courts invalidated thirty-five percent of all capital judgments. State post-appellate process undid a few more. The federal district and appeals courts overturned another ten percent, and last Term the Supreme Court reversed three of the four capital sentences it reviewed. Altogether, about forty-five percent of capital judgments which were reviewed during this period were set aside by one court or another. One index of the vitality of litigation to reverse executions is that while legal attacks on capital punishment began as a coordinated effort by civil rights lawyers, they now come from a variety of segments of the bar.

States not only execute convicted killers rarely, but they do so erratically. Spenkelink's execution, the nation's first involuntary execution since 1967, did not

---

[1] I call an execution "involuntary" if the defendant has contested actual implementation of the death penalty. Conversely, a "voluntary" execution is one in which the defendant at some point has voluntarily ceased efforts to resist.

augur well for new systems of guided discretion designed to produce evenhanded capital justice in which only the worst murderers would be executed. Spenkelink was a drifter who killed a traveling companion who had sexually abused him. The Assistant Attorney General of Florida in charge of capital cases described him as "probably the least obnoxious individual on death row in terms of the crime he committed."

The current round of invalidations highlights the erratic imposition of the death penalty. These invalidations have been based largely on grounds unrelated to the heinousness of the crime or the reprehensibility of the criminal. Thus, the most abhorrent perpetrators of the most execrable crimes have escaped the penalty on grounds wholly unrelated to moral desert—for example, because defense counsel, the prosecutor, or the judge acted ineffectively or improperly on some matter of evidence. By contrast, criminals far less detestable by any rational moral standard—like Spenkelink, "the least obnoxious individual on death row"—have gone to their deaths because their trials "went well." Of course, when errors occur in securing a death penalty, the sentence should be invalidated, particularly because "there is a significant constitutional difference between the death penalty and lesser punishments." The corollary of this imperative is that the current system of capital punishment violates a central tenet of capital justice—that the most reprehensible criminals deserve execution and others deserve lesser sentences.

It is troubling as well that the current level of executions has been attained only by using expedited procedures that undermine confidence in the fairness of the death penalty process. Recent executions have occurred during a period in which some federal judges, frustrated with the slow pace of capital justice, have taken extraordinary measures to expedite capital cases in federal courts. For example, the Fifth Circuit has quickened habeas corpus appeals in capital cases by accelerating the dates of arguments and greatly compressing the time for briefing cases. Increasingly, the Supreme Court has encouraged this hurry-up justice. The Court has not only denied stay applications, but it has also vacated stays entered by lower courts in cases in which stays would have been routine in earlier times. In sum, the recent invalidation rate seems unlikely to change significantly, thereby perpetuating the current system of erratic and haphazard executions.

Of course, one major difference exists between the period 1982 to 1985 and earlier years: increasingly, the death penalty has been concentrated geographically, not applied evenly across the United States. In the most recent period, there were forty-three involuntary executions. Quite strikingly, all occurred in the states of the Old Confederacy. Thirty-four of the forty-three were in four states, and more than a quarter were in a single state, Florida, with thirteen. In all but four cases, the defendants killed white persons. In no case was a white executed for killing a black person.

Why are there so few executions? Convictions and sentences are reversed, cases move slowly, and states devote relatively meager resources to pursuing *actual* executions. Even Florida, which above all other states has shown that it can execute almost any death row inmate it wants to, has killed only 13 of 221 inmates since 1979, 12 since 1982. (It now has 233 convicts on death row.) Outside the former slave-holding states, more than half the states are now abolitionist either de jure (fourteen states) or de facto (five states have no one on death row). Moreover, past experience suggests that the execution level will not go very high. Before the 1967–76 moratorium the number of executions exceeded fifty only once after 1957—fifty-six in 1960. At that time there were fewer abolitionist states and more capital crimes. This experience suggests that executions will not deplete the death row population.

The limited number of actual executions seems to me to reflect the very deep ambivalence that Americans feel about capital punishment. We are the only nation of the Western democratic world that has not abolished capital punishment. By contrast, countries with whose dominant value systems we ordinarily disagree, like the Soviet Union, China, Iran, and South Africa, execute prisoners in great numbers.

II. The Failures of Capital Punishment

We have a system of capital punishment that results in infrequent, random, and erratic executions, one that is structured to inflict death neither on those who have committed the worst offenses nor on defendants of the worst character. This is the "system"—if that is the right descriptive term—of capital punishment that must be defended by death penalty proponents. *This* system may not be justified by positing a particularly egregious killer like Charles Manson. Our commitment to the rule of law means that we need an acceptable *general* system of capital justice if we are to have one at all. However, the real American system of capital punishment clearly fails when measured against the most common justifications for the infliction of punishment, deterrence, and retribution.

If capital punishment can be a deterrent greater than life imprisonment at all, the American system is at best a feeble one. Studies by Thorsten Sellin showed no demonstrable deterrent effect of capital punishment even during its heyday. Today's death penalty, which is far less frequently used, geographically localized, and biased according to the race of the victim, cannot possibly upset that conclusion. The forty-three persons who were involuntarily executed from 1982 to 1985 were among a death row population of more than 1600 condemned to execution out of about 20,000 who committed nonnegligent homicides per year. While forty-three percent of the victims were black, the death penalty is so administered that it overwhelmingly condemns and executes those who have killed whites.

Very little reason exists to believe that the present capital punishment system deters the conduct of others any more effectively than life imprisonment.[2] Potential

---

[2] In the sense of specific deterrence or incapacitation, of course, the forty-three who were put to death indeed have been deterred. But those serving life sentences or terms of years, of course, occasionally kill. That fact would not be accepted as grounds for having sentenced them to death in lieu of the original prison term. Recidivism by convicted murderers and killings by prisoners generally are discussed in Bedau, *Recidivism, Parole, and Deterrence*, in THE DEATH PENALTY IN AMERICA, *supra* note 31, at 173, and Wolfson, *The Deterrent Effect of the Death Penalty Upon Prison Murder*, in THE DEATH PENALTY IN AMERICA, *supra* note 31, at 159, respectively. Wolfson concludes: "Given that the deterrent effect of the death penalty for prison homicide is to be seriously doubted, it is clear that management and physical changes in the prison would do more than any legislated legal sanction to reduce the number of prison murders." *Id.* at 172.

killers who rationally weigh the odds of being killed themselves must conclude that the danger is nonexistent in most parts of the country and that in the South the danger is slight, particularly if the proposed victim is black. Moreover, the paradigm of this kind of murderer, the contract killer, is almost by definition a person who takes his chances like the soldier of fortune he is.[3]

But most killers do not engage in anything like a cost-benefit analysis. They are impulsive, and they kill impulsively. If capital punishment is to deter them, it can do so only indirectly: by impressing on potential killers a standard of right and wrong, a moral authority, an influence on their superegos that, notwithstanding mental disorder, would inhibit homicide. This conception of general deterrence seems deeply flawed because it rests upon a quite implausible conception of how this killer population internalizes social norms. Although not mentally disturbed enough to sustain insanity as a defense, they are often highly disturbed, of low intelligence, and addicted to drugs or alcohol. In any event, the message, if any, that the real American system of capital punishment sends to the psyches of would-be killers is quite limited: you may in a rare case be executed if you murder in the deepest South and kill a white person.[4]

The consequences of the real American system of capital justice are no more favorable as far as retribution is concerned. Retributive theories of criminal punishment draw support from several different moral theories that cannot be adequately elaborated here. While some of the grounds of retribution arguments resemble the conscience-building argument underlying general deterrence theory,[5] all retribution theories insist that seeking retribution constitutes a morally permissible use of governmental power. To retribution theorists, the death penalty makes a moral point: it holds up as an example worthy of the most severe condemnation one who has committed the most opprobrious crime.

As with many controversies over moral issues, these purely moral arguments may appear to end any real possibility for further discussion. For those who believe

---

[3] It might be argued that even the rare execution is dramatic and unduly publicized and consequently has great effect. Ironically, the slight increase in the number of executions in the past few years has robbed them of much dramatic effect.

[4] As to an asserted salutary influence on the healthy mind, tending to cause it to shun lethal violence, one can only respond that no evidence has been offered. Religious, social, moral, and noncapital legal requirements all teach us not to murder. If the death penalty were needed as an incremental influence to persuade noncriminals to abjure killing, there would be elevated murder rates in abolitionist states and nations; these have not been demonstrated.

[5] The reply to this argument is the same as to the arguments that the death penalty deters by teaching not to kill. Retribution is also said to have another utilitarian by-product distinct from a Kantian eye-for-an-eye justification: it satisfies demands for vengeance, preventing retaliatory killing. Yet, during the period of no executions (1967–1977) and in the overwhelming number of states that have abolished the death penalty, have not sentenced anyone to death, or have not carried out executions, it is difficult to find an instance of vengeance killing, although during this time there have been perhaps 360,000 murders (about 20,000 per year for 18 years).

It is also argued that, particularly for those who have been close to the victim, who are members of his or her family, or who are fellow police officers, or for those members of the public who somehow feel an identification with the deceased, the death penalty provides personal satisfaction, repaying in some measure the loss they felt in the death of the victim. This hardly justifies the present system.

in them, they persuade, just as the moral counter-arguments persuade abolitionists. But discussion should not end at this point. Those who claim a moral justification for capital punishment must reconcile that belief with other moral considerations. To my mind, the moral force of any retribution argument is radically undercut by the hard facts of the actual American system of capital punishment. This system violates fundamental norms because it is haphazard, and because it is regionally and racially biased. To these moral flaws, I would add another: the minuscule number of executions nowadays cannot achieve the grand moral aims that are presupposed by a serious societal commitment to retribution.

Some retribution proponents argue that it is the pronouncement of several hundred death sentences followed by lengthy life imprisonment, not the actual imposition of a few executions, that satisfies the public's demand for retribution. Of course, the public has not said that it wants the death penalty as it exists—widely applicable but infrequently used. Nor, to the best of my knowledge, is there any solid empirical basis for such a claim. Like other statutes, death penalty laws are of general applicability, to be employed according to their terms. Nothing in their language or legislative history authorizes the erratic, occasional, racially biased use of these laws. But my objections to this argument go much deeper. I find morally objectionable a system of many pronounced death sentences but few actual executions, a system in which race and region are the only significant variables in determining who actually dies. My objection is not grounded in a theory that posits any special moral rights for the death row population. The decisive point is my understanding of the basic moral aspirations of American civilization, particularly its deep commitment to the rule of law. I cannot reconcile an erratic, racially and regionally biased system of executions with my understanding of the core values of our legal order.

Death penalty proponents may respond to this argument by saying that if there is not enough capital punishment, there should be more. If only killers of whites are being executed, then killers of blacks should be killed too; and if many sentences are being reversed, standards of review should be relaxed. In the meantime, they might urge, the death penalty should go on. But this argument is unavailing, because it seeks to change the terms of the debate in a fundamental way. It seeks to substitute an imaginary system for the real American system of capital punishment. If there were a different kind of system of death penalty administration in this country, or even a reasonable possibility that one might emerge, we could debate its implications. But any current debate over the death penalty cannot ignore the deep moral deficiencies of the present system.

III. The Constitution and the Death Penalty

This debate about whether we should have a death penalty is a matter on which the Supreme Court is unlikely to have the last say now or in the near future. Yet, the Court's decisions have some relevance. The grounds that the Court has employed in striking down various forms of the death penalty resemble the arguments

I have made. Freakishness was a ground for invalidating the death penalty as it was administered throughout the country in 1972. Rarity of use contributed to invalidation of the death penalty for rape and felony murder, and to invalidation of the mandatory death penalty. That constitutional law reflects moral concerns should not be strange: concepts of cruel and unusual punishment, due process, and equal protection express contemporary standards of decency.

Moreover, the whole development of the fourteenth amendment points to the existence of certain basic standards of decency and fairness from which no state or region can claim exemption. One such value is, of course, the racially neutral administration of justice. No one disputes that one of the fourteenth amendment's central designs was to secure the evenhanded administration of justice in the southern state courts and that the persistent failure to achieve that goal has been one of America's greatest tragedies. We cannot be blind to the fact that actual executions have taken place primarily in the South and in at least a racially suspect manner. In light of our constitutional history, the race-specific aspects of the death penalty in the South are profoundly unsettling.

Given the situation as I have described it, and as I believe it will continue so long as we have capital punishment, one could argue that the death penalty should be declared unconstitutional in all its forms. But the Court is unlikely to take that step soon. Only ten years have passed since the type of death statute now in use was upheld, and some states have had such laws for an even shorter period. Thirty-seven states have passed laws showing they want some sort of death penalty. Public opinion polls show that most Americans want capital punishment in some form. Having only recently invalidated one application of the death penalty in *Furman v. Georgia* in 1972, the Court is unlikely soon to deal with the concept wholesale again. But, if the way capital punishment works does not change materially, I think that at some point the Court will declare the overall system to be cruel and unusual. If this prediction is correct—and it is at least arguably so—an additional moral factor enters the debate. Is it right to kill death row inmates during this period of experimentation? There is, of course, an element of bootstrapping to my argument: exercising further restraint in killing death-sentenced convicts reinforces arguments of freakishness and rarity of application. But unless one can assure a full and steady stream of executions, sufficient to do the jobs the death penalty proponents claim that it can do, there is further reason to kill no one at all.

QUESTIONS FOR ANALYSIS AND DISCUSSION

1. Greenberg focuses on the uneven distribution of capital punishment as a sign of its immorality. Do you think Greenberg would agree that an even distribution of capital punishment is morally acceptable? Why, or why not?

2. When you drive fast, you know there is a chance of getting caught, but that does not deter you from pushing the pedal harder. However, since the emergence of Mothers Against Drunk Driving (MADD) as a national organization, many people have altered their driving habits. The penalties for driving under

the influence have been tightly enforced, and many people do not want to risk a heavy fine or having their license suspended. This seems to be a case where the likelihood of stiff punishment changed our behavior. Yet Greenberg insists that the threat of execution does not act as a deterrent on the potential murderer. Is murder a special sort of exception in deterrence logic, or is Greenberg incorrect in his description of the rational murderer?

3. In his review of the contrasting opinions on capital punishment, Greenberg cites both changes in public opinion and Supreme Court decisions. Do you think the Supreme Court should decide on the rightness of capital punishment based on popular opinion, the meaning of the Constitution, or its own ideas of morality? How do you think Greenberg would answer this question?

4. Recently, a white woman was executed in Texas for her part in the brutal slaying of a teenager. She was the first woman to be executed in Texas in over one hundred years. Does this fact weaken or strengthen Greenberg's case about the inconsistent application of the death penalty?

36.

ERNEST VAN DEN HAAG

The Ultimate Punishment: A Defense

One of the four essential virtues in ancient Greek culture was justice. (Courage, temperance, and prudence are generally considered the other three.) In the view of Ernest van den Haag (b. 1914), a professor of jurisprudence and public policy at Fordham University, capital punishment is primarily about justice. Although he takes seriously the argument that disproportionate distribution of the death penalty warrants careful review, he does not take this to mean that the death penalty itself is immoral. Other objections to capital punishment are also addressed by van den Haag. He pays special attention to those who contend that the death penalty is not an effective deterrent, or that it prevents the opportunity to correct a mistaken judgment of guilt, or that it tarnishes the civil decency of a country.

"The Ultimate Punishment: A Defense," *Harvard Law Review* 99 (1986): 1662–1669. Some notes have been omitted.

┤ **CRITICAL READING QUESTIONS** ├

1. What is van den Haag's response to the moral and factual arguments about the discriminatory aspects of capital punishment?
2. Does van den Haag agree that evidence supports the deterrence theory?
3. Which of the following is the basic reason for punishment: to compensate victims for their losses, to vindicate the law and protect the social order, to teach offenders responsibility, or to satisfy the passions of vengeance in a civilized fashion?
4. Toward the end of his essay van den Haag discusses the degradation of punishment. What is meant by degradation? In the death penalty debate, who are the candidates for degradation?

In an average year about 20,000 homicides occur in the United States. Fewer than 300 convicted murderers are sentenced to death. But because no more than thirty murderers have been executed in any recent year, most convicts sentenced to death are likely to die of old age. Nonetheless, the death penalty looms large in discussions: it raises important moral questions independent of the number of executions.

The death penalty is our harshest punishment. It is irrevocable: it ends the existence of those punished, instead of temporarily imprisoning them. Further, although not intended to cause physical pain, execution is the only corporal punishment still applied to adults. These singular characteristics contribute to the perennial, impassioned controversy about capital punishment.

I. Distribution

Consideration of the justice, morality, or usefulness, of capital punishment is often conflated with objections to its alleged discriminatory or capricious distribution among the guilty. Wrongly so. If capital punishment is immoral *in se,* no distribution among the guilty could make it moral. If capital punishment is moral, no distribution would make it immoral. Improper distribution cannot affect the quality of what is distributed, be it punishments or rewards. Discriminatory or capricious distribution thus could not justify abolition of the death penalty. Further, maldistribution inheres no more in capital punishment than in any other punishment.

Maldistribution between the guilty and the innocent is, by definition, unjust. But the injustice does not lie in the nature of the punishment. Because of the finality of the death penalty, the most grievous maldistribution occurs when it is imposed upon the innocent. However, the frequent allegations of discrimination and capriciousness refer to maldistribution among the guilty and not to the punishment of the innocent.

Maldistribution of any punishment among those who deserve it is irrelevant to its justice or morality. Even if poor or black convicts guilty of capital offenses suffer capital punishment, and other convicts equally guilty of the same crimes do not, a more equal distribution, however desirable, would merely be more equal. It would not be more just to the convicts under sentence of death.

Punishments are imposed on persons, not on racial or economic groups. Guilt is personal. The only relevant question is: does the person to be executed deserve the punishment? Whether or not others who deserved the same punishment, whatever their economic or racial group, have avoided execution is irrelevant. If they have, the guilt of the executed convicts would not be diminished, nor would their punishment be less deserved. To put the issue starkly, if the death penalty were imposed on guilty blacks, but not on guilty whites, or, if it were imposed by a lottery among the guilty, this irrationally discriminatory or capricious distribution would neither make the penalty unjust, nor cause anyone to be unjustly punished, despite the undue impunity bestowed on others.

Equality, in short, seems morally less important than justice. And justice is independent of distributional inequalities. The idea of equal justice demands that justice be equally distributed, not that it be replaced by equality. Justice requires that as many of the guilty as possible be punished, regardless of whether others have avoided punishment. To let these others escape the deserved punishment does not do justice to them, or to society. But it is not unjust to those who could not escape.

These moral considerations are not meant to deny that irrational discrimination, or capriciousness, would be inconsistent with constitutional requirements. But I am satisfied that the Supreme Court has in fact provided for adherence to the constitutional requirement of equality as much as is possible. Some inequality is indeed unavoidable as a practical matter in any system. But, *ultra posse nemo obligatur*. (Nobody is bound beyond ability.)

Recent data reveal little direct racial discrimination in the sentencing of those arrested and convicted of murder. The abrogation of the death penalty for rape has eliminated a major source of racial discrimination. Concededly, some discrimination based on the race of murder victims may exist; yet, this discrimination affects criminal victimizers in an unexpected way. Murderers of whites are thought more likely to be executed than murderers of blacks. Black victims, then, are less fully vindicated than white ones. However, because most black murderers kill blacks, black murderers are spared the death penalty more often than are white murderers. They fare better than most white murderers. The motivation behind unequal distribution of the death penalty may well have been to discriminate against blacks, but the result has favored them. Maldistribution is thus a straw man for empirical as well as analytical reasons.

II. Miscarriages of Justice

In a recent survey Professors Hugo Adam Bedau and Michael Radelet found that 7000 persons were executed in the United States between 1900 and 1985 and that 25 were innocent of capital crimes. Among the innocents they list Sacco and Vanzetti as well as Ethel and Julius Rosenberg. Although their data may be questionable, I do not doubt that, over a long enough period, miscarriages of justice will occur even in capital cases.

Despite precautions, nearly all human activities, such as trucking, lighting, or construction, cost the lives of some innocent bystanders. We do not give up these activities, because the advantages, moral or material, outweigh the unintended losses. Analogously, for those who think the death penalty just, miscarriages of justice are offset by the moral benefits and the usefulness of doing justice. For those who think the death penalty unjust even when it does not miscarry, miscarriages can hardly be decisive.

III. Deterrence

Despite much recent work, there has been no conclusive statistical demonstration that the death penalty is a better deterrent than are alternative punishments. However, deterrence is less than decisive for either side. Most abolitionists acknowledge that they would continue to favor abolition even if the death penalty were shown to deter more murders than alternatives could deter. Abolitionists appear to value the life of a convicted murderer or, at least, his non-execution, more highly than they value the lives of the innocent victims who might be spared by deterring prospective murderers.

Deterrence is not altogether decisive for me either. I would favor retention of the death penalty as retribution even if it were shown that the threat of execution could not deter prospective murderers not already deterred by the threat of imprisonment. Still, I believe the death penalty, because of its finality, is more feared than imprisonment, and deters some prospective murderers not deterred by the threat of imprisonment. Sparing the lives of even a few prospective victims by deterring their murderers is more important than preserving the lives of convicted murderers because of the possibility, or even the probability, that executing them would not deter others. Whereas the lives of the victims who might be saved are valuable, that of the murderer has only negative value, because of his crime. Surely the criminal law is meant to protect the lives of potential victims in preference to those of actual murderers.

Murder rates are determined by many factors; neither the severity nor the probability of the threatened sanction is always decisive. However, for the long run, I share the view of Sir James Fitzjames Stephen: "Some men, probably, abstain from murder because they fear that if they committed murder they would be hanged. Hundreds of thousands abstain from it because they regard it with horror. One great reason why they regard it with horror is that murderers are hanged." Penal sanctions are useful in the long run for the formation of the internal restraints so necessary to control crime. The severity and finality of the death penalty is appropriate to the seriousness and the finality of murder.

IV. Incidental Issues: Cost, Relative Suffering, Brutalization

Many nondecisive issues are associated with capital punishment. Some believe that the monetary cost of appealing a capital sentence is excessive. Yet most comparisons of the cost of life imprisonment with the cost of execution, apart from their dubious relevance, are flawed at least by the implied assumption that life prisoners will generate no judicial costs during their imprisonment. At any rate, the actual monetary costs are trumped by the importance of doing justice.

Others insist that a person sentenced to death suffers more than his victim suffered, and that this (excess) suffering is undue according to the *lex talionis* (rule of retaliation). We cannot know whether the murderer on death row suffers more than his victim suffered; however, unlike the murderer, the victim deserved none of the suffering inflicted. Further, the limitations of the *lex talionis* were meant to restrain private vengeance, not the social retribution that has taken its place. Punishment—regardless of the motivation—is not intended to revenge, offset, or compensate for the victim's suffering, or to be measured by it. Punishment is to vindicate the law and the social order undermined by the crime. This is why a kidnapper's penal confinement is not limited to the period for which he imprisoned his victim; nor is a burglar's confinement meant merely to offset the suffering or the harm he caused his victim; nor is it meant only to offset the advantage he gained.

Another argument heard at least since Beccaria is that, by killing a murderer, we encourage, endorse, or legitimize unlawful killing. Yet, although all punishments are meant to be unpleasant, it is seldom argued that they legitimize the unlawful imposition of identical unpleasantness. Imprisonment is not thought to legitimize kidnaping; neither are fines thought to legitimize robbery. The difference between murder and execution, or between kidnapping and imprisonment, is that the first is unlawful and undeserved, the second a lawful and deserved punishment for an unlawful act. The physical similarities of the punishment to the crime are irrelevant. The relevant difference is not physical, but social.[1]

V. Justice, Excess, Degradation

We threaten punishments in order to deter crime. We impose them not only to make the threats credible but also as retribution (justice) for the crimes that were not deterred. Threats and punishments are necessary to deter and deterrence is a sufficient practical justification for them. Retribution is an independent moral jus-

---

[1] Some abolitionists challenge: if the death penalty is just and serves as a deterrent, why not televise executions? The answer is simple. The death even of a murderer, however well-deserved, should not serve as public entertainment. It so served in earlier centuries. But in this respect our sensibility has changed for the better, I believe. Further, television unavoidably would trivialize executions, wedged in, as they would be, between game shows, situation comedies and the like. Finally, because televised executions would focus on the physical aspects of the punishment, rather than the nature of the crime and the suffering of the victim, a televised execution would present the murderer as the victim of the state. Far from communicating the moral significance of the execution, television would shift the focus to the pitiable fear of the murderer. We no longer place in cages those sentenced to imprisonment to expose them to public view. Why should we so expose those sentenced to execution?

tification. Although penalties can be unwise, repulsive, or inappropriate, and those punished can be pitiable, in a sense the infliction of legal punishment on a guilty person cannot be unjust. By committing the crime, the criminal volunteered to assume the risk of receiving a legal punishment that he could have avoided by not committing the crime. The punishment he suffers is the punishment he voluntarily risked suffering and, therefore, it is no more unjust to him than any other event for which one knowingly volunteers to assume the risk. Thus, the death penalty cannot be unjust to the guilty criminal.

There remain, however, two moral objections. The penalty may be regarded as always excessive as retribution and always morally degrading. To regard the death penalty as always excessive, one must believe that no crime—no matter how heinous—could possibly justify capital punishment. Such a belief can be neither corroborated nor refuted; it is an article of faith.

Alternatively, or concurrently, one may believe that everybody, the murderer no less than the victim, has an imprescriptible (natural?) right to life. The law therefore should not deprive anyone of life. I share Jeremy Bentham's view that any such "natural and imprescriptible rights" are "nonsense upon stilts."

Justice Brennan has insisted that the death penalty is "uncivilized," "inhuman," inconsistent with "human dignity" and with "the sanctity of life," that it "treats members of the human race as nonhumans, as objects to be toyed with and discarded," that it is "uniquely degrading to human dignity" and "by its very nature, [involves] a denial of the executed person's humanity." Justice Brennan does not say why he thinks execution "uncivilized." Hitherto most civilizations have had the death penalty, although it has been discarded in Western Europe, where it is currently unfashionable probably because of its abuse by totalitarian regimes.

By "degrading," Justice Brennan seems to mean that execution degrades the executed convicts. Yet philosophers, such as Immanuel Kant and G. F. W. Hegel, have insisted that, when deserved, execution, far from degrading the executed convict, affirms his humanity by affirming his rationality and his responsibility for his actions. They thought that execution, when deserved, is required for the sake of the convict's dignity. (Does not life imprisonment violate human dignity more than execution, by keeping alive a prisoner deprived of all autonomy?)

Common sense indicates that it cannot be death—our common fate—that is inhuman. Therefore, Justice Brennan must mean that death degrades when it comes not as a natural or accidental event, but as a deliberate social imposition. The murderer learns through his punishment that his fellow men have found him unworthy of living; that because he has murdered, he is being expelled from the community of the living. This degradation is self-inflicted. By murdering, the murderer has so dehumanized himself that he cannot remain among the living. The social recognition of his self-degradation is the punitive essence of execution. To believe, as Justice Brennan appears to, that the degradation is inflicted by the execution reverses the direction of causality.

Execution of those who have committed heinous murders may deter only one murder per year. If it does, it seems quite warranted. It is also the only fitting retribution for murder I can think of.

QUESTIONS FOR ANALYSIS AND DISCUSSION

1. Van den Haag treats capital punishment as an extension of other punishments society has a right to inflict. Do you agree that there is no qualitative distinction between the death penalty and other penalties?

2. Critics of the death penalty remind us that at least one qualitative difference — executing an innocent person — cannot be undone. Van den Haag's rejoinder notes that mistakes in nearly all human activities sadly involve the loss of innocent life. Constructing new buildings, increasing speed limits, and engaging in thrilling adventures also invariably lead to death in some instances, but that does not mean we should outlaw these activities. Do you think van den Haag's defense of this issue is adequate?

3. Van den Haag disputes the evidence supporting the discriminatory application of the death penalty. According to Coppin State College social theorist and criminologist Richard C. Monk, the facts about capital punishment are rarely treated with the objectivity one expects of scholarly disputants. "Each side ritualistically marshals empirical evidence to support their respective position," he wryly observes. In light of Monk's point, are the arguments about capital punishment ultimately about the passion of anger, hate, or vengeance?

37.

SENECA

On Clemency

How can we overcome the destructive tendencies of human vice? For Seneca (2 B.C.–A.D. 65), one of the best known Stoic philosophers, the virtue of clemency (or mercy) offers the surest antidote to the cruelty and carnage that highlighted exercises of vengeance in his own time. In this selection Seneca addresses the Roman emperor Nero, widely known for his tyrannical barbarisms. Seneca implores the leader to consider the social and moral value of clemency in light of the power of cruelty to corrupt everyday life. Deeds of savagery are not limited to occasional and festive public punishments; rather they pervade the lives of all citizens. Everyone fears that even minor offenses may be

"On Clemency," from *The Stoic Philosophy of Seneca*, translated and edited by Moses Hadas (Garden City, NY: Doubleday, 1958), pp. 140–147, 162–165.

subject to torture or execution. Incidentally, Seneca eventually had a large political influence as consul. However, under suspicion of conspiring against the emperor, Seneca was forced to commit suicide.

┤ **CRITICAL READING QUESTIONS** ├

1. Why does Seneca think a leader has the greatest responsibility to embrace clemency?
2. What is Seneca's point in making the analogy that the gods treat a leader as the leader treats the people?
3. How does virtue fit the argument that the populace is like the body to the soul of the leader?
4. Does Seneca believe cruelty is a natural attribute of humans?

---

[2] I know there are some who hold that clemency is a prop for villains, since it has room only after crime and is the sole virtue which has no function among innocent men. But first of all, just as medicine functions among the diseased but is esteemed among the sound, so do the innocent, too, respect clemency, though only punishable culprits invoke it. Secondly, this virtue has scope even in the case of the guiltless because misfortune is sometimes a substitute for guilt. And it is not innocence alone that clemency succors but also virtue, for our circumstances give rise to cases where praiseworthy actions are liable to punishment. Furthermore, a large portion of mankind might be restored to innocence if punishment is remitted. Still, pardon should not be general, for if the distinction between bad men and good is abolished, chaos will follow and an eruption of vice. We must therefore apply a moderation capable of distinguishing the curable from the hopeless. The clemency we practice should neither be promiscuous and general nor yet exclusive; to pardon everyone is as cruel as to pardon none. We must keep measure, but since it is difficult to maintain the exact proportion, any departure from the balance should weigh on the kindlier scale.

[3] But it will be better to speak of these things in their proper place. Now I shall divide the material as a whole into three sections. The first will deal with remissions. The second will exhibit the nature and disposition of clemency, for since there are vices which resemble virtues they cannot be separated unless you take good note of the signs by which they can be distinguished. In the third place we shall ask how the mind is introduced to this virtue, how it gives it validity and by habit assimilates it.

That none of the other virtues is more becoming to a human, none being more humane, must be accepted as axiomatic not only by us (Stoics) who hold that man is a social animal born for the common good, but also by those (Epicureans) who subordinate man to pleasure and all of whose words and deeds aim at personal advantage. If quiet and repose is what the Epicurean seeks, he finds this virtue, which loves peace and eschews violence, suited to his constitution. But of all men clemency is most becoming to a king or prince. Mighty strength is comely and glorious only if its power is beneficent; it is a pestilential force which is powerful only for mischief. A ruler's greatness is stable and secure when all men know that he is *for* them as much as *above* them, when experience shows them his vigilant and unremitting solicitude for the welfare of one and all, at whose approach they do not disperse as though some malignant and noxious beast had sprung from its lair but vie in flocking forward as to a shining and beneficent planet. For him they are perfectly ready to fling themselves upon the daggers of assassins and to pave his way with their bodies if human carriage is his path to safety, his sleep they protect with night-long vigils, his person they defend by interposing their bodies round about him, and they expose themselves to dangers that assail him.

The accepted practice of peoples and cities of rendering their kings such protection and such affection, of sacrificing their persons and property whenever the safety of their ruler requires it, is not unreasonable; nor do men hold themselves cheap or suffer madness when many thousands accept wounds and ransom a single life, not infrequently the life of a sick old man, by many deaths. The whole body's service to the soul is analogous. The body is much bigger and showier, while the soul is impalpable and is hidden we know not where, yet hands, feet, and eyes do its business and the skin furnishes it protection; at its bidding we lie still or scurry restlessly about; when it gives command we scour the sea for gain, if it is an avaricious master, or if it is ambitious we unhesitatingly thrust our right arm into the flame or willingly plunge into the pit. Similarly, this enormous populace which is the shell for the soul of one man is regulated by his spirit and guided by his reason; if it were not propped by his intelligence it would bruise itself by its own strength and crumble to fragments.

[4] It is their own safety they are in love with, therefore, when men marshal ten legions in a single battle line for one man, when they charge to the fore and expose their breasts to wounds to keep their general's standard from turning tail. He is the link which holds the commonwealth together, he is the breath of life which the many thousands draw; by themselves, if the intelligence of the empire were withdrawn, they would be only a burden and a prey.

> Their king safe, single-minded are all [the bees];
> Their king lost, they shatter fealty.
> (Vergil, *Georgics* 4.212)

The end of the Roman peace would bring such a disaster, it would ruin the prosperity of so mighty a people. But this people will be far from such danger so long as it will understand submission to the reins; for if ever it severs them or does not suffer them to be replaced if some accident shakes them off, then this unity, this mighty fabric of empire, will explode into many fragments. The end of the capital's obedience will be the end of its domination. It is not remarkable, therefore, that princes and kings and guardians of the public order by whatever title are more beloved than are private connections. If sensible men put public interest ahead of private, it follows that the personage upon whom the public weal turns is also dearer to them. Long ago Caesar so welded himself to the state that neither could be separated without the ruin of both, for the one needs power and the other a head.

[5] My discourse seems to have stayed quite a distance from its theme, but actually, I swear, it is hard on the track. For if, as we have concluded, you are the soul of your state and it your body, you will realize, I fancy, how essential mercy is: it is yourself you spare when you appear to be sparing another. Reprehensible subjects must be spared precisely like ineffective limbs, and if ever blood is to be let the hand must be prevented from cutting deeper than necessary. In all men, as I remarked, mercy is a natural quality, but it especially becomes monarchs, for in them it has greater scope for salvation and ampler opportunity to show its effect. How petty the mischief private cruelty can work! But when princes are savage it is war. The virtues are, to be sure, in concord with one another and none is better or more honorable than another, yet one may be more appropriate to certain individuals. Magnanimity becomes every human being, even the lowliest of the low, for what could be grander or sturdier than to beat misfortune back? Even so magnanimity has freer scope at a higher level and shows to better advantage on the judge's bench than among the groundlings.

Mercy will make whatever house she enters happy and serene, but she is more admirable in the palace in the degree that she is rarer. What could be more memorable than that the man whose wrath nothing can block, to whose harsher sentences the doomed themselves give assent, whom no one will overrule, nay, if his anger flares hot no one will even supplicate—what could be more memorable than that this man should lay a hand upon himself and put his power to better and calmer use, and should reflect, "To kill contrary to law is in any man's power, to save only in mine"? For a high fortune a high spirit is appropriate, and if the spirit does not rise to the fortune's level and stand above it, it will drag the fortune to the ground also. Now the distinguishing marks of a high spirit and composure and serenity and a lofty disregard of insult and injury. To fume with anger is a womanish thing, and beasts (but not the nobler sort) bite and worry the prostrate. Elephants and lions pass by those they have struck down, relentlessness is a trait of ignoble animals. Savage and inexorable anger is not becoming to a king, for then he loses his superiority; anger reduces him to his victim's level. But if he grants life, if he grants their dignities to persons in jeopardy who have deserved to lose them, he does what none but a sovereign could do. Life may be taken even from a superior; it can be given only to an inferior. To save life is the prerogative of high estate, which is never so much to be revered as when it is privileged to emulate the power of the gods, by whose beneficence we are brought into the world, good and bad alike. Adopting the spirit of the gods, therefore, the prince should regard some of his subjects with pleasure because they are useful and good, some he should leave to fill out the number; he should be glad of some, and tolerate the others.

[6] Think of this city: the throng that streams through its broad boulevards is continuous and if the traffic is blocked there is a crush as when a rushing torrent is dammed; three spacious theaters fill up simultaneously; it consumes the produce of all the world's tilth. How deserted and desolate it would be if only those a strict judge would acquit were left! How many a prosecutor would be liable by the very

laws they enforce! How rare an accuser would be free of guilt! I rather think no one is more obdurate in granting pardon than a man who repeatedly should have begged it for himself. We have all sinned, some grievously, some less so, some of set intent and some by chance impulse or by the misleading of others' wickedness; some have not been steadfast in good resolutions and have lost innocence reluctantly and after a struggle. Not only have we been derelict but we shall continue to be so to the end of our time. And even if a man has purged his soul so thoroughly that nothing can now upset or deceive him, yet it is by sinning that he has reached that innocence.

[7] Since I have mentioned the gods I might propose that the ideal to which a prince might best mold himself is to deal with his subjects as he would wish the gods to deal with him. Is it expedient to have deities who are inexorable in the face of sins and derelictions? Is it expedient to have them intransigent to the point of ruination? What king would then be safe? Whose blasted limbs would the soothsayers not have to collect? But if the placable and equable deities do not instantly blast the derelictions of the mighty with their thunderbolts, how much more equable is it for a human given charge over humans to exercise his authority in a mild spirit and to ponder whether the state of the world is fairer and better pleasing to the eyes on a clear and serene day or when all is aquake with repeated crashes of thunder, and lightnings flash from this quarter and that! Yet a quiet and deliberate reign has precisely the same aspect as a serene and shining sky. A cruel regime is turbulent and befogged in darkness; while fear is general and men shudder at any sudden sound not even the author of the confusion is unaffected. It is easy to pardon private citizens who assert their claims tenaciously: they can be injured, and wrong gives rise to resentment; besides, they are afraid of being despised, for not to return blow for blow is interpreted as weakness rather than mercy. But where vengeance is easy the man who overlooks it secures unqualified praise for gentleness. Men in humbler station have greater freedom to use force, to go to law, to quarrel, to indulge their anger. Where rivals are well matched blows fall light; but for a king even a raised voice and intemperate language are a degradation of majesty.

[8] You suppose it is a disability for kings to be deprived of free speech, which the humblest citizens enjoy. "That is servitude," you say, "not sovereignty." Have you not found out that the sovereignty is ours and yours the servitude? The situation of men in the crowd is different. If they do not range above the level they are unnoticed; they must struggle long for their virtues to show, and their vices are sheltered in darkness. But your deeds and words are caught up by rumor, and no one must have greater care for his reputation than the man sure to have a large one whatever his deserts may be. How many things are taboo for you but not, thanks to you, for us! I can stroll alone in any quarter of the city without fear, though no one attends me and I have no sword at my side or at home; but in the peace you have created you must live armed. You cannot stray from your eminence; it besets you, and its grand pomp follows you wherever you step down. Inability to descend is the bondage of supreme greatness; it is a disability you share with the gods. They too are bound to heaven and are no more free to step down; you are fettered to

your pinnacle. Few are aware of our movements; we can come forward or step back or change our dress without public notice; you can no more hide than the sun. A brilliant light plays about you, and all eyes are focused on it. Do you suppose you walk out of your door? You dawn like the sun. You cannot speak without nations the world over hearing your voice; you cannot be angry without setting the world atremble, because you can strike no one without making all about him quake. Lightning's stroke imperils few but frightens all; so chastisement by a mighty power terrifies more widely than it hurts, and with good reason, for where power is absolute men think not of what it has done but of what it might do. There is another consideration. Patience under injuries received lays private persons open to further injury, but gentleness enhances the security of kings, because while frequent punishment does crush the hatred of a few, it provokes the hatred of all. The will to harsh measures must therefore subside before harsh measures do; otherwise a king's sternness will multiply enemies by destroying them, just as the lopped branches of trees shoot out many twigs, and many species of vegetation grow thicker when they are cut back. Parents and children, relatives and friends, step into the place of individuals who are put to death.

. . .

[23] You will observe, furthermore, that sins frequently punished are sins frequently committed. Within five years your father sewed more men into the sack than are recorded to have been sewn in all history. Children did not venture on the ultimate enormity [of parricide] when the law did not envisage such a crime. Very wisely those lofty souls who understood human nature so well preferred to ignore the crime as a thing incredible and surpassing all limits of audacity rather than show that it could be committed by legislating a penalty for it. Parricide thus began when a law was passed about it; the penalty pointed the way to the crime. Filial piety reached its nadir when the sack was a commoner sight than the cross. In a state where men are seldom punished innocence becomes the rule and is encouraged as a public good. If a state think itself innocent, it will be; it will be more indignant with those who transgress the accepted level of sobriety when it sees that they are few. It is dangerous, believe me, to show a community that the wicked are preponderant.

[24] A motion was once made in the senate to distinguish slaves from free men by dress; but then it was discovered how dangerous it might be if our slaves began to count us. You must understand that we would incur a similar danger if no one was pardoned; it would quickly become apparent how much the worse element in the state was in the majority. For a prince many executions are as discreditable as many funerals are for a doctor; one who governs less strictly is better obeyed. The human mind is naturally contumacious, it is refractory and strives against opposition; it follows more readily than it is led. And just as spirited thoroughbreds are better ridden with a loose rein, so clemency begets a spontaneous and unprodded innocence. Such innocence the state thinks worth preserving for its own interest; this is the path of greater progress.

[25] The vice of cruelty is not innate to man and is unworthy man's kindly temper; it is a bestial kind of madness to delight in blood and wounds, to cast off

humanity and be transformed into a creature of the forest. I ask you, Alexander, what difference does it make whether you throw Lysimachus to a lion or mangle him with your own teeth? The mouth is yours, the fierceness yours. How you would have liked to have claws and a maw that could gape wide enough to devour men! We do not insist that the hand which is the inexorable destruction of your intimates should bring healing to anyone, or that your fierce temper, the insatiable bane of nations, should be satisfied short of slaughter and massacre: we will call it mercy if you choose some human executioner to butcher a friend.

This is the reason why cruelty is most abominable: first it exceeds ordinary limits, and then human limits; it finds exquisite modes of execution, retains talent to devise instruments for diversifying and prolonging pain, and takes pleasure in human suffering. The diseased mind of our notorious tyrant reached the ultimate of madness when cruelty became a pleasure and murder a delight. Hard on the heels of such a man follow repugnance and loathing, poison and the sword. He is assailed by perils as numerous as the men he imperils; sometimes a private plot corners him, sometimes a general insurrection. An insignificant or individual disaster does not stir whole cities; but when it begins to rage abroad and menace all comers, weapons begin to prick it from every side. Little snakes go unnoticed and society does not hunt them down; but when one exceeds the ordinary measure and grows into a monster, when it infects springs with its venom, scorches with its breath, and crushes everything in its path, artillery is brought to bear against it. Petty evils may cheat and elude us, but we march out to meet great ones. A solitary invalid does not upset even his own household, but when a rapid succession of fatalities shows that plague is abroad there is a general outcry and men flee the city and shake their fists at the very gods. If a fire breaks out under a single roof, the family and neighbors douse it with water, but a wide conflagration which has fed on many houses can be smothered only by the ruin of a whole quarter.

[26] The cruelty of private citizens even slaves have taken it upon themselves to avenge, where the indubitable penalty is crucifixion. The cruelty of tyrants whole races and nations, people touched by the evil and people threatened by it, have taken steps to extirpate. Sometimes their own guards have risen against them and brought to bear upon the tyrant the perfidy and disloyalty and savagery which they learned from him. What can anyone expect from a man he has taught to be evil? Wickedness does not stay docile long and sin only as it is bidden.

But imagine that cruelty is safe: what is its kingdom like? Like the shape of stormed cities, like the awful show of general terror. Everything is gloomy, panicky, confused; men fear even their pleasures. It is not safe to go to a dinner party, for even the tipsy must watch their tongues; it is not safe to go to the shows, for they are the hunting grounds of informers. Though they are most lavishly mounted, with regal opulence and a cast of stars, how can a man enjoy shows in jail?

To kill, to rage, to take pleasure in clanking chains and lopped heads, to shed streams of blood at every turn, to terrify and scatter people at a look—good heavens, what a bane! Would life be any different if lions and bears ruled over us, if serpents and every noxious beast were given power over us? Those same beasts, irrational though they are and outlawed by us for their ferocity, nevertheless spare their own kind; among wild creatures likeness is a safeguard. But the tyrant's fury does not abstain even from kin; it treats strangers and familiars alike, and increases in intensity with use. From the slaughter of individuals it creeps on to the destruction of nations, and thinks firing houses and plowing over ancient cities is a sign of power. To order one death or a second, it believes, is to belittle its lordliness; unless a whole gang of wretches stands to the stroke it thinks its cruelty is reduced to the ranks.

Happiness is vouchsafing safety to many, calling back to life from the brink of death, deserving a civic crown for clemency. No decoration is fairer or worthier a prince's eminence than the crown awarded "for saving the lives of fellow citizens"—not trophies torn from the vanquished, not chariots bloodied with barbarian gore, not spoils won in war. To save men in crowds and in the exercise of duty is a godlike power; to kill in multitudes and without discrimination is the power of fire and ruin.

QUESTIONS FOR ANALYSIS AND DISCUSSION

1. Seneca acknowledges that the argument for clemency could seem a ruse perpetrated by wrongdoers trying escape the possibility of harsh punishment. How does Seneca respond to this argument so that decent citizens can support clemency without thinking they are being taken advantage of? Do you agree with his view?

2. Fearful citizens are unhappy citizens, and that is a sign of an unjust society or an immoral leader. What brings about everyday fear, according to Seneca, is the perception that increased penalties mean not less but more crime! "You will observe," writes Seneca, "that sins frequently punished are sins frequently committed." We assume that more laws and punishments decrease crime, but Seneca anticipates our modern concerns by noting that law is only part of the effort to live without unrelenting fear. Citizens must feel or perceive the everyday world as safe. "It is dangerous," Seneca admonishes, "to show a community that the wicked are preponderant." In your understanding of Seneca, how do you think he might decide whether members of our society feel that the wicked are preponderant? If you get your news about the world from television, radio talk shows, newspapers, or the Internet, would you conclude that the media portray a community where the members have little fear of one another and are not overly worried about the wicked? Explain your answer, keeping in mind that Seneca believes clemency is part of the moral answer.

3. One is tempted to conclude that only those who have never experienced being a victim could so easily endorse clemency as an essential virtue. Is this a sufficient rebuttal of Seneca's argument? If so, can any legal punishment be fair since the courts cannot have experienced the pain of the victim? If you say no to the rebuttal, how do we know the right times to punish and the right times to offer clemency or show mercy?

38.

JOHN RAWLS

The Problem of Envy

Envy poses a social danger similar to that of anger. Each is aimed at others and is not sated until others go through a downfall. Envy is different from anger because it is less direct. For John Rawls (b. 1921), envy is the one vice that poses the largest threat to his theory of justice. Envy involves psychological notions of well-being and inequality. For Rawls, striving for justice relies on two fundamental principles. The first principle holds that each person has an "equal right to the most extensive total system of equal basic liberties compatible with a similar system of liberty for all." The second principle, sometimes called the difference principle, holds that social and economic inequalities should be arranged so they produce the "greatest benefit for the least advantaged" and that opportunities should be open to all fairly and equally. In Rawls's view these two principles form the basis for each person to enjoy the basic social goods, such as liberty, opportunity, wealth, and self-respect. Envy, then, could mean one of two things. It could be a sign of an unjust society, or it could be an obstacle to striving for a just and fair society. It is the latter that most worries Rawls.

CRITICAL READING QUESTIONS

1. What is the difference between general and particular envy?
2. According to Rawls, what are the key components of envy?
3. How does Rawls distinguish envy from resentment, jealousy, and spite?
4. Is strict egalitarianism the best antidote to envy?

[S]ince envy is generally regarded as something to be avoided and feared, at least when it becomes intense, it seems desirable that, if possible, the choice of principles should not be influenced by this trait. Therefore, for reasons both of simplicity and

---

"The Problem of Envy," from *Theory of Justice* (Cambridge, MA: Harvard University Press, 1971), pp. 530–540. Notes have been omitted.

306

moral theory, I have assumed an absence of envy and a lack of knowledge of the special psychologies.

Nevertheless these inclinations do exist and in some way they must be reckoned with. Thus I have split the argument for the principles of justice into two parts: the first part proceeds on the presumptions just mentioned, and is illustrated by most of the argument so far; the second part asks whether the well-ordered society corresponding to the conception adopted will actually generate feelings of envy and patterns of psychological attitudes that will undermine the arrangements it counts to be just. At first we reason as if there is no problem of envy and the special psychologies; and then having ascertained which principles would be settled upon, we check to see whether just institutions so defined are likely to arouse and encourage these propensities to such an extent that the social system becomes unworkable and incompatible with human good. If so, the adoption of the conception of justice must be reconsidered. But should the inclinations engendered support just arrangements, or be easily accommodated by them, the first part of the argument is confirmed. The essential advantage of the two-step procedure is that no particular constellation of attitudes is taken as given. We are simply checking the reasonableness of our initial assumptions and the consequences we have drawn from them in the light of the constraints imposed by the general facts of our world.

I shall discuss the problem of envy as an illustration of the way in which the special psychologies enter into the theory of justice. While each special psychology raises no doubt different questions, the general procedure may be much the same. I begin by noting the reason why envy poses a problem, namely, the fact that the inequalities sanctioned by the difference principle may be so great as to arouse envy to a socially dangerous extent. To clarify this possibility it is useful to distinguish between general and particular envy. The envy experienced by the least advantaged towards those better situated is normally general envy in the sense that they envy the more favored for the kinds of goods and not for the particular objects they possess. The upper classes say are envied for their greater wealth and opportunity; those envying them want similar advantages for themselves. By contrast, particular envy is typical of rivalry and competition. Those who lose out in the quest for office and honor, or for the affections of another, are liable to envy the success of their rivals and to covet the very same thing that they have won. Our problem then is whether the principles of justice, and especially the difference principle with fair equality of opportunity, is likely to engender in practice too much destructive general envy.

I now turn to the definition of envy that seems appropriate for this question. To fix ideas, suppose that the necessary interpersonal comparisons are made in terms of the objective primary goods, liberty and opportunity, income and wealth, which for simplicity I have normally used to define expectations in applying the difference principle. Then we may think of envy as the propensity to view with hostility the greater good of others even though their being more fortunate than we are does not detract from our advantages. We envy persons whose situation is superior to ours (estimated by some agreed index of goods as noted above) and we are willing to deprive them of their greater benefits even if it is necessary to give up something ourselves. When others are aware of our envy, they may become jealous of their better circumstances and anxious to take precautions against the hostile acts to which our envy makes us prone. So understood envy is collectively disadvantageous: the individual who envies another is prepared to do things that make them both worse off, if only the discrepancy between them is sufficiently reduced. Thus Kant, whose definition I have pretty much followed, quite properly discusses envy as one of the vices of hating mankind.

This definition calls for comment. First of all, as Kant observes, there are many occasions when we openly speak of the greater good of others as enviable. Thus we may remark upon the enviable harmony and happiness of a marriage or a family. Similarly, one might say to another that one envies his greater opportunities or attainments. In these cases, those of benign envy as I shall refer to them, there is no ill will intended or expressed. We do not wish, for example, that the marriage or family should be less happy or harmonious. By these conventional expressions we are affirming the value of certain things that others have. We are indicating that, although we possess no similar good of equal value, they are indeed worth striving for. Those to whom we address these remarks are expected to receive them as a kind of praise and not as a foretaste of our hostility. A somewhat different case is that of emulative envy which leads us to try to achieve what others have. The sight of their greater good moves us to strive in socially beneficial ways for similar things for ourselves. Thus envy proper, in contrast with benign envy which we freely express, is a form of rancor that tends to harm both its object and its subject. It is what emulative envy may become under certain conditions of defeat and sense of failure.

A further point is that envy is not a moral feeling. No moral principle need be cited in its explanation. It is sufficient to say that the better situation of others catches our attention. We are downcast by their good fortune and no longer value as highly what we have; and this sense of hurt and loss arouses our rancor and hostility. Thus one must be careful not to conflate envy and resentment. For resentment is a moral feeling. If we resent our having less than others, it must be because we think that their being better off is the result of unjust institutions, or wrongful conduct on their part. Those who express resentment must be prepared to show why certain institutions are unjust or how others have injured them. What marks off envy from the moral feelings is the different way in which it is accounted for, the sort of perspective from which the situation is viewed.

We should note also the nonmoral feelings connected with envy but not to be mistaken for it. In particular, jealousy and grudgingness are reverse, so to speak, to envy. A person who is better off may wish those less fortunate than he to stay in their place. He is jealous of his superior position and begrudges them the greater advantages that would put them on a level with himself. And should this propensity extend to denying them benefits that he does not need and cannot use himself, then he is moved by spite. These inclinations are collectively harmful in the way that envy is, since the grudging and spiteful man is willing to give up something to maintain the distance between himself and others.

So far I have considered envy and grudgingness as vices. As we have seen, the moral virtues are among the broadly based traits of character which it is rational for persons to want in one another as associates. Thus vices are broadly based traits that are not wanted, spitefulness and envy being clear cases, since they are to everyone's detriment. The parties will surely prefer conceptions of justice the realization of which does not arouse these propensities. We are normally expected to forbear from the actions to which they prompt us and to take the steps necessary to rid ourselves of them. Yet sometimes the circumstances evoking envy are so compelling that given human beings as they are no one can reasonably be asked to overcome his rancorous feelings. A person's lesser position as measured by the index of objective primary goods may be so great as to wound his self-respect; and given his situation, we may sympathize with his sense of loss. Indeed, we can resent being made envious, for society may permit such large disparities in these goods that under existing social conditions these differences cannot help but cause a loss of self-esteem. For those suffering this hurt, envious feelings are not irrational; the satisfaction of their rancor would make them better off. When envy is a reaction to the loss of self-respect in circumstances where it would be unreasonable to expect someone to feel differently, I shall say that it is excusable. Since self-respect is the main primary good, the parties would not agree, I shall assume, to count this sort of subjective loss as irrelevant. Therefore the question is whether a basic structure which satisfies the principles of justice is likely to arouse so much excusable envy that the choice of these principles should be reconsidered.

Envy and Equality

We are now ready to examine the likelihood of excusable general envy in a well-ordered society. I shall only discuss this case, since our problem is whether the principles of justice are a reasonable undertaking in view of the propensities of human beings, in particular their aversion to disparities in objective goods. Now I assume that the main psychological root of the liability to envy is a lack of self-confidence in our own worth combined with a sense of impotence. Our way of life is without zest and we feel powerless to alter it or to acquire the means of doing what we still want to do. By contrast, someone sure of the worth of his plan of life and his ability to carry it out is not given to rancor nor is he jealous of his good fortune. Even if he could, he has no desire to level down the advantages of others at some expense to himself. This hypothesis implies that the least favored tend to be more envious of the better situation of the more favored the less secure their self-respect and the greater their feeling that they cannot improve their prospects. Similarly, the particular envy aroused by competition and rivalry is likely to be stronger the worse one's defeat, for the blow to one's self-confidence is more severe and the loss may seem irretrievable. It is general envy, however, that mainly concerns us here.

There are three conditions, I assume, that encourage hostile outbreaks of envy. The first of these is the psychological condition we have just noted: persons lack a sure confidence in their own value and in their ability to do anything worthwhile.

Second (and one of two social conditions), many occasions arise when this psychological condition is experienced as painful and humiliating. The discrepancy between oneself and others is made visible by the social structure and style of life of one's society. The less fortunate are therefore often forcibly reminded of their situation, sometimes leading them to an even lower estimation of themselves and their mode of living. And third, they see their social position as allowing no constructive alternative to opposing the favored circumstances of the more advantaged. To alleviate their feelings of anguish and inferiority, they believe they have no choice but to impose a loss on those better placed even at some cost to themselves, unless of course they are to relapse into resignation and apathy.

. . .

Finally, considering the last condition, it would seem that a well-ordered society as much as any other offers constructive alternatives to hostile outbreaks of envy. The problem of general envy anyway does not force us to reconsider the choice of the principles of justice. As for particular envy, to a certain extent it is endemic to human life; being associated with rivalry, it may exist in any society. The more specific problem for political justice is how pervasive is the rancor and jealousy aroused by the quest for office and position, and whether it is likely to distort the justice of institutions. It is difficult to settle this matter in the absence of the more detailed knowledge of social forms available at the legislative stage. But there seems to be no reason why the hazards of particular envy should be worse in a society regulated by justice and fairness than by any other conception.

. . .

The importance of separating envy from the moral feelings can be seen from several examples. Suppose first that envy is held to be pervasive in poor peasant societies. The reason for this, it may be suggested, is the general belief that the aggregate of social wealth is more or less fixed, so that one person's gain is another's loss. The social system is regarded, it might be said, as a conventionally established and unchangeable zero-sum game. Now actually, if this belief were widespread and the stock of goods were generally thought to be given, then a strict opposition of interests would be assumed to obtain. In this case, it would be correct to think that justice requires equal shares. Social wealth is not viewed as the outcome of mutually advantageous cooperation and so there is no fair basis for an unequal division of advantages. What is said to be envy may in fact be resentment which might or might not prove to be justified.

. . . That persons have opposing interests and seek to advance their own conception of the good is not at all the same thing as their being moved by envy and jealousy. As we have seen, this sort of opposition gives rise to the circumstances of justice. Thus if children compete for the attention and affection of their parents, to which one might say they justly have an equal claim, one cannot assert that their sense of justice springs from jealousy and envy. Certainly children are often envious and jealous; and no doubt their moral notions are so primitive that the necessary distinctions are not grasped by them. But waiving these difficulties, we could equally well say that their social feeling arises from resentment, from a sense that they are unfairly treated. And similarly one could say to conservative writers that it is mere grudgingness when those better circumstanced reject the claims of the less advantaged to greater equality. But this contention also calls for careful argument. None of these charges and countercharges can be given credence without first examining the conceptions of justice sincerely held by individuals and their understanding of the social situation in order to see how far these claims are indeed founded on these motives.

QUESTIONS FOR ANALYSIS AND DISCUSSION

1. When envy turns to resentment, notes Rawls, there is a moral concern about the fairness of society. Do you agree with Rawls? Can you find other indicators of fairness or unfairness that do not involve resentment?

2. In distinguishing general from particular envy, Rawls uses rivalry and competition as benign examples of particular envy. General envy involves advantages and benefits one group enjoys over another group. If you consider your workplace or a college course as a microcosm (little model) of society, does Rawls's distinction help make sense of the differences you see among colleagues or fellow students? Do we compete not only in games but also for social goods such as greater opportunities, higher grades, and so forth?

3. Rawls connects the emergence of envy with a decrease of self-esteem. Self-esteem is often seen as a psychological notion, but Rawls claims that a well-ordered society is partly measured by the extent to which its citizens have self-esteem. Jordan-Smith (Chapter 3) observes that modern society encourages many vices, particularly envy. If Jordan-Smith is right, do you think Rawls's account indicates a moral failing in American society?

39.

FRIEDRICH NIETZSCHE

Schadenfreude and Envy *and*
Of the Bestowing Virtue

*Is envy an avoidable feeling? Can we develop a way of life that diminishes or eliminates
envy? Friedrich Nietzsche (1844–1900) claims that envy provides meaning in the lives
of many people. This is best illustrated in the phenomenon of* Schadenfreude—*the
delight we experience in hearing of or seeing the misfortunes of others. This malicious joy*

"*Schadenfreude* and Envy," from *Human, All-Too-Human*, Part II, translated by Paul V. Cohn (Edinburgh & London: T. N. Foulis, 1911), pp. 207–217. Notes have been omitted.

appears in many forms, according to Nietzsche. Moreover, he notes, the intensity of the passion of envy is denigrated by moralists. It is possible that humans seek not so much a just society but rather a variety of intense passions.

Although many critics contend that Nietzsche is a moral nihilist—one who either denigrates and mocks conventional moral beliefs or has no positive ethic of his own—in other writings he offers more affirmative views. In Thus Spoke Zarathustra, *a lyrical and philosophical work, Nietzsche introduces the bestowing virtue. This virtue is found in a kind of selfishness that contrasts with the more familiar selfishness of those who are greedy or envious. The selection ends with one of the controversial ideas raised by Nietzsche, the Superman* (Ubermensch).

CRITICAL READING QUESTIONS

1. What is the relation between envy and equality?
2. How does Nietzsche understand the desire for revenge?
3. What is the antagonism between social virtues and individual virtues?
4. Why does Zarathustra compare the bestowing virtue to gold?
5. How does Nietzsche distinguish between a healthy or sick selfishness?

Schadenfreude and Envy

27. Explanation of Malicious Joy

Malicious joy arises when a man consciously finds himself in evil plight and feels anxiety or remorse or pain. The misfortune that overtakes B. makes him equal to A., and A. is reconciled and no longer envious.—If A. is prosperous, he still hoards up in his memory B.'s misfortune as a capital, so as to throw it in the scale as a counter-weight when he himself suffers adversity. In this case too he feels "malicious joy" (*Schadenfreude*). The sentiment of equality thus applies its standard to the domain of luck and chance. Malicious joy is the commonest expression of victory and restoration of equality, even in a higher state of civilisation. This emotion has only been in existence since the time when man learnt to look upon another as his equal—in other words, since the foundation of society.

28. The Arbitrary Element in the Award of Punishment

To most criminals punishment comes just as illegitimate children come to women. They have done the same thing a hundred times without any bad consequences.

Suddenly comes discovery, and with discovery punishment. Yet habit should make the deed for which the criminal is punished appear more excusable, for he has developed a propensity that is hard to resist. Instead of this, the criminal is punished more severely if the suspicion of habitual crime rests on him, and habit is made a valid reason against all extenuation. On the other hand, a model life, wherein crime shows up in more terrible contrast, should make the guilt appear more heavy! But here the custom is to soften the punishment. Everything is measured not from the standpoint of the criminal but from that of society and its losses and dangers. The previous utility of an individual is weighed against his one nefarious action, his previous criminality is added to that recently discovered, and punishment is thus meted out as highly as possible. But if we thus punish or reward a man's past (for in the former case the diminution of punishment is a reward) we ought to go farther back and punish and reward the cause of his past—I mean parents, teachers, society. In many instances we shall then find the *judges* somehow or other sharing in the guilt. It is arbitrary to stop at the criminal himself when we punish his past: if we will not grant the absolute excusability of every crime, we should stop at each individual case and probe no farther into the past—in other words, isolate guilt and not connect it with previous actions. Otherwise we sin against logic. The teachers of free will should draw the inevitable conclusion from their doctrine of "free will" and boldly decree: "No action has a past."

29. Envy and Her Nobler Sister

Where equality is really recognised and permanently established, we see the rise of that propensity that is generally considered immoral, and would scarcely be conceivable in a state of nature—envy. The envious man is susceptible to every sign of individual superiority to the common herd, and wishes to depress every one once more to the level—or raise himself to the superior plane. Hence arise two different modes of action, which Hesiod designated good and bad Eris. In the same way, in a condition of equality there arises indignation if A. is prosperous above and B. unfortunate beneath their deserts and equality. These latter, however, are emotions of nobler natures. They feel the want of justice and equity in things that are independent of the arbitrary choice of men—or, in other words, they desire the equality recognised by man to be recognised as well by Nature and chance. They are angry that men of equal merits should not have equal fortune.

30. The Envy of the Gods

"The envy of the Gods" arises when a despised person sets himself on an equality with his superior (like Ajax), or is made equal with him by the favour of fortune (like Niobe, the too favoured mother). In the social class system this envy demands that no one shall have merits above his station, that his prosperity shall be on a level with his position, and especially that his self-consciousness shall not outgrow the limits of his rank. Often the victorious general, or the pupil who achieves a masterpiece, has experienced "the envy of the gods."

31. Vanity As an Anti-Social Aftergrowth

As men, for the sake of security, have made themselves equal in order to found communities, but as also this conception is imposed by a sort of constraint and is entirely opposed to the instincts of the individual, so, the more universal security is guaranteed, the more do new offshoots of the old instinct for predominance appear. Such offshoots appear in the setting-up of class distinctions, in the demand for professional dignities and privileges, and, generally speaking, in vanity (manners, dress, speech, and so forth). So soon as danger to the community is apparent, the majority, who were unable to assert their preponderance in a time of universal peace, once more bring about the condition of equality, and for the time being the absurd privileges and vanities disappear. If the community, however, collapses utterly and anarchy reigns supreme, there arises the state of nature: an absolutely ruthless inequality as recounted by Thucydides in the case of Corcyra. Neither a natural justice nor a natural injustice exists.

32. Equity

Equity is a development of justice, and arises among such as do not come into conflict with the communal equality. This more subtle recognition of the principle of equilibrium is applied to cases where nothing is prescribed by law. Equity looks forwards and backwards, its maxim being, "Do unto others as you would that they should do unto you." *Aequum* means: "This principle is conformable to our equality; it tones down even our small differences to an appearance of equality, and expects us to be indulgent in cases where we are not compelled to pardon."

33. Elements of Revenge

The word "revenge" is spoken so quickly that it almost seems as if it could not contain more than one conceptual and emotional root. Hence we are still at pains to find this root. Our economists, in the same way, have never wearied of scenting a similar unity in the word "value," and of hunting after the primitive root idea of value. As if all words were not pockets, into which this or that or several things have been stuffed at once! So "revenge" is now one thing, now another, and sometimes more composite. Let us first distinguish that defensive counter-blow, which we strike almost unconsciously, even at inanimate objects (such as machinery in motion) that have hurt us. The notion is to set a check to the object that has hurt us, by bringing the machine to a stop. Sometimes the force of this counter-blow, in order to attain its object, will have to be strong enough to shatter the machine. If the machine be too strong to be disorganised by one man, the latter will all the same strike the most violent blow he can—as a sort of last attempt. We behave similarly towards persons who hurt us, at the immediate sensation of the hurt. If we like to call this an act of revenge, well and good: but we must remember that here self-preservation alone has set its cog-wheels of reason in motion, and that after all we do not think of the doer of the injury but only of ourselves. We act without any idea of doing injury in return, only with a view to getting away safe and sound.—It needs time to pass in thought from oneself to one's adversary and ask oneself at what point he is most vulnerable. This is done in the second variety of revenge, the preliminary idea of which is to consider the vulnerability and susceptibility of the other. The intention then is to give pain. On the other hand, the idea of securing himself against further injury is in this case so entirely outside the avenger's horizon, that he almost regularly brings about his own further injury and often foresees it in cold blood. If in the first sort of revenge it was the fear of a second blow that made the counter-blow as strong as possible, in this case there is an almost complete indifference to what one's adversary will do: the strength of the counter-blow is only determined by what he has *already* done to us. Then what has he done? What profit is it to us if he is now suffering, after we have suffered through him? This is a case of readjustment, whereas the first act of revenge only serves the purpose of self-preservation. It may be that through our adversary we have lost property, rank, friends, children—these losses are not recovered by revenge, the readjustment only concerns a subsidiary loss which is added to all the other losses. The revenge of readjustment does not preserve one from further injury, it does not make good the injury already suffered—except in one case. If our honour has suffered through our adversary, revenge can restore it. But in any case honour *has* suffered an injury if intentional harm has been done us, because our adversary proved thereby that he was not afraid of us. By revenge we prove that we are not afraid of him either, and herein lies the settlement, the readjustment. (The intention of showing their complete lack of fear goes so far in some people that the dangers of revenge—loss of health or life or other losses—are in their eyes an indispensable condition of every vengeful act. Hence they practice the duel, although the law also offers them aid in obtaining satisfaction for what they have suffered. They are not satisfied with a safe means of recovering their honour, because this would not prove their fearlessness.)—In the first-named variety of revenge it is just fear that strikes the counter-blow; in the second case it is the absence of fear, which, as has been said, wishes to manifest itself in the counter-blow.—Thus nothing appears more different than the motives of the two courses of action which are designated by the one word "revenge." Yet it often happens that the avenger is not precisely certain as to what really prompted his deed: perhaps he struck the counter-blow from fear and the instinct of self-preservation, but in the background, when he has time to reflect upon the standpoint of wounded honour, he imagines that he has avenged himself for the sake of his honour—this motive is in any case more *reputable* than the other. An essential point is whether he sees his honour injured in the eyes of others (the world) or only in the eyes of his offenders: in the latter case he will prefer secret, in the former open revenge. Accordingly, as he enters strongly or feebly into the soul of the doer and the spectator, his revenge will be more bitter or more tame. If he is entirely lacking in this sort of imagination, he will not think at all of revenge, as the feeling of "honour" is not present in him, and accordingly cannot be wounded. In the same way, he will not think of revenge if he despises the offender and the spectator; because as objects of his contempt they cannot give him honour, and accordingly cannot rob him of honour. Finally, he will forego revenge in the not uncommon case of his loving the offender. It is true that he then suffers loss of honour in the other's eyes, and will perhaps become less worthy of having his love returned. But even to renounce all requital of love is a sacrifice that love is ready to make when its only object is to avoid hurting the beloved object: this would mean hurting oneself more than one is hurt by the sacrifice.—Accordingly, every one will avenge himself, unless he be bereft of honour or inspired by contempt or by love for the offender. Even if he turns to the law-courts, he desires revenge as a private individual; but also, as a thoughtful, prudent man of society, he desires the revenge of society upon one who does not respect it. Thus by legal punishment private honour as well as that of society is restored— that is to say, punishment is revenge. Punishment undoubtedly contains the first-mentioned element of revenge, in as far as by its means society helps to preserve itself, and strikes a counter-blow in self-defence. Punishment desires to prevent further injury, to scare other offenders. In this way the two elements of revenge, different as they are, are united in punishment, and this may perhaps tend most of all to maintain the above-mentioned confusion of ideas, thanks to which the individual avenger generally does not know what he really wants.

34. The Virtues That Damage Us

As members of communities we think we have no right to exercise certain virtues which afford us great honour and some pleasure as private individuals (for example, indulgence and favour towards miscreants of all kinds)—in short, every mode of action whereby the advantage of society would suffer through our virtue. No bench of judges, face to face with its conscience, may permit itself to be gracious. This privilege is reserved for the king as an individual, and we are glad when he makes use of it, proving that we should like to be gracious individually, but not collectively. Society recognises only the virtues profitable to her, or at least not injurious to her—virtues like justice, which are exercised without loss, or, in fact, at compound interest. The virtues that damage us cannot have originated in society, because even now opposition to them arises in every small society that is in the making. Such virtues are therefore those of men of unequal standing, invented by the superior individuals; they are the virtues of rulers, and the idea underlying them is: "I am mighty enough to put up with an obvious loss; that is a proof of my power." Thus they are virtues closely akin to pride.

35. The Casuistry of Advantage

There would be no moral casuistry if there were no casuistry of advantage. The most free and refined intelligence is often incapable of choosing between two alternatives in such a way that his choice necessarily involves the greater advantage. In such cases we choose because we must, and afterwards often feel a kind of emotional sea-sickness.

36. Turning Hypocrite

Every beggar turns hypocrite, like every one who makes his living out of indigence, be it personal or public.—The beggar does not feel want nearly so keenly as he must make others feel it, if he wishes to make a living by mendicancy.

37. A Sort of Cult of the Passions

You hypochondriacs, you philosophic blind-worms talk of the formidable nature of human passions, in order to inveigh against the dreadsomeness of the whole world-structure. As if the passions were always and everywhere formidable! As if this sort of terror must always exist in the world!—Through a carelessness in small matters, through a deficiency in observation of self and of the rising generation, you have yourselves allowed your passions to develop into such unruly monsters that you are frightened now at the mere mention of the word "passion"! It rests with you and it rests with us to divest the passions of their formidable features and so to dam them that they do not become devastating floods.—We must not exalt our errors into eternal fatalities. Rather shall we honestly endeavour to convert all the passions of humanity into sources of joy.

Of the Bestowing Virtue

1

When Zarathustra had taken leave of the town to which his heart was attached and which was called "The Pied Cow" there followed him many who called themselves his disciples and escorted him. Thus they came to a cross-road: there Zarathustra told them that from then on he wanted to go alone: for he was a friend of going-alone. But his disciples handed him in farewell a staff, upon the golden haft of which a serpent was coiled about a sun. Zarathustra was delighted with the staff and leaned upon it; then he spoke thus to his disciples:

Tell me: how did gold come to have the highest value? Because it is uncommon and useless and shining and mellow in lustre; it always bestows itself.

Only as an image of the highest virtue did gold come to have the highest value. Gold-like gleams the glance of the giver. Gold-lustre makes peace between moon and sun.

The highest virtue is uncommon and useless, it is shining and mellow in lustre: the highest virtue is a bestowing virtue.

"Of the Bestowing Virtue," from *Thus Spoke Zarathustra,* translated by R. J. Hollingdale (Harmondsworth, England: Penguin Books, Ltd., 1961), pp. 99–103.

Truly, I divine you well, my disciples, you aspire to the bestowing virtue, as I do. What could you have in common with cats and wolves?

You thirst to become sacrifices and gifts yourselves; and that is why you thirst to heap up all riches in your soul.

Your soul aspires insatiably after treasures and jewels, because your virtue is insatiable in wanting to give.

You compel all things to come to you and into you, that they may flow back from your fountain as gifts of your love.

Truly, such a bestowing love must become a thief of all values; but I call this selfishness healthy and holy.

There is another selfishness, an all-too-poor, a hungry selfishness that always wants to steal, that selfishness of the sick, the sick selfishness.

It looks with the eye of a thief upon all lustrous things; with the greed of hunger it measures him who has plenty to eat; and it is always skulking about the table of the givers.

Sickness speaks from such craving, and hidden degeneration; the thieving greed of this longing speaks of a sick body.

Tell me, my brothers: what do we account bad and the worst of all? Is it not *degeneration?*—And we always suspect degeneration where the bestowing soul is lacking.

Our way is upward, from the species across to the superspecies. But the degenerate mind which says "All for me" is a horror to us.

Our mind flies upward: thus it is an image of our bodies, an image of an advance and elevation.

The names of the virtues are such images of advances and elevations.

Thus the body goes through history, evolving and battling. And the spirit— what is it to the body? The herald, companion, and echo of its battles and victories.

All names of good and evil are images: they do not speak out, they only hint. He is a fool who seeks knowledge from them.

Whenever your spirit wants to speak in images, pay heed; for that is when your virtue has its origin and beginning.

Then your body is elevated and risen up; it enraptures the spirit with its joy, that it may become creator and evaluator and lover and benefactor of all things.

When your heart surges broad and full like a river, a blessing and a danger to those who live nearby: that is when your virtue has its origin and beginning.

When you are exalted above praise and blame, and your will wants to command all things as the will of a lover: that is when your virtue has its origin and beginning.

When you despise the soft bed and what is pleasant and cannot make your bed too far away from the soft-hearted: that is when your virtue has its origin and beginning.

When you are the willers of a single will, and you call this dispeller of need your essential and necessity: that is when your virtue has its origin and beginning.

Truly, it is a new good and evil! Truly, a new roaring in the depths and the voice of a new fountain!

It is power, this new virtue; it is a ruling idea, and around it a subtle soul: a golden sun, and around it the serpent of knowledge.

2

Here Zarathustra fell silent a while and regarded his disciples lovingly. Then he went on speaking thus, and his voice was different:

Stay loyal to the earth, my brothers, with the power of your virtue! May your bestowing love and your knowledge serve towards the meaning of the earth! Thus I beg and entreat you.

Do not let it fly away from the things of earth and beat with its wings against the eternal walls! Alas, there has always been much virtue that has flown away!

Lead, as I do, the flown-away virtue back to earth—yes, back to body and life: that it may give the earth its meaning, a human meaning!

A hundred times hitherto has spirit as well as virtue flown away and blundered. Alas, all this illusion and blundering still dwells in our bodies: it has there become body and will.

A hundred times has spirit as well as virtue experimented and gone astray. Yes, man was an experiment. Alas, much ignorance and error has become body in us!

Not only the reason of millennia—the madness of millennia too breaks out in us. It is dangerous to be an heir.

We are still fighting step by step with the giant Chance, and hitherto the senseless, the meaningless, has still ruled over mankind.

May your spirit and your virtue serve the meaning of the earth, my brothers: and may the value of all things be fixed anew by you. To that end you should be fighters! To that end you should be creators!

The body purifies itself through knowledge; experimenting with knowledge it elevates itself; to the discerning man all instincts are holy; the soul of the elevated man grows joyful.

Physician, heal yourself: thus you will heal your patient too. Let his best healing-aid be to see with his own eyes him who makes himself well.

There are a thousand paths that have never yet been trodden, a thousand forms of health and hidden islands of life. Man and man's earth are still unexhausted and undiscovered.

Watch and listen, you solitaries! From the future come winds with a stealthy flapping of wings; and good things go out to delicate ears.

You solitaries of today, you who have seceded from society, you shall one day be a people: from you, who have chosen out yourselves, shall a chosen people spring—and from this chosen people, the Superman.

Truly, the earth shall yet become a house of healing! And already a new odour floats about it, an odour that brings health—and a new hope!

QUESTIONS FOR ANALYSIS AND DISCUSSION

1. Nietzsche suggests that *Schadenfreude* is part of the beginnings of social life. Develop an argument to support or reject his suggestion.
2. Rawls mentions how children almost naturally feel envy and jealousy. Does this support Nietzsche's observations about the frequency of envy among

humans? Is Nietzsche simply outlining some truths about people but avoiding the more difficult task of developing a moral view about these truths?

3. In his analysis of revenge, Nietzsche distinguishes two kinds of fear. The first is mostly self-protection, but the second kind of fear involves reputation. Do you think Nietzsche is right that revenge has little to do with retribution or deterrence but is primarily a case of the injured party seeking to reestablish his or her honor? If so, is that a morally worthy reason? If not, how can we account for revenge when both the threats and the pains brought by an offender no longer exist?

4. Throughout much of the Western tradition of virtue ethics, the moral life is depicted as a kind of battle. Vice brings the soul to its downfall. Virtue triumphs over vice. Humility or love direct the soul past vanity or avarice. In this pair of selections from Nietzsche, you catch a glimpse of how one thinker sees this battle. In light of these two selections and others in this chapter, how do you understand the struggle between envy or anger and clemency or the bestowing virtue? Can one endorse both righteous anger and mercy? Can an envious person also illustrate a bestowing virtue? Offer your own example to develop your response.

5. What is the relation between the bestowing virtue and selfishness? and the meaning of the earth? and solitaries?

CHAPTER SIX

Is It All You Need?
Variations on the Love Ethic

Since she is always doomed to dependence, she will prefer to serve a god rather than obey tyrants—parents, husband, or protector. . . . Love becomes for her a religion.

—Simone de Beauvoir, *The Second Sex*

When you first meet, you can have the hots twenty-four hours a day for each other. But after fifteen or twenty years, a different kind of sexual and intellectual relationship develops, right? It's still love, but it's different.

—John Lennon, 1980 Interview

If anger is the best candidate for bringing out the bestial in humans, love ranks at the top for bringing out our divine qualities. The discussants in Plato's *Symposium* debate whether love is the youngest or oldest god. One speech talks of a god who punishes the human species by splitting their members into halves so that their search for true love is only complete upon finding their other half. Socrates' own speech is an account of his lesson on love from the goddess Diotima. Nearly every religion contains a tenet on the importance of love. A believer learns from the Ten Commandments that there is a relation between divine love and divine mercy.

Like anger, however, there is ample room for love to move quickly toward its opposite. Oddly, their directions contrast. Whereas anger begins achieving some sense of moral approval when invoked in terms of God's will, love's decline leads humans to a state of existence that is barely describable. As depicted in allegorical terms in folklore, art, and moral tales, the downfall of love can take humans not only to a bestial level but to something more horrific—Satan, eternal damnation, Hell.

Even in nonreligious portrayals, love can look fairly dismal. In literature and movies love invariably includes heartbreak and emotional confusion. As Wendy Doniger notes (see Chapter 4), expressions of love often disguise more selfish or harmful thoughts. Why do we not protest the disguise? To expose the disguise would risk even greater dangers, such as cynicism and distrust. Lately, more scientifically minded observers of human behavior contend that love is little more than a chemical or genetic matchup. As science writer Gail Vines notes in her recent book, *Raging Hormones,* many researchers work on the assumption that the complexities of human love are explicable in terms of testosterone, biorhythms, and anatomical structures of male and female brains.

In any event, love does not always fulfill its promise. One plausible reason for this cloudy picture is that love's most direct antagonist for many moralists is another universal—lust. Unlike anger, however, lust seeks to enjoy rather than destroy. This enjoyment is necessary to the continuation of the species. As the late Michel Foucault pointed out in his studies of the history of sexuality, many moralists also consider lust as the source of the greatest or most intense enjoyment. How intense? Important thinkers as diverse as Augustine and Freud believe the pleasures of lust are so powerful that they often escape or overwhelm human awareness or self-control. Other moralists, as expressed by thinkers as different as Plato and Nancy Mairs, claim that lust has the power to spark other forms of love—the love in friendship or family, for example. It is these creative and multiple expressions of love that make it essential to any notion of the good life. Only love has such a godlike power to bring out the best in humans.

It is understandable that today's students, like students in past generations, are uneasy about the relation between lust and love. Both lust and love blur the sense of self; and each promises the greatest joy. The selections in this chapter highlight some of the complexities regarding the extent to which the virtuous person understands or lives by the meaning of love as a moral good. The writers do not always address love and lust as an either-or issue but often view it as a how-why concern.

The case study by essayist and poet Nancy Mairs invites you to listen to the various voices she adroitly interweaves. Sounding like an academic, then a feminist or cocktail party intellectual, Mairs mixes self-deprecating insights in a distinct voice that deserves a close reading.

St. Augustine, who with Origen is the most influential thinker among the Church Fathers, believes lust is the most troublesome vice. Lust can escape the control of the rational or moral person and transform him so that he momentarily forgets himself or the Lord.

In the *Kama Sutra,* Vatsyayana illustrates the place of lust differently. Sexual pleasure is one of the three components making up the way to happiness. Dharma (righteousness, duty), Artha (pursuit of social or material goods), and Kama (pursuit of pleasures) are not antagonistic but complementary in terms of seeking the good or liberation. This component involves a virtuous spouse, an obedient wife in Vatsyayana's case.

Does that arrangement bring about earthly joy? According to French existentialist Simone de Beauvoir, a central problem in philosophical speculations about love is that men and women have sharply contrasting views of the very meaning of love. The disparity of views should remind us that when two happy and carefree lovers finally say to one another, "I love you" they might mean two completely different things.

Nigel Warburton, a philosopher at the Open University, offers a different slant on the nature of lust. He examines whether a spouse who finds sexual pleasure while exchanging messages in electronic chat rooms could be counted as morally questionable. For example, if a husband is chatting with Bombshell Betty in cyber-space and has an orgasm from it, and his wife discovers him in the act, does that constitute infidelity? For Warburton, this is a philosophically interesting issue with moral implications.

A different kind of faithfulness is articulated in Theano's letter to a young friend whose husband is behaving badly in an affair. How can you help your friend so that she does the good even though you know she now wants to harm someone? It is more than a contest between wife and mistress, implies Theano. It is a battle within oneself about which virtues or vices will triumph.

The Greek Stoic philosopher Epictetus shifts focus to examine the moral nature of friendship. For many Greek moralists the experience of friendship rather than erotic pleasure provides the exemplary human bond. Here Epictetus points out the strengths and weaknesses of friendship as a moral experience. Compare this view of friendship with that of David Nyberg (see Chapter 4). In his eyes moral philos-ophers have overestimated their own beliefs and underestimated everyday experi-ence when it comes to appreciating the value of deceit in friendship. Good friends are truthful, acknowledges Nyberg, but also know when not to be too truthful.

The social value of lust and love is addressed by Plato. Although some believe Plato is being sardonic, in *The Republic* Plato clarifies an argument that supports the idea of communal families. The private or, in our terms, nuclear family brings about an attitude in love in which people begin to distinguish ownership and per-sonal pride. They give more weight to what is mine rather than what is ours. To this problem Plato offers a solution that sounds incredulous.

Lin Yutang has a somewhat gentler perspective on family life. Recounting Chi-nese traditions and lessons, Lin Yutang believes there is a moral good to a close-knit family. This is realized in part by the moral regard given to one's elders, such as grandparents and parents.

According to philosophers Mary Midgely and Judith Hughes, the ideal of the close-knit family is a distortion of the variety of family structures that succeed in giving society a supply of responsible members. Yet the responsibility of rearing children involves hard work. To enhance family life and the values it can teach, argue Midgely and Hughes, society and government must offer active support rather than homilies to help citizens embrace the virtuous life.

40.

NANCY MAIRS

Case Study: On Not Liking Sex

Can a liberated woman admit to not liking sex? Essayist and poet Nancy Mairs (b. 1943) takes this odd question as the departure point for an insightful and adventurous medita-tion on her life in the United States. Her perspectives range from academic to feminist to teenager to cocktail party intellectual to middle-aged woman gradually crippled by mul-tiple sclerosis. By shifting perspectives Mairs invites you to consider the multiple ways of thinking and talking about the erotic experience. However, Mairs devotes her attention more to the idea rather than to the act of love.

CRITICAL READING QUESTIONS

1. How does Mairs distinguish "liking sex" from "enjoying sex"?
2. Why has erotic pleasure been associated with death?
3. Who is Caleb, and what does Mairs learn from him?
4. What is meant by calling sex a political deed or act of war?

"The other day, sitting in a tweed chair with my knees crossed, drinking a cup of coffee and smoking a cigarette, I looked straight at my therapist and said, 'I don't like sex.' I have known this man for years now. I have told him that I don't like my husband, my children, my parents, my students, my life. I may even have said at some time, 'I don't like sex very much.' But the difference between not liking sex very much and not liking sex is vast, vaster even than the Catholic Church's gulf between salvation and damnation, because there's no limbo, no purgatory. An irony here: For in another age (perhaps in this age within the bosom of the Holy Mother Church) I would be the woman whose price is above rubies, pure and virtuous, purity and virtue having always attached themselves, at least for women, to the matter of sex. As it is, I am, in my metaphor, one of the damned. My thera-pist has a homelier metaphor. I have, he says, what our society considers 'the worst wart.' In 1981 in the United States of America one cannot fail to like sex. It's not normal. It's not nice."

"On Not Liking Sex," from *Plaintext* (Tucson: University of Arizona Press, 1986), pp. 70–92.

This paragraph opened a brief essay I wrote a couple of years ago entitled "On Not Liking Sex." The essay, which I have preserved here in quotation marks, was a brittle, glittery piece, a kind of spun confection of the verbal play I'd like to engage in at cocktail parties but can muster only at a solitary desk with a legal-size yellow pad in front of me. It was, in fact, as you can see if you read it straight through, cocktail party chatter. And yet it was true, insofar as any truth can be translated into words. That is, it said some things, and suggested others, about me and the times I live in which were accurate enough as far as they went.

But they certainly didn't go very far. Hardly to the end of the block. Certainly not across the street. This essay is an almost perfect example of a phenomenon I've only recently become aware of, though clearly at a deeper level I've understood its workings for a very long time, a kind of pretense at serious writing which I use to keep busy and out of trouble: the kind of trouble you get when you run smack into an idea so significant and powerful that the impact jars you to the bone. It's a way of staying out of the traffic. It is not babble, and it is not easy. On the contrary, it requires painstakingly chosen diction, deliberately controlled syntax, and seamless organization. A rough spot is a trouble spot, a split, a crack, out of which something dreadful (probably black, probably with a grin) may leap and squash you flat.

If this essay was an exercise in making careful statements that would ensure that I never said what I really had to say, then what did I have to say? I don't know. If I'd known then, I couldn't have written such a piece in the first place. And the only progress I've made since then is to have gained a little courage in the face of things that leap out of cracks in the pavement. If I look at the essay again closely, if I listen for the resonances among the words with the not-yet-words, perhaps I can discover some portion of the significance—for the woman just turned forty in the 1980s in the United States of America—of not liking sex.

The title and the first paragraph, by using words as though, like algebraic notation, they had fixed meanings in the context of a given problem, claim to have signified an attitude they have in fact obscured. Even if *on* and *not* may be allowed a certain fixity as they function here, *liking* and *sex* may not. *Sex,* in its most general sense, is simply the way one is: male or female just as black or brown, blue- or hazel-eyed, long- or stubby-fingered, able or not to curl one's tongue into a tube. The genes take care of it. One may dislike one's sex, apparently, just as my daughter dislikes her nose, which is round and tends toward rosy under the sun; some people, thanks to the technological genius of modern medicine, even change theirs. But I like my sex. I suffer from penis envy, of course, to the extent that freedom and privilege have attached themselves to this fleshy sign; I've never wished for the actual appendage, however, except on long car trips through sparsely populated areas. In fact, looked at this way, *not liking sex* doesn't make sense to me at all, any more than do *having sex, wanting sex, demanding sex, refusing sex.* Such phrases clarify the specialized use of the word as shorthand for sexual activity, particularly sexual intercourse.

So I don't like sexual activity. But *like* can mean both to take pleasure in, enjoy, and to wish to have, want; and wanting something seems to me quite a different matter from enjoying it. The former is volitional, a reaching out for experience, whereas the latter is a response to an experience (whether sought for or not) already in progress. In these terms I can and often do enjoy sex. But I do not necessarily want to engage in sexual activity even though I may enjoy doing so.

"The human psyche being the squirmy creature that it is, I have trouble pinning down my objections to sex. I do not seem to object to the act itself which, if I can bring myself to commit it, I like very well. I object to the idea. My objections are undoubtedly, in part, Puritanical. Not for nothing did John Howland, Stephen Hopkins, Thomas Rogers, and Elder William Brewster bring on the Mayflower the seed that would one day bloom in me. If it feels good, it's bad. Sex feels good. My objections may also be aesthetic: It's a sweaty, slimy business. Certainly they are mythic, Eros and Thanatos colliding in the orgasm to explode the frail self back into the atoms of the universe. Love is Death."

The human psyche squirms indeed, especially when it is striving to distance itself from its desires by creating platonic distinctions between things in themselves and the ideas of things. I don't object to the idea of sex. In fact, I don't feel any particular response one way or the other to the idea of sex. Sex for me as for most, I should think, is not ideational but sensual, and it is this distinction that gives me trouble, a distinction that resembles that between wanting and enjoying. I don't object to the *idea* of sex: I object to the *sense* of sex. An act is a sign. Directly apprehended, it has always at least one meaning and usually a multiplicity of meanings. These I must sort out—their implications, their resonances—in order to understand how I, with a singularly human perversity, can not want what I enjoy.

Puritanism, aesthetics, and myth all play a part in this response, no doubt, though the reference to the Mayflower is misleading (the Pilgrims were not Puritans, though many of their descendants were), and as far as I know, the Puritans did not prohibit the sex act—no matter what it felt like—so long as it was confined to the marriage bed. The kind of puritanism that has dogged me is more diffuse than that of my foremothers, perhaps the inevitable legacy of their hard-scrabble existence in tiny communities clinging to the flinty, bitter-wintered New England coast, no longer a religion but still a code of conduct, close-mouthed, grudging of joy, quick to judge and reject. We conducted ourselves at all levels with restraint. Our disapproval of Catholics was not particularly theological; rather, we thought them primitive, childishly taken with display, with their candles and crosses and croziers, play-acting at religion. We painted our houses white with black or green shutters, grey with blue shutters, sometimes soft yellow or dark brown, and we shuddered at the pink and turquoise and lime green on the little capes and ranches that belonged, we assumed, to the Italians. When we met, we greeted one another with a nod, perhaps a small smile, a few words, a firm handshake, even a kiss on the cheek, depending on the degree of our intimacy, but we did not fall into each other's arms with loud smackings, everybody jabbering at once. As a child I was given to fits of weeping and outbursts of delight which to this day my mother refers to with a sigh as "Nancy's dramatics"; I do not, of course, have them now.

Here is the real aesthetics of the matter: the refinement of decoration and gesture to a state so etiolated that voices pierce, perfumes smother, colors clash and scream and shout. I still dislike wearing red and certain shades of pink and orange. The entire sensory world impinges—presses, pinches, pummels—unless one keeps a distance. Touch comes, eventually, to burn. Sex isn't bad so much because it feels good as because it's poor form—the kind of rowdy, riotous behavior one squelches in children as they become young ladies (honest to God, I was never permitted to refer to female human beings as women but only as ladies) and gentlemen. Sex is indecorous.

As for the sweat and slime, the basis for this objection strikes me as more medical than aesthetic. After all, one can get a good deal grubbier on a hike up a small mountain, which is just good clean fun. But the body itself is not clean. It is, according to pathologists like my ancestor Rudolf Virchow, a veritable pesthouse. I grew up knowing that my breath was pestilent ("cover your mouth when you sneeze"), that my mouth was pestilent ("don't kiss me—you've got a cold"). And then along came men, themselves crawling with germs, who breathed on me, who wanted to put their mouths on mine and make me sick. Rudolf may have done wonders for German public health, but he sure put a kink in my private sex life. Oddly enough, this phobia of germs did not include my genitalia, perhaps because they lay untouched and unpondered until long after it had been formed. Nowadays, with the threat of venereal disease widely published, I don't suppose one can be so insouciant. The terms lurk at every orifice, and sex is simply contrary to good sanitary practices.

Poor sanitary practices may give you a cold or a stomach flu or herpes, but they are not, in Tucson in 1983, likely to do you in. The equation of sex with death is of another order altogether, though not the less dreadful for not being literal. As late as the Renaissance *to die* was used as we use *to come* to signify orgasm; and although we have abandoned the explicit connection, we have not lost the construct that underlies it. Orgasm shares, briefly, the characteristics we imagine death to have, the annihilation (or at least the transmogrification) of consciousness, the extinction of the *I* that forms and controls being. The loss of my hard-won identity, even for an instant, risks forfeiture of self: not perhaps the death that ends in the coffin but certainly the death that ends in the cell: I am afraid of going away and never coming back.

❧ ❧ ❧

"But most strongly, my objections are what I reluctantly term 'political.' My reluctance stems from the sense that 'political' in this context implies the kind of radical lesbianism that suggests that medical technology is sufficiently advanced to permit the elimination of the male entirely. I learned, in one of the most poignant affairs of my life, that I am not lesbian. Nor am I even a good feminist, since I seldom think abstractly and tend to run principles together like the paints on a sloppy artist's palette, the results being colorful but hardly coherent. No, when I say 'political,' I mean something purely personal governing the nature of the relationship between me and a given man. In this sense, sex is a political act. In it, I lose power, through submission or, in one instance, through force. In either case, my integrity is violated; I become possessed."

❧ ❧ ❧

Here's the heart of the matter—politics—and I've dashed it off and done it up with ribbons of lesbianism and feminism so that the plain package hardly shows. True, I'm not lesbian, but thanks to the fundamental heterosexual bias of our culture no one would be likely to assume that I was. And I am, in fact, a perfectly good if unsystematic feminist. Who in my audience, I wonder, was I worried about when I made that self-deprecatory moue, as if to say, "Don't expect too much of me; I'm just a nonradical heterosexual little woman, a bit daffy perhaps, but harmless"? And what the hell (now that I've got the ribbons off) is in the box that made me wrap it up so tight?

Politics. Power. Submission. Force. Violation. Possession. Sex is not merely a political act; it is an act of war. And no act is ever "purely personal." It is a nexus that accretes out of earlier and other acts older than memory, older than dreams: the exchange of women, along with goods, gestures, and words, in the creation of allies; the ascription to women of all that lurks terrible in the darkened brain; the protection and penetration of the maidenhead in rituals for ensuring paternity and perpetuating lineage; the conscription of women's sons for the destruction of human beings, of women's daughters for their reproduction; enforcement of silence; theft of subjectivity; immurement; death. If I think that what I do, in or out of bed, originates in me, I am a much madder woman that I believe myself to be. I am no original but simply a locus of language in a space and time that permits one—in politics as in sex—to fuck or get fucked. Aggression is the germ in all the words.

From such an angle, sex is always rape, and indeed I tangle the two words at the level just below articulation. Perhaps I do so because my first sexual intercourse was a rape. At least it occurred in the safety of my own bed by someone I knew intimately, so that although I was furious, I was never in fear for my life. We were both nineteen, had been high-school sweethearts grown apart, and he had come to spend a weekend at the Farm, where I was working as a mother's helper for the summer. We spent the evening deep in conversation, I remember, and after I went to bed, he came into my room, jumped on top of me, deflowered me, and went away again. I don't believe we ever exchanged a word or an embrace. I felt some pain, and in the morning I found blood on my thighs and on the sheets, which I had secretly to wash, so I know that all of this really happened, but I never permitted myself the least feeling about it, not as much as I might have given a nightmare. I *knew* that I was furious, but I *felt* nothing. I don't know what response he expected, but he got none at all. He left the next day, without my ever having spoken to him, and we never met again.

Nor do I know what effect he intended his act to have. I'm sure that he was marking me, for we grew up at the tail end of the time when virginity had real significance, and in defloration he claimed me in only a slightly more subtle manner than incising his initials into some hidden area of my flesh. He knew that I was in love with another man, that I planned to be married within a year, and for a long time I believed that he was trying, through some sort of magical thinking, to force me to marry him instead. We really did believe that a woman belonged to the man who first "had" her. But now I think that he wasn't marking me for himself so much as spoiling me for George. Whatever its true interpretation, his act makes clear my absence from the transaction. The business was between him and George, the item of exchange one tarnished coin.

To sense myself such a cipher robs me of power. In sex, as in many other instances, I feel powerless. Part of this feeling arises from the fact that, as new symptoms of multiple sclerosis appear and worsen, my power literally drains away. But to what extent is multiple sclerosis merely the physical inscription of my way of being in the world? In sex, as in the rest of my life, I am acted upon. I am the object, not the agent. I live in the passive voice. The phallus penetrates me; I do not surround, engulf, incorporate the phallus. No wonder Caleb raped me. Rape was his only grammatical option.

Thus, I see that in a queer and cruel way I raped him by forcing him to rape me. I always made myself the object of his desire. How many times, I remember now, we came to the brink of intercourse, and always at the last I turned him away, pretending that I couldn't overcome my moral scruples. What I really couldn't overcome was a barrier so ludicrous that I don't expect you to believe it: my underpants. I couldn't figure out how to get rid of them. The women in films and romantic novels, where I'd gotten my impressions of the mechanics of intercourse, didn't struggle with underpants. Did I think they just melted away? After all, I took my underpants off ever day as matter-of-factly as I kicked them under the bed to drive my mother wild with despair over my inability to keep some man a decent house. Why then could I not just take them off an extra time? The gesture seemed too overt, too clumsy and pedestrian for the occasion. I couldn't bear to look a fool. So I lay in bondage to the concept of woman as image, not agent, kept a virgin till I was nineteen by Carter Lollipop Pants, red ones and navy ones, their combed cotton grim as iron through my crotch. But for Caleb, who knew nothing of my quandary, I was withholding a treasure that must have seemed of great worth, since I guarded it so jealously. I think I can understand his fury when I threatened to give it to someone else.

Ah, but I'm so old now. I can't blame myself for having been a fool, or him for having believed me a pearl of great price instead of a human being, for whatever she was worth. We were both too young to give tongue to the grammar of our intercourse. All I can do now is use the leverage of my understanding to pry open the box I have stripped and look at the contents squarely. In sex, that political act, I lose power because I have still not learned what it might be and how to claim it.

"For this reason, I have preferred casual lovers to a permanent, long-term partner. They have fewer expectations, thus minimizing possession and obligation. Less is at stake. With them, I can concentrate on the act itself without worrying about its implications. They will be gone long before they learn enough about me to threaten my privacy or come to consider sexual access a right or even a privilege. But even lovers, the romantic ones at least, are risky. They can be more interested in being in love than in bed. My latest lover pitched me out on the grounds that he wasn't in love with me (don't ask me why he took me in—life is complicated enough as it is); and with the irony that won't work in fiction but does splendidly in life, I had fallen in love with him, only the second time that I have done so and the only time that doing so was a mistake. The experience was so nearly disastrous that I learned precipitously the lesson that had long been floating just outside the periphery of my vision: Celibacy is power."

❦ ❦ ❦

An agoraphobe, a depressive, I have long since learned that avoidance is the most comfortable way to cope with situations that make me uneasy, and God knows sex makes me uneasy. In the playfulness of the opening of a sexual relationship, the issue of power is eclipsed by curiosity, exhilaration, voluptuousness. I find my delight in the process chronicled in my journal: "I sit beside Richard. It is terribly hot—I can feel the steam from both our bodies. We play the touching game— arms touch, knees brush, shoulders press together—at first by 'accident,' testing for response, then deliberately. I love this game, as often as I've played it and as silly as it is; it has a kind of rhythm and elegance when played properly, with good humor, without haste. Richard is very good at it. When, at one point, we have looked at one another for a long moment, he smiles a little and I say, 'What?' He starts to say something, then breaks off: 'You know.' I laugh and say, 'I've been wondering what would happen if I leaned over and kissed you.' It is a dumb idea— I don't know most of the people there very well, but Richard does, and they all know that I'm married. 'I think we'd better wait to do that on our own,' he replies. 'Soon,' 'Yes,' I say, 'yes, soon.' If I hadn't driven my own car, it could have been right then. Wasn't. The kiss is yet to come."

But in truth I do not like sex, even in brief affairs. In the rush of excitement I think I do, but afterwards I am always embarrassed by it. If I could stay balanced in the delicious vertigo of flirtation, I might not feel ashamed, but I can't. I always want to tumble dizzily into bed. And after I've been there, even once, my privacy has been not merely threatened but ruptured. My privacy I carry around me as a bubble of space. Quite literally. I hate to be touched. I hate to be known. If the bubble is pricked, I may disintegrate, leaking out vaporously and vanishing on the wind. The man who has even once seen me up close, naked and transported, knows more about me than I can bear for him to know. For this reason, I have not, in fact, preferred casual lovers to a permanent, long-term partner; if I had, I wouldn't still be married after twenty years. I have taken a casual lover every now and then in the hope that I can reduce sex to pure, unfreighted fun; but the baggage always catches up with me.

One of the cases, of course, carries love. Lovers and husbands alike are risky to a woman who cannot bear to be loved any more than to be touched. I can feel love creep around me, pat me with soft fingers, and I stiffen and struggle for breath. By contrast, I quite readily fall in love and have loved, in some way, all but one of the men I've slept with. So what all the bobbing and weaving about my "latest lover" might mean I'm not sure. I hadn't, at the time I wrote the essay, got over him, and my immediate judgment now is that one oughtn't to try to write the truth while in the kind of turmoil that at that time was threatening my sanity and therefore my life. But on second thought I see that here are simply two truths. I wrote the truth when I said that I'd fallen in love with only two lovers in my life, though I can't think now who I had in mind; I write the truth when I say that I've fallen in love with all but one. Quod scripsi, scripsi. Anyway, I must have learned some lesson from the bitterness the last one brought me, for I have not taken another.

All the same, celibacy is not power. Celibacy is celibacy: the withholding of oneself from sexual union. When it is actively chosen as a means of redirecting one's attention, as it is by some religious, it may both reflect and confer personal power. But when it is clutched at as a means of disengaging oneself from the tentacles of human conflict, it is simply one more technique for avoiding distress. As I stay at home to avoid agoraphobic attacks, I stay out of bed to avoid claustrophobic ones. I am celibate not for the love of God but for the fear of love.

"Avoiding sex altogether is not difficult. You must simply rent a tiny apartment, large enough only for yourself and possibly a very small black cat, and let no one into it. If you want friends, meet them at their houses, if they'll have you, at bars and restaurants, at art galleries, poetry readings, concerts. But don't take them home with you. Keep your space inviolate. During attacks of loneliness and desire, smoke cigarettes. Drink Amaretto. Throw the I Ching. Write essays. Letting someone into your space is tantamount to letting him between your legs, and more dangerous, since you risk his touching the inner workings of your life, not merely your body. Ask him if he wouldn't rather drive into the country for a picnic."

This advice is sound. I have tested all of it. Then I swallowed a handful of Elavil one Hallowe'en and almost succeeded in avoiding sex altogether.

"All this I have learned. What I haven't learned is what to do with the grief and guilt that not liking sex inevitably arouses. The grief is so protean and private that I will not attempt to articulate it. But the guilt is a decidedly public matter, since it could not exist—not in its present form anyway—in the absence of post-Freudian social pressure to regard sex as the primary source not of joy (I doubt that contemporary society knows much about joy) but of satisfaction. If I don't like sex, I am abnormal, repressed, pathetic, sick—the labels vary but the significance is consistent—I do not belong in the ranks of healthy human beings, health requiring as one of its terms sexual activity and fulfillment."

By separating out grief from the complex of responses I feel to not wanting sex, and by tying it off as a "private" matter, I hoped perhaps that, like a vestigial finger or toe, it would drop away. But the dissociation is not authentic, because in fact all my responses are private insofar as the construct they form is my peculiar *I*, and all are public insofar as that *I* is a linguistic product spoken by a patriarchal culture that insists that my God-created function is to rejoice, through my person, the heart of a man. Moreover, failure to do so results not in guilt, as I have stated it, but in shame, which is a truly protean (and, say some feminists, distinctively feminine) emotion, pervasive and inexpiable. About guilt one can do something: Like a wound in the flesh, with proper cleansing it will heal, the scar, however twisted and lumpy, proof against infection. Shame, like the vaginal wound always open to invasion, is an inoperable state. My tongue has given me these distinctions. With it I must acknowledge my shame.

Shamelessness, like shame, is not a masculine condition. That is, there is no *shameless man* as there is a *shameless woman* or, as my grandmother used to say, a *shameless hussy:* A man without shame is in general assumed simply to have done nothing he need feel guilty about. A woman without shame is a strumpet, a trollop, a whore, a witch. The connotations have been, immemorially, sexual. Here is the thirteenth-century author of the *Ancrene Riwle,* a priest instructing three anchoresses in the correct manner of confession: "A woman will say, 'I have been foolish' or 'I had a lover,' whereas she should confess, 'I am a stud mare, a stinking whore.'" And somewhat later, in the *Malleus Maleficarum,* a warning to Inquisitors: "All witchcraft comes from carnal Lust which is in Women insatiable." My sexuality has been the single most powerful disruptive force mankind has ever perceived, and its repression has been the work of centuries.

Now, suddenly, the message has changed. Now, after ages of covering my face and my genitals—St. Paul's veil over my hair, my breasts bound, my waist girded in whalebone, my face masked with kohl and rouge, my length swathed in white cambric pierced by a lace-edged buttonhole through which to guide the erect penis to my hidden treasure—I am supposed to strip to the skin and spread my legs and strive for multiple orgasm.

Knowing what The Fathers have given me to know of the dangers of female sexuality, how could I dare?

"If I got this message from one person at a time, I might be able to deal with it with rationality, distance, even amusement. But I get it impersonally, from all sides, in a barrage so relentless that the wonder is that I survive my guilt, let alone cope with it. I get the message from the bookshelves, where I find not only *The Joy of Sex* but also *More Joy of Sex,* written by a man whose very name promises physical contentment. (I have read some of these books. They contain many instructions on how to do it well. I know how to do it well. I just don't know whether I want to do it at all.) The message comes with my jeans, which I may buy no longer merely for durability and comfort but for the ache they will create in some man's crotch. It foams in my toothpaste, my bath soap, even my dish detergent. It follows me through the aisles of the supermarket and the drugstore. It ridicules my breastless body, my greying hair."

Or has the message really changed? The body swaddled has become the body naked but it is, all the same, the female body, artifice of desire, still inscribed after stripping with the marks of straps cut into the shoulders, underwires into the breasts, zipper into the belly, squeezed and shaved and deodorized until it is shapely and sanitary enough to arouse no dread of its subjective possibilities. The mechanics of its eroticism have been altered so that, instead of receiving male desire as a patient vessel, it is supposed to validate male performance by resonating when it is played upon. Nonetheless, it remains a thing, alien, "other," as Simone de Beauvoir has pointed out, to the man who dreams of it—and also to the woman who wears it, sculpturing it to the specifications of the male-dominated advertising, publishing, fashion, and cosmetic industries.

An object does not know its own value. Even a sentient being, made into an object, will feel uncertain of her worth except as it is measured by the standards of the agora, the market place, which will reflect whatever male fantasies about women are current. Thanks to astonishing technological advances in the broadcasting of these standards, almost everyone in the world knows what they are and can weigh his object or her self against them, no matter how bizarre the means for their attainment may be. Somewhere I read that it takes the concerted pushing and pulling of three people to get a high-fashion model zipped into her jeans and propped into position for photographing. We all see the photographs, though not the three laborers behind them, and believe that the ideal woman looks like that. Thus a standard has been fixed, and most of us, lacking the appropriate sturdy personnel, won't meet it.

Through such manipulation I have learned to despise my body. I have, perhaps, more reason than most for doing so, since my body is not merely aging but also crippled. On the fair market, its value is slipping daily as the musculature twists and atrophies, the digestive system grinds spasmodically, the vision blurs, the gait lurches and stumbles. But long before I knew I had multiple sclerosis, I hadn't much use for it. Nor have I had much use for the man who desires it. He lacks taste, it seems to me: the kind of man who prefers formica to teak, Melmac to Limoges, canned clam chowder to bouillabaisse. Who wants to have sex with a man who can't do better than you?

"Were I living in the Middle Ages, my difficulty could be quickly solved. I would become an anchoress, calling from my cell, 'And all shall be well, and all manner of thing shall be well.' God would love me. My fellow creatures would venerate me. But the wheel has turned and tipped me into a time when God has been dead for a century and my fellow creatures are likely to find me more pitiable than venerable. I shall no doubt be lonelier than any anchoress.

Nonetheless, my bed will stay narrow."

I love closure. Especially in any kind of writing. I like to tie off the tale with some statement that sounds as though nothing further can be said. Never mind the Princess's hysterical weeping on the morning after her wedding night, her later infidelities, the first son's cleft palate, the Prince's untimely death during an ill-advised raid on the neighboring kingdom, the old King's driveling madness: They lived happily ever after, or, if the tale is a modern one like mine, unhappily ever after. But their development ceased. I love closure enough to pretend that quick resolution lies along the length of a cell (in which I might prostrate myself praying not "All shall be well" but "I am a stud mare, a stinking whore"), enough to believe that virtue lies easy in a narrow bed. True, at the time I wrote the essay I was sleeping alone in a narrow bed, but it's widened again now to queen size, with George in one half, or sometimes two thirds, and often Vanessa Bell and Lionel Tigress too.

My sexuality is too complicated a text to be truncated neatly at any point. What has woven it together until now, I see, to prevent it from being a mere tangle of random terror and revulsion, has been my coherent inverse equation of autonomy with physical violation. Such a connection is predicated upon the denial of my own subjectivity in sexual experience. Afraid of being reduced by another to an object, I have persisted in seeing myself as such. Why did I lie, limp as a doll, while Caleb butted at me? Why didn't I writhe, scratch, bite? Why didn't I at least give him a thorough tongue-lashing the next morning before he left my life forever? Over and over I have demanded that I be raped and have then despised both the rapist and myself.

I understand now some of the teachings that helped me compose such a tale of invasion, illness, self-immolation. And I will not close it off with an *ever after,* happy or unhappy. Tomorrow the Princess gets out of bed again: She washes her hair, drinks her coffee, scribbles some pages, tells a joke to her son, bakes a spinach quiche. And the day after. And the day after that. All the while she is telling herself a story. In it, she is aging now, and she drags one foot behind her when she walks. These are changes she can scrutinize in her mirror. They tell her that the true texts are the ones that do not end but revolve and reflect and spin out new constellations of meaning day after day, page after page, joke after joke, quiche after quiche. She has been learning much about vision and revision. She has been learning much about forgiveness. In this story, she is the writer of essays. She has a black typewriter and several reams of paper. One day, she thinks she could find herself writing an essay called "On Liking Sex." There's that to consider.

QUESTIONS FOR ANALYSIS AND DISCUSSION

1. Mairs introduces and intersperses this essay with quoted paragraphs from another essay. Some of these passages conclude with a shocking tone, such as "love is death" or "celibacy is power." What purpose does this format serve? Select one of the quoted passages and clarify its relation to the essay.

2. Mairs recounts beliefs of the Puritans, Church Fathers, and sundry other moralists who presumed that good girls do not think about their bodies as sources of erotic joy. Do you think she is blaming these moral influences for her own uncertainty and misgivings? Cite passages to support your answer.

3. What is meant by the ideal woman? Given Mairs's criteria for the cultural shaping of this ideal, could there also be an ideal man that has the effect of diminishing men's self-respect? Why, or why not?

4. What is the importance of Mairs's relation to Caleb? What is your impression of her reflections on Caleb?

41.

ST. AUGUSTINE

Lust

For Augustine (354–430), one of the most influential Christian thinkers, lust presents humans with the severest dangers. Unlike other vices, lust seems to thrive when we are least suspecting of its presence. Hence, virtuous persons and religious believers are especially vulnerable to the powers of lust; sexual desire and pleasure often induce one to forget about oneself or about God. Lust is a most dangerous vice—it can ruin all the good done by a person's virtuous efforts. Some historians of moral thought recognize Augustine as representing a turning point in ethics. Pagan ethics did not assume that sexual love was inherently evil; after Augustine and still today, people have trouble separating acts of lust from sin, guilt, or immorality.

⊢ CRITICAL READING QUESTIONS ⊢

1. Why does Augustine introduce sleep when talking about the pleasures of lust?
2. For Augustine, what is the relation between the flesh and the spirit?
3. Why is lust described as a disease?
4. Where does Augustine think the self contains a monstrousness?

"Lust," from *Confessions*, translated by F. J. Sheed (Indianapolis: Hackett, 1993), pp. 135–142. Notes have been omitted.

V

Now when this man of Yours, Simplicianus, had told me the story of Victorinus, I was on fire to imitate him: which indeed was why he had told me. He added that in the time of the emperor Julian, when a law was made prohibiting Christians from teaching Literature and Rhetoric, Victorinus had obeyed the law, preferring to give up his own school of words rather than Your word, by which You make eloquent the tongues of babes. In this he seemed to me not only courageous but actually fortunate, because it gave him the chance to devote himself wholly to You. I longed for the same chance, but I was bound not with the iron of another's chains, but by my own iron will. The enemy held my will; and of it he made a chain and bound me. Because my will was perverse it changed to lust, and lust yielded to become habit, and habit not resisted became necessity. These were like links hanging one on another—which is why I have called it a chain—and their hard bondage held me bound hand and foot. The new will which I now began to have, by which I willed to worship You freely and to enjoy You, O God, the only certain Joy, was not yet strong enough to overcome that earlier will rooted deep through the years. My two wills, one old, one new, one carnal, one spiritual, were in conflict and in their conflict wasted my soul.

Thus, with myself as object of the experiment, I came to understand what I had read, how the *flesh lusts against the spirit and the spirit against the flesh*. I indeed was in both camps, but more in that which I approved in myself than in that which I disapproved. For in a sense it was now no longer I that was in this second camp, because in large part I rather suffered it unwillingly than did it with my will. Yet habit had grown stronger against me by my own act, since I had come willingly where I did not now will to be. Who can justly complain when just punishment overtakes the sinner? I no longer had the excuse which I used to think I had for not yet forsaking the world and serving You, the excuse namely that I had no certain knowledge of the truth. By now I was quite certain; but I was still bound to earth and refused to take service in Your army; I feared to be freed of all the things that impeded me, as strongly as I ought to have feared the being impeded by them. I was held down as agreeably by this world's baggage as one often is by sleep; and indeed the thoughts with which I meditated upon You were like the efforts of a man who wants to get up but is so heavy with sleep that he simply sinks back into it again. There is no one who wants to be asleep always—for every sound judgment holds that it is best to be awake—yet a man often postpones the effort of shaking himself awake when he feels a sluggish heaviness in the limbs, and settles pleasurably into another doze though he knows he should not, because it is time to get up. Similarly I regarded it as settled that it would be better to give myself to Your love rather than go on yielding to my own lust; but the first course delighted and convinced my mind, the second delighted my body and held it in bondage. For there was nothing I could reply when You called me: *Rise, thou that sleepest and arise from the dead: and Christ shall enlighten thee;* and whereas You showed me by every evidence that Your words were true, there was simply nothing I could answer save only laggard lazy words: "Soon," "Quite soon," "Give me just a little while." But "soon" and "quite soon" did not mean any particular time; and "just a little while" went on for a long while. It was in vain that *I delighted in Thy law according to the inner man, when that other law in my members rebelled against the law of my mind and led me captive in the law of sin that was in my members.* For the law of sin is the fierce force of habit, by which the mind is drawn and held even against its will, and yet deservedly because it had fallen wilfully into the habit. *Who then should deliver me from the body of this death, but Thy grace only, through Jesus Christ Our Lord?*

VI

Now, O Lord, my Helper and my Redeemer, I shall tell and confess to Your name how You delivered me from the chain of that desire of the flesh which held me so bound, and the servitude of worldly things. I went my usual way with a mind ever more anxious, and day after day I sighed for You. I would be off to Your church as often as my business, under the weight of which I groaned, left me free. Alypius was with me, at liberty from his legal office after a third term as Assessor and waiting for private clients, to whom he might sell his legal advice––just as I sold skill in speaking, if indeed this can be bought. Nebridius had yielded to our friendship so far as to teach under Verecundus, a great friend of all of us, a citizen and elementary school teacher of Milan, who had earnestly asked and indeed by right of friendship demanded from our company the help he badly needed. Nebridius was not influenced in the matter by any desire for profit, for he could have done better had he chosen, in a more advanced school; but he was a good and gracious friend and too kindly a man to refuse our requests. But he did it all very quietly, for he did not want to draw the attention of those persons whom the world holds great; he thus avoided distraction of mind, for he wanted to have his mind free and at leisure for as many hours as possible to seek or read or hear truths concerning wisdom.

On a certain day—Nebridius was away for some reason I cannot recall—there came to Alypius and me at our house one Ponticianus, a fellow countryman of ours, being from Africa, holder of an important post in the emperor's court. There was something or other he wanted of us and we sat down to discuss the matter. As it happened he noticed a book on a gaming table by which we were sitting. He picked it up, opened it, and found that it was the apostle Paul, which surprised him because he had expected that it would be one of the books I wore myself out teaching. Then he smiled a little and looked at me, and expressed pleasure but surprise too at having come suddenly upon that book, and only that book, lying before me. For he was a Christian and a devout Christian; he knelt before You in church, O our God, in daily prayer and many times daily. I told him that I had given much care to these writings. Whereupon he began to tell the story of the Egyptian monk Antony, whose name was held in high honour among Your servants, although Alypius and I had never heard it before that time. When he learned this, he was the more intent upon telling the story, anxious to introduce so great a man to men ignorant of him, and very much marvelling at our ignorance. But Alypius and I stood amazed to hear of Your wonderful works, done in the true faith and in the Catholic Church so recently, practically in our own times, and with such numbers of witnesses. All three of us were filled with wonder, we because the deeds we were now hearing were so great, and he because we had never heard them before.

From this story he went on to the great groups in the monasteries, and their ways all redolent of You, and the fertile deserts of the wilderness, of all of which we knew nothing. There was actually a monastery at Milan, outside the city walls. It was full of worthy brethren and under the care of Ambrose. And we had not heard of it. He continued with his discourse and we listened in absolute silence. It chanced that he told how on one occasion he and three of his companions—it was at Treves, when the emperor was at the chariot races in the Circus—had gone one afternoon to walk in the gardens close by the city walls. As it happened they fell into two groups, one of the others staying with him, and the other two likewise walking their own way. But as those other two strolled on they came into a certain house, the dwelling of some servants of Yours, poor in spirit, of whom is the king-dom of God. There they found a small book in which was written the life of An-tony. One of them began to read it, marvelled at it, was inflamed by it. While he was actually reading he had begun to think how he might embrace such a life, and give up his worldly employment to serve You alone. For the two men were both state officials. Suddenly the man who was doing the reading was filled with a love of holiness and angry at himself with righteous shame. He looked at his friend and said to him: "Tell me, please, what is the goal of our ambition in all these labours of ours? What are we aiming at? What is our motive in being in the public service? Have we any higher hope at court than to be friends of the emperor? And at that level, is not everything uncertain and full of perils? And how many perils must we meet on the way to this greater peril? And how long before we are there? But if I should choose to be a friend of God, I can become one now." He said this, and all troubled with the pain of the new life coming to birth in him, he turned back his eyes to the book. He read on and was changed inwardly, where You alone could see; and the world dropped away from his mind, as soon appeared outwardly. For while he was reading and his heart thus tossing on its own flood, at length he broke out in heavy weeping, saw the better way and chose it for his own. Being now Your servant he said to his friend, "Now I have broken from that hope we had and have decided to serve God; and I enter upon that service from this hour, in this place. If you have no will to imitate me, at least do not try to dissuade me."

The other replied that he would remain his companion in so great a service for so great a prize. So the two of them, now Your servants, built a spiritual tower at the only cost that is adequate, the cost of leaving all things and following You. Then Ponticianus and the man who had gone walking with him in another part of the garden came looking for them in the same place, and when they found them suggested that they should return home as the day was now declining. But they told their decision and their purpose, and how that will had arisen in them and was now settled in them; and asked them not to try to argue them out of their decision, even if they would not also join them. Ponticianus and his friend, though not changed from their former state, yet wept for themselves, as he told us, and congratulated them in God and commended themselves to their prayers. Then with their own heart trailing in the dust they went off to the palace, while the other two, with their heart fixed upon heaven, remained in the hut. Both these men, as it happened, were betrothed, and when the two women heard of it they likewise dedicated their virginity to You.

VII

This was the story Ponticianus told. But You, Lord, while he was speaking, turned me back towards myself, taking me from behind my own back where I had put myself all the time that I preferred not to see myself. And You set me there before my own face that I might see how vile I was, how twisted and unclean and spotted and ulcerous. I saw myself and was horrified; but there was no way to flee from myself. If I tried to turn my gaze from myself, there was Ponticianus telling what he was telling; and again You were setting me face to face with myself, forcing me upon my own sight, that I might see my iniquity and loathe it. I had known it, but I had pretended not to see it, had deliberately looked the other way and let it go from my mind.

But this time, the more ardently I approved those two as I heard of their determination to win health for their souls by giving themselves up wholly to Your healing, the more detestable did I find myself in comparison with them. For many years had flowed by—a dozen or more—from the time when I was nineteen and was stirred by the reading of Cicero's Hortensius to the study of wisdom; and here was I still postponing the giving up of this world's happiness to devote myself to the search for that of which not the finding only but the mere seeking is better than to find all the treasures and kingdoms of men, better than all the body's pleasures though they were to be had merely for a nod. But I in my great worthlessness—for it was greater thus early—had begged You for chastity, saying: "Grant me chastity and continence, but not yet." For I was afraid that You would hear my prayer too soon, and too soon would heal me from the disease of lust which I wanted satisfied rather than extinguished. So I had gone wandering in my sacrilegious superstition through the base ways of the Manicheans: not indeed that I was sure they were right but that I preferred them to the Christians, whom I did not inquire about in the spirit of religion but simply opposed through malice.

I had thought that my reason for putting off from day to day the following of You alone to the contempt of earthly hopes was that I did not see any certain goal towards which to direct my course. But now the day was come when I stood naked in my own sight and my conscience accused me: "Why is my voice not heard? Surely you are the man who used to say that you could not cast off vanity's baggage for an uncertain truth. Very well: now the truth is certain, yet you are still carrying the load. Here are men who have been given wings to free their shoulders from the load, though they did not wear themselves out in searching nor spend ten years or more thinking about it."

Thus was I inwardly gnawed at. And I was in the grip of the most horrible and confounding shame, while Ponticianus was telling his story. He finished the tale and the business for which he had come; and he went his way, and I to myself. What did I not say against myself, with what lashes of condemnation did I not scourge my soul to make it follow me now that I wanted to follow You! My soul hung back. It would not follow, yet found no excuse for not following. All its arguments had already been used and refuted. There remained only trembling silence: for it feared as very death the cessation of that habit of which in truth it was dying.

VIII

In the midst of that great tumult of my inner dwelling place, the tumult I had stirred up against my own soul in the chamber of my heart, I turned upon Alypius, wild in look and troubled in mind, crying out: "What is wrong with us? What is this that you heard? The unlearned arise and take heaven by force, and here are we with all our learning, stuck fast in flesh and blood! Is there any shame in following because they have gone before us, would it not be a worse shame not to follow at once?" These words and more of the same sort I uttered, then the violence of my feeling tore me from him while he stood staring at me thunderstruck. For I did not sound like myself. My brow, cheeks, eyes, flush, the pitch of my voice, spoke my mind more powerfully than the words I uttered. There was a garden attached to our lodging, of which we had the use, as indeed we had of the whole house: for our host, the master of the house, did not live there. To this garden the storm in my breast somehow brought me, for there no one could intervene in the fierce suit I had brought against myself, until it should reach its issue: though what the issue was to be, You knew, not I: but there I was, going mad on my way to sanity, dying on my way to life, aware how evil I was, unaware that I was to grow better in a little while. So I went off to the garden, and Alypius close on my heels: for it was still privacy for me to have him near, and how could he leave me to myself in that state? We found a seat as far as possible from the house. I was frantic in mind, in a frenzy of indignation at myself for not going over to Your law and Your covenant, O my God, where all my bones cried out that I should be, extolling it to the skies. The way was not by ship or chariot or on foot: it was not as far as I had gone when I went from the house to the place where we sat. For I had but to will to go, in order not merely to go but to arrive: I had only to will to go—but to will powerfully and wholly, not to turn and twist a will half-wounded this way and that, with the part that would rise struggling against the part that would keep to the earth.

In the torment of my irresolution, I did many bodily acts. Now men sometimes will to do bodily acts but cannot, whether because they have not the limbs, or because their limbs are bound or weakened with illness or in some other way unable to act. If I tore my hair, if I beat my forehead, if I locked my fingers and clasped my knees, I did it because I willed to. But I might have willed and yet not done it, if my limbs had not had the pliability to do what I willed. Thus I did so many things where the will to do them was not at all the same thing as the power to do them: and I did not do what would have pleased me incomparably more to do—a thing too which I could have done as soon as I willed to, given that willing means willing *wholly*. For in that matter, the power was the same thing as the will, and the willing *was* the doing. Yet it was not done, and the body more readily obeyed the slightest wish of the mind, more readily moved its limbs at the mind's mere nod, than the mind obeyed itself in carrying out its own great will which could be achieved simply by willing.

IX

Why this monstrousness? And what is the root of it? Let Your mercy enlighten me, that I may put the question: whether perhaps the answer lies in the mysterious punishment that has come upon men and some deeply hidden damage in the sons of Adam. Why this monstrousness? And what is the root of it? The mind gives the body an order, and is obeyed at once: the mind gives itself an order and is resisted. The mind commands the hand to move and there is such readiness that you can hardly distinguish the command from its execution. Yet the mind is mind, whereas the hand is body. The mind commands the mind to will, the mind is itself, but it does not do it. Why this monstrousness? And what is the root of it? The mind I say commands itself to will: it would not give the command unless it willed: yet it does not do what it commands. The trouble is that it does not totally will: therefore it does not totally command. It commands in so far as it wills; and it disobeys the command in so far as it does not will. The will is commanding itself to be a will— commanding itself, not some other. But it does not in its fullness give the command, so that what it commands is not done. For if the will were so in its fullness, it would not command itself to will, for it would already will. It is therefore no monstrousness, partly to will, partly not to will, but a sickness of the soul to be so weighted down by custom that it cannot wholly rise even with the support of truth. Thus there are two wills in us, because neither of them is entire: and what is lacking to the one is present in the other.

QUESTIONS FOR ANALYSIS AND DISCUSSION

1. How does Augustine view the basic components of the self? Are they in harmony or conflict? Does Augustine's portrayal of the self reflect something about human beings in general? about men? or only about Augustine?

2. The power of lust is illustrated as a kind of unstoppable force, for it escapes the powers of the will or mind. Why should the power of lust be viewed in such negative moral terms? Is there a form of lust that deserves praise in Augustine's view?

3. One of Augustine's best known lines is "Grant me chastity and continence, but not yet." How do you understand this quote in light of Augustine's confessions about his inner turmoil?

4. Examine Augustine's concerns outside a religious context. Do you think his depiction of the struggle between the temptations of the flesh, particularly sexual desire, and the rational control expected of a moral person is a problem for many human beings still today? Explain your answer.

42.

VATSYAYANA

Behavior of a Virtuous Woman

Augustine's views are expressed with dramatic flair, but his opposition between morality and lust is hardly universal. In the renowned Kama Sutra, *Hindu thinker Vatsyayana (c. 200 B.C.–A.D. 100) combines the work of numerous writers in delineating the arts of sexual pleasure as part of the moral life. Indeed, along with Dharma (religious duty or service) and Artha (acquisition of worldly goods, from property to friends), Kama (the enjoyment of sensual pleasures) is a central component to the highest goal in Hindu life— Moksha (enlightenment and liberation). This view is a clear contrast to the moral tradition of Christianity so indebted to Augustine. The* Kama Sutra *is a text meant for all. Its sexual pedagogy ranges from the right spices and foods to the variations on effective nibbles and bites when kissing. Yet its universal appeal does not mean egalitarianism. The* Kama Sutra *clearly distinguishes the duties and contributions of men from those of women. This selection illustrates that distinction.*

"Behavior of a Virtuous Woman," from *Kama Sutra*, translated by Richard Burton (New York: The Medical Press of New York, 1962), pp. 161–167.

CRITICAL READING QUESTIONS

1. Can you identify at least three duties of the virtuous woman that have nothing to do with sexual pleasure?
2. What is the difference between a virtuous woman's public and private behavior?
3. Does a virtuous woman seek Moksha, serve her assigned roles, or define the good only in terms of pleasing her man?

A virtuous woman, who has affection for her husband, should act in conformity with his wishes as if he were a divine being, and with his consent should take upon herself the whole care of his family. She should keep the whole house well cleaned, and arrange flowers of various kinds in different parts of it, and make the floor smooth and polished so as to give the whole a neat and becoming appearance. She should surround the house with a garden, and place ready in it all the materials required for the morning, noon, and evening sacrifices. Moreover she should herself revere the sanctuary of the Household Gods, for says Gonardiya, "nothing so much attracts the heart of a householder to his wife as a careful observance of the things mentioned above."

Towards the parents, relations, friends, sisters, and servants of her husband she should behave as they deserve. In the garden she should plant beds of green vegetables, bunches of the sugar cane, and clumps of the fig tree, the mustard plant, the parsley plant, the fennel plant, and the xanthochymus pictorius. Clusters of various flowers such as the trapa bispinosa, the jasmine, the gasminum grandiflorum, the yellow amaranth, the wild jasmine, the taberna montana coronaria, the nadyaworta, the china rose and others, should likewise be planted, together with the fragrant grass andropogon schænanthus, and the fragrant root of the plant andropogon miricatus. She should also have seats and arbours made in the garden, in the middle of which a well, tank, or pool should be dug.

The wife should always avoid the company of female beggars, female buddhist mendicants, unchaste and roguish women, female fortune tellers and witches. As regards meals, she should always consider what her husband likes and dislikes, and what things are good for him, and what are injurious to him. When she hears the sound of his footsteps coming home she should at once get up, and be ready to do whatever he may command her, and either order her female servant to wash his feet, or wash them herself. When going anywhere with her husband she should put on her ornaments, and without his consent she should not either give or accept invitations, or attend marriages and sacrifices, or sit in the company of female friends, or visit the temples of the Gods. And if she wants to engage in any kind of games or sports, she should not do it against his will. In the same way she should always sit down after him, and get up before him, and should never awaken him when he is asleep. The kitchen should be situated in a quiet and retired place, so as not to be accessible to strangers, and should always look clean.

In the event of any misconduct on the part of her husband, she should not blame him excessively, though she be a little displeased. She should not use abusive language towards him, but rebuke him with conciliatory words, whether he be in the company of friends or alone. Moreover, she should not be a scold, for says Gonardiya "there is no cause of dislike on the part of a husband so great as this characteristic in a wife." Lastly she should avoid bad expressions, sulky looks, speaking aside, standing in the doorway, and looking at passers-by, conversing in pleasure groves, and remaining in a lonely place for a long time; and finally she should always keep her body, her teeth, her hair and everything belonging to her tidy, sweet, and clean.

When the wife wants to approach her husband in private her dress should consist of many ornaments, various kinds of flowers, and a cloth decorated with different colours, and some sweet-smelling ointments or unguents. But her everyday dress should be composed of a thin, close-textured cloth, a few ornaments and flowers, and a little scent, not too much. She should also observe the fasts and vows of her husband, and when he tries to prevent her doing this, she should persuade him to let her do it.

At appropriate times of the year, and when they happen to be cheap, she should buy earth, bamboos, firewood, skins, and iron pots, as also salt and oil. Fragrant substances, vessels made of the fruit of the plant wrightea antidysenterica, or oval leaved wrightea, medicines, and other things which are always wanted, should be obtained when required and kept in a secret place of the house. The seeds of the radish, the potato, the common beet, the Indian wormwood, the mangoe, the cucumber, the egg plant, the kushmanda, the pumpkin gourd, the surana, the bignonia indica, the sandal wood, the premna spinosa, the garlic plant, the onion, and other vegetables, should be bought and sown at the proper seasons.

The wife, moreover, should not tell to strangers the amount of her wealth, nor the secrets which her husband has confided to her. She should surpass all the women of her own rank in life in her cleverness, her appearance, her knowledge of cookery, her pride, and her manner of serving her husband. The expenditure of the year should be regulated by the profits. The milk that remains after the meals should be turned into ghee or clarified butter. Oil and sugar should be prepared at home: spinning and weaving should also be done there; and a store of ropes and cords, and barks of trees for twisting into ropes should be kept. She should also attend to the pounding and cleaning of rice, using its small grain and chaff in some way or other. She should pay the salaries of the servants, look after the tilling of the fields, the keeping of the flocks and herds, superintend the making of vehicles, and take care of the rams, cocks, quails, parrots, starlings, cuckoos, peacocks, monkeys, and deer; and finally adjust the income and expenditure of the day. The worn-out clothes should be given to those servants who have done good work, in order to show them that their services have been appreciated, or they may be applied to some other use. The vessels in which wine is prepared, as well as those in which it is kept, should be carefully looked after, and put away at the proper time. All sales and purchases should also be well attended to. The friends of her husband she should welcome by presenting them with flowers, ointment, incense, betel leaves, and betel nut. Her father-in-law and mother-in-law she should treat as they deserve, always remaining dependent on their will, never contradicting them, speaking to them in few and not harsh words, not laughing loudly in their presence, and acting with their friends and enemies as with her own. In addition to the above she should not be vain, or too much taken up with her enjoyments. She should be liberal towards her servants, and reward them on holidays and festivals; and not give away anything without first making it known to her husband.

Thus ends the manner of a virtuous woman.

During the absence of her husband on a journey the virtuous woman should wear only her auspicious ornaments, and observe the fasts in honour of the Gods. While anxious to hear the news of her husband, she should still look after her household affairs. She should sleep near the elder women of the house, and make herself agreeable to them. She should look after and keep in repair the things that are liked by her husband, and continue the works that have been begun by him. To the abode of her relations she should not go except on occasions of joy and sorrow, and then she should go in her usual travelling dress, accompanied by her husband's servants, and not remain there for a long time. The fasts and feasts should be observed with the consent of the elders of the house. The resources should be increased by making purchases and sales according to the practice of the merchants, and by means of honest servants, superintended by herself. The income should be increased, and the expenditure diminished as much as possible. And when her husband returns from his journey, she should receive him at first in her ordinary clothes, so that he may know in what way she has lived during his absence, and should bring to him some presents, as also materials for the worship of the Deity.

Thus ends the part relating to the behaviour of a wife during the absence of her husband on a journey.

There are also some verses on the subjects as follows.

"The wife, whether she be a woman of noble family, or a virgin widow[1] remarried, or a concubine, should lead a chaste life, devoted to her husband, and doing every thing for his welfare. Women acting thus, acquire Dharma, Artha, and Kama, obtain a high position, and generally keep their husbands devoted to them."

QUESTIONS FOR ANALYSIS AND DISCUSSION

1. Vatsyayana marks a contrast between public and private behavior. Do you agree that any moral values of erotic behavior must distinguish private from public expressions of love and pleasure? Why, or why not?

2. Augustine and Vatsyayana disagree about the place of erotic pleasure within the religious life. Develop your own thoughts about whether a moral person can celebrate religious belief and erotic pleasure. Does belief rely on the authority of sacred texts or experts? Should that make a difference?

---

[1] This probably refers to a girl married in her infancy, or when very young, and whose husband had died before she arrived at the age of puberty. Infant marriages are still the common custom of the Hindoos.

3. The *Kama Sutra* is a manual on the art of love meant for a variety of audiences, yet it outlines different responsibilities for men and women. Does that make it outdated? Is it fair to accuse the many writers compiled by Vatsyayana of sexual bias? Can an ethical or cultural relativist be consistent in making any moral judgments about the content of the *Kama Sutra?* Explain your answer.

43.

SIMONE DE BEAUVOIR

The Woman in Love

According to Simone de Beauvoir, one reason for the perennial disputes about love is that men and women have completely different conceptions in mind. This is notably evident when men and women reflect on the relation of the self to the experience of love. A man in love does not alter his identity. A woman in love, however, undergoes a transformation. This contrast underscores the various moral and social practices and values men and women attribute to love. The selection here is from de Beauvoir's classic work, The Second Sex, still considered by many to be the foundation for contemporary feminist thought.

CRITICAL READING QUESTIONS

1. What are some of the key differences between a man in love and a woman in love?
2. Why does de Beauvoir remark that for a woman love is a kind of religion?
3. Which moment marks the happiness of a woman in love? Why does this moment set her up for disappointment?
4. How does de Beauvoir describe genuine love?

"The Woman in Love," from *The Second Sex*, translated by H. M. Parshley (New York: Alfred A. Knopf, Inc., 1952, 1980), pp. 642–669. Some notes have been omitted.

The word *love* has by no means the same sense for both sexes, and this is one cause of the serious misunderstandings that divide them. Byron well said: "Man's love is of man's life a thing apart; 'Tis woman's whole existence." Nietzsche expresses the same idea in *The Gay Science:*

> The single word love in fact signifies two different things for man and woman. What woman understands by love is clear enough: it is not only devotion, it is a total gift of body and soul, without reservation, without regard for anything whatever. This unconditional nature of her love is what makes it a *faith,* the only one she has. As for man, if he loves a woman, what he *wants* is that love from her; he is in consequence far from postulating the same sentiment for himself as for woman; if there should be men who also felt that desire for complete abandonment, upon my word, they would not be men.

Men have found it possible to be passionate lovers at certain times in their lives, but there is not one of them who could be called "a great lover"; in their most violent transports, they never abdicate completely; even on their knees before a mistress, what they still want is to take possession of her; at the very heart of their lives they remain sovereign subjects; the beloved woman is only one value among others; they wish to integrate her into their existence and not to squander it entirely on her. For woman, on the contrary, to love is to relinquish everything for the benefit of a master. As Cécile Sauvage puts it: "Woman must forget her own personality when she is in love. It is a law of nature. A woman is nonexistent without a master. Without a master, she is a scattered bouquet."

The fact is that we have nothing to do here with laws of nature. It is the difference in their situations that is reflected in the difference men and women show in their conceptions of love. The individual who is a subject, who is himself, if he has the courageous inclination toward transcendence, endeavors to extend his grasp on the world: he is ambitious, he acts. But an inessential creature is incapable of sensing the absolute at the heart of her subjectivity; a being doomed to immanence cannot find self-realization in acts. Shut up in the sphere of the relative, destined to the male from childhood, habituated to seeing in him a superb being whom she cannot possibly equal, the woman who has not repressed her claim to humanity will dream of transcending her being toward one of these superior beings, of amalgamating herself with the sovereign subject. There is no other way out for her than to lose herself, body and soul, in him who is represented to her as the absolute, as the essential. Since she is anyway doomed to dependence, she will prefer to serve a god rather than obey tyrants—parents, husband, or protector. She chooses to desire her enslavement so ardently that it will seem to her the expression of her liberty; she will try to rise above her situation as inessential object by fully accepting it; through her flesh, her feelings, her behavior, she will enthrone him as supreme value and reality: she will humble herself to nothingness before him. Love becomes for her a religion.

As we have seen, the adolescent girl wishes at first to identify herself with males; when she gives that up, she then seeks to share in their masculinity by having one of them in love with her; it is not the individuality of this one or that one which attracts her; she is in love with man in general. "And you, the men I shall love, how I await you!" writes Irène Reweliotty. "How I rejoice to think I shall know you soon: especially You, the first." Of course the male is to belong to the same class and race as hers, for sexual privilege is in play only with this frame. If man is to be a demigod, he must first of all be a human being, and to the colonial officer's daughter the native is not a man. If the young girl gives herself to an "inferior," it is for the reason that she wishes to degrade herself because she believes she is unworthy of love; but normally she is looking for a man who represents male superiority. She is soon to ascertain that many individuals of the favored sex are sadly contingent and earthbound, but at first her presumption is favorable to them; they are called on less to prove their worth than to avoid too gross a disproof of it—which accounts for many mistakes, some of them serious. A naïve young girl is caught by the gleam of virility, and in her eyes male worth is shown, according to circumstances, by physical strength, distinction of manner, wealth, cultivation, intelligence, authority, social status, a military uniform; but what she always wants is for her lover to represent the essence of manhood.

Familiarity is often sufficient to destroy his prestige; it may collapse at the first kiss, or in daily association, or during the wedding night. Love at a distance, however, is only a fantasy, not a real experience. The desire for love becomes a passionate love only when it is carnally realized. Inversely, love can arise as a result of physical intercourse; in this case the sexually dominated woman acquires an exalted view of a man who at first seemed to her quite insignificant.

But it often happens that a woman succeeds in deifying none of the men she knows. Love has a smaller place in woman's life than has often been supposed. Husband, children, home, amusements, social duties, vanity, sexuality, career, are much more important. Most women dream of a *grand amour,* a soul-searing love. They have known substitutes, they have been close to it; it has come to them in partial, bruised, ridiculous, imperfect, mendacious forms; but very few have truly dedicated their lives to it. The *grandes amoureuses* are most often women who have not frittered themselves away in juvenile affairs; they have first accepted the traditional feminine destiny: husband, home, children; or they have known pitiless solitude; or they have banked on some enterprise that has been more or less of a failure. And when they glimpse the opportunity to salvage a disappointing life by dedicating it to some superior person, they desperately give themselves up to this hope. Mlle Aïssé, Juliette Drouet, and Mme d'Agoult were almost thirty when their love-life began, Julie de Lespinasse not far from forty. No other aim in life which seemed worth while was open to them, love was their only way out.

Even if they can choose independence, this road seems the most attractive to a majority of women: it is agonizing for a woman to assume responsibility for her life. Even the male, when adolescent, is quite willing to turn to older women for guidance, education, mothering; but customary attitudes, the boy's training, and his own inner imperatives forbid him to content himself in the end with the easy solution of abdication; to him such affairs with older women are only a stage through which he passes. It is man's good fortune—in adulthood as in early childhood—to be obliged to take the most arduous roads, but the surest; it is woman's misfortune to be surrounded by almost irresistible temptations; everything incites her to follow the easy slopes; instead of being invited to fight her own way up, she is told that she has only to let herself slide and she will attain paradises of enchantment. When she perceives that she has been duped by a mirage, it is too late; her strength has been exhausted in a losing venture.

. . .

Many examples have already shown us that this dream of annihilation is in fact an avid will to exist. In all religions the adoration of God is combined with the devotee's concern with personal salvation; when woman gives herself completely to her idol, she hopes that he will give her at once possession of herself and of the universe he represents. In most cases she asks her lover first of all for the justification, the exaltation, of her ego. Many women do not abandon themselves to love unless they are loved in return; and sometimes the love shown them is enough to arouse their love. The young girl dreamed of herself as seen through men's eyes, and it is in men's eyes that the woman believes she has finally found herself. Cécile Sauvage writes:

> To walk by your side, to step forward with my little feet that you love, to feel them so tiny in their high-heeled shoes with felt tops, makes me love all the love you throw around me. The least movements of my hands in my muff, of my arms, of my face, the tones of my voice, fill me with happiness.

. . .

In one of her letters to Middleton Murry, Katherine Mansfield wrote that she had just bought a ravishing mauve corset; she at once added: "Too bad there is no one to *see* it!" There is nothing more bitter than to feel oneself but the flower, the perfume, the treasure, which is the object of no desire: what kind of wealth is it that does not enrich myself and the gift of which no one wants? Love is the developer that brings out in clear, positive detail the dim negative, otherwise as useless as a blank exposure. Through love, woman's face, the curves of her body, her childhood memories, her former tears, her gowns, her accustomed ways, her universe, everything she is, all that belongs to her, escape contingency and become essential: she is a wondrous offering at the foot of the altar of her god.

This transforming power of love explains why it is that men of prestige who know how to flatter feminine vanity will arouse passionate attachments even if they are quite lacking in physical charm. Because of their lofty positions they embody the Law and the Truth: their perceptive powers disclose an unquestionable reality. The woman who finds favor in their sight feels herself transformed into a priceless treasure. D'Annunzio's success was due to this, as Isadora Duncan explains in the introduction to *My Life:*

> When D'Annunzio loves a woman, he lifts her spirit from this earth to the divine region where Beatrice moves and shines. In turn he transforms each woman to a part of the divine essence, he carries her aloft until she believes herself really with Beatrice. . . .
> He flung over each favorite in turn a shining veil. She rose above the heads of ordinary mortals and walked surrounded by a strange radiance. But when the caprice of the poet ended, this veil vanished, the radiance was eclipsed, and the woman turned again to common clay. . . . To hear oneself praised with that magic peculiar to D'Annunzio is, I imagine, something like the experience of Eve when she heard the voice of the serpent in Paradise. D'Annunzio can make any woman feel that she is the centre of the universe.

Only in love can woman harmoniously reconcile her eroticism and her narcissism; we have seen that these sentiments are opposed in such a manner that it is very difficult for a woman to adapt herself to her sexual destiny. To make herself a carnal object, the prey of another, is in contradiction to her self-worship: it seems to her that embraces blight and sully her body or degrade her soul. Thus it is that some women take refuge in frigidity, thinking that in this way they can preserve the integrity of the ego. Others dissociate animal pleasure and lofty sentiment. In one of Stekel's cases the patient was frigid with her respected and eminent husband and, after his death, with an equally superior man, a great musician, whom she sincerely loved. But in an almost casual encounter with a rough, brutal forester she found complete physical satisfaction, "a wild intoxication followed by indescribable disgust" when she thought of her lover. Stekel remarks that "for many women a descent into animality is the necessary condition for orgasm." Such women see in physical love a debasement incompatible with esteem and affection.

But for other women, on the contrary, only the esteem, affection, and admiration of the man can eliminate the sense of abasement. They will not yield to a man unless they believe they are deeply loved. A woman must have a considerable amount of cynicism, indifference, or pride to regard physical relations as an exchange of pleasure by which each partner benefits equally. As much as woman—and perhaps more—man revolts against anyone who attempts to exploit him sexually; but it is woman who generally feels that her partner is using her as an instrument. Nothing but high admiration can compensate for the humiliation of an act that she considers a defeat.

We have seen that the act of love requires of woman profound self-abandonment; she bathes in a passive langour; with closed eyes, anonymous, lost, she feels as if borne by waves, swept away in a storm, shrouded in darkness: darkness of the flesh, of the womb, of the grave. Annihilated, she becomes one with the Whole, her ego is abolished. But when the man moves from her, she finds herself back on earth, on a bed, in the light; she again has a name, a face: she is one vanquished, prey, object.

This is the moment when love becomes a necessity. As when the child, after weaning, seeks the reassuring gaze of its parents, so must a woman feel, through the man's loving contemplation, that she is, after all, still at one with the Whole from which her flesh is now painfully detached. She is seldom wholly satisfied even if she has felt the orgasm, she is not set completely free from the spell of her flesh; her desire continues in the form of affection. In giving her pleasure, the man increases her attachment, he does not liberate her. As for him, he no longer desires her; but she will not pardon this momentary indifference unless he has dedicated to her a timeless and absolute emotion. Then the immanence of the moment is transcended; hot memories are no regret, but a treasured delight; ebbing pleasure becomes hope and promise; enjoyment is justified; woman can gloriously accept her sexuality because she transcends it; excitement, pleasure, desire are no longer a state, but a benefaction; her body is no longer an object: it is a hymn, a flame.

. . .

The supreme goal of human love, as of mystical love, is identification with the loved one. The measure of values, the truth of the world, are in his consciousness;

hence it is not enough to serve him. The woman in love tries to see with his eyes; she reads the books he reads, prefers the pictures and the music he prefers; she is interested only in the landscapes she sees with him, in the ideas that come from him; she adopts his friendships, his enmities, his opinions; when she questions herself, it is his reply she tries to hear; she wants to have in her lungs the air he has already breathed; the fruits and flowers that do not come from his hands have no taste and no fragrance. Her idea of location in space, even, is upset: the center of the world is no longer the place where she is, but that occupied by her lover; all roads lead to his home, and from it. She uses his words, mimics his gestures, acquires his eccentricities and his tics. "I am Heathcliffe," says Catherine in *Wuthering Heights;* that is the cry of every woman in love; she is another incarnation of her loved one, his reflection, his double: she is *he.* She lets her own world collapse in contingence, for she really lives in his.

The supreme happiness of the woman in love is to be recognized by the loved man as a part of himself; when he says "we," she is associated and identified with him, she shares his prestige and reigns with him over the rest of the world; she never tires of repeating—even to excess—this delectable "we." As one necessary to a being who is absolute necessity, who stands forth in the world seeking necessary goals and who gives her back the world in necessary form, the woman in love acquires in her submission that magnificent possession, the absolute. It is this certitude that gives her lofty joys; she feels exalted to a place at the right hand of God. Small matter to her to have only second place if she has *her* place, forever, in a most wonderfully ordered world. So long as she is in love and is loved by and necessary to her loved one, she feels herself wholly justified: she knows peace and happiness. Such was perhaps the lot of Mlle Aïsse with the Chevalier d'Aydie before religious scruples troubled his soul, or that of Juliette Drouet in the mighty shadow of Victor Hugo.

But this glorious felicity rarely lasts. No man really is God. The relations sustained by the mystic with the divine Absence depend on her fervor alone; but the deified man, who is not God, is present. And from this fact are to come the torments of the woman in love. Her most common fate is summed up in the famous words of Julie de Lespinasse:[1] "Always, my dear friend, I love you, I suffer and I await you." To be sure, suffering is linked with love for men also; but their pangs are either of short duration or not overly severe. Benjamin Constant wanted to die on account of Mme Récamier: he was cured in a twelvemonth. Stendhal regretted Métilde for years, but it was a regret that perfumed his life without destroying it. Whereas woman, in assuming her role as the inessential, accepting a total dependence, creates a hell for herself. Every woman in love recognizes herself in Hans Andersen's little mermaid who exchanged her fishtail for feminine legs through love and then found herself walking on needles and live coals. It is not true that the loved man is absolutely necessary, above chance and circumstance, and the woman

---

[1] Famous intellectual woman of the eighteenth century, noted for her salon and her fervid correspondence with the rather undistinguished military officer and writer Count Guibert, mentioned below.—TR.

is not necessary to him; he is not really in a position to justify the feminine being who is consecrated to his worship, and he does not permit himself to be possessed by her.

An authentic love should assume the contingence of the other; that is to say, his lacks, his limitations, and his basic gratuitousness. It would not pretend to be a mode of salvation, but a human interrelation. Idolatrous love attributes an absolute value to the loved one, a first falsity that is brilliantly apparent to all outsiders. "*He* isn't worth all that love," is whispered around the woman in love, and posterity wears a pitying smile at the thought of certain pallid heroes, like Count Guibert. It is a searing disappointment to the woman to discover the faults, the mediocrity of her idol. Novelists, like Collette, have often depicted this bitter anguish. The disillusion is still more cruel than that of the child who sees the father's prestige crumble, because the woman has herself selected the one to whom she has given over her entire being.

Even if the chosen one is worthy of the profoundest affection, his truth is of the earth, earthy, and it is no longer this mere man whom the woman loves as she kneels before a supreme being; she is duped by that spirit of seriousness which declines to take values as incidental—that is to say, declines to recognize that they have their source in human existence. Her bad faith[2] raises barriers between her and the man she adores. She offers him incense, she bows down, but she is not a friend to him since she does not realize that he is in danger in the world, that his projects and his aims are as fragile as he is; regarding him as the Faith, the Truth, she misunderstands his freedom—his hesitancy and anguish of spirit. This refusal to apply a human measuring scale to the lover explains many feminine paradoxes. The woman asks a favor from her lover. Is it granted? Then he is generous, rich, magnificent; he is kingly, he is divine. Is it refused? Then he is avaricious, mean, cruel; he is a devilish or a bestial creature. One might be tempted to object: if a "yes" is such an astounding and superb extravagance, should one be surprised at a "no"? If the "no" discloses such abject selfishness, why wonder so much at the "yes"? Between the superhuman and the inhuman is there no place for the human?

A fallen god is not a man: he is a fraud; the lover has no other alternative than to prove that he really is this king accepting adulation—or to confess himself a usurper. If he is no longer adored, he must be trampled on. In virtue of that glory with which she has haloed the brow of her beloved, the woman in love forbids him any weakness; she is disappointed and vexed if he does not live up to the image she has put in his place. If he gets tired or careless, if he gets hungry or thirsty at the wrong time, if he makes a mistake or contradicts himself, she asserts that he is "not himself" and she makes a grievance of it. In this indirect way she will go so far as to take him to task for any of his ventures that she disapproves; she judges her judge, and she denies him his liberty so that he may deserve to remain her master. Her worship sometimes finds better satisfaction in his absence than in his presence; as we have seen, there are women who devote themselves to dead or otherwise

---

[2] In Sartre's existentialist terminology, "bad faith" means abdication of the human self with its hard duty of choice, the wish therefore to become a thing, the flight from the anguish of liberty.—TR.

inaccessible heroes, so that they may never have to face them in person, for beings of flesh and blood would be fatally contrary to their dreams. Hence such disillusioned sayings as: "One must not believe in Prince Charming. Men are only poor creatures," and the like. They would not seem to be dwarfs if they had not been asked to be giants.

. . .

Waiting can be a joy; to the woman who watches for her beloved in the knowledge that he is hastening toward her, that he loves her, the wait is a dazzling promise. But with the fading of the confident exaltation that can change absence itself into presence, tormenting uneasiness begins to accompany the absence: he may never come back. I knew a woman who received her lover each time with astonishment: "I thought you wouldn't come back any more," she would say. And if he asked why: "You might not return; when I wait for you I always get the feeling that I shall never see you again."

Worst of all, he may cease to love her: he may love another woman. For the intensity of a woman's effort to create her illusion—saying to herself: "He loves me madly, he can love me alone"—does not exclude the tortures of jealousy. It is characteristic of bad faith to permit passionate and contradictory affirmations. Thus the madman who obstinately insists he is Napoleon is not embarrassed in admitting that he is also a barber. Woman rarely consents to ask herself the question: does he really love me? but she asks herself a hundred times: does he love someone else? She does not admit that the fervor of her lover can have died down little by little, nor that he values love less than she does: she immediately invents rivals.

She regards love as a free sentiment and at the same time a magic spell; and she supposes that "her" male continues, of course, to love her as a free agent while he is being "bewitched," "ensnared," by a clever schemer. A man thinks of a woman as united with him, in her immanence; that is why he readily plays the Boubouroche;[3] it is difficult for him to imagine that she is also another person who may be getting away from him. Jealousy with him is ordinarily no more than a passing crisis, like love itself; the crisis may be violent and even murderous, but it is rare for him to acquire a lasting uneasiness. His jealousy is usually derivative: when his business is going badly, when he feels that life is hurting him, then he feels his woman is flouting him.

Woman, on the other hand, loving her man in his alterity and in his transcendence, feels in danger at every moment. There is no great distance between the treason of absence and infidelity. From the moment when she feels less than perfectly loved, she becomes jealous, and in view of her demands, this is always pretty much her case; her reproaches and complaints, whatever the pretexts, come to the surface in jealous scenes; she will express in this way the impatience and ennui of waiting, the bitter taste of her dependence, her regret at having only a mutilated existence. Her entire destiny is involved in each glance her lover casts at another

---

[3] A naïve, easygoing character in a novel and a play by Courteline, deceived by his mistress and exploited by his friends.—Tr.

woman, since she has identified her whole being with him. Thus she is annoyed if his eyes are turned for an instant toward a stranger; but if he reminds her that she has just been contemplating some stranger, she firmly replies: "That is not the same thing at all." She is right. A man who is looked at by a woman receives nothing; no gift is given until the feminine flesh becomes prey. Whereas the coveted woman is at once metamorphosed into a desirable and desired object; and the woman in love, thus slighted, is reduced to the status of ordinary clay. And so she is always on the watch. What is he doing? At whom is he looking? With whom is he talking? What a desire has given her, a smile can take away from her; it needs only an instant to cast her down from "the pearly light of immortality" to the dim light of the everyday. She has received all from love, she can lose all in losing it. Vague or definite, ill-founded or justified, jealousy is maddening torture for the woman, because it is radically at variance with love: if the treason is unquestionable, she must either give up making love a religion or give up loving. This is a radical catastrophe and no wonder the woman in love, suspicious and mistaken in turn, is obsessed by the desire to discover the fatal truth and the fear that she will.

. . .

Genuine love ought to be founded on the mutual recognition of two liberties; the lovers would then experience themselves both as self and as other: neither would give up transcendence, neither would be mutilated; together they would manifest values and aims in the world. For the one and the other, love would be revelation of self by the gift of self and enrichment of the world. In his work on self-knowledge George Gusdorf sums up very exactly what *man* demands of love.

> Love reveals us to ourselves by making us come out of ourselves. We affirm ourselves by contact with what is foreign and complementary to us. . . . Love as a form of perception brings to light new skies and a new earth even in the landscape where we have always lived. Here is the great secret: the world is different, I myself *am different*. And I am no longer alone in knowing it. Even better: someone has apprised me of the fact. Woman therefore plays an indispensable and leading role in man's gaining knowledge of himself.

This accounts for the importance to the young man of his apprenticeship in love; we have seen how astonished Stendhal, Malraux, were at the miracle expressed in the phrase: "I myself, I am different." But Gusdorf is wrong when he writes: "And *similarly* man represents for woman an indispensable intermediary between herself and herself," for today her situation is not *similar;* man is revealed in a different aspect but he remains himself, and his new aspect is integrated with the sum total of his personality. It would be the same with woman only if she existed no less essentially than man as *pour-soi;* this would imply that she had economic independence, that she moved toward ends of her own and transcended herself, without using man as an agent, toward the social whole. Under these circumstances, love in equality is possible, as Malraux depicts it between Kyo and May in *Man's Fate.* Woman may even play the virile and dominating role, as did Mme de Warens with Rousseau, and, in Colette's *Chéri,* Léa with Chéri.

But most often woman knows herself only as different, relative; her *pour-autrui,* relation to others, is confused with her very being; for her, love is not an intermediary "between herself and herself" because she does not attain her subjective existence; she remains engulfed in this loving woman whom man has not only revealed, but created. Her salvation depends on this despotic free being that has made her and can instantly destroy her. She lives in fear and trembling before this man who holds her destiny in his hands without quite knowing it, without quite wishing to. She is in danger through an other, an anguished and powerless onlooker at her own fate. Involuntary tyrant, involuntary executioner, this other wears a hostile visage in spite of her and of himself. And so, instead of the union sought for, the woman in love knows the most bitter solitude there is; instead of cooperation, she knows struggle and not seldom hate. For woman, love is a supreme effort to survive by accepting the dependence to which she is condemned; but even with consent a life of dependency can be lived only in fear and servility.

Men have vied with one another in proclaiming that love is woman's supreme accomplishment. "A woman who loves as a woman becomes only the more feminine," says Nietzsche; and Balzac: "Among the first-rate, man's life is fame, woman's life is love. Woman is man's equal only when she makes her life a perpetual offering, as that of man is perpetual action." But therein, again, is a cruel deception, since what she offers, men are in no wise anxious to accept. Man has no need of the unconditional devotion he claims, nor of the idolatrous love that flatters his vanity; he accepts them only on condition that he need not satisfy the reciprocal demands these attitudes imply. He preaches to woman that she should give — and her gifts bore him the distraction; she is left in embarrassment with her useless offerings, her empty life. On the day when it will be possible for woman to love not in her weakness but in her strength, not to escape herself but to find herself, not to abase herself but to assert herself — on that day love will become for her, as for man, a source of life and not of mortal danger. In the meantime, love represents in its most touching form the curse that lies heavily upon woman confined in the feminine universe, woman mutilated, insufficient unto herself. The innumerable martyrs to love bear witness against the injustice of a fate that offers a sterile hell as ultimate salvation.

QUESTIONS FOR ANALYSIS AND DISCUSSION

1. De Beauvoir relies on classic literary sources to document many of her observations. She also enlists the ideas of modern social scientists to account for the discrepancies between men and women on their views of love. Although de Beauvoir does not describe each and every kind of love men and women have shared, she accounts for a prevailing attitude and cultural value that helps us understand why men and women are often disappointed in love. As one who has observed, experienced, or studied these attitudes and values, how do you assess de Beauvoir's contrast of men and women in love?

2. A woman says "we" when in love. What does a man in love say? Can you find other linguistic changes among those who are in the throes of a new love?

3. Review de Beauvoir's notion of genuine love. Specifically, what do you think is meant by the "mutual recognition of two liberties"? Do you find this a good or practical meaning of love?

4. In light of de Beauvoir's conclusion envisioning a woman loving not out of weakness but out of strength, how do you think she would view the ideas of Augustine or Vatsyayana? How would they view de Beauvoir's ideas?

44.

NIGEL WARBURTON

Virtual Fidelity

A different slant on the moral aspects of erotic love can be illustrated by the emergence of sexual conduct in cyberspace. The idea that a spouse may be having an orgasm while exchanging sexual messages over the computer with a nonspouse strikes British philosopher Nigel Warburton (b. 1962) as a challenging test for understanding the limits of monogamous fidelity. In a careful analysis Warburton applies conventional worries of infidelity to unconventional forms of erotic encounters. To reach his interesting conclusion, Warburton clarifies key terms, such as reality, desire, sex, and fidelity.

⊢ CRITICAL READING QUESTIONS ⊣

1. What are the three main risks of infidelity? What particular dangers do they pose?
2. How does Warburton understand the importance of fantasy?
3. For Warburton, is the physical presence of two people essential for their having sex?
4. What is the key difference between fidelity and nonfidelity?

The subject of this article is sexual fidelity in the context of a monogamous relationship, homo- or hetero-sexual. It is worth stating at the outset that I am not in

"Virtual Fidelity," *Cogito*, November 1996: 193–199. Notes have been omitted.

any way arguing that, for instance, promiscuity or casual sex are morally blame-worthy, nor am I attempting to promote heterosexual marriage-type relationships above other approaches to human sexuality. My aim is to look at the justifications offered for an agreement of fidelity within a relationship and their implications; if individuals have found other strategies for managing their sexual relationships which, given their particular drives, personalities, and so on, allow them to interact sexually with other people without harming anyone, that is beyond my scope here.

I use the term "non-fidelity" to refer to sex with someone other than your estab-lished partner outside the context of an agreement, or else within an agreement which permits you to have sex with other people; in contrast "infidelity" (about which I have very little to say here) is the breaking of an agreement; "fidelity," keeping it.

The usual justifications for entering into a contract of fidelity are of two major kinds: one based on the consequences of non-fidelity; the other on a picture of what human sexual relationships ought to be like (in a categorical sense)—often based on religious teaching, or derived from secular versions of it. I am only con-cerned here with the former class—the consequence-based approach. I reject any transcendental or natural foundation that could underpin the notion that fidelity is unconditionally the right approach in long-term sexual relationships. I am as-suming that if an agreement of fidelity is the right option, then it is right because of its consequences and that there would be consequential justification for keeping to the agreement once it was made.

There are three main consequences of non-fidelity which most people would rather avoid

1. Physical risks.
2. Emotional risks.
3. Relationship risks.

1. Physical Contamination

There are prudential considerations of health which can sometimes be thought to justify a policy of absolute sexual fidelity. Clearly in an age where there is quite a reasonable chance of contracting the HIV virus and other sexually transmitted diseases through unprotected sexual contact of various kinds, there are good grounds for minimizing such unprotected contact. One effective means of doing so is only to have unprotected sexual contact with people whom you are certain not to be carriers of the virus or disease. In practice the only effective way of doing this (apart from avoiding sex altogether) is to restrict your unprotected sexual contact to a partner who is likewise restricting his or her sexual contact, and whom you know well enough to trust in this respect.

One obvious criticism of this view is that it is extremely simple to practise vari-ous forms of safe sex using prophylactics: the argument from physical hygiene won't work if you use hygienic methods of having sex with other people. However, in reply it can be said that safe sex is a misnomer; it is only *safer sex*—there is always the possibility of infection. A version of Pascal's Wager might convince us that the slightest possibility of a painful death by AIDS, with all the consequences for those around you, should far outweigh the intense but often transient sexual pleasures that may be involved in contracting the condition: a rational person would minimize (and if possible eliminate) the chance of such a terrible death, especially if there was the further risk of passing the virus on to one's long-term partner. The only problem with this line of thought is that it might lead to the advocacy of complete chastity.

Yet the Argument from Physical Contamination would permit sexual contact outside the main relationship provided it was with people one could be certain were not carriers of any sexually transmitted diseases. So risk of physical contamination alone will not justify making a contract of complete fidelity, though it will justify fidelity in a wide range of circumstances and will give a good reason for not indulging in certain more dangerous sexual activities outside of the central relationship.

Another type of physical consequence of non-fidelity for fertile women is conception as a result of heterosexual intercourse with a non-partner. Although historically important, this is less relevant where effective means of contraception are used. However, in cases of heterosexual fertile couples performing intrinsically reproductive sexual acts without the use of contraception—as some orthodox Catholics, and plenty of others no doubt would—the question of paternity worries might play a significant role in the assessment of the consequences of non-fidelity. Obviously there are many forms of sexual contact which would circumvent this sort of consequence.

2. Emotional Risks

A second consequential argument for an agreement of fidelity is that the consequences of non-fidelity would be likely to involve emotional confusion and in the worst cases, turmoil. The emotional problems of non-fidelity in the context of a long-term relationship centre on two main emotions: guilt and jealousy.

Guilt

Many people will feel guilty if they have sexual contact outside their established relationship regardless of whether or not this guilt is appropriate. This is because most of us have been indoctrinated about the virtues of fidelity from an early age, and also because of a general tendency to feel guilty about sexual matters, exacerbated by the sense that being non-faithful you may have wronged the person you care most about in the world. Fidelity avoids the emotional pain of extreme feelings of guilt.

However, there may be good grounds for trying to eliminate such guilty feelings in cases where no fidelity contract has been made, thus freeing oneself to have guilt-free non-monogamous sexual relations. If the guilt is inappropriate, surely it is better to eliminate it wherever possible, particularly if it is an obstacle to realizing your freedom. In principle this may be so, but for many people it is extremely difficult to eliminate the tendency to feel guilty about sexual relations of an extra-relationship kind: such feelings can easily ruin the pleasure of the affair outside the relationship (even if permitted within the terms of the relationship agreement) and at the same time introduce emotional problems in the long-term relationship. If you are the kind of person who has a tendency to feel guilty in such situations, fidelity is one way of avoiding the guilt-evoking situations.

If you do eliminate the inappropriate guilty feelings that you would otherwise feel when being non-faithful, then you may run the risk of a generalised emotional numbness: people who shut down one emotion often find that they experience a general emotional distancing. So even if there are good grounds for trying to eliminate inappropriate guilt, then you might still find the knock-on effect in the rest of your life too costly.

Jealousy

A potentially more serious consequence of non-fidelity is the jealousy characteristically experienced by the partner, an emotion which is often strong enough to destroy a relationship (most murderers in Broadmoor committed their crimes as a result of morbid jealousy). Consequently it may be better if either partner has a tendency to jealousy to establish a strictly adhered-to policy of fidelity.

Against this it might be argued that if you don't know that your partner was unfaithful, you are unlikely to feel jealousy; so all that the argument from jealousy should lead to is secrecy about your sexual activity rather than fidelity. (This raises the question about the degree to which you can be harmed by events of which you have no knowledge.) However, the Othello syndrome is sufficiently common to undermine this conclusion: the mere suspicion that your partner has had sex with someone else is often enough to arouse extreme jealousy. By making a contract of fidelity a couple should reduce the likelihood of jealousy-inducing situations occurring (as compared with the situation in which there is a genuine possibility that your partner has had sex with someone else).

The problem of jealousy frequently arises in relationships which are set up as alternatives to the marriage ideal, e.g. in open marriages. The resulting tumult of emotions may be so unpleasant that any potential gains from increased sexual liberty are lost. Suppressing jealousy in such circumstances may have the same general emotion-numbing effect as suppressing guilt. Also, partners in such circumstances frequently have affairs with the sole aim of evoking jealousy in their partner, even if it is a strictly inappropriate emotion within the context of their relationship agreement.

Against both arguments from guilt and arguments from jealousy a defender of non-fidelity might maintain that suppressing a desire to have extra-relationship sex was not only an unacceptable infringement on personal liberty but would also result in more emotional turmoil than would occur through subsequent feelings of guilt or jealousy; and of course there are vast individual differences in these matters. However, I suggest that this would only very rarely be true and that self-justifying rationalizations abound in this area.

3. Relationship Risks

Fidelity is often a policy adopted pre-emptively to preserve the relationship between two people. It is felt that sexual contact with other people can involve a level of intimacy which could easily undermine the central relationship. This danger of loss can take many forms: for instance, it may break up a relationship simply through pressures on time—if both members of a couple are having extra-relationship affairs, they may have very little time (or energy) left to spend together; or else, as often happens, the outside relationship develops into a more fulfilling one than the original, and eventually supersedes it: in this case avoiding the first step reduces the chance of this form of break up. A kept contract of fidelity avoids the first steps being taken which might well lead to the eventual destruction of a relationship.

Even sexual liaisons which do not overtly threaten a relationship (e.g. a casual one-off sexual encounter), may make it easier to enter into a more long-term relationship next time. Once an initial resistance to intimate relations with others is lowered it can become easier to indulge in a relationship which would be genuinely threatening to the central one. In other words there is often a slippery slope from casual encounter to a long-term affair: one step down this slope and you might well end up at the bottom. The risk of loss is often coupled with the feeling that the extra-relationship affair is far more dangerous than could be justified by the pleasures it gives, that somehow it is an act of selfish greed. If you really valued this relationship you wouldn't jeopardize it for the sake of such transient pleasures. The combination of these three risk factors gives consequentialist justification for most established couples to enter into a contract of fidelity.

So far I have not really addressed the question of what fidelity might reasonably be taken to be. A simple agreement of sexual fidelity would involve the promise not to have sex with other people—but what does this mean, and where is it reasonable to draw the line? Would it be reasonable to include what you fantasize about as well as what you actually do in the contract of fidelity?

Rather than address these questions in an abstract way, I want to look at them in the context of moral questions which are raised by the invention of a particular branch of virtual reality technology. Virtual Reality is a form of computer simulation. The experiencer of VR puts on a pair of goggles which contain miniature TV screens and a body stocking wired with pressure detectors and stimulators capable of monitoring bodily position and giving a wide range of tactile stimulation. On the screens in the goggles a virtual world appears through which the experiencer can move—any movement he or she makes results in a corresponding change in what he or she sees, feels and hears (in principle any of the senses can be simulated). The virtual world is usually known as cyberspace. The creators of cyberspace can, like Descartes' evil demon, people it with virtual people or objects of any shape, size or character. At present the technology of VR is relatively unsophisticated—it produces a virtual world that resembles the images on arcade computer games—but in the near future much more sophisticated virtual reality machines will undoubtedly be created, machines which will provide realistic simulations of a whole range of experiences.

One of the more obvious commercial applications of such technology is in the realm of sex. Virtual reality sex, dubbed 'teledildonics' by Howard Rheingold, would in principle allow two people to have virtual sex via a telephone line, experiencing a realistic simulation of any tactile stimulation that the physical act would normally involve. Indeed, in such a case, there would be no need for the virtual bodies experienced by the participants (the ones they seem to see, touch, and feel) to resemble the bodies of their sources: you could be having sex with a simulation of John Major when in fact the body wired up at the other end of the 'phone line was David Mellor's. Clearly such a set up allows great scope for the realization of fantasy.

I want to look at three questions that arise about such VR sex.

a. Would it be sex or just interactive pornography?
b. Would it involve any of the negative consequences usually associated with nonfidelity?
c. Would it involve other negative consequences because it is a kind of realized fantasy?

(a) Crude Biological Argument

It could be argued that VR sex isn't really sex at all in any relevant sense—it is more like a form of masturbation than a complex interaction between two people. One simplistic argument which might be used to support this view is that real sex necessarily involves intrinsically reproductive acts; this is because its biological function is passing on genes to offspring. In other words, any act which could not in principle result in reproduction is not really sex. This sort of argument has unacceptable consequences: it would make oral sex, homosexual sex, and many other varieties not really sex. From the point of view of an agreement of fidelity whether we choose to call them real sex or not is largely irrelevant, since these activities could have most of the consequences of non-fidelity by means of an intrinsically reproductive act.

Another reason for thinking that VR sex might not be real sex is that it does not involve direct physical contact. Since paradigm cases of sex do involve direct physical contact of an extremely intimate kind, it might be felt that it would be wrong to call VR sex sex at all. However, a consequence of taking this line would seem to be that two people each entirely wrapped in clingfilm would be incapable of having sex with each other (which they clearly can). What is important about contact in sex is not its directness, but two other features: its capacity to stimulate and its interactive potential. A VR machine allows two people to stimulate each other via reasonably direct causal pathways. Familiarity with how the machine works would allow each participant's virtual body to be the equivalent of a prosthetic device. It also permits interaction between the participants. Interaction of a specific kind—reciprocity—has been singled out by Thomas Nagel as central to normal (as opposed to perverted) sex. In his article on sexual perversion he declared that normal sex:

> involves a desire that one's partner be aroused by the recognition of one's desire that he or she be aroused.

VR sex would allow just such subtle reciprocity to be expressed through indirect physical contact. In principle your body stocking could be equipped with touch sensors and stimulators for every nerve ending—this would allow precisely the same touch-sensitive reciprocity with a virtual body as would be possible in the flesh. However, as several commentators have pointed out, Nagel's account goes too far in making escalating Gricean desires about desires essential to normal sex. A simpler kind of reciprocity may be sufficient for real sexual interaction: the knowledge that there is someone else at the other end of the machine responding interactively to what I do at my end of the machine, and that at least one of us is being sexually aroused by this interaction, is sufficient to make it a sexual interaction. And in many cases the knowledge that you are arousing someone else can be a cause of your own arousal.

It might be objected that my experience of the machine would be just the same if there was no one on the other end of the line, just a sophisticated sex computer that had passed a novel version of the Turing Test; in contrast with sex of the old-fashioned kind you would not always be able to tell whether or not you were having sex with another person. But this might just be a hazard of having indirect as opposed to direct sex with people: in the former case you could be more easily deceived about whether you are having sex than in the latter: but it doesn't stop VR sex being real sex when there is someone else on the other end of the machine.

It might also be objected that because you would know so little about your sexual partner—partly because their virtual body may be significantly different from their real one—your interaction barely deserves the label sex at all. However, the same sort of argument would have to apply to casual sex with someone who was wearing a disguise (which sounds implausible).

(b) Negative Consequences of Virtual Non-Fidelity

I want now to consider whether or not sex with an anonymous and unidentifiable non-partner via a machine should be prohibited under a reasonable agreement of sexual fidelity, one made because of the undesirable consequences of non-fidelity. Quite clearly, such VR sex would not have any of the physical consequences currently endangering conventional forms of sexual liaison, unless, of course, the equipment you used was unhygienic.

The question of whether or not there would be a risk of guilt or jealousy is a harder one to answer. Certainly many users of such virtual reality technology would be likely to have guilty twinges in the same way that they might if using pornography to fuel their masturbatory fantasies: the psychological link between sex and guilt is not easy to sever. But the guilt feelings would be unlikely to be as severe as with physical non-fidelity given that the risk of physical contamination is nil. Similarly, partners might well feel jealous if their partner spent a lot of time using VR machines. However, assuming anonymity was respected, there does not seem to be a serious risk to any relationship involved in the use of such machines, apart from the risk that, the partner will come to prefer the machine to sex in the flesh, or else might find a way to meet up with the flesh behind the screen.

(c) Fantasy

So does the VR machine look to provide a safe way of preserving relationships? There might be further objections to it; such as that it relies on fantasy surrogates. An objection to VR sex could be constructed from Roger Scruton's writing on fantasy. For him, sexual fantasy aims to approach as nearly as possible to a substitute for the absent object, but a substitute that is free from danger. Sexual relationships are notoriously fraught with dangers, physical and emotional—hence the tendency to avoid them and move off into the safe realms of fantasy. Sexual fantasy, according to Scruton, feeds upon modes of representation which approach substitution, such as photographs and videos, and, though he doesn't mention them, sophisticated VR machines would surely be the next stage. Fantasy, he says:

> eschews style and convention, since these constitute impediments to the construction of the surrogate object, ways of veiling it and confusing it in a mask of thought. The ideal fantasy object is perfectly "realized," while remaining wholly unreal. It "leaves nothing to the imagination": at the same time it is to be understood only as a simulacrum and not as the thing itself.

This could almost be a description of the aim of teledildonics. Scruton believes that such fantasy detracts from deeper human satisfaction; his reason is as follows:

> It seems to me that the fantasy-ridden soul will tend to have a diminished sense of the objectivity of his world, and a diminished sense of his own agency within it. The habit of pursuing the "realized unreal" seems to conflict with the habit, which we all, I believe, have reason to acquire, of pursuing what is real.

Normal passions are "disciplined" by the world: they change as understanding changes. Passions felt in the presence of realized fantasy objects, such as those on the cinema screen, are not modified by the real world and so tend to diminish the experiencer's sense of agency and ultimately undermine his or her habit of pursuing what is real. Scruton writes:

> In love, all my fantasy is destroyed just so soon as it is erected, by the deeper desire to understand and respond to a being whose essence resides in his independence, in his freedom from me. It seems to be no accident that people have repeatedly described sexual fantasy as "loveless."

If we apply Scruton's ideas to the virtual reality sex machine, we see that it would be very likely to threaten the relationship by rewarding the user for engaging in the world in an escapist way that would be an obstacle to love in the real world: fantasy works against true understanding of another person. In which case, given that the usual context of a sexual fidelity contract is in a loving relationship, it would tend to put VR sex in the category of sexual relationships that are risky to the main relationship.

But Scruton's argument about fantasy and its relation to the real world doesn't hold up when applied to the VR sex machine. Take the analogy of a flight simulator. The best flight simulators are VR machines of a kind which give the closest approximation possible to the experience of flying a plane, yet without the obvious dangers of being several miles high in a fast moving bit of metal. Yet flight simulators prepare would-be pilots for interaction with the real world far better than "throwing them in at the deep-end" would. The lack of danger allows new approaches to be explored, and yet protects the pilot from the more serious consequences of mistakes. Analogously, controlled use of VR sex machines could help individuals to explore their sexuality in a safe environment without most of the more risky consequences that that would involve if interacting directly with real people. What's more it might indulge desire for sexual freedom without grave consequences. In fact, it is the lack of danger inherent in fantasy experiences which, far from preventing them being learning experiences, makes them particularly useful for acquiring the kinds of self-knowledge which can make for a more satisfactory interaction with people in the real world (though, obviously, fantasy has great power to initiate harm as well as pleasure).

In conclusion, although sex with other people via VR machines is certainly real sex, it seems likely that it would present fewer risks to a relationship than would most other forms of non-fidelity; in addition it could considerably improve the quality of an existing sexual relationship because of its potential for risk-free interactions leading to greater self-understanding. In view of this, it seems reasonable that fidelity agreements made on consequentialist grounds should have an exception clause permitting moderate anonymous use of virtual reality sex machines.

QUESTIONS FOR ANALYSIS AND DISCUSSION

1. Warburton is careful to define his key terms. Do you agree with his definitions of fidelity, sex, and jealousy? If you have a better definition or believe his is wrong, how will this affect his argument?

2. The advent of virtual sex is hailed as a safe but innovative way for humans to explore new pleasures. Imagine if you either discovered your lover enjoying virtual sex or were discovered by your lover having virtual sex with someone else. In either scenario if a partner feels jealousy, guilt, embarrassment, or anger, does that mean the relationship is on shaky grounds? According to Warburton, a rational couple would find no objections to this scenario. What are your thoughts on Warburton's argument?

3. Imagine you are feeling amorous one evening but your lover or spouse deflects your overtures with, "Not tonight, dear. . . . I'm exhausted from a wild fling this afternoon on the Internet." According to Warburton's analysis, should you: (a) be disappointed, but treat it just as you would if your lover was too tired from a long day at work; (b) be disappointed, but treat yourself to some pleasure anyway by heading for the computer and checking out the most licentious chat rooms; (c) be glad that your lover is enjoying modern life; (d) be glad that your lover is not cavorting with real sleazeballs and risking giving you a sexual disease; or (e) feel betrayed. Briefly justify your choice.

4. Much of de Beauvoir's discussion involves the sense of self and body one gains in matters of love. In *The War of Desire and Technology*, Allecquere Stone articulates the position of those who delight in cyberspace, which allows partici-

pants to change or create all sorts of fantasies about themselves. Warburton seems to support this in his praise of the innovative pleasures offered by virtual sex. Do you think de Beauvoir's ideas can make sense of this new technology? Can she help us make any moral judgments about virtual sex? Clarify your response.

45.

THEANO

Letter on Marriage and Fidelity

A different approach to the question of fidelity is outlined by Theano in her letter to a friend who is troubled by her husband's affair with a courtesan (or mistress). Nikostrate is weighing her options in getting back at her husband. Sympathetic to her friend's anguish, Theano nevertheless cautions Nikostrate from doing more harm than good. Thus her letter can be read as a piece of advice on the conduct of a virtuous person when confronted with the unhappiness caused by the vicious deeds of others. Jealousy, lust, love, grace, and anger are among the moral concerns highlighted in Theano's letter.

CRITICAL READING QUESTIONS

1. What is the difference between being loved on the basis of good judgment or on the basis of passion?
2. Why does Theano caution Nikostrate from battling the courtesan on her own terms?
3. Is divorce a practical option? Why, or why not?

Theano to Nikostrate: Greetings. I hear repeatedly about your husband's madness: he has a courtesan; also that you are jealous of him. My dear, I have known many men with the same malady. It is as if they are hunted down by these women and

"Letter on Marriage and Fidelity," from *A History of Women Philosophers*, Vol. 1, edited by Mary Ellen Waithe, translated by Vicki Lynn Harper (Dordrecht: Martinus Nijhoff, 1987), pp. 46–48.

held fast; as if they have lost their minds. But you are dispirited by night and by day, you are sorely troubled and contrive things against him. Don't *you*, at least, be that way, my dear. For the moral excellence of a wife is not surveillance of her husband but companionable accommodation; it is in the spirit of accommodation to bear his folly.

If he associates with the courtesan with a view towards pleasure, he associates with his wife with a view towards the beneficial. It is beneficial not to compound evils with evils and not to augment folly with folly. Some faults, dear, are stirred up all the more when they are condemned, but cease when they are passed over in silence, much as they say fire quenches itself if left alone. Besides, though it seems that you wish to escape notice yourself, by condemning him you will take away the veil that covers your own condition.

Then you will manifestly err: You are not convinced that love of one's husband resides in conduct that is noble and good. For this *is* the grace of marital association. Recognize the fact that he goes to the courtesan in order to be frivolous but that he abides with you in order to live a common life; that he loves you on the basis of good judgment, but her on the basis of passion. The moment for this is brief; it almost coincides with its own satisfaction. In a trice it both arises and ceases. The time for a courtesan is of brief duration for any man who is not excessively corrupt. For what is emptier than desire whose benefit of enjoyment is unrighteousness? Eventually he will perceive that he is diminishing his life and slandering his good character.

No one who understands persists in self-chosen harm. Thus, being summoned by his just obligation towards you and perceiving the diminution of his livelihood [he will take notice of you,] unable to bear the outrage of moral condemnation, he will soon repent. My dear, this is how you must live: not defending yourself against courtesans but distinguishing yourself from them by your orderly conduct towards your husband, by your careful attention to the house, by the calm way in which you deal with the servants, and by your tender love for your children. You must not be jealous of that woman (for it is good to extend your emulation only to women who are virtuous); rather, you must make yourself fit for reconciliation. Good character brings regard even from enemies, dear, and esteem is the product of nobility and goodness alone. In this way it is even possible for the power of a woman to surpass that of a man. It is possible for her to grow in his esteem instead of having to serve one who is hostile towards her.

If he has been properly prepared for it by you, he will be all the more ashamed; he will wish to be reconciled sooner and, because he is more warmly attached to you, he will love you more tenderly. Conscious of his injustice towards you, he will perceive your attention to his livelihood and make trial of your affection towards himself. Just as bodily illnesses make their cessations sweeter, so also do differences between friends make their reconciliations more intimate. As for you, do resist the passionate resolutions of your suffering. Because he is not well, he excites you to share in his plight; because he himself misses the mark of decency, he invites you to fail in decorum; having damaged his own life, he invites you to harm what is beneficial to you. Consequently you will seem to have conspired against him and, in reproving him will appear to reprove yourself.

If you divorce yourself from him and move on, you will change your first husband only to try another and, if he has the same feelings, you will resort to yet another (for the lack of a husband is not bearable for young women); or else you will abide alone without any husband like a spinster. Do you intend to be negligent of the house and to destroy your husband? Then you will share the spoils of an anguished life. Do you intend to avenge yourself upon the courtesan? Being on her guard, she will circumvent you; but, if she actively wards you off, a woman who has no tendency to blush is formidable in battle. Is it good to fight with your husband day after day? To what advantage? The battles and reproaches will not stop his licentious behavior, but they will increase the dissension between you by their escalations. What, then? Are you plotting something against him? Don't do it, my dear. Tragedy teaches us to conquer jealousy, encompassing a systematic treatise on the actions by which Medea was led to the commission of outrage. Just as it is necessary to keep one's hands away from a disease of the eyes, so must you separate your pretension from your pain. By patiently enduring you will quench your suffering sooner.

QUESTIONS FOR ANALYSIS AND DISCUSSION

1. Theano encourages Nikostrate to remain true to her good character. Do you think this is the kind of advice that is easier to give than to follow? If so, can anyone offer moral advice to Nikostrate? If not, what is the role of Theano that makes her possibly invaluable to her friend?

2. How does Theano understand the difference between the husband's relation to his wife and his relation to his mistress? Is this understanding relevant to her moral advice to Nikostrate? Be specific in your response.

3. Consider the times when a friend of yours may have gone through a situation similar to Nikostrate. If the opportunity arose, would you advise your friend as Theano does? offer different advice? or conclude that your duty is to ignore your friend's confusion and sorrow? Explain your choice.

4. What is Theano's understanding of the significance of her friend's suffering? Auden (see Chapter 5) thinks one source of excessive suffering is pride insofar as we inflate our own pain. In your view, when is the anger of those betrayed in love excessive?

46.

EPICTETUS

Of Friendship

Another view on the importance of friendship is elucidated by one of the great Stoic phi-
losophers, Epictetus (60–138). He believes that the good life derives largely from internal
rather than external sources. Love is more an internal source, for it is based on one's own
choices and appreciates the true character rather than the appearance of the beloved. In
this light friendship is one of the exemplary models of the good life. Yet Epictetus recog-
nizes the fragility of friendship. Offering a variety of examples where even the most en-
during friendships are easily destroyed by the vices of the friends, Epictetus encourages the
pursuit of self-interest by leading a virtuous life.

CRITICAL READING QUESTIONS

1. Why is only the prudent person capable of loving?
2. What is Epictetus's point in offering the analogy about dogs playing with one another?
3. Why does Epictetus cite Plato's doctrine that the soul never willingly avoids the truth?

---

1. To whatever objects a person devotes his attention, these objects he probably loves. Do men ever devote their attention, then, to evils?—By no means. Or even to what doth not concern them?—No, nor this. It remains, then, that good must be the sole object of their attention; and, if of their attention, of their love too. Whoever, therefore, understands good is capable likewise of love; and he who cannot distinguish good from evil, and things indifferent from both, how is it possible that he can love? The prudent person alone, then, is capable of loving.

How so? I am not this prudent person, yet I love my child.

I protest it surprises me that you should, in the first place, confess yourself imprudent. For in what are you deficient? Have you not the use of your senses? Do not you distinguish the appearance of things? Do not you provide such food and clothing and habitation as are suitable to you? Why, then, do you confess that you

---

"Of Friendship," from *The Moral Discourses of Epictetus*, translated by Elizabeth Carter (New York: Dutton, 1913), pp. 119–123. Notes have been omitted.

want prudence? In truth, because you are often struck and disconcerted by appearances, and their speciousness gets the better of you; and hence you sometimes
suppose the very same things to be good, then evil, and lastly, neither; and, in a
word, you grieve, you fear, you envy, you are disconcerted, you change. Is it from
hence that you confess yourself imprudent? And are you not changeable too in
love? Riches, pleasure, in short, the very same things, you at some times esteem
good, and at others evil; and do not you esteem the same persons, too, alternately
good and bad? And at one time treat them with kindness, at another with enmity?
one time commend, and at another censure them?

Yes. This too is the case with me.

Well, then, can he who is deceived in another be his friend, think you?

No, surely.

Or doth he who loves him with a changeable affection bear him genuine
goodwill?

Nor he, neither.

Or he, who now vilifies, then admires him?

Nor he.

Do you not often see little dogs caressing and playing with each other, that you
would say nothing could be more friendly; but, to learn what this friendship is,
throw a bit of meat between them, and you will see. Do you too throw a bit of an
estate betwixt you and your son, and you will see that he will quickly wish you
underground, and you him: and then you, no doubt, on the other hand, will exclaim, What a son have I brought up! He would bury me alive! Throw in a pretty
girl, and the old fellow and the young one will both fall in love with her; or let
fame or danger intervene, the words of the father of Admetus will be yours:

You hold life dear; doth not your father too?

Do you suppose that he did not love his own child when he was a little one?
That he was not in agonies when he had a fever, and often wished to undergo that
fever in his stead? But, after all, when the trial comes home, you see what expressions he uses. Were not Eteocles and Polynices born of the same mother and of the
same father? Were they not brought up, and did they not live and eat and sleep,
together? Did not they kiss and fondle each other? So that any one who saw them
would have laughed at all the paradoxes which philosophers utter about love.
And yet, when a kingdom, like a bit of meat, was thrown betwixt them, see what
they say, and how eagerly they wish to kill each other. For universally, be not deceived, no animal is attached to anything so strongly as to its own interest. Whatever therefore appears a hindrance to that—be it brother, or father, or child, or
mistress, or friend—is hated, abhorred, execrated; for by nature it loves nothing
like its own interest. This is father, and brother, and family, and country, and God.
Whenever, therefore, the gods seem to hinder this, we vilify even them, and throw
down their statues and burn their temples, as Alexander ordered the temple of
Æsculapius to be burnt, because he had lost the man he loved.

2. Whenever, therefore, any one makes his interest to consist in the same thing
with sanctity, virtue, his country, parents, and friends, all these are secured; but
wherever they are made to interfere, friends, and country, and family, and justice

itself, all give way, borne down by the weight of self-interest. For wherever *I* and *mine* are placed, thither must every animal gravitate. If in body, that will sway us; if in choice, that; if in externals, these. If, therefore, I be placed in a right choice, then only I shall be a friend, a son, or a father, such as I ought. For in that case it will be for my interest to preserve the faithful, the modest, the patient, the abstinent, the beneficent character; to keep the relations of life inviolate. But, if I place myself in one thing, and virtue in another, the doctrine of Epicurus will stand its ground, That virtue is nothing, or mere opinion.

3. From this ignorance it was that the Athenians and Lacedemonians quarreled with each other; and the Thebans with both; the Persian king with Greece; and the Macedonians with both: and now the Romans with the Getes. And in still remoter times, the Trojan war arose from the same cause. Paris was the guest of Menelaus; and whoever had seen the mutual proofs of goodwill that passed between them would never have believed that they were not friends. But a tempting bit, a pretty woman, was thrown in between them; and for this they went to war. At present, therefore, when you see dear brothers have, in appearance, but one soul, do not immediately pronounce upon their friendship; not though they should swear it, and affirm it was impossible to live asunder. (For the governing faculty of a bad man is faithless, unsettled, injudicious; successively vanquished by different appearances.) But inquire, not as others do, whether they were born of the same parents, and brought up together, and under the same preceptor; but this thing only, in what they place their interest—in externals, or in choice. If in externals, no more call them friends, than faithful, or constant, or brave, or free; nay, nor even men, if you are wise. For it is no principle of humanity that makes them bite and vilify each other, and take possession of public assemblies as wild beasts do of solitudes and mountains; and convert courts of justice into dens of robbers; nor that prompts them to be intemperate, adulterers, seducers; or leads them into other offences that men commit against each other, from the one single principle by which they place themselves and their own concerns in things independent on choice.

4. But if you hear that these men in reality suppose good to be placed only in choice, and in a right use of the appearances of things, no longer take the trouble of inquiring if they are father and son, or old companions and acquaintance; but as boldly pronounce that they are friends, as that they are faithful and just. For where else can friendship be met but with fidelity and modesty, and a communication of virtue; and of no other thing?

Well; but such a one paid me the utmost regard for so long a time, and did not he love me?

How can you tell, wretch, if that regard be any other than he pays to his shoes, or his horse, when he cleans them? And how do you know but when you cease to be a necessary utensil, he may throw you away, like a broken stool?

Well; but it is my wife, and we have lived together many years.

And how many did Eriphyle live with Amphiaraus, and was the mother of children, and not a few? But a bracelet fell in between them. What was this bracelet? The principle [she had formed] concerning such things. This turned her into a savage animal; this cut asunder all love, and suffered neither the wife nor the mother to continue such.

5. Whoever, therefore, among you studies to be or to gain a friend, let him cut up all these principles by the root; hate them; drive them utterly out of his soul. Thus, in the first place, he will be secure from inward reproaches and contests; from change of mind and self-torment. Then, with respect to others: to every one like himself he will be unreserved. To such as are unlike he will be patient, mild, gentle, and ready to forgive them, as failing in points of the greatest importance: but severe to none; being fully convinced of Plato's doctrine, That the soul is never willingly deprived of truth. Without all this you may, in many respects, live as friends do; and drink and lodge and travel together; and be born of the same parents; and so may serpents too; but neither they nor you can ever be friends, while you have these brutal and execrable principles.

QUESTIONS FOR ANALYSIS AND DISCUSSION

1. For many people loving involves some passion. Why do you think Epictetus emphasizes prudence and neglects passion when discussing love? Consider his comments on appearance, change, and deceit.

2. Epictetus illustrates his points with examples where even the happiest friendships were quickly destroyed by the introduction of a desireable object. Do you agree with his contention that most friendships are vulnerable? That is, many of us like to think of ourselves as true friends, but are we, as Epictetus implies, true friends only to the extent that our own interests are not threatened? Review some of the present or former friendships in your own life. Do they reflect or reject the basic points made by Epictetus?

3. Friendship should include "fidelity and modesty, and a communication of virtue," says Epictetus. At the same time he admits that it is unclear whether you are respected as a friend or merely as an object who offers an occasional service. How can you know whether another person is a true friend?

4. Which principle does Epictetus offer as the guide to a true friendship? Can you think of an alternative? Or do you think friends do not need to share a common principle or value?

47.

DAVID NYBERG

Friendship and Altruism: Be Untruthful to Others As You Would Have Others Be Untruthful to You

Ask most people about the central values of friendship, and they will likely talk about trust and honesty. David Nyberg, who in Chapter 4 discusses the tendency of moralists to overrate truthfulness, continues to explore the relation of truthfulness to the good life. Here he readily acknowledges that friendship is also essential to the good life but argues that what sustains friendship involves something more than complete candor. A true friendship also involves deceit. This deceit does not come at the cost of sacrificing trust. Rather, contrary to what most moral thinkers believe, Nyberg thinks trust and deceit go hand in hand. The responsibility of a virtuous person is to decide when deceit is a justifiable way of doing something good for a friend.

CRITICAL READING QUESTIONS

1. How is Nyberg's notion of trust different from the more familiar notion that trust refers to credibility?
2. What is Nyberg's point in raising the example of a king needing his court jester?
3. How does an episode on the television show *L.A. Law* illustrate the idea of a compassionate lie?
4. What is the distinction between trusting the truth and trusting the person?

As scarce as truth is, the supply has always been in excess of the demand.

—Josh Billings

It's a rare person who wants to hear what he doesn't want to hear.

—Dick Cavett

"Friendship and Altruism: Be Untruthful to Others As You Would Have Others Be Untruthful to You," from *The Varnished Truth* (Chicago: University of Chicago Press, 1994), pp. 137–146. Notes have been omitted.

Here's a story about two friends, both wonderful writers. One of them is Bernard Malamud, a frail and very sick old man. The other is Philip Roth. After lunch together with their wives, Malamud asks if he might read aloud from the opening chapters of a work in progress, to get Roth's opinion. Here is Roth's description of what happened:

> After coffee Bern went to his study for the manuscript, a thin sheaf of pages perfectly typed and neatly clipped together. I noticed when he sat down that all around his chair, on the porch floor, were scattered crumbs from his lunch. A tremor had made eating a little bit of an adventure, too, and yet he had driven himself to undertake once again this ordeal.
>
> It turned out that not too many words were typed on each page and that the first-draft chapters were extremely brief. I didn't dislike what I heard because there was nothing yet to like or dislike—he hadn't got started, really, however much he wanted to think otherwise. It was like having been led into a dark hold to see by torchlight the first Malamud story ever scratched upon a cave wall. What was awesome wasn't what was on the wall but, rather, contemplating the power of the art that had been generated by such simple markings. I didn't want to lie to him but, looking at the thin sheaf of pages in the hands of that very frail man, I couldn't tell the truth, even if he was expecting it of me. I said simply, and only a little evasively, that it seemed to me a beginning like all beginnings. That was quite truthful enough for a man of 71 who had published 12 of the most original works of fiction written by an American in the past 35 years. Trying to be constructive, I suggested that perhaps the narrative opened too slowly and that he might begin better further on, with one of the later chapters. Then I asked where it was all going. "What comes next?" I said, hoping we could pass on to what it was he had in mind if not yet down on the page.
>
> But he wouldn't let go of what he'd written—at such cost—as easily as that. Nothing was ever as easy as that, least of all the end of things. In a soft voice suffused with fury, he said, "What's next isn't the point."
>
> In the silence that followed, before Claire eased him gently into a discussion of the kind of character he was imagining as his hero, he was perhaps as angry at failing to master the need for assurance so nakedly displayed as he was with me for having nothing good to say. He wanted to be told that what he had painfully composed while enduring all his burdens was something more than he himself must have known it to be in his heart. He was suffering so, I wished I could have said that it *was* something more, and that if I'd said it, he could have believed me.
>
> Before I left for England in the fall I wrote him a note telling him that I was off, and inviting him and Ann to come down to Connecticut the next summer—it was our turn to entertain them. The response that reached me in London some weeks later was pure, laconic Malamudese. They'd be delighted to visit, but he reminded me, "next summer is next summer."
>
> He died on March 18, three days before spring.

What is the desirable balance of truth telling and deceiving in this story? Roth avoided lying. That's good. We should do that when we can. But he also avoided telling the truth. More accurately, he avoided telling exactly that part of the truth that was uppermost in his mind, the part that best represented the reality of the situation as he saw it. He judged that part of the truth to be unsuitable in the circumstances. Instead, he tried to be constructive by redirecting his friend's attention from the central point, by consciously misrepresenting his honest answer to the question of how good the writing was. Is that good, too? Should Roth have told the dying man, whose memory and vision were seriously clouded, that his writing now came to nothing? Is that what Malamud deserved to hear? Was Malamud really asking for Roth's candid critical opinion of his draft or was he asking for some kind of assurance to help him endure a crumbly end to his life? We can never know for sure what is in other people's minds, and it is presumptuous to assume to know what other people "really" need. Nevertheless, it's a fair guess that Roth did do the right thing when he varnished the truth he had to tell, and that what passed between the two friends was an understanding more valuable and constructive than the unequivocal truth would have been.

Frankness in the Stable

In his journal entry for Thursday, March 8, 1849, the painter Eugène Delacroix made a similar observation about the character of frank opinions.

> In the evening, Chopin. At his house, met an original who has come from Quimper to admire him and cure him for he is or has been a doctor and has a great contempt for the homeopaths of all colors. He is a rabid music lover: but his admiration is limited, particularly to Beethoven and Chopin. Mozart does not seem to him on their height; Cimarosa is old hat, etc. You've got to come from Quimper to have ideas like that and express them with such nerve: that passes for the frankness of a Breton. I detest that kind of character. That so-called frankness, which permits people to utter cutting or wounding opinions, is the thing for which I have the greatest antipathy. Relationships among men are no longer possible if frankness like that is a sufficient answer to everything. To speak frankly, one should, with a disposition like that, live in a stable, where relationships are established by thrusts of a pitchfork or by horns; that's the kind of frankness I prefer.
>
> In the morning, at the studio of Couder, to talk about the picture at Lyons. He is witty, and his wife is very good-looking. If we had been frank with each other, along the lines of my Breton, we should have had a fight before the end of the meeting; on the contrary, we parted in perfect agreement.

What is frankness that makes it such a highly placed but controversial virtue? It is defined by candor, honesty, sincerity, truthfulness—and is taken often to be a mark of integrity. However, it can just as often be offensive and wounding, as Delacroix found his Breton to be. If causing offense and injury is sometimes the price of frankness, then perhaps, in cases when there is no greater benefit to outweigh the loss, it would be better to forego frankness—candor, honesty, sincerity, and truthfulness—in favor of some less direct means of expression. All for the sake of preserving and enhancing relationships with other people.

Friends have the right to expect the truth from one another, but they have the right to expect more than that when the truth gets them headed down a path with no affirmative sense of destination.

Trust, Truth, and Friendship

What does it mean when I say, "I trust you," or "Trust me"? First of all, "it is not possible to demand the trust of others; trust can only be offered and accepted." If the offer is accepted, there must be some reason other than the offer itself that accounts for the acceptance. Perhaps we already know something about a person's background, through experience or reputation, which disposes us to trust, and so the present offer acts as reassurance; or perhaps we ask why we should trust and reasons are given that satisfy the question. Acceptance of personal trust is risky, but the risk can be reduced a good deal through the "verbal magic" of promises:

> Part of what makes promises the special thing they are, and the philosophically intriguing thing they are, is that we *can* at will accept *this* sort of invitation to trust, whereas in general we cannot trust at will. Promises are puzzling because they seem to have the power, by verbal magic, to initiate real voluntary short-term trusting.

What have we done when we have decided to trust someone? I like Annette Baier's definition of trust as "reliance on others' competence and willingness to look after, rather than harm, things one cares about which are entrusted to their care." I trust you if I rely upon you to look after what I have entrusted to your care. In friendship, what I entrust is myself (and at least some of that which I value): I rely upon you to look after me. Whatever happens in friendship, then, happens in an atmosphere of reciprocal trust.

I think that trust is part of what friendship means; it is not easy to imagine having a friend whom one cannot generally trust (though there may be specific areas in which the trust is weak, or has even been abused in the past). There is no friendship without a strong sense of trust: trust is necessary to friendship. But it is easy to imagine trusting someone who is not a friend—a surgeon, for example, who is about to operate on you. So, while trust is necessary to friendship, it is by no means exclusive to friends.

Now I want to make a suggestion that may at first sound ironic: Given the nature of trust in friendship there is an important and serious role for deception to play in keeping a friendship going. How could I seriously suggest that deception has anything to do with trust and is necessary for success in friendship? As Kathryn Morgan, one of my friends, wrote after she had heard my arguments for this point of view:

> Friendship is a paradigm of a personal relation constructed in a context of intimacy, trust, mutual vulnerability, and caring. The condition for such a relationship over time is deep, detailed knowledge of another's life, character, desires, ends, and interests in a mutually understood context of trusting openness which is incompatible with the

principled intent to deceive. Such conditions are built in because friendship, ideally, is the paradigm of a simultaneously disinterested and caring relationship where the relationship itself is the *raison d'être* for the pact of truth telling.

She went on to ask, "Why does the king *need* a jester? To tell him crucial truths about himself, to prick the balloons of self-deception *through* the sharpness of his jests." The point she wanted to make was that a friend is someone who is willing to hurt you with the truth when it is in your interest to know it. "Ideally," she argued, "we rely on our friends for sincerity, for insight because of the knowledge and caring that previous compassionate acts of truth telling have both constructed and protected." The point is well taken, but the two qualifications she adds make all the difference: a friend will tell you the truth *when it is in your interest* to hear it, and he will tell it *compassionately.* That's what I think, and under her formal objections, I suspect that's what my friend thinks, too. Friendship is not defined by disinterested truth telling alone, but by compassionate acts performed in the friend's interests. Friendship is based upon trust that your friend will look after you and what you value. There is plenty of room in compassion for handling the truth, for being less than frank, for not telling all of the right story, for playing with some of the balloons of self-deception to keep them aloft instead of pricking them all.

This discussion has been limited by the unspoken assumption that friendship is a two-party relationship, rather than a network of several people who are involved to differing degrees with each other. In some cases, friendship may involve just two people at a time, but mostly friends know each other. Thus, what I say to one affects the others. There may well be conflicts among friends that become exacerbated by truth telling; in telling *this* truth about you to *that* friend, I fail in my obligation to look after your friendship with him. While honoring his trust in my veracity, I may dishonor your trust in my good judgment and discretion.

My friend has read approvingly Sissela Bok's book on lying and agrees with her that "*whatever* matters to human beings, trust is the atmosphere in which it thrives." It would be hard to argue with that, and I'm not sure I want to; but still, I wonder what we are getting at with the metaphoric "atmosphere of trust"? Bok actually suggests that "trust is a social good to be protected just as much as the air we breathe or the water we drink. When it is damaged, the community as a whole suffers; and when it is destroyed, societies falter and collapse."

The irony that goes unappreciated in this thinking is that an "atmosphere" of trust is itself a delicately balanced mixture of the essential gases of communication, namely, truth telling and deceiving. An atmosphere of pure truth telling is no more fit to support friendship than an atmosphere of pure oxygen is fit to support life.

Compassionate Truth, Compassionate Lie

Recently on the television program "L.A. Law," I saw an illustration of a compassionate admixture of truth telling and deception that strengthened a friendship. Abby, a young attorney trying to make it on her own, asks her friend Stuart, a very good tax lawyer in a prestigious firm, to become co-attorney and advise her on a case. Her client has received an offer for a $40,000 settlement. As she is serving the client on a contingency basis, she will earn a percentage of the settlement without the costs of a trial if her client accepts the offer. The prospect of some immediate income is extremely attractive to Abby since she has pressing debts to pay. She is a little uncertain about the fairness of the offer, though, so she asks Stuart to go over the facts and figures and give his opinion. He does so and tells her that he thinks she has a case to support a $65,000 settlement and that she should go to court if necessary. Abby knows a court proceeding will take a long time, doesn't want to take the risk of losing, and angrily accuses Stuart of trying to undermine her. Stuart sticks with his honest assessment and adds his belief that a good lawyer doesn't sell a client short in order to pay the bills. He offers to loan Abby the money she needs to see her through. She tells him to stick his money, and his moralizing, and fires him on the spot to relieve him of his professional obligation as co-attorney to inform the client of his opinion on the case.

As her friend, Stuart had told her the truth, because it was in her best interests.

The following day, the client comes to Stuart to ask what has happened, why he is no longer on the case. Stuart does not give a straight answer, though he does not lie, because he wants the client to stay with Abby and work things out. He reiterates that Abby is a good attorney, that they don't have any serious differences but have disagreed on some figures. The client asks if Stuart thinks the settlement should be higher. Stuart says he should talk to Abby about that, and brushes off further questions.

As Abby's friend, he did not tell her client the whole truth, again because he thought it was in her best interests, and because he was under no formal obligation to say more than he did say.

As it happened, Abby lost the client and received no fee. She later came to Stuart's office to make a full and humble apology for her anger at him for telling her what she now recognized as the truth and as the right thing for him to have said. She was ashamed of herself, grateful to him, as they were closer as friends after the reconciliation. Their relationship was deepened and even more solidly based on trust, intimacy, mutual vulnerability, and caring. You see, my friend would say, that's the role of truth telling in friendship. It's that simple. Friends tell the truth to each other.

Right. But let me tell you what happened next. Before Abby left his office, Stuart told her that he had given her name to another prospective client, a very big copyright case. Stuart was afraid Abby was still hurt by his criticism, was losing confidence in herself, and he was still worried about her financial well-being. He felt he had to do something. This news visibly brightened Abby's mood, and she left in a hurry to start reading up on the technical details of copyright, with visions of a rosier future just ahead; more importantly, she had proof that Stuart still believed in her. His timing was perfect. When she left, Stuart made a phone call. He was relieved to find the prospective client in so he could now really give him Abby's name and recommend her.

In telling Abby that he had already recommended her, he actually had lied to her, and he lied for the very same reason he had for telling her the truth earlier: he thought it was in her best interests. He deceived her into thinking what he wanted her to think by saying something that was not true at the time he said it. Then he did what he could to make it true after the fact. What shall we call this if not deception? Retroactive truth telling? Leveraged truth telling? Lag time truth telling? However we qualify it, it's deception. And in this case, it's an act of friendship, too.

Stuart has given us, by saying something that was not true at the time, but later fortunately becomes true, an example of a deception created for the sake of friendship, intended to serve his friend's best interests. In fact, Abby has greater reason to trust Stuart now than she did before he lied to her. Why is that? It's because he has proved himself imaginative in figuring out ways to help her without causing harm; with her best interest at heart, he was able to rise above the principle of truth telling and do something that really made her life better. She can trust him to look after her, and that's a far greater and profounder gift of friendship than mere truth telling.

Trust in the Truth and Trust in the Person

The function of trust, I think, is to provide some confident expectation in a relationship. My friend would agree with me on that, I trust. Still, we differ, and our difference lies in a further distinction to be made in the definition of the word "trust." The *Shorter Oxford English Dictionary* helps point out this distinction when it explains that trust means "confidence in or reliance on some quality or attribute of a person or thing, *or* the truth of a statement." The key is that little word "or." Trust in friendship does not *exclusively* mean trust in the truth of your friend's statements. It also means reliance on some quality or attribute of your friend, a quality such as discretion, which is having tact with regard to the truth, or wisdom, which is having the good sense to know that not everything that *could* be said *should* be said, or resourcefulness, which is the capacity to make happen what should happen but won't happen unless somebody does something to nudge it along. Of course there is a role for truth telling in all of this, but as Stuart showed in his shrewd way of taking care of Abby, there is a role for deception, too. Trusting a person to look after your best interests is different from trusting a person never to deceive you. There are *some* things the jester should not tell his king.

QUESTIONS FOR ANALYSIS AND DISCUSSION

1. Nyberg begins the selection with two epigraphs. How do they fit the tone and content of his discussion?

2. Paternalism involves the practice of making moral decisions on behalf of another person. This practice is justified based on the other person's inability to make moral decisions on his or her own behalf. Acting paternalistically is supposed to be benevolent, having the well-being of the other person as the primary end. A parent choosing on behalf of a child is a traditional example of paternalism. Standard criticisms of paternalism contend it takes away a person's moral autonomy and presumes to know what makes another person happy. Do you think Nyberg's defense of deceit in friendship amounts to a

version of paternalism? If yes, is it morally defensible? If no, specify why it is not a form of paternalism.

3. Central to Nyberg's case is a careful interpretation of the meaning of trust: "the function of trust . . . is to provide some confident expectation in a relationship." Lore Segal's case study (Chapter 3) recounts the dilemma between choosing truthfulness and hope; there are times, usually tragic, she notes, when the virtue of hope supersedes the value of truth. Is Nyberg's argument a variation of this dilemma? Or is Nyberg highlighting a different virtue (or vice) that outweighs truthfulness? For example, does love or prudence outweigh the virtues of honesty or sincerity? Cite passages in Nyberg to support your answer.

48.

PLATO

Communal Families

Is friendship or the family the ideal form of love? Plato (428–348 B.C.) dramatizes this philosophical contest in many of his dialogues. Though the popular notion of Platonic love refers to affection that contains no sexual pleasure—hence, friendship seems to be the best model—in The Republic *Plato introduces an even stronger experience of love, that of a parent for a child. So strong is this love that it—not lust or friendship— can threaten social justice. Plato's solution, whether serious or sarcastic, is nonetheless striking.*

┤ CRITICAL READING QUESTIONS ├

1. Why does Plato have the women guardians exercising naked with the male guardians?
2. What is Plato's point in talking about breeding dogs or birds?
3. What is the relation between having a festival and drawing lotteries? How is this a political ceremony?
4. In talking about the public hymeneal, why does Plato not want parents to recognize their biological offspring?

"Communal Families," from *The Republic and Other Works*, translated by Benjamin Jowett (Oxford, England: Clarendon Press, 1875).

We had to consider, first, whether our proposals were possible, and secondly whether they were the most beneficial?

Yes.

And the possibility has been acknowledged?

Yes.

The very great benefit has next to be established?

Quite so.

You will admit that the same education which makes a man a good guardian will make a woman a good guardian; for their original nature is the same?

Yes.

I should like to ask you a question.

What is it?

Would you say that all men are equal in excellence, or is one man better than another?

The latter.

And in the commonwealth which we were founding do you conceive the guardians who have been brought up on our model system to be more perfect men, or the cobblers whose education has been cobbling?

What a ridiculous question!

You have answered me, I replied: Well, and may we not further say that our guardians are the best of our citizens?

By far the best.

And will not their wives be the best women?

Yes, by far the best.

And can there be anything better for the interests of the State than that the men and women of a State should be as good as possible?

There can be nothing better.

And this is what the arts of music and gymnastic, when present in such manner as we have described, will accomplish?

Certainly.

Then we have made an enactment not only possible but in the highest degree beneficial to the State?

True.

Then let the wives of our guardians strip, for their virtue will be their robe, and let them share in the toils of war and the defence of their country; only in the distribution of labors the lighter are to be assigned to the women, who are the weaker natures, but in other respects their duties are to be the same. And as for the man who laughs at naked women exercising their bodies from the best of motives, in his laughter he is plucking

"*A fruit of unripe wisdom,*"

and he himself is ignorant of what he is laughing at, or what he is about;—for that is, and ever will be, the best of sayings, *That the useful is the noble and the hurtful is the base.*

Very true.

Here, then, is one difficulty in our law about women, which we may say that we have now escaped; the wave has not swallowed us up alive for enacting that the guardians of either sex should have all their pursuits in common; to the utility and also to the possibility of this arrangement the consistency of the argument with itself bears witness.

Yes, that was a mighty wave which you have escaped.

Yes, I said, but a greater is coming; you will not think much of this when you see the next.

Go on; let me see.

The law, I said, which is the sequel of this and of all that has preceded, is to the following effect,—"that the wives of our guardians are to be common, and their children are to be common, and no parent is to know his own child, nor any child his parent."

Yes, he said, that is a much greater wave than the other; and the possibility as well as the utility of such a law are far more questionable.

I do not think, I said, that there can be any dispute about the very great utility of having wives and children in common; the possibility is quite another matter, and will be very much disputed.

I think that a good many doubts may be raised about both.

You imply that the two questions must be combined, I replied. Now I meant that you should admit the utility; and in this way, as I thought, I should escape from one of them, and then there would remain only the possibility.

But that little attempt is detected, and therefore you will please to give a defence of both.

Well, I said, I submit to my fate. Yet grant me a little favor: let me feast my mind with the dream as day dreamers are in the habit of feasting themselves when they are walking alone; for before they have discovered any means of effecting their wishes—that is a matter which never troubles them—they would rather not tire themselves by thinking about possibilities; but assuming that what they desire is already granted to them, they proceed with their plan, and delight in detailing what they mean to do when their wish has come true—that is a way which they have of not doing much good to a capacity which was never good for much. Now I myself am beginning to lose heart, and I should like, with your permission, to pass over the question of possibility at present. Assuming therefore the possibility of the proposal, I shall now proceed to inquire how the rulers will carry out these arrangements, and I shall demonstrate that our plan, if executed, will be of the greatest benefit to the State and to the guardians. First of all, then, if you have no objection, I will endeavor with your help to consider the advantages of the measure; and hereafter the question of possibility.

I have no objection; proceed.

First, I think that if our rulers and their auxiliaries are to be worthy of the name which they bear, there must be willingness to obey in the one and the power of command in the other; the guardians must themselves obey the laws, and they must also imitate the spirit of them in any details which are entrusted to their care.

That is right, he said.

You, I said, who are their legislator, having selected the men, will now select the women and give them to them;—they must be as far as possible of like natures with them; and they must live in common houses and meet at common meals. None of them will have anything specially his or her own; they will be together, and will be brought up together, and will associate at gymnastic exercises. And so they will be drawn by a necessity of their natures to have intercourse with each other—necessity is not too strong a word, I think?

Yes, he said;—necessity, not geometrical, but another sort of necessity which lovers know, and which is far more convincing and constraining to the mass of mankind.

True, I said; and this, Glaucon, like all the rest, must proceed after an orderly fashion; in a city of the blessed, licentiousness is an unholy thing which the rulers will forbid.

Yes, he said, and it ought not to be permitted.

Then clearly the next thing will be to make matrimony sacred in the highest degree, and what is most beneficial will be deemed sacred?

Exactly.

And how can marriages be made most beneficial?—that is a question which I put to you, because I see in your house dogs for hunting, and of the nobler sort of birds not a few. Now, I beseech you, do tell me, have you ever attended to their pairing and breeding?

In what particulars?

Why, in the first place, although they are all of a good sort, are not some better than others?

True.

And do you breed from them all indifferently, or do you take care to breed from the best only?

From the best.

And do you take the oldest or the youngest, or only those of ripe age?

I choose only those of ripe age.

And if care was not taken in the breeding, your dogs and birds would greatly deteriorate?

Certainly.

And the same of horses and animals in general?

Undoubtedly.

Good heavens! my dear friend, I said, what consummate skill will our rulers need if the same principle holds of the human species!

Certainly, the same principle holds; but why does this involve any particular skill?

Because, I said, our rulers will often have to practise upon the body corporate with medicines. Now you know that when patients do not require medicines, but have only to be put under a regimen, the inferior sort of practitioner is deemed to be good enough; but when medicine has to be given, then the doctor should be more of a man.

That is quite true, he said; but to what are you alluding?

I mean, I replied, that our rulers will find a considerable dose of falsehood and deceit necessary for the good of their subjects: we were saying that the use of all these things regarded as medicines might be of advantage.

And we were very right.

And this lawful use of them seems likely to be often needed in the regulations of marriages and births.

How so?

Why, I said, the principle has been already laid down that the best of either sex should be united with the best as often, and the inferior with the inferior, as seldom as possible; and that they should rear the offspring of the one sort of union, but not of the other, if the flock is to be maintained in first-rate condition. Now these goings on must be a secret which the rulers only know, or there will be a further danger of our herd, as the guardians may be termed, breaking out into rebellion.

Very true.

Had we not better appoint certain festivals at which we will bring together the brides and bridegrooms, and sacrifices will be offered and suitable hymeneal songs composed by our poets: the number of weddings is a matter which must be left to the discretion of the rulers, whose aim will be to preserve the average of population? There are many other things which they will have to consider, such as the effects of wars and diseases and any similar agencies, in order as far as this is possible to prevent the State from becoming either too large or too small.

Certainly, he replied.

We shall have to invent some ingenious kind of lots which the less worthy may draw on each occasion of our bringing them together, and then they will accuse their own ill-luck and not the rulers.

To be sure, he said.

And I think that our braver and better youth, besides their other honors and rewards, might have greater facilities of intercourse with women given them; their bravery will be a reason, and such fathers ought to have as many sons as possible.

True.

And the proper officers, whether male or female or both, for offices are to be held by women as well as by men—

Yes—

The proper officers will take the offspring of the good parents to the pen or fold, and there they will deposit them with certain nurses who dwell in a separate quarter; but the offspring of the inferior, or of the better when they chance to be deformed, will be put away in some mysterious, unknown place, as they should be.

Yes, he said, that must be done if the breed of the guardians is to be kept pure.

They will provide for their nurture, and will bring the mothers to the fold when they are full of milk, taking the greatest possible care that no mother recognizes her own child; and other wet-nurses may be engaged if more are required. Care will also be taken that the process of suckling shall not be protracted too long; and the mothers will have no getting up at night or other trouble, but will hand over all this sort of thing to the nurses and attendants.

You suppose the wives of our guardians to have a fine easy time of it when they are having children.

Why, said I, and so they ought. Let us, however, proceed with our scheme. We were saying that the parents should be in the prime of life?

Very true.

And what is the prime of life? May it not be defined as a period of about twenty years in a woman's life, and thirty in a man's?

Which years do you mean to include?

A woman, I said, at twenty years of age may begin to bear children to the State, and continue to bear them until forty; a man may begin at five-and twenty, when he has passed the point at which the pulse of life beats quickest, and continue to beget children until he be fifty-five.

Certainly, he said, both in men and women those years are the prime of physical as well as of intellectual vigor.

Any one above or below the prescribed ages who takes part in the public hymeneals shall be said to have done an unholy and unrighteous thing; the child of which he is the father, if it steals into life, will have been conceived under auspices very unlike the sacrifices and prayers, which at each hymeneal priestesses and priests and the whole city will offer, that the new generation may be better and more useful than their good and useful parents, whereas his child will be the offspring of darkness and strange lust.

Very true, he replied.

And the same law will apply to any one of those within the prescribed age who forms a connection with any woman in the prime of life without the sanction of the rulers; for we shall say that he is raising up a bastard to the State, uncertified and unconsecrated.

Very true, he replied.

This applies, however, only to those who are within the specified age: after that we allow them to range at will, except that a man may not marry his daughter or his daughter's daughter, or his mother or his mother's mother; and women, on the other hand, are prohibited from marrying their sons or fathers, or son's son or father's father, and so on in either direction. And we grant all this, accompanying the permission with strict orders to prevent any embryo which may come into being from seeing the light; and if any force a way to the birth, the parents must understand that the offspring of such an union can not be maintained, and arrange accordingly.

That also, he said, is a reasonable proposition. But how will they know who are fathers and daughters, and so on?

They will never know. The way will be this:—dating from the day of the hymeneal, the bridegroom who was then married will call all the male children who are born in the seventh and the tenth month afterwards his sons, and the female children his daughters, and they will call him father, and he will call their children his grandchildren, and they will call the elder generation grandfathers and grandmothers. All who were begotten at the time when their fathers and mothers came together will be called their brothers and sisters, and these, as I was saying, will be forbidden to intermarry. This, however, is not to be understood as an absolute prohibition of the marriage of brothers and sisters; if the lot favors them, and they receive the sanction of the Pythian oracle, the law will allow them.

Quite right, he replied.

Such is the scheme, Glaucon, according to which the guardians of our State are to have their wives and families in common. And now you would have the argument show that this community is consistent with the rest of our polity, and also that nothing can be better—would you not?

Yes, certainly.

Shall we try to find a common basis by asking of ourselves what ought to be the chief aim of the legislator in making laws and in the organization of a State,—what is the greatest good, and what is the greatest evil, and then consider whether our previous description has the stamp of the good or of the evil?

By all means.

Can there be any greater evil than discord and distraction and plurality where unity ought to reign? or any greater good than the bond of unity?

There can not.

And there is unity where there is community of pleasures and pains—where all the citizens are glad or grieved on the same occasions of joy and sorrow?

No doubt.

Yes; and where there is no common but only private feeling a State is disorganized—when you have one half of the world triumphing and the other plunged in grief at the same events happening to the city or the citizens?

Certainly.

Such differences commonly originate in a disagreement about the use of the terms "mine" and "not mine," "his" and "not his."

Exactly so.

And is not that the best-ordered State in which the greatest number of persons apply the terms "mine" and "not mine" in the same way to the same thing?

Quite true.

Or that again which most nearly approaches to the condition of the individual—as in the body, when but a finger of one of us is hurt, the whole frame, drawn towards the soul as a centre and forming one kingdom under the ruling power therein, feels the hurt and sympathizes all together with the part affected, and we say that the man has a pain in his finger; and the same expression is used about any other part of the body, which has a sensation of pain at suffering or of pleasure at the alleviation of suffering.

Very true, he replied; and I agree with you that in the best-ordered State there is the nearest approach to this common feeling which you describe.

Then when any one of the citizens experiences any good or evil, the whole State will make his case their own, and will either rejoice or sorrow with him?

Yes, he said, that is what will happen in a well-ordered State.

It will now be time, I said, for us to return to our State and see whether this or some other form is most in accordance with these fundamental principles.

Very good.

Our State like every other has rulers and subjects?

True.

All of whom will call one another citizens?

Of course.

But is there not another name which people give to their rulers in other States?

Generally they call them masters, but in democratic States they simply call them rulers.

And in our State what other name besides that of citizens do the people give the rulers?

They are called saviours and helpers, he replied.

And what do the rulers call the people?

Their maintainers and foster-fathers.

And what do they call them in other States?

Slaves.

And what do the rulers call one another in other States?

Fellow-rulers.

And what in ours?

Fellow-guardians.

Did you ever know an example in any other State of a ruler who would speak of one of his colleagues as his friend and of another as not being his friend?

Yes, very often.

And the friend he regards and describes as one in whom he has an interest, and the other as a stranger in whom he has no interest?

Exactly.

But would any of your guardians think or speak of any other guardian as a stranger?

Certainly he would not; for every one whom they meet will be regarded by them either as a brother or sister, or father or mother, or son or daughter, or as the child or parent of those who are thus connected with him.

Capital, I said; but let me ask you once more: Shall they be a family in name only; or shall they in all their actions be true to the name? For example, in the use of the word "father," would the care of a father be implied and the filial reverence and duty and obedience to him which the law commands; and is the violator of these duties to be regarded as an impious and unrighteous person who is not likely to receive much good either at the hands of God or of man? Are these to be or not to be the strains which the children will hear repeated in their ears by all the citizens about those who are intimated to them to be their parents and the rest of their kinsfolk?

These, he said, and none other; for what can be more ridiculous than for them to utter the names of family ties with the lips only and not to act in the spirit of them?

Then in our city the language of harmony and concord will be more often heard than in any other. As I was describing before, when any one is well or ill, the universal word will be "with me it is well" or "it is ill."

Most true.

And agreeably to this mode of thinking and speaking, were we not saying that they will have their pleasures and pains in common?

Yes, and so they will.

And they will have a common interest in the same thing which they will alike call "my own," and having this common interest they will have a common feeling of pleasure and pain?

Yes, far more so than in other States.

And the reason of this, over and above the general constitution of the State, will be that the guardians will have a community of women and children?

That will be the chief reason.

And this unity of feeling we admitted to be the greatest good, as was implied in our own comparison of a well-ordered State to the relation of the body and the members, when affected by pleasure or pain?

That we acknowledge, and very rightly.

Then the community of wives and children among our citizens is clearly the source of the greatest good to the State?

Certainly.

QUESTIONS FOR ANALYSIS AND DISCUSSION

1. Plato often uses analogies to make his argument. An analogy is persuasive to the extent that its key similarities outweigh any significant dissimilarities. Part of Plato's argument for the regulated breeding of human beings is that other animals are also bred for certain purposes. Do you accept the case for breeding humans? If not, which significant dissimilarities arise in Plato's analogy? Be specific.

2. What does Plato describe as the troubling aspect of parental love? Do you agree? Do you accept his proposal? Why, or why not?

3. There has been some dispute whether Plato's *Republic* should always be taken at face value. Some of the things proposed cannot be taken seriously, so some conclude that Plato engages in bits of humor, irony, or sarcasm to make his points. Given the vivid descriptions of these communal families, how do you interpret this portion of *The Republic?* If Plato is serious, is his proposal practical? If Plato is being facetious, what do you think is his underlying point?

49.

LIN YUTANG

Growing Old Gracefully

Can the love the parent has for a child be two-directional? For Chinese thinker Lin Yutang (1895–1976), the love a child has for a parent or grandparent can be as important and intense as the love a parent offers a child. Citing the Chinese tradition of respecting the elderly, Lin Yutang depicts the love an adult child shows an aging parent as reflecting

"On Growing Old Gracefully," from *The Importance of Living* (England: William Heinemann, Ltd., 1931), pp. 751–757.

gratitude and loyalty. These virtues are not only personal but need to be encouraged as part of being a social creature. If attending to the elderly is left to institutions and personal choice, then we might look to America's treatment of the elderly to see if gratitude or loyalty are needed for the elderly to live well.

CRITICAL READING QUESTIONS

1. How does Lin Yutang characterize American cultural attitudes toward the elderly?
2. What is the key moral difference between modern Western culture and traditional Chinese culture when it comes to showing respect for parents or grandparents?
3. Which is preferable: that the elderly announce their right to be cared for by their children, that the government ensures their well-being, that the government makes laws and policies to persuade children to take care of the elderly, or that children want to care for their parents?

The Chinese family system, as I conceive it, is largely an arrangement of particular provision for the young and the old, for since childhood and youth and old age occupy half our life, it is important that the young and the old live a satisfactory life. It is true that the young are more helpless and can take less care of themselves, but on the other hand, they can get along better without material comforts than the old people. A child is often scarcely aware of material hardships, with the result that a poor child is often as happy as, if not happier than, a rich child. He may go barefooted, but that is a comfort, rather than a hardship to him, whereas going barefooted is often an intolerable hardship for old people. This comes from the child's greater vitality, the bounce of youth. He may have his temporary sorrows, but how easily he forgets them. He has no idea of money and no millionaire complex, as the old man has. At the worst, he collects only cigar coupons for buying a pop-gun, whereas the dowager collects Liberty Bonds. Between the fun of these two kinds of collection there is no comparison. The reason is the child is not intimidated by life as all grown-ups are. His personal habits are as yet unformed, and he is not a slave to a particular brand of coffee, and he takes whatever comes along. He has very little racial prejudice and absolutely no religious prejudice. His thoughts and ideas have not fallen into certain ruts. Therefore, strange as it may seem, old people are even more dependent than the young because their fears are more definite and their desires are more delimited.

Something of this tenderness toward old age existed already in the primeval consciousness of the Chinese people, a feeling that I can compare only to the Western chivalry and feeling of tenderness toward women. If the early Chinese people had any chivalry, it was manifested not toward women and children, but toward the old people. That feeling of chivalry found clear expression in Mencius in some such saying as, "The people with grey hair should not be seen carrying burdens on the street," which was expressed as the final goal of a good government. Mencius also described the four classes of the world's most helpless people as: "The widows, widowers, orphans, and old people without children." Of these four classes, the first two were to be taken care of by a political economy that should be so arranged that there would be no unmarried men and women. What was to be done about the orphans Mencius did not say, so far as we know, although orphanages have always existed throughout the ages, as well as pensions for old people. Every one realizes, however, that orphanages and old age pensions are poor substitutes for the home. The feeling is that the home alone can provide anything resembling a satisfactory arrangement for the old and the young. But for the young, it is to be taken for granted that not much need be said, since there is natural parental affection. "Water flows downwards and not upwards," the Chinese always say, and therefore the affection for parents and grandparents is something that stands more in need of being taught by culture. A natural man loves his children, but a cultured man loves his parents. In the end, the teaching of love and respect for old people became a generally accepted principle, and if we are to believe some of the writers, the desire to have the privilege of serving their parents in their old age actually became a consuming passion. The greatest regret a Chinese gentleman could have was the eternally lost opportunity of serving his old parents with medicine and soup on their deathbed, or not to be present when they died. For a high official in his fifties or sixties not to be able to invite his parents to come from their native village and stay with his family at the capital, "seeing them to bed every night and greeting them every morning," was to commit a moral sin of which he should be ashamed and for which he had constantly to offer excuses and explanations to his friends and colleagues. This regret was expressed in two lines by a man who returned too late to his home, when his parents had already died:

> The tree desires repose, but the wind will not stop;
> The son desires to serve, but his parents are already gone.

It is to be assumed that if man were to live his life like a poem, he would be able to look upon the sunset of his life as his happiest period, and instead of trying to postpone the much feared old age, be able actually to look forward to it, and gradually build up to it as the best and happiest period of his existence. In my efforts to compare and contrast Eastern and Western life, I have found no differences that are absolute except in this matter of the attitude towards age, which is sharp and clearcut and permits of no intermediate positions. The differences in our attitude towards sex, toward women, and toward work, play, and achievement are all relative. The relationship between husband and wife in China is not essentially different from that in the West, nor even the relationship between parent and child. Not even the ideas of individual liberty and democracy and the relationship between the people and their ruler are, after all, so very different. But in the matter of our attitude toward age, the difference is absolute, and the East and West take exactly opposite points of view. This is clearest in the matter of asking about a person's age or telling one's own. In China, the first question a person asks the other on an official call, after asking about his name and surname is, "What is your glorious age?" If the person replies apologetically that he is twenty-three or twenty-eight, the other party generally comforts him by saying that he has still a glorious future, and that one day he may become old. But if the person replies that he is thirty-five or thirty-eight, the other party immediately exclaims with deep respect, "Good luck!"; enthusiasm grows in proportion as the gentleman is able to report a higher and higher age, and if the person is anywhere over fifty, the inquirer immediately drops his voice in humility and respect. That is why all old people, if they can, should go and live in China, where even a beggar with a white beard is treated with extra kindness. People in middle age actually look forward to the time when they can celebrate their fifty-first birthday, and in the case of successful merchants or officials, they would celebrate even their forty-first birthday with great pomp and glory. But the fifty-first birthday, or the half-century mark, is an occasion of rejoicing for people of all classes. The sixty-first is a happier and grander occasion than the fifty-first and the seventy-first is still happier and grander, while a man able to celebrate his eighty-first birthday is actually looked upon as one specifically favored by heaven. The wearing of a beard becomes the special prerogative of those who have become grandparents, and a man doing so without the necessary qualifications, either of being a grandfather or being on the other side of fifty, stands in danger of being sneered at behind his back. The result is that young men try to pass themselves off as older than they are by imitating the pose and dignity and point of view of the old people, and I have known young Chinese writers graduated from the middle schools, anywhere between twenty-one and twenty-five, writing articles in the magazines to advise what "the young men ought and ought not to read," and discussing the pitfalls of youth with a fatherly condescension.

This desire to grow old and in any case to appear old is understandable when one understands the premium generally placed upon old age in China. In the first place, it is a privilege of the old people to talk, while the young must listen and hold their tongue. "A young man is supposed to have ears and no mouth," as a Chinese saying goes. Men of twenty are supposed to listen when people of thirty are talking, and these in turn are supposed to listen when men of forty are talking. As the desire to talk and to be listened to is almost universal, it is evident that the further along one gets in years, the better chance he has to talk and to be listened to when he goes about in society. It is a game of life in which no one is favored, for everyone has a chance of becoming old in his time. Thus a father lecturing his son is obliged to stop suddenly and change his demeanor the moment the grandmother opens her mouth. Of course he wishes to be in the grandmother's place. And it is quite fair, for what right have the young to open their mouth when the old men can say, "I have crossed more bridges than you have crossed streets!" What right have the young got to talk?

In spite of my acquaintance with Western life and the Western attitude toward age, I am still continually shocked by certain expressions for which I am totally unprepared. Fresh illustrations of this attitude come up on every side. I have heard an old lady remarking that she has had several grandchildren, but, "It was the first one that hurt." With the full knowledge that American people hate to be thought of as old, one still doesn't quite expect to have it put that way. . . .

I have no doubt that the fact that the old men of America still insist on being so busy and active can be directly traced to individualism carried to a foolish extent. It is their pride and their love of independence and their shame of being dependent upon their children. But among the many human rights the American people have provided for in the Constitution, they have strangely forgotten about the right to be fed by their children, for it is a right and an obligation growing out of service. How can any one deny that parents who have toiled for their children in their youth, have lost many a good night's sleep when they were ill, have washed their diapers long before they could talk and have spent about a quarter of a century bringing them up and fitting them for life, have the right to be fed by them and loved and respected when they are old? Can one not forget the individual and his pride of self in a general scheme of home life in which men are justly taken care of by their parents and, having in turn taken care of their children, are also justly taken care of by the latter? The Chinese have not got the sense of individual independence because the whole conception of life is based upon mutual help within the home; hence there is no shame attached to the circumstance of one's being served by his children in the sunset of one's life. Rather it is considered good luck to have children who can take care of one. One lives for nothing else in China.

In the West, the old people efface themselves and prefer to live alone in some hotel with a restaurant on the ground floor, out of consideration for their children and an entirely unselfish desire not to interfere in their home life. But the old people have the right to interfere, and if interference is unpleasant, it is nevertheless natural, for all life, particularly the domestic life, is a lesson in restraint. Parents interfere with their children anyway when they are young, and the logic of non-interference is already seen in the results of Behaviorists, who think that all children should be taken away from their parents. If one cannot tolerate one's own parents when they are old and comparatively helpless, parents who have done so much for us, whom else can one tolerate in the home? One has to learn self-restraint anyway, or even marriage will go on the rocks. And how can the personal service and devotion and adoration of loving children ever be replaced by the best hotel waiters?

The Chinese idea supporting this personal service to old parents is expressly defended on the sole ground of gratitude. The debts to one's friends may be numbered, but the debts to one's parents are beyond number. Again and again, Chinese essays on filial piety mention the fact of washing diapers, which takes on significance when one becomes a parent himself. In return, therefore, is it not right that in their old age, the parents should be served with the best food and have their favorite dishes placed before them? The duties of a son serving his parents are pretty hard, but it is sacrilege to make a comparison between nursing one's own parents and nursing a stranger in a hospital. For instance, the following are some of the duties of the junior at home, as prescribed by Tu Hsishih and incorporated in a book of moral instruction very popular as a text in the old schools:

In the summer months, one should, while attending to his parents, stand by their side and fan them, to drive away the heat and the flies and mosquitoes. In winter, he should see that the bed quilts are warm enough and the stove fire is hot enough, and see that it is just right by attending to it constantly. He should also see if there are holes or crevices in the doors and windows, that there may be no draft, to the end that his parents are comfortable and happy.

A child above ten should get up before his parents in the morning, and after the toilet go to their bed and ask if they have had a good night. If his parents have already gotten up, he should first curtsy to them before inquiring after their health, and should retire with another curtsy after the question. Before going to bed at night, he should prepare the bed, when the parents are going to sleep, and stand by until he sees that they have fallen off to sleep and then pull down the bed curtain and retire himself.

Who, therefore, wouldn't want to be an old man or an old father or grandfather in China?

This sort of thing is being very much laughed at by the proletarian writers of China as "feudalistic," but there is a charm to it which makes many old gentlemen inland cling to it and think that modern China is going to the dogs. The important point is that every man grows old in time, if he lives long enough, as he certainly desires to. If one forgets this foolish individualism which seems to assume that an individual can exist in the abstract and be literally independent, one must admit that we must so plan our pattern of life that the golden period lies ahead in old age and not behind us in youth and innocence. For if we take the reverse attitude, we are committed without our knowing to a race with the merciless course of time, forever afraid of what lies ahead of us—a race, it is hardly necessary to point out, which is quite hopeless and in which we are eventually all defeated. No one can really stop growing old; he can only cheat himself by not admitting that he is growing old. And since there is no use fighting against nature, one might just as well grow old gracefully. The sympathy of life should end with a grand finale of peace and serenity and material comfort and spiritual contentment, and not with the crash of a broken drum or cracked cymbals.

QUESTIONS FOR ANALYSIS AND DISCUSSION

1. Lin Yutang's argument rests in part on the contrast between American and Chinese traditional attitudes on family and individualism. If a sociological survey of the current quality of life of elderly Americans and Chinese found that the latter were considerably worse off, should that affect Lin Yutang's argument? Why, or why not?

2. Is his discussion one-sided? Many people acknowledge that children should appreciate all their parents have done. However, should this appreciation include the pressures and difficulties of taking care of a parent who is sickly, or whose changing personality begins to upset the grandchildren, or who wants

to maintain some authority in how the children lead their lives or rear their own children? Imagine that you face the choice of what kind of care to provide an aging parent or grandparent. How does Lin Yutang offer moral and practical guidance? Does American morality offer better or worse guidance? Develop your response in light of Lin Yutang's observations.

3. What do you think Lin Yutang means by growing old "gracefully"? Do you think growing old gracefully is a matter of good luck or a result of one's moral choices?

4. How do you think an ethical egoist would respond to Lin Yutang's position? or a defender of the idea that morality is dictated by the genetic drive to improve the species? or a believer in the Ten Commandments where God tells us to honor our mothers and fathers? Select one or two readings from Chapter 1 and develop a debate with Lin Yutang's moral outlook.

50.

MARY MIDGELY AND JUDITH HUGHES

Trouble with Families?

It is tempting to avoid the debate over families by treating families as we treat individuals—leaving them alone until they start bothering us. It is also tempting to conclude that the family is the most important social institution and hence needs careful structuring and monitoring. For philosophers and social critics Mary Midgely (b. 1919) and Judith Hughes, both temptations misconstrue the meaning of family life and the love that underscores it. Midgely and Hughes remind us that the family, in all its forms—heterosexual couples, single parents, homosexual couples, extended families—is critically important for children. In family life children learn of the virtues and vices, which are learned poorly or not at all in other social arenas. Given this importance, Midgely and Hughes address the issue of political and social policies regarding family life.

"Trouble with Families?" from *Introducing Applied Ethics*, edited by Brenda Almond (Oxford, England and Cambridge, MA: Blackwell Publishers Ltd., 1995), pp. 17–32. Notes have been omitted.

CRITICAL READING QUESTIONS

1. What is the difference between a sociologist's and a philosopher's study of the family?
2. How do Midgely and Hughes interpret Plato's discussion of the "mine" and "not mine" that underlies family life?
3. What is meant by individualism, and how does it relate to family life?
4. What do Hughes and Midgely see as the peculiar problem of modern Western societies in terms of helping young people prepare for family life?
5. How do they see the value of family life? Is there a single ideal of family?

Distress Signals

The family, it is said, is in a state of crisis. From the right and from the left the lamentations pour thick and fast. Agreeing that the family has "broken down," experts lay the blame, singly or severally, on irresponsible fathers, selfish mothers, poverty and deprivation, politicians, the decline of religious belief, incompetent teachers, lax law courts or junk food. Whatever the cause or causes, the state, it is said, can no longer support feckless women who have babies out of wedlock. And in any case, there is something terribly wrong going on in contemporary western societies. We need (these critics argue) a return to basics, which includes a return to the image—projected in a thousand Hollywood movies of the mid-twentieth century—of happy wedded couples producing children in their twenties and staying together in conjugal bliss until death do them part. This is recommended as the main, perhaps the only, way to solve the problem of juvenile crime and to cut the rising social security bill at a stroke. It will also make the children happy and self-fulfilled.

That, anyway, is the story. And even those who do not share the partisan beliefs fuelling parts of it may still share a general unease and suspect a moral decline. Old values of respect for age, privacy and property, care of the young, politeness to those in authority, loyalty, truthfulness and patriotism are seen every day to have lost their force. And now we mourn them.

It is the job of sociologists, not philosophers, to enquire into the facts supporting these allegations, and the job of historians to decide how far the golden past age that is now invoked ever existed. But when the decline of the family is identified with a moral decline, philosophers need to ask what such a thing would be. They need, too, to question just what model or ideal of the family is at issue here. For when we think of moral decline as identical with the decline of traditional family structures, values and practices we need first to note that all these have been under attack from many quarters, at least since the time of Plato.

The firm pronouncements of public figures today rarely reflect those past criticisms. For instance, the British Home Secretary Michael Howard, speaking at the Conservative Party Conference in October 1993, said flatly, "We must emphasize our belief that the traditional two-parent family is best. Best for the parents, best for society, and above all best for children." But many philosophers, political theorists, psychologists and social reformers have not shared that confidence. From all these quarters, families have been castigated as undermining the state and society and as causing harm to the individuals within them. Precisely because the family is seen as a powerful element in society, it has the resources to subvert it; precisely because it is thought to hold so much sway over individuals, it has the power to oppress them. More recently, the premisses, though not the conclusion, have changed to suggest that, far from being all-powerful, the family is positively incompetent to undertake those roles which its advocates claim it fulfils.

Plato's suggestion in the *Republic* that the Guardians, though not the general populace, should hold wives and children in common was prompted partly by his eugenic beliefs, but mainly by his hope that eliminating family ties and interests would remove a major cause of quarrels. Quarrels debilitate not just the individuals but the state itself, for the good state, like the good man, is a harmonious whole. What binds the state is that individuals in a community experience pleasures and pains in unison. And this is indeed a phenomenon which we see repeatedly in contemporary communities who have a common reaction of horror to a child murder or a terrorist bombing, a shared sense of jubilation as the local football team makes good. Communities bound, as Plato says, by shared pleasure or pain are strong and united and remain so as long as the individuals within them do not cut the bonds by the simple expedient of having each "his own feelings apart."

That city, says Plato, is best managed "in which the greatest number say 'mine' and 'not mine' with the same meaning about the same thing." Hence the Guardians would couple only at the behest of the state and would not know who their own parents or children were. Women would suckle any baby as it was handed to them. All would treat all as fathers, mothers, sons and daughters. They would then "not use the word 'mine' each of different things, but of the same; one will not drag into his own house whatever goods he can get apart from the rest; another will not drag into his own separate house a separate wife and separate children." This is to make them "free from quarrels and factions, as far as human quarrels come from possessing wealth or children or kindred."

Plato is not saying that we should not say "mine" and "not mine" at all, but that we should say these things of the same things, not different ones. This is the thinking behind all genuine movements which aim to establish communes. The idea is not to abolish the family but to extend it. The same values of loyalty and concern, affection and responsibility are not removed but applied to a wider community.

These values run into serious trouble only when the community is extended beyond the grasp of the moral imagination so that the language of family relationship can no longer signify, or when the state itself claims entirely to replace the other individuals with whom one is in community. There is then a corresponding shift in values. Communism and fascism reduce the terminology of relationship to "brother" and "sister" or replace it with words like "citizen" or "comrade" or "fellow countryman." At this point, concepts such as filial duty, parental protectiveness, family loyalty finally vanish.

These moves can be, and usually are, made on nationalistic or party grounds. But there is a different, more drastic kind of rationale which has developed along philosophical rather than political lines and which attacks more deeply the insidiousness of the possessive "my" and "mine." On this account, the problem with strong personal emotions such as love, which are known to occur sometimes in families, is that they destroy the impartiality needed for being a truly moral agent. A graphic illustration of this view is the celebrated ruling of the political philosopher William Godwin that "pure unadulterated justice" compels one to save from a burning building a gifted benefactor of mankind, such as Archbishop Fénelon, rather than his chambermaid, even if that chambermaid happens to be one's own wife or mother. Godwin asks,

> What magic is there in the pronoun "my" to overturn the decision of everlasting truth? My wife or my mother may be a fool or a prostitute, malicious, lying or dishonest. If they be, of what consequence is it that they are mine?

This second line of attack shifts the focus from the harm which families may do to outsiders to their power to corrupt their own members, though some people might think that the denial of such ties was itself also a form of corruption.

Bad for Everybody?

Other theorists, however, have taken a still more drastic line, seeing family ties, not just as corrupting, but as deadly to the whole personality. Thus the British "anti-psychiatrist" R. D. Laing argued, in his study of neuroses, that families, far from helping to cure the mental breakdowns of their members, were to a large extent the cause of them. Even schizophrenia and other psychoses were, in Laing's view, to be understood as simply natural responses to unbearable family pressures.

Plenty of other arguments have been used to show how unsuitable a social environment families can provide for men, for women and for children—how they can destroy all three. Until recently, sympathy was usually reserved for the males, for whom marriage was held to mark the end of most of the desirable features of life. "Times are changed with him who marries," wrote R. L. Stevenson; "there are no more by-path meadows, where you may innocently linger, but the road lies long and straight and dusty to the grave." But it is not only pleasure which flees. "In marriage, a man becomes slack and selfish, and undergoes a fatty degeneration of his moral being." Disraeli's maxim that "Every woman should marry—and no man" echoed this view. Not until the twentieth century was there a popular and sustained counter-claim made by women themselves. But if the family limits and represses creativity and individuality in men, how much more must it do this to women? For women not only take on extra responsibilities at marriage but change their names, may lose their jobs, and are likely to bear and rear children. Married women, it is claimed, are more likely to suffer mental breakdown than married men, while unmarried women are less likely than bachelors to suffer the same fate.

As for children, more of them are abused by members of their own families than by outsiders. For them, the family is a dangerous lottery whose closeness and privacy can hide and protect abuses just as surely as it can provide a safe and reassuring haven. Cycles of abuse and of criminality may perpetuate themselves through generations. According to this argument, if the family can be a force for great moral good through its inculcation of high moral standards, so it can be an equal force for bad, and it often is.

As if all this were not enough, the family also faces the opposite charge, not that it does bad things well, but that it does good things badly. The professionalization of education and child-rearing has steadily undermined the role of parents in the upbringing of children to the point where they have been deliberately excluded from playing traditional roles. For centuries, parents who could do so taught their children to read, inculcated moral values, socialized infants and passed on skills and folk wisdom. The state, quite rightly, stepped in to help those whose own skills or knowledge were deficient in these areas. But of course, it did not stop there. The professionals, not content merely to fill the gaps, began to claim exclusive rights and expertise over the whole business. Parents are still often discouraged from teaching their pre-school children to read, and sometimes expressly forbidden to do so. Nursery education is increasingly seen, not just as a desirable option for children without siblings or for children of working parents, but as a prerequisite of anyone's happy and successful development. State and Church sometimes ignore the role of parents in disputing over which of them ought to be teaching moral values to children. Through increasing professionalization, then, the family escapes the charge of wickedness only to face the lesser accusation of incompetence.

Locating the Trouble

So, if families are damaging, damaged or both, we may wonder why there should now be complaints that all these efforts to destroy or undermine them seem to have succeeded. Yet the "breakdown of the family" is indeed now seen as the central problem. Is it emerging that the benefits which families bestow on individuals and society do, after all, outweigh the catalogue of ills which we have been considering? This "breakdown" is currently often identified with the increase in divorce, separation and single parenthood, but we should notice that the concern is not new. In an earlier generation, the move from the extended to the nuclear family was seen as a cause of isolation, bad manners and a diminishing sense of respect for the old. It then seemed that it was not the absence of a particular individual, father or mother, which was the problem but the absence of a network of related individuals. Moreover, the messages of distress are mixed; is the family too extended or too nuclear? Divorce sometimes helps to recreate extended families by generating wider, looser networks of step-relatives. But far from being welcomed, divorce is in general blamed as a cause of disaster.

Modern Mobility

What, then, is the central trouble? It is certainly not only that the state has to pay more for the upkeep of children. People do feel that something important is fading. Essentially, this important thing is surely the closeness, the emotional security, the firm sense of belonging that families everywhere have usually had.

But if we ask what has loosened that closeness, we see at once that huge changes in the wider world during the last two centuries were bound to weaken such links. Before the Industrial Revolution, nearly all human beings stayed put throughout their lives with a single set of people. Though there were always some traders and travellers and administrators who knew about matters at a distance, most people neither saw nor envisaged any other way of life than that of their parents. Now, most people in the wealthier nations feel mobile from the very start of their lives. They see many alternative ways of life and meet any number of strangers. They are brought up knowing that they may go anywhere, and also that customs in their own lands are constantly changing.

All this mobility is no doubt seen as a welcome freedom, but of course people do not move just for pleasure. Industry sucks people from place to place, dropping them at its own convenience, not theirs. Workless people drift into big towns. And the sheer numbers who are swirling around in this way are constantly growing. Neighbourhoods, which used to back and strength family bonds, are weakened and replaced by crowds of strangers. Networks of various sizes, both formal and informal, that used to structure life in clans, villages, churches, schools, clubs, societies, political parties and other groupings have become weaker, more transient, harder to maintain. Workplaces have an increasingly fast turnover of staff. As all these wider patterns shift around, families are tending to be left as the last remaining unit that is available to maintain whatever stability is needed. This naturally puts great strain on personal affection, which is often left to do, in isolation, the connective work that used to be shared over a whole social network.

Individualist Euphoria

In this way, practical changes tend strongly to break up groups and to loosen bonds of all kinds. But at the level of theory too, powerful ideas have been working to justify, encourage and celebrate this shift. Since the early Enlightenment, individualism has had great influence both in right-wing and left-wing thought. Western civilization has, in fact, developed a most unusual ideal of personal freedom, an ideal which often startles people from other sophisticated civilizations such as those of Asia. This ideal of freedom has powered the West's highest achievements and has certainly also produced theorists from Rousseau through Mill to Sartre, and modern right-wing thinkers have celebrated the value of independence and the dignity of isolation. As Nietzsche put it,

> Do I counsel you to love your neighbour? I rather counsel you to flee from your neighbour and to love that which is farthest.

> Higher than love for one's neighbour is love for the remote and for the future. And
> I hold love for things and phantoms higher than love for men.

In that spirit, during the twentieth century, a whole flood of anti-family novels,
plays and films has warned the young of the need to isolate themselves and to reject
interfering relatives, particularly parents. As Samuel Butler complained in *The Way
of All Flesh*,

> Why should the generations overlap one another at all? Why cannot we be buried as
> eggs in neat little cells with ten or twenty thousand pounds each wrapped round us in
> Bank of England notes, and wake up, as the sphex wasp does, to find that its papa and
> mamma have not only left ample provision at its elbow, but have been eaten by spar-
> rows some time before it began to live consciously on its own account?

More seriously, the sociologist Edmund Leach laid it down in his 1967 Reith Lecture that, "far from being the basis of the good society, the family, with all its
narrow privacy and tawdry secrets, is the source of all our discontent." Or, as the
English poet Philip Larkin put it (in "This Be The Verse"),

> They fuck you up, your mum and dad.
>   They may not mean to, but they do.
> They fill you with the faults they had
>   And add some extra, just for you.

This warning is certainly worth having. They may indeed do so. But if they were
not there, would whoever else was in charge of us have done things any better?
The memoirs of those brought up in orphanages do not suggest so. Small children
everywhere form strong attachments, invariably expecting more attention than
their carers can possibly give, and absorbing their faults as well as their virtues.
They cannot, however, be left alone. Unlike wasps, we human beings need to be
looked after and inducted into a culture. This is a most difficult, complex and
exhausting process, one which stretches many parents' endurance beyond its limit.
And culture itself is not an assault on our freedom, as romantics have often suggested. Without a culture, we would not be human at all. It is the deep, indispensable mine from which we draw most of our treasures, including, of course, our
distinctive conception of freedom itself, and the concepts we use in criticizing current customs.

Should Families Be Wider?

One-sided moralizing of the kind we have been considering is common. There is
nothing unusual even about the individualistic humbug of claiming that radically
dependent creatures such as ourselves can exist in social isolation. Pendulums,
however, need to come back gently from these extremes if the point of the original
campaign is not to be lost. Today, we certainly do still value individual freedom
highly. We want to control domestic as well as political tyranny. But that does not
mean we must endorse the violent exaltation of solitude urged on us by philosophical prophets of individualism.

Not all philosophical attacks on "the family," however, have aimed at this complete isolation of the individual. Instead, theorists such as Plato and Marx wanted to widen the sense of belonging to include the whole community. They were protesting against the narrow, exclusive selfishness of the bourgeois family, which wasted people's efforts in strife. It was *in order to* cure this quarrelsome narrowness that Plato wanted all his Guardians to form one vast, undifferentiated family. His methods were extreme, but not his aims. Many of those who set up the Israeli kibbutzim and other communal groups have also wished to widen family feeling rather than to destroy it. So do many feminists, though some of them are indeed more radical, more individualistic libertarians.

Notoriously, however, actual attempts to put Plato's principles into practice always founder on the unregenerate partiality of human emotions. Neither parents nor children can play their roles without strong individual attachments. In orphanages, carers who try to be impartial find that the babies themselves frustrate them by attaching themselves firmly from the earliest age to one particular carer. We are born profoundly partial. Stoic philosophers tried very hard to eradicate these special attachments, calling for *apatheia*, a general, equable absence of passion. Thus Epictetus:

> The will of nature is to be learnt from matters which do not concern ourselves . . . Has another man's child died, or his wife? Who is there will not say, *It is the lot of humanity?* But when his own may die, then straightway it is, *Alas, wretched that I am!* But we should bethink ourselves of what we felt on hearing of others in the same plight.

The Stoic idea was not that we should extend our strong feeling to include others, but that we should extend indifference from their case to our own. This singularly negative ideal had a deep and long-lasting effect on Enlightenment thinking, an effect that is most obvious in Spinoza (1632–1677) but is still potent in Kant (1724–1804). Bishop Butler (1692–1752), however, shrewdly remarked that it is much easier to suppress affection in this way than it is to produce justice. As he put it,

> In general, experience will show that, as want of appetite to food supposes and proceeds from some bodily disease, so the apathy the Stoics talk of as much supposes or is accompanied with somewhat amiss in the moral character, in that which is the health of the mind. Those who formerly aimed at this upon the foot of philosophy appear to have had better success in eradicating the affections of tenderness and compassion than they had with the passions of envy, pride and resentment: these latter, at best, were but concealed, and that imperfectly too.

Humans, it seems, can reach wider loyalties only through a gradual, careful expansion which has to start from vigorous personal and local bonds. Genuine, Buddhist-style non-attachment which converts affection into universal compassion may be the terminus of human striving, but it cannot possibly be its starting-point.

Normally, human loyalties must develop through a widening series of interlinked circles, starting with those around one, who are usually relatives, and following out wider networks of connections. Explicit reasons for preferring one network over another only emerge later when conflicts arise between different loyalties. Thus, someone brought up inside a positive, articulate family, political party, Church and state is likely to be provided with plenty of conflicts between the various ideals which these units represent, but also with plenty of material for resolving these conflicts and finding a way forward. Frictions between the various units can be fruitful sources of reform. By contrast, people who are brought up in a family that is socially isolated will lack that material, and they may have much more difficulty in understanding their whole social situation.

What Is It to Be Mine or Yours?

The dilemma about families is, then, a real one. Close personal relations do involve ambivalence. They make possible the worst as well as the best in human life. People brought near to each other do collide and often hurt one another gravely. The psychiatrist R. D. Laing and the campaigners against child-abuse are right to stress the risks involved in individual parenting. The difficulty is that no one has ever found a real alternative, an infallible, impartial, non-intimate way of rearing babies.

Can the concept of intimacy be cleared of its connection with the notion of *possession?* Is there, as Godwin suggested, something hopelessly corrupting about the use of the pronoun "my" here? Is there something wrong with the whole concept of "belonging" when it is applied to people?

Certainly owning or possessing people can sound wrong. Yet nobody, surely, wants to be "disowned," or to belong nowhere? The trouble seems to be that this idea of possession or belonging covers an enormously wide spectrum. Plato was right to draw attention to the use of possessive pronouns such as "mine." These words range from unalarming examples such as *my shoes* and *my cup,* through *my house, my trees* and *my land* to much more mysterious cases like *my cat, my colleagues, my friends, my mother, my children* and *my country.* At one end, there seems to be a simple property relation based on contract, a relation that gives total control and no duties. At the other end lies a set of most complex personal relations involving deep respect and responsibility. And these relations unavoidably bind us to the wider community.

But even at the narrow end—the apparently neutral relation with shoes and cups—matters are not really so simple. Attachment comes in and plays its part. A small child who does not learn to care for its belongings, a child who is encouraged to treat them with casual contempt, misses something vital. Our shoes and cups are not just items that we have bought by contract so that we can smash them when we feel like it. They link us with the wider community. Perhaps Kant was wrong to rule that respect belongs only to persons, not to things. Things have meaning. They are tokens binding us into our culture, and also into the wider realm of nature. Contempt for things has in fact played a great part in our recent destruction of the environment. Perhaps the whole notion of belonging is one that we should treat more seriously.

Can Individualism Be Made Family-Friendly?

Individualism is certainly here to stay, and we have reason to be thankful for that. When individuals are harmed, by their families or anything else, we do need to insist that they matter, that they should not be sacrificed to an ideal, however lofty, that their freedom is indeed a precious thing for which it is worth struggling. For those who are oppressed, freedom comes first, because without it nothing else seems possible. But there are other goods to consider as well as freedom. "Bonds" are not just fetters; they are also life-lines.

Enlightenment thinking has tended to ignore the deep human need to balance freedom by love and co-operation, independence by sociability. In particular, certain philosophers, themselves celibate, have been disastrously blind to the intense, specific social needs of small children—and indeed of their parents too.

Britain, like some other western societies, seems now to be reaching a stage where many people fear the evils of loneliness and emotional insecurity more than the pains of traditional constraint. Philosophers need to help in articulating this feeling, in rephrasing individualism in more human, less antisocial terms. They need to talk less about freedom in the abstract and more about the balance between particular freedoms and between the particular evils from which people need to be free. In our view, that is perhaps the main philosophical issue emerging from this topic.

The idea that life would be better without close, lasting attachments such as those that arise in families seems a foolish one. But how can people today organize the individualistic world in a less isolating way? How can we control our civilization's current fluidity so as to leave pockets of refuge in which people can safely bring up their children?

Various suggestions seem to surface as important. For instance, since children do make these intense demands for stable support, we surely need to help adolescents who cannot yet provide that support to avoid having babies too early. Unwanted and unconsidered teenage pregnancies are a real and serious evil. So it seems to us that making contraception, and an understanding of it, freely available to the young ought to be considered as among the duties of a responsible government. It is extremely unfortunate that, in some countries, governments have attempted to do this in a heavy-handed and overbearing manner which has discredited the whole project. But there are also countries, such as Mexico, where family-planning campaigns conducted by local people have proved both popular and effective. Their example should surely be followed.

For older people who already have children, the question is rather whether the parents will stay together. Here again, the conventions that used to enforce this stability undoubtedly caused a good deal of misery. It is neither possible nor desirable to revive them. Even within those conventions, however, it was not necessarily thought that upbringing by a mother alone—say, a widow or a sailor's wife—must be disastrous, though it was always recognized that her work was hard and she would need outside support.

The reformers who made divorce and separation easier no doubt thought that children would do better if the parents parted than if they stayed together while quarreling. And it does seem that what upsets children most is not so much absence as discord. Unfortunately, however, current arrangements tend to provide both these things, since separated parents tend to continue to quarrel over the difficulties of disentangling their lives, and particularly over the children themselves. The importance of conciliation services here does now seem to be being recognized, along with the danger of letting adversarial lawyers inflame disputes. Family courts, devoted to resolving difficulties rather than allotting blame, are now being established. All this is surely a step in the right direction.

Undoubtedly, however, there is still a general dilemma here. At many points we today, in all kinds of societies, have to ask which we want more: secure social bonding or complete individual freedom? How shall we balance these ideals? It is not a single black-or-white choice between going into moral decline and returning to old ways. Instead, each society has a range of problems, some much harder than others, concerned with finding ways in which people can live together. Those ways will not necessarily produce familiar patterns. In many countries, family arrangements have changed a great deal over the ages, and they can very well change again.

Bring Back the Fathers?

Recently, discussions of family "breakdown" have mainly treated the absence of fathers as the central cause. In particular, apparent increases in the criminality and irresponsibility of young males have been attributed to the absence of their fathers. The existence and strength of this particular causal link are at present much disputed, and, unfortunately, ideological commitments on both sides make considerable caution necessary in interpreting the evidence. Recent attempts by administrators to extract maintenance from these fathers have become a political issue in a number of western countries, including Britain and the USA. But these moves seem aimed rather at saving public money than at domesticating these young men.

More seriously, however, it begins to seem that many young women are not prepared to take the trouble of domesticating them either. Substantial numbers of mothers do now seem to be choosing to be lone parents, rather than relying on the support of a man. We need to ask why they should make this choice.

In the economic climate of industrialized countries today, one answer is obvious. High unemployment means that many men are simply unable to provide financial support. And the kind of unemployment now prevailing, in which low-paid, insecure, part-time jobs for women replace full-time ones for men, has an evident tendency to break up families. But it seems that more is at stake than money. After all, men and women have always lived together in situations of extreme poverty and deprivation. Women do not refuse to live with men simply because they are poor. The reasons they are now giving have more to do with the attitudes of the men themselves than with their inability to be providers.

One young woman interviewed on a British television programme in September 1993 describe how the father of her child occasionally came round to visit, stayed a while and then went off to his mother's house when he felt like it. She complained that he had no sense of responsibility and just wanted to do as he pleased. She was clear that he did not play a significant part in her life or the life of her child. She did not seem to think this a desirable situation, but rather a sorry fact. And no doubt she had reason to be sorry. When the two parent arrangement does work it has obvious great advantages. Effort and worry can then be divided, the partners can support each other, and the children can get two satisfactory role models. But when it doesn't work, all this fails to happen.

Does the young male's inability to be a financial provider somehow deprive him of that sense of responsibility in any walk of life which comes with having a real role to play in the family? This surely cannot be inevitable. Many men have learnt to take on other responsibilities in the family than that of breadwinner. What does seem to have happened is that young men are facing these responsibilities earlier and earlier and are finding that they simply are not ready to handle them.

There was perhaps some common sense behind Aristotle's recommendation that a man should marry and begin to produce children at the age of 37 while a woman should do so at 18. Aristotle may have been wrong to think that these respective ages indicated the physical peak of the two sexes, but his suggestion that men need to mature—in other words, grow up—before taking on family responsibilities is one which is echoed through the ages. It has appeared in many forms. When men were obliged to soldier or to save or to learn before they were in a position to support a family, they married at a suitably late age. The need to delay starting a family became celebrated and tied to a notion of carefree bachelorhood which was tolerantly regarded as a necessary period of "sowing wild oats."

Obviously, a great deal of hypocrisy surrounded these attitudes. Men were not expected to do without sexual activity during this period and they were not legally obliged to provide for the children that they then fathered. But what was recognized, in the case of men, was that sexual proclivity and readiness to discharge family obligations do not necessarily go hand in hand. Neither perhaps do they with women, and the concern about teenage pregnancies and motherhood is sometimes tied to a concern that 14- or 15-year-old girls are not psychologically or practically fitted to motherhood.

Modern western society adds a special difficulty here for both sexes in its remarkable segregation of different age-groups, which tends to keep current teenagers more ignorant than they are in most societies about what child-rearing will actually involve. Girls as well as boys now confront this problem, but they seem to manage their responsibilities better and at an earlier age than men do. They do not, on the whole, choose to give up their children for adoption or abandon them, nor to abuse them. Nor do these young single mothers produce an undue proportion of criminals or psychopaths.

The problem seems to be, not so much that we in the West are demanding less of young men but that we are demanding considerably more of them than previous ages did, and that they simply do not or cannot meet those demands. This is a serious difficulty, and it is certainly not going to go away quickly. Like the tendency of marriages to break down, it results in large part from a general, deliberate loosening of bonds and it is therefore an integral part of the current culture.

Conclusion

Whatever may eventually be done about these things, it seems clear that for some considerable time many children in Britain, the USA, and similar countries will be being brought up in one-parent families, or in what has been described as "the mother-state-child family." We need, therefore, to find ways of making life tolerable for them, as well as ways of helping parents to stay together. Everything that tends to revive neighbourhoods, to reintegrate social contexts, to provide some sort of permanence within which these networks can grow and prosper, is urgently called for.

This support is not just a pragmatic, economic need, a device for keeping down crime, disease and protest. It is needed morally. The sort of provision that a society makes for families is indeed a moral matter, an aspect of its structure of ideals. If some kind of social Darwinist belief in the universal value of competition leads us to treat families as just one kind of unit among many, a unit that will survive or not according as it is fit to do so, then we shall be handing on an unbalanced, absurdly individualistic morality to our children.

If, too, that kind of competitive ethic leads us to treat the interests of men and women as necessarily competing, then we shall fail to look for ways in which they can be reconciled and can live harmoniously together. But living together is something absolutely essential for humans. It has to be made possible for the two sexes, just as it does across every other division where people often find it hard to understand one another. It is surely open to us to look for a more balanced form of individualism, a more human kind of freedom, that can make this possible.

QUESTIONS FOR ANALYSIS AND DISCUSSION

1. Which moral values do people learn in family life? Why are they better learned in a family setting rather than outside it?

2. As Midgely and Hughes point out, social and political theorists have frequently disputed the value of family life. Many target the family as the source not of happiness but of misery. Is this true only of bad families? Could a good family be the source of an unhappy person, just as a good person could still emerge from a bad family setting?

3. Which practical directions raised by Midgely and Hughes do you agree or disagree with? Could you add other practical solutions? Consider easier or stricter regulations on divorce, more or less public stigma on having children out of wedlock, and tighter legal constraints on divorced parents who avoid financial support of their children in addition to the solutions you may propose. Finally, are these practical directions consistent or inconsistent with traditional beliefs in personal rights, individualism, and privacy?

CHAPTER SEVEN

Self-Regarding Virtues

"Know Thyself!"

—Delphic Oracle to Socrates

Most of us do love to talk about ourselves, although I've always regarded it as a slightly illicit pleasure or one you pay for by the hour.

—Wendy Kaminer, *I'm Dysfunctional, You're Dysfunctional*

More than any other topic, the morality of how to treat oneself is complicated by a thorny philosophical issue. What exactly is the self? Religious believers have a version that usually involves a soul. Sociologists tend to focus on the self performing a role. Psychologists often view the self as dissatisfied whole. As several of the selections in Chapter 1 remind us, dispute remains over whether the self is primarily a biological entity, an entity largely molded by cultural influences, or a unique creation. In the history of philosophy no single concept of the self has overwhelmed all others. Indeed, the question that sparks much of a child's philosophical wonderment—"Who am I?"—has not been fully answered even by those who devote their careers to studying this topic. With these metaphysical reservations in mind, moralists continue to debate to what extent a person does or should do good for him- or herself.

The ethical questions about the self are not any easier to resolve then the metaphysical concerns. One of the first moral lessons for children is tempering their own selfish desires and learning to show concern for others. The child who laughs at the misfortune of a playmate is scolded; the child who offers a piece of candy to a classmate is praised. At the same time, moral persons are encouraged to take care of themselves. As Hiriyanna and Jordan-Smith point out in Chapter 3, one of the motivations for following a particular moral direction lies in the likelihood that this will be the best way to achieve a good life, or at least to avoid a miserable one. Although people tend to think that the first principle of most ethical theories involves a component of altruism, many moral traditions also emphasize the proper respect and treatment of oneself. After all, other people can do only so much—we need to take care of ourselves.

Does this mean that people who go to health clubs, walking on treadmills while staring into the mirror to see if their svelte bodies still need some muscle tone, are moral exemplars? Do people who bemoan social policies aimed at helping the downtrodden represent the true morality, demanding that we take care of number

406

one first? When talk shows flood the airwaves with stories of dysfunctional friendships and families, is the audience's attention focused on a traditional concern for
developing self-esteem? Is my sense of my own importance sufficient that the world
should address my despair or failings? At what point does the virtue of self-regard
become the vice of pridefulness?

Pride is distinguished in its moral ambivalence. As Aristotle observes, pride is
the crown virtue for it makes other virtues possible. Yet in Christian morality pride
is often considered the fundamental vice, for the failings of pride (or vanity) open
the door for the other vices to threaten the self with moral decay. The selections in
this chapter address the various forms of pride and their moral significance.

In the case study social critic and essayist Wendy Kaminer invites us to tour the
world of television talk shows. As part of her larger inquiry into the contemporary
fascination with selfhood, Kaminer discovers that talk shows have a curious appeal for those trying to understand the nature of self-respect.

Aristotle outlines the value of a magnanimous character, or great soul. Pride
reflects the proper sense of proportion attained by a moral person. This sense of
proportion underscores the proud person's well-being and his or her relations with
the world.

His Holiness the Dalai Lama, a Buddhist leader exiled from his native Tibet,
questions the centrality of pride. He points out that a virtue such as courage does
not spring from pride; moreover, pride risks an overvaluation of the self.

Essayist Edith Sitwell acknowledges the moral ambivalence of pride and tends
to favor Aristotle's position, noting that a certain amount of self-respect is needed
to give the person the confidence to try to accomplish something. Finally, Sitwell
describes how humility and pride are interrelated rather than opposed.

Philosopher Norvin Richards believes humility has been widely misunderstood.
Call someone a humble person and people are likely to conclude either that the
person has done nothing worthwhile or that humility is a pose to disguise overweening pride. According to Richards, humility is central to the good life insofar
as it helps the moral person overcome the temptations of jealousy, envy, and other
vices.

Much of the debate about self-regarding virtues, as well as many moral issues,
has to do with the possibility that humans can change their ways. In the view of
Voltaire, one of the best known writers and thinkers of the French Enlightenment,
both character and self-love are ingenious instruments for self-preservation rather
than virtues leading to a moral life.

Joyce Carol Oates, widely known American essayist and novelist, suggests that
we should entertain a new candidate for the list of vices—despair. Despair partly
involves the regard one has for oneself. More important, despair is about one's
relation to the world, to life in general. Unlike other vices, which corrupt, despair
paralyzes the moral person.

Philosopher Gabriele Taylor looks at the distinction between self-regarding and
other-regarding virtues, drawing out the importance of self-respect or self-love.
The value of these self-regarding virtues should not be associated with egoism.
Rather, Taylor argues, these virtues are the worthiest instruments for combating
the vices that most threaten the self, such as sloth and its helpers.

Joan Didion, essayist and novelist, wittily reminds us of much of the silliness that goes along with a preoccupation with the self. Nevertheless, she observes, self-respect is essential for any person who wishes to avoid something worse—alienation from oneself.

51.

WENDY KAMINER

Case Study: Testifying: Television

Wendy Kaminer is, as far as I know, the only writer in this text to appear as a guest on a talk show. (Sissela Bok has appeared on Nightline, *but that's not what is meant here by* talk show.) *A widely published essayist with a sardonic wit, Kaminer was intrigued enough by the recent phenomenon of television talk that she conducted her own empirical investigations. One of her striking discoveries is the approach deliberately taken by all those who participate in the world of television talk—they all dramatize the value of self-esteem while trivializing it with rambling confessions, anecdotes, and wistful sentiments.*

CRITICAL READING QUESTIONS

1. What is the traditional difference between confession and testimony?
2. What accounts for the popularity of talk shows where ordinary people reveal intimate and embarrassing aspects of their lives?
3. Why are talk shows not really debates?
4. What is the talk show name for gluttony? What is the problem behind the name?
5. Why does Kaminer say that talk shows "substitute sentimentality for thought"?

Recovering substance abuser Kitty Dukakis once called a press conference to announce her descent into alcoholism and request respect for her privacy. It was

"Testifying: Television," from *I'm Dysfunctional, You're Dysfunctional* (Reading, MA: Addison Wesley Longman, Inc., 1992).

shortly after her husband's defeat in the 1988 presidential race, when she was less newsworthy than the pearls adorning Barbara Bush's neck. I marveled only briefly at the spectacle of a woman seeking privacy in a press conference and public confession of an addiction. Some people, especially famous and formerly famous ones, seem to enjoy their privacy only in public. *Now You Know,* Kitty Dukakis called her book, in case you cared.

Still, millions of readers who don't care about Dukakis and all the other recovering personalities who write books are curious, I guess. Confessional autobiographies by second-string celebrities are publishing staples (and where would the talk shows be without them?). Ali MacGraw exposes her sex addiction and the lurid details of her marriage to Steve McQueen. Suzanne Somers chronicles her life as an ACOA. Former first children Michael Reagan and Patti Davis reveal their histories of abuse.

"I truly hope my book will help others to heal," the celebrity diarists are likely to say. Or they assure us that writing their books was therapeutic (and if they pay me to read them, I will). But the celebrities don't really have to explain the decision to go public. In our culture of recovery we take their confessions for granted. Talking about yourself is "part of the process." Suggesting to someone that she is talking too much about herself is a form of abuse. If you can't feign interest in someone else's story, you're supposed to maintain respectful or, better yet, stunned silence. In recovery, where everyone gets to claim that she's survived some holocaust of family life, everyone gets to testify.

The tradition of testifying in court, church, or the marketplace for justice, God, or the public good is a venerable one that I would not impugn. But it is also a tradition I'd rather not debase by confusing testifying with advertisements for yourself or simple plays for sympathy and attention. The recovery movement combines the testimonial tradition that serves a greater good, like justice, with the therapeutic tradition in which talking about yourself is its own reward. It also borrows liberally from the revivalist tradition of testifying to save your soul and maybe others: in recovery, even the most trivial testimony is sanctified.

I'm not impugning therapy or religion either, but I wish that people would keep them off the streets. Religion has, of course, a complicated, controversial history of public uses and abuses, which are beyond the scope of this book. But therapy was conceived as a private transaction between doctors and patients (experts and clients) or between groups of patients, clients, seekers of psychic well-being. Testimony was public. By blurring the distinction between confession and testimony, recovery transforms therapy into a public process too. People even do it on TV.

Most of us do love to talk about ourselves, although I've always regarded it as a slightly illicit pleasure or one you pay for by the hour. Etiquette books dating back over a century gently admonish readers to cultivate the art of listening, assuming that, unmannered in their natural states, most people are braggarts and bores. Success primers have always stressed that listening skills will help you get ahead: Listen raptly to someone in power who loves talking about himself in order to impress him with your perspicacity. Listening is a useful form of flattery, Dale Carnegie advised, sharing with men what women have always known. Flirting is a way of listening. (Feminism is women talking.)

For women who were socialized to listen, uncritically, talking too much about themselves may feel like an act of rebellion. Maybe Kitty Dukakis felt liberated by her book. Personal development passes for politics, and what might once have been called whining is now exalted as a process of asserting selfhood; self-absorption is regarded as a form of self-expression, as if creative acts involved no interactions with the world. Feminists did say that the personal was political, but they meant that private relations between the sexes reflected public divisions of power, that putatively private events, like wife beating, were public concerns. They didn't mean that getting to know yourself was sufficient political action. Consciousness raising was supposed to inspire activism. Feminism is women talking, but it is not women only talking and not women talking only about themselves.

Talk shows and the elevation of gossip to intellectual discourse are, after all, postfeminist, postmodern phenomena. In academia, where gossip is now text, poststructural scholars scour history for the private, particular experiences of ordinary "unempowered" people; and like denizens of daytime TV, they also talk a lot about themselves, deconstructing their own class, racial, or ethnic biases in perverse assertions of solidarity with what are presumed to be other entirely subjective selves. On talk shows, ordinary people, subject of tomorrow's scholars, find their voice. Men and most women distinguished only by various and weird infidelities or histories of drug abuse and overeating get equal time with movie actors, soap stars, and the occasional hair stylist. Now everyone can hope for sixty minutes of fame, minus some time for commercials.

I never really wonder anymore why people want to talk about themselves for nearly an hour in front of millions of strangers. They find it "affirming"; like trees that fall in the forest, they're not sure that they exist when no one's watching. I've accepted that as postmodern human nature. I do wonder at the eagerness and pride with which they reveal, on national television, what I can't help thinking of as intimacies—sexual and digestive disorders; personal conflicts with parents, children, spouses, lovers, bosses, and best friends. I wonder even more at the intensity with which the audience listens.

Why aren't they bored? It may be that listening is simply the price they pay for their turn to grab the mike and have their say, offering criticism or advice, just like the experts. But they seem genuinely intrigued by the essentially unremarkable details of other people's lives and other people's feelings. Something in us likes soap operas, I know, but watching the talks is not like watching "Dallas" or "Days of Our Lives." The guests aren't particularly articulate, except on "Geraldo" sometimes, where they seem to be well coached; they rarely finish their sentences, which trail off in vague colloquialisms, you know what I mean? Most guests aren't witty or perceptive or even telegenic. They aren't artful. They are the people you'd ignore if you saw them on line at the supermarket instead of on TV.

I'm not sure how we got to the point of finding anyone else's confessions, obsessions, or advertisements for herself entertaining. I'm not sure why watching other people's home movies became fun; the appeal of "America's Funniest Home Videos" eludes me. But it's clear that the popularity of "real people" television— talk shows and home videos—has little to do with compassion and the desire to connect. If an average person on the subway turns to you, like the ancient mariner, and starts telling you her tale, you turn away or nod and hope she stops, not just because you fear she might be crazy. If she tells her tale on camera, you might listen. Watching strangers on television, even responding to them from a studio audience, we're disengaged—voyeurs collaborating with exhibitionists in rituals of sham community. Never have so many known so much about people for whom they cared so little.

⚘ ⚘ ⚘

A woman appears on "Oprah Winfrey" to tell the nation that she hates herself for being ugly. Oprah and the expert talk to her about self-esteem and the woman basks, I think, in their attention. The spectacle is painful and pathetic, and watching it, I feel diminished.

Oprah, I suspect, regards her show as a kind of public service. The self-proclaimed ugly woman is appearing on a segment about our obsession with good looks. We live in a society that values pretty people over plain, Oprah explains; and maybe she is exploring a legitimate public issue, by exploiting a private pathology.

Daytime TV, however, is proudly pathological. On "Geraldo" a recovering sex addict shares a story of incest—she was raped by her father and stepfather; her husband and children are seated next to her on the stage. This is family therapy. (The family that reveals together congeals together.) Her daughter talks about being a lesbian. Two sex addiction experts—a man and a woman, "professional and personal partners"—explain and offer commentary on sex and love addictions. "It's not a matter of frequency," they say in response to questions about how often sex addicts have sex. Anonymous addicts call in with their own tales, boring and lurid: "I do specifically use sex to make myself feel better," one caller confesses. Who doesn't?

Geraldo, his experts, and the members of his audience address the problem of promiscuity with the gravity of network anchors discussing a sub-Saharan famine. If I were a recovering person, I might say that they're addicted to melodrama. In fact, Geraldo does a show on people "addicted to excitement—drama, danger, and self-destruction"—people who create crises for themselves. He offers us a self-evaluation tool—eleven questions "to determine whether you're a soap opera queen." Do you get mad at other drivers on the road? Do you talk about your problems with a lot of other people? Questions like these make addicts of us all, as experts must hope. Labeling impatience in traffic a symptom of disease creates a market for the cure; and Joy Davidson, the expert/author who identified the "soap opera syndrome" for us is here on "Geraldo," peddling her book.

The audience is intrigued. People stand up to testify to their own experiences with drama and excitement addictions. With the concern of any patient describing her symptoms, one woman says that she often disagrees with her husband for no good reason. Someone else confesses to being a worrier.

No one suggests to Davidson that calling the mundane concerns and frustrations of daily life symptoms of the disease of overdramatizing is, well, overdramatizing. In the language of recovery, we might say that Davidson is an enabler, encouraging her readers to indulge in their melodrama addictions, or we might say that she too is a practicing melodrama addict. One man does point out that there are "people in the ghetto" who don't have to fabricate their crises. But if Davidson gets the point, she successfully eludes it. Yes, she admits, the crises in the ghetto are real, but what matters is the way you deal with them. As Norman Vincent Peale might say, people in crisis have only to develop a happiness habit.

Meanwhile, on daytime TV, middle-class Americans are busy practicing their worry habits, swapping stories of disease and controversial eccentricities. Here is a sampling of "Oprah": Apart from the usual assortment of guests who eat, drink, shop, worry, or have sex too much, there are fathers who sleep with their sons' girlfriends (or try to), sisters who sleep with their sisters' boyfriends, women who sleep with their best friends' sons, women who sleep with their husbands' bosses (to help their husbands get ahead), men who hire only pretty women, and men and women who date only interracially. Estranged couples share their grievances while an expert provides on-air counseling: "Why are you so afraid to let your anger out at her?" he asks a husband. "Why don't you let him speak for himself," he chides the wife. Couples glare at each other, sometimes the women cry, and the expert keeps advising them to get in touch with their feelings and build up their self-esteem. The chance to sit in on someone else's therapy session is part of the appeal of daytime TV. When Donahue interviews the children of prostitutes, he has an expert on hand to tell them how they feel.

The number of viewers who are helped by these shows is impossible to know, but it's clear that they're a boon to several industries—publishing, therapy, and, of course, recovery. Commercials often tie in to the shows. A segment on food addiction is sponsored by weight-loss programs: "It's not what you're eating. It's what's eating you," the ads assure anxious overeaters. Shows on drug and alcohol abuse are sponsored by treatment centers, set in sylvan glades. Standing by lakes, leaning on trees, the pitchmen are soft and just a little somber—elegiac; they might be selling funeral plots instead of a recovery lifestyle and enhanced self-esteem.

On almost every show, someone is bound to get around to self-esteem; most forms of misconduct are said to be indicative of low self-esteem. On every other show, someone talks about addiction. The audiences usually speak fluent recovery. You can talk about your inner child or your grief work on "Oprah" and no one will ask you what you mean. "I follow a twelve-step program that helps me deal with the disease concept, the addiction [to overeating]," a man in the audience announces, and people nod. No one asks, "What's a twelve-step program?" or "What do you mean by addiction?" Oprah testifies too: "I'm still addicted [to food]. I'll never be free."

Onstage, a panel of recovering food addicts, all women, is vowing never to diet again. "We have to allow ourselves to love ourselves," they say, and Oprah agrees. "I'm never going to weigh another piece of chicken." Tired of "seeking control," these women want to accept their weight, not constantly struggle to lose it, and I wish them luck. Beauty may lack moral value, but it's useful, and what has been labeled beastly—obesity or really bad skin—is a painful liability, as the women on "Oprah" make clear. They've apparently spent much of their lives embarrassed by their bodies; now, in recovery, they talk about the "shame" of fatness. They find some self-esteem in victimhood. They aren't gluttons but "victims of a disease process." Being fat is not their fault. Recovering from obesity "is not about self-control," one woman says, voicing the ethos of recovery that dispenses with will. "It's about self-love."

But the next day, when Oprah does a show on troubled marriages, some sort of therapist, Dr. Ron, advises a woman who is self-conscious about her small breasts to have implants. He berates her unfaithful husband for not supporting her in this quest for a better body, for her own good, for the sake of her self-esteem, and to help save their marriage: her poor self-image was one of the reasons he strayed. That a woman with small breasts can't be expected to improve her self-esteem without implants is apparently evident to Dr. Ron and everyone else on the show. No one questions his wisdom, not even learning-to-love-herself Oprah, recovering dieter.

I digress, but so do Geraldo, Donahue, and Oprah. Talking about these shows, I find it hard to be entirely coherent, and coherence would not do justice to the kaleidoscope of complaints, opinions, prejudices, revelations, and celebrations they comprise: Geraldo discusses celibacy with a panel of virgins and Helen Gurley Brown. "There are no medical risks associated with virginity," a doctor assures us. Adopted children and their biological parents as well as siblings separated from birth for over twenty years meet, for the first time, on "Geraldo" ("Reunions of the Heart: Finding a Lost Love," the show is called). "Welcome long-lost brother Brian," Geraldo commands, to wild applause, as Brian emerges from backstage, and in a TV minute people are hugging and sobbing on camera as they did years ago on "This Is Your Life." I want someone in the audience to ask them why they're not having their reunions in private, but I already know the answer. "We want to share the love and joy of this moment," they'd say. "We want to inspire other people from broken families not to give up the search." I suspect that the audience knows these answers too. Clapping and crying (even Geraldo is teary), reached for and touched, they offer support and validation: "It's a real blessing to see how you've all been healed of your hurts," one woman in the audience declares. Geraldo makes a plea for open adoption, grappling with an issue, I guess.

. . .

This is the new journalism—issues packaged in anecdotes that may or may not be true. As an occasional, alternative approach to news and analysis, it is affecting; as the predominant approach, it is not just trite but stupefying. If all issues are personalized, we lose our capacity to entertain ideas, to generalize from our own or someone else's experiences, to think abstractly. We substitute sentimentality for thought.

TV talk shows certainly didn't invent the new journalism and are hardly the only abusers of it. But they are emblematic of the widespread preference for feelings over ideas that is celebrated by recovery and other personal development movements. It is no coincidence that the two trends—talk shows and recovery—have fueled each other. The shows often seem like orchestrated support groups; the groups seem like rehearsals for the shows.

Accusing talk shows of not providing critical analysis of issues is, I know, like accusing "Ozzie and Harriet" of idealizing the nuclear family. "He wrestles with the obvious," a friend once said of an especially boring pundit, and I don't mean to wrestle with TV. I just wanna testify too.

Once, I appeared on the "Oprah Winfrey" show. I was one of six alleged experts participating in what was billed as a "debate" on codependency. Joining me on-stage were two against-codependency allies and three for-codependency opponents. (The two sides were driven in separate limousines and kept in separate rooms before the show.) Oprah was more or less pro-codependency too—someone said she had just returned from one of John Bradshaw's retreats—and the audience seemed filled with evangelical twelve steppers.

"Just jump in. Don't wait to be called on," one of Oprah's people told us when she prepped us for the show. "You mean you want us to interrupt each other?" I asked; the woman nodded. "You want us to be really rude and step on each other's lines?" She nodded again. "You want us to act as if we're at a large, unruly family dinner on Thanksgiving?" She smiled and said, "You got it!"

I had a good time on "Oprah." Being chauffeured around in a limo and housed in a first-class hotel, I felt like Cinderella, especially when I got home. I liked being on national television, almost as much as my mother liked watching me. I also like unruly family dinners, but I'd never call what goes on over the turkey a debate.

The trouble with talk shows is that they claim to do so much more than entertain; they claim to inform and explain. They dominate the mass marketplace and help make it one that is inimical to ideas.

That's probably not a startling revelation, but appearing on a talk show, you are hit hard with the truth of it. Being on "Oprah" was still a shock, although not a surprise. I watch a fair amount of talk shows and understand the importance of speaking in sound bites, although I don't always succeed in doing so. I know that talk show "debates" are not usually coherent; they don't usually follow any pattern of statement and response. They don't make sense. The host is less a moderator than a traffic cop. People don't talk to each other; they don't even talk at each other. They talk at the camera. . . .

It should be needless to say that individual preferences are not always the best measures of what is generally good. A tax provision that saves you money may still be generally unfair. Of course, the recovery movement is not analogous to the tax code. It is not imposed on us. It is not a public policy that demands deliberation and debate. I don't want to gloss over the difference between public acts and private experiments with personality development. Indeed, I want to highlight it.

A self-referential evaluation of a self-help movement is probably inevitable and, to some extent, appropriate. A self-referential evaluation of public policies can be disastrous. What is disturbing about watching the talk shows is recognizing in discussions of private problems a solipsism that carries over into discussions of public issues. What you see on "Oprah" is what you see in the political arena. We choose our elected officials and formulate policies on the basis of how they make us feel about ourselves. (Jimmy Carter's biggest mistake was in depressing us.) We even evaluate wars according to their effect on our self-esteem: Vietnam was a downer. The Persian Gulf War, like a good self-help program, cured us of our "Vietnam syndrome" and "gave us back our pride," as General Motors hopes to do with Chevrolets. Norman Schwarzkopf and Colin Powell satisfied our need for heroes, everyone said. The networks stroked us with video montages of handsome young soldiers, leaning on tanks, staring off into the desert, wanting to "get the job done" and go home. By conservative estimates, 150,000 people were killed outright in the war; the number who will die from disease, deprivation, and environmental damage may be incalculable. Whether or not the war was necessary, whether or not the victory was real, we shouldn't consider it a great success because it gave us parades and a proud Fourth of July. The culture of recovery is insidious: now the moral measure of a war is how it makes us feel about ourselves.

"Try and put aside your own experiences in recovery and the way it makes you feel," I suggested to the audience on "Oprah." "Think about what the fascination with addiction means to us as a culture. Think about the political implications of advising people to surrender their will and submit to a higher power." People in the audience looked at me blankly. Later, in the limo, one of my copanelists (against codependency) shook his head at me and smiled and said, "That was a PBS comment."

Some two months later I showed my "Oprah" tape to a group of college friends, over a bottle of wine. None of them is involved in the recovery movement or familiar with its programs or jargon. Listening to six panelists and a studio audience compete for air time, in eight-minute segments between commercials, none of them thought the "Oprah" show made any sense. Like the man in the audience who asked, "What are you all recovering from?" they didn't have a clue. "You have to think with your hearts and not your heads," a for-codependency expert exhorted us at the end of the show, as the credits rolled.

QUESTIONS FOR ANALYSIS AND DISCUSSION

1. "Sham communities" and "perverse assertions of solidarity" are two phrases Kaminer uses to describe the sociability of the talk show atmosphere. What does she mean by this indictment? From your own watching of talk shows, do you mostly agree with her assessment? Is it possible for television to conduct a talk show that allows people suffering from low self-esteem to gain recovery? Why, or why not?

2. One of the problems that concerns Kaminer is how the attitudes that underlie the appeal of talk shows pervade social thought. Wars and public policies are discussed as if everyone's self-esteem is the most sensitive issue in life, and Kaminer cites the Gulf War in 1991 as an example. Can you find a current example to support her claim? Do you think she is exaggerating and that social and political discourse is more serious than she contends?

3. Pride, gluttony, anger, lust, compassion, and hope are among the virtues and vices often discussed on television talk shows. Given that fact, can one argue

that they are not sham communities, as Kaminer asserts, but little morality plays that offer important lessons to the viewing audience? Explain your response.

52.

ARISTOTLE

Pride As the Crown Virtue

Aristotle does what talk shows avoid. He examines the meaning of pride and its relation to a moral person. By understanding the meaning of pride we can also grasp the problems of those who lack pride. Aristotle emphasizes how pride involves honor, but he also illustrates how the proud man is more able than an unproud man to embrace the other virtues and to avoid the vices. Note Aristotle's attention to how the proud man relates to other human beings and perceives the good things life has to offer.

CRITICAL READING QUESTIONS

1. What is the difference between how a proud and an unproud man handle the goods of life?
2. Which is more opposed to pride—vanity or humility? Why?
3. What does Aristotle mean by honor?
4. Who are "mock-modest" people? What is Aristotle's view of them?
5. Is one who boasts a proud person?

---

3. Pride seems even from its name[1] to be concerned with great things; what sort of great things, is the first question we must try to answer. It makes no difference whether we consider the state of character or the man characterized by it. Now the

---

"Pride As the Crown Virtue," *Nicomachean Ethics,* Book IV, Chapters 3–9, translated by W. D. Ross (Oxford, England: Oxford University Press, 1925). Some notes have been omitted.

[1]"Pride" of course has not the etymological associations of *megalopsychia,* but seems in other respects the best translation.

man is thought to be proud who thinks himself worthy of great things, being worthy of them; for he who does so beyond his deserts is a fool, but no virtuous man is foolish or silly. The proud man, then, is the man we have described. For he who is worthy of little and thinks himself worthy of little is temperate, but not proud; for pride implies greatness, as beauty implies a good-sized body, and little people may be neat and well-proportioned but cannot be beautiful. On the other hand, he who thinks himself worthy of great things, being unworthy of them, is vain; though not every one who thinks himself worthy of more than he really is worthy of is vain. The man who thinks himself worthy of less than he is really worthy of is unduly humble, whether his deserts be great or moderate, or his deserts be small but his claims yet smaller. And the man whose deserts are great would seem *most* unduly humble; for what would he have done if they had been less? The proud man, then, is an extreme in respect of the greatness of his claims, but a mean in respect of the rightness of them; for he claims what is in accordance with his merits, while the others go to excess or fall short.

If, then, he deserves and claims great things, and above all the greatest things, he will be concerned with one thing in particular. Desert is relative to external goods; and the greatest of these, we should say, is that which we render to the gods, and which people of position most aim at, and which is the prize appointed for the noblest deeds; and this is honour; that is surely the greatest of external goods. Honours and dishonours, therefore, are the objects with respect to which the proud man is as he should be. And even apart from argument it is with honor that proud men appear to be concerned; for it is honour that they chiefly claim, but in accordance with their deserts. The unduly humble man falls short both in comparison with his own merits and in comparison with the proud man's claims. The vain man goes to excess in comparison with his own merits, but does not exceed the proud man's claims.

Now the proud man, since he deserves most, must be good in the highest degree; for the better man always deserves more, and the best man most. Therefore the truly proud man must be good. And greatness in every virtue would seem to be characteristic of a proud man. And it would be most unbecoming for a proud man to fly from danger, swinging his arms by his sides, or to wrong another; for to what end should he do disgraceful acts, he to whom nothing is great? If we consider him point by point, we shall see the utter absurdity of a proud man who is not good. Nor, again, would he be worthy of honour if he were bad; for honour is the prize of virtue, and it is to the good that it is rendered. Pride, then, seems to be a sort of crown of the virtues; for it makes them greater, and it is not found without them. Therefore it is hard to be truly proud; for it is impossible without nobility and goodness of character. It is chiefly with honours and dishonours, then, that the proud man is concerned; and at honours that are great and conferred by good men he will be moderately pleased, thinking that he is coming by his own or even less than his own; for there can be no honour that is worthy of perfect virtue, yet he will at any rate accept it since they have nothing greater to bestow on him; but honour from casual people and on trifling grounds he will utterly despise, since it is not this that he deserves, and dishonour too, since in his case it cannot be just. In the first place, then, as has been said, the proud man is concerned with honours;

yet he will also bear himself with moderation towards wealth and power and all good or evil fortune, whatever may befall him, and will be neither over-joyed by good fortune nor over-pained by evil. For not even towards honour does he bear himself as if it were a very great thing. Power and wealth are desirable for the sake of honour (at least those who have them wish to get honour by means of them); and for him to whom even honour is a little thing the others must be so too. Hence proud men are thought to be disdainful.

The goods of fortune also are thought to contribute towards pride. For men who are well-born are thought worthy of honour, and so are those who enjoy power or wealth; for they are in a superior position, and everything that has a superiority in something good is held in greater honour. Hence even such things make men prouder; for they are honoured by some for having them; but in truth the good man alone is to be honoured; he, however, who has both advantages is thought the more worthy of honour. But those who without virtue have such goods are neither justified in making great claims nor entitled to the name of "proud"; for these things imply perfect virtue. Disdainful and insolent, however, even those who have such goods become. For without virtue it is not easy to bear gracefully the goods of fortune; and, being unable to bear them, and thinking themselves superior to others, they despise others and themselves do what they please. They imitate the proud man without being like him, and this they do where they can; so they do not act virtuously, but they do despise others. For the proud man despises justly (since he thinks truly), but the many do so at random.

He does not run into trifling dangers, nor is he fond of danger, because he honours few things; but he will face great dangers, and when he is in danger he is unsparing of his life, knowing that there are conditions on which life is not worth having. And he is the sort of man to confer benefits, but he is ashamed of receiving them; for the one is the mark of a superior, the other of an inferior. And he is apt to confer greater benefits in return; for thus the original benefactor besides being paid will incur a debt to him, and will be the gainer by the transaction. They seem also to remember any service they have done, but not those they have received (for he who receives a service is inferior to him who has done it, but the proud man wishes to be superior), and to hear of the former with pleasure, of the latter with displeasure; this, it seems, is why Thetis did not mention to Zeus the services she had done him, and why the Spartans did not recount their services to the Athenians, but those they had received. It is a mark of the proud man also to ask for nothing or scarcely anything, but to give help readily, and to be dignified towards people who enjoy high position and good fortune, but unassuming towards those of the middle class; for it is a difficult and lofty thing to be superior to the former, but easy to be so to the latter, and a lofty bearing over the former is no mark of ill-breeding, but among humble people it is as vulgar as a display of strength against the weak. Again, it is characteristic of the proud man not to aim at the things commonly held in honour, or the things in which others excel; to be sluggish and to hold back except where great honour or a great work is at stake, and to be a man of few deeds, but of great and notable ones. He must also be open in his hate and in his love (for to conceal one's feelings, i.e. to care less for truth than for what people will think, is a coward's part), and must speak and act openly; for he is free of speech because he is contemptuous, and he is given to telling the truth, except when he speaks in irony to the vulgar. He must be unable to make his life revolve round another, unless it be a friend; for this is slavish, and for this reason all flatterers are servile and people lacking in self-respect are flatterers. Nor is he given to admiration; for nothing to him is great. Nor is he mindful of wrongs; for it is not the part of a proud man to have a long memory, especially for wrongs, but rather to overlook them. Nor is he a gossip; for he will speak neither about himself nor about another, since he cares not to be praised nor for others to be blamed; nor again is he given to praise; and for the same reason he is not an evil-speaker, even about his enemies, except from haughtiness. With regard to necessary or small matters he is least of all men given to lamentation or the asking of favours; for it is the part of one who takes such matters seriously to behave so with respect to them. He is one who will possess beautiful and profitless things rather than profitable and useful ones; for this is more proper to a character that suffices to itself.

Further, a slow step is thought proper to the proud man, a deep voice, and a level utterance; for the man who takes few things seriously is not likely to be hurried, nor the man who thinks nothing great to be excited, while a shrill voice and a rapid gait are the results of hurry and excitement.

Such, then, is the proud man; the man who falls short of him is unduly humble, and the man who goes beyond him is vain. Now even these are not thought to be bad (for they are not malicious), but only mistaken. For the unduly humble man, being worthy of good things, robs himself of what he deserves, and seems to have something bad about him from the fact that he does not think himself worthy of good things, and seems also not to know himself; else he would have desired the things he was worthy of, since these were good. Yet such people are not thought to be fools, but rather unduly retiring. Such a reputation, however, seems actually to make them worse; for each class of people aims at what corresponds to its worth, and these people stand back even from noble actions and undertakings, deeming themselves unworthy, and from external goods no less. Vain people, on the other hand, are fools and ignorant of themselves, and that manifestly; for, not being worthy of them, they attempt honourable undertakings, and then are found out; and they adorn themselves with clothing and outward show and such things, and wish their strokes of good fortune to be made public, and speak about them as if they would be honoured for them. But undue humility is more opposed to pride than vanity is; for it is both commoner and worse.

Pride, then, is concerned with honour on the grand scale, as has been said.

4. There seems to be in the sphere of honour also, as was said in our first remarks on the subject, a virtue which would appear to be related to pride as liberality is to magnificence. For neither of these has anything to do with the grand scale, but both dispose us as is right with regard to middling and unimportant objects; as in getting and giving of wealth there is a mean and an excess and defect, so too honour may be desired more than is right, or less, or from the right sources and in the right way. We blame both the ambitious man as aiming at honour more than is right and from wrong sources, and the unambitious man as not willing to be honoured even for noble reasons. But sometimes we praise the ambitious man as being manly and a lover of what is noble, and the unambitious man as being moderate and self-controlled, as we said in our first treatment of the subject. Evidently, since "fond of such and such an object" has more than one meaning, we do

not assign the term "ambition" or "love of honour" always to the same thing, but when we praise the quality we think of the man who loves honour more than most people, and when we blame it we think of him who loves it more than is right. The mean being without a name, the extremes seem to dispute for its place as though that were vacant by default. But where there is excess and defect, there is also an intermediate; now men desire honour both more than they should and less; therefore it is possible also to do so as one should; at all events this is the state of character that is praised, being an unnamed mean in respect of honour. Relatively to ambition it seems to be unambitiousness, and relatively to unambitiousness it seems to be ambition, while relatively to both severally it seems in a sense to be both together. This appears to be true of the other virtues also. But in this case the extremes seem to be contradictories because the mean has not received a name.

. . .

6. In gatherings of men, in social life and the interchange of words and deeds, some men are thought to be obsequious, viz. those who to give pleasure praise everything and never oppose, but think it their duty "to give no pain to the people they meet"; while those who, on the contrary, oppose everything and care not a whit about giving pain are called churlish and contentious. That the states we have named are culpable is plain enough, and that the middle state is laudable—that in virtue of which a man will put up with, and will resent, the right things and in the right way; but no name has been assigned to it, though it most resembles friendship. For the man who corresponds to this middle state is very much what, with affection added, we call a good friend. But the state in question differs from friendship in that it implies no passion or affection for one's associates; since it is not by reason of loving or hating that such a man takes everything in the right way, but by being a man of a certain kind. For he will behave so alike towards those he knows and those he does not know, towards intimates and those who are not so, except that in each of these cases he will behave as is befitting; for it is not proper to have the same care for intimates and for strangers, nor again is it the same conditions that make it right to give pain to them. Now we have said generally that he will associate with people in the right way; but it is by reference to what is honourable and expedient that he will aim at not giving pain or at contributing pleasure. For he seems to be concerned with the pleasures and pains of social life; and wherever it is not honourable, or is harmful, for him to contribute pleasure, he will refuse, and will choose rather to give pain; also if his acquiescence in another's action would bring disgrace, and that in a high degree, or injury, *on that other,* while his opposition brings a little pain, he will not acquiesce but will decline. He will associate differently with people in high station and with ordinary people, with closer and more distant acquaintances, and so too with regard to all other differences, rendering to each class what is befitting, and while for its own sake he chooses to contribute pleasure, and avoids the giving of pain, he will be guided by the consequences, if these are greater, i.e. honour and expediency. For the sake of a great future pleasure, too, he will inflict small pains.

The man who attains the mean, then, is such as we have described, but has not received a name; of those who contribute pleasure, the man who aims at being pleasant with no ulterior object is obsequious, but the man who does so in order that he may get some advantage in the direction of money or the things that money buys is a flatterer; while the man who quarrels with everything is, as has been said, churlish and contentious. And the extremes seem to be contradictory to each other because the mean is without a name.

7. The mean opposed to boastfulness is found in almost the same sphere; and this also is without a name. It will be no bad plan to describe these states as well; for we shall both know the facts about character better if we go through them in detail, and we shall be convinced that the virtues are means if we see this to be so in all cases. In the field of social life those who make the giving of pleasure or pain their object of associating with others have been described; let us now describe those who pursue truth or falsehood alike in words and deeds and in the claims they put forward. The boastful man, then, is thought to be apt to claim the things that bring glory, when he has not got them, or to claim more of them than he has, and the mock-modest man on the other hand to disclaim what he has or belittle it, while the man who observes the mean is one who calls a thing by its own name, being truthful both in life and in word, owing to what he has, and neither more nor less. Now each of these courses may be adopted either with or without an object. But each man speaks and acts and lives in accordance with his character, if he is *not* acting for some ulterior object. And falsehood is *in itself* mean and culpable, and truth noble and worthy of praise. Thus the truthful man is another case of a man who, being in the mean, is worthy of praise, and both forms of untruthful man are culpable, and particularly the boastful man.

Let us discuss them both, but first of all the truthful man. We are not speaking of the man who keeps faith in his agreements, i.e. in the things that pertain to justice or injustice (for this would belong to another virtue), but the man who in the matters in which nothing of this sort is at stake is true both in word and in life because his character is such. But such a man would seem to be as a matter of fact equitable. For the man who loves truth, and is truthful where nothing is at stake, will still more be truthful where something is at stake; he will avoid falsehood as something base, seeing that he avoided it even for its own sake; and such a man is worthy of praise. He inclines rather to understate the truth; for this seems in better taste because exaggerations are wearisome.

He who claims more than he has with no ulterior object is a contemptible sort of fellow (otherwise he would not have delighted in falsehood), but seems futile rather than bad; but if he does it for an object, he who does it for the sake of reputation or honour is (for a boaster) not very much to be blamed, but he who does it for money, or the things that lead to money, is an uglier character (it is not the capacity that makes the boaster, but the purpose; for it is in virtue of his state of character and by being a man of a certain kind that he is a boaster); as one man is a liar because he enjoys the lie itself, and another because he desires reputation or gain. Now those who boast for the sake of reputation claim such qualities as win praise or congratulation, but those whose object is gain claim qualities which are of value to one's neighbours and one's lack of which is not easily detected, e.g. the powers of a seer, a sage, or a physician. For this reason it is such things as these that most people claim and boast about; for in them the above-mentioned qualities are found.

Mock-modest people, who understate things, seem more attractive in character; for they are thought to speak not for gain but to avoid parade; and here too it is qualities which bring reputation that they disclaim, as Socrates used to do. Those who disclaim trifling and obvious qualities are called humbugs and are more contemptible; and sometimes this seems to be boastfulness, like the Spartan dress; for both excess and great deficiency are boastful. But those who use understatement with moderation and understate about matters that do not very much force themselves on our notice seem attractive. And it is the boaster that seems to be opposed to the truthful man; for he is the worse character.

8. Since life includes rest as well as activity, and in this is included leisure and amusement, there seems here also to be a kind of intercourse which is tasteful; there is such a thing as saying—and again listening to—what one should and as one should. The kind of people one is speaking or listening to will also make a difference. Evidently here also there is both an excess and a deficiency as compared with the mean. Those who carry humour to excess are thought to be vulgar buffoons, striving after humour at all costs, and aiming rather at raising a laugh than at saying what is becoming and at avoiding pain to the object of their fun; while those who can neither make a joke themselves nor put up with those who do are thought to be boorish and unpolished. But those who joke in a tasteful way are called ready-witted, which implies a sort of readiness to turn this way and that; for such sallies are thought to be movements of the character, and as bodies are discriminated by their movements, so too are characters. The ridiculous side of things is not far to seek, however, and most people delight more than they should in amusement and in jesting, and so even buffoons are called ready-witted because they are found attractive; but that they differ from the ready-witted man, and to no small extent, is clear from what has been said.

To the middle state belongs also tact; it is the mark of a tactful man to say and listen to such things as befit a good and well-bred man; for there are some things that it befits such a man to say and to hear by way of jest, and the well-bred man's jesting differs from that of a vulgar man, and the joking of an educated man from that of an uneducated. One may see this even from the old and the new comedies; to the authors of the former indecency of language was amusing, to those of the latter innuendo is more so; and these differ in no small degree in respect of propriety. Now should we define the man who jokes well by his saying what is not unbecoming to a well-bred man, or by his not giving pain, or even giving delight, to the hearer? Or is the latter definition, at any rate, itself indefinite, since different things are hateful or pleasant to different people? The kind of jokes he will listen to will be the same; for the kind he can put up with are also the kind he seems to make. There are, then, jokes he will not make; for the jest is a sort of abuse, and there are things that lawgivers forbid us to abuse; and they should, perhaps, have forbidden us even to make a jest of such. The refined and well-bred man, therefore, will be as we have described, being as it were a law to himself.

Such, then, is the man who observes the mean, whether he be called tactful or ready-witted. The buffoon, on the other hand, is the slave of his sense of humour, and spares neither himself nor others if he can raise a laugh, and says things none of which a man of refinement would say, and to some of which he would not even listen. The boor, again, is useless for such social intercourse; for he contributes nothing and finds fault with everything. But relaxation and amusement are thought to be a necessary element in life.

The means in life that have been described, then, are three in number, and are all concerned with an interchange of words and deeds of some kind. They differ, however, in that one is concerned with truth, and the other two with pleasantness. Of those concerned with pleasure, one is displayed in jests, the other in the general social intercourse of life.

QUESTIONS FOR ANALYSIS AND DISCUSSION

1. One of the disputes in virtue ethics is whether virtues are universal. In Aristotle's discussion of pride and honor, is moral character, in principle, universal, or is it limited to only one segment of the population? Cite passages from the text to support your answer.

2. Aristotle writes that the goods of fortune are better given to those with pride than to those without pride. Imagine that someone lacking pride wins the lottery jackpot. Why should that be construed as a blessing? Do you agree with Aristotle's view?

3. To what extent does a person know that he or she is proud? Could this be known by introspection, through the acknowledgments or praises of others, by the honor one receives, or by the fact that one is happy with one's life? Or is it possible that a proud person does not describe her- or himself as proud?

4. What are Aristotle's opinions of the boaster, the buffoon, and the boor? They all bring attention to themselves, but what is their moral status? Can you find any current examples of each type? Do your examples strengthen or weaken Aristotle's opinions?

53.

DALAI LAMA

On Pride, Courage, and Self

The Dalai Lama (b. 1935) lives in exile from his native land, Tibet, and his early years are the subject of a recent film. The Dalai Lama states that if pride is the crown virtue, then no other virtue could be opposed to pride. Courage is clearly a virtue. Yet, according

---

"On Pride and Courage," from *The Dalai Lama at Harvard: Lectures on the Buddhist Path to Peace* (Ithaca, NY: Snow Lion Publications, 1988), pp. 57–61, 67–69, 119–124, 179–188. Notes have been omitted.

to His Holiness the Dalai Lama, courage is often opposed to pride. Hence, his argument concludes, pride cannot be the crown virtue. Indeed, pride may not even be that important a virtue, if it is one at all. Pride is, by any sensible use of the term, a matter of the self. And whatever form we give to this matter, the result is that we always take the self too seriously, as if it is the center. This leads to a confusion about the self. It takes a certain amount of courage and insight, not the honors of pride, for the wise and moral person to realize the good of this truth.

CRITICAL READING QUESTIONS

1. What are two types of virtue? How does the Dalai Lama distinguish between them?
2. How are pride and courage two different modes of thought?
3. What are the true paths? Where do they lead?
4. What are the nonvirtues? How do they relate to emotions and the self?
5. Why is patience or tolerance important in the ethical life? From whom do we best learn tolerance?

The Sources of Suffering

Yesterday, we discussed true sufferings; today, let us discuss true sources of suffering. The fact that sufferings are not *always* produced but are produced in *some* places at *some* times and cease at *some* times and in *some* places indicates that they are caused. Logically, it can be said that sufferings are caused because of being produced occasionally. If sufferings were produced causelessly, either they would never exist or they would always exist.

Since sufferings are caused, one needs to look into what their causes are. In the Buddhist systems, the causes are explained to be contaminated actions and afflictive emotions. In the non-Buddhist systems of India, there are many different presentations of what the causes of suffering are. In general, there are many non-Buddhist systems, which are condensed into five main systems; among them, the chief seem to be the Sāṃkhyas and the Jainas. The Sāṃkhyas enumerate twenty-five categories of objects of knowledge—of existents; according to them, the basic cause of both pleasure and pain is the fundamental nature, also called the general principal, and the experiencer of pleasure and pain is the person. They say that through understanding that the varieties of pleasure and pain are created by the general principal, the general principal is, so to speak, flushed with shame and ceases its transformations with respect to that person, whereby the person attains liberation.

The Jainas, on the other hand, posit a state of liberation that is like an upside down umbrella on top of the world system. There are many such systems of explanation, which engage in critical discussion with each other. In the Buddhist systems, once the effects—true sufferings—are compounded phenomena, their causes must be compounded, impermanent phenomena and could not be permanent factors.

For instance, if I had an angry feeling, this could serve as a motivating force that would lead to a harsh attitude, harsh speech, and harsh physical gestures. Since the anger that serves as the motivating factor is a defilement—an afflictive emotion—the physical and verbal actions done through that motivating force are negative karmas, negative actions. Through them, the atmosphere immediately changes into one of tension. Right away, I might not feel the effects of those actions, perhaps even feeling that I had gained a victory over someone, even shouting, "I have won." However, later I will feel very sorry and shy, deep down experiencing a guilty conscience. Similarly, those around me would immediately lose their tranquility and peace. These are painful results of actions impelled by a bad motivation. This is the law of karma—motivation, action, result.

Conversely, a good, open, sincere motivation such as compassion with a deep respect for others impels verbal and physical actions that immediately create a peaceful, harmonious, enjoyable atmosphere. Due to that, I feel happy and calm, enjoying that atmosphere, and others around me also enjoy the same. Therefore, bad motivation creates problems, suffering, and pain, whereas good motivation creates happiness and peacefulness—something good.

This is the general explanation. On a deeper level, right at the time of an action, predisposing potencies are instilled in the consciousness. The performance of an action establishes a predisposing potency in the mind that, in the future, will serve as the causal condition for one's experiencing a good or bad effect.

Karma

With respect to actions, karma, there are two types—actions of intention and intended actions, that is to say, motivations and actions motivated. With respect to intended actions, the Proponents of the Great Exposition and the Consequentialists posit physical, verbal, and mental actions, whereas the Proponents of Sūtra and Proponents of Mind Only hold that all intended actions are only mental since physical and verbal actions are, for them, the mental factor of intention at the time of the performance of these actions.

In terms of the avenues by which actions are displayed, there are actions of body, speech, and mind. In terms of their effects, there are two types, virtuous and non-virtuous actions. Within the virtuous, there are again two types, actions of merit that impel rebirth in happy transmigrations in the Desire Realm and non-fluctuating actions that impel rebirth in the Form and the Formless Realms.

In terms of the experience or non-experience of the effect, there are two types— those of which the effect is definite to be experienced and those of which the effect is not definite to be experienced. These can be understood through discussing another division into four types by way of motivation and accomplishment—those done deliberately, those deliberated but not done, those done but not deliberately, and those neither deliberated nor done. An example of the first would be to deliberately kill a mosquito. Then, let us suppose that an insect was bothering you, and you wanted very much to kill it, but someone distracts you. In this case, you have karmically accumulated the motivation but you did not carry out the action; this is an action deliberated but not done. An example of an action done but without deliberation would be to kill a mosquito by just moving one's hand without having intended to do so; you killed it, but not deliberately. The fourth type is when one neither has the motivation nor carries out the action.

Of these four types, the first two—those done deliberately and those deliberated but not done—are actions the effects of which are definite to be experienced. The other two—those done without deliberation and those neither deliberated nor done—are actions the effects of which are not definite to be experienced. For instance, if a person who does want to kill is inducted into an army and ordered to kill, even when that person kills someone, as long as he or she has an immediate sense of very strong regret, that action is one of which the experience of its effect is indefinite.

From this, one can see that the action is not as important as the motivation. Thus, a big general or leader of a country, who, out of a motivation to destroy all the opposing forces, actually orders that war be made accumulates all the sins of killings that occur during the war, even if his physical body is not involved in carrying out the action that he orders. Similarly, if ten persons make plans for a feast that involve buying an animal and slaughtering it, only one animal is killed, but since all ten have the motivation to kill and eat the animal, each of the ten persons accumulate the complete sin of killing that sentient being.

Again, with respect to those actions of which the effects are definite to be experienced, there are different divisions from the viewpoint of the time when the effect is experienced. With some actions, their effects are begun to be experienced in this very lifetime. For others, their effects are begun to be experienced in the next lifetime. Again, there are others of which the effects are begun to be experienced in lifetimes after the next lifetime.

Also, with respect to virtues, there are many types. A true cessation of a level of suffering, for instance, is an *ultimate virtue*. Faith and compassion, for instance, are *virtues by way of their own nature*. Mental factors such as mindfulness and introspection that accompany a virtuous consciousness are *virtues by way of association*. If, with a helpful motivation, one walked from one area to another, although the walking itself is not a virtuous activity, each step would be a *virtue by way of motivation*. Also, the virtuous predispositions established by virtuous minds and mental factors are *virtues through subsequent relation*.

That concludes a short discussion of karma. For a Buddhist practitioner, the basis of the various types of ethical practices is the abandonment of the ten nonvirtues, many of which are like the ten commandments.

. . .

More about Consciousness and Karma

Question and Answer Period

QUESTION: Those who have been denied a sense of self-worth seem to benefit from gaining self-identity through therapy, support groups, and self-assertiveness training. Are such therapeutic approaches to self-validation increasing illusion and suffering even though they seem to do the opposite? How can the need for individual integrity and power be reconciled with the spiritual principle of self-lessness? In our practice, how can we avoid the state of pride from accomplishment and depression caused by disintegration of the ego?

ANSWER: This question meets back to not understanding well the fact that the self, the person, is indeed asserted to exist conventionally. There are two types of elevated attitudes. One is an elevated or confident attitude that is well reasoned—has a reasonable foundation; this is a state of courage and is definitely needed. Another type is an elevated or proud attitude, which is actually based on misconception; it is pride. However, if one engages in a practice and experiences the true imprint or result of that practice, it is suitable to be proud of this in the sense of taking delight in it.

Shāntideva speaks of various types of elevated attitudes in his *Engaging in the Bodhisattva Deeds*. One type is to have the courage of thinking that you can do what others cannot do; this is strength of will, not pride, and is not contradictory with taking a humble or lower position when meeting others. For instance, the second of the *Eight Stanzas on Training* the Mind speaks of the need to take the lowest position when meeting with any others:

> Whenever I associate with others, I will learn
> To think of myself as the lowest among all
> And respectfully hold others to be supreme
> From the very depths of my heart.

The modes of thought in pride and in courageous thought are entirely different.

Depression caused by disintegration of the ego probably comes from not being able to posit a conventionally existent I. Still, when some understanding of emptiness develops, you have a different feeling of I than that to which you previously were accustomed. Our usual feeling is that the I is something solid, really independent, and very forceful. Such no longer remains, but at the same time there is a sense of a mere I that accumulates karma and performs actions. Such a sense of self is not at all a source of depression.

If you have difficulty positing a merely nominal I as well as merely nominal cause and effect of actions—if you get to the point where if you assert selflessness, you cannot posit dependent-arising—then it would be better to assert dependent-arising and give up selflessness. Indeed, there are many levels of understanding selflessness, and Buddha, out of great skillfulness in method, taught many different schools of tenets that posit coarser levels of selflessness for those temporarily unable to understand the more subtle levels. It is not the case that only if the most profound level is immediately accessible, it is suitable, and if it is not accessible, the whole endeavor should be thrown away. You have to proceed step by step with whatever accords with your level of mind. Between emptiness and dependent-arising, you should value dependent-arising more highly.

. . .

True Paths

We have spoken about nirvana. In the eighteenth chapter of his *Treatise on the Middle* Nāgārjuna says:

> Once the self does not exist,
> How could the mine exist?

When the self does not inherently exist, the mine could not possibly inherently exist. He also says:

> When thoughts of self and mine are extinguished
> With regard to the internal and the external,
> Appropriation [of new mental and physical aggregates] ceases.
> Through the extinction of this, rebirth is extinguished.

When, with respect to internal and external phenomena, one extinguishes the conception of inherently existent I and mine, the appropriation of mental and physical aggregates is extinguished. Due to this, rebirth is extinguished.

In brief, when the accumulation of new karma is extinguished and there are no afflictive emotions to nourish the remaining old karma, at that time there is liberation from cyclic existence. Contaminated karmas are produced from afflictive emotions, and afflictive emotions are generated from improper conceptuality. Improper conceptuality, in turn, is generated from the elaborations of the conception of inherent existence. Consciousnesses conceiving inherent existence are ceased by emptiness. This is how Nāgārjuna explains the process of achieving liberation.

This brings us to the fourth noble truth, paths. Those which directly induce true cessations are true paths directly realizing emptiness. According to the Consequence School, a Superior of any of the three vehicles—Hearer, Solitary Realizer, or Bodhisattva—has necessarily realized emptiness directly. Even direct perception of the four noble truths cannot harm the conception of inherent existence.

In order to generate in one's continuum such an actual true path of direct realization of emptiness in which all dualistic appearance has vanished, one needs the wisdom arisen from meditation that realizes emptiness within dualistic appearance. To generate this, one first needs to form an understanding of emptiness—ascertaining its meaning with the wisdoms arisen from hearing and from thinking.

As one advances over the five paths as either a Hearer, Solitary Realizer, or Bodhisattva, one proceeds from a lower path to a higher—from a lower realization to higher—within meditative equipoise realizing emptiness. Thus, the five paths are set forth in terms of the ever-increasing profundity of the practice of emptiness.

The path of accumulation is a period when one has wisdoms arisen from hearing and thinking. Then, the path of preparation begins with the attainment of wisdom arisen from meditation that realizes emptiness. After that, the path of seeing begins with the initial direct perception of emptiness. Then, the path of meditation is a period of repeated familiarizing with the direct perception of emptiness. The fifth and last path is the period when one has completed training in the respective series of paths, and thus it is called the path of no more learning. It is the object one is seeking to attain; for the two lower paths of Hearers and Solitary Realizers, it is a *temporary* attainment, leading to entry into the Great Vehicle.

Mere realization of emptiness is not sufficient; it must be conjoined with method. The chief scriptures of the Great Vehicle, the Perfection of Wisdom Sūtras, teach in an explicit way about emptiness but, in a hidden way, also teach about the types of method that assist the various levels of realization of emptiness as well as the levels of clear realization that are generated. These sūtras were set forth mainly for disciples who are Bodhisattvas, but Bodhisattvas—in order to bring about others' welfare—must know the many and various paths of Hearers, Solitary Realizers, and Bodhisattvas; they must know all paths, and this is why these sūtras speak about all of these paths.

What is the mode of procedure of the paths of Hearers and Solitary Realizers for actualizing nirvana? These are the paths of the thirty-seven harmonies with enlightenment. When these are condensed in terms of practice, there come to be the three trainings. The first is the training in higher ethics. In the scriptures of the Hearers, eight types of vows of individual liberation are described. The first three are for householders, and the latter five are for those who have left the householder life. If one looks at it superficially, it seems that the celibacy required in some vows of individual liberation and the use of sex in the path in Highest Yoga Mantra would be contradictory, but they are not. This is because these practices are set forth appropriate to the level of realization and capacity of individual persons; at the beginning level of training, celibacy is very important, but when one develops to the point where one can realistically have the confidence that other practices can be utilized properly, then the situation is different.

The union that is described in Highest Yoga Tantra is not a matter of engaging in sexual union from being afflicted with the pangs of desire. Rather, within perceiving the disadvantages of desire, the practitioner understands that another, higher level of the path can be induced through sexual union. It is within such a context of perceiving the faults of desire and a special purpose in union that practices utilizing union are set forth.

The root of all the vows for laypersons and for monks and nuns is the ethics of the abandonment of the non-virtues. Three physical actions (killing, stealing, and sexual misconduct), four verbal actions (lying, divisive talk, harsh speech, and senseless chatter), and three mental actions (covetousness, harmful intent, and wrong views) are to be abandoned. I will not elaborate on these here.

When one restrains ill deeds of body and speech, coarse mental distractions are also restrained, and from this viewpoint the mind becomes a little withdrawn inside. A second factor is that one has to use constant introspection, built on conscientiousness, to determine whether physical and verbal ill deeds are arising or not, and thereby the power of mindfulness and introspection is generated. These two—the withdrawal of the mind inside and the generation of the power of mindfulness and introspection—are indispensable factors in the development of meditative stabilization. This is the relationship between ethics and meditative stabilization.

When practicing the ethics of individual liberation, the main point is to refrain from harming others. When practicing the Bodhisattva ethics, the main point is to refrain from self-centeredness. Again, in the mantric system of ethics, the main point is to refrain from ordinary appearances and the conception of being ordinary.

For all the vehicles, higher and lower, the procedure of the three trainings is similar. One reason why there are just three trainings is in terms of taming the mind: the training in ethics is for the sake of causing the distracted mind not to be distracted; the training in meditative stabilization is for the sake of causing the unequipoised mind to be set in meditative equipoise; and the training in wisdom is for the sake of freeing the unfreed mind. Another reason why there are just three trainings is in terms of their respective effects: an effect of not letting ethics degenerate is the attainment of rebirths in happy transmigrations within the Desire Realms as humans and gods; an effect of the training in meditative stabilization is the attainment of rebirths in happy transmigrations within the Form and Formless Realms; and an effect of training in wisdom is the attainment of liberation.

Another reason why there are just three trainings is in terms of the afflictive emotions that they cause to be abandoned: ethics suppress afflictive emotions; for example, when one gets angry at someone and thinks to harm that person, the memory that one formerly decided to refrain from harming others stops such behavior. Meditative stabilization suppresses the manifest form of afflictive emotions, and the training in wisdom removes afflictive emotions down to the level of their seeds.

The Buddhist teachings repeatedly indicate that we must control ourselves, but nowadays some people say that when one generates a mind of desire or hatred, one should not hold it in but instead should let it out, display it. I feel that, for instance, in cases of depression that are due to trauma, it indeed is very helpful to express openly one's feelings, but with consciousnesses such as desire and hatred, if you express them as soon as they are generated, the expression does not clear them away; they will be produced again and again.

From your own experience, you can understand that if you try to control your mind with self-discipline and self-awareness, even though at the beginning you may still be very short-tempered, over time as years pass, it will improve—the amount of anger will decrease. However, if you leave your irritableness without paying attention to it and without taking care, it will increase. Now, after all, nobody wants anger. Once anger comes, you go mad; you will even break your own beautiful possessions. Again, afterwards, you will really feel sorry, at least about your broken articles. Therefore, no one loves anger; it is far better to control it. Of course, in the beginning, it is not at all easy, but through determination, realization, and will-power, gradually the situation will change, if you work at it wisely and not just with stubbornness. The mind is such that if we make a plan—that in the next five years I should reach such and such a stage—and carry it out with strong determination, the mind definitely will change.

. . .

Training in Altruism

Yesterday, we discussed the altruistic intention to become enlightened, reaching the topic of the equalizing and switching of self and other. As Shāntideva says about equalizing self and other, everybody—oneself and all others—wants happiness and does not want suffering. For example, just as every part of our body is equally considered to be our body and to be equally protected from pain, so all sentient beings are equally to be protected from suffering.

From our own viewpoint, we can understand that the only reason why we must be separated from suffering is that we do not want suffering. There is no further reason; we have a wish that naturally comes from within—a wish to be free from suffering. All sentient beings have the same wish. Since this is the case, what is the difference between self and other? There is a great difference in number. No matter how important you are, you are just one simple person; for example, in my own case I am just a single Buddhist monk. But other people are infinite in number. Even without counting other planets, in this world alone others are limitless—several billions. Now, if we consider which is more important, the benefit of the majority or the benefit of a minority of one, there is no argument, no question. The benefit of the majority is much more important than myself, a single person.

Like yourself, everyone else from their own side equally does not want suffering and equally wants happiness. For example, among ten ill people, each of them just wants happiness; from their side they are all ill, and they all want to be freed from their illness. Hence there is no possible reason for making a biased exception, treating a certain one better and neglecting the others. It is impossible to select one out for better treatment. Moreover, from your own viewpoint, all sentient beings, in terms of their connection with you over the course of lifetimes, have in the past helped you and in the future will help again. Thus, you also cannot find any reason from your own side to treat some better and others worse.

Also, from the viewpoint of the nature of yourself and others, both have a nature of suffering, a nature of impermanence, and so forth. Once all of us have a similar nature of deprivation, there is no sense in our being belligerent with each other; it is not worthwhile. Take, for example, a group of prisoners who are about to be executed. During their stay together in the prison, all of them will meet their end; thus, during their remaining few days there is no sense in quarrelling with each other. Similarly, all of us are bound within the same nature of suffering and impermanence, conquered by ignorance; under such circumstances, it is clear that both self and other are in the same basic condition; thus, there is no reason to fight with each other. If oneself were completely pure and other beings were impure, then this might be a reason for looking down on others. But this is not the case! This is another reason to consider self and other to be equal.

We have the bias of considering some people to be enemies and others to be friends. If this really were true such that an enemy always remained an enemy and a friend always remained a friend, then there might be a reason to hate certain people and love others. But, again, this is not the case. As was mentioned earlier, there is no certainty in relationships.

Also, if we hate other people, the result is not good either for others or for ourselves. Nothing helpful comes from it. Anger ultimately will not harm others; actually it hurts us. When you are very angry, even though you have good food, it is not tasty. You may even get irritated at food that otherwise would be tasty. Also, when you become angry, even the beautiful faces of your friends—your husband, wife, or children—give you irritation, not because they are bad but because something is wrong with your own attitude. This is very clear. Using common sense, consider what the usefulness of anger and hatred is.

If we think along these lines, there is absolutely no reason to be angry. When an unfortunate event happens, we can face and handle a problem or tragedy more effectively without anger. The usefulness of anger is practically zero. As I mentioned earlier, it is possible within a compassionate causal motivation for an action to be done with an immediate motivation of hatred; however, that is a different situation. The type of upset that comes within affection and the type of upset that comes within hatred are different. With a causal motivation of deep love and compassion, it is possible—in order to bring about a certain action—for the immediate motivation at the time of the action itself to involve anger; however, the action basically comes out of concern for the particular person. In order to stop the person from a stupid deed, sometimes a harsh word is needed, in the course of which anger may be needed, but this anger is not the basic, causal motivation. On the other hand, strong actions that come solely out of hatred are of no use at all.

We are always talking about how human beings are superior to animals since animals cannot think as humans can; our human brain, therefore, is an endowment. Animals also can practice anger and attachment very well, but only human beings can judge and reason; this is a real human quality. Also, humans can develop infinite love, whereas animals such as dogs or cats can have only a limited form of affection and love for their offspring and so forth. Also, their affection is present for a certain period of time, but when a puppy, for instance, becomes grown up, the sense of affection disappears. Human beings, on the other hand, can think much more deeply and much more in the distance. When you become angry, however, all of these fine potentialities are lost. Thus, anger is the real destroyer of our good human qualities; an enemy with a weapon cannot destroy these qualities, but anger can. Anger is our real enemy.

Again, if we consider the other side—love, compassion, and concern for other people—these are *real* sources of happiness. With love and compassion, even if you are living in a very uncomfortable place, the external circumstances will not disturb you. With hatred, however, even if you have the best of facilities, you will not be happy. Thus, since we all want happiness, if we really do want it, we must follow a right method to achieve it. This type of thought is not particular to Buddhist or religious thinking but is common sense.

With a selfish attitude, oneself is important, and others are not so important. According to Shāntideva's advice, a technique to help in turning this attitude around is to imagine—in front of yourself as an unbiased observer—your own selfish self on one side and a limited number of other beings on the other side—ten, fifty, or a hundred. On one side is your proud, selfish self, and on the other side are a group of poor, needy people. You are, in effect, in the middle—as an unbiased, third person. Now, judge. Is this one, single, selfish person more important? Or is the group of people more important? Think. Will you join this side or that side? Naturally, if you are a real *human* being, your heart will go with the group because the number is greater and they are more needy. The other one is just a single person, proud and stupid. Your feeling naturally goes with the group. By thinking, thinking, thinking in this way, selfishness gradually decreases, and respect for others grows. This is the way to practice.

I usually advise that even if you want to be selfish, then be wisely selfish, not narrowly selfish! Wise people think of others, serve others sincerely as much as they can—not in order to cheat them, but sincerely. Regard yourself as a secondary factor. The ultimate result will be that you will get the maximum benefit. Clear? This is how to be wisely selfish!

Through fighting, killing, stealing, or harsh words—forgetting other people's welfare, always thinking of yourself, "I, I, I,"—the result will be your own loss; you will become a loser. Others may speak nice words in front of you, but behind your back they will not speak so nicely. This itself shows that you are losing. Therefore, the practice of altruism is not religious but the authentic way of human life, the real human quality. Being a believer or a non-believer, a Buddhist or non-Buddhist, is secondary, not important. The important thing is that, as human beings, we live purposeful, meaningful lives. Eating just makes excrement; that is not the purpose of our life! The purpose of life is the development of a good, warm heart, whereby we become good human beings. With this quality, you will lead your whole life meaningfully, purposefully; you will be the friend of everyone, the helper of everyone.

Through such thought, we can get a real sense of being brothers and sisters. Full of hatred, "brothers" and "sisters" are just words, nothing, but with an altruistic motivation, our big human community will become one harmonious, friendly, just, and honest family. This is our aim. Whether we achieve it in this life or not is a different matter; in any case, the attempt is worthwhile. This is my belief; I usually call such an attitude a universal religion. Not necessarily this or that religion, it is universal. Do you agree that these things are important? Complicated theories are not necessary; think with common sense. By thinking properly, we can convince ourselves that the practice of altruism, of love and compassion, is worthwhile, necessary, and most important.

Taking and Giving

When a Buddhist practitioner who has thought in this way sees sentient beings troubled by suffering, he or she wonders what can be done to help these beings. All of these sufferings are due to their own karma, and thus one is limited in how

much one can help them directly. However, one can voluntarily and enthusiasti-
cally, from the depths of the heart, make the wish and imagine with great will,
"May their suffering as well as its causes ripen within me." This is called the practice of taking others' suffering within emphasizing compassion.

Correspondingly, from the depths of one's heart one can wish and imagine that
whatever few virtues one has accumulated, which will produce pleasurable effects,
be given to other sentient beings, without the slightest regret. This is called the
practice of giving away one's own happiness within emphasizing love. Although
such mental imagining does not actually bring about these results, it helps with
regard to increasing determination and will power.

A person who has become accustomed to this practice can, at the time of an
illness or unfortunate happening, implement it, thereby both keeping one's suffering from getting worse and developing courage. In my limited experience, these
practices are really sources of courage, sources of inner strength. I think that this
may have some connection with the question earlier today about why Buddhist
teachers can be jovial. If you worry, it does not help, does it?

As far as my own motivation is concerned, I am sincere; I will do whatever I
can. Whether something is achieved or not is a different matter; thus, I have no
regret. It is better to be focused on larger issues than smaller ones; a lifetime even
of a hundred years is very small, not important. Now I am forty-six; if I remain
another forty or even fifty years, that time will not be very important compared to
the infinite future. Also, compared to the problems of limitless sentient beings, my
own are nothing. If you look at problems, suffering, very closely, they become very
big, complicated, and unbearable. But when you look from a distance, they become smaller, not worth too much worry. When you concentrate on the bigger
issues, the small ones come and go, come and go—that is their nature; they do not
cause much concern.

Patience

As I mentioned yesterday, one of the most important practices is that of tolerance,
patience. Tolerance can be learned only from an enemy; it cannot be learned from
your guru. At these lectures, for instance, you cannot learn tolerance, except perhaps when you are bored! However, when you meet your enemy who is really
going to hurt you, then, at that moment you can learn tolerance. Shāntideva makes
a beautiful argument; he says that one's enemy is actually a good spiritual guide
because in dependence upon an enemy one can cultivate patience, and in dependence upon patience one accumulates great power of merit. Therefore, it is as if an
enemy were purposefully getting angry in order to help you accumulate merit.

However, Shāntideva posits someone who objects—this person being a manifestation of one's own inner afflictive emotions. The objector says, "That is not so.
The enemy does not have an attitude of helping me; thus, there is no reason for me
to be nice to him/her." Shāntideva answers, "It is not necessary for something to
have an intention to help in order for it to help; for instance, we have faith in and
very much want true cessations of sufferings and the true paths that bring these

about, but they do not have any intention to help. Nevertheless, because they help, we respect them."

Then, the manifestation of one's own afflictive emotions, seeming to accept this, makes a further objection, "But an enemy has an intention to harm, whereas true cessations and true paths, even if they do not have an intention to help, also do not have an intention to harm. Therefore, I cannot respect an enemy." Shāntideva answers, "Because they have an intention to harm, they are called harmers, enemies. If they did not have an intention to harm, they would not even be called by that name. If they were like doctors, you would not get upset and thus would not have a chance to practice patience. Thus, since enemies are necessary for the practice of patience, an enemy is needed, and for someone to be an enemy, that person needs an intention to harm. Consequently, it us unsuitable to respond angrily; rather, an enemy should be respected."

Also, when someone strikes us, we immediately get angry at that person, but Shāntideva reasons differently: "If you consider what is actually harming you by creating suffering, then it is not the person but the weapon, be this a stick, the person's arm, or whatever. Still, even if you consider what indirectly brings about harm, the main source is not the person, it is the afflictive emotions in that person's mental continuum. Therefore, if you are going to get angry, either you should get angry at the weapon or at the motivation, the person's anger, not the person him/herself." This is very true. The actual pain is created by the weapon, but we foolishly do not get angry at the weapon, though indeed we sometimes do this as when bumping into an object! In the past when I was occupied with fixing up cars, I had a friend who, while working under a car, hit his head on the chassis; he yelled, "Yah! Yah!" He got so angry he hit the car twice with his head!

Besides such exceptions, generally we do not get upset at the weapon; we particularly choose the person. However, without anger, the person will not hit you; thus, it is because of the anger that he/she took the action. Therefore, if we think properly about the real source, the troublemaker is anger. We should get upset, not at the person, but at the afflictive emotion in the person.

Also, about angry persons, Shāntideva gives advice to consider whether anger is the nature of the person or is something adventitious—peripheral to the person's nature. If it is the nature of the person, then just as we do not get angry at fire even if it burns our hand because it is the very nature of fire to burn, so we should not get angry at the person. Again, if it is adventitious or peripheral, then just as when a cloud covers the sun, we do not get angry at the sun but see that the problem is with the cloud, so one should not get angry at the person but get upset with the person's afflictive emotion.

Also, one can think that one's own body has a nature of suffering and that the weapon has a nature of suffering, and thus when these two come together, pain is produced. Hence, half the fault is one's own. Then, just as one gets angry at the other person, so one should get angry at oneself.

Thus, as you can see, many worthwhile and meaningful ideas can be gained from reading Shāntideva's work—very useful for self-discipline and self-awareness. I practice according to Shāntideva's book; it is very, very helpful.

Through such reflections, one can develop a very strong sense of altruism. It is not absolutely necessary that you recognize other sentient beings as mothers. In contemplations such as those just discussed, the main reason for altruism is just that others want happiness; since this is sufficient, there is no fault even if you do not put emphasis on recognizing other beings as mothers. For, even in recognizing other beings as mothers, they come to be valued because they are *your own* mothers, and this involves considering yourself to be important. However, when the cherishing of others is achieved with the sole reason being that others want happiness and do not want suffering, there is no connection with considering yourself to be important. In particular, when you are able to generate a strong sense of respect for an enemy, all the rest of the people are easy since it is hardest to engender a sense of cherishing enemies.

That completes discussion of cultivating altruism by way of the equalizing and switching self and other.

Bodhisattva Deeds

Then, when one has trained in such an altruistic intention to become enlightened to the point where a moderate degree of experience has been developed, one makes a promise never to forsake it. Through making such a promise, the aspirational intention to become enlightened becomes more steady.

Having done this, one trains in causes to keep this aspiration from deteriorating in this and future lifetimes, after which one trains in the wish to engage in the Bodhisattva deeds, the six perfections—giving, ethics, patience, effort, concentration, and wisdom. There are many explanations about the six perfections in terms of their entities, precise enumeration, precise order, coarse and subtle forms, etc., but I will not go into these here. All of the practices of Bodhisattvas are contained in the six perfections, which, in turn, are contained in the three types of ethics—restraining ill deeds, the composite of virtuous practices, and bringing about others' welfare. The root of the ethics of Bodhisattvas is the restraining of self-centeredness. Thus, it is said that the root of all of Buddha's teaching is compassion, for in the vehicles of Hearers and Solitary Realizers it is within the context of compassion that they restrain from harming others, and Bodhisattvas not only refrain from not harming others but also seek to help others. In this way, the whole of Buddhism can be included in two sentences: "If you can, help others. If you cannot, at least do not harm them." The essence of the Buddhist vehicles is contained, in an abbreviated way, in this advice.

QUESTIONS FOR ANALYSIS AND DISCUSSION

1. For many moral thinkers, pride and courage go together. Why does the Dalai Lama separate the two? Do you think his understanding of pride is different from Aristotle's?

2. Review the nonvirtues. How similar are they to codes of conduct or principles of morality in Western ethics as articulated, for example, by the Ten Commandments? Are there notable differences? Clarify your response.

3. Imagine a student of the Dalai Lama watching one of the talk shows described in Kaminer's case study. What conclusions do you think the student would draw? Why?

4. Many of the Dalai Lama's ethical points are elaborated in the context of a goal in which the self reaches an enlightened view of no-self. How do you understand this view? Does it accord with other ethical views in that the happiness of individuals is morally significant? Clarify your response using a practical example from everyday life.

54.

EDITH SITWELL

Pride

For Edith Sitwell (1887–1964) much of the confusion about the status of pride can be attributed to bad press. The language we use to discuss pride either mocks pride or fears it. We tend to make fun of those with inflated egos, people who are so full of themselves they are about to explode. We enjoy the shame of celebrities caught in scandal or the rumors of the egotistical colleague facing a downfall. We hate and fear the person whose pride can be likened only to a tyrant, oblivious to anything in life outside her- or himself. Sitwell richly illustrates the dangers and strengths of pride. Moreover, she helps us consider whether pride is closer to love, humility, or temperance.

CRITICAL READING QUESTIONS

1. How does Sitwell distinguish stupid vanity from true pride?
2. Why does she despise anything that reduces human pride?
3. What is the difference between the examples that clarify Sitwell's contrast of proper and wicked pride?

Pride has always been one of my favourite virtues. I have never regarded it, except in certain cases, as a major sin.

"Pride," from *The Seven Deadly Sins* (New York: William Morrow, 1970), pp. 14–23.

Owing to a gradual debasement, a weakening of language, certain words do not, at this time, bear their original meaning. The word Pride is sometimes used when what is meant is a silly, useless vanity. Nor have I an affection for a pride which is simply the result of obstinacy.

There is, of course, a deadly sin of Pride—that which caused Hitler to say, "I walk with the certainty of the somnambulist." But there is also the Pride which can yet inspire love and admiration, such as Dante felt for his dear former tutor Brunetto Latini (said Professor Jacques Maritain in that great book, *Creative Intuition in Art and Poetry*), who even in Hell "seemed like him who wins and not him who loses."

Such was the tragic grandeur of

> *. . . that first archetype*
> *Of pride the paragon of all creation*
> *Who, of the light impatient, fell unripe.*
> —Dante, *Paradiso XIX*

A very great man (one of the greatest of our time) is reputed, I do not know with how much truth, to have said that his political opponents (who simply would not move and get out of the way, but persisted in being obstructions to every form of progress) were "lion-hearted limpets." I hope he said it. If he did not, he deserved to have said it, for the description could not be bettered. I have never been a limpet, lion-hearted or otherwise. My pride, which is great, is not of the kind that forbids me to move from any untenable position.

I have never minded being laughed at. All original artists *are* laughed at. But sometimes I laugh back, and that is not appreciated.

When I was a very young woman, I sat to Roger Fry (a most delightful man) for several portraits. Our appearance, as we crossed from his studio to his house for luncheon, caused a certain amount of interest. Roger wore, over his bushy grey hair, a very wide felt hat. I wore a leaf-green evening dress. With the result that the younger members of the crowd surveying us inquired:

A: Where did you get that hat, Where did you get that tile?

B: Does your mother know you're out?

—and, finally, suggested, benevolently, that a certain day in November would have been a more suitable day for our appearance.

Apropos of this date in November, my grandmother, Lady Londesborough, a most formidable lady, was the centre-piece of one of the worst falls from pride that I remember. It happened on that auspicious day, the Fifth of November. My grandmother was sitting in a bathchair, surrounded by captive daughters, outside the gate of the Londesborough Lodge gardens.

A young curate approached, accompanied by his wife. Struck by my grandmother's remarkable appearance, and remembering the date, he placed two pennies in her lap, and made his way into the gardens (which were private). The gift was *not* appreciated. In fact, there was an appalling storm, and the donor was chased by footmen through the gardens.

I have always enjoyed those frequent occasions on which I have been put in a place that is not mine. When I was about twenty-two years old, I went to a house belonging to some very rich people, in order to play the accompaniments on the piano for Helen Rootham, an admirable musician who had been engaged to sing at an afternoon party.

When the music was over, I was hastily removed from the drawing-room, as it was not thought suitable that I should have tea with gentry. The butler advanced upon me, "Follow me, if you please, Miss." And I found myself in a small room where, I must admit, a most delicious tea was awaiting me—everything that a girl of twenty-two would enjoy most—meringues, chocolate éclairs, etc. Of these I ate a great many. Then the butler reappeared, and I was led back into the drawing-room in order to accompany Helen on her farewell tour of the gentry.

There were a few moments of desultory conversation before the farewells were over.

"I do hope," said my hostess's daughter, "that Lady Londesborough is going to invite me to her ball." (Lady Londesborough was the wife of my mother's brother, and was, at that time, one of the most important London hostesses.)

"I'll remind her," I said. "Lord Londesborough is my uncle, and I am staying with them at the moment."

There was a short silence. Then we said goodbye.

I have never seen any of the gentry since.

It is sad when one's pride, which may be a form of love—perhaps one of the highest forms of love—receives a fall. When I was four years old, before the birth of either of my brothers, my pride and love were concentrated on the Renishaw peacock. This love was, *at the moment*, returned.

Every morning, punctually at nine o'clock (it is strange how birds and animals have an accurate sense of time), the peacock would stand on the leads outside my mother's bedroom, waiting for me to come and say good morning to her. When he saw me, he would let out a harsh shriek of welcome. (I do not, as a rule, appreciate ugly voices, but I loved him so much that in this case I did not care.) He would wait until I left my mother's room, and then, with another harsh shriek, would fly down into the garden to wait for me. We would walk round and round the large garden, not arm in arm, since that was impossible, but side by side, with my arm round his lovely shining neck. If it had not been for his crown, which made him slightly taller than me, we should have been of exactly the same size.

My nurse said to me, "Why do you love Peaky so much?"

I replied "Because he is beautiful and wears a heavenly crown."

—"The pride of the peacock," wrote William Blake, "is the glory of God."

This lovely innocent romance lasted for months. Then my father found Peaky a wife, after which he never looked at me, but occupied himself completely with teaching his children to unfurl the fans with which they had been endowed for tails. I do not think it was the injury to my pride, being jilted by a peacock, that I minded. It was the injury to my affections.

True pride has no connection with the stupid vanity of the person who believes the world was created for his convenience, or to prove some theory of his.

"I am afraid, sir," said the young author in *Lavengro*, "it was very wrong to write such trash, and yet more, to allow it to be published."

"Trash! Not at all," replied his publisher. "A very pretty piece of speculative philosophy. Of course you were wrong in saying there is no world. The world must exist, to have the shape of a pear. And that the world is shaped like a pear, and not like an apple, as the fools of Oxford say, I have satisfactorily proved in my book. Now, if there were no world, what would become of my system?" (Incidentally, if I remember rightly, in *The First Five Books of America,* we read that at one moment Christopher Columbus believed the world was shaped like a pear.)

In Mr Malcolm Letts's remarkable book about the real or imaginary Sir John Mandeville, he speaks of the belief held by medieval geographers that "Jerusalem was the centre of the earth . . . Mandeville was concerned about the Antipodes because of the suggestion by the supporters of the flat earth theory that if, in fact, the earth were a sphere, the men on the sides and lower surface, would be living sideways or upside down, even if they did not fall off into space. . . . As Mandeville implies, if a man thinks he is walking upright, he is in fact walking the right way up, as God meant him to do, and that is all that matters." This delightful suggestion seems to me to hold endless possibilities for the exercise of pride, and also conceit.

There is also a want of proper pride—which is ugly and evil, and ugly humility.

Blake said, "Modesty is only the cloak of pride."

I regard with disfavour the natural crawler—persons like the North American Indian who, according to Charleston's *Histoire de la Nouvelle France,* was found fondling a dead mouse, in the hope of appeasing the genius of mice.

When, after the Serpent's intolerable interference in the Garden of Eden, the Lord God said to him, "Upon thy belly shalt thou go," surely the Serpent was being condemned to an ugly form of humility.

I despise anything which reduces the pride of Man. In January, 1959, I read in a daily paper that in a certain town, "A plan to lock a man in a cage for eight days and put him in a show in a public park as the carnival feature, is to be put before the Health Committee. . . . He would stay in the 12 feet by 12 feet cage day and night, the town's Carnival Committee was told." The Carnival Committee's secretary said . . . "We are looking for a volunteer who will play the part of a human ape. We will offer him a gratuity of £25, plus food, during the eight days and nights he will lie in the cage. Feeding times will be posted up outside the cage as in a zoo."

I find it difficult to express my feelings about this hideous debasement of the pride of mankind.

We may remember, also, the praise bestowed upon an actress in America, of whom a critic wrote: "Now I'm saying she will be the sensation of New York . . . she walked off the stage on all fours, with elbows and knees straighter than pokers."

Is it *really* necessary to walk on all fours?

We should, like Goethe, regard man as "the first conversation that nature holds with God." And if this does not give us proper pride, we deserve to go with the gait of the Serpent.

Pride may be my own besetting sin; but it is also my besetting virtue. I take pride in the glory of mankind, and it would please me to think that like the Horse of which God spoke to Job, "my neck is clothed with thunder." (Wyclif dwarfed this, in his translation, down to "don about his necke with neiynge.") Certainly my life has been spent in saying "Ha ha among the trumpets."

A *proper* pride is a necessity to an artist in any of the arts. Only this will save an artist's work and his private life from the attacks and intrusions made on these by those unfortunate persons who have been unable to attract attention to themselves except by incessant bawling. Alexander Pope wrote in a letter:

> I will venture to say that no man ever rose to any degree of perfection in writing, but through obstinacy and an inveterate resolution against the stream of mankind; so that if the world has received any benefit from the labours of the learned, it was in its own despite. For when first they essay their parts, all people in general are prejudiced against new beginners: and when they have got a little above contempt, then some particular persons who were before unfortunate in their own attempts are sworn foes to them only because they succeed.

Socrates said to some carping person, "I would rather die having spoken in my manner, than speak in your manner and live."

This is the proper pride of the artist.

Iago is, I think, the greatest epitome in all literature of wicked pride. This is his element, his climate, his eternity, the whole of his being.

"If of that which this heart of mine is feeling, one drop were to fall into hell, hell itself would become all life eternal. . . ." Thus spoke St Catherine of Genoa . . . the life eternal is union with God.

One drop from the pride of Iago would raise all hell to rebellion against God. But that drop from the pride of Iago would come from a heart that had no feeling. He would, indeed, hardly know the difference between those pains and the pleasures of heaven. For he is not a damned soul. He is a devil.

Much of Shakespeare is concerned with the humbling of pride, as in certain speeches of Hamlet:

> A man may fishe with the Worme that hath eat of a King, and eat of the fishe that had fed of that Worme.

> King: What dost thou meane by this?

> Hamlet: Nothing but to show you how a King may goe a Progresse through the guts of a Begger.

> —*Hamlet*, iv, 3

But death has its pride, as well as its humility. Epiharnus of Syracuse (who was in his prime between 485 and 467 B.C.) told of a dead man saying "I am a corpse.

A corpse is dung, and dung is earth. Earth is a God; then am I not a corpse, but a God."

The greatest poet of our time, W. B. Yeats, writing of pride in humility, said:

O what a sweetness strayed
Through barren Thebaid
Or by the Mareotic sea .
When that exultant Anthony
And twice a thousand more
Starved upon the shore
And withered to a bag of bones!
What had the Caesars but their thrones?

QUESTIONS FOR ANALYSIS AND DISCUSSION

1. Many of Sitwell's examples involve artists and their works. Do you think these examples also represent or characterize the struggles most ordinary people have with pride?

2. When describing the opposite of pride, Sitwell talks not only of evil but also of the ugly. What do you think she means by wicked pride as also being ugly? Can you clarify her point with your own example? Keep in mind that "evil" and "ugly" are distinct ideas.

3. Sitwell closes her essay with three quotes. One, from Epiharnus, appears to be a straightforward argument. It links being a corpse with dung, dung with earth, and then earth with God. Hence, the dead person is not a corpse but a God. Do you agree or disagree with this conclusion? Explain your position. Why would many find Epiharnus's conclusion preposterous?

4. Imagine a dialogue among Sitwell, the Dalai Lama, and Aristotle. On which of the main points about pride do you think they would agree? What might be the main source of disagreement? Review your own beliefs about pride and self and consider whether any of the essays have encouraged you to examine those beliefs. Do those who appear on talk shows debating low self-esteem reflect any of the ideas raised by the essays? Clarify your answers.

55.

NORVIN RICHARDS

The Virtue of Humility

One alternative to the debate on pride focuses on humility. A common perception of humility is that it either expresses a sense of pretense or smugness, or it reveals a sign of weakness. According to University of Alabama philosopher Norvin Richards (b. 1943), humility is actually a much stronger virtue. It is part of the good life. As Richards understands it, a virtuous person is humble for positive rather than negative or cynical reasons. Humility is the best antidote to personal and social vices such as anger and jealousy. In addition, humility involves an effort to "live simply." As with the discussions on pride, Richards asks to what extent a virtuous person either strives for or is aware of being humble.

⊣ CRITICAL READING QUESTIONS ⊢

1. What are three distinct features of humility as outlined by Richards?
2. How does a humble person weigh his or her fortunes or misfortunes when compared to others?
3. What two things are required of a humble person when faced with the distress suffered by others?
4. How does humility overcome envy and jealousy?
5. What is the relation between humility and pride? Do both encourage one to live simply?

. . . [H]umility is not what it is often taken to be. Humility is not a meek lack of self-respect or low self-esteem or the undervaluing of one's good qualities. If it were any of these, then to be humble would be pitiable at best. There is an element of resignation in the attitudes mentioned, a hopelessness so resistant to encouragement as eventually to try the most sympathetic patience. Such an outlook should be no one's ideal, surely.

"The Virtue of Humility," from *Humility* (Philadelphia: Temple University Press, 1992), pp. 187–196, 201–202, 208–209. Notes have been omitted.

A different complaint about humility construed in these ways is that it would often embody a mistake. Anyone who undervalues his good qualities is thereby wrong about them; no one should lack self-respect; and, although there are people whose low opinion of themselves would be accurate enough, there are also a great many for whom a low opinion would be quite mistaken. Hence, a humble attitude would embody an error about oneself if it were the attitude described. That makes it hard, once again, to see why anyone should value humility: why should it be virtuous to have a false view of yourself?

Finally, consider for a moment the person of great accomplishment or great virtue who has retained her humility, despite the over-excited praise of others. Hers is the kind of humility we most admire, having come to expect heroes to be a bit full of themselves instead. But if humility consists in thinking one amounts to very little, has done nothing, and so on, it does not even seem possible for these heroes to be humble. We lesser types know that this is not the truth about them; surely they would know it too? Surely they could not fail to notice that they were very good people, or that they had done something of great difficulty or great benefit to mankind, or whatever. So their humility would have to be *false* humility, then; it would have to be that annoying pretense that spoils our pleasure in contemplating someone excellent and dampens our admiration for him.

In short, this conception of humility is difficult to retain if we believe that there are good and accomplished people in the world and that such people are capable of humility. It is impossible to retain if, as we think, their humility is especially admirable. Finally, it makes very puzzling the high esteem in which humility is commonly held. Why so many of us consider it a virtue at all is hard to see, if being humble amounts to lacking self-respect or undervaluing one's good qualities or having a low opinion of oneself that is somehow more praiseworthy the more mistaken it is.

I have offered a different analysis, according to which humility consists, roughly, in having oneself and one's accomplishments in perspective. On this view, to be humble is to understand yourself and your moral entitlements sufficiently clearly that you are disposed not to exaggerate about these. How that could be a good thing in a person is not puzzling, I take it; nor is our admiration for it. It does not seem impossible, either, for an especially accomplished person to retain this perspective (unlike his holding the clearly false belief that he had done very little). It seems only a *difficult* thing to do: which, in turn, explains why humility might be especially admirable in such a person. In sum, humility is no longer paradoxical in the ways mentioned, if we construe it as suggested.

What would it be like to have this unexaggerated perspective on yourself and what you had done? In part, it would involve understanding certain facts about yourself. You would be realistic about your abilities and your limitations, rather than thinking yourself abler than you were. Similarly, you would understand rightly the things you had accomplished, rather than believing them to have been more difficult or more nobly motivated or more far reaching in their consequences than they actually were. You would not exaggerate the part that (as a matter of fact) you play in the lives of others. You would not overestimate the contributions you had made to their achievements or the extent to which what they did was meant to affect you (as opposed to affecting you only in passing) or the extent to which you were in competition with them.

Getting these facts straight is one part of what it is to be humble. What humility works against is not simply thinking of the facts about you as *different* from what they are but thinking of them as *better*. Humility works against believing yourself more able than you actually are, for example, thinking you can accomplish things that are well beyond your reach. Humility also works against overestimating yourself morally: against believing that you merit more praise and gratitude than you actually do, for example, or considering yourself entitled to behave in ways in which you are not. Those are flattering pictures of oneself, but false ones; a humble person grasps the truth sufficiently clearly to resist them.

Humility also provides an understanding that one is not special, from the point of view of the universe, not an exception to be treated differently from the others. "Of course I'm not an exception," we may be inclined to think, "only an utter loon would believe himself the universe's chosen child." But, in fact, the mistake is much more common: it occurs whenever we expect mistreatment and misfortune to be taken more seriously when they happen to us than we would think appropriate when they happen to others. The mistake occurs, too, whenever someone acts as if she may do things that others in similar situations may not do. For, these are ways of taking oneself to be exceptional, and they are hardly rare.

So humility protects us from a mistake life offers us many opportunities to make. To say more specifically how it affords this protection describes what it is to be humble. Now to pull together some elements of that description.

1

No one is always treated exactly as he or she should be. The luckiest do not suffer deeds of great violence or wrenching betrayals or smothering subjugation, but even the luckiest sometimes find that they have been cheated or deceived or treated unjustly. How would humility incline a person to respond to whatever mistreatment came his way? Would it dispose him not to take offense, for example? And, if he did take offense, would it make him hasten to extend forgiveness to the wrongdoer?

So it might appear, and this seems to some to render humility indistinguishable from a lack of self-respect. For the most part, however, self-respect requires only that we not demote ourselves beneath the class in which we place others. Humility would certainly not foster such a demotion. Instead it would foster the reverse: understanding yourself and your accomplishments should incline you to recognize that you are certainly not some lesser being who must accept mistreatment as your due.

While humility therefore does not require a meek submissiveness, as noted, it does require that we take whatever happens to us to be no more important intrinsically than it would be if it befell another. Your being shortchanged at the store calls for no stronger reaction than would anyone else's being shortchanged: no stronger reaction, that is, from the victim, from strangers, from those who penalize wrongdoers, from the wrongdoer himself. So, the properly humble attitude is to be no more resentful than you would consider it appropriate for anyone to be, and not to expect any more sympathy or support or remorse from the others, either.

This view permits the humble person to be resentful, of course, and to withhold forgiveness, unlike the view that we must never take offense and must always forgive. There is no self-elevation in taking offense, as long as we are consistent. Nor is there any in being unforgiving, as long as we regard that as a suitable attitude for any victim of the same mistreatment. It is essential that this consistency hold across cases in which we are the wrongdoer rather than the victim: we must take the wrong equally seriously then, if we are not to be taking ourselves too seriously. When we do not, our attitude is that what happens to us has a unique importance to it, however blind others might be to this fact.

We lack humility in a different fashion when we take what is really only indifference to our interests to be something more focused on us. A good deal of mistreatment is like that, I believe. It involves no intention to do us harm, that is, but only a certain lack of interest in how we might be affected. To think there is more to an episode than that is to overestimate your centrality to the great flow of events: a mistake against which humility provides protection.

2

Another fact of life is that there are people in great misery in the world because of natural disasters and the like. We could help them, and we know it. Mostly we do not do so, though, but go about our own lives. What does humility require of a person here?

A thesis modeled on Peter Singer's work would be that not to be greatly alive to the needs of others is a failure of humility. Specifically, we should be moved to sacrifice anything to help them, up to the point of doing comparable harm in making the sacrifice. On this view, to fall short of such sacrifice is to act as if lesser benefits to ourselves were more important than greater benefits to others: as if our having a new suit or a weekend at the beach were more important than several other human beings' being rescued from miserable starvation. That would be to act as if we were more important than they, the argument continues: since we are not, this is a failure of moral humility on our part.

I have argued instead that humility requires two things of us in our compassion for those in distress: consistency like that required in our reactions to wrongdoing and avoidance of self-absorption. To be consistent we need not be as upset over the plight of those in distress as we would be if it were our own (or as upset as if it were the plight of "a neighbor's child ten yards from me," in Singer's phrase), any more than we need be as outraged over their being assaulted as we would be if we were assaulted ourselves. What is necessary instead is that we not take distress to be any more significant intrinsically because it is we who suffer it, just as a moral wrong is not any more significant intrinsically because we are its victim. Most of us take our being in even *minor* trouble to be something strangers should take very seriously. So, humility requires most of us to take the *major* troubles of strangers very seriously. Our usual indifference to them is a failure of moral humility.

Humility demands as well that we avoid self-absorption. To call someone self-absorbed is to say she is fascinated by such matters as her own appearance, her image, her personality or character, her progress up life's ladder, her evening's entertainment, and so on. What fascinates the self-absorbed person is herself; to say she is *fascinated* means that she is very difficult to distract from attending to herself, in the same way as a child absorbed in a game is difficult to draw away into other pursuits. There is a level of self-absorption that amounts to taking oneself too seriously, relative to other matters. To do so is to exaggerate one's own importance, and therefore to lack humility.

Which failures to respond compassionately would qualify as unhumbly self-absorbed? The clearest examples verge on the pathological: Singer's man who would let a child drown rather than muddy his clothes, James Rachels's diners who would let a child starve at their feet rather than interrupt their repast. The underlying idea is one of being undiverted from self-centered pursuits even when the calls to compassion are loud and clear. What makes a call to compassion "loud and clear" is a complicated matter of human psychology, but some of its elements seem identifiable, along the following lines.

Generally, suffering in one's presence is more vivid than suffering that is only described, and the suffering of someone who has been a part of your life is more vivid to you than the suffering of some imagined member of a future generation. Even the most wrenching agony can fail to grip us if it is described only statistically, and something much less serious can be depicted far more compellingly by focusing our attention on some particular waif. There may also be a loss of vividness when the call on our compassion is one among many, rather than one standing alone in stark contrast.

No doubt, there is much more to all this. The main point here is that whatever the particulars turn out to be, for a person to be undistracted from self-centered pursuits by even the more vivid and desparate calls on her compassion is for her to take herself too seriously. That is a moral mistake a humble person would not make.

3

Although the world contains many who are far worse off than we, it also contains many who are far better off. And not only wealthier than we, of course: there are plenty who are better philosophers, plenty who are nicer people, and Lord *knows* there are plenty who are better looking. What is more, others sometimes get the recognition we would like to have, or the respect, or the affection.

This means there are many occasions for bitterness: for feeling unjustly treated by life or injured by a rival or envious or jealous of those who are doing better. It is possible to admire those who surpass you instead, or, at least, to take their superiority in stride. Nearly all of us are capable of these nobler-sounding reactions at times. For someone *always* to be so mature when surpassed would seem almost inhuman, however. How would humility dispose a person toward those who seem to put him in the shade?

Notice here how often the hard feelings we have on these occasions are unreasonable, in one way or another. It is not as if those who surpass us were to blame for our relative positions, as if they had held us back while they surged ahead, and might sensibly be resented as people who had done us wrong. Nor are we always realistic when our envy passes quickly into complaints about injustice, as if the gap between us were due to some unfair third party who has not taken our merit properly into account. These reactions evince a certain unwillingness to believe the truth about oneself, an inclination to substitute some grander person who is never surpassed except through chicanery. A humble person would know herself better than that, and thus her humility would protect her against hard feelings that are unreasonable in this way.

Similarly, both jealousy and envy can be imbued with a lack of realism about one's possibilities. Thus, some are greatly upset when surpassed by individuals against whom they quite wrongly suppose they should be able to compete on equal terms. If they knew themselves better, they would not take these to be failures that call for self-reproach, or for special explanations preserving the false picture of themselves. Yet another element of understanding oneself is to be realistic about one's place in the lives of others, rather than presuming there to be commitments and relationships of intimacy when none is present. That spares a person the jealous rages and hurt feelings of those who feel betrayed, despite not being entitled to any such feelings.

Even when hard feelings are appropriate, there is still a matter of keeping them in proportion, moreover, and here too humility comes into play: overreacting to defeat or to displacement is a failure of humility. Suppose that whatever else we have been to each other, I now think of you mainly, if not exclusively, as the person who received the bigger raise or confided in someone else rather than in me, and this puts a distance and reserve between us. Clearly, this can exaggerate the importance of these things happening to me, taking them to be far more significant events in the history of the universe than they are. Clearly too, it may be that I would consider this reaction excessive if someone else were to carry on in the same way. Humility inclines us not to elevate ourselves in either of these ways.

One further benefit of humility is an understanding that you are not in nearly so many competitions as those prone to envy seem to think they are in. Ordinarily, the success of another person does not put you behind in a race in the way the envious person takes it to. Ordinarily, their success has nothing to do with you at all. Similarly, the fact that someone else is wonderful in some way does not ordinarily mean that you are losing in some cosmic competition for best in show. This false picture of the world sees many connections between you and others that are simply not there: as if there were a web connecting you with them, so that any shift in their position had something to do with you. That is a very unhumble picture, surely. Those who view their place in the universe more realistically gain protection from the envy and jealousy that afflict those who consider life a constant competition on multiple fronts.

. . .

6

There are several respects in which we associate humility with living simply, unencumbered by possessions beyond the bare minimum. We expect a humble person to live in a humble dwelling, not in opulence, and to eat humble fare, not rich dishes. Is there anything to this? Would genuine humility incline one to forego whatever is beyond the essentials, so that our own more luxurious lives betray the extent to which we have not achieved it?

That might well be the truth of the matter, if the fathers of the Roman Catholic church were correct in thinking that every good thing about a person is God's gift and every bad one that person's own doing. For, it might well follow that understanding yourself would incline you to make your life as hard as you could manage, in penance for misusing your gifts. And similarly, if not overestimating your place in the larger scheme of things meant realizing that all earthly pleasures are a snare and a delusion, then someone with the right attitude would avoid such pleasures, presumably. In short, if this Catholic metaphysics is correct about what is understood by those who do not overestimate themselves, then such an understanding might very well incline a person to live not merely a simple life but one he or she intentionally made hard.

This may not be the correct metaphysical view, however. The truth may be what many of us believe: that we sometimes deserve credit for the things we do and become, that a life wholly devoted to worship is not the only proper one for us, and that earthly pleasures are not intrinsically wicked. It is interesting to consider what would follow if *that* were the truth of the matter: would a humble perspective still incline a person to live simply?

There are several reasons to think so, I believe, but it is important not to overstate their implications. A humble person will not be thoroughly self-absorbed, but this is far from saying he must give up his substance for the good of others. A humble person will not have certain exaggerated ambitions, but this does not mean he will so lack ambition that a simple life will suit him fine and will be all he can hope to achieve. A humble person will not live boastfully or in hopes of making others envious, but this allows for creature comforts well beyond the minimal. A humble person will be disinclined to live opulently, but this is not the same as being inclined to make one's life intentionally hard or to limit one's goods to the barest necessities.

Just as we might exaggerate the extent to which humility calls for austerity in one's life, we might also exaggerate the extent to which it forbids us to be proud of anything. Richard Taylor does so in the following passage: "Pride is quite correctly perceived to be incompatible with . . . the supposed virtue of humility that is so congenial to the devout mind and so foreign to the pagan temperament." By "the supposed virtue of humility that is so congenial to the devout mind," however, Taylor means the conviction that we are utterly worthless. No doubt that conviction *is* incompatible with being proud of anything, just as he asserts, but, as we have seen, there are good reasons for taking humility to be something else altogether.

On the account offered here, humility does not preclude our taking what is sometimes called *proper* pride in ourselves and our accomplishments, but only guards against our being foolishly or excessively proud. To say only this much is rather abstract and uninformative, however. It would be nice to have some idea of *when* pride is foolish or excessive, and therefore not the humble person's style, and when it is pride of a kind a humble person might take.

We should start our thoughts about this by considering what pride is. As many have noted, to be proud of something is not the same as simply taking pleasure in it. You might take pleasure in the lovely view from a secluded hillside, for example, taking every opportunity to visit and enjoy it, without being at all *proud* of the view. If you had managed to complete a marathon, on the other hand, you might be not merely pleased by this but also proud of it. The difference lies in your taking completing the marathon to speak well of you, in some way, and *not* thinking of the view from the hillside in those terms. You regard the view only as a pleasure, while you take completing the marathon to be something to your credit.

If this is the correct account of pride, we should be proud of exactly those things that we would be right to regard as to our credit. We would be wrong to be proud of things that do not speak well of us, or that we have insufficient reason to take to do so. And our pride would be excessive, insofar as we drew grander implications than we had grounds to draw. What humility does, in general terms, is to protect us against errors of each kind. Humility inclines us to be proud only of what actually is to our credit and only when we are justified in thinking of it in that way, and it keeps our pride proportionate rather than exaggerated.

. . .

Freedom from elitism is among the advantages of humility, then. There are many others. A person who does not overestimate his abilities is less likely to undertake projects that are beyond him, or to fret impatiently when difficult tasks are not easily completed. There is protection here as well against frustration over lost competitions, derived from a good sense as to when we simply would not be in the running and so ought not to feel sure someone must have cheated or to reproach ourselves for not having done better. A humble person is free to admire rather than to envy or to burn in some other way.

As another part of understanding themselves, the humble are aware that they do not necessarily know what course would be in another person's best interests. This alone should make them cautious about pressing their unwanted expertise upon others—to be bewildered, sometimes, by its rejection. By the same token, to understand ourselves is to know better than to think we are nothing, that others may treat us as they wish or that we must allow them to make the decisions that shape our lives. Having self-respect in this way is not what we think of as an *expression* of humility, but the two have a natural connection.

Although humility involves having a sense of one's worth, it also acquaints a person with the fact that she is not *uniquely* worthy. She will know she is not so important to the universe as she is to herself: although she may be first in her own heart, she will not take it that others must somehow *err* by having different priorities. That may seem an obvious thing to know, but many seem not to know it. To live in accordance with the knowledge that you are not uniquely important enhances the ability to manage the mistreatment you suffer, rather than having it disrupt your life out of all proportion. To live in accordance with this knowledge enhances the ability to tolerate minor human error when it affects you, as opposed to considering everytime you are wronged so outrageous that all must take notice and the miscreant must be made to suffer. To know you are not uniquely important makes extending forgiveness a possibility, by enabling you to see that not every time you are wronged has the status of a sacrilege.

On the other hand, to know that you have no unique intrinsic importance is to know that others are entitled to take their mistreatment every bit as seriously as you are entitled to take yours. What is more, others are entitled to the same concern about their mistreatment from the rest of the world as well. This should mean recognizing that you must take some care regarding others, insofar as you feel entitled to have them take care regarding you. Indeed, you should see that the more intimate your relationship with others the greater they merit your concern. For, the more intimate the relationship, the more concern you feel entitled to expect from them. The evenhandedness of humility's perspective thus removes one obstacle to intimacy, as well as erasing more generally the self-aggrandizement of the egotist.

Nor will anyone who knows herself be greatly self-absorbed, for she will see that she is not so much more fascinating than other subjects. That will free her to be compassionate, among other things, without of course meaning that she must take no greater interest in herself than she takes in remote strangers. It means instead that she will be distractable from self-interested pursuits, that her heart will not be entirely closed.

Martin Luther once asserted that humility is so wonderful a virtue that one can never be aware of having it, for the awareness would surely turn one's head. I doubt the advantages cited above are quite so dazzling as that. They do seem, however, to make humility both a valuable asset to the person who has it and something we should welcome in those who cross our path. Being humble is a good way for a person to be.

QUESTIONS FOR ANALYSIS AND DISCUSSION

1. Richards is concerned with the distinct ability of humility to help moral persons resist self-absorption. Why is self-absorption such a problem? How can we distinguish between proper and improper self-regard?

2. A humble person is not meek and submissive, as common perception has it, but rather may be quite accomplished. What is important is the amount of personal credit taken for accomplishments. Suppose you get an "A" in your ethics course. Being a humble person as depicted by Richards, how would you

decide how much credit should be given to you and to others? Moreover, is it possible to credit fairly or accurately all those who have contributed to your getting an "A"? Why, or why not?

3. Richards argues that humility overcomes envy and jealousy because it recognizes that life is not always constant competition. The envious person invariably sees the good fortunes of others as affecting his or her own prospects and self-regard. This is a dangerous misconception, one a humble person strives to avoid by understanding that not everything that happens in the world also happens to the self. Given Richards's conclusion that humility is central to the good life, which of the following do you think encourage (or have no influence on) humility or envy: (a) television talk shows, (b) commercials and advertisements, (c) college courses that distribute grades according to the bell curve, (d) sociobiologists who contend that most of our character is attributed to our genetic makeup, (e) religious believers who give credit to a benevolent deity for the good fortune that befalls us, (f) parents who praise us when we are good and admonish us when we are bad, (g) love, or (h) death? Briefly justify your answers in light of Richards's discussion.

4. Near the end of his essay Richards connects humility with the simple life. What do you think constitutes living simply? Consider the things you and your friends and family have. To what extent do they reflect a simple or luxurious life? If you believe in humility, should you strive for the simple life?

56.

VOLTAIRE

Character and Self-Love

A contrasting and sardonic take on self-regarding virtues comes from Voltaire (1694–1778), one of the best known thinkers of the French Enlightenment. A voluminous writer (known to work in stretches of 18 to 20 hours a day), Voltaire wonders whether humans exaggerate their own powers when engaging in moral speculations. For him, self-love is a natural rather than a moral given. Any creature seeks to preserve its own existence. If this protection includes some pleasure, how can any moral theory demand otherwise? This is

"Character" and "Self-Love," Philosophical Dictionary, from *Portable Voltaire*, edited by Ben Ray Redman (New York: Viking Penguin, 1977), pp. 93–95, 199–200.

from Voltaire's Philosophical Dictionary, *a compendium of his witty observations on human life.*

┤ **CRITICAL READING QUESTIONS** ├

1. What is Voltaire's point in comparing one's character with one's physical attributes?
2. How does he understand the relation between reflection and mastery of one's life?
3. What is the lesson on the passions in the story about the farmer and the ninety-year-old general?
4. How do the parables of the beggar in Madrid and the fakir having himself whipped illustrate Voltaire's points about self-love?

Character

(From the Greek word *impression, engraving.* It is what nature has graved in us.)

Can one change one's character? Yes, if one changes one's body. It is possible for a man to be born a mischief-maker of tough and violent character, and, as a result of being stricken with apoplexy in his old age, to become a foolish, tearful child, timid and peaceable. His body has changed. But as long as his nerves, his blood and his marrow remain the same, his nature will not change any more than will a wolf's and a marten's instinct.

Our character is composed of our ideas and our feelings: and, since it has been proved that we give ourselves neither feelings nor ideas, our character does not depend on us.

If it did depend on us, there is nobody who would not be perfect.

We cannot give ourselves tastes or talents; why should we be able to give ourselves qualities?

If one does not reflect, one thinks oneself master of everything; but when one does reflect, one realizes that one is master of nothing.

Should you wish to change a man's character completely, purge him daily with diluents until you have killed him. Charles XII, in his suppurative fever on the road to Bender, was no longer the same man. He was as tractable as a child.

If I have a crooked nose and two cat's eyes, I can hide them with a mask. Can I do more with the character which nature has given me?

A man who was naturally violent and impetuous presented himself before François I, King of France, to complain of an injustice. The prince's countenance, the respectful bearing of the courtiers, the very place in which he found himself, made a powerful impression on this man. Mechanically he lowered his eyes, his rough voice softened, he presented his petition humbly; one would have thought him as gentle as were the courtiers themselves, whom he found so disconcerting. But François I understood physiognomy, he easily discovered in the lowered eyes, still burning with somber fire, in the strained facial muscles and the compressed lips, that this man was not as gentle as he was forced to appear. This man followed the king to Pavia, was captured with him, and put in the same prison in Madrid. François I's majesty no longer made the same impression on him; he grew familiar with the object of his respect. One day when he was pulling off the king's boots— and pulling them off badly—the king, embittered by his misfortune, became angry; whereupon my man sent the king about his business, and threw his boots out of the window.

Sixtus V was born petulant, stubborn, haughty, impetuous, vindictive, and arrogant. This character, however, seemed softened during the trials of his novitiate, and he began to enjoy a certain credit in his order. Then he flew into a passion with a guard, and battered him with his fist. As an inquisitor at Venice, he performed his duties insolently. Behold him a cardinal—he is possessed *dalla rabbia papale.* This passionate desire triumphs over his nature: he buries his person and his character in obscurity; he apes the humble and the dying man. Then he is elected Pope, and this moment gives back all its long-curbed elasticity to the spring which politics have bent. He is the haughtiest and most despotic of sovereigns.

> *Naturam expellas furca, tamen usque recurret.*
> —Horace, *Epistolae,* 1, 10

> Drive away nature, it returns at the gallop.
> —Destouches, *Glorieux,* Act 3, Sc. 5

Religion, morality put a brake on a nature's strength; they cannot destroy it. The drunkard in a cloister, reduced to a half-setier of cider at each meal, will no longer get drunk, but he will always like wine.

Age enfeebles character; it is a tree that produces only degenerate fruit, but the fruit is always of the same nature; the tree is knotted and covered with moss, it becomes worm-eaten, but it is always an oak or a pear tree. If one could change one's character, one would give oneself a character; one would be master of nature. But can one give oneself anything? Do we not receive everything? Try to arouse an indolent man to sustained activity; try to freeze with apathy the boiling soul of an impetuous fellow; or try to inspire someone who has neither ear nor taste with a taste for music and poetry, and you will no more succeed than if you undertook to give sight to a man born blind. We perfect, we soften, we conceal what nature has put in us, but we ourselves do not put in anything at all.

Someone says to a farmer: "You have too many fish in this pond, they will not prosper; there are too many cattle in your meadows, grass is lacking, and they will grow thin." After this exhortation it happens that the pike eat half my man's carp, and the wolves half of his sheep, while the rest grow fat. Will he not congratulate himself on his economy? This countryman is yourself: one of your passions has devoured the others, and you think that you have triumphed over yourself. Do not most of us resemble that old general of ninety who, having come on some young officers who were having a bit of fun with some girls, said to them angrily: "Gentlemen, is that the example I give you?"

Self-Love

Nicole in his *Essais de Morale*—written on top of two or three thousand other volumes of ethics—says that "by means of the wheels and gibbets which people erect in common, the tyrannous thoughts and designs of each individual's self-love are repressed."

I shall not inquire whether or not people have gibbets in common, as they have meadows and woods in common, and a common purse, or if one represses ideas with wheels; but it seems very strange to me that Nicole should take highway robbery and assassination for self-love. One should distinguish shades of difference a little better. The man who said that Nero had his mother assassinated through self-love, and that Cartouche had an excess of self-love, would not be expressing himself very correctly. Self-love is not wickedness, it is a sentiment that is natural to all men; it is much nearer vanity than crime.

A beggar in the suburbs of Madrid was nobly begging charity. A passer-by said to him: "Are you not ashamed to practice this infamous calling when you are able to work?"

"Sir," answered the beggar, "I ask for money, not advice." And he turned on his heel with full Castilian dignity.

This gentleman was a proud beggar, his vanity was wounded by a trifle. He asked charity out of love for himself, and could not tolerate the reprimand out of further love for himself.

A missionary traveling in India met a fakir laden with chains, naked as a monkey, lying on his stomach, who was having himself whipped for the sins of his compatriots, the Indians, who gave him a few farthings.

"What self-denial!" said one of the spectators.

"Self-denial!" answered the fakir. "I have myself flogged in this world in order to give this flogging back to you in the next world, when you will be horses and I a horseman."

Those who have said that love of ourselves is the basis of all our opinions and all our actions, have therefore been quite right in India, Spain, and all the habitable world: and as one does not write to prove to men that they have faces, it is not necessary to prove to them that they have self-love. Self-love is our instrument of preservation; it resembles the instrument which perpetuates the species. It is necessary, it is dear to us, it gives us pleasure, and it has to be hidden.

QUESTIONS FOR ANALYSIS AND DISCUSSION

1. Voltaire doubts that humans can change their character. This runs counter to one of the central themes in virtue ethics, that of moral education, which stresses the development of moral character. What is Voltaire's reasoning? Do you agree or disagree? Specify which points of Voltaire you question.

2. Voltaire is also suspicious of the power of religion or morality to change our nature. We are born with a set of basic abilities and functions. To change our nature is as odd a task as changing what a tree is supposed to do. Do you

agree with his analogy? Can you identify any relevant or significant differences between the natures of humans and trees in terms of Voltaire's primary issue?

3. Concluding his observations about self-love, Voltaire writes, "It is necessary, it is dear to us, it gives us pleasure, and it has to be hidden." Why must self-love be hidden? Is Voltaire praising humility, proper pride, or deception? Develop your response in light of his examples and your own.

57.

JOYCE CAROL OATES

Despair

The list of the seven cardinal virtues and the seven deadly sins continues to be questioned and amended. In the view of widely known essayist and novelist Joyce Carol Oates (b. 1938), we should entertain a new candidate for a major sin—despair. As Oates portrays it, despair is not a sin you want to experience too closely. If you experience the other sins, you have a chance for forgiveness. Despair does not allow this possibility. Despair offers the image that the individual self really is "no-thing." As Oates eloquently puts it, "despair seems to bleed out beyond the confines of the immediate ego-centered self and to relate to no desire, no-thing." In a concise review of religious, literary, and existential answers to the question of despair, Oates concludes by citing several poetic voices on the evil or moral wrongness of despair.

⊣ CRITICAL READING QUESTIONS ⊢

1. Just as we see how it is possible that anger leads to killing or torture, envy threatens justice and goodwill, or lust risks adultery or AIDS, which specific morally controversial action does despair generally include?

2. What is distinct about literary despair? Which individuals can be affected by literary despair?

3. What is the importance for Oates of Kafka's writing?

"Despair," from *Deadly Sins* (New York: Morrow, 1993), pp. 107–116.

What mysterious cruelty in the human soul, to have invented despair as a "sin"! Like the Seven Deadly Sins employed by the medieval Roman Catholic Church to terrify the faithful into obedience, despair is most helpfully imagined as a mythical state. It has no quantifiable existence; it "is" merely allegory, yet no less lethal for the fact. Unlike other sins, however, despair is by tradition the sole sin that cannot be forgiven: it is the conviction that one may be damned absolutely, thus a refutation of the Christian savior and a challenge to God's infinite capacity for forgiveness. The sins for which one may be forgiven—pride, anger, lust, sloth, avarice, gluttony, envy—are all firmly attached to objects of this world, but despair seems to bleed out beyond the confines of the immediate ego-centered self and to relate to no desire, no-thing. The alleged sinner has detached himself even from the possibility of sin as a human predilection, and this the Church as the self-appointed voice of God on earth cannot allow.

Religion is organized power in the seemingly benevolent guise of the "sacred" and power is, as we know, chiefly concerned with its own preservation. Its structures, its elaborate rituals and customs and scriptures and commandments and ethics, its very nature, objectify human experience, insisting that what is *out there* in the world is of unquestionably greater significance than what is *in here* in the human spirit. Despair, surely the least aggressive of sins, is dangerous to the totalitarian temperament because it is a state of intense inwardness, thus independence. The despairing soul is a rebel.

So, too, suicide, the hypothetical consequence of extreme despair, has long been a mortal sin in Church theology, in which it is equivalent to murder. Suicide has an element of the forbidden, the obscene, the taboo about it, as the most willful and the most defiantly antisocial of human acts. While thinkers of antiquity condoned suicide, in certain circumstances at least—"In all that you do or say or think, recollect that at any time the power of withdrawal from life is in your hands," Marcus Aurelius wrote in the *Meditations*—the Church vigorously punished suicides in ways calculated to warn others and to confirm, posthumously, their despair: bodies were sometimes mutilated, burial in consecrated soil was of course denied, and the Church, ever resourceful, could confiscate goods and land belonging to suicides.

Yet how frustrating it must have been, and be, the attempt to outlaw and punish *despair*—of all sins!

(In fact, one wonders: is "despair" a pathology we diagnose in people who seem to have repudiated our own life-agendas, as "narcissism" is the charge we make against those who fail to be as intrigued by us as we had wished?)

At the present time, despair as a "sin" is hardly convincing. As a state of intense inwardness, however, despair strikes us as a spiritual and moral experience that cuts across superficial boundaries of language, culture, and history. No doubt, true despair is mute and unreflective as flesh lacking consciousness; but the *poetics* of despair have been transcendentally eloquent:

> The difference between Despair
> And Fear—is like the One—
> Between the instant of a Wreck—
> And when the Wreck has been—

The Mind is smooth—no Motion—
Contented as the Eye
Upon the Forehead of a Bust—
That knows—it cannot see—
                    —Emily Dickinson

This condition, which might be called a stasis of the spirit, in which life's energies are paralyzed even as life's physical processes continue, is the essence of literary despair. The plunging world goes its own way, the isolated consciousness of the writer splits from it, as if splitting from the body itself. Despair as this state of keenly heightened inwardness has always fascinated the writer, whose subject is after all the imaginative reconstruction of language. The ostensible subject *out there* is but the vehicle, or the pretext, for the ravishing discoveries to be made *in here* in the activity of creating.

Literary despair is best contemplated during insomniac nights. And perhaps most keenly savored during adolescence, when insomnia can have the aura of the romantic and the forbidden; when sleepless nights can signal rebellion against a placidly sleeping—un-conscious—world. At such times, inner and outer worlds seem to merge; insights that by day would be lost define themselves like those phosphorescent minerals coarse and ordinary in the light that yield a mysterious glimmering beauty in the dark. Here is the "Zero at the Bone" of which Emily Dickinson, our supreme poet of inwardness, writes, with an urgency time has not blunted.

❧ ❧ ❧

My first immersion in the Literature of Despair came at a time of chronic adolescent insomnia, and so the ravishing experience of reading certain writers—most of them, apart from Dickinson and William Faulkner, associated with what was called European existentialism—is indelibly bound up with that era in my life. Perhaps the ideal reader *is* an adolescent: restless, vulnerable, passionate, hungry to learn, skeptical and naïve by turns; with an unquestioned faith in the power of the imagination to change, if not life, one's comprehension of life. To the degree to which we remain adolescents we remain ideal readers to whom the act of opening a book can be a sacred one, fraught with psychic risk. For each work of a certain magnitude means the assimilation of a new voice—that of Dostoyevsky's Underground Man, for instance, or Nietzsche's Zarathustra—and the permanent altering of one's own interior world.

Literary despair, as opposed to "real" despair, became fashionable at mid-century with a rich, diverse flood of English translations of European writers of surpassing originality, boldness, and genius. Misleadingly linked by so-called "Existentialist" themes, these highly individual writers—among them Dostoyevsky, Kafka, Kierkegaard, Mann, Sartre, Camus, Pavese, Pirandello, Beckett, Ionesco— seemed to characterize the very mission of literature itself: never in the service of "uplifting," still less "entertaining," but with a religious ideal of penetrating to the most inward and intransigent of truths. Despair at the randomness of mankind's fate and of mankind's repeatedly demonstrated inhumanity was in a sense celebrated, that we might transcend it through the symbolic strategies of art. For no fate, however horrific, as in the graphically detailed execution of the faithful officer of Kafka's great story "In the Penal Colony," or the ignominious execution of Joseph K. of Kafka's *The Trial*—cannot be transmogrified by its very contemplation; or redeemed, in a sense, by the artist's visionary fearlessness. It is not just that despair is immune to the comforts of the ordinary—despair *rejects* comfort. And Kafka, our exemplary artist of despair, is one of our greatest humorists as well. The bleakness of his vision is qualified by a brash, unsettling humor that flies in the face of expectation. Is it tragic that Gregor Samsa is metamorphosed into a giant cockroach, suffers, dies, and is swept out with the trash?—is it tragic that the Hunger Artist starves to death, too finicky to eat the common food of humanity?— no, these are ludicrous fates, meant to provoke laughter. The self-loathing at the heart of despair repudiates compassion.

I would guess that my generation, coming of age at the very start of the Sixties and a national mood of intense political and moral crisis, is the last American generation to so contemplate *inwardness* as a romantic state of being; the last generation of literary-minded young men and women who interiorized the elegiac comedy of Beckett's characters, the radiant madness of Dostoyevsky's self-lacerated God-haunted seekers, the subtle ironies of Camus's prose. I doubt that contemporary adolescents can identify with Faulkner's Quentin Compson of *The Sound and the Fury* as, a Harvard freshman, he moves with the fatedness of a character in a ballad to his suicide by drowning in the Charles River—"People cannot do anything that dreadful they cannot do anything very dreadful at all they cannot even remember tomorrow what seemed dreadful today," Quentin's alcoholic father tells him, as if urging him to his doom. For even tragedy, in Faulkner's vision of a debased twentieth-century civilization, is "second-hand."

That this is a profound if dismaying truth, or an outrageous libel of the human spirit, either position to be confirmed by history, seems beside the point today, in a country in which politics has become the national religion. The Literature of Despair may posit suicide as a triumphant act of rebellion, or a repudiation of the meanness of life, but our contemporary mood is one of compassionate horror at any display of self-destruction. We perceive it, perhaps quite accurately, as misguided politics; a failure to link *in here* with *out there*.

For Americans, the collective belief, the moral imperative is an unflagging optimism. We want to believe in the infinite elasticity of the future: what *we will*, we can *enact*. Just give us time—and sufficient resources. Our ethos has always been hardcore pragmatism as defined by our most eminent philosopher, William James: "truth" is something that happens to a proposition, "truth" is something that works. It is a vehicle empowered to carry us to our destination.

Yet there remains a persistent counterimpulse; an irresistible tug against the current; an affirmation of those awkward truths that, in Melville's words, will not be comforted. At the antipode of American exuberance and optimism there is the poet's small, still, private voice; the voice, most powerfully, of Emily Dickinson who, like Rilke, mined the ideal vocabulary for investigating those shifting, penumbral states of consciousness that do, in the long run, constitute our lives. Whatever our public identities may be, whatever our official titles, our heralded or derided achievements and the statistics that accrue to us like cobwebs, this is the voice we trust. For, if despair's temptations can be resisted, surely we become more human and compassionate; more like one another in our common predicament.

> There is a pain—so utter—
> It swallows substance up—
> Then covers the Abyss with Trance—
> So Memory can step
> Around—across—upon it—
> As one within a Swoon—
> Goes safely—where an open eye—
> Would drop Him—Bone by Bone.
> —Emily Dickinson

The self's resilience in the face of despair constitutes its own transcendence. Even the possibility of suicide is a human comfort—a "carrion" comfort. In the Jesuit Gerard Manley Hopkins, extreme states of mind are confronted, dissected, overcome by the poet's shaping language:

> I am gall, I am heartburn. God's most deep decree
> Bitter would have me taste: my taste was me;
> Bones built in me, flesh filled, blood brimmed the curse.
> Selfyeast of spirit a dull dough sours. I see
> The lost are like this, and their scourge to be
> As I am mine, their sweating selves; but worse.
> —"I Wake and Feel"

> Not, I'll not, carrion comfort, Despair, not feast on thee;
> Not untwist—slack they may be—these last strands of man
> In me or, most weary, cry *I can no more*. I can;
> Can something, hope, wish day come, not choose not to be.
> But ah, but O thou terrible, why wouldst thou rude on me
> Thy wring-earth right foot rock? lay a lionlimb against me? scan
> With darksome devouring eyes my bruised bones? and fan,
> O in turns of tempest, me heaped there; me frantic to avoid thee and flee?
> —"Carrion Comfort"

These poems are among the most unsettling ever written; yet, in the way of all great art, they so passionately transcend their subject as to be a statement of humankind's strength, and not weakness.

QUESTIONS FOR ANALYSIS AND DISCUSSION

1. Oates writes that "the despairing soul is a rebel." Then she discusses the moral status of suicide. Does despair lead to immoral rebellion? Or, for example, could rebellion lead to a moral or immoral despair? If you don't agree with these possible connections, what connection do you believe could exist among despair, suicide, and morality?

2. Why is suicide or despair a frustrating sin to outlaw? (For more on suicide see the essays by Quill and Bogen in Chapter 9.) Can you imagine a law that

could or should decrease the likelihood of suicide? Be specific. How would such a law affect despair?

3. Oates recognizes Emily Dickinson as one of the great teachers of despair. Why? Do the excerpts from Dickinson support Oates's praise? Be specific.

4. Oates illustrates human life in dark tones but concludes with an enthusiastic spotlight on human strength. Which qualities make up this strength? Do you think these qualities involve moral virtues? Do you think these qualities describe (a) the exception, (b) the few, (c) the majority, or (d) nearly all human beings? Briefly explain your choice.

58.

GABRIELE TAYLOR

Deadly Vices?

Though philosopher Gabriele Taylor does not address the essay by Joyce Carol Oates, in many ways Taylor's distinction between self-regarding and other-regarding virtues involves despair. Taylor focuses on sloth as a kind of human life with little worth. (See Chapter 10 for additional essays on sloth.) How can we tell if a life has little worth? Boredom, indolence, hopelessness, and despair are some of the moods or attitudes about the world that reflect a life of little worth, and these are aspects of sloth, Taylor argues. The counter to the life of sloth is a version of love, but one not traditionally considered a cardinal virtue.

CRITICAL READING QUESTIONS

1. Is idleness always a sign of sloth? If so, why? If not, when is it not?
2. What is the difference between a mood and an emotion?
3. What does Taylor have in mind when talking about the daughters of acedia?
4. Which new candidate for a major virtue does Taylor nominate? Why?

"Deadly Vices?" from *How Should One Live*, edited by Roger Crisp (Oxford, England: Oxford University Press, 1996). Notes have been omitted.

The vices, I take it, are the opposites of the virtues. This does not imply that every vice can neatly be paired off with a virtue. But it does imply that where virtues are thought to be beneficial, vices are harmful; while virtues are thought to contribute to human good and to be needed in human life, vices on the contrary are corruptive of such good and are an obstacle to human flourishing. Given these general descriptions both may then be classified according to who precisely benefits or is harmed by the exercise of a particular virtue or vice, whether or not its exercise requires a certain type of motivation, or what sorts of unfortunate human inclination they respectively counterbalance or encourage. So we may for instance identify a class of "social virtues" necessary for the smooth running of society; a class of "other-regarding virtues" the exercise of which is intended to benefit particular persons other than the agent herself, and where each exercise has to be motivated by concern for that other in order to count as an instance of a relevant virtue; and a class of what are sometimes labelled "self-regarding virtues," which do not require such motivation and which, while they may or may not benefit others, are thought to profit primarily the agent herself. The vices may be grouped similarly: some may be undermining of a harmonious life in society, some may harm individuals other than the person acting viciously, and some may be destructive mainly of that person herself.

An account of the virtues should explain in precisely what way they are needed in human life, and the extent to which we have reason for cultivating this or that particular virtue. Presumably some are needed more than are others. In certain cases, I think, this is best done negatively, i.e. by investigating the vice(s) which a cultivation of some virtue is designed to prevent. It seems to be true particularly of some members of the "self-regarding" class that an account of the nature and degree of damage engendered by the vice serves to demonstrate the need for countervailing virtues, the importance of which might otherwise be underestimated. I shall therefore concentrate on those vices which are thought to harm primarily the person possessing them, and ask what exactly that harm might amount to. By being harmful to her they are, probably inevitably, also harmful to others. But the harm to others is not necessarily prompted by malicious motives on the part of the agent. The coward, for example, may harm others in that she will fail to help them on those occasions when doing so would involve facing danger, which she cannot bring herself to do however compassionate her thoughts and intentions may be. A person possessing such vices, therefore, need not be immoral or wicked in the sense of denying that the well-being of others need ever be a reason for action, or of thinking that in the cause of her own advancement any means is justified. Since the harm is principally to the agent herself, and since it is unlikely that any sane person would want to harm herself, it seems that these vices must be unwanted by those prone to them. So what has here gone wrong?

There is a familiar pattern of faulty practical reasoning into which some self-regarding vices may quite plausibly be fitted. A person acts in a cowardly fashion, for instance, if believing herself to have an overriding reason for facing the danger confronting her she nevertheless does not do so; she is a coward if in such circumstances she mostly or always does not act as she herself believes she should; she acts against her own better judgement. Alternatively, she may be less clear-sighted about what she ought to do for either prudential or moral reasons: she may mis-read the situation and inaccurately weight the reasons she has for or against facing the danger precisely because her timidity prevents her from being clear about what it is more or less worth while for her do to. Her judgement is clouded, her reason-ing based on faulty premises. The disadvantages of either form of cowardice are obvious: she will not achieve what she herself wants to achieve; her life will by her own standards not be as good as it might have been. She will fail herself and others on all those occasions where she should act in spite of what she perceives as some risk. In extreme cases, seeing danger everywhere and not facing it, her life will be in a mess. This will have repercussions: she will be a nuisance to others, which will worsen her position, contribute to her misery, and so on. There are therefore good practical reasons for cultivating the virtue of courage.

If the coward nevertheless does not act on, or does not see, these reasons, then maybe the answer to the paradox of persisting in a course of conduct which is harmful to oneself is that in being weak or muddled she is a helpless victim of her feelings rather than an agent in control of her life. To accept, or dispute, this type of answer is to raise a problem I shall not deal with here, viz. that of responsibility. The vices, as well as being harmful, are thought to share with the virtues the char-acteristic of being subject to the will. This must be so, for we blame people for their vices and thereby imply that the exercise of control is possible, so that they can fairly be held responsible, at least to a degree, for their possessing them. Perhaps the notion of control has been given too much prominence. To make this aspect the focus of attention tends to result in undue emphasis being placed on matters of the will, on intention, choice, decision, and consequent action. But to isolate merely these features is to ignore the complexity of the phenomenon and leave quite unexplained the nature of the kinds of harm inflicted by characteristics we pick out as vices.

The two cases of cowardice as I have described them may give the impression that, if not in practice then at any rate theoretically, they can be clearly separated from one another, the flaw of one type of coward being in the will, that of the other in their faculty of judgement. But notoriously, the phenomenon of weakness of will needs explaining: the person concerned is in the paradoxical position of both accepting that she has an overriding reason for acting in a certain way and yet, since she does not act accordingly, also rejecting it as overriding. Her ac-ceptance seems intellectual merely, without emotional backing; there is a lack of whole-heartedness in her assessments of and attitudes towards her circumstances. If so, then there is here a connection with the second case envisaged, for the clouded judgement, too, was linked with emotional attitudes.

In some cases, at least, a more detailed scrutiny of these interrelated features is of interest in itself, as well as yielding a clearer picture of the nature of the harm entailed by some specific vice. This, I think, is so in the case of the so-called "deadly sins," given that label because they are said to bring death to the soul, and thus to constitute the most fundamental ways in which human beings may go wrong: pride, envy, covetousness, gluttony, sloth, lust, and anger are to be seen as different forms of corruption of the self and so totally destructive of a flourishing life. To think of these (or any other) vices as so fundamentally damaging must mean that

the kind of harm elicited from the model used for cowardice is relatively superficial. That harm was, after all, contingent on the circumstances of the person's life.
It is at least conceivable that she may encounter only a few and unimportant occasions where danger should be faced, that she has "moral luck" either in this
respect or in that the consequences of her timidity are not as harsh as has been
envisaged; maybe her charm is such that there are always friends ready to help.
For anything to count as a *deadly* vice such contingencies are presumably beside
the point. In order at least to indicate the complexity of this type of vice I shall
concentrate on only one of the traditional deadly sins. Though occupying perhaps
a unique place among them, it is nevertheless representative of the group in showing the undermining flaws to be in a person's inner emotional life and attitudes
rather than in her intention and action.

II

Looking at the history of the concept of acedia or sloth, it is clear that it has been
used to refer to many different though presumably related phenomena. In the
course of the Middle Ages, the understanding of acedia as a sin shifted from viewing it as a kind of depression and boredom with a specifically monastic form of life
to seeing it as a moral perversion of human nature in general, which might be
manifested by anybody. Naturally enough, cutting across this development, the
features of acedia emphasized by the scholastics differed from those expounded
in the more popular literature, designed to be practical and concrete. The latter
tended to look at the vice from an "external" point of view, as it shows itself in
behaviour. The slothful neglect their religious duties, they do not say their prayers,
they sleep through the sermon. They are lazy and idle. The "internal," scholarly
viewpoint, by contrast, concerns itself with the state of the person's soul or mind:
it is, after all, possible that she may be outwardly punctilious in performing her
duties but do so in the wrong spirit, full of doubt or without joy, for example.
"Sloth" therefore spans a wide range of both behavioural and mental phenomena,
of which among the most commonly mentioned are laziness, idleness, compla-
cency, cowardice, lack of imagination, irresponsibility, boredom, uneasiness of
mind, restlessness of body, verbosity, idle curiosity, melancholy, and despair. Only
some of these characteristics are likely to be associated with slothfulness today,
where (if we think in these terms at all) we think of the slothful as being generally
inactive, lazy, and indolent. If sloth is a vice, then it seems a wholly negative and
relatively harmless one: the slothful may not do much good, but they do not do
much harm, either. Our view of it tends to pick out the behavioural features of the
sin rather than internal states like boredom or despair, which makes it hard to see
why it should have been regarded as a deadly sin at all.

Behaviour by itself is not a good indicator of the vice, for what is seen as laziness
or idleness may not at all connect with a slothful state of mind, and conversely, the
relevant state of mind may not express itself in that type of behaviour. To be slothful is to be in an inactive and indolent state, but again, not all such states need be

destructive in the sense required for there to be a vice. It is a specific form of indolence which has to be identified.

A person may be in an indolent mood: she does not feel like doing anything at all. The mood itself may be felt as pleasant or unpleasant. At one extreme of the range of possible responses she may feel pleasantly lazy and relaxed, at the other feel unpleasantly inert, unable to move herself. Either way, short-lived and infrequent moods of this kind are unlikely to do much harm; feeling pleasantly lazy and free from demands may on the contrary be a healthy state which it is good every now and then to experience. The person who possesses the vice is not merely occasionally in the relevant mood of indolence; she has the character-trait slothfulness. To ascribe a character-trait is to label and so try to impose some order on a whole complex of behaviour and states of mind. We take ourselves to be isolating certain dominant tendencies to behave and dispositions to have certain thoughts and feelings which will help us to explain particular actions and reactions and to predict how she will behave and feel on other occasions. Such "explanations" may be quite minimal and tell us no more than that such behaviour and thoughts are only to be expected. But explanations in terms of character-traits may also be more substantial, in that they may shed light on conduct or feelings which are not usually thought typical of the character-trait in question. Those who are slothful may tend to be in the relevant mood for prolonged periods and behave in a manner expressive of this mood. But while I shall treat this position as the paradigm case of the vice, it is not the only way in which sloth may manifest itself.

Being in the mood of not wanting to do anything that needs effort may or may not be accompanied by the thought that none the less the situation is such that some effort is required. In each case further distinctions may be drawn. In the first case, the person who believes that no effort is required of her may do so on the grounds that, as it happens, there are at present no demands on her, that at the moment at least there are no duties to fulfil or prudential steps to be taken. It is this view of the situation which is most likely that of the person feeling pleasantly lazy. Alternatively, she may view the situation not as providing a temporary respite from such demands, but as being typical of many in her life in simply not offering anything worth making an effort for.

In the second case, those who believe that they should make some effort and resist their present state of indolence may see the demand to exert themselves as either externally or internally imposed. The protagonist of Goncharov's novel *Oblomov* will serve as an example to illustrate the difference. When we first meet Oblomov, in a state of complete physical and mental indolence, he is inclined to take the first, external, view of the situation. He can see that there is some urgency for him to bestir himself if various catastrophes are to be averted: unfortunately, the world is so arranged that he cannot do what he wants to do without having to expend some effort. But any kind of effort, in his view, interferes with enjoyment and should be avoided at all cost. The best he can do, therefore, is to forget about the demands of everyday life and return to his bed and enjoyable day-dreams. But although in this way he manages for much of the time to escape from thoughts of the unpleasantness of everyday demands on him and to enjoy his idleness, his state is clearly a precarious one. It seems that effort is required to ensure a more or less

effortless enjoyment of life, and this effort he will not make because it will interfere with his enjoyment of an effortless life. There is something irrational in this
state of affairs, an indication, perhaps, that here we have one form of sloth the vice.
On the other hand, the irrationality of his situation is a contingent one, depending
on the particular circumstances of his life. If the manager of his estate were an
honest man, if his landlord were more considerate and his servant not so lazy, he
might be able simply to enjoy his idleness. It is at least not clear that in such circumstances his indolence would amount to sloth.

Sometimes, however, Oblomov's mood changes: occasionally he sees that there
are worthwhile things to achieve in life, which he will not achieve because he will
not make the effort, because he cannot get himself sufficiently engaged with what
he thinks worth while to push him into activity. When in these moods, the demand
for effort is of the second, "internal," type and is not contingent on the specific
unfortunate states of affairs which happen to obtain. The external demands were
just a nuisance, but what he now sees as requiring effort is the achieving of something which is worth while in itself. When in this mood, he sees himself, rather
than his specific circumstances, as being the obstacle to his ever leading an admirable sort of life.

A person who tends to remain in a state of indolence in spite of recognizing that
there are urgent external demands will no doubt possess a number of failings: she
will be typically self-indulgent and weak-willed and probably cowardly in failing
to face up to the realities of life. All these are serious defects, but not, perhaps,
deadly sins. Given such demands she will be unable to enjoy the kind of idle existence she plans for herself. At a later period in his life, however, Oblomov appears
to have achieved just that. His circumstances have altered: an energetic friend
keeps an eye on his estates for him and secures a steady income; a devoted woman
is prepared to look after him without asking anything in return. There are no more
demands on him; he remains totally inactive and, it seems, is content. There is, on
the face of it, nothing destructive about this state, so it may be that, though hardly
admirable, this form of indolence does not add up to the vice. I shall return to this
point.

Where, however, the demands are internal ones, the person herself believes that
there is a worthwhile life for her to lead if only she could make the requisite effort.
Since she does not do so she is a failure in her own eyes and cannot be content. She
does not or cannot move herself sufficiently to make her life worth living. But a self
seen as failing to be engaged in worthwhile activities presents itself as a worthless
self. Hence a person in that state will take a gloomy view of herself, which will
tend to be self-perpetuating: a worthless self is not worth taking trouble over, so
there is no point in making any kind of effort on its behalf by finding worthwhile
things for it to do. So she may as well give up the thought of leading a worthwhile
life; there is no reason for her to bestir herself.

In all essentials this state of mind is also that of the person who acknowledged
no internal demands at all, who could see nothing in the situation worth making
any effort for. This is so because forms of evaluative awareness of the world cannot
be separated from conceptions of one's own position in the world so assessed, and
vice versa. Seeing nothing in the world worth engaging with, she also sees no rea-

son to engage herself with such a world. So she, too, is confronted by a self not meaningfully employed. The difference in the two states described is merely one of emphasis: in the first case the person concerned will be more likely to blame herself for this dismal state of affairs; in the second she may tend to see the fault in what she finds is on offer. Their common feature is that both are in a state of boredom.

We may be bored by this or that, on some specific occasion. Boredom, in this case, has an "object": the lecture, her chatter, the interminable play. If I am bored by the lecture then I see nothing in it to engage my attention and interest, maybe because it offers nothing new, maybe because it is above my head. But here I am; I have to do something with the time I was supposed to fill by listening. I may be able to divert myself by thinking about something else and so keep myself occupied. If so, then, although bored by the lecture, I am not bored. But I may not succeed in diverting myself. In that case the "object" of my boredom, the lecture, figures in my thoughts as an irritant, as an obstacle to not being bored; it is that which prevents me from doing something with this time which, as things are, hangs heavy on my hands. So I feel caught: that which is supposed to occupy my time does not in fact do so but merely prevents me from making a better use of it. I naturally want to escape from this situation.

The state of boredom is a negative one which we experience as unpleasant and so want to avoid if possible. In all cases time is the enemy. It is there to be done something with, but no content offers itself, and without content it passes extremely slowly, making it even more difficult to find something to fill it with. Of course, on those occasions where there is an "object" perceived by me to be causally responsible for my inability to deal with time, it is relatively straightforward to remedy my state by removing myself physically from the obstacle or by developing techniques for preventing the object of boredom from inducing a state of boredom. Boredom threatens to be a serious evil only when neither type of escape is possible, and this is paradigmatically the case when boredom is "objectless," when it is a mood rather than an emotion.

Moods are objectless in the sense that there is no specific thing, situation, or event which can be picked out and described independently of the mood itself and which the state is "about." This is not to say that the mood in question may not have been caused by some specific event, but even where it is so caused, and even where the person is aware of her mood's causal antecedents, it is not *felt* as motivated by particular situations. While she may be aware of causal links, she does not experience them as such, and consequently her state is not "about" what she may recognize as its cause. When in a mood-state, therefore, it is not a specific situation she will see in a certain light, as, e.g. threatening or insulting; her mood will colour everything in her perception. It is a constitutive feature of moods that they involve a way of seeing the world. They are distinguished from each other by the particular way in which the world is seen: in moods of elation everything is perceived as attractive and attainable, in moods of depression everything appears gloomy or irritating, the worthwhile out of one's reach. The difference between emotions and moods is reflected also, of course, in the person's actions and reactions. When in a mood-state, her tendency to behave in certain ways will not have a specific focus but will manifest itself more generally in an increased or decreased interest in the world around her, a greater readiness to be provoked, discouraged, or encouraged.

A person who is bored by some specific situation finds nothing of interest in that situation, sees nothing in it she can engage with. If she is in the mood-state of boredom then she can see nothing at all in the world to interest her, nothing that is worth engaging with. But if there is nothing to engage and interest her then life will seem quite meaningless. "[T]he only thing I see is emptiness, the only thing I move about in is emptiness. I do not even suffer pain," says Kierkegaard's aestheticist. Nothing is seen as either pleasurable or painful, so that nothing is seen as differentiated from anything else. In a world so seen no particular course of action will seem more attractive than another; there is nothing to engage one's desires and move one to act. Hence the bored will also tend to be indolent; not seeing any point in doing anything, they are inclined to do nothing and experience themselves as inert, as being heavy on their own hands.

It is this experience which is typical of that form of indolence which is sloth. To be in a slothful mood is to be in a state of which the interrelated components are feelings of physical and mental inertness and a cognitive appraisal of the world as not worth engaging with. And so, maybe, a slothful person is one who is inclined to be in that state. But this move is too simple; to pinpoint the vice, more needs to be said about the nature and dimensions of this form of indolence. Aquinas, in reply to the objection that sloth cannot be a mortal sin since even the virtuous may suffer from it, makes the point that there may be an inclination towards such a state even in holy men, but they are not therefore sinful because they withhold rational consent. I want to incorporate this point by offering one possible interpretation of what it is to consent to one's state.

In order to do so, further distinctions between mental states need to be drawn: I have spoken of moods of boredom and indolence. But moods may be thought of either as occurrent or as standing. For a person to be in some occurrent mood is for her to see the world in the relevant way and to have the experience of so seeing it, to have the appropriate feeling. To have the experience of seeing nothing worth making an effort for, for example, is to feel inert. I shall speak of a person who is in an occurrent indolent mood as being in a state of indolence.

It is occurrent moods which have the two elements spoken of earlier: a form of awareness and an experienced consciousness on the agent's part of this awareness. A "standing mood" refers to the former only. Occurrent moods are changeable and may be quite short-lived. The standing mood, the relevant form of awareness, may live and die with the person's experience of it. But it may also outlast it; it is compatible with a whole range of other occurrent moods. I shall refer to a person's standing mood as her frame of mind. A frame of mind which is long-lasting may be called an attitude, and if that attitude is dominant in a person's life in that it governs a high proportion of her moods and behaviour, then it will be a character-trait.

Reference to a standing mood will be explanatory. It will be explanatory in the minimal sense if what is "explained" is the corresponding occurrent mood; but it will offer a more substantial explanation when the occurrent mood is a different one. Not thinking anything worth making an effort for minimally explains her present inertness, but more substantially explains, for example, her present hopelessness or despair. The claim here is that her frame of mind is causally responsible for her present state of mind; a causal connection not hard to explain since the given view of the world and herself is naturally undermining of all hope and joy. In this sense despair and hopelessness are indeed "daughters" of acedia.

The distinction between occurrent and standing moods was introduced to explain how "consenting to one's state" might be understood: it is to let the state of mind turn into a frame of mind which comes to dominate one's life. It is to be uncritical of that form of awareness and hence not to try to modify it in any way but to let it become established. The slothful, then, are not those who are merely inclined to be in the occurrent mood of indolence, but are those who do not oppose such inclination even in thought, who by not attempting to alter their vision of the world encourage those occurrent states which are causally dependent on that frame of mind.

The most important aspect of this form of consent is to allow oneself to take the relevant particular view of oneself: that the self is a worthless one. There is no point in engaging such a self. The form of awareness is that of boredom. As earlier it was the lecture or play that was seen by the person as the obstacle to her doing something with the time there was, it is now herself in the state of inertness that is the obstacle. Evidently, she cannot remove herself from herself as she could remove herself from the lecture, nor can she comfort herself with the thought that the spell of boredom will end when the lecture is over. It is the self so perceived which is the "object" of sloth and is the source of its destructiveness. The slothful person will not be able to respect or like herself and thereby precludes even the possibility of her leading a flourishing life.

III

Constitutive of the vice, on this account, is a certain view of the world and of the self, and hence a shift in vision the only remedy. In the paradigm case the slothful person's frame of mind will be operative in states of indolence and tend to manifest itself also in states of hopelessness and despair. But there are other, less obviously destructive cases of sloth. At one period in his life Oblomov appears to be no longer in the grip of indolence. He is attracted to Olga, and under her influence seems to be leading a more or less normally active life. Nevertheless, although no longer idle, there has, I think, been no fundamental change; basically he is as indolent as he has ever been. Yet activity, on the face of it, is incompatible with indolence, and is often prescribed as its cure. Kant, as is only to be expected, speaks of activity as part of life's sustenance. "It is by his activities and not by enjoyment that man feels that he is alive," he says. Kierkegaard's aestheticist, however, expresses the opposite view: he thinks of activity as being a kind of restlessness which is incompatible with the spiritual life. Seen in this way, idleness is a good rather than an evil. Hence merely being active or non-idle is not a desirable state. It is, according to him, enjoyment rather than activity with which we should fill our lives.

Both sides have a point, and their respective points are acceptable once their different understandings of "activity" are disentangled. Kant thinks of being active as implying a whole-hearted and rationally justified commitment on the part of the agent. The aestheticist, by contrast, has in mind a "being busy," a form of being active which lacks the implication of fully engaging the agent and being worth the effort expended on it. It is activity and not busyness which is incompatible with indolence. This is not to deny that busyness may well be a way of not consenting to one's state, if embarked on in the hope that it will turn into activity. But I shall ignore this possibility and assume no such motivation.

The person who is merely busy may or may not believe at the time that what she is doing is worth while. In the latter case she knows herself to be unengaged and is only superficially different from the slothful person so far described. But even temporary engagement is no indication of activity rather than busyness. Kant remarks that "The present may, indeed, seem full to us, but if we have filled it with play, etc., the appearance of fullness will be confined to the present. Memory will find it empty." The valid point here is not whether we have filled the time with play or work but whether looking back we think of it as a superficial filling only, and so a waste of time. Looking back we find that what we took to be a worthwhile engagement was nothing of the sort.

The person's own view, either at the time or in retrospect, is then one indication of her being busy rather than active. But the superficiality of the engagement may also show itself in a lock of being goal-directed: since her commitment to whatever she is doing is a merely shallow one it will not generate reasons for embarking on a coherent, life-guiding plan of action. Oblomov is stimulated or bullied by Olga into periods of non-idleness, but his engagements remain isolated occurrences with no aim or cohesion. A person who is busy, therefore, while not outwardly idle, is nevertheless indolent. Her frame of mind has not changed, though she may be more successful in avoiding the corresponding state of mind. In such a case her life is quite likely to exhibit that form of restlessness which in medieval literature was cited as a consequence of sloth.

The possibility of busyness has introduced a variation and complication into the paradigmatic case of slothfulness initially discussed. The indolent person is not now totally unengaged, but her engagement is a shallow one. If aware of its super-ficiality she will still tend to find time heavy on her hands, and experience herself as inert and bored; consequently she, too, is prey to depression and despair. On the other hand, being engaged at all, if only temporarily and superficially, may offer a distraction, a way of avoiding such low states of mind, and in particular may enable her to avoid taking such a grim view of herself. The obvious disadvantages of living with a wholly negative view of oneself make it tempting and natural to try to persuade oneself that one is active and not merely busy. But if, as claimed earlier, the requisite view of the self is an essential ingredient of the vice, then busyness would after all seem to offer an escape, provided she manages to hide her lack of proper engagement from herself. For such self-deception to succeed she would have to make it appear to herself and others that her engagements are not merely shallow, that they do generate life-guiding commitments. If it is possible so to deceive oneself then it would be impossible to tell that she is merely busy. But given that her frame of mind is that of the slothful, the coherence in her life will be sham; she will not really care.

But why should this matter? If no one, including the person herself, can tell whether her life is sham and her engagement shallow, then it seems that it will make no difference at all to her, and the remedy to suggest to those who are disposed towards sloth is to try to practice self-deception until they are perfect at it. It would certainly prevent them from suffering hopelessness and despair, which are consequent only on facing the situation. But it seems paradoxical to suggest that possession of a vice can be avoided by such means. On the contrary, deceiving oneself should surely make matters even worse?

It is, however, not possible for a person in the given frame of mind to deceive herself to the extent envisaged. In her view there is nothing worth taking trouble over, and this includes herself. It is true that this frame of mind need not manifest itself in certain specific states of mind, such as hopelessness and despair. But it will have some causal efficacy: some states or attitudes are incompatible with it. It is a frame of mind which precludes doing anything with joy, and in particular, it makes it impossible to respect or love oneself. Consequently, the self-deceived person will not be able to avoid taking a negative view of herself. It is indeed part of her self-deception that she will not articulate this view, that she will not spell it out to herself, but it will nevertheless be operative in everything she does. It is in this sense that self-deception cannot be complete. While self-deception may save the person concerned some actual suffering, it does not enable her to lead a flourishing life; and rather than being a means of escape from the vice it constitutes a form of consenting to it.

IV

Traditionally the seven deadly sins are thought of as exhibiting misguided or deficient love. It is a consequence of the characteristics of the vice outlined above that the slothful, not being engaged with anything, do not love anything, and this includes themselves. Self-love does not normally appear on any list specifying virtues, for it is thought that we can be trusted to love ourselves anyway, the danger being that we love ourselves too much rather than too little. But the nature of the harm suffered by the slothful seems to imply that such a virtue is required, though of course not any kind of love will do. Self-concern is presumably that kind of love which we are so prone to that it is more likely to be an obstacle to virtuous behaviour than itself a virtue. Equally, the self-indulgence of an Oblomov is the wrong type of love, if love at all. Self-indulgence is not only compatible with self-contempt, it may even be its ground; it is constitutive of one manifestation of sloth.

This suggests that it is perhaps self-respect rather than self-love that is required. The slothful's lack of self-respect is indeed fundamentally damaging, and the possession of it, therefore, secures freedom from the vice. A Kantian notion of respect, however, with its requirement that it be based on admirable characteristics and hence universalizable, implies a degree of detachment and rationality which seems inappropriate in the virtue set in opposition to a vice anchored in the person's affective state. The characteristics of the opposing virtue should be such that they counter the emotional as well as the cognitive aspects of the vice, the feelings of inertia as well as the specific mode of awareness. The person possessing the virtue will, therefore, not only differentiate between the more or less worthwhile and hence think of some things as being more worth achieving than others, she will in particular experience herself as being engaged with the worthwhile, with what she thinks worth caring for. Sloth and its countervailing virtue may then be seen as manifesting themselves in opposing forms of self-consciousness.

One implication of the form of consciousness constitutive of the virtue is that it will generate self-respect, not in the sense of a favourable self-assessment, but in that a self discriminating between the more or less worthwhile will at the same time be self-discriminating, i.e. be aware of what is more and what is less worth her making an effort for. If engaged accordingly she will necessarily respect herself: to respect oneself is to be conscious of being valuably employed. It does not require a self-consciousness in the sense of being aware of oneself as being so employed; her consciousness is directed rather at what she cares for, not at herself as caring for these things. But in being self-discriminating she cannot be indifferent as to whether or not she is engaged with what strikes her as worth while, and so she cares about her caring. Since in this sense she may be said to care for herself, there is here one reason why "self-love" is not an inappropriate label for this virtue.

Possession of the virtue, corresponding to possession of the vice, has two interrelated aspects: a certain perspective on the world and a feeling response. The fact that she believes what she is doing worth while provides her with reason for further pursuing it and for embarking on related projects. Particularly relevant in the present context is her being (obliquely) aware of herself being so engaged. She will, as a consequence, be feeling alive. At the very least she will not be in the grip of feelings of apathy and inertia, for she will be doing something with herself rather than be an obstacle in her way. Awareness of doing something with oneself is itself a source of pleasure and a stimulation for further activity, thus providing further reason for remaining involved, and a sense of being in control. In contrast to the slothful she not only is able to live with herself, she is in a position to enjoy living with herself. For this reason, too, the virtue opposing the vice of sloth may be spoken of as self-love.

Considerations of this kind indicate that self-deception cannot be a way of escaping from the vice. For the inertness and lack of all pleasure in anything one does and hence in oneself, which is consequent on the given frame of mind, will remain and affect one's being, however much one may try to shut one's mind to it. The self-deceived suffer from that malady of spirit of which one indication is the lack of harmony between motivation and evaluation: they do not care for what moves them to act, and consent to their state by disguising this split from themselves. Nor is contentment with one's state an indication that all is well with one's life. If it is true that a degree of self-love, in the sense given, is a necessary antidote to sloth, then an Oblomov undisturbed by external demands has not escaped from the vice, even if he is content with his state. He, too, has consented to his indolence by his having reconciled himself to the withering away of whatever internal demands he once experienced.

QUESTIONS FOR ANALYSIS AND DISCUSSION

1. In the Jordan-Smith essay on "saligia" (Chapter 3), sloth was at the bottom of the vices, for it was considered the deadliest. A central reason lies in the sloth-ful person's spiritual death. Do you think Taylor has a similar explanation in mind, even though she hardly talks about God or religion? In developing your answer, consider what is meant by "spiritual death."

2. Incorporating some of the thoughts of existentialists such as Soren Kierke-gaard, Taylor writes that sloth is more than a mood that overcomes the mor-ally troubled person. Rather, sloth reflects a *choice* made by the person. How do you understand her claim? Do you agree that sloth is a choice? Would a rational person make such a choice? Why, or why not?

3. Taylor introduces self-love as a new virtue. What qualities make up self-love? Compare Taylor's view of self-love with the virtues of humility, pride, vanity, and courage discussed in other readings in this chapter.

59.

JOAN DIDION

On Self-Respect

If television talk shows trivialize or sensationalize the value of self-respect, that does not mean we should stop considering its moral importance. According to essayist and novelist Joan Didion (b. 1934), self-respect is something like the bed we make for ourselves. The extent to which the bed is comfortable or uncomfortable reflects the kind of character and life we have made. The sense of comfort, however, should not be construed as a kind of

---

"On Self-Respect," from *Slouching Towards Bethlehem* by Joan Didion (New York: Farrar, Straus, & Giroux, 1968), pp. 729–733.

pleasure. Rather, writes Didion, it involves our willingness to face up to both the successes and the failures for which we are responsible. This responsibility becomes, in turn, the source for developing the virtuous qualities that help us gain a sense of self-worth and prepare for the future. Echoing Aristotle's thought that pride is the crown of the virtues, Didion adds her own twist in showing how self-respect is the basis for living by other virtues, such as courage and love, and avoiding vices, such as sloth.

⊢ CRITICAL READING QUESTIONS ⊢

1. What is Didion's point in retelling her Phi Beta Kappa story?
2. Why is a person without self-respect compared to an "interminable documentary"?
3. What kind of courage do persons of self-respect have?
4. How is the problem of self-deception related to self-respect?

Once, in a dry season, I wrote in large letters across two pages of a notebook that innocence ends when one is stripped of the delusion that one likes oneself. Although now, some years later, I marvel that a mind on the outs with itself should have nonetheless made painstaking record of its every tremor, I recall with embarrassing clarity the flavor of those particular ashes. It was a matter of misplaced self-respect.

I had not been elected to Phi Beta Kappa. This failure could scarcely have been more predictable or less ambiguous (I simply did not have the grades), but I was unnerved by it; I had somehow thought myself a kind of academic Raskolnikov, curiously exempt from the cause-effect relationships which hampered others. Although even the humorless nineteen-year-old that I was must have recognized that the situation lacked real tragic stature, the day that I did not make Phi Beta Kappa nonetheless marked the end of something, and innocence may well be the word for it. I lost the conviction that lights would always turn green for me, the pleasant certainty that those rather passive virtues which had won me approval as a child automatically guaranteed me not only Phi Beta Kappa keys but happiness, honor, and the love of a good man; lost a certain touching faith in the totem power of good manners, clean hair, and proven competence on the Stanford-Binet scale. To such doubtful amulets had my self-respect been pinned, and I faced myself that day with the nonplused apprehension of someone who has come across a vampire and has no crucifix at hand.

Although to be driven back upon oneself is an uneasy affair at best, rather like trying to cross a border with borrowed credentials, it seems to me now the one condition necessary to the beginnings of real self-respect. Most of our platitudes notwithstanding, self-deception remains the most difficult deception. The tricks that work on others count for nothing in that very well-lit back alley where one keeps assignations with oneself: no winning smiles will do here, no prettily drawn lists of good intentions. One shuffles flashily but in vain through one's marked cards—the kindness done for the wrong reason, the apparent triumph which involved no real effort, the seemingly heroic act into which one had been shamed. The dismal fact is that self-respect has nothing to do with the approval of others—who are, after all, deceived easily enough; has nothing to do with reputation, which, as Rhett Butler told Scarlett O'Hara, is something people with courage can do without.

To do without self-respect, on the other hand, is to be an unwilling audience of one to an interminable documentary that details one's failings, both real and imagined, with fresh footage spliced in for every screening. *There's the glass you broke in anger, there's the hurt on X's face; watch now, this next scene, the night Y came back from Houston, see how you muff this one.* To live without self-respect is to lie awake some night, beyond the reach of warm milk, phenobarbital, and the sleeping hand on the coverlet, counting up the sins of commission and omission, the trusts betrayed, the promises subtly broken, the gifts irrevocably wasted through sloth or cowardice or carelessness. However long we postpone it, we eventually lie down alone in that notoriously uncomfortable bed, the one we make ourselves. Whether or not we sleep in it depends, of course, on whether or not we respect ourselves.

To protest that some fairly improbable people, some people who *could not possibly respect themselves,* seem to sleep easily enough is to miss the point entirely, as surely as those people miss it who think that self-respect has necessarily to do with not having safety pins in one's underwear. There is a common superstition that "self-respect" is a kind of charm against snakes, something that keeps those who have it locked in some unblighted Eden, out of strange beds, ambivalent conversations, and trouble in general. It does not at all. It has nothing to do with the face of things, but concerns instead a separate peace, a private reconciliation. Although the careless, suicidal Julian English in *Appointment in Samarra* and the careless, incurably dishonest Jordan Baker in *The Great Gatsby* seem equally improbable candidates for self-respect, Jordan Baker had it, Julian English did not. With that genius for accommodation more often seen in women than in men, Jordan took her own measure, made her own peace, avoided threats to that peace: "I hate careless people," she told Nick Carraway. "It takes two to make an accident."

Like Jordan Baker, people with self-respect have the courage of their mistakes. They know the price of things. If they choose to commit adultery, they do not then go running, in an access of bad conscience, to receive absolution from the wronged parties; nor do they complain unduly of the unfairness, the undeserved embarrassment, of being named co-respondent. In brief, people with self-respect exhibit a certain toughness, a kind of moral nerve; they display what was once called *character,* a quality which, although approved in the abstract, sometimes loses ground to other, more instantly negotiable virtues. The measure of its slipping prestige is that one tends to think of it only in connection with homely children and United States senators who have been defeated, preferably in the primary, for reelection. Nonetheless, character—the willingness to accept responsibility for one's own life—is the source from which self-respect springs.

Self-respect is something that our grandparents, whether or not they had it, knew all about. They had instilled in them, young, a certain discipline, the sense that one lives by doing things one does not particularly want to do, by putting fears and doubts to one side, by weighing immediate comforts against the possibility of larger, even intangible, comforts. It seemed to the nineteenth century admirable, but not remarkable, that Chinese Gordon put on a clean white suit and held Khartoum against the Mahdi; it did not seem unjust that the way to free land in California involved death and difficulty and dirt. In a diary kept during the winter of 1846, an emigrating twelve-year-old named Narcissa Cornwall noted coolly: "Father was busy reading and did not notice that the house was being filled with strange Indians until Mother spoke about it." Even lacking any clue as to what Mother said, one can scarcely fail to be impressed by the entire incident: the father reading, the Indians filing in, the mother choosing the words that would not alarm, the child duly recording the event and noting further that those particular Indians were not, "fortunately for us," hostile. Indians were simply part of the *donnée*.

In one guise or another, Indians always are. Again, it is a question of recognizing that anything worth having has its price. People who respect themselves are willing to accept the risk that the Indians will be hostile, that the venture will go bankrupt, that the liaison may not turn out to be one in which *every day is a holiday because you're married to me*. They are willing to invest something of themselves; they may not play at all, but when they do play, they know the odds.

That kind of self-respect is a discipline, a habit of mind that can never be faked but can be developed, trained, coaxed forth. It was once suggested to me that, as an antidote to crying, I put my head in a paper bag. As it happens, there is a sound physiological reason, something to do with oxygen, for doing exactly that, but the psychological effect alone is incalculable; it is difficult in the extreme to continue fancying oneself Cathy in *Wuthering Heights* with one's head in a Food Fair bag. There is a similar case for all the small disciplines, unimportant in themselves; imagine maintaining any kind of swoon, commiserative or carnal, in a cold shower.

But those small disciplines are valuable only insofar as they represent larger ones. To say that Waterloo was won on the playing fields of Eton is not to say that Napoleon might have been saved by a crash program in cricket; to give formal dinners in the rain forest would be pointless did not the candlelight flickering on the liana call forth deeper, stronger disciplines, values instilled long before. It is a kind of ritual, helping us to remember who and what we are. In order to remember it, one must have known it.

To have that sense of one's intrinsic worth which constitutes self-respect is potentially to have everything: the ability to discriminate, to love and to remain indifferent. To lack it is to be locked within oneself, paradoxically incapable of either love or indifference. If we do not respect ourselves, we are on the one hand forced to despise those who have so few resources as to consort with us, so little perception as to remain blind to our fatal weaknesses. On the other, we are peculiarly in thrall to everyone we see, curiously determined to live out—since our self-image is untenable—their false notions of us. We flatter ourselves by thinking this compulsion to please others an attractive trait: a gist for imaginative empathy, evidence of our willingness to give. Of *course* I will play Francesca to your Paolo, Helen Keller to anyone's Annie Sullivan: no expectation is too misplaced, no role too ludicrous. At the mercy of those we cannot but hold in contempt, we play roles doomed to failure before they are begun, each defeat generating fresh despair at the urgency of divining and meeting the next demand made upon us.

It is the phenomenon sometimes called "alienation from self." In its advanced stages, we no longer answer the telephone, because someone might want something; that we could say *no* without drowning in self-reproach is an idea alien to this game. Every encounter demands too much, tears the nerves, drains the will, and the specter of something as small as an unanswered letter arouses such disproportionate guilt that answering it becomes out of the question. To assign unanswered letters their proper weight, to free us from the expectations of others, to give us back to ourselves—there lies the great, the singular power of self-respect. Without it, one eventually discovers the final turn of the screw: one runs away to find oneself, and finds no one at home.

QUESTIONS FOR ANALYSIS AND DISCUSSION

1. What is meant by "alienation from self"? How can you tell if you or someone else suffers from self-alienation? Do you agree with Didion that someone without self-respect is unhappy?

2. Self-deception is a tricky issue, yet it is a central problem to developing moral character and ethical conduct. What is Didion's description of self-deception? Can self-deception ever be a good thing? Why, or why not?

3. How does self-respect lead to other virtues and help us avoid other vices? If you were to set up your own ranking of the virtues (or vices), would you agree with Aristotle and Didion that self-respect is the most important virtue? Do you agree with Richards that humility is the key to the good life? Do you share the flavor of skepticism or cynicism sketched by Kaminer or Voltaire? If you think that none of the self-regarding virtues discussed in this chapter deserve the top rank, what virtue is most important? Why?

CHAPTER EIGHT

Morality and the Other

The Other becomes my neighbor precisely through the way the face summons me, calls for me, begs for me, and in so doing recalls my responsibility, and calls me into question.
— Emmanuel Levinas, "Ethics As First Philosophy"

The third form stood outside the well and beneath the stone. It was clothed in a daz-zlingly white garment, and its countenance radiated such splendor that my own face had to draw back from it. Before and above these three (forms) appeared — like clouds — the blessed ranks of the saints, who gazed intently down at them.
— Hildegard von Bingen, "Eighth Vision"

I walk over to the nearby 7-Eleven for a soda. "Have some spare change?" a beggar asks. I decline, thinking to myself that any change left will go to my lottery ticket rather than the beggar's fund for cheap wine that will keep him warm tonight.

You are sitting on the front steps when a car suddenly pulls over. The driver jumps out and yells at you in barely recognizable English. You panic and call 911. The cops arrive, talk to the driver, then ask why you wasted their time over some-one who is asking for directions to a friend's house.

A neighbor brings her children home from school. The little girl sings a lyric her classmates just learned: "Home is on the ranger, don't trust a stranger."

These observations take on philosophical and moral importance when we con-sider how and why we treat certain people differently from others. The source of intense debate among social and political thinkers, otherness is a central theme in modern life. Which policies and institutions marginalize others? How does a coun-try's culture and history exclude those not like ourselves? Which forms of differ-ence do we resist, and which do we assimilate — and at what price? These are the kinds of questions that highlight controversies about which literary books to as-sign in schools, whether various forms of sexual or gender identities should be part of the school curriculum or be broadcast on prime time television or whether fa-miliar cultural icons as diverse as Christopher Columbus, the *Enola Gay,* Thanks-giving, the Miss America pageant, or Independence Day should be recognized.

Important as these disputes are, they are not entirely new. In his trial for impi-ety, Socrates explained how part of his mission involved answering the Delphic Oracle's riddle that he is the wisest of all. Socrates learned that only he was aware of his ignorance after realizing how others made their reputation by concealing their ignorance. The golden rule emphasizes consideration of what you do to others when thinking about how you want others to treat you. Many passages in the Bible call for hospitality and kindness to strangers. And thinkers outside the Western philosophical tradition, such as the Dalai Lama and Lao Tzu, encourage questioning yourself by thinking of other ways of being.

What recent philosophers have added to this important theme in moral thought is the idea that our concern for others might not be anchored by our knowledge of them. This, of course, is directly contrary to the reasoning of moral egoists such as Harry Browne (see Chapter 1) who assert we should attend to our own interests because we know best what our interests are. Utilitarians acknowledge the limitations of moral egoism (see Chapter 2). Their outlook largely dismisses moral sanctions rooted in superstition or passion. They neglect the rational ability humans have in knowing what their common interests are. Under the umbrella of "the other," moral thinkers address those aspects of life that we may not be able to know. Others are unlike ourselves, yet their pull on our moral conduct is undeniable.

The readings in this chapter were selected in large part for their ability to introduce and examine the significance of others in our lives. The case study by the Reverend Daniel Berrigan, political activist and writer, invites you to a meditation on helping those who are dying. Here we learn of a woman calling Berrigan to attend her son who is dying from AIDS.

The selections following this case study are organized into sets of three. The first three selections focus on the human others. Philosopher Nel Noddings outlines some of the central features of what she calls the virtue of care. For her, this virtue is exemplified by women as they attend to the needs of others regardless of self-interest. Feminist philosopher Sarah Hoagland characterizes the care ethic as formulated by Noddings as historically and politically naive. That women seem to be the model for care should be construed as a negative rather than a positive virtue, says Hoagland, for it represents the sustained exploitation of women in the name of moral goodness. Two feminist philosophers, Alisa Carse and Hilde Nelson, offer a rejoinder to Nodding's critics. They believe the virtue of care contains a model of moral conduct that is historically embraced by women and that deserves to be emulated by all moral persons.

The second set of readings addresses nature as the other. British philosopher Ray Racy clarifies the moral concern we owe to animals as a matter of justice. How we treat humans should be the basis for how we treat animals, excepting minor qualifications. Bill Shaw, a professor of business and law, goes further than Racy, proposing that virtue ethics should respect all of nature. This respect, according to Shaw, includes two familiar virtues: prudence and practical judgment. The problem with these moral attitudes lies in their confusing sense of nature. According to historian William Cronon, the idea of nature as other has undergone a rather sudden transformation from wild to tame. Though Cronon is sympathetic to moral concerns for the ecology, he cautions against an intellectual misunderstanding of humanity's view of nature.

The final threesome introduce what we might call the intangible or abstract other. American philosopher Josiah Royce promotes loyalty to a cause greater than the self as the key to a meaningful life. Though he does not endorse a specific cause, Royce believes there are enough values or movements in the world to give every moral person a chance to live a life guided by loyalty. Medieval visionary and composer Hildegard von Bingen portrays a life devoted to spiritual goodness. The virtues of love, humility, and peace underscore this life in which one discovers something greater than the conventional self. Finally, Plato speculates on the love that goes beyond the changing dynamics of human passion to the love for something eternal—truth. We are so attached to our worldly selves, Socrates suggests in *The Symposium*, that we have difficulty appreciating the beauty that results from the love of truth.

60.

DANIEL BERRIGAN

Case Study: In the Evening We Will Be Judged by Love

Father Berrigan (b. 1921), with his brother Philip and other friends, is a well-known peace activist. He has been jailed numerous times protesting military programs. Berrigan also devotes considerable effort to accompanying those who are dying. How does one do this? Here Berrigan retells the last days of Luke, a friend's nephew, who is dying from AIDS, likely caught by "deviant conduct."

⊢ CRITICAL READING QUESTIONS ⊢

1. What is meant by the world's cornucopia?
2. How does Berrigan clarify the term *catholic*?
3. Why is the nurse reviewing the hospital menu with Luke in his death-bed an irony?
4. Which virtues does Berrigan learn from Luke?

"In the Evening We Will Be Judged by Love," from *Sorrow Built a Bridge: Friendship and AIDS* (Baltimore, MD: Fortkamp Publishing,1989), pp. 3–14.

It started with a phone call from a nun. There was trouble in her family.

It would seem that the affliction she alluded to should at very least be given a name; especially when, as in this instance, an urgent SOS was being issued.

Eventually the affliction was named by the caller, with fear and trembling. But the illness was by no means dwelt on, as to effect, symptom; above all, cause. Only the terror, the grief.

It was clear once more; the illness in question is more than a disease. It carries a baleful light of the supernatural, it stands oblique and blind and menacing outside medical category. In the mind of the beholder it is mated with deviant conduct, it conjures up dark corners where the unspeakable festers away.

I must add that the voice on the phone held none of this dark coloration of innuendo. It was as though the caller were, in the midst of great suffering, reaching out to a last resort. Fairly straightforwardly: "My nephew has AIDS. You were on a college faculty with his uncle, a Jesuit, Father So-and-so. Luke has survived for a matter of three years. The latest bout seems final; both cancer and pneumonia. Will you visit him?"

Other talents, other strokes. Our world is a wondrous cornucopia indeed; it contains cardsharpers and belly dancers, poets, flamenco guitarists, hang gliders and money-market players—stars of the firmament all, native winners. And then other sorts, drawn, for reasons that utterly escape them (us, me)—drawn to such scenes as AIDS.

These latter will bear scrutiny. They are cursed with a very connoisseurship in such summonses as I describe. They are even found useful there.

To speak shortly, it seems as though the world of pain is their turf; native, never moony or distant. On that planet where humans are born only to go under, they are granted a royal welcome. The world is, alas, densely populated; the planet as terminal ward.

What does the planet look like? Well, for one thing, and here and now—like the ravaged landscape of a single face. Telltale splotches, the color of damp soil. Lazarine, as though the grave spots still clung to the risen. (But here we have the bitter reverse of a miracle, death claiming the young and vigorous.)

❦ ❦ ❦

Luke's hospital room was altogether familiar. I could have entered it blindfolded. Nor was it a stranger who languished there; I knew him. Something of a recognition scene, old Walt Whitman or the Latin poet Horace; nothing human foreign to me.

Human indeed. A face pressed by an unseen hand into a new form, new contours of bones, cheek, socket. Death looked out of him, that old taker and giver, mortality and then presto! immortality. I thought, not of death but of Yeats and "the face I had before the world was made."

His face was cleared for action, no missing it. Or it was a pro tem face, borrowed. On consignment, was that the phrase?

There would be a day, and not far distant, when the claim fell due.

❦ ❦ ❦

Most days his parents made their way into Manhattan.

They were more or less bewildered, a low voltage panic. In such a world, will someone make sense of it all? Please?

As far as could be judged, there was no God around to tell them the score. There was only brute fact. Reasoning stopped here, solutions there were none. There was only ruin, disaster, blighted hope.

And the priest standing there, what of him?

If truth were told, he was as ignorant as they. An ignorance that was something more than a hiatus in the mind. It was more like a working principle. You might even call it a source of endurance, if not courage.

It went something like this. He knew nothing of the why of God, or the why of AIDS. And he came to the hospital, and stood with the parents and their dying son.

There was a strange kinship here, of ignorance. He knew nothing as they knew nothing; or as near nothing as to make no difference.

The so-called working principle, it went to work. One might even say in a sorry sense, it worked.

In this way: being almost dumb, having little to say, he would not offer false comfort or a quick fix.

Nor would he play God. He knew the only god one could mime in such circumstances was an inferior one, a ventriloquist's doll mouthing someone else's platitudes. So he kept quiet.

Why not? He could offer no formulas to comfort their suffering.

Any more than God did. True God that is, merciless God, the God of Jesus on the cross and "Why have you forsaken me?" The God of silence, of turning aside, the God of "not yet," the God of no comment. The God who bore with extermination camps and torture rooms and the disappeared. The God of this world; a world of contras and wicked judges and drug kingpins and police beatings and abortion abattoirs and electric chairs.

Dare we say: the God who walks this world, who bears with all this, who groans and weeps? who is patient—even with the likes of us?

In any case. The priest's strength (or what passed muster for strength) was a simple act of the will. At least it set the priest free, it relieved his dumb and heavy ignorance, made it bearable. He wanted to be there. To be with this afflicted pair and their son. To go through it all with them. This, he thought, might be the substance of that "answer" we lust after, and in so lusting, forget to frame the question aright.

A question such as—have You really abandoned us, left us to our sorry resources and sorrier outcomes? Or are You really here, in our midst, helping us find a human way together, two added to two, parents, priest, son? and so doing, come to a peace, a lightness of heart, even laughter now and then?

And summoning a laugh or a cheerful face, can we let the ominous undercurrent flow along, but kept under, where it belongs? I mean that stream, icy and scalding, tears, stalemate, onset of grief, outcries.

These too. But in their time and place.

Meantime, in this place, meeting for the first time, without a word we came to a common resolve. To forbid that current a takeover, determining mood and word, owning us. Like the shadow of a lamprey in a free-running stream. Let it keep its distance.

❧ ❧ ❧

A parallel occurs to me, a scene in the gospel. The Lord enters a room where the daughter of the house has died. The family are mourning uncontrollably. And He comes in.

He has no word of comfort. Indeed he speaks sharply, in reproof. As though to ask indignantly, why do you pay unseemly tribute to necessity and nature? As though the Lord of Life could, to any right understanding, arrive "too late."

Then it blazes out: "She is not dead, but sleeping."

They break out in derision, but he puts them to the door. And proceeds to raise the child from death.

It is that diagnosis of His that clings in the mind. Not dead, but sleeping. Not dying, but going toward life.

❧ ❧ ❧

I thought also of a visit a few years back, to Northern Ireland. We arrived in Belfast in the midst of the crisis in Long Kesh prison. We lodged with the families of prisoners, we witnessed their grief and pain; and in those humble homes were treated royally.

And now and again, in this or that pub, we celebrated together.

And this transpired, it must be understood, in the midst of the prisoners' fast, and the death eventually of twelve of them. There we sat with the families and the pub crowd, lifting our ale in salute, singing.

It seemed right to do so. Despite all. Some sixth sense in us went deeper than the brute fact of impending death. Something about surpassing death by celebrating life.

A matter of hope in a bad time. Of hope against a wall, and in that testing, that stalemate, vindicating itself; hope, and no illusion, no base or frivolous substitute.

Those we love (so our hope went) may be taken from us by death. Indeed they will be. But this is hardly the last word; there is more to be said, the Savior has said so. More, he has gone through it all, and come out. He knows whereof he speaks. So we, in face of death, act in the world as though this great thing were true.

The grave is a hole reversed, an empty pocket.

Thus we and the prisoners' families raised our glasses, and sang together, and toasted the dying. Whom we loved and mourned. And more.

This is the strength of that thing we name, and now and again see in its grandeur and strength, "catholic."

❧ ❧ ❧

Well, there he lay, Luke, master chef, trained in France, lately owner of his own restaurant in Brooklyn.

Now everything was "lately," everything on hold. You couldn't miss it in his eyes, in the calm level blur of a voice, bled of emotion. He knew. In his best moments (which were most of them), he was—accepting. Taking what came with a laconic, understated nobility.

He spoke now and then of the good days, the cafe, overseeing waiters, marketing, trying out recipes, pleasing and teasing those finicky New York palates. Mindful, remembering. But not lustful, not nostalgic or resentful. Done with all that.

His hand and foot were swollen and empurpled and twice their normal size. Useless, they lay on pillows like limbs become ikons or relics.

And the parents in the background, greeting the priest. "Of course we remember you. God knows we heard you preach last New Year's at Saint Francis Xavier."

Well well.

We had a few memories in common, no great thing. But enough to distill some half-hour into a semblance of reason, the small talk that saves.

I walked with them to the elevator. "He'll never leave here. Nothing to do but prepare him for a good death." The mother mourned.

Nothing indeed.

"He's fought so long and so hard." She looked me longingly in the eye, awaiting something; reassurance. Would he die a "good catholic"? Would I see to that?

Know it or not, the son was already seeing to that. On his own, with their goodness at his side. Therefore say nothing, for now.

Against all expectations he went home, swollen limbs and all, the lungs still congested.

I visited his apartment, a small cove in Chelsea. It was snug and neat; in the living room, unusual urban amenities; a fine brick wall and a fireplace.

There he held court, grayfaced, his hair a mere wisp of coarse straw. Death nearing, but on his phiz a smile that turned the heart over. And stuck on his head, visor reversed, the most rakish baseball cap of that or any season.

A fading pro, a dying ballplayer. And no giving up. The season was over, pennants were out, life was a holiday. Hail to the champ!

I brought flowers and a wedge of brie. On the phone, when I asked what I should bring along, he said; "Of course, brie. I'm not supposed to have it, but what the hell."

"Tell me about that restaurant of yours."

"Well, I came back from France with a bit of money. I wanted to open my own place. So I took out an ad in the *Times*, seeking a partner, and found someone with cash in hand. We rented a storefront in a tough neighborhood. We wanted to do something other than chic, a French and Italian menu, good food at decent prices.

"We took a big chance. And we lost, lasted only a year. I can see now the mistakes we made."

A faint, lurking regret. That was all.

A day later, on the phone. "You know that cheese you brought. I was sick for twenty-four hours afterward."

"What an ending to a party!"

"Yeah. But didn't we have a good time!"

The news was, he had to go back to hospital. "I haven't told the folks yet. They'll know soon enough."

What was it (my heart sinking) this time?

"They want to do an implant in the chest. Something about direct chemotherapy."

Then; "Daniel, how did you know when to phone? Your timing's perfect."

How come?

"Well, I'm alone today, a mixup with the visiting help. I've been trying to reach her, but no go. I worry about her, she has kids."

I was learning. Down and out is strictly relative. More, down and out is a spiritual matter. It says something about One Body, All of Us.

And relative. Put it this way: when life is seen whole and steady, someone else is always downer and outer.

Some thirty-six years ago I was ordained. Shortly thereafter, I remember preaching on a text of St. John of the Cross; "In the evening we will be judged by love."

I think of Luke; and of what a mild and gentle judgment that will be.

My friend will be judged by love. Which is to say, he will not be judged, but embraced.

What draws us to the embrace of love is a courage akin to his. The courage to believe, church and state notwithstanding, the only judgment will be that of love.

Luke, in his flat New York brogue. In the middle of a discussion on the latest symptomatic horror, he'll suddenly break off, "Now what about you? What're you up to?"

Courage, he seems to say, no big deal. Thereby indicating by indirection how big a deal it is. Courage sums him up, that sparse, barely ambulatory shadow of a figure, as he makes an old man's way from chair to bed and back again.

He is much on my mind.

I learn from him. To believe. To say, as seldom before, I believe in the resurrection of the body.

The present state of that body, awful as it is, and appalling as it must be to its person—that body is all the more dazzling and beautiful in its import. For all of that, all taken in account.

His sores are a kind of stunning negative apologia.

The least likely event in all creation is that this frame of his, ruined and rent as it is, and utterly bereft of temporal prospect, should be the subject of apotheosis.

That this wasted weakened frame should become a resurrected body, lithe and weightless and free of the awful necessities of mortal flesh?

Nothing less likely, goes the holy illogic. Therefore nothing more true.

So near removal he is, soon to be thrust out of time and place. He is in a truly spectacular position, a kind of box seat adjacent to eternity. Able from there, from that extraordinary vantage point, to tell what shall shortly be. To tell of resurrection.

Not by dying, certainly (anyone can die; most of us will)—but by living as he does.

Another visit. He's bound hand and foot to that wheel of grief known as time. In his case, hospital time.

But for his eyes, still lively and watchful, he could already have been consigned to the permanent underground.

I enter. Someone unidentifiable, masked, is addressing the patient in a high pitched singsong. She is, it appears, the hospital dietitian. Her tones are punishing, she stands at safe distance from the bed and its hypothetical contaminations. Rants on of this and that, and mainly nothing at all.

The scene is hilarious, if one has heart for it. She is revealing as to a little child, certain esoteric information concerning hospital menus. The difference, otherwise unattainable by mortals like him, between pureed and ground food! And all conveyed with deadly seriousness. How to relieve dry fowl "with a spot of butter or gravy." And so on.

I listen, my jaw hangs witless. The woman is instructing, apparently without knowing or caring, the quondam chef of a gourmet restaurant of some note.

She departs. We grin like two goblins in the night.

I venture a word of praise for his patience. He receives the tribute equably.

I tell him there is something of his Jesuit uncle about him; I remember a modest man of scholarly achievement, and a splendid teacher.

"Too bad I never got to know him well, he was always the scholar and I had no talent in that direction."

I returned one day, he was sleeping. I sat within range of his eyes. His poor sunken eyes opened and slowly focused. I was wearing a white shirt, Indian fashion, against the heat of the season.

"Good God," he quipped hoarsely. "That beautiful shirt! I thought for a moment we'd both made it."

I was not to see him again. Within days he was in better hands than ours. Faith, though blind with tears, assures us it is so.

His mother wrote, "Luke was the peacemaker in our family. He had great courage and a wonderful sense of humor. . . . Just in the last weeks of his life, when he and I had a quiet moment alone, he took my hand in his and said, 'I know I'm not leaving the hospital, but I've accepted it. It's all right, but I'm concerned for you and Dad. Please don't grieve for me.'"

He meant the request with all his rugged failing heart. And he knew it could not be honored.

"We grieve for him," his mother continued, "but we know that he is with the Lord and at peace and freed from his terrible suffering."

QUESTIONS FOR ANALYSIS AND DISCUSSION

1. In which ways is Luke much different from Berrigan, or you, or me? Do you think these differences would be enough for most people not to worry about Luke? Why, or why not?

2. Is everyone entitled to accompaniment when dying? Or should only moral persons receive such accompaniment?

3. Before the nineteenth century, one criterion for being a moral person was preparation for another's dying. Though this often had religious intent—last rites, final confession, declaration of one's belief in God—even nonreligious people believed we should accompany those who are dying. Historians call this the *ars moriendi* tradition. Indeed, an unwanted or immoral death was one in which an individual died alone or suddenly. Nowadays people are more likely to express a desirable death as one that happens suddenly, preferably in one's sleep so the person is not even aware of the imminence of death. In such cases one is likely to die in isolation. What are your thoughts on accompanying the dying? How is this a moral effort to help the other? Do you agree with Berrigan that such accompaniment is moral? Can it make sense without a belief in the soul or God? Clarify your views.

61.

NEL NODDINGS

Caring

In Chapter 1 Nel Noddings articulates a view of the self as fundamentally related to others. This contrasts with the moral theories of egoism and utilitarianism, which assume that individuals are self-contained or independent of one another. Here Noddings develops a consequence of that position, what she calls the virtue of care. Religious moralists understand the care ethic as a combination of love and charity, but Noddings notes several distinctions that, in her view, show that the virtue of care is an entirely new way of approaching moral life. It includes both a personal and a social good. Moreover, notes Noddings, the virtue of care should not be relegated to a minor status because historically it has been associated with women. Rather, caring requires some of the most important virtues, such as courage, and is difficult to carry out.

⊢ CRITICAL READING QUESTIONS ⊢

1. Which does Noddings favor, a morality of attitude or a morality of judgment? Why?

2. What is the difference between natural caring and ethical caring?

3. Why does Noddings reject the virtues embodied by a monk or religious ascetic?

4. How does the biblical story of Abraham's sacrifice of Isaac reflect a male's approach to ethics in contrast to a woman's approach to ethics?

5. If a juror adopts the care ethic, how should the juror decide in a trial that involves the possible execution of the guilty party?

"Caring," from *Caring: A Feminine Approach to Ethics and Moral Education* (Berkeley: University of California Press, 1984), chapter 1 with deletions. Notes have been omitted.

Ethics and Caring

It is generally agreed that ethics is the philosophical study of morality, but we also speak of "professional ethics" and a "personal ethic." When we speak in the second way, we refer to something explicable—a set of rules, an ideal, a constellation of expressions—that guides and justifies our conduct. One can, obviously, behave ethically without engaging in ethics as a philosophical enterprise, and one can even put together an ethic of sorts—that is, a description of what it means to be moral—without seriously questioning what it means to be moral. Such an ethic, it seems to me, may or may not be a guide to moral behavior. It depends, in a fundamental way, on an assessment of the answer to the question: What does it mean to be moral? This question will be central to our investigation. I shall use "ethical" rather than "moral" in most of our discussions but, in doing so, I am assuming that to behave ethically is to behave under the guidance of an acceptable and justifiable account of what it means to be moral. To behave ethically is not to behave in conformity with just any description of morality, and I shall claim that ethical systems are not equivalent simply because they include rules concerning the same matters or categories.

In an argument for the possibility of an objective morality (against relativism), anthropologist Ralph Linton makes two major points that may serve to illuminate the path I am taking. In one argument, he seems to say that ethical relativism is false because it can be shown that all societies lay down rules of some sort for behavior in certain universal categories. All societies, for example, have rules governing sexual behavior. But Linton does not seem to recognize that the content of the rules, and not just their mere existence, is crucial to the discussion of ethicality. He says, for example, ". . . practically all societies recognize adultery as unethical and punish the offenders. The same man who will lend his wife to a friend or brother will be roused to fury if she goes to another man without his permission." But, surely, we would like to know what conception of morality makes adultery "wrong" and the lending of one's wife "right." Just as surely, an ethical system that renders such decisions cannot be equivalent to one that finds adultery acceptable and wife lending unacceptable.

In his second claim, Linton is joined by a substantial number of anthropologists. Stated simply, the claim is that morality is based on common human characteristics and needs and that, hence, an objective morality is possible. That morality is rooted somehow in common human needs, feelings, and cognitions is agreed. But it is not clear to me that we can move easily or swiftly from that agreement to a claim that objective morality is possible. We may be able to describe the moral impulse as it arises in response to particular needs and feelings, and we may be able to describe the relation of thinking and acting in relation to that impulse; but as we tackle these tasks, we may move farther away from a notion of objective morality and closer to the conviction that an irremovable subjective core, a longing for goodness, provides what universality and stability there is in what it means to be moral.

I want to build an ethic on caring, and I shall claim that there is a form of caring natural and accessible to all human beings. Certain feelings, attitudes, and memories will be claimed as universal. But the ethic itself will not embody a set of universalizable moral judgments. Indeed, moral judgment will not be its central concern. It is very common among philosophers to move from the question: What is morality? to the seemingly more manageable question: What is a moral judgment? Fred Feldman, for example, makes this move early on. He suggests:

> Perhaps we can shed some light on the meaning of the noun "morality" by considering the adjective "moral." Proceeding in this way will enable us to deal with a less abstract concept, and we may thereby be more successful. So instead of asking "What is morality?" let us pick one of the most interesting of these uses of the adjective "moral" and ask instead, "What is a moral judgment?"

Now, I am not arguing that this move is completely mistaken or that nothing can be gained through a consideration of moral judgments, but such a move is not the only possibility. We might choose another interesting use of the adjective and ask, instead, about the moral impulse or moral attitude. The choice is important. The long-standing emphasis on the study of moral judgments has led to a serious imbalance in moral discussion. In particular, it is well known that many women— perhaps most women—do not approach moral problems as problems of principle, reasoning, and judgment. . . . If a substantial segment of humankind approaches moral problems through a consideration of the concrete elements of situations and a regard for themselves as caring, then perhaps an attempt should be made to enlighten the study of morality in this alternative mode. Further, such a study has significant implications, beyond ethics, for education. If moral education, in a double sense, is guided only by the study of moral principles and judgments, not only are women made to feel inferior to men in the moral realm but also education itself may suffer from impoverished and one-sided moral guidance.

So building an ethic on caring seems both reasonable and important. One may well ask, at this point, whether an ethic so constructed will be a form of "situation ethics." It is not, certainly, that form of act-utilitarianism commonly labeled "situation ethics." Its emphasis is not on the consequences of our acts, although these are not, of course, irrelevant. But an ethic of caring locates morality primarily in the pre-act consciousness of the one-caring. Yet it is not a form of agapism. There is no command to love nor, indeed, any God to make the commandment. Further, I shall reject the notion of universal love, finding it unattainable in any but the most abstract sense and thus a source of distraction. While much of what will be developed in the ethic of caring may be found, also, in Christian ethics, there will be major and irreconcilable differences. Human love, human caring, will be quite enough on which to found an ethic.

We must look even more closely at that love and caring.

An Ethic of Caring

From Natural to Ethical Caring

David Hume long ago contended that morality is founded upon and rooted in feeling—that the "final sentence" on matters of morality, "that which renders morality an active virtue"—". . . this final sentence depends on some internal sense or feeling, which nature has made universal in the whole species. For what else can have an influence of this nature?"

What is the nature of this feeling that is "universal in the whole species"? I want to suggest that morality as an "active virtue" requires two feelings and not just one. The first is the sentiment of natural caring. There can be no ethical sentiment without the initial, enabling sentiment. In situations where we act on behalf of the other because we want to do so, we are acting in accord with natural caring. A mother's caretaking efforts in behalf of her child are not usually considered ethical but natural. Even maternal animals take care of their offspring, and we do not credit them with ethical behavior.

The second sentiment occurs in response to a remembrance of the first. Nietzsche speaks of love and memory in the context of Christian love and Eros, but what he says may safely be taken out of context to illustrate the point I wish to make here:

> There is something so ambiguous and suggestive about the word love, something that speaks to memory and to hope, that even the lowest intelligence and the coldest heart still feel something of the glimmer of this word. The cleverest woman and the most vulgar man recall the relatively least selfish moments of their whole life, even if Eros has taken only a low flight with them.

This memory of our own best moments of caring and being cared for sweeps over us as a feeling—as an "I must"—in response to the plight of the other and our conflicting desire to serve our own interests. There is a transfer of feeling analogous to transfer of learning. In the intellectual domain, when I read a certain kind of mathematical puzzle, I may react by thinking, "That is like the sailors, monkey, and coconuts problem," and then, "Diophantine equations" or "modulo arithmetic" or "congruences." Similarly, when I encounter an other and feel the natural pang conflicted with my own desires—"I must—I do not want to"—I recognize the feeling and remember what has followed it in my own best moments. I have a picture of those moments in which I was cared for and in which I cared, and I may reach toward this memory and guide my conduct by it if I wish to do so.

Recognizing that ethical caring requires an effort that is not needed in natural caring does not commit us to a position that elevates ethical caring over natural caring. Kant has identified the ethical with that which is done out of duty and not out of love, and that distinction in itself seems right. But an ethic built on caring strives to maintain the caring attitude and is thus dependent upon, and not superior to, natural caring. The source of ethical behavior is, then, in twin sentiments—

one that feels directly for the other and one that feels for and with that best self, who may accept and sustain the initial feeling rather than reject it.

We shall discuss the ethical ideal, that vision of best self, in some depth. When we commit ourselves to obey the "I must" even at its weakest and most fleeting, we are under the guidance of this ideal. It is not just any picture. Rather, it is our best picture of ourselves caring and being cared for. It may even be colored by acquaintance with one superior to us in caring, but, as I shall describe it, it is both constrained and attainable. It is limited by what we have already done and by what we are capable of, and it does not idealize the impossible so that we may escape into ideal abstraction.

Now, clearly, in pointing to Hume's "active virtue" and to an ethical ideal as the source of ethical behavior, I seem to be advocating an ethic of virtue. This is certainly true in part. Many philosophers recognize the need for a discussion of virtue as the energizing factor in moral behavior, even when they have given their best intellectual effort to a careful explication of their positions on obligation and justification. When we discuss the ethical ideal, we shall be talking about "virtue," but we shall not let "virtue" dissipate into "the virtues" described in abstract categories. The holy man living abstemiously on top of the mountain, praying thrice daily, and denying himself human intercourse may display "virtues," but they are not the virtues of one-caring. The virtue described by the ethical ideal of one-caring is built up in relation. It reaches out to the other and grows in response to the other.

Since our discussion of virtue will be embedded in an exploration of moral activity we might do well to start by asking whether or under what circumstances we are obliged to respond to the initial "I must." Does it make sense to say that I am obliged to heed that which comes to me as obligation?

Obligation

There are moments for all of us when we care quite naturally. We just do care; no ethical effort is required. "Want" and "ought" are indistinguishable in such cases. I want to do what I or others might judge I ought to do. But can there be a "demand" to care? There can be, surely, no demand for the initial impulse that arises as a feeling, an inner voice saying "I must do something," in response to the need of the cared-for. This impulse arises naturally, at least occasionally, in the absence of pathology. We cannot demand that one have this impulse, but we shrink from one who never has it. One who never feels the pain of another, who never confesses the internal "I must" that is so familiar to most of us, is beyond our normal pattern of understanding. Her case is pathological, and we avoid her.

. . .

Let me try to make plausible my contention that the moral imperative arises directly. And, of course, I must try to explain how caring and what I am calling the "moral imperative" are related. When my infant cries in the night, I not only feel that I must do something but I want to do something. Because I love this child, because I am bonded to him, I want to remove his pain as I would want to remove my own. The "I must" is not a dutiful imperative but one that accompanies the "I want." If I were tied to a chair, for example, and wanted desperately to get free, I might say as I struggled, "I must do something; I must get out of these bonds." But this "must" is not yet the moral or ethical "ought." It is a "must" born of desire.

The most intimate situations of caring are, thus, natural. I do not feel that taking care of my own child is "moral" but, rather, natural. A woman who allows her own child to die of neglect is often considered sick rather than immoral; that is, we feel that either she or the situation into which she has been thrust must be pathological. Otherwise, the impulse to respond, to nurture the living infant, is overwhelming. We share the impulse with other creatures in the animal kingdom. Whether we want to consider this response as "instinctive" is problematic, because certain patterns of response may be implied by the term and because suspension of reflective consciousness seems also to be implied (and I am not suggesting that we have no choice), but I have no difficulty in considering it as innate. Indeed, I am claiming that the impulse to act in behalf of the present other is itself innate. It lies latent in each of us, awaiting gradual development in a succession of caring relations. I am suggesting that our inclination toward and interest in morality derives from caring. In caring, we accept the natural impulse to act on behalf of the present other. We are engrossed in the other. We have received him and feel his pain or happiness, but we are not compelled by this impulse. We have a choice; we may accept what we feel, or we may reject it. If we have a strong desire to be moral, we will not reject it, and this strong desire to be moral is derived, reflectively, from the more fundamental and natural desire to be and to remain related. To reject the feeling when it arises is either to be in an internal state of imbalance or to contribute willfully to the diminution of the ethical ideal.

But suppose in a particular case that the "I must" does not arise, or that it whispers faintly and disappears, leaving distrust, repugnance, or hate. Why, then, should I behave morally toward the object of my dislike? Why should I not accept feelings other than those characteristic of caring and, thus, achieve an internal state of balance through hate, anger, or malice?

The answer to this is, I think, that the genuine moral sentiment (our second sentiment) arises from an evaluation of the caring relation as good, as better than, superior to, other forms of relatedness. I feel the moral "I must" when I recognize that my response will either enhance or diminish my ethical ideal. It will serve either to increase or decrease the likelihood of genuine caring. My response affects me as one-caring. In a given situation with someone I am not fond of, I may be able to find all sorts of reasons why I should not respond to his need. I may be too busy. He may be undiscerning. The matter may be, on objective analysis, unimportant. But, before I decide, I must turn away from this analytic chain of thought and back to the concrete situation. Here is this person with this perceived need to which is attached this importance. I must put justification aside temporarily. Shall I respond? How do I feel as a duality about the "I" who will not respond?

I am obliged, then, to accept the initial "I must" when it occurs and even to fetch it out of recalcitrant slumber when it fails to awake spontaneously. The source of my obligation is the value I place on the relatedness of caring. This value itself arises as a product of actual caring and being cared-for and my reflection on the goodness of these concrete caring situations.

Now, what sort of "goodness" is it that attaches to the caring relation? It cannot be a fully moral goodness, for we have already described forms of caring that are natural and require no moral effort. But it cannot be a fully nonmoral goodness either, for it would then join a class of goods many of which are widely separated from the moral good. It is, perhaps, properly described as a "premoral good," one that lies in a region with the moral good and shades over into it. We cannot always decide with certainty whether our caring response is natural or ethical. Indeed, the decision to respond ethically as one-caring may cause the lowering of barriers that previously prevented reception of the other, and natural caring may follow.

. . .

Before turning to a discussion of "right" and "wrong" and their usefulness in an ethic of caring, we might try to clear up the problem earlier mentioned as a danger in any ethic of virtue; the temptation to withdraw from the public domain. It is a real danger. Even though we rejected the sort of virtue exhibited by the hermit-monk on the mountaintop, that rejection may have been one of personal choice. It still remains possible that an ethic of caring is compatible with the monk's choice, and that such an ethic even induces withdrawal. We are not going to be able to divide cases clearly. The monk who withdraws only to serve God is clearly under the guidance of an ethic that differs fundamentally from the ethic of caring. The source of his ethic is not the source of ours, and he might deny that any form of human relatedness could be a source for moral behavior. But if, when another intrudes upon his privacy, he receives the other as one-caring, we cannot charge him with violating our ethic. Further, as we saw in our discussion of the one-caring, there is a legitimate dread of the proximate stranger—of that person who may ask more than we feel able to give. We saw there that we cannot care for everyone. Caring itself is reduced to mere talk about caring when we attempt to do so. We must acknowledge, then, that an ethic of caring implies a limit on our obligation.

Our obligation is limited and delimited by relation. We are never free, in the human domain, to abandon our preparedness to care; but, practically, if we are meeting those in our inner circles adequately as ones-caring and receiving those linked to our inner circles by formal chains of relation, we shall limit the calls upon our obligation quite naturally. We are not obliged to summon the "I must" if there is no possibility of completion in the other. I am not obliged to care for starving children in Africa, because there is no way for this caring to be completed in the other unless I abandon the caring to which I am obligated. I may still choose to do something in the direction of caring, but I am not obliged to do so. When we discuss our obligation to animals, we shall see that this is even more sharply limited by relation. We cannot refuse obligation in human affairs by merely refusing to enter relation; we are, by virtue of our mutual humanity, already and perpetually in potential relation. Instead, we limit our obligation by examining the possibility of completion. In connection with animals, however, we may find it possible to refuse relation itself on the grounds of a species-specific impossibility of any form of reciprocity in caring.

Now, this is very important, and we should try to say clearly what governs our obligation. On the basis of what has been developed so far, there seem to be two criteria: the existence of or potential for present relation, and the dynamic potential for growth in relation, including the potential for increased reciprocity and, perhaps, mutuality. The first criterion establishes an absolute obligation and the second serves to put our obligations into an order of priority.

If the other toward whom we shall act is capable of responding as cared-for and there are no objective conditions that prevent our receiving this response—if, that is, our caring can be completed in the other—then we must meet that other as one-caring. If we do not care naturally, we must call upon our capacity for ethical caring. When we are in relation or when the other has addressed us, we must respond as one-caring. The imperative in relation is categorical. When relation has not yet been established, or when it may properly be refused (when no formal chain or natural circle is present), the imperative is more like that of the hypothetical: I must if I wish to (or am able to) move into relation.

The second criterion asks us to look at the nature of potential relation and, especially, at the capacity of the cared-for to respond. The potential for response in animals, for example, is nearly static; they cannot respond in mutuality, nor can the nature of their response change substantially. But a child's potential for increased response is enormous. If the possibility of relation is dynamic—if the relation may clearly grow with respect to reciprocity—then the possibility and degree of my obligation also grows. If response is imminent, so also is my obligation. This criterion will help us to distinguish between our obligation to members of the nonhuman animal world and, say, the human fetus. We must keep in mind, however, that the second criterion binds us in proportion to the probability of increased response and to the imminence of that response. Relation itself is fundamental in obligation.

I shall give an example of thinking guided by these criteria, but let us pause for a moment and ask what it is we are trying to accomplish. I am working deliberately toward criteria that will preserve our deepest and most tender human feelings. The caring of mother for child, of human adult for human infant, elicits the tenderest feelings in most of us. Indeed, for many women, this feeling of nurturance lies at the very heart of what we assess as good. A philosophical position that has difficulty distinguishing between our obligation to human infants and, say, pigs is in some difficulty straight off. It violates our most deeply cherished feeling about human goodness. This violation does not, of course, make the position logically wrong, but it suggests that especially strong grounds will be needed to support it. In the absence of such strong grounds—and I shall argue in a later chapter that they are absent—we might prefer to establish a position that captures rather than denies our basic feelings. We might observe that man (in contrast to woman) has continually turned away from his inner self and feeling in pursuit of both science and ethics. With respect to strict science, this turning outward may be defensible; with respect to ethics, it has been disastrous.

Now, let's consider an example: the problem of abortion. Operating under the guidance of an ethic of caring, we are not likely to find abortion in general either right or wrong. We shall have to inquire into individual cases. An incipient embryo is an information speck—a set of controlling instructions for a future human being. Many of these specks are created and flushed away without their creators' awareness. From the view developed here, the information speck is an information speck, it has no given sanctity. There should be no concern over the waste of "human tissue," since nature herself is wildly prolific, even profligate. The one-caring is concerned not with human tissue but with human consciousness—with pain, delight, hope, fear, entreaty, and response.

But suppose the information speck is mine, and I am aware of it. The child-to-be is the product of love between a man deeply cared-for and me. Will the child have his eyes or mine? His stature or mine? Our joint love of mathematics or his love of mechanics or my love of language? This is not just an information speck; it is endowed with prior love and current knowledge. It is sacred, but I—humbly, not presumptuously—confer sacredness upon it. I cannot, will not destroy it. It is joined to loved others through formal chains of caring. It is linked to the inner circle in a clearly defined way. I might wish that I were not pregnant, but I cannot destroy this known and potentially loved person-to-be. There is already relation albeit indirect and formal. My decision is an ethical one born of natural caring.

But suppose, now, that my beloved child has grown up; it is she who is pregnant and considering abortion. She is not sure of the love between herself and the man. She is miserably worried about her economic and emotional future. I might like to convey sanctity on this information speck; but I am not God—only mother to this suffering cared-for. It is she who is conscious and in pain, and I as one-caring move to relieve the pain. This information speck is an information speck and that is all. There is no formal relation, given the breakdown between husband and wife, and with the embryo, there is no present relation; the possibility of future relation—while not absent, surely—is uncertain. But what of this possibility for growing response? Must we not consider it? We must indeed. As the embryo becomes a fetus and, growing daily, becomes more nearly capable of response as cared-for, our obligation grows from a nagging uncertainty—an "I must if I wish"—to an utter conviction that we must meet this small other as one-caring.

If we try to formalize what has been expressed in the concrete situations described so far, we arrive at a legal approach to abortion very like that of the Supreme Court; abortions should be freely available in the first trimester, subject to medical determination in the second trimester, and banned in the third, when the fetus is viable. A woman under the guidance of our ethic would be likely to recognize the growing possibility of relation; the potential is clearly dynamic. Further, many women recognize the relation as established when the fetus begins to move about. It is not a question of when life begins but of when relation begins.

But what if relation is never established? Suppose the child is born and the mother admits no sense of relatedness. May she commit infanticide? One who asks such questions misinterprets the concept of relatedness that I have been struggling to describe. Since the infant, even the near-natal fetus, is capable of relation—of the sweetest and most unselfconscious reciprocity—one who encounters the infant is obligated to meet it as one-caring. Both parts of this claim are essential; it is not only the child's capability to respond but also the encounter that induces obligation. There must exist the possibility for our caring to be completed in the other. If the mother does not care naturally, then she must summon ethical caring to support her as one-caring. She may not ethically ignore the child's cry to live.

The one-caring, in considering abortion as in all other matters, cares first for the one in immediate pain or peril. She might suggest a brief and direct form of counseling in which a young expectant mother could come to grips with her feelings. If the incipient child has been sanctified by its mother, every effort must be made to help the two to achieve a stable and hopeful life together; if it has not, it should be removed swiftly and mercifully with all loving attention to the woman, the conscious patient. Between these two clear reactions is a possible confused one: the young woman is not sure how she feels. The one-caring probes gently to see what has been considered, raising questions and retreating when the questions obviously have been considered and are now causing great pain. Is such a view "unprincipled"? If it is, it is boldly so; it is at least connected with the world as it is, at its best and at its worst, and it requires that we—in espousing a "best"—stand ready to actualize that preferred condition. The decision for or against abortion must be made by those directly involved in the concrete situation, but it need not be made alone. The one-caring cannot require everyone to behave as she would in a particular situation. Rather, when she dares to say, "I think you should do X," she adds, also, "Can I help you?" The one under her gaze is under her support and not her judgment.

One under the guidance of an ethic of caring is tempted to retreat to a manageable world. Her public life is limited by her insistence upon meeting the other as one-caring. So long as this is possible, she may reach outward and enlarge her circles of caring. When this reaching out destroys or drastically reduces her actual caring, she retreats and renews her contact with those who address her. If the retreat becomes a flight, an avoidance of the call to care, her ethical ideal is diminished. Similarly, if the retreat is away from human beings and toward other objects of caring—ideas, animals, humanity-at-large, God—her ethical ideal is virtually shattered. This is not a judgment, for we can understand and sympathize with one who makes such a choice. It is more in the nature of a perception: we see clearly what has been lost in the choice.

Our ethic of caring—which we might have called a "feminine ethic"—begins to look a bit mean in contrast to the masculine ethics of universal love or universal justice. But universal love is illusion. Under the illusion, some young people retreat to the church to worship that which they cannot actualize; some write lovely poetry extolling universal love; and some, in terrible disillusion, kill to establish the very principles which should have entreated them not to kill. Thus are lost both principles and persons.

. . .

Women and Morality: Virtue

Many of us in education are keenly aware of the distortion that results from undue emphasis on moral judgments and justification. Lawrence Kohlberg's theory, for example, is widely held to be a model for moral education, but it is actually only a hierarchical description of moral reasoning. It is well known, further, that the description may not be accurate. In particular, the fact that women seem often to be "stuck" at stage three might call the accuracy of the description into question. But perhaps the description is accurate within the domain of morality conceived as moral justification. If it is, we might well explore the possibility that feminine nonconformity to the Kohlberg model counts against the justification/judgment paradigm and not against women as moral thinkers.

Women, perhaps the majority of women, prefer to discuss moral problems in terms of concrete situations. They approach moral problems not as intellectual problems to be solved by abstract reasoning but as concrete human problems to be lived and to be solved in living. Their approach is founded in caring. Carol Gilligan describes the approach:

> . . . women not only define themselves in a context of human relationship but also judge themselves in terms of their ability to care. Woman's place in man's life cycle has been that of nurturer, caretaker, and helpmate, the weaver of those networks of relationships on which she in turn relies.

Faced with a hypothetical moral dilemma, women often ask for more information. It is not the case, certainly, that women cannot arrange principles hierarchically and derive conclusions logically. It is more likely that they see this process as peripheral to or even irrelevant to moral conduct. They want more information, I think, in order to form a picture. Ideally, they need to talk to the participants, to see their eyes and facial expressions, to size up the whole situation. Moral decisions are, after all, made in situations; they are qualitatively different from the solution of geometry problems. Women, like act-deontologists in general, give reasons for their acts, but the reasons point to feelings, needs, situational conditions, and their sense of personal ideal rather than universal principles and their application.

As we have seen, caring is not in itself a virtue. The genuine ethical commitment to maintain oneself as caring gives rise to the development and exercise of virtues, but these must be assessed in the context of caring situations. It is not, for example, patience itself that is a virtue but patience with respect to some infirmity of a particular cared-for or patience in instructing a concrete cared-for that is virtuous. We must not reify virtues and turn our caring toward them. If we do this, our ethic turns inward and is even less useful than an ethic of principles, which at least remains indirectly in contact with the acts we are assessing. The fulfillment of virtue is both in me and in the other.

A consideration of caring and an ethic built upon it give new meaning to what Kohlberg assesses as "stage three" morality. At this stage, persons behave morally in order to be thought of —or to think of themselves as—"good boys" or "good girls." Clearly, it makes a difference whether one chooses to be good or to be thought of as good. One who chooses to be good may not be "stuck," as Kohlberg suggests, in a stage of moral reasoning. Rather, she may have chosen an alternative route to moral conduct.

It should be clear that my description of an ethic of caring as a feminine ethic does not imply a claim to speak for all women or to exclude men. As we shall see in the next chapter, there is reason to believe that women are somewhat better equipped for caring than men are. This is partly a result of the construction of psychological deep structures in the mother-child relationship. A girl can identify with the one caring for her and thus maintain relation while establishing identity. A boy must, however, find his identity with the absent one—the father—and thus disengage himself from the intimate relation of caring.

. . .

Let me say a little more here, because I know the position is a hard one for many—even for many I love. In our earlier discussion of Abraham, we saw a fundamental and deeply cut chasm between male and female views. We see this difference illustrated again in the New Testament. In Luke 16, we hear the story of a rich man who ignored the suffering of Lazarus, a beggar. After death, Lazarus finds peace and glory, but the rich man finds eternal torment. He cries to Abraham for mercy:

> Father Abraham, have mercy on me, and send Lazarus, that he may dip the tip of his finger in water, and cool my tongue; for I am tormented in this flame.
>
> But Abraham said, Son, remember that thou in thy lifetime receivedst thy good things, and likewise Lazarus evil things: but now he is comforted and thou art tormented.
>
> And beside all this, between us and you there is a great gulf fixed: so that they which would pass from hence to you cannot; neither can they pass to us, that would come from thence.

But what prevents their passage? The judgmental love of the harsh father establishes the chasm. This is not the love of the mother, for even in despair she would cast herself across the chasm to relieve the suffering of her child. If he calls her, she will respond. Even the wickedest, if he calls, she must meet as one-caring. Now, I ask again, what ethical need has woman for God?

In the stories of Abraham, we hear the tragedy induced by the traditional, masculine approach to ethics. When Kierkegaard defends him in an agonized and obsessive search for "something beyond" to which he can repeatedly declare his devotion, he reveals the emptiness at the heart of his own concrete existence. If Abraham is lost, he, Kierkegaard, is lost. He observes: "So either there is a paradox, that the individual as the individual stands in an absolute relation to the absolute/ or Abraham is lost."

Woman, as one-caring, pities and fears both Abraham and Kierkegaard. Not only are they lost, but they would take all of us with them into the lonely wilderness of abstraction.

The Toughness of Caring

An ethic built on caring is thought by some to be tenderminded. It does involve construction of an ideal from the fact and memory of tenderness. The ethical sentiment itself requires a prior natural sentiment of caring and a willingness to sustain tenderness. But there is no assumption of innate human goodness and, when we move to the construction of a philosophy of education, we shall find enormous differences between the view developed here and that of those who find the child innately good. I shall not claim that the child is "innately wise and good," or that the aim of life is happiness, or that all will be well with the child if we resist interfering in its intellectual and moral life. We have memories of caring, of tenderness, and these lead us to a vision of what is good—a state that is good-in-itself and a commitment to sustain and enhance that good (the desire and commitment to be moral). But we have other memories as well, and we have other desires. An ethic of caring takes into account these other tendencies and desires; it is precisely because the tendency to treat each other well is so fragile that we must strive so consistently to care.

Far from being romantic, an ethic of caring is practical, made for this earth. Its toughness is disclosed in a variety of features, the most important of which I shall try to describe briefly here.

First, since caring is a relation, an ethic built on it is naturally other-regarding. Since I am defined in relation, I do not sacrifice myself when I move toward the other as one-caring. Caring is, thus, both self-serving and other-serving. Willard Gaylin describes it as necessary to the survival of the species: "If one's frame of reference focuses on the individual, caring seems self-sacrificing. But if the focus is on the group, on the species, it is the ultimate self-serving device—the sine qua non of survival."

Clearly, this is so. But while I am drawn to the other, while I am instinctively called to nurture and protect, I am also the initiator and chooser of my acts. I may act in accordance with that which is good in my deepest nature, or I may seek to avoid it—either by forsaking relation or by trying to transform that which is feeling and action into that which is all propositional talk and principle. If I suppose, for example, that I am somehow alone and totally responsible for either the apprehension or creation of moral principles, I may find myself in some difficulty when it comes to caring for myself. If moral principles govern my conduct with respect to others, if I must always regard the other in order to be moral, how can I properly meet my own needs and desires? How can I, morally, care for myself?

An ethic of caring is a tough ethic. It does not separate self and other in caring, although, of course, it identifies the special contribution of the one-caring and the cared-for in caring. In contrast to some forms of agapism, for example, it has no problem in advocating a deep and steady caring for self. In a discussion of other-regarding forms of agapism, Gene Outka considers the case of a woman tied to a demanding parent. He explores the possibility of her finding justification for leaving in an assessment of the greatest good for all concerned, and he properly recommends that her own interests be included. In discussing the insistence of some agapists on entirely other-regarding justification, he explores the possibility of her breaking away "to become a medical doctor," thereby satisfying the need for multilateral other-interests. The one-caring throws up her hands at such casting about for reasons. She needs no special justification to care for herself for, if she is not supported and cared-for, she may be entirely lost as one-caring. If caring is to be maintained, clearly, the one-caring must be maintained. She must be strong, courageous, and capable of joy.

When we [look] at the one-caring in conflict (e.g., Mr. Jones and his mother), we [see] that he or she can be overwhelmed by cares and burdens. The ethical responsibility of the one-caring is to look clear-eyed on what is happening to her ideal and how well she is meeting it. She sees herself, perhaps, as caring lovingly for her parent. But perhaps he is cantankerous, ungrateful, rude, and even dirty. She sees herself becoming impatient, grouchy, tired, and filled with self-pity. She can stay and live by an honestly diminished ideal—"I am a tired, grouchy, pitiful caretaker of my old father"—or she can free herself to whatever degree she must to remain minimally but actually caring. The ethical self does not live partitioned off from the rest of the person. Thinking guided by caring does not seek to justify a way out by means of a litany of predicted "goods," but it seeks a way to remain one-caring and, if at all possible, to enhance the ethical ideal. In such a quest, there is no way to disregard the self, or to remain impartial, or to adopt the stance of a disinterested observer. Pursuit of the ethical ideal demands impassioned and realistic commitment.

We see still another reason for accepting constraints on our ethical ideals. When we accept honestly our loves, our innate ferocity, our capacity for hate, we may use all this as information in building the safeguards and alarms that must be part of the ideal. We know better what we must work toward, what we must prevent, and the conditions under which we are lost as ones-caring. Instead of hiding from our natural impulses and pretending that we can achieve goodness through lofty abstractions, we accept what is there—all of it— and use what we have already assessed as good to control that which is not-good.

Caring preserves both the group and the individual and, as we have already seen, it limits our obligation so that it may realistically be met. It will not allow us to be distracted by visions of universal love, perfect justice, or a world unified under principle. It does not say, "Though shalt not kill," and then seek other principles under which killing is, after all, justified. If the other is a clear and immediate danger to me or to my cared-fors, I must stop him, and I might need to kill him. But I cannot kill in the name of principle or justice. I must meet this other—even this evil other—as one-caring so long as caring itself is not endangered by my doing so. I must, for example, oppose capital punishment. I do not begin by saying, "Capital punishment is wrong." Thus I do not fall into the trap of having to supply reasons for its wrongness that will be endlessly disputed at a logical level. I do not say, "Life is sacred," for I cannot name a source of sacredness. I may point to the irrevocability of the decision, but this is not in itself decisive, even for me, because in many cases the decision would be just and I could not regret the demise of the condemned. (I have, after all, confessed my own ferocity; in the heat of emotion, I might have torn him to shreds if I had caught him molesting my child.)

My concern is for the ethical ideal, for my own ethical ideal and for whatever part of it others in my community may share. Ideally, another human being should be able to request, with expectation of positive response, my help and comfort. If I am not blinded by fear, or rage, or hatred, I should reach out as one-caring to the proximate stranger who entreats my help. This is the ideal one-caring creates. I should be able to respond to the condemned man's entreaty, "Help me." We must ask, then, after the effects of capital punishment on jurors, on judges, on jailers, on wardens, on newspersons "covering" the execution, on ministers visiting the condemned, on citizens affirming the sentence, on doctors certifying first that the condemned is well enough to be executed and second that he is dead. What effects have capital punishment on the ethical ideals of the participants? For me, if I had to participate, the ethical ideal would be diminished. Diminished. The ideal itself would be diminished. My act would either be wrong or barely right—right in a depleted sense. I might, indeed, participate ethically—rightly—in an execution but only at the cost of revising my ethical ideal downward. If I do not revise it and still participate, then my act is wrong, and I am a hypocrite and unethical. It is the difference between "I don't believe in killing, but . . ." and "I did not believe in killing cold-bloodedly, but now I see that I must and for these reasons." In the latter case, I may retain my ethicality, but at considerable cost. My ideal must forever carry with it not only what I would be but what I am and have been. There is no unbridgeable chasm between what I am and what I will be. I build the bridge to my future self, and this is why I oppose capital punishment. I do not want to kill if other options are open to me, and I do not want to ask others in the community to do what may diminish their own ethical ideals.

While I must not kill in obedience to law or principle, I may not, either, refuse to kill in obedience to principle. To remain one-caring, I might have to kill. Consider the case of a woman who kills her sleeping husband. Under most circumstances, the one-caring would judge such an act wrong. It violates the very possibility of caring for the husband. But as she hears how the husband abused his wife and children, about the fear with which the woman lived, about the past efforts to solve the problem legally, the one-caring revises her judgment. The jury finds the woman not guilty by reason of an extenuated self-defense. The one-caring finds her ethical, but under the guidance of a sadly diminished ethical ideal. The woman has behaved in the only way she found open to protect herself and her children and, thus, she has behaved in accord with the current vision of herself as one-caring. But what a horrible vision! She is now one-who-has-killed once and who would not kill again, and never again simply one who would not kill. The test of ultimate blame or blamelessness, under an ethic of caring, lies in how the ethical ideal was diminished. Did the agent choose the degraded vision out of greed, cruelty, or personal interest? Or was she driven to it by unscrupulous others who made caring impossible to sustain?

We see that our own ethicality is not entirely "up to us." Like Winston in *Nineteen Eighty-Four,* we are fragile; we depend upon each other even for our own goodness. This recognition casts some doubt on Immanuel Kant's position:

> It is contradictory to say that I make another person's *perfection* my end and consider myself obliged to promote this. For the *perfection* of another man, as a person, consists precisely of *his own* power to adopt his end in accordance with his own concept of

duty; and it is self-contradictory to demand that I do (make it my duty to do) what only the other person himself can do.

In one sense, we agree fully with Kant. We cannot define another's perfection; we, as ones-caring, will not even define the principles by which he should live, nor can we prescribe the particular acts he should perform to meet that perfection. But we must be exquisitely sensitive to that ideal of perfection and, in the absence of a repugnance overwhelming to one-caring, we must as ones-caring act to promote that ideal. As parents and educators, we have perhaps no single greater or higher duty than this.

The duty to enhance the ethical ideal, the commitment to caring, invokes a duty to promote skepticism and noninstitutional affiliation. In a deep sense, no institution or nation can be ethical. It cannot meet the other as one-caring or as one trying to care. It can only capture in general terms what particular ones-caring would like to have done in well-described situations. Laws, manifestos, and proclamations are not, on this account, either empty or useless; but they are limited, and they may support immoral as well as moral actions. Only the individual can be truly called to ethical behavior, and the individual can never give way to encapsulated moral guides, although she may safely accept them in ordinary, untroubled times.

Everything depends, then, upon the will to be good, to remain in caring relation to the other. How may we help ourselves and each other to sustain this will?

QUESTIONS FOR ANALYSIS AND DISCUSSION

1. The virtue of care strongly embraces a notion of love, yet Noddings says her notion is not like the Christian notion of universal love. What is her argument? Do you find her version of love an improvement over the Christian version? Why, or why not?

2. In criticizing the so-called monkish virtues, Noddings claims they are not anchored by the self-in-relation. In contrast, the virtue of care "reaches out to the other and grows in response to the other." Do you think the conduct of Daniel Berrigan as depicted in the case study reflects a monkish virtue or a caring virtue? In your own life, which individuals do you think best exemplify the caring virtue as described by Noddings? Do you agree with her that moral persons can be virtuous but not caring? Using your own examples, develop a position on whether those who care make fewer, equal, or more contributions to the good life than those who emphasize a contrasting moral approach.

3. Is the care virtue teachable? Much of Noddings's discussion highlights examples that clearly represent deeds of caring. In her distinction between natural caring and ethical caring, Noddings gives greater moral worth to the latter. Yet if someone does not care about others in any significant sense—but does them no harm—should we teach that person the virtue of care? If not, why not? if yes, how?

4. Noddings is one of a growing number of feminist philosophers who see the care virtue as a redeeming rather than a demeaning factor of a prototypical woman's moral experience. This argument has two edges. First, it undercuts

what seem to be divisive moral and political values held by other feminists—
the caring is more inclusive than exclusive. Second, there must be a sense of a
prototypical man's moral experience that allows one to clarify the meaning of
the woman's moral experience. How does Noddings support each side of this
argument?

62.

SARAH LUCIA HOAGLAND

Some Thoughts about "Caring"

*Philosopher Sarah Hoagland (b. 1945) appreciates the efforts of Noddings but concludes
that the care ethic remains misguided and incomplete. It is misguided in that the care ethic
portrays women, not as women see themselves but as men characterize them. Noddings
inadvertently falls into this trap. The care ethic is also inadequate in that it fails to address the issues of social and political injustice that precede and create the conditions in
which we experience fear of the stranger. A more radical moral view is needed, Hoagland
proposes. This view should help us rethink the shortcomings of heterosexualism and the
need to challenge all moral values representing the prototypical father.*

CRITICAL READING QUESTIONS

1. What is meant by "heterosexualism"? Which three feminine virtues
   does it spawn?
2. For Hoagland, which type of woman is the model for Noddings's virtue of care?
3. How are reciprocal and unequal relationships distinguished?
4. What point is made by introducing the image of amazons?
5. Who are the typical recipients of caring women? Do these recipients
   exploit, appreciate, or misunderstand caring women?

"Some Thoughts about 'Caring,'" from *Feminist Ethics,* edited by Claudia Card (Lawrence, KS: University of Kansas Press, 1991), pp. 246–261. Notes have been omitted.

I wrote *Lesbian Ethics* after years of observing and participating in lesbian community. The analysis I developed yielded a critique of traditional anglo-european ethics as, among other things, designed to coerce "cooperation" among antagonists. In focusing on the concept "lesbian," I found myself challenging heterosexualism. What I call "heterosexualism" is not simply males having procreative sex with females but rather an entire way of living:

> Heterosexualism is men dominating and de-skilling women in any of a number of forms; from outright attack to paternalistic care, and women devaluing (of necessity) female bonding as well as finding inherent conflicts between commitment and autonomy, and consequently valuing an ethics of dependence. Heterosexualism is a way of living (which actual practitioners exhibit to a greater or lesser degree) that normalizes the dominance of one person in a relationship and the subordination of another. As a result it undermines female agency.

I found that one central problem resulting from heterosexualism is the question of female agency. (By "agency" I simply mean the ability to make choices and act in situations.)

Under the heterosexual model of femininity, the feminine virtues are self-sacrifice, vulnerability, and altruism. Female actions are to be directed toward others, thus the female ability to act is located in others. Consequently, the primary mode of female agency is manipulation. And this, of course, is the stereotype men use to dismiss and criticize women when they behave in ways men have prescribed. The resulting situation is one of the double binds discovered as feminists developed an analysis of sexism.

The independence of the male agent, the model for anglo-european ethics, is possible in real life only presuming the dependence of the female agent who provides the necessary services to allow the male agent to pretend autonomy. The anglo-european model of male ethical agency is that of one who is isolated, egoistic, competitive, and antagonistic. And as a result of this model, Alison Jaggar notes, the central question of anglo-european political theory is, How do we ever get people to cooperate? Further, if we start with such a model of moral agency, it is no wonder that male philosophers will argue that if there is no altruism, there is no ethics. Nevertheless, as one might suspect, altruism accrues to those with lesser power. It is a feminine virtue.

To counter this ethics of independence, some heterosexual women philosophers have developed an ethics of dependence, partially in an attempt, I believe, to capture and explore the idea of community beyond the collection of independent antagonists attempted in much masculinist ethics. Significantly, this ethics of dependence is often explored within the framework of mothering in which the idea of dependency can be explored and is often romanticized, but in which the women as mothers are not the ones who are dependent. I question the mother model as a model for female agency as much as I question the masculine egoistic model.

What I want to do in this [selection] is examine some of the pitfalls of using mothering as the model of female moral agency. I chose Nel Noddings's work because it is perhaps most directly involved in developing the masculine model of the feminine.

Introduction

Nel Noddings's book, *Caring,* has many fine points that I consider central to ethical theory and that I find missing for the most part from traditional, masculinist ethics. Perhaps most central is her shift of the source of ethical sentiment from rules to natural sentiment—especially, caring. This shift includes two elements of particular importance. First, there is a refusal to rely on principles and rules. In discussing a situation in which she lies to an authority about her son's absence from school, or another one in which she refuses to spy on a neighbor, Nel Noddings explains how considering the particulars of a situation helps one make a decision about what to do in that situation. In short, principles don't tell us when to apply them, and in the long run, they work only when we don't really need them.

She argues that to accept the universalizability of principles, "we would have to establish that human predicaments exhibit sufficient sameness, and this we cannot do without abstracting away from concrete situations those qualities that seem to reveal sameness. In doing this, we often lose the very qualities or factors that gave rise to the moral question in the situation." This does not mean, however, that we reject principles altogether. It is just that we regard them as guidelines, not ultimate arbiters of behavior. "The one-caring displays a characteristic variability in her actions—she acts in a nonrule-bound fashion in behalf of the cared-for."

The second aspect of Nel Noddings's shift from rule-oriented ethics to an ethics of caring is her focus on interaction between ethical parties. Her position is that relation is ontologically basic and the caring relation is ethically basic. She argues: "Taking *relation* as ontologically basic simply means that we recognize human encounter and affective response as a basic fact of human existence." She contrasts the philosopher who begins with a supremely free consciousness, one who has an aloneness and emptiness at the heart of existence, with one who recognizes and longs for relatedness. She suggests that our efforts must be "directed to the maintenance of conditions that will permit caring to flourish." And she suggests her concern is not on the judgment or the acts, but how we meet each other morally.

In particular, she introduces in caring the idea of receiving the other, of apprehending their reality. "Caring involves stepping out of one's own personal frame of reference into the other's. When we care, we consider the other's point of view."

As a result of this focus on caring, Nel Noddings offers many valuable insights about relatedness—for example, that caring requires maintenance of self and that knowledge of what gives us pain and pleasure precedes caring for others. She also discusses how caring for others can become an assumption of burdens whereby one is only focused on oneself—when caring becomes simply a matter of "cares and burdens" and I have become the object of my own caring. Of particular interest is her notion that our moral agency is affected by others and that in certain respects we depend on others to enhance our moral self. And there is something to be said for the idea of interacting with others by acknowledging only good motives.

In many respects I agree with this focus. However, if such a focus is going to serve us morally, it must have a way of assessing the values we reinforce through our interactions and a vision of how values can change. My criticism stems from Nel Noddings's analysis of caring, an analysis that uses mothering as a model, and from implications that derive from this analysis. My concern is twofold. First, I object to the unidirectional description of caring. Second, I do not think mothering can be properly used as the model for an ethics of caring.

I take time with this because my concern is not to challenge caring as a pivotal point for ethical theory but rather to question a particular portrayal of caring. Nel Noddings's analysis of caring involves several elements: acting, engrossment, and motivational displacement on the part of the one who cares (the one-caring) and reciprocity on the part of the one who is cared for (the cared-for).

The action component is the most elusive as it cannot be defined in terms of behavioral indications. It is here that the move away from rule-bound behavior is most significant. One must determine one's course of action in terms of the person and the situation: "To care is to act not by fixed rule but by affection and regard."

Engrossment, receiving, and motivational displacement concern the way we involve ourselves with an other. Engrossment and receiving involve apprehending the other's reality, and Nel Noddings distinguishes this from empathy—I need to apprehend the other's reality not as I would feel it in their shoes but as they feel it. This is close to what María Lugones calls "playful world travel," through which we can learn to love cross-culturally and cross-racially. It involves being able to go into the world of another quite different from our own without trying to conquer or destroy it (men's idea of play).

According to Nel Noddings, the element of motivational displacement enters because if I go into another's world, then "I am impelled to act as though in my own behalf, but in behalf of the other." Or again: "I allow my motive energy to be shared; I put it at the service of the other."

Finally, reciprocity on the part of the cared-for is crucial to caring because caring must be completed in the other. Reciprocity is not a matter of the cared-for responding as one-caring. Rather, "caring is completed in all relationships through the apprehension of caring by the cared-for." A baby wiggling in delight as she is bathed exhibits the reciprocal efforts of the cared-for.

Unequal Relationships

Certainly there are arguments for focusing on mothering in considering ethical (and political) questions. Alison Jaggar argues that if we stop viewing individuals as isolated, solitary, and essentially rational and consider the facts of biology—namely, that mothers need cooperative effort in raising infants—then liberals would be puzzled by the existence of egoism, competitiveness, and aggressiveness rather than the existence of community and cooperation. Yet Nel Noddings's focus is not on the cooperation necessary among adults for child-rearing but rather on the unequal relationship between mother and child. She also brings in teacher/student and, later, therapist/client relationships.

Nel Noddings's interest in these relationships seems to be a matter of the child/student/client having a need the mother/teacher/therapist can fill. In some respects, she equates caring with teaching, and her focus on the mother/child relationship as primary seems to be a matter of the dependency of the child, which elicits a response from the mother. Thus the mother cares—a natural caring that can be turned into a moral caring. This relationship is unequal, however, because the child or student is "incapable of perceiving or understanding what the parent or teacher wants for herself."

Now, in the first place, the very purpose of parenting, teaching, and providing therapy is to wean the cared-for of dependency. Consequently, an ethics of caring whose model is a dependency relationship, ideally transitory, provides at best for an incomplete analysis of caring. More significantly, to the extent that it is true that the cared-for cannot understand what the one-caring needs or wants, the conclusion I draw is that such a relationship is ipso facto a diminished caring relationship. Second, Nel Noddings argues elsewhere that the authorization of the parent/teacher/therapist, combined with the situation of the cared-for, justifies the inequality and, by extension, the lack of expectation of real reciprocity from the cared-for. But this portrays only one party as needing help in the relationship; unless we are talking about a mere development of skills, this is false.

Third, there tends to be an assumption that we value unequal relationships because they afford a means of addressing differences in ability. That is, we tend to justify relationships unequal in power by assuming that their function is acknowledgment of differences in abilities. Along with this goes the further assumption that in equal relationships, we treat our peers as having abilities equal to our own. However, this is not the case. When interacting with those we consider our peers, we do not treat each other as if our abilities were the same, and we do not treat each other as lesser or unequal because of it. More likely, we just treat one another as normal and get on with helping or teaching each other. My friend who is an accountant helps me with my accounting, but the relationship is not an unequal one. So when we interact with someone in a way that is premised on a difference of power, it is not simply because we perceive them as not having abilities we have. Often it is because we perceive them as incompetent or less competent than we are in being able to make decisions in general. Consequently, we must ask ourselves what values we promote when we encourage unequal relationships as an ideal rather than as something to be worked out of or even overcome.

In my opinion, caring must find its grounding in a relationship that is not "authorized" and indeed serve as a check on the power exercised in these "authorized" relationships. For we live in a society premised on dominance and subordination, and oppression emerges in many forms—from parental all the way to colonial relationships—when decisions are made "for another's own good."

. . .

Further, the unidirectional ideal of mothering undermines reciprocal interaction beyond acknowledgment between mothers and daughters and so also encourages incompetency and ageism among us. Recipients of unconditional loving—children and husbands—combine in exploiting mothers, helping to create an ageist response to older women:

> The children learned an assumption of privilege from their father, and he in turn became one of the children—legitimately passive, irresponsible. . . . [M]y older daughters

never witnessed an *exchange* of nurturance. In their view of how the world worked, mothers gave, and men/daughters received. Ours was such an isolated nuclear family that they literally never had an opportunity to witness me being nourished, sustained, taken care of, or emotionally supported. . . . My own daughters, now in their thirties, are dutiful wives but still do not know how to extend nurturance to me, or to negotiate when we have a difference of interest. . . . As the children grow up, they continue to relate to older women with the clear expectations of service. By then they have laid claim to a place of privilege in the power hierarchy.

María Lugones writes of her failure to love her mother and suggests that until she became basically one-caring herself toward her mother and thereby met her mother in care, meaning could not arise fully between them.

To pursue the feminine (a part of whose essence is agape and unconditional loving), to pursue this sense of female agency, is to pursue oppression. The masculine and the feminine are not significantly different in what they engender.

Insularism

Nel Noddings's analysis of caring appeals to the feminine, to receptiveness. A truly radical ethics will challenge not only the masculine but also the feminine, for the feminine is born of a masculinist framework and so does not, at a deep level, represent any change. Both the masculine and the feminine are central to heterosexualism. In general, I do not find the society of mothers preferable to the society of fathers. In contrasting mothers and amazons, Monique Wittig and Sande Zeig suggest, mythically, that there came a time when some would no longer ride with the amazons and instead stayed in the city and watched their abdomens grow, refusing other interests and calling themselves "mothers":

During the Golden Age, everyone in the terrestrial garden was called amazon. Mothers were not distinct from daughters. They lived in harmony and shared pleasures. They enumerated every beautiful and pleasant place in the terrestrial garden and invited one another to visit them. They hunted together. They gathered together and they wandered together. They described their deeds and exploits in epics. There were no limits to their adventures and age had no meaning in their lives or in their poems. Everyone thought of herself as an amazon.

After the first settlements in the cities everything continued as before. The amazons lived far from, rather than inside, their cities. After hunting or gathering, the food was prepared out of doors and a festival was held. Very often the city was completely deserted and vacant for several days.

Then came a time when some daughters and some mothers did not like wandering anymore in the terrestrial garden. They began to stay in the cities and most often they watched their abdomens grow. This activity brought them, it is said, great satisfaction. Things went so far in this direction that they refused to have any other interests. In vain, their friends asked them to join them in their travels. They always had a new abdomen to watch. Thus they called themselves mothers. And they found qualifications corresponding to this function of childbearing, for example, mother the plenary, mother the one who engenders. The first generation of static mothers who refused to leave their cities, began. From then on, they called the others "eternal, immature daughters, amazons."

They did not welcome them cordially when they came back from their travels. They did not listen to their accounts of discoveries or explorations anymore. The joy of hunting, gathering, and wandering had disappeared. At that time the mothers stopped calling themselves amazons and the mothers and the amazons began to live separately.

In a sense I am charging the one-caring as Nel Noddings describes her with a lack of experience in the world—indeed, with a withdrawal from the public domain. I am suggesting that hers is the focus of one who has limited her attention and who will not leave the city. But my criticism is not a criticism from the masculine ethics Nel Noddings abandons, because I am not appealing to principles to solve these problems. Acting from principle can be acting from an equal or even greater lack of experience. It is a lesbian criticism: Caring cannot be insular and it cannot ignore the political reality, material conditions, and social structure of the world.

Although I applaud Nel Noddings's focus on care and situations and away from rules and principles, as well as the care she exhibits in detailing her examples, I question her particular analysis of caring because it does not adequately challenge the proximate intimate, because it fears the proximate stranger, and because it ignores the distant stranger. An ethics that leaves starving people in a distant land outside the realm of moral consideration is inadequate, especially when, as Claudia Card notes, we have had a hand in creating these conditions. And a stance that fears the proximate stranger means the caring is not capable of crossing politically and socially imposed barriers, such as racism, to promote change. In discussing the failure of love between white anglo women and women of color, María Lugones writes: "I am particularly interested . . . in those cases in which White/Anglo women . . . ignore us, ostracize us, render us invisible, stereotype us, leave us completely alone, interpret us as crazy. All of this *while we are in their midst.*"

If an ethics of caring is going to be morally successful in replacing an ethics located in principles and duty, particularly within the context of oppression, then it must provide for the possibility of ethical behavior in relation to what is foreign, it must consider analyses of oppression, it must acknowledge a self that is both related and separate, and it must have a vision of, if not a program for, change. In my opinion, care stripped of these elements isn't a caring that benefits us. Further, as long as we exist within a context of oppression, an ethics relevant to us must function under oppression. If we are to have a female-focused caring central to an ethical theory, a theory of value, particularly one functioning in a patriarchal society, I suggest it be the caring of amazons, a caring of those concerned with challenging the inequities resulting from the values of the fathers.

QUESTIONS FOR ANALYSIS AND DISCUSSION

1. In her definition of "heterosexualism" Hoagland identifies an inherent assault on women that is nevertheless upheld as a model of virtue. This model is the mother. Why does Hoagland, who is generally appreciative of Noddings's

goals, criticize her moral idealization of the mother? Do you agree or disagree
with Hoagland's view?

2. According to Hoagland, Noddings is right in questioning the isolated individual as the foundation for moral theories. This foundation has fostered
many modern political theories dominated by the worry about getting people
to cooperate with one another. But it is men, not women, according to Hoagland, who are dominated by this worry. Hence, men's moral dramatics about
altruism. From a woman's perspective in which cooperation is a matter of fact,
the men's primary worry is actually secondary. What points of Hoagland's position do you agree or disagree with? Clarify your view of those points and
how they affect your general assessment of her argument.

3. Hoagland says that Noddings conceives of caring as lacking a sense of reciprocity. Review the case study by Berrigan or the essay by Noddings. Do you
agree that there are clear-cut examples of caring in which reciprocity does not
exist or is drastically unequal? If not, why not? If so, is the lack of reciprocity
morally relevant? Clarify your answer.

4. How does Hoagland explain the moral problem of the father's relation to the
mother's embodiment of the care virtue? From your observations of friends
and acquaintances or through personal experiences, to what extent do you
support or question Hoagland's account of the father? In light of Hoagland's
conclusion, who will be the model for moral education? Do you think her
proposal is a worthy alternative to more conventional models? Clarify your
reasons.

63.

ALISA L. CARSE AND HILDE LINDEMANN NELSON

Rehabilitating Care

Philosophers Alisa Carse and Hilde Nelson offer a defense of the care ethic on several
fronts. Although granting the importance of the general concerns of Noddings's critics,
Carse and Nelson describe how these critics have distorted or miscast the arguments for
the virtue of care. In defending Noddings they concede the labor that goes into a woman's

"Rehabilitating Care," *Kennedy Institute of Ethics Journal*, March 1996, 6(1): 19–35. Notes have
been omitted.

efforts to care for others. But this is not a mark of derision, say Carse and Nelson. Caring is worthy of emulation by all because the virtue of care is the basis not only for personal morality but also for social justice. Deeds of care contribute to human flourishing and the good life.

⊢ CRITICAL READING QUESTIONS ⊢

1. What are the four central points Carse and Nelson address to defend the care ethic from its critics?
2. What is meant by integrity? Why is integrity a virtue?
3. What is Carse and Nelson's position on the dispute about women's dependence or independence in relation to moral life?
4. Why is the relation between care and strangers a special moral issue?

The ethic of care validates skills and virtues traditionally associated with women and women's roles. This presents feminists in particular with a dilemma. On the one hand, there is a vital need for an ethic that takes the experiences of women seriously, and the ethic of care does just that, capturing certain features of our moral lives that other, more standard approaches to morality underplay or ignore. On the other hand, the ethic threatens to support and sustain the subordinate status of women in society, contributing to the exploitation and denigration of women with which feminist ethics is more broadly concerned. If it can be shown that the threat is real, feminists may feel obliged to repudiate the approach.

Can the ethic of care be saved? In this essay we examine four standard complaints that are lodged against the care orientation in ethics, namely, complaints concerning the exploitation of care givers, the challenges of care taking to caregiver integrity, the potential perils of conceiving the mother-child dyad normatively as a paradigm for human relationships, and the inadequacy of the care ethic in securing social justice among relative strangers. We find that much can be done to address all four complaints and that progress can thus be made toward rehabilitating care. We close by discussing why and how the ethic might be further developed.

Self-Sacrifice: The Problem of Exploitation

Broadly construed, the care ethic poses a challenge to prevailing models of moral knowledge and responsibility, especially the tendency in ethical theory to construe as paradigmatic those forms of judgment and response that abstract away from the concrete identities of others and our relationships to them. An adequate grasp of the moral contours of specific situations, especially as they concern other people and our responsibilities to them, requires an acute attentiveness to particularity and to the situation-specific nature of others' needs. As Margaret Walker writes, "The others I need to understand . . . are actual others in a particular case at hand, and not repeatable instances or replaceable occupants of a general status." Such attention to particularity competes uneasily and sometimes irreconcilably with the movement toward abstraction and generalization characterized by the impartial, principled deliberation and justification emphasized in dominant moral theoretical models, particularly those rooted in Kant and liberal contractarianism.

The rejection of impartiality and principlism that characterizes much care-oriented ethical theory is one source of the criticisms that have been raised against care theory. The emphasis within care theory on attunement to concrete others, their situations, and their relationships to us is rooted in an axiology centered on our moral responsibility to understand and attend to the needs of others. Care theory's insistence on the importance of acute sensitivity to concrete circumstances, and on the cultivation of those capacities necessary for sympathetic, imaginative projection into the perspectives and situations of others, derives from the view that such sensitivity and the capacities it entails are crucial to achieving an understanding of the way others see and experience their needs, and thus to the ability to care for them effectively.

These emphases raise the first set of worries. Though care-oriented theory is permeated with metaphors of sight and perception, the activity of caring can be blind and indiscriminate. A conception of the care ethic that includes no general normative constraints to regulate its force or direct it toward worthy objects only reinforces existing stereotypes of selfless, womanly sacrifice. If we are to protect against exploitative, abusive, demeaning, or otherwise unfair patterns of distribution and responsibility in our roles and relationships, we must have some way of reflecting critically on our roles and relationships and of determining which of the expressed needs, expectations, and demands with which they confront us are morally legitimate ones. And since we cannot respond to every legitimate claim on our care, we require a means of distinguishing between the care we *may* give and the care we *must* give.

Some would argue that the ethic of care is an ethic of intimate relationships, in which there is no need for justice. We will suggest later that this circumscription of the care ethic underestimates its potential. The point we want to emphasize here is that care giving that is servile or exploitative should not be morally condoned in *any* relational context. The scope of justice properly extends not only to formal relations between distant strangers, but also to our more proximate relational spheres. The vulnerability invited by intimacy and mutual concern can, along with the fact that family members and friends (or proximate strangers) differ in strength, power, and degrees of dependency, make these relationships particularly susceptible to problems of exploitation and injustice. As Jean Hampton warns:

> A moral agent has to have a good sense of her own moral claims if she is going to be . . . a real partner in a morally sound relationship. She must also have some sense of what it is to make a legitimate claim if she is to understand and respond to the legitimate claims of others and resist attempts to involve herself in relationships that will make her the mere servant of others' desires.

To facilitate the task of recognizing a servile relationship—whether "in the family, the marketplace . . . political society, or the workplace"—Hampton looks to a justice perspective and proposes a "contractarian test." She invokes David Gauthier's claim that our sociality "becomes a source of exploitation if it induces persons to acquiesce in institutions and practices that but for their fellow-feeling would be costly to them." In assessing our relationships, we are to ask whether we could "reasonably accept the distribution of costs and benefits . . . that are not themselves side effects of any affective or duty-based ties between us . . . if [the relationship] were the subject of an informed, unforced agreement in which we think of ourselves as motivated solely by self-interest." The point is not to ensure relations of equal reciprocity where this is impossible, but to prohibit relational arrangements in which one party exploits another by *taking advantage of* his or her affections. This test is intended in effect to introduce the Kantian constraint that no member of a relationship be treated as a mere instrument of others.

Now, there is no question that an ethic emphasizing responsiveness to others' needs risks reinforcing our vulnerability to others' unfair demands. Indeed, it is precisely in the interest of setting just limits on our obligations to others that many critics of care theory insist that acceptable forms of caring presuppose that prior conditions of justice are met. We want, however, to suggest ways in which care theory itself can enrich our notions of relational justice, thereby better accommodating the different kinds of relationships and roles we inhabit.

It is clear that Hampton's contractarian test can offer limited guidance at best. As she notes, it does not apply to relationships of "radical inequality," such as those between a parent and infant, or a care taker and someone seriously ill or infirm—i.e., relationships in which one party is "incapable of reciprocating the benefit[s]" provided by the other. And yet many of our most demanding relationships are of just this sort. Moreover, there is a wide range of relationships between those of "radical inequality" on the one hand and those of material equality on the other. Consider relationships of material inequality in which limited forms of reciprocity are possible, especially forms of affectionate expression and exchange. An adult who cares for her ill father may well derive a significant benefit from the relationship through the love and appreciation he expresses, even though he may be too incapacitated by illness to return care taking of the same kind. Both the quality of the affection and the balance of affection exchanged should play a role in our moral assessments of the justice of such relationships.

Furthermore, the care giver–recipient dyad rarely exists in isolation from other relationships; the care giver is generally nested in a cluster of relationships from which she in turn can draw care. Suppose an individual cares for her sister, whose Alzheimer's disease has progressed beyond the point where even affection is possible. If her family expects her to provide the labor of care simply because she is the wife or the mom, or because they do not want to do it themselves, or because they are indifferent to her situation, she is arguably exploited, not because she gets nothing in exchange for the care she gives, or because she yields to her sister's needs out of affection, but because capable members of her family ignore the burdens they impose on her by failing to be concerned with *her* welfare and thus to do their share. To argue along these lines is to see the fact of familial relationship as having at least *prima facie* importance for the care we owe others.

An acceptable account of relational justice must require respect, concern, and support for the well-being and flourishing of *all* parties within relational structures. Respect from a care perspective will, as Robin Dillon argues, see "individuals as equally worthy of attention, consideration, and concern, equally worthy of understanding and care." On this view, justice prevails when each is attended to, each is heard, each is recognized, and—crucially—no one's welfare is ignored or dismissed. The able husband who tenderly acknowledges how hard his wife works, but never lends a hand to help, fails to manifest the respectful concern this understanding of justice would demand, for he does not actively support his wife's flourishing. This suggests that it is not sufficient, in ensuring relational justice, that one refrain from degrading others or from treating others as mere instruments to one's own ends; within a care orientation, respectful caring requires the mutual, active promotion of one another's well-being. As Dillon writes, such caring joins "individuals together in a community of mutual concern and mutual aid."

This notion of respect differs from the Kantian notion: In a care perspective, people are to be valued and respected directly, as concrete, particular selves, not because they are taken universally to possess an abstract and generic capacity for rational autonomous agency. Moral focus is placed on individuals' idiosyncracies and vulnerabilities and on the quality and particularity of specific interpersonal relationships; the fact of human interdependency is recognized as morally fundamental. Within a care ethic, a decent solution to the problem of exploitation will refer us both to an examination of the balance of relational goods exchanged by individuals (including affection, concern, humor, and the like) and to the broader structure of the relational networks in which we live. It will challenge us to reflect on the care we *may* give when our proximate relationships are marked by respectful love and to explore further how facts of relational distance and proximity ought bear on the care we *must* give as a matter of relational justice.

Self-Effacement and the Problem of Integrity

The need to set limits on care is an important problem for the care ethic not only because of the danger of exploitation, but also because of the danger of oppressing the recipient of care. The imposition of care on another without consulting her wishes or trying to understand her needs from her own point of view is rightly excoriated as paternalism; when we care for another solely on our own terms, we act arrogantly. The desire to avoid arrogant and invasive caring prompts many care theorists to insist on the requirement that the care giver enter imaginatively and empathically into the world of the person being cared for. As Nel Noddings writes, caring "involves stepping out of one's own personal frame of reference into the other's." As a care taker, "I set aside my temptation to analyze and to plan. I do not project; I receive the other into myself, and I see and feel with the other." The care taker actively assimilates the other's values and ideas and "affectively interiorizes" an alien perspective, supplanting her own. She undergoes what Noddings calls "motivational displacement," in which she grasps what the person receiving her care wants for himself and allows that want to supersede her own motives for action; she also adopts the interpretive framework of the other, yielding her own understanding of the situation and its moral stakes.

But this motivational and interpretive "displacement" raises a second set of problems. As crucial as the skills of receptivity are to care taking, they can pose serious risks in their own right—among other things, the risk of morally problematic self-effacement. Sandra Bartky offers a trenchant exploration of ways in which care giving can threaten care givers with what she calls "epistemic" and "ethical disempowerment." She writes:

> An "epistemic lean" in the direction of the object of her solicitude is part of the care giver's job. . . . There is, then, a risk for women's epistemic development in our unreciprocated care giving. . . . Many of us, I suspect, have been morally silenced or morally compromised in small ways because we thought it more important to provide emotional support than to keep faith with our own principles. . . . More corrosive is a danger that inheres in the very nature of intimate care giving—the danger of an "ethical lean" that, like the epistemic lean . . . may rob the care giver herself of a place to stand.

Bartky does not deny that care taking has its attendant powers. Indeed, one may be and feel tremendously efficacious as a healer, consoler, and sustainer, the source of "a great reservoir of restorative power." This, she claims, helps to explain why women, among others, have persisted with little protest in roles and relationships that have exacted from them high epistemic and ethical costs. Her example is that of Teresa Stangl, who, though herself devoutly religious and opposed to Nazism, paid homage to her husband, Fritz, comforting and succoring him in ways that made it possible for him to continue in the capacity of Kommandant at Treblinka, even while she found his work morally repugnant.

Less dramatic but more familiar is the example of the health professional—the nurse, who, in wrestling with the conflict between her patient's desires and her own sense of what is right, can resolve the conflict with her conscience only by quieting it. If she takes herself to be obligated to step outside her own moral beliefs and commitments in order to serve her patient well, she may thereby be engaging in moral and ideational modes that reinforce her self-estrangement and subservience as a care taker.

Responsiveness to another's needs, however, ought not involve overidentification with the other or assumed possession of the other's condition. Indeed, this can compromise care, by bringing one's focus onto one's self—one's own fears, felt needs, or aspirations. It thus risks being disrespectful and blind to the other as a separate locus of experience and agency. A viable ethic of care must address the profoundly important moral challenge of healthy receptivity. It must acknowledge how traits that are in some contexts clearly virtues can be distorted and transformed, how tenderness, imagination, empathy, and sympathy—though often essential to caring effectively for others—can chip away at the integrity of the care giver, promote moral compromise or even complicity in moral wrongdoing, and thus be potentially both destructive of the care giver and morally pernicious in their effects.

One theoretical solution to the problem is to incorporate self-care into the ethic of care and so keep it from being an ethic of self-effacement. The success of this solution, however, depends on the theoretical motivation for self-care. If the point of self-care is to enable the care giver to care better for others, self-care is, as Rosemarie Tong observes, nothing more than "a disguised form of other-directed care." If the one who cares has dedicated herself to another so completely that she sets even care of herself at the other's service, she stands in danger of losing herself. For this reason, self-care must have its ethical basis in an affirmation of the care giver's integrity. Cheshire Calhoun has recently suggested that integrity is not only a personal virtue, by which one acts to protect the boundaries of the self, but also centrally a social virtue in that it involves standing for something *to other people*. As one among many deliberators, each of us uses her best moral judgment to answer the question, "What is worth doing?" We try to answer this correctly not only for ourselves, but "for, and before, all deliberators who share the goal of determining what is worth doing."

By offering us a picture of integrity that reminds us that we are social selves, selves in relationship, Calhoun builds accountability to others directly into her understanding of what it is to "be oneself." Being oneself is being responsible to, and before, others for one's moral judgments, which requires that one take one's own judgments seriously. A self of the kind presupposed by Calhoun's picture of integrity cannot easily be lost by empathic caring for others because it is the self of a morally developed person. When we hold the other's felt needs or desires to be deeply at odds with our own conception of the good, or of the other's interests, integrity requires that we follow our conscience and refuse to yield to the other's demands. However, it also requires that we take the other person's perspective seriously, consider it openly, and understand its potentially important connection to her self-conception, even if we ultimately reject it.

Receptivity to the other must not be confused with self-abnegating absorption into the other. An empathetic care taker must be able to survive as a strong, intact, self-respecting person in her own right. If Calhoun's account of integrity is correct, the nurse who faces the problem of doing something morally questionable because her patient desires it must ask, "How, when I care for others, can I stand for what in my considered opinion is ethical care?" She thus represents both to her patient and to herself her own best judgment of what is worth doing.

Material Inequality:
The Problem of the Mother-Child Paradigm

Some care theorists take its moral paradigm to be relationships of material inequality and unidirectional dependency, such as that found in the mother-child dyad. For Nel Noddings, for example, the ideal image of care—the mother nursing her child—is unidirectional care that asks for nothing in return. Sara Ruddick looks to a normative account of the structure of maternal practice for a characterization of the virtues and modes of being that are crucial to fostering the preservation, growth, and socialization of a child. She sees a great need to cultivate in people such traits as "attentive love," "resilient cheerfulness," innovation, and responsiveness to others in their singularity. Virginia Held also focuses on the mother-child dyad in her examination of the moral contours of relationships characterized by nonvoluntary participation, mutual support, dependency, and irreplaceability. Held argues that marketplace models of "rational man," on which ethical concerns pertain to constraints on voluntary, cooperative interaction and ways of ensuring mutual noninterference, cannot adequately address the morality of relationships of inequality and dependence.

Many critics have rejected maternal-child (and other familial) models of moral relationship, claiming that, at best, they represent perilous paradigms. Unrequited care, romanticized as a model for human relationships, can only reinforce oppressive roles and practices, teaching those who are cared for to receive without giving and doing nothing to promote the self-respect and equal moral standing of the care taker. It is also argued that the forms of material inequality, unidirectional dependency, and asymmetrical concern that characterize relations such as that between a mother and her child are to be outgrown or transcended rather than celebrated.

Moreover, it has been pointed out that construing unequal, emotionally engaged dependency relationships as morally paradigmatic fails to provide adequate moral protection against arbitrary and abusive uses of care-taker power; we need to be on guard against the potential for cruel or disabling exercises of maternal authority and discretionary leeway. It is precisely the asymmetries of power, authority, and vulnerability in parent-child relationships that lead many to deem them ill-suited as moral paradigms, for they permit—even require—forms of domination that are morally inappropriate in relations between equal adults.

It would indeed be a mistake to see the mother-child dyad as a sole and sufficient moral paradigm. But it does not follow that there is no moral wisdom to be gained from normative models of relationships—such as that of mother and child—that are in fact characterized, often ineluctably, by inequalities of power, knowledge, vulnerability, and dependency. We need not think of such relational models as exhaustive in order to take them seriously as sources of moral insight and key objects of ethical attention. As Annette Baier has argued, the relative weight given to relations among "equals" in moral theory has led to a damaging "moral myopia." Baier writes that modern moral philosophers have managed

> to focus their philosophical attention . . . single-mindedly on cool, distanced relations between more or less free and equal adult strangers. . . . Philosophers who remember what it was like to be a dependent child or who know what it is like to be a parent or to have a dependent parent, an old or handicapped relative, friend, or neighbor will find it implausible . . . [to] see morality as essentially a matter of keeping to the minimal moral traffic rules, designed to restrict close encounters between autonomous persons to self-chosen ones. . . . For those most of whose daily dealings are with the less powerful or the more powerful, a moral code designed for those equal in power will be at best nonfunctional, at worst an offensive pretense of equality as a substitute for its actuality.

The fact remains that we are, as humans, deeply interdependent; it is not uncommon to be in need of care and expertise that we cannot reciprocate fully or at all. The vulnerability we experience when we are ill, for example, is often intensified by our lack of medical expertise; we must hand our lives and welfare over to others who have knowledge, training, and experience that we do not have. We are in a similar state of dependence when we submit to the judgment and skill of pharmacists, nurses, train conductors, or the teachers who oversee our children each day.

Although we can retain broad rights of refusal and request, contract models for relationships of material inequality are inherently impoverished, given the material realities of need, on the one hand, and limited knowledge and expertise, on the other. We are often not in a position to negotiate the terms of our relationships as equal partners; we must yield discretionary power to others. Nor can we rely on negotiation to assure that our welfare will be sought. Relationships with those who care for us or for our loved ones, those on whose wisdom, skill, and good will we depend, must of necessity be bound by *trust*. When we are in conditions of dependency, we must often place presumptive faith in those entrusted with our welfare, relying on them not to exploit our vulnerability or to abuse the power we have given them.

This is not to deny that some of the material inequalities and imbalances that structure our relationships are themselves morally suspect and avoidable, and thus are to be overcome. Nor is it to maintain that we should blindly and dumbly trust all who come our way. It is, rather, to insist that our moral models and guides realistically acknowledge the full extent of our mutual interdependence as human beings and to suggest that a large measure of merited trust is necessary to the survival and flourishing of all of us, most of the time. This, in turn, raises crucial questions for political morality, concerning how our practices and institutions succeed or fail to sustain trustworthy relations between us.

The Scope of Care: The Problem of Strangers

Many critics argue that care, which is naturally extended to intimates and others with whom we come into direct contact, cannot help us to resist the evil that strangers do to strangers. Claudia Card notes, for example, that when all of morality is subsumed under the care we provide to our families, friends, and others in proximity, too much of the world is left out; we are too easily tempted to sexism, racism, xenophobia, homophobia, and disregard for future generations. In the absence of principles that can show us toward whom our care ought to be directed, we can only care for those with whom we happen to be in relation, and although a care ethic might bid us individually to care for those social causes we find most worthwhile, it cannot help us revise the institutions and ideological and economic forces that play a large role in such evils as world hunger or homelessness. The solutions of care theory are likely to be patchwork solutions rather than the radical reconfigurations of social structures that these endemic ills require. To be sure, a care ethic alone cannot address all of morality. Because it focuses on the particularistic and the personal, it is especially well-designed to do the work of fine detail, and thus is too delicate an instrument for some large-scale problems posed by social justice. Nonetheless, the ethic can play a role in addressing both the conditions of social justice and the directions we must take in reframing our conceptions of it.

In understanding how an ethic of care can affect our conception of social justice, it is useful to draw a distinction between "caring for" and "caring about" others. "Caring about" can be seen to presuppose a position in value theory—i.e., What makes x worth caring about?—and this position need not be divided along intimate/stranger or private/public lines. We can care about the needs of future generations, the suffering of Bosnian Muslims, or the health of children far away and unknown to us personally. "Caring for," on the other hand, is an activity involving moral skill; we must decide how best to care for what we care about, and act accordingly. Marilyn Friedman gives examples of what care might look like outside of more intimate spheres: "In its more noble manifestation, care in the public realm would show itself . . . in foreign aid, welfare programs, famine or disaster relief, or other social programs designed to relieve suffering and attend to human needs."

Justice is undermined, among other things, by forces of bigotry and hatred, by competitive desire for unilateral advantage, by more seemingly innocuous forms of "tunnel vision" that emerge from blindness or indifference toward others or ignorance about them, and by the many often unconscious and unacknowledged aversions and biases that are in fact at play in our resistance to receiving each other in welcome partnership. These include prejudices about "funny" accents; discomfort with scarred faces, personal odors, or body types; and negative preconceptions about race, ethnicity, religion, sexual orientation, and the like. The harm we do to strangers often is founded not only in bigotry and hatred, but also in forms of indifference that render us uninclined even to treat them justly. The extension of justice requires that others be on our "radar screen." They get there by being cared about. An ethic of care that propels us to extend the scope of our attentiveness and responsiveness might go a long way—even if not all the way—toward undercutting crucial impediments to social justice. As Margaret Walker notes, we need to encourage just those virtues and capacities necessary "to defend ourselves against dispositions to keep strangers strange and outsiders outside."

More fundamentally, while many have urged the importance of conceptualizing justice as "blind" to particulars of race, gender, religion, and the like, in order to provide protection against prejudice and parochialism, the ethic of care challenges us to resist the human tendencies to remain blind and unconcerned about what is unfamiliar or more relationally and personally distant and to develop a sensitivity to differences in perspective and need *as a demand of justice.* Crucial to this end is a normative conception of care that does not ground it solely in love and affection for those whose connections to us are visible, but that urges respectful, compassionate concern for the welfare of others even in the absence of bonds of affection, or of relational, geographic, or cultural familiarity. We underestimate the care ethic when we confine it to dyadic relationships or to proximate spheres of social relationship and interaction.

Why Should We Care?

Much of our discussion has *assumed* that the ethic of care introduces important dimensions into ethical discourse. The question we need to pursue further is why we should regard the care ethic as a serious moral contender. It is not sufficient to claim that it reflects many women's lived experiences in ways that standing moral theories cannot, as this invites the objection that something is wrong with women's lives and the norms and demands structuring them, rather than with the standing theories and the norms and demands that they set out. Such a claim need not blame women; it might simply express the view that women have been so oppressed and their lives so distorted that little of moral value can be gained from studying them. We must ask, therefore, whether there is an argument independent of a simple gender-bias thesis for maintaining that the care perspective and the norms and standards it engenders ought to be granted moral legitimacy.

To this question we reply that the ethic of care ought to be granted moral legitimacy because we need such an ethic if we are to be honest about what is required for human flourishing. Women's traditional labor—a vastly disproportionate share of the work of caring—has been important moral labor. It is labor that underscores the moral significance of human *interdependence,* raising ethical concerns about aloneness, abandonment, neglect, and isolation—concerns that arise especially when we are in special states of vulnerability, as are those who are young, ill, frail, disabled, or otherwise in need of others' care. Human thriving requires a world in which there are loving parents and caring citizens: trustworthy and responsible nurses, physicians, political representatives, teachers, neighbors, and cabbies. A stable social order depends on the presence in many of us, at least, of benevolence, compassion, kindness, imagination, and trustworthiness—traits that diminish conflict, promote cooperation, and secure the nurturance we all need. In the absence of a robust ethic of care, no one would ensure that children were tended and educated, that the needy and powerless were protected against neglect and abandonment, that we would receive attentive care when we were ill or downtrodden. Standard moral theories can continue to underplay these tasks of care only if they keep turning a blind eye toward those whom Annette Baier has dubbed "the long unnoticed moral proletariat . . . mostly female" who do so much of the unacknowledged work on which our survival and flourishing depend.

Precisely because this work is so morally valuable, retaining a vivid sense of its potential dangers remains a crucial task for care theorists. We need to construct a frame of discourse that extends beyond the "lived experience" of the daily round of care or we will find ourselves without the conceptual and theoretical resources required to protect women and other care givers from further exploitation and disrespect.

Central to this reconstructive project will be the de-gendering of the care ethic: the extension of its norms and prescriptions to men as well as to women and to the traditionally male domains of our social world. This will require, as Patrocinio Schweickart asserts, "the incorporation of the moral values traditionally associated with femininity into the authoritative discourses of the community, into the way we reflect on, judge, and articulate the worthiness or unworthiness of actions, relations, laws, and institutions." It will engage us in critical reflection about many social and cultural practices and expectations concerning who takes on the responsibilities of caring for those in need, under what conditions, and at what cost. Given our social roles, practices, and institutions, how does the work of care taking, which is necessary to society, affect the distribution of benefits and burdens within society? How, that is, does this work affect economic status and stability, job security and promotion, the ability to pursue projects of one's own, or to contribute as an equal in the constitution and evaluation of our shared moral life? It is only after we bring the moral work of caring to the table that we can begin to articulate unromanticized, realistic, and just conceptions of what this ethic should entail.

QUESTIONS FOR ANALYSIS AND DISCUSSION

1. Central to the dispute surrounding Noddings's theory is the role of mothers as exemplars or fools of the virtue of care. How do you understand the main points of the dispute? Are the views of the mother based on historical, sociological, psychological, or anecdotal evidence? Think of the various mothers of friends you have known, as well as your own. Do you share the reflections about the moral importance of motherhood? Do you agree with the ethical egoists that women become and remain mothers out of self-interest?

2. One way of appreciating the exchange of the discussants of the care ethic is to consider those who have been your moral teachers. Do your moral teachers share the qualities discussed by Noddings, Hoagland, or Carse and Nelson? Develop your response.

3. How do you understand the philosophical problem of the virtue of care and the moral regard for strangers? Do you think Carse and Nelson have provided an acceptable account of our moral regard for strangers? Does Hoagland? What moral concern should we have for strangers?

64.

RAY RACY

In Justice to Animals

Philosophers and religious thinkers have always contemplated our relation to animals and to the earth, but environmental ethics is a fairly new branch of ethics. Addressing a range of complex issues that includes animal experimentation, vegetarianism, pollution, the greenhouse effect, use or misuse of natural resources, and even building zoos or keeping pets, environmental ethics helps us rethink fundamental philosophical questions about humanity's rightful place in the world. British philosopher Ray Racy succinctly reviews the case for treating animals justly. He looks at several familiar moral perspectives and concludes that each demands greater moral respect for nonhuman creatures, particularly those who are sentient.

CRITICAL READING QUESTIONS

1. What is the distinction between objective and subjective interests?
2. Which sorts of animals, according to Racy, have objective interests, subjective interests, or neither?
3. How does Racy use three moral perspectives to support the proper treatment of animals?
4. Should animals be treated in equal or reciprocal fashion?

There can be no serious dispute that animals and other non-human creatures get a raw deal in our world. We slaughter them for food, confine them in batteries, laboratories and zoos, pursue and kill them in the name of "sport," perform damaging and often painful experiments on them in the name of medical science and frequently for more trivial ends, poison them with pesticides, deprive wild creatures of their natural habitat, and abuse them in every conceivable way as if they were no more than inanimate objects. An increasing number of publications demonstrate a growing concern over our abuse of other species. They provide mounting evidence that this ought to be regarded as unacceptable as human sacrifice, cannibalism, child labour and slavery.

I want to argue that since animals as sentient creatures can be shown to have sensations and interests, it follows that the moral status of animals is logically

---

"In Justice to Animals," *Cogito*, Autumn 1989: 217–223. Notes have been omitted.

equivalent to that of human beings, and they should therefore be treated with proper consideration for their interests and be accorded appropriate equivalent rights.

Sentience and Interests

We know from subjective experience and also by inference from other people's behavior that human beings are sentient creatures. That is to say, they have sense perceptions and sensory responses which do not necessarily involve intelligence or mental activities. In short they have sensations and feelings. As sentient creatures they also have interests—primarily in life and some degree of autonomy, and a multitude of other interests far too numerous and diverse to mention.

What do we ordinarily mean by interests? Two principal usages can be distinguished. To say that someone has an interest in something is to say that he actively pays attention to it, or at least that it is of some concern to him, without necessarily implying any overt action on his part. It usually takes the form of "A takes an interest in Y," or "A is interested in Y." For example, "Jane takes a lively interest in modern ballet." In this sense it has a predominantly subjectivist use insofar as it indicates the subject's disposition. It is also used objectively, as when we say that something is *in* someone's interest. This normally takes the form "X is in A's interest." Both uses can be illustrated in the example: "Smith is interested in weight-lifting, but as a result of a hernia it would not be in his interest to carry on with it." In other words he has a subjective interest in it, but it would do him no good.

Clearly only sentient creatures can be said to have interests. Non-sentient entities cannot have interests in either the subjective or the objective sense. As inanimate objects they can have no subjective sensations or inclinations. Nothing that happens to an inanimate object can be either in its objective interest or against it. If a computer breaks down, the disadvantage accrues not to the computer but to its user or anyone affected by it. If its performance can be technologically enhanced, that can only be in the interest of the user or those affected by it.

Given that human beings are sentient creatures and as such have subjective and objective interests, can it be claimed that nonhuman species—i.e. animals—are also sentient creatures in the same sense and that they also have interests in one or both senses of the word? Let us look first at what evidence there is for animal sentience.

To raise the question at all might seen absurd were it not often maintained that it cannot be proved that animals have sensations, and that even if they do, it cannot be proved that they are similar to our own. That is true so far as conclusive proof is concerned. All we can ever get in the practical world is a high degree of probability by way of rational inferences based on empirical evidence. So far as the question of animal sentience is concerned, the only reliable evidence is to be obtained by analogical inference, that is, inferences based on the observations of relevant similarities in the things compared.

In discussing animal sentience we have to remember that the term "animal" covers a very wide spectrum of species, from mammals through birds, reptiles and fish to insects and other living organisms normally characterized by voluntary movement. What can be said about mammals in terms of sentience may not apply to fish, insects or grubs in the same degree, or it may apply differently. However, let us consider what evidence there is for sentience in those creatures with zoological characteristics most like our own, namely mammals.

To begin with, evolutionary theory provides strong evidence of structural and behavioural similarities between human beings and other mammals. One example of this is that animals' responses to stimuli which normally cause pain is similar to that of humans. Another is that stress, in the form of persistent threats to normal behaviour, extreme frustration, overcrowding, confinement, and other factors, can cause ulcers in animals as well as in humans. It has been shown that the electro-encephalograms (brain patterns) of mice, rats, rabbits, cats, dogs, monkeys, goats, sheep and cows are broadly analogous to those of humans. Whilst such inferences as these cannot be conclusive, they are as reliable as we can expect in empirical issues of this kind.

Significant evidence is the fact that laboratory experiments are carried out on animals precisely because it is recognized that their organisms respond in similar ways to our own. It is held to be scientifically predictable that what causes injury and pain to animals will have a similar effect on human beings. This amounts to a tacit admission of a scientific belief in the essential similarity of human and animal sentience, at least so far as mammals are concerned.

There is, of course, genuine doubt about the degree of animal sensitivity and whether birds, reptiles, fish and insects can have the same sort of sensations as we have or as it can be rationally maintained that mammals have. Pragmatically, however, there can be no serious justification for doubting that mammals, and probably other species, can suffer physical and psychological pain. So far as mammals are concerned, their physical constitution suggests that their sensory and psychological characteristics are not entirely dissimilar from our own. There is abundant evidence that they have subjective psychosomatic states such as pain and pleasure, fear, desire, satisfaction and frustration, and that they not only respond to, but pay active attention to, their physical and social environment. A dog shows a subjective response when it leaps about when its master indicates it's time for "walkies," in much the same way a cat stalking a bird is clearly showing an active subjective interest in it.

More importantly, it is equally apparent that various kinds of things can be said to be in their objective interest: for example, adequate food supplies, a congenial environment, appropriate liberty, association with others of their own kind, and many other factors which can contribute to their well-being. By the same token the lack or deprivation of such factors as these can operate against their objective interests. I would want to maintain that liberty is a factor of fundamental importance to animals, as it is to human beings, on the grounds that it is a defining characteristic of animals as distinct from plants that they are capable of voluntary movement. Confinement, whether in an extreme or a limited form, denies them the ability to function appropriately according to their nature. Whilst reptiles, fish and insects are clearly sentient creatures in the sense defined, that is as having sense perceptions and sensory responses, though not necessarily sensations of pleasure and pain, we cannot be altogether certain whether they can be said to have interests in the subjectivist sense of having or taking an interest in something.

However that may be, it does not follow that they do not all have vital objective interests. If we pull the wings off a fly or boil a lobster alive it may, or may not, feel pain in much the same way as we would if a leg were torn off or we were plunged into boiling water. But clearly it is not in the fly's objective interest to have its primary means of locomotion removed, nor in the lobster's interest to have its life arbitrarily cut short, painfully or even painlessly. Either way we deprive it of its ability to function as a living creature. Objective interests of course, are not confined to bodily states only, but may include many other factors such as food, environment, liberty, community, and doubtless special conditions which we may be unaware of which apply to particular species.

Ethical Issues

To cause any creature unnecessary pain, to prevent it from functioning naturally, or to deprive it arbitrarily of its life, is a moral issue. Such treatment raises the whole question of the ethical status of animals in relation to human beings.

It is only in comparatively recent history that the issue has begun to be seriously addressed. Prehistoric man in his earlier forms was no doubt as intimately involved in and subject to the laws and processes of nature as were other species alongside which he had evolved. His status would, in effect, have been that of an animal among other animals, and his perception of men much the same as their perceptions of him—that is as both a threat and a possible meal. In recorded history, at least from Genesis onwards, human ascendancy over other creatures had become well established, and along with it there began to be recognized the need to care for and respect the other creatures in God's creation, or at least those which were not actually harmful to human interests. However, man's intellectual ascendancy only reinforced the belief that man was a unique and entirely separate form of life. This reached its most exaggerated form in the bizarre Cartesian-type notion of animals as no more than insensitive machines. Only in the last two hundred years or so has man's relationship to animals begun to be more widely recognized as a moral issue. Bentham's observation that "the question is not, Can they reason? nor, Can they talk? but Can they *suffer*?" is a landmark in our slowly developing awareness of animal sensibility and its ethical implications.

Given, as I have indicated, that there are certain relevant similarities between human beings and animals in terms of sensations and interests, and between humans and birds, reptiles, fish and insects at least in terms of interests, it follows both logically and as a moral imperative that we ought to treat animals with a respect for their sensations and interests equivalent to that accorded to our own species. In practical terms it has to be counted as morally wrong to cause other creatures to suffer without some special moral justification. It should not be assumed that an animal's interest is always or necessarily to be counted as inferior. In situations where a conflict occurs between human and animal interests, both interests should be given fair consideration and a decision made as to which should be given preference. Exactly what every other species' interests may be it would tax human knowledge to define in detail, but broadly speaking they may be subsumed under the general headings already given, namely that they have, as we have, a fundamental interest in life, liberty and wellbeing, and freedom from abuse. I have suggested that equal respect for other creatures' interests as for our own should be regarded as a moral imperative. How can that be justified?

The Golden Rule

It is not necessary to invoke any esoteric ideas to do so. The justification lies readily to hand in the well-known principle of the golden rule. This usually takes the form that one ought to treat others as one would wish to be treated oneself. It might at once be objected that if one happens to be a masochist, it would be permissible to inflict pain on others since that is one of the things one wants for oneself. But that interpretation misses the essentially moral point of the principle. It does not imply action in favour of the agent's inclinations or interests, which would be a form of special pleading. It implies action in favour of others' inclinations or interests. To comply with the principle, the agent has to project himself imaginatively into the other party's situation and appreciate how he or she would feel in those circumstances. The principle is sometimes formulated negatively, namely that one ought not to treat others as one would not wish to be treated oneself, on the grounds that the avoidance of evil is ethically more fundamental than the promotion of good.

It is not difficult to see how the golden rule, in either of its forms, ought to be applied by human beings to other species, as well as to their own kind. The argument can be briefly outlined as follows. Suffering, whether physical, psychological, social or of whatever kind, is something we do not like. If I, as a sentient being, dislike certain kinds of suffering, I must, to be consistent, assume that other sentient beings with similar or equivalent basic feelings and interests to my own can suffer in much the same way as I do in similar circumstances. Moreover, I have to put myself imaginatively into another creature's situation to understand how it would feel if it were caused unnecessary pain or its interests were harmed. For example, I have to consider how a badger would feel when it is savaged by dogs in its sett, or a monkey if it is deprived of its natural and social environment and isolated in a clinical laboratory for experimental purposes. The moral imperative requires that we ought not to inflict on others what we could not accept for ourselves if we were in their situation.

The moral principle can also be validated by its consonance with the purely logical principle of universalizability, which requires that if we are to be consistent, we cannot make different moral judgments about actions and situations which we admit to be exactly or relevantly similar.

Clearly the golden rule can be adopted only by human beings, that is beings capable of making rational choices and of using imagination. We cannot require that it should be reciprocated by animals, or indeed by very young children or mental defectives, as none of these is capable of making rational choices or of conceptual thought.

Justice

The issue can be given additional support by appeal to the principle of justice. If, as I have tried to show, humans and animals share certain relevant similarities in terms of sensations and interests, it follows that according to the ordinary principle of justice they should be entitled to equivalent treatment appropriate to their sensibilities and interests. If justice is to be understood in its ordinary meaning of "fairness," it implies consistency in treating relevantly similar cases alike. If it is considered morally unacceptable to perform potentially painful or harmful experiments on human beings without their knowledge or without their consent, it must be even more unacceptable to perform such experiments on other sentient creatures who cannot know what is being done to them and who cannot refuse.

However, a somewhat different interpretation of justice throws light on the issue and reinforces the case for the moral valuation of animals. This is the formal principle which requires that each individual is to be given his due. It is a formal principle in that it does not specify *what* individuals are due. The specific question arises therefore as to what that would be. According to Tom Regan, who advances this view, the most satisfactory answer is the one based on the principle of equality. What individuals are due is respect for their equal inherent value. By inherent value he means having value as a being in one's own right, or as Kant puts it, as an end in oneself. He distinguishes this from intrinsic value, by which he refers to an individual's pleasures, preferences, experiences, culture, etc. I would, however, understand intrinsic value somewhat differently. I would take it to mean that for an individual to have intrinsic value is to say that he is commendable for some personal quality such as knowledge, ability, disposition, integrity or some other human characteristic. To say that an individual has inherent value is not to imply any kind of praise for some value associated with him, but to value him simply as an individual being, regardless of whether he is rated as good, bad or indifferent.

I would agree with Tom Regan that every individual has inherent value, but I do not think it can be satisfactorily claimed that every individual has that value equally, as he maintains. Can it be held that an ant has the same inherent value as a human being? If by inherent value is meant value as a being in its own right, apart from any utility it may or may not have for others, it is surely the case that a human being is altogether richer in inherent characteristics of an intellectual, aesthetic, moral and religious kind as well as having more complex sensibilities and a more extensive variety of projects and relationships than can be attributed to an ant, still less to an amoeba. It would not be difficult to draw up a rough hierarchy of life forms, from micro-organisms and plants, through insects, fish, reptiles and birds upwards to mammals and human beings in terms of their inherent value, that is in terms of the richness of their inherent characteristics. All forms of life may be said to have inherent value, but I would want to contend that they have it in different degrees.

According to the criterion of a hierarchy of inherent characteristics it can be seen how a distinction can be made between plants and other creatures, and indeed between insects and other animals, particularly mammals. Such a distinction is most apparent in terms of sentience. Animals, as already defined, are sentient creatures characterized by voluntary movement and having sensations and interests. As far as we know plants do not experience sensations as we understand the terms since they have no nervous system. The same may apply, as I have suggested, to insects. To the extent, therefore, that plants are endowed with more primitive characteristics, they cannot be rated as highly in inherent value as, say, birds and mammals. But that does not exclude them from having inherent value at all. As I have argued above, just as insects have an interest in functioning according to their genetic programme, whether or not they experience any kind of sensations in doing so, plants may also be said to have an objective interest in functioning according to their nature and fulfilling their respective programmes. The moral implications which arise would appear to be much the same as for other living creatures— namely that we should not harm or destroy them arbitrarily, that is, without sufficient reason. We may not be able to cause them pain, but at least we ought not to stunt their growth or destroy them wantonly. Just such an attitude to the natural world is exemplified in Blake's declaration that "Everything that lives is Holy."

Noxious Creatures

The concept of inherent value has significant implications for our attitude to creatures which we regard as harmful, from scorpions and rats to house flies and lice. From our characteristically anthropocentric viewpoint we classify creatures as noxious if they harm our interests as human beings. Of course most species are harmful to some others—carnivores to their prey, herbivores to their competitors for food supplies, parasites to their host, and man to most other forms of life. Respect for inherent value in other creatures does not, however, imply that we should tolerate infestation by cockroaches, or flies walking over children's eyes. It does not imply absolute liberty for any species or individuals, including humans. Liberty for all necessarily imposes reciprocal limitations on the liberty of all. If any species multiplies indiscriminately it becomes a threat to others. Normally, natural processes maintain a system of checks and balances. This has been so far disrupted by human dominance that we alone are in a position to restore a viable equilibrium for all. Our ecological awareness and practical capability impose on us the responsibility for ensuring that no species is allowed to multiply or dominate at the expense of others. It is only in superabundance that any species becomes a pest— humanity not excluded. Given an acceptable numerical limitation which we alone are able to secure for ourselves and others, there seems to be no valid reason why every existing species should not have its place on earth. The principle of justice requires us to respect the inherent value of species as species and of individual creatures as individuals. Every creature that is born, human and non-human, should be regarded as having a *prima facie* right to exist. We cannot justify exterminating any species or harming any individual if doing so contravenes the principle of justice—i.e. treating others as if they were objects whose value was simply their usefulness to ourselves.

Rights

It is of course one thing to make the case for the identity of fundamental human and animal interests; it is another to protect those interests. Important human interests are acknowledged and protected by corresponding rights, expressed in general terms as the right to life, liberty and the pursuit of happiness, however that ambiguous term may be interpreted. To have a right to something implies that it would be morally wrong to deprive anyone of it without sufficient justification. It would be wrong to deprive anyone of his liberty unless it became a threat to others. Whilst such rights are sometimes referred to as *natural* rights, in fact no rights exist in nature. They have to be recognized by others and safeguarded by law. There can be no real rights without the ultimate sanction of laws to uphold them. Clearly not all human beings can establish rights for themselves, for example children, mental defectives and primitive tribes, but that does not count against their moral entitlement to certain basic rights and their protection in law. The case is no different in principle with animals. Other creatures which have fundamental interests of a similar kind must be equally entitled to have those interests recognized as rights and safeguarded by legislation. Our situation of dominance over other species entails on us a unique and increasingly urgent responsibility for their protection and well-being.

It does not of course follow that animal rights should be regarded as equal in all respects to our own. If an unequivocal choice had to be made between saving the life of an animal or a human being, other things being equal, giving preference to the human life would be justified on the grounds that a person's interests, which would include his activities, expectations, projects, relationships and other factors, would be infinitely richer and he would therefore stand to lose far more. But it should not be assumed that human rights should always or necessarily take precedence. As stated above in connection with interests, where a conflict between human and animal rights occurs, no hard and fast ruling in favour of either would be in order. In justice, consideration ought to be given to the interests of both parties and equitable decisions made accordingly.

The weight of evidence is clearly against there being any rational doubt that sentient creatures, from the so-called "higher" mammals to insects and other more primitive forms of life, are subject to factors which can operate either in or against their interests. It follows that their moral status is logically equivalent to our own in respect of these interests and the corresponding rights which are designed to protect them. As a matter of logic and justice, the case for animal rights can be defined as no more nor less than a logical extension of ordinary human ethics.

QUESTIONS FOR ANALYSIS AND DISCUSSION

1. Racy proposes that the human mistreatment of animals should be morally equivalent to and "as unacceptable as human sacrifice, cannibalism, child labour, and slavery." Consider an ordinary event. Between classes you are eating tender fried chicken for lunch; the classmate who joins you is munching on a juicy bacon/cheeseburger. Your friend the nutrition major joins you, admon-

ishes your dietary indulgences and begins nibbling on a tuna salad. Midway through lunch your friend the philosophy major stops by, pulls a veggieburger sandwich out of his book bag, and lectures you not on your dietary but on your immoral indulgences. Using Racy's essay as the model, explain how the three of you can continue your lunch in good conscience.

2. Racy distinguishes animals from plants by claiming that animals have sentience and liberty. Yet some have claimed that plants are sensitive too. Horticulturalists and home gardeners often relate tales of how plants thrive in tranquil circumstances. Blossoms are more colorful and leaves are healthier if plants grow in a musical climate featuring Mozart rather than heavy metal. How do you think Racy would respond to these claims?

3. Though plants are qualitatively different from animals (that is, different in kind), most animals are only quantitatively different from humans (that is, different by degrees), according to Racy. Moreover, those areas where humans might be clearly distinct from animals, such as their use of symbols or construction of artificial systems of life, are not morally significant. Do you agree or disagree with Racy's distinctions? Be specific.

4. Racy states that the golden rule dictates a moral regard for animals, yet he acknowledges that we cannot expect animals to reciprocate. Hence, animals are the other, and we should show them a respect that is not attached to our understanding of them. In Hoagland's critique of the virtue of care, she says that any moral attitude that emphasizes a one-directional ethic exploits and subjugates the moral person. If Racy is correct about nonreciprocity, is he setting humans up for exploitation and subjugation by animals? If not, what is the relevant difference between the model of the caring mother and the model of the human who cares for animals?

65.

BILL SHAW

A Virtue Ethics Approach to Aldo Leopold's Land Ethic

Anthropocentrism is the belief that humans are the center of the universe in terms of value or moral worth. Utilitarian philosopher Peter Singer labels this belief a form of speciesism, the unwarranted claim that other species are inherently inferior to humans. For Bill

"A Virtue Ethics Approach to Aldo Leopold's Land Ethic," *Environmental Ethics*, Spring 1997: 53–57, 61–67. Notes have been omitted.

Shaw (b. 1940), a professor of law and business ethics at the University of Texas–
Austin, virtue ethics provides a richer understanding of moral relations between humans
and nature, avoiding the extremes of those who contend that humans are either equal to or
naturally superior to the nonhuman world. Using the ideas of early environmentalist
Aldo Leopold as a departure point, Shaw clarifies the relevance of three virtues: respect,
prudence, and practical judgment. These virtues provide a model by which both the natu-
ral world and the human community can flourish.

⊣ CRITICAL READING QUESTIONS ⊢

1. For many virtue-based moralists, the good is defined as human happiness. How does Shaw define the good from an ecological perspective?
2. What is the difference between a biotic and a human community?
3. How does Shaw distinguish the force of moral virtues from moral
   rules?
4. How are prudence and practical judgment related?
5. What is the point in introducing slave girls near the end of the essay?

1. Introduction

Moral philosophers tend to approach the subject of environmental ethics from the
same two perspectives that they approach every other subject within their domain.
The perspectives center on issues of "the good," i.e., the good for the human community, and "the right," i.e., the rules of right conduct. Their mission, so to speak,
is to "search for knowledge of the good life and right conduct." This approach
certainly includes the common understanding of the word *ethics*, but it is not at all
clear that these perspectives are sufficient for environmental ethics.

In a broad sense, an ethic is a way of life or an attitude towards life. It distinguishes social from antisocial behavior on the basis of a commitment to certain
values of the human community—values that underlie any attempt to understand
and articulate the right and the good. The ethical life as we live it day-to-day is
guided by a sense of meaning and purpose that has in part to do with feeling and
emotion and in part with rational processes.

If we conceive of ethics as a system of values or a set of attitudes that differentiates between the good for the community and the bad, we might conceive of the
project of environmental ethics as an attempt to extend the notion of the good to
embrace a community beyond that of human beings. Such a project engages both
our emotional and our rational resources as we reflect upon, and develop, a moral

concern toward the natural world as a whole. This concern, and the ethics it engenders, leads us to explore our relationships with the world around us.

Relationships, specifically ecological relationships, are clearly the centerpiece of environmental ethics. After all, ecology is the study of the relationships of organisms with one another and with the environment. A good place to begin this study is with the work of a person who was an ecologist rather than a moral philosopher. I am referring to Aldo Leopold and to his famous essay, "The Land Ethic." Leopold has long been recognized as one of the most significant figures in the development of the environmental ethics—especially the more controversial, non-human-centered strain of this movement identified with preservationist theories, ecocentrism, deep ecology, and the like. In this paper, I use some of the basic principles at work in "The Land Ethic" to launch a discussion of two things. First, I examine the possibility of a paradigm shift in everyday ethical attitudes. This examination focuses on the interests that are at stake in such a shift, and the difficulties inherent in a modification of our ethical perception. Second, I consider the possibility of "land virtues" that may provide us with an avenue for circumventing some of the difficulties inherent in a paradigm shift.

One way to understand "The Land Ethic" is to look upon it as a set of attitudes and practices toward the unfolding or blossoming of natural systems (ecosystems) in accordance with their purpose or *telos*. This naturalistic trajectory is, of course, highly controversial as a general approach to ethical theory. With regard to environmental ethics in particular, the observation that the environment evolves continuously (rather than crystallizing at a particular stage) has served to challenge this idea. It should be noted, however, that human communities evolve as well, and no one has thought to jettison virtue ethics for that reason alone. Further, it appears that an Aristotelian conception of the "good" of natural systems, in reference to their nature and *telos,* is operating in Leopold's notion of the "integrity" of natural systems. I have more to say about this later.

Because ecosystems include nonhuman as well as human subjects among its "citizens," Leopold's ethic does indeed demand a reevaluation and a reorientation in our thinking. The object of this process is to bring into harmony these nonhuman and human subjects by bestowing a special status upon those systems exhibiting a *telos* (in Aristotle's terms, a "nature," a "way of being"). A forest, no less than a human, exhibits the capacity for internal self-direction—for growth, for blossoming, for achieving its *telos*—and for that reason forests and other natural systems are respected as citizens in this new paradigm. Of great significance is the corollary of this proposition: human beings are reduced from masters of the land to "plain member and fellow citizens." How might something like this notion of citizenship be rendered plausible, and desirable—that is, in the interests of human and nonhuman subjects alike?

The attitudes and practices that serve the ultimate good in this new paradigm—the land virtues—tend to preserve the integrity, stability, and beauty of natural systems. Vices tend to destabilize and to destroy these characteristics of natural systems. They send shock waves through the environment—the greenhouse effect, ozone depletion, eutrophication, loss of species, and desertification—that jeopardize all living systems. I discuss the significance of adopting virtue language and its relation to these problems below.

II. The Land Ethic

Clearly, an environmental ethic is an intangible thing. In an effort to explore it further, it is necessary to consider what is "good" from a different perspective—an environmental perspective. The next step then is to ask what might count as the "good" in an ethic based upon a fundamental moral regard for the environment.

The Good

Leopold envisions "the ultimate good" not as happiness but as *harmony* within the biotic, or living, community. The biotic community is one that is composed of natural, living systems including nonhuman and human members. In Leopold's scheme of things, the word *land* stands proxy for life and for the source of life, e.g., the soil, water, plants, and animals. Harmony within this community—specifically, the integrity, stability, beauty of the community—is the ultimate good. Everything aims at harmony, but, given its scope and complexity, it is not one of those subjects that can be specified with precision.

Because humans are included in this community, Leopold evidently views "the good for humanity" as compatible with, or a subset of, "the good for the biotic community." This point is obviously a crucial issue, and the connection between the entirety of the biotic community and the subcommunities within it (including the human community) has to be addressed, as does the question of the status of individual members of the biotic community vis-à-vis the whole. The fear, if well grounded, that neither the human community or any of its members nor any individual member of any other biotic community has any value apart from the whole, certainly constitutes a radical departure from the standard course of ethical theory.

Bentham admits into the moral community any being capable of feeling pain; thus, animals with a nervous system less developed than ours could get in. Albert Schweitzer extends this community by advocating a "reverence for life," but these views have been largely ignored by mainstream philosophy. Bentham, Schweitzer, and more recently Peter Singer and Tom Regan all appear to be arguing for an extentionist approach, but one that maintains a human center. What *seems* to be implied in Leopold, however, is much more holistic. With the biotic community as a whole occupying the center, human rights, interests, and preferences can no longer dominate the stage as a privileged and unqualified "trump."

Clearly then, we need to address two major issues before we can continue. The first concerns the question of extending the boundary of the moral universe to biotic communities, to beings with a *telos*. Why is doing so morally just? The second issue revolves around the question of the status of the human component within an expanded moral community. Is there any room for a hierarchical conception of moral worth within the "land ethic," or should such a vision be dismissed as unjustifiably anthropocentric? If human beings are obliged to abandon the center of the moral universe, then Leopold's vision surely seems to be at odds with the interests of the most articulate citizens of this universe. First, however, let us approach the issue of the extension of the boundaries of moral standing.

We might ask, why let "them" in? Why admit something as intangible as "the land" into the moral community? One would not have to go far to hear arguments that there is not enough harmony within the moral community now. How is that going to change for the better by granting something like citizenship to "land?" Finally, what does it mean as a practical matter to admit land into full citizenship? Would it mean that the "land" gets a voice, a vote, a veto? Would it hold the ultimate "trump"?

(1) *Why let "them" in?* Leopold views the admission of land into the moral community as a natural extension of ethics. In the evolutionary or historical sense, as we understand it, family groups of humans and certain nonhuman animals survive and prosper by developing modes of cooperation within the group. It has been the natural or evolutionary development for groups with the greatest internal harmony and cooperation to flourish, and to be successful in extending their boundaries.

Group bonds, group loyalty, or group identification—the internal harmony or cohesion that forestalls splintering or deterioration within the group—also fosters or enhances the group's success in competition with other groups (the gentlest and most cooperative member of the group may be its fiercest defender). Through the process of natural selection, cohesive groups (and group members with the most highly developed sense of cooperation) are the "fittest." Consequently they "survive" in competition with others.

These "modes of cooperation," observable in other and lower life forms (i.e., in natural systems or biotic communities), can be articulated as an "ethic" only with the imaginative and intellectual powers of human beings, but they are nevertheless real and valid processes. These instinctive or genetic forces at work in nonhuman systems find their near counterpart, though not their exact mirror image, in the human "affective domain" (i.e., the "emotional" side). Human feeling, sentiment, and emotion, then, account for the origin of ethics in the Darwinian sense.

. . .

The Land Virtues

Why introduce virtue language at this point? I believe it can be helpful for a number of reasons. Clearly, this examination of the land ethic has opened up a myriad of difficulties. On what grounds are we attributing intrinsic value to participants in the biotic community? What could possibly be the basis for the claim that the land has a "right" to continued existence, as Leopold suggests? Is this a moral right, a legal right, or perhaps both? Moreover, even if we grant such rights, on the basis of value or interests, for example, how do we begin to develop a theory to guide us through the process of adjudicating between competing sets of interests and rights? Do we really want to frame the notion of an environmental ethic in terms of a litany of who has claims against whom, and who has a right to what?

Virtue language, I believe, allows us to circumvent, or at least to place on the back burner, some of these divisive issues. In order to begin addressing these concerns, we need the mediation of virtue ethics analysis to explore the sorts of attitudes and habits that we are in fact cultivating toward the environment, or, perhaps more importantly, to explore the sorts of attitudes and habits that we should be cultivating.

In virtue ethics we are able to stop fretting about what claims the environment has against us, what rights we may be impinging upon, and concentrate on the more important question of how we as moral agents ought to relate to other environmental communities. From this perspective, the fundamental moral question is not "who has what against me?" but rather "what kind of person should I be?" and, given the enormous complexities and uncertainties of ecological relationships, "how should a person act to foster the well-being of all living communities?" Leopold, prophetically I believe, underscores the necessity of changing attitudes before changing laws: "Obligations have no meaning without conscience," he relates, "and the problem we face is the extension of the social conscience from people to land."

(1) *Virtues and Rules.* To begin with, virtues are stable propensities to excel or character habits that are instilled into us from our early years and for as long as we are capable of moral growth. Second, virtues are "means" or midpoints between excess and deficit. A person who exhibits the virtue of honesty is discrete enough not to "spill his guts" at every opportunity to be heard, but forthcoming enough to volunteer information that is relevant to a discussion and not privileged. Finally, virtues are not the same as rules, and the person of virtue is not a mere rule follower living in blind obedience to a fixed position. A virtuous person is a person of character and judgment. Virtues cannot be formulated with the precision of a rule because they require decisions to be made under unique and challenging circumstances. In making these decisions, a virtuous person harnesses the emotional (affective) and the cognitive (rational) aspects of his or her psyche.

It is wrong, however, to suggest that virtue ethics is hostile to rules, even if, at bottom, virtues are contextual. Good rules for children to learn include "Never tell a lie," "Be kind to animals," and "Don't play with matches." A virtuous person has been conditioned for so long and so well by parents and friends that such a rule has become internalized—it has become a "natural" habit, that is, second nature. In educating children, rules have their place. However, in the life of an adult, rules are either too rigid or narrow for the kinds of judgments that have to be made, or are too abstract to give any valuable guidance.

(2) *Land Virtues and Social or Interpersonal Virtues.* Honesty, thoughtfulness, and prudence, the examples utilized above, are very important social or interpersonal virtues. Honesty and thoughtfulness are frequently characterized as moral virtues (character habits that are good in themselves) and prudence as a nonmoral virtue (generally equated with enlightened self-interest). These and other such internalized virtues are constituents of the good, but the good consists of external

elements as well (good laws, good fortune, good health, good climate). All of these goods relate in some way to Leopold's vision of a land ethic—an ethic in which the good of the biotic community is "integrity, stability, and beauty." The role of the land virtues should be to foster or advance that good. If they were, we could then use them to instill in our children such great respect for those virtues that it would become natural, or second nature, for them to act in ways that supported the well-being of biotic communities.

These land virtues would not repeal or replace the social or interpersonal virtues. Instead, the land virtues would exist in phase with them. The virtues of courage, temperance, truthfulness, and justice as we have come to know them, or the Christian virtues of faith, hope, and charity, have little to say to us about how to treat the owl. However, Leopold's new concept of the good (a new order or new paradigm) gives us a clue—the owl and other members of the biotic community should be treated with respect as citizens—citizens who have intrinsic value or value in themselves—as citizens they should not be put in jeopardy for any but the most compelling reasons.

(3) *Land Virtues.* Beginning with the notion that it is the community rather than the individual community member that takes precedence in "The Land Ethic," and that the "good" of the community consists in the harmony of its elements—integrity, stability, and beauty—the "land virtues" should be those character traits (habits) that foster the "good." This kind of regard for the land, sometimes even approaching a spiritual regard, is commonplace in other, supposedly less advanced cultures, and, to borrow a familiar example, is classically illustrated by the attitudes of the North American native peoples. Such regard represents "simpler times," to be sure, but this window into the past gives exposure to a heritage that seems worthy of recapture and of adapting to a contemporary setting.

What are the virtues, then, that we could call "land virtues"? I advance here no more than three, though others can also be advanced. Each of the three I want to consider is an adaptation of a traditional virtue: respect (ecological sensitivity), prudence, and practical judgment.

(a) The first of these, respect for biotic communities (hence, ecosystems and ultimately the biosphere), equates with a respect for things with a *telos*. The human community is not isolated from the environment, but a part of it—part of a greater whole that functions in very complex and dynamic, if not fully understood, ways. This dynamic and complex interaction is something that we must bear in mind when we try to cultivate an appropriate attitude toward the environment and deliberate about ethical choices. After all, things with a telos are, literally, things with a purpose, things with intrinsic value. Respect for this intrinsic value cautions us that they are not merely for our play, but are placed here by nature for purposes that we may not even fully understand.

Thus, although the well-being of the community comes first, it does not mean that individual members of the community can be sacrificed for merely trivial ends. While the deer, quail, and trout communities can survive with fewer members, they are not purely "game," that is, they are not candidates for waste, depletion, or extinction by hunters and fishers. Concerning the supposition that hunting and fishing are a significant need (a physical need such as food or shelter or even a psychic need), such a justification holds only so long as it does not undermine the "good," which incorporates the "integrity, stability, and beauty" of the species or biotic community.

(b) The virtue of prudence embodies the age-old wisdom that enlightened, long-term well-being, rather than immediate preference gratification, is more likely to advance the good. There is always the risk, however, that the perceived long-term good may never materialize, and that the short-term gain, in retrospect, may have been the better choice. This prospect serves to remind us of the deficiency of our science and of our lack of understanding of human and ecological affairs. Setbacks of this nature, nevertheless, do not undermine the virtue of prudence. Although prudence is heir to many such setbacks, our experience teaches that on the whole we should cultivate the habit of "not rushing to judgment." On the contrary, we should be thoughtful, considerate, and sometimes even plodding on how best to advance the good. Prudence, being the midpoint between "a mad rush into oblivion" and an "intransigent do-nothingness," has particular relevance to the good of ecosystems.

> [E]cosystems that are stable relative to characteristic fluctuations or stresses in which they have evolved may not be stable relative to human-induced stress no matter how diverse they are, simply because shifts in the characteristic diversity induced by high technology or large population influxes are not the kinds of stress to which even the most diverse ecosystems have evolved a resistance.

The prudent course of action for the human species, or the course of action exhibiting a high degree of "enlightened self-interest," surely links the well-being of the ecosystem with its own. Nevertheless, we must make this realization a part of our general moral outlook before we can begin to sort out issues of genuinely competing interests. Otherwise, the short-term, bottom-line, cost-benefit approach will win out again and again.

Finally, in regard to the virtue of prudence, there is no apology for the pursuit of self-interest. Self-interest, identified closely with the interest of the community (and most of the time even identified as the community interest) has its place, and is not to be confused with selfishness and the radical pursuit of freedom that is certain to be destructive of community bonds.

(c) Practical wisdom or judgment is the third of my "land virtues," and it should be understood as permeating the other two. Judgment is involved in showing "sensitivity" to ecological communities and their members and in sorting out the rival claims and interests within and among communities. The same is true of acting with "prudence." In face of the uncertain environmental consequences of clearing the Brazilian rain forests, or of logging "old forests" in Washington and Oregon, what weight should an enlightened decision maker place on real human needs for food, clothing, and employment and what weight on the preservation of those ecosystems? Surely there are no rules here that guarantee a single right answer. It is, of course, important to proceed with sensitivity and with prudence, but when one has to make choices and the consequence of those choices cannot be known, what should guide that decision? For a person committed to "The Land Ethic," (i) the decision should advance a concept of the good that welcomes the "integrity, stability, and beauty" of biotic communities within its sphere, and it should exhibit the land virtues (respect, prudence, and practical judgment) in mediating the welfare of this expanded network of communities, and (ii) the decision should not rest on the uncritical assumption that in all of its aspects the human community is the most highly evolved and that it always exhibits the greatest degree of "integrity, stability, and beauty" (housing developments and golf courses piled upon aquifers are good evidence that certain preferences should be reexamined).

III. Conclusion: Citizenship and the Land Ethic

Leopold's controversial work should not be taken as a political treatise or as an original work of ethical theory. He speaks of *citizenship,* commonly understood as a political concept, and *respect,* a term familiar to ethicists, but his overriding message pushes the language of these traditions to the limits—even beyond those limits. Central to his thought, however, is the compelling need to reconceptualize the "land," that is, to enter into a new relationship with the network of biotic communities that metaphorically compose the land.

In Leopold's view, land is community. More precisely, land is a web of interrelated and interdependent communities, and those relationships and dependencies are exposed to ever-increasing pressure, and sometimes even to extinction, by the human community. The human community is not the sole intruder on this web, however; it is only the most recent and the most dangerous.

Mankind's intrusions upon other biotic communities are led by the assumption that land is a resource. These forays are sometimes characterized by prudence (a virtue which includes a survival component), but also, and too frequently, by indifference, by ignorance, and by a materialistic, economic imperative. At some time or another, every biotic community treats one or more of its neighbors as a resource, and this exploitation is taken to be the "survival" mode in a Darwinian sense that is beyond any moral condemnation. It is the human community alone (or a substantial segment of that community) that sees itself as virtually unrestrained in its pursuit of material well-being and looks upon all choices as economically driven.

Leopold arrived upon the scene as a modest but insightful professional, a forest and game manager. He doesn't invite us into a world of deep ecology. He does, however, urge upon us a different way of thinking, a different mindset or paradigm. It may not be "new under the sun," and he makes no such claim. Leopold understands his ethic to be an extension of an anthropocentric vision. In a way that parallels the admission of "slave girls" into the human fold, he sees the protective cloak of the land ethic drawn warmly about the borders of neighboring communities. Communities that were once mere instruments, mere resources, mere property, are valued in a different light.

Leopold makes it clear enough that the new paradigm is not a new set of commandments or an ecological golden rule. Right and wrong, good and bad, are assessed in terms of the tendency to produce or preserve "the integrity, beauty, and stability of the biotic community." This standard can be understood as a component of "the good," and "the good," since Aristotle's time, is the thing to be aimed for.

It would, of course, advance Leopold's case, and Aristotle's, if the components of the good were stationary targets and were profiled in stark clarity. Then we could correct our aim, or even perfect it. But this degree of clarity is not one of the attributes of this good, which is an evolving target, in which elements that Leopold conjoins must take their place alongside other constituents of the good.

Beyond that, the land ethic, and the virtues that advance it, simply take time to do their work. This approach is no quick fix. The tradition of virtue ethics, so long absorbed with the good for humankind, is being asked to extend its territory, and to enfold the good of biotic communities as well. As once it received into its realm the descendants of Odysseus' slave girls, and elevated their status from chattel property to personhood, it now stands ready to welcome the "integrity, stability, and beauty" of biotic communities into its borders.

QUESTIONS FOR ANALYSIS AND DISCUSSION

1. Central to Shaw's position is a value for community. Do you accept his meaning of community? If it is true that the human community threatens the biotic community, does that necessarily mean the human community is treading on morally weak ground? Why, or why not?

2. According to J. A. Baker in *The Peregrine*, only humans have terrorized the natural world. "No pain," he writes, "no death is more terrible to a wild creature than its fear of man. . . . A poisoned crow, gaping and helplessly floundering in the grass, bright yellow foam bubbling from its throat, will dash itself up again and again onto the descending wall of air, if you try to catch it." Given this scenario, is there any reason to expect animals and nature to trust the human community? If not, is environmental ethics a lost cause? If trust is possible, which specific steps should humans take to reestablish this trust?

3. Three virtues are described as best able to treat nature morally. Which vices do you think best describe how humans have developed their sovereignty—and misuse—of nature? excessive pride? gluttony? sloth? Consider the vices you think are the likely candidates and assess whether Shaw's virtues are strong enough to overcome them. Be specific in your view of this moral tension.

66.

WILLIAM CRONON

The Trouble with Wilderness

On one hand, it is easy to support the efforts of environmentalists. At least since Jeremy Bentham's version of utilitarianism weighed the pains and pleasures of animals as part of moral practice, philosophers have been careful when addressing the value of the natural world. Indeed, in the nineteenth century a number of social utopians and critics of industrialism—Henry David Thoreau and Ralph Waldo Emerson among them—articulated a respect for nature. On the other hand, it is difficult to support the moral ambitions of environmentalists if they rest on shaky intellectual foundations. According to William Cronon (b. 1954), history professor at the University of Wisconsin, the shaky foundations of the current ecology movement include a weak and limited sense of how humans have for centuries held a rather fearful attitude toward nature. Cronon's lucid account of the idea of nature shows that only in recent times has nature been viewed as sacred. In earlier times nature was better known as wilderness. In earlier times a trip to the mountains or forests was not the occasion for a pleasant guided tour but was an encounter with the unpredictable and the dangerous. Nature was truly the other. These days, observes Cronon, nature has become assimilated or tamed. This shift has gone largely unnoticed in environmental ethics.

CRITICAL READING QUESTIONS

1. What were some of the main descriptions of wilderness 250 years ago?
2. What does Cronon mean in saying that wilderness is in many ways a creation of culture?
3. Why are our views of nature like a mirror?
4. If nature exists for everyone, why does Cronon suggest that the environmental movement could be seen as a form of cultural imperialism?
5. How are the terms *home*, *wild*, and *other* used by Cronon?

"The Trouble with Wilderness: or, Getting Back to the Wrong Nature," from *Uncommon Ground: Toward Inventing Nature*, edited by William Cronin (New York: W. W. Norton & Company, Inc., 1995), pp. 83–88, 94–98, 105–109.

The time has come to rethink wilderness.

This will seem a heretical claim to many environmentalists, since the idea of wilderness has for decades been a fundamental tenet—indeed, a passion—of the environmental movement, especially in the United States. For many Americans wilderness stands as the last remaining place where civilization, that all too human disease, has not fully infected the earth. It is an island in the polluted sea of urban-industrial modernity, the one place we can turn for escape from our own too-muchness. Seen in this way, wilderness presents itself as the best antidote to our human selves, a refuge we must somehow recover if we hope to save the planet. As Henry David Thoreau once famously declared, "In Wildness is the preservation of the World."

But is it? The more one knows of its peculiar history, the more one realizes that wilderness is not quite what it seems. Far from being the one place on earth that stands apart from humanity, it is quite profoundly a human creation—indeed, the creation of very particular human cultures at very particular moments in human history. It is not a pristine sanctuary where the last remnant of an untouched, endangered, but still transcendent nature can for at least a little while longer be encountered without the contaminating taint of civilization. Instead, it is a product of that civilization, and could hardly be contaminated by the very stuff of which it is made. Wilderness hides its unnaturalness behind a mask that is all the more beguiling because it seems so natural. As we gaze into the mirror it holds up for us, we too easily imagine that what we behold is Nature when in fact we see the reflection of our own unexamined longings and desires. For this reason, we mistake ourselves when we suppose that wilderness can be the solution to our culture's problematic relationships with the nonhuman world, for wilderness is itself no small part of the problem.

To assert the unnaturalness of so natural a place will no doubt seem absurd or even perverse to many readers, so let me hasten to add that the nonhuman world we encounter in wilderness is far from being merely our own invention. I celebrate with others who love wilderness the beauty and power of the things it contains. Each of us who has spent time there can conjure images and sensations that seem all the more hauntingly real for having engraved themselves so indelibly on our memories. Such memories may be uniquely our own, but they are also familiar enough to be instantly recognizable to others. Remember this? The torrents of mist shoot out from the base of a great waterfall in the depths of a Sierra canyon, the tiny droplets cooling your face as you listen to the roar of the water and gaze up toward the sky through a rainbow that hovers just out of reach. Remember this too: looking out across a desert canyon in the evening air, the only sound a lone raven calling in the distance, the rock walls dropping away into a chasm so deep that its bottom all but vanishes as you squint into the amber light of the setting sun. And this: the moment beside the trail as you sit on a sandstone ledge, your boots damp with the morning dew while you take in the rich smell of the pines, and the small red fox—or maybe for you it was a raccoon or a coyote or a deer—that suddenly ambles across your path, stopping for a long moment to gaze in your direction with cautious indifference before continuing on its way. Remember the feelings of such moments, and you will know as well as I do that you were in the presence of something irreducibly nonhuman, something profoundly Other than yourself. Wilderness is made of that, too.

And yet: what brought each of us to the places where such memories became possible is entirely a cultural invention. Go back 250 years in American and European history, and you do not find nearly so many people wandering around remote corners of the planet looking for what today we would call "the wilderness experience." As late as the eighteenth century, the most common usage of the word "wilderness" in the English language referred to landscapes that generally carried adjectives far different from the ones they attract today. To be a wilderness then was to be "deserted," "savage," "desolate," "barren"—in short, a "waste," the word's nearest synonym. Its connotations were anything but positive, and the emotion one was most likely to feel in its presence was "bewilderment"—or terror.

Many of the word's strongest associations then were biblical, for it is used over and over again in the King James Version to refer to places on the margins of civilization where it is all too easy to lose oneself in moral confusion and despair. The wilderness was where Moses had wandered with his people for forty years, and where they had nearly abandoned their God to worship a golden idol. "For Pharaoh will say of the Children of Israel," we read in Exodus, "They are entangled in the land, the wilderness hath shut them in." The wilderness was where Christ had struggled with the devil and endured his temptations: "And immediately the Spirit driveth him into the wilderness. And he was there in the wilderness for forty days tempted of Satan; and was with the wild beasts; and the angels ministered unto him." The "delicious Paradise" of John Milton's Eden was surrounded by "a steep wilderness, whose hairy sides / Access denied" to all who sought entry. When Adam and Eve were driven from that garden, the world they entered was a wilderness that only their labor and pain could redeem. Wilderness, in short, was a place to which one came only against one's will, and always in fear and trembling. Whatever value it might have arose solely from the possibility that it might be "reclaimed" and turned toward human ends—planted as a garden, say, or a city upon a hill. In its raw state, it had little or nothing to offer civilized men and women.

But by the end of the nineteenth century, all this had changed. The wastelands that had once seemed worthless had for some people come to seem almost beyond price. That Thoreau in 1862 could declare wildness to be the preservation of the world suggests the sea change that was going on. Wilderness had once been the antithesis of all that was orderly and good—it had been the darkness, one might say, on the far side of the garden wall—and yet now it was frequently likened to Eden itself. When John Muir arrived in the Sierra Nevada in 1869, he would declare, "No description of Heaven that I have ever heard or read of seems half so fine." He was hardly alone in expressing such emotions. One by one, various corners of the American map came to be designated as sites whose wild beauty was so spectacular that a growing number of citizens had to visit and see them for themselves. Niagara Falls was the first to undergo this transformation, but it was soon followed by the Catskills, the Adirondacks, Yosemite, Yellowstone, and others.

Yosemite was deeded by the U.S. government to the state of California in 1864 as the nation's first wildland park, and Yellowstone became the first true national park in 1872.

By the first decade of the twentieth century, in the single most famous episode in American conservation history, a national debate had exploded over whether the city of San Francisco should be permitted to augment its water supply by damming the Tuolumne River in Hetch Hetchy valley, well within the boundaries of Yosemite National Park. The dam was eventually built, but what today seems no less significant is that so many people fought to prevent its completion. Even as the fight was being lost, Hetch Hetchy became the battle cry of an emerging movement to preserve wilderness. Fifty years earlier, such opposition would have been unthinkable. Few would have questioned the merits of "reclaiming" a wasteland like this in order to put it to human use. Now the defenders of Hetch Hetchy attracted widespread national attention by portraying such an act not as improvement or progress but as desecration and vandalism. Lest one doubt that the old biblical metaphors had been turned completely on their heads, listen to John Muir attack the dam's defenders. "Their arguments," he wrote, "are curiously like those of the devil, devised for the destruction of the first garden—so much of the very best Eden fruit going to waste; so much of the best Tuolumne water and Tuolumne scenery going to waste." For Muir and the growing number of Americans who shared his views, Satan's home had become God's own temple.

The sources of this rather astonishing transformation were many, but for the purposes of this essay they can be gathered under two broad headings: the sublime and the frontier. Of the two, sublime is the older and more pervasive cultural construct, being one of the most important expressions of that broad transatlantic movement we today label as romanticism; the frontier is more peculiarly American, though it too had its European antecedents and parallels. The two converged to remake wilderness in their own image, freighting it with moral values and cultural symbols that it carries to this day. Indeed, it is not too much to say that the modern environmental movement is itself a grandchild of romanticism and post-frontier ideology, which is why it is no accident that so much environmentalist discourse takes its bearings from the wilderness these intellectual movements helped create. Although wilderness may today seem to be just one environmental concern among many, it in fact serves as the foundation for a long list of other such concerns that on their face seem quite remote from it. That is why its influence is so pervasive and, potentially, so insidious.

To gain such remarkable influence, the concept of wilderness had to become loaded with some of the deepest core values of the culture that created and idealized it: it had to become sacred. This possibility had been present in wilderness even in the days when it had been a place of spiritual danger and moral temptation. If Satan was there, then so was Christ, who had found angels as well as wild beasts during his sojourn in the desert. In the wilderness the boundaries between human and nonhuman, between natural and supernatural, had always seemed less certain than elsewhere. This was why the early Christian saints and mystics had often emulated Christ's desert retreat as they sought to experience for themselves the visions and spiritual testing he had endured. One might meet devils and run the risk of losing one's soul in such a place, but one might also meet God. For some that possibility was worth almost any price.

By the eighteenth century this sense of the wilderness as a landscape where the supernatural lay just beneath the surface was expressed in the doctrine of the *sublime*, a word whose modern usage has been so watered down by commercial hype and tourist advertising that it retains only a dim echo of its former power. In the theories of Edmund Burke, Immanuel Kant, William Gilpin, and others, sublime landscapes were those rare places on earth where one had more chance than elsewhere to glimpse the face of God. Romantics had a clear notion of where one could be most sure of having this experience. Although God might, of course, choose to show himself anywhere, he would most often be found in those vast, powerful landscapes where one could not help feeling insignificant and being reminded of one's own mortality. Where were these sublime places? The eighteenth-century catalogue of their locations feels very familiar, for we still see and value landscapes as it taught us to do. God was on the mountaintop, in the chasm, in the waterfall, in the thundercloud, in the rainbow, in the sunset. One has only to think of the sites that Americans chose for their first national parks—Yellowstone, Yosemite, Grand Canyon, Rainier, Zion—to realize that virtually all of them fit one or more of these categories. Less sublime landscapes simply did not appear worthy of such protection; not until the 1940s, for instance, would the first swamp be honored, in Everglades National Park, and to this day there is no national park in the grasslands.

. . .

There were other ironies as well. The movement to set aside national parks and wilderness areas followed hard on the heels of the final Indian wars, in which the prior human inhabitants of these areas were rounded up and moved onto reservations. The myth of the wilderness as "virgin," uninhabited land had always been especially cruel when seen from the perspective of the Indians who had once called that land home. Now they were forced to move elsewhere, with the result that tourists could safely enjoy the illusion that they were seeing their nation in its pristine, original state, in the new morning of God's own creation. Among the things that most marked the new national parks as reflecting a post-frontier consciousness was the relative absence of human violence within their boundaries. The actual frontier had often been a place of conflict, in which invaders and invaded fought for control of land and resources. Once set aside within the fixed and carefully policed boundaries of the modern bureaucratic state, the wilderness lost its savage image and became safe: a place more of reverie than of revulsion or fear. Meanwhile, its original inhabitants were kept out by dint of force, their earlier uses of the land redefined as inappropriate or even illegal. To this day, for instance, the Blackfeet continue to be accused of "poaching" on the lands of Glacier National Park that originally belonged to them and that were ceded by treaty only with the proviso that they be permitted to hunt there.

The removal of Indians to create an "uninhabited wilderness"—uninhabited as never before in the human history of the place—reminds us just how invented, just how constructed, the American wilderness really is. To return to my opening argument: there is nothing natural about the concept of wilderness. It is entirely a creation of the culture that holds it dear, a product of the very history it seeks to deny. Indeed, one of the most striking proofs of the cultural invention of wilderness is its thoroughgoing erasure of the history from which it sprang. In virtually all of its manifestations, wilderness represents a flight from history. Seen as the original garden, it is a place outside of time from which human beings had to be ejected before the fallen world of history could properly begin. Seen as the frontier, it is a savage world at the dawn of civilization, whose transformation represents the very beginning of the national historical epic. Seen as the bold landscape of frontier heroism, it is the place of youth and childhood, into which men escape by abandoning their pasts and entering a world of freedom where the constraints of civilization fade into memory. Seen as the sacred sublime, it is the home of a God who transcends history by standing as the One who remains untouched and unchanged by time's arrow. No matter what the angle from which we regard it, wilderness offers us the illusion that we can escape the cares and troubles of the world in which our past has ensnared us.

. . .

This, then, is the central paradox: wilderness embodies a dualistic vision in which the human is entirely outside the natural. If we allow ourselves to believe that nature, to be true, must also be wild, then our very presence in nature represents its fall. The place where we are is the place where nature is not. If this is so—if by definition wilderness leaves no place for human beings, save perhaps as contemplative sojourners enjoying their leisurely reverie in God's natural cathedral—then also by definition it can offer no solution to the environmental and other problems that confront us. To the extent that we celebrate wilderness as the measure with which we judge civilization, we reproduce the dualism that sets humanity and nature at opposite poles. We thereby leave ourselves little hope of discovering what an ethical, sustainable, *honorable* human place in nature might actually look like.

Worse: to the extent that we live in an urban-industrial civilization but at the same time pretend to ourselves that our *real* home is in the wilderness, to just that extent we give ourselves permission to evade responsibility for the lives we actually lead. We inhabit civilization while holding some part of ourselves—what we imagine to be the most precious part—aloof from its entanglements. We work our nine-to-five jobs in its institutions, we eat its food, we drive its cars (not least to reach the wilderness), we benefit from the intricate and all too invisible networks with which it shelters us, all the while pretending that these things are not an essential part of who we are. By imagining that our true home is in the wilderness, we forgive ourselves the homes we actually inhabit. In its flight from history, in its siren song of escape, in its reproduction of the dangerous dualism that sets human beings outside of nature—in all of these ways, wilderness poses a serious threat to responsible environmentalism at the end of the twentieth century.

By now I hope it is clear that my criticism in this essay is not directed at wild nature per se, or even at efforts to set aside large tracts of wild land, but rather at the specific habits of thinking that flow from this complex cultural construction called wilderness. It is not the things we label as wilderness that are the problem—for nonhuman nature and large tracts of the natural world *do* deserve protection—

but rather what we ourselves mean when we use that label. Lest one doubt how pervasive these habits of thought really are in contemporary environmentalism, let me list some of the places where wilderness serves as the ideological underpinning for environmental concerns that might otherwise seem quite remote from it. Defenders of biological diversity, for instance, although sometimes appealing to more utilitarian concerns, often point to "untouched" ecosystems as the best and richest repositories of the undiscovered species we must certainly try to protect. Although at first blush an apparently more "scientific" concept than wilderness, biological diversity in fact invokes many of the same sacred values, which is why organizations like the Nature Conservancy have been so quick to employ it as an alternative to the seemingly fuzzier and more problematic concept of wilderness. There is a paradox here, of course. To the extent that biological diversity (indeed, even wilderness itself) is likely to survive in the future only by the most vigilant and self-conscious management of the ecosystems that sustain it, the ideology of wilderness is potentially in direct conflict with the very thing it encourages us to protect.

The most striking instances of this have revolved around "endangered species," which serve as vulnerable symbols of biological diversity while at the same time standing as surrogates for wilderness itself. The terms of the Endangered Species Act in the United States have often meant that those hoping to defend pristine wilderness have had to rely on a single endangered species like the spotted owl to gain legal standing for their case—thereby making the full power of sacred land inhere in a single numinous organism whose habitat then becomes the object of intense debate about appropriate management and use. The ease with which anti-environmental forces like the wise-use movement have attacked such single-species preservation efforts suggests the vulnerability of strategies like these.

Perhaps partly because our own conflicts over such places and organisms have become so messy, the convergence of wilderness values with concerns about biological diversity and endangered species has helped produce a deep fascination for remote ecosystems, where it is easier to imagine that nature might somehow be "left alone" to flourish by its own pristine devices. The classic example is the tropical rain forest, which since the 1970s has become the most powerful modern icon of unfallen, sacred land; a veritable Garden of Eden—for many Americans and Europeans. And yet protecting the rain forest in the eyes of First World environmentalists all too often means protecting it from the people who live there. Those who seek to preserve such "wilderness" from the activities of native peoples run the risk of reproducing the same tragedy—being forcibly removed from an ancient home—that befell American Indians. Third World countries face massive environmental problems and deep social conflicts, but these are not likely to be solved by a cultural myth that encourages us to "preserve" peopleless landscapes that have not existed in such places for millennia. At its worst, as environmentalists are beginning to realize, exporting American notions of wilderness in this way can become an unthinking and self-defeating form of cultural imperialism.

Indeed, my principal objection to wilderness is that it may teach us to be submissive or even contemptuous of such humble places and experiences. Without our quite realizing it, wilderness tends to privilege some parts of nature at the expense of others. Most of us, I suspect, still follow the conventions of the romantic sublime in finding the mountaintop more glorious than the plains, the ancient forest nobler than the grasslands, the mighty canyon more inspiring than the humble marsh. Even John Muir, in arguing against those who sought to dam his beloved Hetch Hetchy valley in the Sierra Nevada, argued for alternative dam sites in the gentler valleys of the foothills—a preference that had nothing to do with nature and everything with the cultural traditions of the sublime. Just as problematically, our frontier traditions have encouraged Americans to define "true" wilderness as requiring very large tracts of roadless land—what Dave Foreman calls the Big Outside. Leaving aside the legitimate empirical question in conservation biology of how large a tract of land must be before a given species can reproduce on it, the emphasis on big wilderness reflects a romantic frontier belief that one hasn't really gotten away from civilization unless one can go for days at a time without encountering another human being. By teaching us to fetishize sublime places and wide open country, these peculiarly American ways of thinking about wilderness encourage us to adopt too high a standard for what counts as "natural." If it isn't hundreds of square miles big, if it doesn't give us God's-eye views or grand vistas, if it doesn't permit us the illusion that we are alone on the planet, then it really isn't natural. It's too small, too plain, or too crowded to be *authentically* wild.

In critiquing wilderness as I have done in this essay, I'm forced to confront my own deep ambivalence about its meaning for modern environmentalism. On the one hand, one of my own most important environmental ethics is that people should always be conscious that they are part of the natural world, inextricably tied to the ecological systems that sustain their lives. Any way of looking at nature that encourages us to believe we are separate from nature— as wilderness tends to do—is likely to reinforce environmentally irresponsible behavior. On the other hand, I also think it no less crucial for us to recognize and honor nonhuman nature as a world we did not create, a world with its own independent, nonhuman reasons for being as it is. The autonomy of nonhuman nature seems to me an indispensable corrective to human arrogance. Any way of looking at nature that helps us remember—as wilderness also tends to do—that the interests of people are not necessarily identical to those of every other creature or of the earth itself is likely to foster responsible behavior. To the extent that wilderness has served as an important vehicle for articulating deep moral values regarding our obligations and responsibilities to the nonhuman world, I would not want to jettison the contributions it has made to our culture's way of thinking about nature.

If the core problem of wilderness is that it distances us too much from the very things it teaches us to value, then the question we must ask is what it can tell us about home, the place where we live. How can we take the positive values we associate with wilderness and bring them closer to home? I think the answer to this question will come by broadening our sense of the otherness that wilderness seeks to define and protect. In reminding us of the world we did not make, wilderness can teach profound feelings of humility and respect as we confront our fellow beings and the earth itself. Feelings like these argue for the importance of self-awareness and self-criticism as we exercise our own ability to transform the world around us, helping us set responsible limits to human mastery—which without such limits too easily becomes human hubris. Wilderness is the place where, symbolically at least, we try to withhold our power to dominate.

Wallace Stegner once wrote of

> the special human mark, the special record of human passage, that distinguishes man from all other species. It is rare enough among men, impossible to any other form of life. *It is simply the deliberate and chosen refusal to make any marks at all.* . . . We are the most dangerous species of life on the planet, and every other species, even the earth itself, has cause to fear our power to exterminate. But we are also the only species which, when it chooses to do so, will go to great effort to save what it might destroy.

The myth of wilderness, which Stegner knowingly reproduces in these remarks, is that we can somehow leave nature untouched by our passage. By now it should be clear that this for the most part is an illusion. But Stegner's deeper message then becomes all the more compelling. If living in history means that we cannot help leaving marks on a fallen world, then the dilemma we face is to decide what kinds of marks we wish to leave. It is just here that our cultural traditions of wilderness remain so important. In the broadest sense, wilderness teaches us to ask whether the Other must always bend to our will, and, if not, under what circumstances it should be allowed to flourish without our intervention. This is surely a question worth asking about everything we do, and not just about the natural world.

When we visit a wilderness area, we find ourselves surrounded by plants and animals and physical landscapes whose otherness compels our attention. In forcing us to acknowledge that they are not of our making, that they have little or no need of our continued existence, they recall for us a creation far greater than our own. In the wilderness, we need no reminder that a tree has its own reasons for being, quite apart from us. The same is less true in the gardens we plant and tend ourselves: there it is far easier to forget the otherness of the tree. Indeed, one could almost measure wilderness by the extent to which our recognition of its otherness requires a conscious, willed act on our part. The romantic legacy means that wilderness is more a state of mind than a fact of nature, and the state of mind that today most defines wilderness is *wonder*. The striking power of the wild is that wonder in the face of it requires no act of will, but forces itself upon us—as an expression of the nonhuman world experienced through the lens of our cultural history—as proof that ours is not the only presence in the universe.

Wilderness gets us into trouble only if we imagine that this experience of wonder and otherness is limited to the remote corners of the planet, or that it somehow depends on pristine landscapes we ourselves do not inhabit. Nothing could be more misleading. The tree in the garden is in reality no less other, no less worthy of our wonder and respect, than the tree in an ancient forest that has never known an ax or a saw—even though the tree in the forest reflects a more intricate web of ecological relationships. The tree in the garden could easily have sprung from the same seed as the tree in the forest, and we can claim only its location and perhaps its form as our own. Both trees stand apart from us; both share our common world. The special power of the tree in the wilderness is to remind us of this fact. It can teach us to recognize the wildness we did not see in the tree we planted in our own back yard. By seeing the otherness in that which is most unfamiliar, we can learn to see it too in that which at first seemed merely ordinary. If wilderness can do this—if it can help us perceive and respect a nature we had forgotten to recognize as natural—then it will become part of the solution to our environmental dilemmas rather than part of the problem.

This will happen, however, only if we abandon the dualism that sees the tree in the garden as artificial—completely fallen and unnatural—and the tree in the wilderness as natural—completely pristine and wild. Both trees in some ultimate sense are wild; both in a practical sense now depend on our management and care. We are responsible for both, even though we can claim credit for neither. Our challenge is to stop thinking of such things according to a set of bipolar moral scales in which the human and the nonhuman, the unnatural and the natural, the fallen and the unfallen, serve as our conceptual map for understanding and valuing the world. Instead, we need to embrace the full continuum of a natural landscape that is also cultural, in which the city, the suburb, the pastoral, and the wild each has its proper place, which we permit ourselves to celebrate without needlessly denigrating the others. We need to honor the Other within and the Other next door as much as we do the exotic Other that lives far away—a lesson that applies as much to people as it does to (other) natural things. In particular, we need to discover a common middle ground in which all of these things, from the city to the wilderness, can somehow be encompassed in the word "home." Home, after all, is the place where finally we make our living. It is the place for which we take responsibility, the place we try to sustain so we can pass on what is best in it (and in ourselves) to our children.

The task of making a home in nature is what Wendell Berry has called "the forever unfinished lifework of our species." "The only thing we have to preserve nature with," he writes, "is culture; the only thing we have to preserve wildness with is domesticity." Calling a place home inevitably means that we will *use* the nature we find in it, for there can be no escape from manipulating and working and even killing some parts of nature to make our home. But if we acknowledge the autonomy and otherness of the things and creatures around us—an autonomy our culture has taught us to label with the word "wild"—then we will at least think carefully about the uses to which we put them, and even ask if we should use them at all. Just so can we still join Thoreau in declaring that "in Wildness is the preservation of the World," for *wild*ness (as opposed to wilderness) can be found anywhere: in the seemingly tame fields and woodlots of Massachusetts, in the cracks of a Manhattan sidewalk, even in the cells of our own bodies. As Gary Snyder has wisely said, "A person with a clear heart and open mind can experience the wilderness anywhere on earth. It is a quality of one's own consciousness. The planet is a wild place and always will be." To think ourselves capable of causing "the end of nature" is an act of great hubris, for it means forgetting the wildness that dwells everywhere within and around us.

Learning to honor the wild—learning to remember and acknowledge the autonomy of the Other—means striving for critical self-consciousness in all of our actions. It means that deep reflection and respect must accompany each act of use, and means too that we must always consider the possibility of non-use. It means looking at the part of nature we intend to turn toward our own ends and asking whether we can use it again and again and again—sustainably—without its being diminished in the process. It means never imagining that we can flee into a mythical wilderness to escape history and the obligation to take responsibility for our own actions that history inescapably entails. Most of all, it means practicing remembrance and gratitude, for thanksgiving is the simplest and most basic of ways for us to recollect the nature, the culture, and the history that have come together to make the world as we know it. If wildness can stop being (just) out there and start being (also) in here, if it can start being as humane as it is natural, then perhaps we can get on with the unending task of struggling to live rightly in the world—not just in the garden, not just in the wilderness, but in the home that encompasses them both.

QUESTIONS FOR ANALYSIS AND DISCUSSION

1. Relative to the arrival of humans, the earth itself is quite old. Considering our youth, does the environmentalist banner "save the planet" strike you as somewhat arrogant and vain? Do you think this idea reflects an emerging voice that will force us to rethink the place of humanity and redirect our compassion to include nonhuman elements?

2. Cronon admits his own ambivalence. He values the otherness of wilderness but cautions against the tendency to experience this otherness in exotic places. Where does Cronon think humans can encounter the wilderness in ordinary settings? Why does he invoke gratitude as a proper response to this encounter? Do you agree or disagree with his conclusion?

3. What do you see as the advantages and disadvantages of the historical perspective? Many philosophers in recent times have been attentive to historical scholarship when addressing current philosophical issues. History often provides a lesson on how ideas that seem so clear and obvious to us have changed in their meaning and value over time. To what extent do you think Cronon provides us with a similar lesson? How does it affect your view on issues relating to environmental ethics?

4. Suppose you are moved by the discussions of Racy, Shaw, or Cronon. You hear of a protest demonstration being planned at a local factory that is not in compliance with pollution regulations. You and a couple of friends attend the rally. Just as you arrive, three leaders of the rally drive up in all-terrain, 4×4 Jeeps. With the air conditioning on, you know they get about 12 miles to the gallon. The leaders use a bullhorn to tell the protestors what to do, especially when the television cameras start filming. You decide to: (a) do what they say because this is your first political rally and you don't want to mess up; (b) do what they say because you are a recent convert to environmental ethics and see the factory as a vicious entity; (c) start talking to some other protestors about whether these demonstrations have any effect; (d) politely confront one

of the leaders and inquire about a possible double standard in protesting the factory while driving a gas guzzler; or (e) do "d," get rudely rebuffed, and wait for the television cameras to roll so you can publicly denounce the hypocrisy of the rally leaders. Provide a brief justification for your choice.

67.

JOSIAH ROYCE

Loyalty

For many moral thinkers the other is best sought as an intangible or abstract form. One way to realize this form in concrete terms is by considering the concept of loyalty. According to California native Josiah Royce (1855–1916), loyalty allows individuals to escape the pessimism that often characterizes excessive individualism. In professing loyalty to a principle or a cause greater than oneself, the moral person participates in a dimension of life that calls on personal resources often neglected in an egoistic life. These resources are part of the virtuous life. In addition, contends Royce, the life of loyalty is available to anyone. There are many principles or causes deserving of people's energy and devotion. In finding the right cause, the loyal person gives meaning of purpose to everyday life.

⊣ CRITICAL READING QUESTIONS ⊢

1. Is patriotism or the war hero an example of loyalty?
2. Why can't individuals find a plan of life within themselves?
3. What is Royce's response to the many examples of those who have been loyal to bad causes?
4. What is meant by "loyalty to loyalty"?

Suppose a being whose social conformity has been sufficient to enable him to learn many skilful social arts,—arts of speech, of prowess in contest, of influence over other men. Suppose that these arts have at the same time awakened this man's pride, his self-confidence, his disposition to assert himself. Such a man will have in

---

"Loyalty," from *Loyalty* (New York: Macmillan, 1924), pp. 38–48, 156–162.

him a good deal of what you can well call social will. He will be no mere anarchist. He will have been trained into much obedience. He will be no natural enemy of society, unless, indeed, fortune has given him extraordinary opportunities to win his way without scruples. On the other hand, this man must acquire a good deal of self-will. He becomes fond of success, of mastery, of his own demands. To be sure, he can find within himself no one naturally sovereign will. He can so far find only a general determination to define some way of his own, and to have his own way. Hence the conflicts of social will and self-will are inevitable, circular, endless, so long as this is the whole story of the man's life. By merely consulting convention, on the one hand, and his disposition to be somebody, on the other hand, this man can never find any one final and consistent plan of life, nor reach any one definition of his duty.

But now suppose that there appears in this man's life some one of the greater social passions, such as patriotism well exemplifies. Let his country be in danger. Let his elemental passion for conflict hereupon fuse with his brotherly love for his own countrymen into that fascinating and blood-thirsty form of humane but furious ecstasy, which is called the war-spirit. The mood in question may nor may not be justified by the passing circumstances. For that I now care not. At its best the war-spirit is no very clear or rational state of anybody's mind. But one reason why men may love this spirit is that when it comes, it seems at once to define a plan of life,—a plan which solves the conflicts of self-will and conformity. This plan has two features: (1) it is through and through a social plan, obedient to the general will of one's country, submissive; (2) it is through and through an exaltation of the self, of the inner man, who now feels glorified through his sacrifice, dignified in his self-surrender, glad to be his country's servant and martyr,—yet sure that through this very readiness for self-destruction he wins the rank of hero.

Well, if the man whose case we are supposing gets possessed by some such passion as this, he wins for the moment the consciousness of what I call loyalty. This loyalty no longer knows anything about the old circular conflicts of self-will and of conformity. The self, at such moments, looks indeed *outwards* for its plan of life. "The country needs me," it says. It looks, meanwhile, *inwards* for the inspiring justification of this plan. "Honor, the hero's crown, the soldier's death, the patriot's devotion—these," it says, "are my will. I am not giving up this will of mine. It is my pride, my glory, my self-assertion, to be ready at my country's call." And now there is no conflict of outer and inner.

How wise or how enduring or how practical such a passion may prove, I do not yet consider. What I point out is that this war-spirit, for the time at least, makes self-sacrifice seem to be self-expression, makes obedience to the country's call seem to be the proudest sort of display of one's own powers. Honor now means submission, and to obey means to have one's way. Power and service are at one. Conformity is no longer opposed to having one's own will. One has no will but that of the country.

As a mere fact of human nature, then, there are social passions which actually tend to do at once two things: (1) to intensify our self-consciousness, to make us more than ever determined to express our own will and more than ever sure of our own rights, of our own strength, of our dignity, of our power, of our value; (2) to make obvious to us that this our will has no purpose but to do the will of some fascinating social power. This social power is the cause to which we are loyal.

Loyalty, then, fixes our attention upon some one cause, bids us look without ourselves to see what this unified cause is, shows us thus some one plan of action, and then says to us, "In this cause is your life, your will, your opportunity, your fulfillment."

Thus loyalty, viewed merely as a personal attitude, solves the paradox of our ordinary existence, by showing us outside of ourselves the cause which is to be served, and inside of ourselves the will which delights to do this service, and which is not thwarted but enriched and expressed in such service.

I have used patriotism and the war-spirit merely as a first and familiar illustration of loyalty. But now, as we shall later see, there is no necessary connection between loyalty and war; and there are many other forms of loyalty besides the patriotic forms. Loyalty has its domestic, its religious, its commercial, its professional forms, and many other forms as well. The essence of it, whatever forms it may take, is, as I conceive the matter, this: Since no man can find a plan of life by merely looking within his own chaotic nature, he has to look without, to the world of social conventions, deeds, and causes. Now, a loyal man is one who has found, and who sees, neither mere individual fellow-men to be loved or hated, nor mere conventions, nor customs, nor laws to be obeyed, but some social cause, or some system of causes, so rich, so well knit, and, to him, so fascinating, and withal so kindly in its appeal to his natural self-will, that he says to his cause: "Thy will is mine and mine is thine. In thee I do not lose but find myself, living intensely in proportion as I live for thee." If one could find such a cause, and hold it for his lifetime before his mind, clearly observing it, passionately loving it, and yet calmly understanding it, and steadily and practically serving it, he would have one plan of life, and this plan of life would be his own plan, his own will set before him, expressing all that his self-will has ever sought. Yet this plan would also be a plan of obedience, because it would mean living for the cause.

Now, in all ages of civilized life there have been people who have won in some form a consciousness of loyalty, and who have held to such a consciousness through life. Such people may or may not have been right in their choice of a cause. But at least they have exemplified through their loyalty one feature of a rational moral life. They have known what it was to have unity of purpose.

And again, the loyal have known what it was to be free from moral doubts and scruples. Their cause has been their conscience. It has told them what to do. They have listened and obeyed, not because of what they took to be blind convention, not because of a fear of external authority, not even because of what seemed to themselves any purely private and personal intuition, but because, when they have looked first outwards at their cause, and then inwards at themselves, they have found themselves worthless in their own eyes, except when viewed as active, as confidently devoted, as willing instruments of their cause. Their cause has forbidden them to doubt; it has said: "You are mine, you cannot do otherwise." And they have said to the cause: "I am, even of my own will, thine. I have no will except thy will. Take me, use me, control me, and even thereby fulfil me and exalt me." That is again the speech of the devoted patriots, soldiers, mothers, and martyrs of our race. They have had the grace of this willing, this active loyalty.

Now, people loyal in this sense have surely existed in the world, and, as you all know, the loyal still exist amongst us. And I beg you not to object to me, at this point, that such devoted people have often been loyal to very bad causes; or that different people have been loyal to causes which were in deadly war with one another, so that loyal people must often have been falsely guided. I beg you, above all, not to interpose here the objection that our modern doubters concerning moral problems simply cannot at present see to what one cause they ought to be loyal, so that just herein, just in our inability to see a fitting and central object of loyalty, lies the root of our modern moral confusion and distraction. All those possible objections are indeed perfectly fair considerations. I shall deal with them in due time; and I am just as earnestly aware of them as you can be. But just now we are getting our first glimpse of our future philosophy of loyalty. All that you can say of the defects of loyalty leaves still untouched the one great fact that, if you want to find a way of living which surmounts doubts, and centralizes your powers, it must be some such a way as all the loyal in common have trodden, since first loyalty was known amongst men. What form of loyalty is the right one, we are hereafter to see. But unless you can find some sort of loyalty, you cannot find unity and peace in your active living. You must find, then, a cause that is really worthy of the sort of devotion that the soldiers, rushing cheerfully to certain death, have felt for their clan or for their country, and that the martyrs have shown on behalf of their faith. This cause must be indeed rational, worthy, and no object of a false devotion. But once found, it must become your conscience, must tell you the truth about your duty, and must unify, as from without and from above, your motives, your special ideals, and your plans. You ought, I say, to find such a cause, if indeed there be any ought at all. And this is my first hint of our moral code.

But you repeat, perhaps in bewilderment, your question: "Where, in our distracted modern world, in this time when cause wars with cause, and when all old moral standards are remorselessly criticised and doubted, are we to find such a cause—a cause, all-embracing, definite, rationally compelling, supreme, certain, and fit to centralize life? What cause is there that for us would rationally justify a martyr's devotion?" I reply: "A perfectly simple consideration, derived from a study of the very spirit of loyalty itself, as this spirit is manifested by all the loyal, will soon furnish to us the unmistakable answer to this question." For the moment we have won our first distant glimpse of what I mean by the general nature of loyalty, and by our common need of loyalty. . . .

. . . Your very loyalty to your own cause will tend to prove infectious. Whoever is loyal to his own therefore helps on the cause of universal loyalty by his every act of devotion, precisely in so far as he refrains from any hostile attack upon the loyalty of other people, and simply lets his example of loyalty work. Whoever makes the furtherance of universal loyalty his cause, lacks, therefore, neither practical means nor present opportunity for serving his cause.

To each man our principle therefore says: *Live in your own way a loyal life and one subject to the general principle of loyalty to loyalty.* Serve your own cause, but so choose it and so serve it that in consequence of your life loyalty amongst men shall prosper. Fortune may indeed make the range of your choice of your calling very narrow. Necessity may bind you to an irksome round of tasks. But sweeten these with whatever loyalty you can consistently get into your life. Let loyalty be your pearl of great price. Sell all the happiness that you possess or can get in disloyal or in non-loyal activities, and buy that pearl. When you once have found, or begun to find, your personal cause, be as steadily faithful to it as loyalty to loyalty henceforth permits. That is, if you find that a cause once chosen does indeed involve disloyalty to loyalty, as one might find who, having sworn fidelity to a leader, afterwards discovered his leader to be a traitor to the cause of mankind, you may have altogether to abandon the cause first chosen. But never abandon a cause except for the sake of some higher or deeper loyalty such as actually requires the change.

Meanwhile, the principle of loyalty to loyalty obviously requires you to *respect loyalty in all men, wherever you find it.* If your fellow's cause has, in a given case, assailed your own, and if, in the world as it is, conflict is inevitable, you may then have to war with your fellow's cause, in order to be loyal to your own. But even then, you may never assail whatever is sincere and genuine about his spirit of loyalty. Even if your fellow's cause involves disloyalty to mankind at large, you may not condemn the loyalty of your fellow in so far as it is loyalty. You may condemn only his blindly chosen cause. All the loyal are brethren. They are children of one spirit. Loyalty to loyalty involves the active furtherance of this spirit wherever it appears. Fair play in sport, chivalrous respect for the adversary in war, tolerance of the sincere beliefs of other men,—all these virtues are thus to be viewed as mere variations of loyalty to loyalty. Prevent the conflict of loyalties when you can, minimize such conflict where it exists, and, by means of fair play and of the chivalrous attitude towards the opponent, utilize even conflict, where it is inevitable, so as to further the cause of loyalty to loyalty. Such maxims are obvious consequences of our principle. Do we not gain, then, a great deal from our principle in the way of unifying our moral code?

II

But next, as to those just-mentioned paradoxes of popular morality, do we not gain from our principle a guide to help us through the maze? "Be just; but also be kind." These two precepts, so far as they are sound, merely emphasize . . . two distinct but inseparable aspects of loyalty. My cause links my fellow and myself by social ties which, in the light of our usual human interpretation of life, appear to stand for super-personal interests,—for interests in property rights, in formal obligations, in promises, in various abstractly definable relations. If I am loyal, I respect these relations. And I do so since, from the very definition of a cause to which one can be loyal, this cause will become nothing unless these ties are preserved intact. But to respect relations as such is to be what men call just. Meanwhile, our common cause also personally interests both my fellow and myself. So far as we both know the cause, we love it, and delight in it. Hence in being loyal to our cause, I am also being kind to my fellow. For hereby I further his delight in just so far as I help him to insight. But kindness which is not bound up with loyalty is as a sounding brass and as a tinkling cymbal, a mere sentimentalism. And abstract justice, apart from loyalty, is a cruel formalism. My fellow wants to be loyal. This is his deepest need. If I am loyal to that need, I therefore truly delight him. But kindness that is not bound up with loyalty may indeed amuse my fellow for a moment. Yet like "fancy," such kindness "dies in the cradle where it lies." Even so, if I am loyal, I am also just. But justice that is no aspect of loyalty has no reason for existence. The true relations of benevolence and justice can therefore be best defined in terms of our conception of loyalty. If any one says, "I will show thee my justice or my kindness without my loyalty," the loyal man may rightly respond, "I will show thee my kindness and my justice by my loyalty."

In a similar fashion, the moral problems regarding the right relations of strictness to generosity, of prudent foresight to present confidence, of self-surrender to self-assertion, of love to the righteous resistance of enemies,—all these moral problems, I say, are best to be solved in terms of the principle of loyalty to loyalty. As to the problem of the true concern and regard for the self, the loyal man cultivates himself, and is careful of his property rights, just in order to furnish to his cause an effective instrument; but he aims to forget precisely so much of himself as is, at any time, an obstruction to his loyalty; and he also aims to be careless of whatever about his private fortunes may be of no importance to his service of the cause. When he asserts himself, he does so because he has neither eyes to see nor tongue to speak save as his cause commands; and it is of precisely such self-sacrificing self-assertion that the foes of his cause would do well to beware. All the paradoxes about the care of self and the abandonment of self are thus soluble in terms of loyalty. Whoever knows and possesses the loyal attitude, *ipso facto* solves these paradoxes in each special case as it arises. And whoever comprehends the nature of loyalty to loyalty, as it is expressed in the form of fair play in sport, of chivalry in war, of tolerance in belief, and of the spirit that seeks to prevent the conflict of loyalties where such prevention is possible,—whoever, I say, thus comprehends what loyalty to loyalty means, holds the key to all the familiar mysteries about the right relation of the love of man to the strenuous virtues, and to the ethics of conflict.

QUESTIONS FOR ANALYSIS AND DISCUSSION

1. One way to characterize the loyal man, says Royce, is by his appeal to the cause: "Thy will is mine and mine is thine. In thee I do not lose but find myself, living intensely in proportion as I live for thee." Do you think this expression captures a meaningful life? Why, or why not?

2. How can you avoid the wrong object of loyalty? Are excessive passions spawned by loyalty? Is loyalty, like love, a virtue that easily transforms the moral person into one whose life is controlled by vice? Do you agree or disagree with

Royce's answer to these questions? Explain your position using specific examples from Royce's argument.

3. Royce claims that the cause that calls for our loyalty "must be indeed rational, worthy, and no object of false devotion." Consider a cause that you have studied in another course or one you have supported in your own life. Does devotion to this cause reflect what Royce means by loyalty?

68.

HILDEGARD VON BINGEN

Eighth Vision: On the Effect of Love

A second way of depicting the moral appeal to an intangible existence is found in the work of the medieval visionary Hildegard von Bingen (1098–1179). In addition to her studies of music, cosmology, and herbal medicines, Hildegard was a prolific writer. Her writings spanned the repertoire from operas to letters to memoirs of her visions, and they covered a variety of areas from theology to painting. In this selection Hildegard discusses her eighth of ten visions. Note how Satan or the Devil appears in this vision, especially in contrast to the portrayal of the saints.

CRITICAL READING QUESTIONS

1. Which three virtues are central to Hildegard's eighth vision?
2. What is the relation between Wisdom and the Devil?
3. How does humility reflect love?
4. Why is arrogance evil?

Vision Eight: 1

I saw three forms in the midst of the above-mentioned southern regions. Two of them stood in a very clear well, which was encircled and crowned by a round,

"Eighth Vision: On the Effect of Love," from *Book of Divine Works*, from *Spiritual Writings*, edited by Mathew Fox (Santa Fe, NM: Bear & Company, 1987), pp. 204–209.

porous stone. They seemed rooted in the well, so to speak, just as trees at times seem to grow in water. One form was encircled by such a purple glimmer and the second by such a dazzlingly white brilliance that I could not bear to look fully at them. The third form stood outside the well and beneath the stone. It was clothed in a dazzlingly white garment, and its countenance radiated such splendor that my own face had to draw back from it. Before and above these three appeared—like clouds—the blessed ranks of the saints, who gazed intently down at them.

Vision Eight: 2

The first figure said:

I am Love, the splendor of the living God. Wisdom has influenced me, and the humility rooted in the living fountain is my helper. Peace is associated with humility. Through the splendor that is my essence, the living light of the blissful angels shines. For just as a ray of light shines, this splendor shines for the blissful angels. It could hardly keep from shining, for there can be no light that does not shine. I have designed the human species, which has its roots in me like a shadow, just as one can see the shadow of every object in water. And so I am a living fountain because all creation is like a shadow within myself. As regards this shadow, the human species is formed from fire and water, just as I am both "fire" and "living water." The human species has within its soul the ability to arrange everything according to its own wish.

Every human creature has a shadow, and what is alive within that creature moves now this way and now that way —just like a shadow. Only a rational form of life can think. Savage beasts do not think, for they exist from day to day and have instincts by which they know what to avoid and what to seek out. Only the human soul that receives life from God is rational.

My splendor has always overshadowed the prophets who in holy inspiration foretold the future, just as everything that God intended to create was only a shadow until it became a reality. But Reason speaks by means of sound, and this sound is, so to speak, a thought and a word and—to a certain degree—a deed (*verbum quasi opus*). Out of this shadow the book *Scivias* emerged. It was composed by a woman who was, so to speak, only a shadow of strength and health because such qualities had no effect in her.

But the living well is also the Spirit of God. God has distributed this Spirit among all divine deeds. From this source they have their life, just as the shadow of all things appears in water. And there is nothing that can know totally and completely whence it derives life. Rather, such a thing feels only obscurely what moves it. And just as water causes everything within it to turn liquid, the soul is a living breath of the spirit (*vivens spiraculum*). This breath is constantly at work within us and causes us to flow, so to speak, through whatever we know, think, say, or do.

In this shadow Wisdom distributes everything to the same degree so that nothing can exceed another thing in weight, and so that nothing can be moved by another thing to become what it is not. Wisdom overcomes all evil deeds caused by the Devil's tricks and places them in chains. For she was before the origin of every beginning and will continue to be in full force after the end of everything, for nothing can resist Wisdom. She has invoked no one's help and needs no help, because she is the First and the Last. From no one has she had a reply because she who is the First has arranged the order of all things. Out of her own being and by herself she has formed all things in love and tenderness. Nor was it possible any more for anything to be destroyed by an enemy. For she oversaw completely and fully the beginning and end of her deeds because she formed everything completely, just as everything was under her guidance.

Wisdom considers her own achievement, which she has arranged in the shadow of the living water in accord with a just decision. She did so by revealing through the untutored woman mentioned above certain "natural powers of various things" (*virtutes naturales diversarum rerum*) as well as writings about the "meritorious life" (*scripta vitae meritorum*) and certain other deep secrets which that woman beheld in a true vision and which exhausted her.

In addition, Wisdom has created from the living source especially the words of the prophets and the other sages as well as those of the evangelists. She has transmitted these words to the disciples of the Son of God so that they might pour out streams of living water over the whole world and so that through these streams we human beings might be taken like fishes in a net and brought back to salvation.

The bubbling source of the living God is the purity in which God's splendor is reflected. Within this brilliance God has enclosed with great love all things whose shadows have appeared in the bubbling source before God caused them to emerge in their own shape.

All being is reflected in myself, who am Love. My brilliance reveals the form of things, just as a shadow indicates a figure. Out of humility, which is my helper, the created universe arises at God's command. In the same humility God has lowered the Divine to me in order to lift up the withered, fallen leaves once again to that bliss by which God can accomplish whatever the Divine desires. For God formed the creatures from the Earth by means of which God redeemed them after the Fall.

For the human species is completely the image of God (*homo pleniter factura Dei*). We human beings look up to the heavens and tread upon the Earth, which we dominate. We command each and every creature because with our soul we behold the heights of heaven. Therefore, we are of a heavenly nature while through our visible body we exist in an earthly way. But God has opposed in humility the human species, which is so low, to the one who was ejected from heaven because of his wickedness. Because the old serpent in its arrogance sought to destroy the harmony of the angels, God's power kept this harmony from being destroyed by the serpent's anger. Satan was well known on high, and he thought that he could do what he wanted without giving up the brilliance of the stars. He wanted everything, and because he made a grab for it all, he lost all he had.

Vision Eight: 3

And once again I heard a voice from heaven say to me:

Everything God has made has been made in love, humility, and peace. Therefore, we too should be fond of love, we should strive for humility, and we should keep the peace so that we do not perish with those who have scorned these virtues from the moment of their birth.

[The three forms represent the following virtues: Love is God, who became a human being in humility. From on high God brought down to us peace, which has to be fought for with difficulty in a changeable world and which can be preserved only with difficulty.]

But the human species, which is God's deed, will praise God because the souls of human beings will live by praising God, just as the angels now do. For as long as we humans live in our earthly time, we act upon the Earth according to our own wishes and desires, and in this way point to God. For we bear the divine seal. In the company of these forms, the hosts of the saints appear, and the saints regard the forms carefully, as they would a cloud. For through love and humility we attain the honor of the heavens on high, while the spirit of believers flies like a cloud from virtue to virtue. This is because love and humility, which are both severe and gentle, direct the spirit through careful consideration and concern toward a longing for higher things.

For love is the adornment of God's deeds, just as a diamond adorns a ring. But humility has revealed itself in the Incarnation of the Son of God, which emerged from the intact Star of the Sea. . . . [Love has always been fertile and was never idle. The Church received these three virtues as an adornment and dowry.]

Vision Eight: 4

. . . And thus humanity is the deed of God's right hand. God's hand clothed us and called us to the heavenly wedding feast. This is what humility did because the highest God looked down upon the center of the Earth and established the divine Church through ordinary people. Those who have fallen should rise up in repentance and renew themselves by a holy change of life through the multiplicity of virtues like fresh-blooming flowers. Yet arrogance is always evil because it oppresses everything, disperses everything, and deprives everything. By way of contrast, humility does not rob people or take anything from them. Rather, it holds together everything in love. God has condescended to the Earth in love and brought together all the powers of the virtues. For the virtues strive toward the Son of God, just as a virgin rejects men and calls Christ her bridegroom. Such virtues are associated with humility when Christ goes with them to the wedding feast of the King.

Believers should accept these words in the humility of their hearts because these words were revealed for the benefit of believers by One who is both the First and the Last.

QUESTIONS FOR ANALYSIS AND DISCUSSION

1. Saints, angels, devils, serpents, God, and Satan all seem to be real figures in Hildegard's discussion of the virtue of love and humility. Do you think these figures exist or are fantasy? How do these figures contribute to Hildegard's portrayal of love, humility, and peace as virtues?

2. Hildegard writes: "Every human creature has a shadow, and what is alive within that creature moves now this way and now that way—just like a shadow." What do you think she has in mind in talking about the shadow inside ourselves? In his *The Community of Those Who Have Nothing in Common*, Alphonso Lingis notes that the "other community" acts like a double or shadow of the rational community. If the shadow is a version of the other that we have in ourselves, do you think all moral persons are condemned to uncertainty? Can we ever be sure of capturing the shadow that holds the secret to the true self? Clarify your response.

3. Humble people are often described as nice, passive, and relatively harmless. We assume that humble people will not harm us, but they won't do much for us, either. Do you think Hildegard believes humility is a virtue because it does no harm? Or does Hildegard believe that humility is a productive force? From your reading of Hildegard's Eighth Vision, do you agree that if a person is humble his or her virtue lies not in the result of harming none but in contributing to the happiness of others? In considering your answer, think about your relation to a deity and whether you are or should be humble.

69.

PLATO

Beauty, Truth, and Immortality

Another version of seeking or respecting an intangible other appears in Plato's Symposium. *This dialogue begins with a series of speeches among Socrates' friends. All the speeches are supposed to explain the meaning of love. One says love is the oldest god;*

"Symposium," from *The Collected Dialogues of Plato*, edited by Edith Hamilton and Huntington Cairns, translated by Michael Joyce (Princeton, NJ: Princeton University Press, 1961, 1989), pp. 554–563.

another holds that love is the youngest god. One believes a love makes for the greatest courage, for the lover will die for the beloved; another describes how love always seeks the other half that completes the self. Socrates speaks last and relates his encounter with the goddess or oracle Diotima. This is where this selection begins. Diotima teaches Socrates about the divine aspects of love. True love, Diotima observes, takes the human mortal beyond his worldly and corporeal concerns.

┤ CRITICAL READING QUESTIONS ├

1. How is love part of Need, Resource, and Craft?
2. What are three things the lover seeks?
3. What are four steps in the progression of love?
4. What is the difference between true and apparent virtue, according to Diotima?

Whereupon, My dear Diotima, I asked, are you trying to make me believe that Love is bad and ugly?

Heaven forbid, she said. But do you really think that if a thing isn't beautiful it's therefore bound to be ugly?

Why, naturally.

And that what isn't learned must be ignorant? Have you never heard of something which comes between the two?

And what's that?

Don't you know, she asked, that holding an opinion which is in fact correct, without being able to give a reason for it, is neither true knowledge—how can it be knowledge without a reason?—nor ignorance—for how can we call it ignorance when it happens to be true? So may we not say that a correct opinion comes midway between knowledge and ignorance?

Yes, I admitted, that's perfectly true.

Very well, then, she went on, why must you insist that what isn't beautiful is ugly, and that what isn't good is bad? Now, coming back to Love, you've been forced to agree that he is neither good nor beautiful, but that's no reason for thinking that he must be bad and ugly. The fact is that he's between the two.

And yet, I said, it's generally agreed that he's a great god.

It all depends, she said, on what you mean by "generally." Do you mean simply people that don't know anything about it, or do you include the people that do?

I meant everybody.

At which she laughed, and said, Then can you tell me, my dear Socrates, how people can agree that he's a great god when they deny that he's a god at all?

What people do you mean? I asked her.

You for one, and I for another.

What on earth do you mean by that?

Oh, it's simple enough, she answered. Tell me, wouldn't you say that all the gods were happy and beautiful? Or would you suggest that any of them were neither?

Good heavens, no! said I.

And don't you call people happy when they possess the beautiful and the good?

Why, of course.

And yet you agreed just now that Love lacks, and consequently longs for, those very qualities?

Yes, so I did.

Then, if he has no part in either goodness or beauty, how can he be a god?

I suppose he can't be, I admitted.

And now, she said, haven't I proved that you're one of the people who don't believe in the divinity of Love?

Yes, but what can he be, then? I asked her. A mortal?

Not by any means.

Well, what then?

What I told you before—halfway between mortal and immortal.

And what do you mean by that, Diotima?

A very powerful spirit, Socrates, and spirits, you know, are halfway between god and man.

What powers have they, then? I asked.

They are the envoys and interpreters that ply between heaven and earth, flying upward with our worship and our prayers, and descending with the heavenly answers and commandments, and since they are between the two estates they weld both sides together and merge them into one great whole. They form the medium of the prophetic arts, of the priestly rites of sacrifice, initiation, and incantation, of divination and of sorcery, for the divine will not mingle directly with the human, and it is only through the mediation of the spirit world that man can have any intercourse, whether waking or sleeping, with the gods. And the man who is versed in such matters is said to have spiritual powers, as opposed to the mechanical powers of the man who is expert in the more mundane arts. There are many spirits, and many kinds of spirits, too, and Love is one of them.

Then who were his parents? I asked.

I'll tell you, she said, though it's rather a long story. On the day of Aphrodite's birth the gods were making merry, and among them was Resource, the son of Craft. And when they had supped, Need came begging at the door because there was good cheer inside. Now, it happened that Resource, having drunk deeply of the heavenly nectar—for this was before the days of wine—wandered out into the garden of Zeus and sank into a heavy sleep, and Need, thinking that to get a child by Resource would mitigate her penury, lay down beside him and in time was brought to bed of Love. So Love became the follower and servant of Aphrodite because he was begotten on the same day that she was born, and further, he was born to love the beautiful since Aphrodite is beautiful herself.

Then again, as the son of Resource and Need, it has been his fate to be always needy; nor is he delicate and lovely as most of us believe, but harsh and arid, barefoot and homeless, sleeping on the naked earth, in doorways, or in the very streets beneath the stars of heaven, and always partaking of his mother's poverty. But, secondly, he brings his father's resourcefulness to his designs upon the beautiful and the good, for he is gallant, impetuous, and energetic, a mighty hunter, and a master of device and artifice—at once desirous and full of wisdom, a lifelong seeker after truth, an adept in sorcery, enchantment, and seduction.

He is neither mortal nor immortal, for in the space of a day he will be now, when all goes well with him, alive and blooming, and now dying, to be born again by virtue of his father's nature, while what he gains will always ebb away as fast. So Love is never altogether in or out of need, and stands, moreover, midway between ignorance and wisdom. You must understand that none of the gods are seekers after truth. They do not long for wisdom, because they are wise—and why should the wise be seeking the wisdom that is already theirs? Nor, for that matter, do the ignorant seek the truth or crave to be made wise. And indeed, what makes their case so hopeless is that, having neither beauty, nor goodness, or intelligence, they are satisfied with what they are, and do not long for the virtues they have never missed.

Then tell me, Diotima, I said, who are these seekers after truth, if they are neither the wise nor the ignorant?

Why, a schoolboy, she replied, could have told you that, after what I've just been saying. They are those that come between the two, and one of them is Love. For wisdom is concerned with the loveliest of things, and Love is the love of what is lovely. And so it follows that Love is a lover of wisdom, and, being such, he is placed between wisdom and ignorance—for which his parentage also is responsible, in that his father is full of wisdom and resource, while his mother is devoid of either.

Such, my dear Socrates, is the spirit of Love, and yet I'm not altogether surprised at your idea of him, which was, judging by what you said, that Love was the beloved rather than the lover. So naturally you thought of Love as utterly beautiful, for the beloved is, in fact, beautiful, perfect, delicate, and prosperous—very different from the lover, as I have described him.

Very well, dear lady, I replied, no doubt you're right. But in that case, what good can Love be to humanity?

That's just what I'm coming to, Socrates, she said. So much, then, for the nature and the origin of Love. You were right in thinking that he was the love of what is beautiful. But suppose someone were to say, Yes, my dear Socrates. Quite so, my dear Diotima. But what do you mean by the love of what is beautiful? Or, to put the question more precisely, what is it that the lover of the beautiful is longing for?

He is longing to make the beautiful his own, I said.

Very well, she replied, but your answer leads to another question. What will he gain by making the beautiful his own?

This, as I had to admit, was more than I could answer on the spur of the moment.

Well then, she went on, suppose that, instead of the beautiful, you were being asked about the good. I put it to you, Socrates. What is it that the lover of the good is longing for?

To make the good his own.

Then what will he gain by making it his own?

I can make a better shot at answering that, I said. He'll gain happiness.

Right, said she, for the happy are happy inasmuch as they possess the good, and since there's no need for us to ask why men should want to be happy, I think your answer is conclusive.

Absolutely, I agreed.

This longing, then, she went on, this love—is it common to all mankind? What do you think, do we all long to make the good our own?

Yes, I said, as far as that goes we're all alike.

Well then, Socrates, if we say that everybody always loves the same thing, does that mean that everybody is in love? Or do we mean that some of us are in love, while some of us are not?

I was a little worried about that myself, I confessed.

Oh, it's nothing to worry about, she assured me. You see, what we've been doing is to give the name of Love to what is only one single aspect of it; we make just the same mistake, you know, with a lot of other names.

For instance . . . ?

For instance, poetry. You'll agree that there is more than one kind of poetry in the true sense of the word—that is to say, calling something into existence that was not there before, so that every kind of artistic creation is poetry, and every artist is a poet.

True.

But all the same, she said, we don't call them all poets, do we? We give various names to the various arts, and only call the one particular art that deals with music and meter by the name that should be given to them all. And that's the only art that we call poetry, while those who practice it are known as poets.

Quite.

And that's how it is with Love. For "Love, that renowned and all-beguiling power," includes every kind of longing for happiness and for the good. Yet those of us who are subject to this longing in the various fields of business, athletics, philosophy, and so on, are never said to be in love, and are never known as lovers, while the man who devotes himself to what is only one of Love's many activities is given the name that should apply to all the rest as well.

Yes, I said, I suppose you must be right.

I know it has been suggested, she continued, that lovers are people who are looking for their other halves, but as I see it, Socrates, Love never longs for either the half or the whole of anything except the good. For men will even have their hands and feet cut off if they are once convinced that those members are bad for them. Indeed I think we only prize our own belongings in so far as we say that the good belongs to us, and the bad to someone else, for what we love is the good and nothing but the good. Or do you disagree?

Good heavens, no! I said.

Then may we state categorically that men are lovers of the good?

Yes, I said, we may.

And shouldn't we add that they long for the good to be their own?

We should.

And not merely to be their own but to be their own forever?

Yes, that must follow.

In short, that Love longs for the good to be his own forever?

Yes, I said, that's absolutely true.

Very well, then. And that being so, what course will Love's followers pursue, and in what particular field will eagerness and exertion be known as Love? In fact, what *is* this activity? Can you tell me that, Socrates?

If I could, my dear Diotima, I retorted, I shouldn't be so much amazed at *your* grasp of the subject, and I shouldn't be coming to you to learn the answer to that very question.

Well, I'll tell you, then, she said. To love is to bring forth upon the beautiful, both in body and in soul.

I'm afraid that's too deep, I said, for my poor wits to fathom.

I'll try to speak more plainly, then. We are all of us prolific, Socrates, in body and in soul, and when we reach a certain age our nature urges us to procreation. Nor can we be quickened by ugliness, but only by the beautiful. Conception, we know, takes place when man and woman come together, but there's a divinity in human propagation, an immortal something in the midst of man's mortality which is incompatible with any kind of discord. And ugliness is at odds with the divine, while beauty is in perfect harmony. In propagation, then, Beauty is the goddess of both fate and travail, and so when procreancy draws near the beautiful it grows genial and blithe, and birth follows swiftly on conception. But when it meets with ugliness it is overcome with heaviness and gloom, and turning away it shrinks into itself and is not brought to bed, but still labors under its painful burden. And so, when the procreant is big with child, he is strangely stirred by the beautiful, because he knows that beauty's tenant will bring his travail to an end. So you see, Socrates, that Love is not exactly a longing for the beautiful, as you suggested.

Well, what is it, then?

A longing not for the beautiful itself, but for the conception and generation that the beautiful effects.

Yes. No doubt you're right.

Of course I'm right, she said. And why all this longing for propagation? Because this is the one deathless and eternal element in our mortality. And since we have agreed that the lover longs for the good to be his own forever, it follows that we are bound to long for immortality as well as for the good—which is to say that Love is a longing for immortality.

So much I gathered, gentlemen, at one time and another from Diotima's dissertations upon Love.

And then one day she asked me, Well, Socrates, and what do you suppose is the cause of all this longing and all this love? Haven't you noticed what an extraordinary effect the breeding instinct has upon both animals and birds, and how obsessed they are with the desire, first to mate, and then to rear their litters and their broods, and how the weakest of them are ready to stand up to the strongest in defense of their young, and even die for them, and how they are content to bear the pinch of hunger and every kind of hardship, so long as they can rear their offspring?

With me, she went on, you might put it down to the power of reason, but how can you account for Love's having such remarkable effects upon the brutes? What do you say to that, Socrates?

Again I had to confess my ignorance.

Well, she said, I don't know how you can hope to master the philosophy of Love, if *that's* too much for you to understand.

But, my dear Diotima, I protested, as I said before, that's just why I'm asking you to teach me—because I realize how ignorant I am. And I'd be more than grateful if you'd enlighten me as to the cause not only of this, but of all the various effects of Love.

Well, she said, it's simple enough, so long as you bear in mind what we agreed was the object of Love. For here, too, the principle holds good that the mortal does all it can to put on immortality. And how can it do that except by breeding, and thus ensuring that there will always be a younger generation to take the place of the old?

Now, although we speak of an individual as being the same so long as he continues to exist in the same form, and therefore assume that a man is the same person in his dotage as in his infancy, yet, for all we call him the same, every bit of him is different, and every day he is becoming a new man, while the old man is ceasing to exist, as you can see from his hair, his flesh, his bones, his blood, and all the rest of his body. And not only his body, for the same thing happens to his soul. And neither his manners, nor his disposition, nor his thoughts, nor his desires, nor his pleasures, nor his sufferings, nor his fears are the same throughout his life, for some of them grow, while others disappear.

And the application of this principle to human knowledge is even more remarkable, for not only do some of the things we know increase, while some of them are lost, so that even in our knowledge we are not always the same, but the principle applies as well to every single branch of knowledge. When we say we are studying, we really mean that our knowledge is ebbing away. We forget, because our knowledge disappears, and we have to study so as to replace what we are losing, so that the state of our knowledge may seem, at any rate, to be the same as it was before.

This is how every mortal creature perpetuates itself. It cannot, like the divine, be still the same throughout eternity; it can only leave behind new life to fill the vacancy that is left in its species by obsolescence. This, my dear Socrates, is how the body and all else that is temporal partakes of the eternal; there is no other way. And so it is no wonder that every creature prizes its own issue, since the whole creation is inspired by this love, this passion for immortality.

Well, Diotima, I said, when she had done, that's a most impressive argument. I wonder if you're right.

Of course I am, she said with an air of authority that was almost professorial. Think of the ambitions of your fellow men, and though at first they may strike you as upsetting my argument, you'll see how right I am if you only bear in mind that men's great incentive is the love of glory, and that their one idea is "To win eternal mention in the deathless roll of fame."

For the same of fame they will dare greater dangers, even, than for their children; they are ready to spend their money like water and to wear their fingers to the bone, and, if it comes to that, to die.

Do you think, she went on, that Alcestis would have laid down her life to save Admetus, or that Achilles would have died for the love he bore Patroclus, or that Codrus, the Athenian king, would have sacrificed himself for the seed of his royal consort, if they had not hoped to win "the deathless name for valor," which, in fact, posterity has granted them? No, Socrates, no. Every one of us, no matter what he does, is longing for the endless fame, the incomparable glory that is theirs, and the nobler he is, the greater his ambition, because he is in love with the eternal.

Well then, she went on, those whose procreancy is of the body turn to woman as the object of their love, and raise a family, in the blessed hope that by doing so they will keep their memory green, "through time and through eternity." But those whose procreancy is of the spirit rather than of the flesh—and they are not unknown, Socrates—conceive and bear the things of the spirit. And what are they? you ask. Wisdom and all her sister virtues; it is the office of every poet to beget them, and of every artist whom we may call creative.

Now, by far the most important kind of wisdom, she went on, is that which governs the ordering of society, and which goes by the names of justice and moderation. And if any man is so closely allied to the divine as to be teeming with these virtues even in his youth, and if, when he comes to manhood, his first ambition is to be begetting, he too, you may be sure, will go about in search of the loveliness—and never of the ugliness—on which he may beget. And hence his procreant nature is attracted by a comely body rather than an ill-favored one, and if, besides, he happens on a soul which is at once beautiful, distinguished, and agreeable, he is charmed to find so welcome an alliance. It will be easy for him to talk of virtue to such a listener, and to discuss what human goodness is and how the virtuous should live—in short, to undertake the other's education.

And, as I believe, by constant association with so much beauty, and by thinking of his friend when he is present and when he is away, he will be delivered of the burden he has labored under all these years. And what is more, he and his friend will help each other rear the issue of their friendship—and so the bond between them will be more binding, and their communion even more complete, than that which comes of bringing children up, because they have created something lovelier and less mortal than human seed.

And I ask you, who would not prefer such fatherhood to merely human propagation, if he stopped to think of Homer, and Hesiod, and all the greatest of our poets? Who would not envy them their immortal progeny, their claim upon the admiration of posterity?

Or think of Lycurgus, she went on, and what offspring he left behind him in his laws, which proved to be the saviors of Sparta and, perhaps the whole of Hellas. Or think of the fame of Solon, the father of Athenian law, and think of all the other names that are remembered in Grecian cities and in lands beyond the sea for the noble deeds they did before the eyes of all the world, and for all the diverse virtues that they fathered. And think of all the shrines that have been dedicated to them in memory of their immortal issue, and tell me if you can of *anyone* whose mortal children have brought him so much fame.

Well now, my dear Socrates, I have no doubt that even you might be initiated into these, the more elementary mysteries of Love. But I don't know whether you could apprehend the final revelation, for so far, you know, we are only at the bottom of the true scale of perfection.

Never mind, she went on, I will do all I can to help you understand, and you must strain every nerve to follow what I'm saying.

Well then, she began, the candidate for this initiation cannot, if his efforts are to be rewarded, begin too early to devote himself to the beauties of the body. First of all, if his preceptor instructs him as he should, he will fall in love with the beauty of one individual body, so that his passion may give life to noble discourse. Next he must consider how nearly related the beauty of any one body is to the beauty of any other, when he will see that if he is to devote himself to loveliness of form it will be absurd to deny that the beauty of each and every body is the same. Having reached this point, he must set himself to be the lover of every lovely body, and bring his passion for the one into due proportion by deeming it of little or of no importance.

Next he must grasp that the beauties of the body are as nothing to the beauties of the soul, so that wherever he meets with spiritual loveliness, even in the husk of an unlovely body, he will find it beautiful enough to fall in love with and to cherish—and beautiful enough to quicken in his heart a longing for such discourse as tends toward the building of a noble nature. And from this he will be led to contemplate the beauty of laws and institutions. And when he discovers how nearly every kind of beauty is akin to every other he will conclude that the beauty of the body is not, after all, of so great moment.

And next, his attention should be diverted from institutions to the sciences, so that he may know the beauty of every kind of knowledge. And thus, by scanning beauty's wide horizon, he will be saved from a slavish and illiberal devotion to the individual loveliness of a single boy, a single man, or a single institution. And, turning his eyes toward the open sea of beauty, he will find in such contemplation the seed of the most fruitful discourse and the loftiest thought, and reap a golden harvest of philosophy, until, confirmed and strengthened, he will come upon one single form of knowledge, the knowledge of the beauty I am about to speak of.

And here, she said, you must follow me as closely as you can.

Whoever has been initiated so far in the mysteries of Love and has viewed all these aspects of the beautiful in due succession, is at last drawing near the final revelation. And now, Socrates, there bursts upon him that wondrous vision which is the very soul of the beauty he has toiled so long for. It is an everlasting loveliness which neither comes nor goes, which neither flowers nor fades, for such beauty is the same on every hand, the same then as now, here as there, this way as that way, the same to every worshiper as it is to every other.

Nor will his vision of the beautiful take the form of a face, or of hands, or of anything that is of the flesh. It will be neither words, nor knowledge, nor a something that exists in something else, such as a living creature, or the earth, or the heavens, or anything that is—but subsisting of itself and by itself in an eternal oneness, while every lovely thing partakes of it in such sort that, however much the parts may wax and wane, it will be neither more nor less, but still the same inviolable whole.

And so, when his prescribed devotion to boyish beauties has carried our candidate so far that the universal beauty dawns upon his inward sight, he is almost within reach of the final revelation. And this is the way, the only way, he must approach, or be led toward, the sanctuary of Love. Starting from individual beauties, the quest for the universal beauty must find him ever mounting the heavenly ladder, stepping from rung to rung—that is, from one to two, and from two to *every* lovely body, from bodily beauty to the beauty of institutions, from institutions to learning, and from learning in general to the special lore that pertains to nothing but the beautiful itself—until at last he comes to know what beauty is.

And if, my dear Socrates, Diotima went on, man's life is ever worth the living, it is when he has attained this vision of the very soul of beauty. And once you have seen it, you will never be seduced again by the charm of gold, of dress, of comely boys, or lads just ripening to manhood; you will care nothing for the beauties that used to take your breath away and kindle such a longing in you, and many others like you, Socrates, to be always at the side of the beloved and feasting your eyes upon him, so that you would be content, if it were possible, to deny yourself the grosser necessities of meat and drink, so long as you were with him.

But if it were given to man to gaze on beauty's very self—unsullied, unalloyed, and freed from the mortal taint that haunts the frailer loveliness of flesh and blood—if, I say, it were given to man to see the heavenly beauty face to face, would you call *his*, she asked me, an unenviable life, whose eyes had been opened to the vision, and who had gazed upon it in true contemplation until it had become his own forever?

And remember, she said, that it is only when he discerns beauty itself through what makes it visible that a man will be quickened with the true, and not the seeming, virtue—for it is virtue's self that quickens him, not virtue's semblance. And when he has brought forth and reared this perfect virtue, he shall be called the friend of god, and if ever it is given to man to put on immortality, it shall be given to him.

This, Phaedrus—this, gentlemen—was the doctrine of Diotima. I was convinced, and in that conviction I try to bring others to the same creed, and to convince them that, if we are to make this gift our own, Love will help our mortal nature more than all the world. And this is why I say that every man of us should worship the god of love, and this is why I cultivate and worship all the elements of Love myself, and bid others do the same. And all my life I shall pay the power and the might of Love such homage as I can. So you may call this my eulogy of Love, Phaedrus, if you choose; if not, well, call it what you like.

QUESTIONS FOR ANALYSIS AND DISCUSSION

1. In the parable on the birth of Love, Diotima notes how Love is the child of Resourcefulness and Need. Love is then likened to someone barefoot and homeless, living on the streets. The resourcefulness of this life of poverty is likened to a hunter, a master of device and artifice, a seeker of wisdom, but also one adept in sorcery and enchantment. How does this portrayal compare with

more conventional notions of love? Why does Diotima describe love as an envoy between the good and the bad, the beautiful and the ugly?

2. In longing for the beautiful and the good, Diotima tells Socrates, Love also longs for immortality. Can you clarify the steps Diotima takes to reach this conclusion? Do you think her idea of immortality implies an individual soul, an abstract spirit, or an eternal truth? Consider your own views of immortality. In what ways are your views similar or dissimilar to Diotima's?

3. How do the steps of love that reach the love of knowledge also lead to a virtuous person? Do you think this rendition of Platonic love respects or condemns the initial experience of love that emphasizes physical attraction and pleasure? Which passages in Socrates' discussion with Diotima support your answer?

4. As with Hildegard von Bingen, Diotima's talk of love includes images of making, begetting, and creating. In the case of the lover of knowledge, the good person seeks the beloved in a peculiar way. "It will be easy for him to talk of virtue to such a listener, and to discuss what human goodness is and how the virtuous should live—in short, to undertake the other's education." Consider those whose education you have undertaken, or those who have educated you. To what extent, in your view, does the one who teaches the good reflect the love characterized by Diotima? Can you teach the good without being a lover of knowledge? Clarify your response.

CHAPTER NINE

The Problems of Burdensome Lives

In the middle of the night, a skull came to Chuang Tzu in a dream and said, "You chatter like a rhetorician and all your words betray the entanglements of a living man. The dead know nothing of these! Would you like to hear a lecture on the dead?" Chuang Tzu answered yes.

The skull said, "Among the dead there are no rulers above, no subjects below, and no chores of the four seasons. With nothing to do, our springs and autumns are as endless as heaven and earth. A king facing south on his throne could have no more happiness than this!"

Chuang Tzu couldn't believe this and said, "If I got the Arbiter of Fate to give you a body again, make you some bones and flesh, return you to your parents and family and your old home and friends, you would want that, wouldn't you?"

The skull frowned severely, wrinkling up its brow. "Why would I throw away more happiness than that of a king on a throne and take on the troubles of a human being again?" it said.

—Chuang Tzu, *"Supreme Happiness"*

Burdensome lives refers to the human task of distinguishing between those lives worth living and those not worth living. The moments that call forth this choice arise in various ways, from the burdens posed by a newborn to the deteriorating health of an elderly relative to the burdens of one's own life that may trigger thoughts of suicide. These issues are familiar to us all. They are taught in a variety of college courses. They provide the focus for television and movie scripts. They are central to our understanding of the law. We cannot escape them.

There is a good chance that you have already made up your mind about some of these issues. Some issues have received so much attention that it is easy to sympathize with the skull's observation that all our words could wind up being "the entanglements of a living man." Can those who directly engage in public debate about these issues demonstrate that they have done more good than harm with their scholarly, emotional, and explosive rhetoric?

Yet while you are sitting in class taking notes on the lecture, you are also worried about your friend who recently learned she is pregnant. She comes to you with a mixture of anger, worry, shame, hope, and love. She wants you to help her sort out these feelings and make a good decision. Can you?

Or think of your new friend diligently taking the history test you both crammed for last night and this morning. He will probably get a good grade, but you know his mind is elsewhere, with his grandfather. Just as the sun was rising, he wearily told you that his family no longer knows what to do about Grandpa, the man who gave your friend the inspiration to be a history major. Is there any way you can help your friend? Is there any moral advice or deed that would do any good?

The selections in this chapter outline some of the ways to look at the ending of a life. For moral thinkers this ending is less a biological event than an ethical one. Which life and which death is justifiable? Who determines when a person is to die? Is this decided by rights, overall pleasure, individual convenience, or in some other way? Is everyone entitled to live as long as technologically or economically feasible, or is there such a thing as wanting to live too long?

Depending on one's proximity, burdensome can mean several things. Some burdens are rewarding—putting up with this semester's course load, for example. Other burdens are not—the boss you want to cuss out, the professor you want to refute, the noisy neighbors, or the annoying colleague. There are also the burdens offered by life itself. They are so troubling that they push us to question the first law of nature—the right to self-preservation.

The case study by Swiss philosopher Max Picard concisely portrays the significance of silence. According to Picard, silence has different meanings in childhood and old age. In both cases silence should be construed as a meaningful or positive value rather than as a mere absence of something to say. The moral issues surrounding silence at the end of life highlight the moral person's desire to do the good.

Four essays on abortion address some of the many perspectives on the morality and legalization of abortion. John Noonan articulates a rejection of abortion based on the idea of universal respect for human life. Judith J. Thomson, an MIT philosopher, offers her well-known defense of abortion using an analogy of a moral patient finding himself the direct source of another patient's survival. Susan Sherwin outlines a feminist perspective on the abortion debate, with special attention to the political aspects of this ongoing controversy. Philosopher Rosalind Hursthouse concludes by articulating the approach a virtuous person would take when considering the morality of having an abortion. Legal and utilitarian minded people, she notes, have not addressed the existential confusions of those considering an abortion.

Many social and moral critics have devoted their attention to how the elderly ought to be treated. For them this demands something more than the gratitude argument given by Lin Yutang (Chapter 6). It involves a cultural decision about how long we should expect to live and whether we should live within those expectations by setting clearly defined limits. Ethics scholar Daniel Callahan and philosophy professor Susan Purviance discuss how social norms and virtue ethics can contribute to moral concerns over the growing burdens of the elderly.

What if our own lives become too burdensome? Timothy Quill, a medical doctor in New York, explains his decision in helping a patient die by means of assisted suicide. Though this help may not yet have the official support of the American Medical Association, Quill suggests that many doctors are sympathetic to his decision. With the recent passage of the Death with Dignity Act in Oregon, citizens are asking doctors to address this evolving moral controversy. Philosopher James Bogen relies on a virtue-based ethic to reflect on what a moral person should consider when confronted with a potential suicide.

70.

MAX PICARD

Case Study: Childhood, Old Age and Silence

What can be said in the face of a life nearing its end? What cannot or should not be said? Swiss philosopher Max Picard (1888–1965) articulates a connection between the twilight of life and the dawn of life by reflecting on the meaning and importance of silence. In silence, and with a respect for silence, one gains a renewed appreciation for human communication. Communication is more than the exchange of information bits. It is also melodious and poetic, as exemplified in the child's early journeys into the world. Communication also resides in those for whom the utterance of words expresses less than the silence shared by those who are aging together. These points are concisely and insightfully captured by Picard in developing a systematic understanding of silence.

CRITICAL READING QUESTIONS

1. Why are children "little hills of silence"?
2. What makes the child's language poetic?
3. How does Picard relate silence to the anticipation of death?
4. What is the difference between the child and the adult when connecting silence with sound?

"Childhood, Old Age and Silence," from *The World of Silence*, translated by Stanley Godman (South Bend, IN: Regnery/Gateway, 1952), pp. 119–122.

The Child

The child is like a little hill of silence. On this little hill of silence suddenly the word appears. The little hill becomes quite small when the first word of the child is spoken. It sinks beneath the pressure of the word as if by magic, and the word tries to make itself look important.

It is as though with the sound that comes from its mouth the child were knocking on the door of silence and silence were replying: Here I am, Silence, with a word for you.

The word has difficulty in coming up from the silence of the child. Just as the child is led by its mother, so, it seems, the word is led by silence to the edge of the child's mouth, and is held so firmly there by silence that it is as though each syllable had to detach itself separately from the silence. More silence than sound comes out through the words of children, more silence than real language.

The words a child speaks do not flow in a straight line, but in a curve, as if they wanted to fall back again into the silence. They make their slow journey from the child to other people, and when they arrive they hesitate a moment, to decide whether they should return to the silence or stay where they are. The child gazes after its word as it might watch its ball in the air, watching to see if it will come back again or not.

The child cannot replace by another word the word it has brought with difficulty out of the silence; it cannot put a pronoun in place of a noun. For each word is there as it were for the first time, and what is there for the first time, what is quite new, naturally has no wish to be replaced by something else.

A child never speaks of itself as "I," but it always says its name: "Andrew wants. . . ." The child would think it were disappearing if it were to replace its own name by a pronoun—its own name that has just come up out of the silence with the word and is there as it were for the first time ever.

The child's language is poetic, for it is the language of the beginning of things, and therefore original and first-hand as the language of poets is original and first-hand. "The moon has got broken," says the child of the new moon. "We must take it to mother to mend it."

The child's language is melodious. The words hide and protect themselves in the melody—the words that have come shyly out of the silence. They almost disappear again in the silence. There is more melody than content in the words of the child.

It is as though silence were accumulating within the child as a reserve for the adult, for the noisy world of the child's later years as an adult. The adult who has preserved within himself not only something of the language of childhood but also something of its silence, too, has the power to make others happy.

The language of the child is silence transformed into sound. The language of the adult is sound that seeks for silence.

Children—the little hills of silence—are scattered about everywhere in the world of words, reminding men of the origin of speech. They are like a conspiracy against the all-too-dynamic world of the words of today. And sometimes it is as though they were not only a reminder of where the word comes from but also a warning as to where it might return: back into silence. But what better thing could happen to the corrupted word than to be brought back into these little hills of silence to become immersed therein? Then there would be only little hills of silence on the earth, and in them the word would try to sink itself deep down into the hills so that out of the depth of the silence the first, the original, word might be born again.

The Old People

The Word climbs up slowly out of the silence in the child, and the words of old men and women are slow, too, as they return to the silence that is the end of life. Like a burden that has grown too heavy the word falls out of the mouth of the old, more down into the silence than outwards to other men, for the old speak more to their own silence than to other men.

They move their words like heavy globules hither and thither between their lips. It is as though they were rolling them back in secret into the silence, as though before they leave the earth themselves, the old men and women were trying to give back to the silence the words they received from the silence almost unnoticed when they were children.

An old man and an old woman sitting beside each other in silence outside their home in the evening. . . . They and every word that comes from them and every action to which the word gives rise, are within the silence. They are not even listening any longer to hear what the silence is saying, for they have already become a part of the silence. Just as they led the cattle to water, they now lead the evening to the watering place of silence and wait till it is satisfied. Then they slowly rise and lead it back into the warming light of the house.

Even before they move into the silence of death, the old have something of that silence within them; their movements are slow, as though they were trying not to disturb the silence at the end of the journey. With their stick to help them they still walk hesitantly as if on a bridge without railings, from both sides of which not language any more, but death, rises up to meet them. They go to meet the silence of death with their own silence within. And the last word of the old is like a ship carrying them over from the silence of life into the silence of death.

QUESTIONS FOR ANALYSIS AND DISCUSSION

1. There is an element of paradox in discussing silence—are we not betraying it when talking about it? Yet Picard is very descriptive in his accounts of silence. How is silence related to words and spoken language? Can the use of words respect as well as betray silence? Clarify your understanding of Picard's use of "silence."

2. "Silence," writes Picard, "has the power to make others happy." What do you think is meant by this remark? Can you offer your own example of what Picard has in mind?

3. How is silence related to noise? Which is the greater enemy of the word: silence, noise, or a third candidate? Briefly explain your answer.

4. Do you think the silence of old age is similar to the silence of childhood? Or is the death that frames the silence of the aging a sharp contrast to the silence of joy characteristic of childhood? Develop your thoughts in light of Picard's descriptions.

71.

JOHN T. NOONAN JR.

An Almost Absolute Value in History

As many historians of morality remind us, abortion has long been an option for women seeking to end a pregnancy. Infanticide has also had a long history as an acceptable means by which men and women could rid themselves of a baby that was deformed, a bastard, conceived in sinful or illicit sex, or a burden for the mother or family too poor to raise it. Despite these widespread practices of discarding unwanted infants, moral thinkers have yet to reach a consensus about the rightness of abortion. Are there stages of a pregnancy during which abortion is morally permissible? Is the morality of abortion dependent on the motives or reasons behind the deed? Is this debate about personal ethics, or is it about cultural and political issues? Do the definitions of fetus, personhood, *and* human life *help resolve or exacerbate the problem?*

John T. Noonan Jr. (b. 1926) argues that abortion is almost always morally wrong. He looks at some of the key issues in the abortion debate and contends that they are too uncertain to reach any clear-cut support of abortion. Given this uncertainty, Noonan says we should stand by the principle that human life is sacred. Noonan emphasizes a religious perspective but interweaves it with careful observations on historical and biological evidence.

"An Almost Absolute Value in History," from *The Morality of Abortion*, edited by John T. Noonan Jr. (Cambridge, MA: Harvard University Press, 1970), pp. 360–365.

CRITICAL READING QUESTIONS

1. What are four distinctions made by those who believe that a fetus is not a human being?

2. Why does Noonan remind us that there are about 200 million spermatozoa in a male ejaculate and a range of 100 thousand to one million oocytes that can become ova?

3. For Noonan, what is the decisive moment of humanity?

4. Under which condition is abortion morally permissible?

The most fundamental question involved in the long history of thought on abortion is: How do you determine the humanity of a being? To phrase the question that way is to put in comprehensive humanistic terms what the theologians either dealt with as an explicitly theological question under the heading of "ensoulment" or dealt with implicitly in their treatment of abortion. The Christian position as it originated did not depend on a narrow theological or philosophical concept. It had no relation to the theories of infant baptism. It appealed to no special theory of instantaneous ensoulment. It took the world's view on ensoulment as that view changed from Aristotle to Zacchia. There was, indeed, theological influence affecting the theory of ensoulment finally adopted, and, of course, ensoulment itself was a theological concept, so that the position was always explained in theological terms. But the theological notion of ensoulment could easily be translated into humanistic language by substituting "human" for "rational soul"; the problem of knowing when a man is a man is common to theology and humanism.

If one steps outside the specific categories used by the theologians, the answer they gave can be analyzed as a refusal to discriminate among human beings on the basis of their varying potentialities. Once conceived, the being was recognized as man because he had man's potential. The criterion for humanity, thus, was simple and all-embracing: if you are conceived by human parents, you are human.

The strength of this position may be tested by a review of some of the other distinctions offered in the contemporary controversy over legalizing abortion. Perhaps the most popular distinction is in terms of viability. Before an age of so many months, the fetus is not viable, that is, it cannot be removed from the mother's womb and live apart from her. To that extent, the life of the fetus is absolutely dependent on the life of the mother. This dependence is made the basis of denying recognition to its humanity.

There are difficulties with this distinction. One is that the perfection of artificial incubation may make the fetus viable at any time: it may be removed and artificially sustained. Experiments with animals already show that such a procedure is possible. This hypothetical extreme case relates to an actual difficulty: there is considerable elasticity to the idea of viability. Mere length of life is not an exact measure. The viability of the fetus depends on the extent of its anatomical and functional development. The weight and length of the fetus are better guides to the state of its development than age, but weight and length vary. . . . If viability is the norm, the standard would vary with . . . many individual circumstances.

The most important objection to this approach is that dependence is not ended by viability. The fetus is still absolutely dependent on someone's care in order to continue existence; indeed a child of one or three or even five years of age is absolutely dependent on another's care for existence; uncared for, the older fetus or the younger child will die as surely as the early fetus detached from the mother. The unsubstantial lessening in dependence at viability does not seem to signify any special acquisition of humanity.

A second distinction has been attempted in terms of experience. A being who has had experience, has lived and suffered, who possesses memories, is more human than one who has not. Humanity depends on formation by experience. The fetus is thus "unformed" in the most basic human sense.

This distinction is not serviceable for the embryo which is already experiencing and reacting. The embryo is responsive to touch after eight weeks and at least at that point is experiencing. At an earlier stage the zygote is certainly alive and responding to its environment. The distinction may also be challenged by the rare case where aphasia has erased adult memory: has it erased humanity? More fundamentally, this distinction leaves even the older fetus or the younger child to be treated as an unformed inhuman thing. Finally, it is not clear why experience as such confers humanity. It could be argued that certain central experiences such as loving or learning are necessary to make a man human. But then human beings who have failed to love or to learn might be excluded from the class called man.

A third distinction is made by appeal to the sentiments of adults. If a fetus dies, the grief of the parents is not the grief they would have for a living child. The fetus is an unnamed "it" till birth, and is not perceived as personality until at least the fourth month of existence when movements in the womb manifest a vigorous presence demanding joyful recognition by the parents.

Yet feeling is notoriously an unsure guide to the humanity of others. Many groups of humans have had difficulty in feeling that persons of another tongue, color, religion, sex, are as human as they. Apart from reactions to alien groups, we mourn the loss of a ten-year-old boy more than the loss of his one-day-old brother or his 90-year-old grandfather. The difference felt and the grief expressed vary with the potentialities extinguished, or the experience wiped out; they do not seem to point to any substantial difference in the humanity of baby, boy, or grandfather.

Distinctions are also made in terms of sensation by the parents. The embryo is felt within the womb only after about the fourth month. The embryo is seen only at birth. What can be neither seen nor felt is different from what is tangible. If the fetus cannot be seen or touched at all, it cannot be perceived as man.

Yet experience shows that sight is even more untrustworthy than feeling in determining humanity. By sight, color became an appropriate index for saying who was a man, and the evil of racial discrimination was given foundations. Nor can touch provide the test; a being confined by sickness, "out of touch" with others, does not thereby seem to lose his humanity. To the extent that touch still has appeal as a criterion, it appears to be a survival of the old English idea of "quickening"—

a possible mistranslation of the Latin *animatus* used in the canon law. To that extent touch as a criterion seems to be dependent on the Aristotelian notion of ensoulment, and to fall when this notion is discarded.

Finally, a distinction is sought in social visibility. The fetus is not socially perceived as human. It cannot communicate with others. Thus, both subjectively and objectively, it is not a member of society. As moral rules are rules for the behavior of members of society to each other, they cannot be made for behavior toward what is not yet a member. Excluded from the society of men, the fetus is excluded from the humanity of men.

By force of the argument from the consequences, this distinction is to be rejected. It is more subtle than that founded on an appeal to physical sensation, but it is equally dangerous in its implications. If humanity depends on social recognition, individuals or whole groups may be dehumanized by being denied any status in their society. Such a fate is fictionally portrayed in *1984* and has actually been the lot of many men in many societies. In the Roman empire, for example, condemnation to slavery meant the practical denial of most human rights; in the Chinese Communist world, landlords have been classified as enemies of the people and so treated as nonpersons by the state. Humanity does not depend on social recognition, though often the failure of society to recognize the prisoner, the alien, the heterodox as human has led to the destruction of human beings. Anyone conceived by a man and a woman is human. Recognition of this condition by society follows a real event in the objective order, however imperfect and halting the recognition. Any attempt to limit humanity to exclude some group runs the risk of furnishing authority and precedent for excluding other groups in the name of the consciousness or perception of the controlling group in the society.

A philosopher may reject the appeal to the humanity of the fetus because he views "humanity" as a secular view of the soul and because he doubts the existence of anything real and objective which can be identified as humanity. One answer to such a philosopher is to ask how he reasons about moral questions without supposing that there is a sense in which he and the others of whom he speaks are human. Whatever group is taken as the society which determines who may be killed is thereby taken as human. A second answer is to ask if he does not believe that there is a right and wrong way of deciding moral questions. If there is such a difference, experience may be appealed to: to decide who is human on the basis of the sentiment of a given society has led to consequences which rational men would characterize as monstrous.

The rejection of the attempted distinctions based on viability and visibility, experience and feeling, may be buttressed by the following considerations: Moral judgments often rest on distinctions, but if the distinctions are not to appear arbitrary fiat, they should relate to some real difference in probabilities. There is a kind of continuity in all life, but the earlier stages of the elements of human life possess tiny probabilities of development. Consider, for example, the spermatozoa in any normal ejaculate: There are about 200,000,000 in any single ejaculate, of which one has a chance of developing into a zygote. Consider the oocytes which may become ova: there are 100,000 to 1,000,000 oocytes in a female infant, of which a maximum of 390 are ovulated. But once spermatozoon and ovum meet and the conceptus is formed, such studies as have been made show that roughly in only 20 percent of the cases will spontaneous abortion occur. In other words, the chances are about 4 out of 5 that this new being will develop. At this stage in the life of the being there is a sharp shift in probabilities, an immense jump in potentialities. To make a distinction between the rights of spermatozoa and the rights of the fertilized ovum is to respond to an enormous shift in possibilities. For about twenty days after conception the egg may split to form twins or combine with another egg to form a chimera, but the probability of either event happening is very small.

It may be asked, What does a change in biological probabilities have to do with establishing humanity? The argument from probabilities is not aimed at establishing humanity but at establishing an objective discontinuity which may be taken into account in moral discourse. As life itself is a matter of probabilities, as most moral reasoning is an estimate of probabilities, so it seems in accord with the structure of reality and the nature of moral thought to found a moral judgment on the change in probabilities at conception. The appeal to probabilities is the most commensical of arguments, to a greater or smaller degree all of us base our actions on probabilities, and in morals, as in law, prudence and negligence are often measured by the account one has taken of the probabilities. If the chance is 200,000,000 to 1 that the movement in the bushes into which you shoot is a man's, I doubt if many persons would hold you careless in shooting; but if the chances are 4 out of 5 that the movement is a human being's, few would acquit you of blame. Would the argument be different if only one out of ten children conceived came to term? Of course this argument would be different. This argument is an appeal to probabilities that actually exist, not to any and all states of affairs which may be imagined.

The probabilities as they do exist do not show the humanity of the embryo in the sense of a demonstration in logic any more than the probabilities of the movement in the bush being a man demonstrate beyond all doubt that the being is a man. The appeal is a "buttressing" consideration, showing the plausibility of the standard adopted. The argument focuses on the decisional factor in any moral judgment and assumes that part of the business of a moralist is drawing lines. One evidence of the nonarbitrary character of the line drawn is the difference of probabilities on either side of it. If a spermatozoon is destroyed, one destroys a being which had a chance of far less than 1 in 200 million of developing into a reasoning being, possessed of the genetic code, a heart and other organs, and capable of pain. If a fetus is destroyed, one destroys a being already possessed of the genetic code, organs, and sensitivity to pain, and one which had an 80 percent chance of developing further into a baby outside the womb who, in time, would reason.

The positive argument for conception as the decisive moment of humanization is that at conception the new being receives the genetic code. It is this genetic information which determines his characteristics, which is the biological carrier of the possibility of human wisdom, which makes him a self-evolving being. A being with a human genetic code is man.

This review of current controversy over the humanity of the fetus emphasizes what a fundamental question the theologians resolved in asserting the inviolability of the fetus. To regard the fetus as possessed of equal rights with other humans was not, however, to decide every case where abortion might be employed. It did decide the case where the argument was that the fetus should be aborted for its own good. To say a being was human was to say it had a destiny to decide for itself which could not be taken from it by another man's decision. But human beings with equal rights often come in conflict with each other, and some decision must be made as whose claims are to prevail. Cases of conflict involving the fetus are different only in two respects: the total inability of the fetus to speak for itself and the fact that the right of the fetus regularly at stake is the right to life itself.

The approach taken by the theologians to these conflicts was articulated in terms of "direct" and "indirect." Again, to look at what they were doing from outside their categories, they may be said to have been drawing lines or "balancing values." "Direct" and "indirect" are spatial metaphors; "line-drawing" is another. "To weigh" or "to balance" values is a metaphor of a more complicated mathematical sort hinting at the process which goes on in moral judgments. All the metaphors suggest that, in the moral judgments made, comparisons were necessary, that no value completely controlled. The principle of double effect was no doctrine fallen from heaven, but a method of analysis appropriate where two relative values were being compared. In Catholic moral theology, as it developed, life even of the innocent was not taken as an absolute. Judgments on acts affecting life issued from a process of weighing. In the weighing, the fetus was always given a value greater than zero, always a value separate and independent from its parents. This valuation was crucial and fundamental in all Christian thought on the subject and marked it off from any approach which considered that only the parents' interests needed to be considered.

Even with the fetus weighed as human, one interest could be weighed as equal or superior: that of the mother in her own life. The casuists between 1450 and 1895 were willing to weigh this interest as superior. Since 1895, that interest was given decisive weight only in the two special cases of the cancerous uterus and the ectopic pregnancy. In both of these cases the fetus itself had little chance of survival even if the abortion were not performed. As the balance was once struck in favor of the mother whenever her life was endangered, it could be so struck again. The balance reached between 1895 and 1930 attempted prudentially and pastorally to forestall a multitude of exceptions for interests less than life.

The perception of the humanity of the fetus and the weighing of fetal rights against other human rights constituted the work of the moral analysts. But what spirit animated their abstract judgments? For the Christian community it was the injunction of Scripture to love your neighbor as yourself. The fetus as human was a neighbor; his life had parity with one's own. The commandment gave life to what otherwise would have been only rational calculation.

The commandment could be put in humanistic as well as theological terms: Do not injure your fellow man without reason. In these terms, once the humanity of the fetus is perceived, abortion is never right except in self-defense. When life must be taken to save life, reason alone cannot say that a mother must prefer a child's life to her own. With this exception, now of great rarity, abortion violates the rational humanist tenet of the equality of human lives.

For Christians the commandment to love had received a special imprint in that the exemplar proposed of love was the love of the Lord for his disciples. In the light given by this example, self-sacrifice carried to the point of death seemed in the extreme situations not without meaning. In the less extreme cases, preference for one's own interests to the life of another seemed to express cruelty or selfishness irreconcilable with the demands of love.

QUESTIONS FOR ANALYSIS AND DISCUSSION

1. The near universal taboo on murder underlies much of the moral interest on abortion. Hence, the controversy about the status of the fetus. Noonan outlines four distinctions made by those who believe the fetus is not human. Select one or two of the distinctions and consider Noonan's rejoinder. Do you agree with his rejoinder? If so, does that mean abortion is murder? Or do you find flaws in his rejoinder? If so, specify them.

2. One of the laws of nature is the right to self-preservation. To override this right requires either a greater right, the moral avenue, or a greater physical force, the coercive or warlike avenue. As Noonan puts it, at the moment of conception there is a distinct creature whose right to self-preservation deserves respect. Do you agree? If so, does this right also extend to all potential forms of life? If not, at what point does a creature deserve to have its right to self-preservation respected?

3. The "almost" in Noonan's title seems to refer to the only exception for a morally permissible abortion. Do you agree with Noonan on this point? What about a pregnancy that results from rape? a pregnancy in which doctors detect severe medical problems for the fetus? a pregnancy that interrupts plans for graduate school or a job promotion? Explain your position.

72.

JUDITH JARVIS THOMSON

A Defense of Abortion

According to Judith Jarvis Thomson, a philosopher from MIT, the human status of the fetus is not the central problem of abortion because this issue cannot be satisfactorily resolved. Even the most conscientious thinkers will have trouble agreeing on where to draw

"A Defense of Abortion," *Philosophy and Public Affairs*, Fall 1971, 1(1): 351–360. Notes have been omitted.

*the line between human and fetus. Thomson adroitly circumvents this issue by raising
an analogy in which a hospital patient awakens from surgery to find himself the blood
source for a famous violinist. The moral question is: Does the patient have a right to sever
the blood lines, or is the patient obligated to endure the experience until the violinist recu-
perates? How one answers this should help in clarifying the problem of abortion.*

| CRITICAL READING QUESTIONS |

1. What are the major similarities between a woman considering an abortion and a patient providing blood to the violinist?
2. How does Thomson respond to the "right to life" argument?
3. Which two kinds of Samaritan does she distinguish? What are their respective qualities?
4. Which kinds of abortion does Thomson call indecent?
5. Which kind of abortion is clearly not the killing of a person?

Most opposition to abortion relies on the premise that the fetus is a human being, a person, from the moment of conception. The premise is argued for, but, as I think, not well. Take, for example, the most common argument. We are asked to notice that the development of a human being from conception through birth into childhood is continuous; then it is said that to draw a line, to choose a point in this development and say "before this point the thing is not a person, after this point it is a person" is to make an arbitrary choice, a choice for which in the nature of things no good reason can be given. It is concluded that the fetus is, or anyway that we had better say it is, a person from the moment of conception. But this conclusion does not follow. Similar things might be said about the development of an acorn into an oak tree, and it does not follow that acorns are oak trees, or that we had better say they are. Arguments of this form are sometimes called "slippery slope arguments"—the phrase is perhaps self-explanatory—and it is dismaying that opponents of abortion rely on them so heavily and uncritically.

I am inclined to agree, however, that the prospects for "drawing a line" in the development of the fetus look dim. I am inclined to think also that we shall probably have to agree that the fetus has already become a human person well before birth. Indeed, it comes as a surprise when one first learns how early in its life it begins to acquire human characteristics. By the tenth week, for example, it already has a face, arms and legs, fingers and toes; it has internal organs, and brain activity is detectable. On the other hand, I think that the premise is false, that the fetus is not a person from the moment of conception. A newly fertilized ovum, a newly implanted clump of cells, is no more a person than an acorn is an oak tree. But I shall not discuss any of this. For it seems to me to be of great interest to ask what happens if, for the sake of argument, we allow the premise. How, precisely, are we supposed to get from there to the conclusion that abortion is morally impermissible? Opponents of abortion commonly spend most of their time establishing that the fetus is a person, and hardly any time explaining the step from there to the impermissibility of abortion. Perhaps they think the step too simple and obvious to require much comment. Or perhaps instead they are simply being economical in argument. Many of those who defend abortion rely on the premise that the fetus is not a person, but only a bit of tissue that will become a person at birth; and why pay out more arguments than you have to? Whatever the explanation, I suggest that the step they take is neither easy nor obvious, that it calls for closer examination than it is commonly given, and that when we do give it this closer examination we shall feel inclined to reject it.

I propose, then, that we grant that the fetus is a person from the moment of conception. How does the argument go from here? Something like this, I take it. Every person has a right to life. So the fetus has a right to life. No doubt the mother has a right to decide what shall happen in and to her body; everyone would grant that. But surely a person's right to life is stronger and more stringent than the mother's right to decide what happens in and to her body, and so outweighs it. So the fetus may not be killed; an abortion may not be performed.

It sounds plausible. But now let me ask you to imagine this. You wake up in the morning and find yourself back to back in bed with an unconscious violinist. A famous unconscious violinist. He has been found to have a fatal kidney ailment, and the Society of Music Lovers has canvassed all the available medical records and found that you alone have the right blood type to help. They have therefore kidnapped you, and last night the violinist's circulatory system was plugged into yours, so that your kidneys can be used to extract poisons from his blood as well as your own. The director of the hospital now tells you, "Look, we're sorry the Society of Music Lovers did this to you—we would never have permitted it if we had known. But still, they did it, and the violinist now is plugged into you. To unplug you would be to kill him. But never mind, it's only for nine months. By then he will have recovered from his ailment, and can safely be unplugged from you." Is it morally incumbent on you to accede to this situation? No doubt it would be very nice of you if you did, a great kindness. But do you *have* to accede to it? What if it were not nine months, but nine years? Or longer still? What if the director of the hospital says, "Tough luck, I agree, but you've now got to stay in bed, with the violinist plugged into you, for the rest of your life. Because remember this. All persons have a right to life, and violinists are persons. Granted you have a right to decide what happens in and to your body, but a person's right to life outweighs your right to decide what happens in and to your body. So you cannot ever be unplugged from him." I imagine you would regard this as outrageous, which suggests that something really is wrong with that plausible-sounding argument I mentioned a moment ago.

In this case, of course, you were kidnapped; you didn't volunteer for the operation that plugged the violinist into your kidneys. Can those who oppose abortion on the ground I mentioned make any exception for a pregnancy due to rape? Certainly. They can say that persons have a right to life only if they didn't come into existence because of rape; or they can say that all persons have a right to life, but that some have less of a right to life than others, in particular, that those who came into existence because of rape have less. But these statements have a rather unpleasant sound. Surely the question of whether you have a right to life at all, or how much of it you have, shouldn't turn on the question of whether or not you are the product of a rape. And in fact the people who oppose abortion on the ground I mentioned do not make this distinction, and hence do not make an exception in case of rape.

Nor do they make an exception for a case in which the mother has to spend the nine months of her pregnancy in bed. They would agree that would be a great pity, and hard on the mother; but all the same, all persons have a right to life, the fetus is a person, and so on. I suspect, in fact, that they would not make an exception for a case in which, miraculously enough, the pregnancy went on for nine years, or even the rest of the mother's life.

Some won't even make an exception for a case in which continuation of the pregnancy is likely to shorten the mother's life; they regard abortion as impermissible even to save the mother's life. Such cases are nowadays very rare, and many opponents of abortion do not accept this extreme view. All the same, it is a good place to begin: a number of points of interest come out in respect to it.

1. Let us call the view that abortion is impermissible even to save the mother's life "the extreme view." I want to suggest first that it does not issue from the argument I mentioned earlier without the addition of some fairly powerful premises. Suppose a woman has become pregnant, and now learns that she has a cardiac condition such that she will die if she carries the baby to term. What may be done for her? The fetus, being a person, has a right to life, but as the mother is a person too, so has she a right to life. Presumably they have an equal right to life. How is it supposed to come out that an abortion may not be performed? If mother and child have an equal right to life, shouldn't we perhaps flip a coin? Or should we add to the mother's right to life her right to decide what happens in and to her body, which everybody seems to be ready to grant—the sum of her rights now outweighing the fetus's right to life?

The most familiar argument here is the following. We are told that performing the abortion would be directly killing the child, whereas doing nothing would not be killing the mother, but only letting her die. Moreover, in killing the child, one would be killing an innocent person, for the child has committed no crime, and is not aiming at his mother's death. And then there are a variety of ways in which this might be continued. (1) But as directly killing an innocent person is always and absolutely impermissible, an abortion may not be performed. Or, (2) as directly killing an innocent person is murder, and murder is always and absolutely impermissible, an abortion may not be performed. Or, (3) as one's duty to refrain from directly killing an innocent person is more stringent than one's duty to keep a person from dying, an abortion may not be performed. Or, (4) if one's only options are directly killing an innocent person or letting a person die, one must prefer letting the person die, and thus an abortion may not be performed.

Some people seem to have thought that these are not further premises which must be added if the conclusion is to be reached, but that they follow from the very fact that an innocent person has a right to life. But this seems to me to be a mistake, and perhaps the simplest way to show this is to bring out that while we must certainly grant that innocent persons have a right to life, the theses in (1) through (4) are all false. Take (2), for example. If directly killing an innocent person is murder, and thus is impermissible, then the mother's directly killing the innocent person inside her is murder, and thus is impermissible. But it cannot seriously be thought to be murder if the mother performs an abortion on herself to save her life. It cannot seriously be said that she *must* refrain, that she *must* sit passively by and wait for her death. Let us look again at the case of you and the violinist. There you are, in bed with the violinist, and the director of the hospital says to you "It's all most distressing, and I deeply sympathize, but you see this is putting an additional strain on your kidneys, and you'll be dead within the month. But you *have* to stay where you are all the same. Because unplugging you would be directly killing an innocent violinist, and that's murder, and that's impermissible." If anything in the world is true, it is that you do not commit murder, you do not do what is impermissible, if you reach around to your back and unplug yourself from that violinist to save your life. . . .

2. The extreme view could of course be weakened to say that while abortion is permissible to save the mother's life, it may not be performed by a third party, but only by the mother herself. But this cannot be right either. For what we have to keep in mind is that the mother and the unborn child are not like two tenants in a small house which has, by an unfortunate mistake, been rented to both: the mother *owns* the house. The fact that she does adds to the offensiveness of deducing that the mother can do nothing from the supposition that third parties can do nothing. But it does more than this: it casts a bright light on the supposition that third parties can do nothing. Certainly it lets us see that a third party who says "I cannot choose between you" is fooling himself if he thinks this is impartiality. If Jones has found and fastened on a certain coat, which he needs to keep him from freezing, but which Smith also needs to keep him from freezing, then it is not impartiality that says "I cannot choose between you" when Smith owns the coat. Women have said again and again "This body is *my* body!" and they have reason to feel angry, reason to feel that it has been like shouting into the wind. Smith, after all, is hardly likely to bless us if we say to him, "Of course it's your coat, anybody would grant that it is. But no one may choose between you and Jones who is to have it."

We should really ask what it is that says "no one may choose" in the face of the fact that the body that houses the child is the mother's body. It may be simply a failure to appreciate this fact. But it may be something more interesting, namely the sense that one has a right to refuse to lay hands on Jones, a right to refuse to do physical violence to people, even where it would be just and fair to do so, even where justice seems to require that somebody do so. Thus justice might call for somebody to get Smith's coat back from Jones, and yet you have a right to refuse to be the one to lay hands on Jones, a right to refuse to do physical violence to him. This, I think, must be granted. But then what should be said is not "no one may choose" but only "*I* cannot choose," and indeed not even this, but "*I* will not *act*," leaving it open that somebody else can or should, and in particular that anyone in a position of authority, with the job of securing people's rights, both can and should. So this is no difficulty. I have not been arguing that any given third party must accede to the mother's request that he perform an abortion to save her life, but only that he may.

I suppose that in some views of human life the mother's body is only on loan to her, the loan not being one which gives her any prior claim to it. One who held this view might well think it impartiality to say "I cannot choose." But I shall simply ignore this possibility. My own view is that if a human being has any just, prior claim to anything at all, he has a just, prior claim to his own body. And perhaps this needn't be argued for here anyway, since, as I mentioned, the arguments against abortion we are looking at do grant that the woman has a right to decide what happens in and to her body.

But although they do grant it, I have tried to show that they do not take seriously what is done in granting it. I suggest the same thing will reappear even more clearly when we turn away from cases in which the mother's life is at stake, and attend, as I propose we now do, to the vastly more common cases in which a woman wants an abortion for some less weighty reason than preserving her own life.

3. Where the mother's life is not at stake, the argument I mentioned at the outset seems to have a much stronger pull. "Everyone has a right to life, so the unborn person has a right to life." And isn't the child's right to life weightier than anything other than the mother's own right to life, which she might put forward as ground for an abortion?

This argument treats the right to life as if it were unproblematic. It is not, and this seems to me to be precisely the source of the mistake.

For we should now, at long last, ask what it comes to, to have a right to life. In some views having a right to life includes having a right to be given at least the bare minimum one needs for continued life. But suppose that what in fact *is* the bare minimum a man needs for continued life is something he has no right at all to be given? If I am sick unto death, and the only thing that will save my life is the touch of Henry Fonda's cool hand on my fevered brow, then all the same, I have no right to be given the touch of Henry Fonda's cool hand on my fevered brow. It would be frightfully nice of him to fly in from the West Coast to provide it. It would be less nice, though no doubt well meant, if my friends flew out to the West Coast and carried Henry Fonda back with them. But I have no right at all against anybody that he should do this for me. Or again, to return to the story I told earlier, the fact that for continued life that violinist needs the continued use of your kidneys does not establish that he has a right to be given the continued use of your kidneys. He certainly has no right against you that *you* should give him continued use of your kidneys. For nobody has any right to use your kidneys unless you give him such a right; and nobody has the right against you that you shall give him this right—if you do allow him to go on using your kidneys, this is a kindness on your part, and not something he can claim from you as his due. Nor has he any right against anybody else that *they* should give him continued use of your kidneys. Certainly he had no right against the Society of Music Lovers that they should plug him into you in the first place. And if you now start to unplug yourself, having learned that you will otherwise have to spend nine years in bed with him, there is nobody in the world who must try to prevent you, in order to see to it that he is given something he has a right to be given.

Some people are rather stricter about the right to life. In their view, it does not include the right to be given anything, but amounts to, and only to, the right not to be killed by anybody. But here a related difficulty arises. If everybody is to refrain from killing that violinist, then everybody must refrain from doing a great many different sorts of things. Everybody must refrain from slitting his throat, everybody must refrain from shooting him—and everybody must refrain from unplugging you from him. But does he have a right against everybody that they shall refrain from unplugging you from him? To refrain from doing this is to allow him to continue to use your kidneys. It could be argued that he has a right against us that *we* should allow him to continue to use your kidneys. That is, while he has no right against us that we should give him the use of your kidneys, it might be argued that he anyway has a right against us that we shall not now intervene and deprive him of the use of your kidneys. I shall come back to third-party interventions later. But certainly the violinist has no right against you that *you* shall allow him to continue to use your kidneys. As I said, if you do allow him to use them, it is a kindness on your part, and not something you owe him.

The difficulty I point to here is not peculiar to the right to life. It reappears in connection with all the other natural rights; and it is something which an adequate account of rights must deal with. For present purposes it is enough just to draw attention to it. But I would stress that I am not arguing that people do not have a right to life—quite to the contrary, it seems to me that the primary control we must place on the acceptability of an account of rights is that it should turn out in that account to be a truth that all persons have a right to life. I am arguing only that having a right to life does not guarantee having either a right to be given the use of or a right to be allowed continued use of another person's body—even if one needs it for life itself. So the right to life will not serve the opponents of abortion in the very simple and clear way in which they seem to have thought it would.

4. There is another way to bring out the difficulty. In the most ordinary sort of case, to deprive someone of what he has a right to is to treat him unjustly. Suppose a boy and his small brother are jointly given a box of chocolates for Christmas. If the older boy takes the box and refuses to give his brother any of the chocolates, he is unjust to him, for the brother has been given a right to half of them. But suppose that, having learned that otherwise it means nine years in bed with that violinist, you unplug yourself from him. You surely are not being unjust to him, for you gave him no right to use your kidneys, and no one else can have given him any such right. But we have to notice that in unplugging yourself, you are killing him; and violinists, like everybody else, have a right to life, and thus in the view we were considering just now, the right not to be killed. So here you do what he supposedly has a right you shall not do, but you do not act unjustly to him in doing it.

The emendation which may be made at this point is this: the right to life consists not in the right not to be killed, but rather in the right not to be killed unjustly. This runs a risk of circularity, but never mind: it would enable us to square the fact that the violinist has a right to life with the fact that you do not act unjustly toward him in unplugging yourself, thereby killing him. For if you do not kill him unjustly, you do not violate his right to life, and so it is no wonder you do him no injustice.

But if this emendation is accepted, the gap in the argument against abortion stares us plainly in the face: it is by no means enough to show that the fetus is a person, and to remind us that all persons have a right to life—we need to be shown also that killing the fetus violates its right to life, i.e., that abortion is unjust killing. And is it?

I suppose we may take it as a datum that in a case of pregnancy due to rape the mother has not given the unborn person a right to the use of her body for food and shelter. Indeed, in what pregnancy could it be supposed that the mother has given the unborn person such a right? It is not as if there were unborn persons drifting about the world, to whom a woman who wants a child says "I invite you in."

But it might be argued that there are other ways one can have acquired a right to the use of another person's body than by having been invited to use it by that person. Suppose a woman voluntarily indulges in intercourse, knowing of the chance it will issue in pregnancy, and then she does become pregnant; is she not in part responsible for the presence, in fact the very existence, of the unborn person inside her? No doubt she did not invite it in. But doesn't her partial responsibility for its being there itself give it a right to the use of her body? If so, then her aborting it would be more like the boy's taking away the chocolates, and less like your unplugging yourself from the violinist—doing so would be depriving it of what it does have a right to, and thus would be doing it an injustice.

And then, too, it might be asked whether or not she can kill it even to save her own life: If she voluntarily called it into existence, how can she now kill it, even in self-defense?

The first thing to be said about this is that it is something new. Opponents of abortion have been so concerned to make out the independence of the fetus, in order to establish that it has a right to life, just as its mother does, that they have tended to overlook the possible support they might gain from making out that the fetus is *dependent* on the mother, in order to establish that she has a special kind of responsibility for it, a responsibility that gives it rights against her which are not possessed by any independent person—such as an ailing violinist who is a stranger to her.

On the other hand, this argument would give the unborn person a right to its mother's body only if her pregnancy resulted from a voluntary act, undertaken in full knowledge of the chance a pregnancy might result from it. It would leave out entirely the unborn person whose existence is due to rape. Pending the availability of some further argument, then, we would be left with the conclusion that unborn persons whose existence is due to rape have no right to the use of their mothers' bodies, and thus that aborting them is not depriving them of anything they have a right to and hence is not unjust killing.

And we should also notice that it is not at all plain that this argument really does go even as far as it purports to. For there are cases and cases, and the details make a difference. If the room is stuffy, and I therefore open a window to air it, and a burglar climbs in, it would be absurd to say, "Ah, now he can stay, she's given him a right to the use of her house—for she is partially responsible for his presence there, having voluntarily done what enabled him to get in, in full knowledge that there are such things as burglars, and that burglars burgle." It would be still more absurd to say this if I had had bars installed outside my windows, precisely to prevent burglars from getting in, and a burglar got in only because of a defect in the bars. It remains equally absurd if we imagine it is not a burglar who climbs in, but an innocent person who blunders or falls in. Again, suppose it were like this: people-seeds drift about in the air like pollen, and if you open your windows, one may drift in and take root in your carpets or upholstery. You don't want children, so you fix up your windows with fine mesh screens, the very best you can buy. As can happen, however, and on very, very rare occasions does happen, one of the screens is defective; and a seed drifts in and takes root. Does the person-plant who now develops have a right to the use of your house? Surely not—despite the fact that you voluntarily opened your windows, you knowingly kept carpets and upholstered furniture, and you knew that screens were sometimes defective. Someone may argue that you are responsible for its rooting, that it does have a right to your house, because after all you *could* have lived out your life with bare floors and furniture, or with sealed windows and doors. But this won't do—for by the same token anyone can avoid a pregnancy due to rape by having a hysterectomy, or anyway by never leaving home without a (reliable!) army.

It seems to me that the argument we are looking at can establish at most that there are *some* cases in which the unborn person has a right to the use of its mother's body, and therefore *some* cases in which abortion is unjust killing. There is room for much discussion and argument as to precisely which, if any. But I think we should sidestep this issue and leave it open, for at any rate the argument certainly does not establish that all abortion is unjust killing.

5. There is room for yet another argument here, however. We surely must all grant that there may be cases in which it would be morally indecent to detach a person from your body at the cost of his life. Suppose you learn that what the violinist needs is not nine years of your life, but only one hour: all you need do to save his life is to spend one hour in that bed with him. Suppose also that letting him use your kidneys for that one hour would not affect your health in the slightest. Admittedly you were kidnapped. Admittedly you did not give anyone permission to plug him into you. Nevertheless it seems to me plain you *ought* to allow him to use your kidneys for that hour—it would be indecent to refuse.

Again, suppose pregnancy lasted only an hour, and constituted no threat to life or health. And suppose that a woman becomes pregnant as a result of rape. Admittedly she did not voluntarily do anything to bring about the existence of a child. Admittedly she did nothing at all which would give the unborn person a right to the use of her body. All the same it might well be said, as in the newly emended violinist story, that she *ought* to allow it to remain for that hour—that it would be indecent of her to refuse.

Now some people are inclined to use the term "right" in such a way that it follows from the fact that you ought to allow a person to use your body for the hour he needs, that he has a right to use your body for the hour he needs, even though he has not been given that right by any person or act. They may say that it follows also that if you refuse, you act unjustly toward him. This use of the term is perhaps so common that it cannot be called wrong; nevertheless it seems to me to be an unfortunate loosening of what we would do better to keep a tight rein on. Suppose that box of chocolates I mentioned earlier had not been given to both boys jointly, but was given only to the older boy. There he sits, stolidly eating his way through the box, his small brother watching enviously. Here we are likely to say "You ought not to be so mean. You ought to give your brother some of those chocolates." My own view is that it just does not follow from the truth of this that the brother has any right to any of the chocolates. If the boy refuses to give his brother any, he is greedy, stingy, callous—but not unjust. I suppose that the people I have in mind will say it does follow that the brother has a right to some of the chocolates, and thus that the boy does act unjustly if he refuses to give his brother any. But the effect of saying this is to obscure what we should keep distinct, namely the difference between the boy's refusal in this case and the boy's refusal in the earlier case, in which the box was given to both boys jointly, and in which the small brother thus had what was from any point of view clear title to half.

A further objection to so using the term "right" that from the fact that A ought to do a thing for B, it follows that B has a right against A that A do it for him, is that it is going to make the question of whether or not a man has a right to a thing turn on how easy it is to provide him with it; and this seems not merely unfortunate, but morally unacceptable. Take the case of Henry Fonda again. I said earlier that I had no right to the touch of his cool hand on my fevered brow even though I needed it to save my life. I said it would be frightfully nice of him to fly in from the West Coast to provide me with it, but that I had no right against him that he should do so. But suppose he isn't on the West Coast. Suppose he has only to walk across the room, place a hand briefly on my brow—and lo, my life is saved. Then surely he ought to do it; it would be indecent to refuse. Is it to be said, "Ah, well, it follows that in this case she has a right to the touch of his hand on her brow, and so it would be an injustice for him to refuse"? So that I have a right to it when it is easy for him to provide it, though no right when it's hard? It's rather a shocking idea that anyone's rights should fade away and disappear as it gets harder and harder to accord them to him.

So my own view is that even though you ought to let the violinist use your kidneys for the one hour he needs, we should not conclude that he has a right to do so—we should say that if you refuse, you are, like the boy who owns all the chocolates and will give none away, self-centered and callous, indecent in fact, but not unjust. And similarly, that even supposing a case in which a woman pregnant due to rape ought to allow the unborn person to use her body for the hour he needs, we should not conclude that he has a right to do so; we should conclude that she is self-centered, callous, indecent, but not unjust, if she refuses. The complaints are no less grave; they are just different. However, there is no need to insist on this point. If anyone does wish to deduce "he has a right" from "you ought," then all the same he must surely grant that there are cases in which it is not morally required of you that you allow that violinist to use your kidneys, and in which he does not have a right to use them, and in which you do not do him an injustice if you refuse. And so also for mother and unborn child. Except in such cases as the unborn person has a right to demand it—and we were leaving open the possibility that there may be such cases—nobody is morally *required* to make large sacrifices, of health, of all other interests and concerns, of all other duties and commitments, for nine years, or even for nine months, in order to keep another person alive.

6. We have in fact to distinguish between two kinds of Samaritan: the Good Samaritan and what we might call the Minimally Decent Samaritan. The story of the Good Samaritan, you will remember, goes like this:

> A certain man went down from Jerusalem to Jericho, and fell among thieves, which stripped him of his raiment, and wounded him, and departed, leaving him half dead.
>
> And by chance there came down a certain priest that way; and when he saw him, he passed by on the other side.
>
> And likewise a Levite, when he was at the place, came and looked on him, and passed by on the other side.
>
> But a certain Samaritan, as he journeyed, came where he was; and when he saw him he had compassion on him.
>
> And went to him, and bound up his wounds, pouring in oil and wine, and set him on his own beast, and brought him to an inn, and took care of him.
>
> And on the morrow, when he departed, he took out two pence, and gave them to the host, and said unto him, "Take care of him; and whatsoever thou spendest more, when I come again, I will repay thee." (Luke 10:30–35)

The Good Samaritan went out of his way, at some cost to himself, to help one in need of it. We are not told what the options were, that is, whether or not the priest and the Levite could have helped by doing less than the Good Samaritan did, but assuming they could have, then the fact they did nothing at all shows they were not even Minimally Decent Samaritans, not because they were not Samaritans, but because they were not even minimally decent.

These things are a matter of degree, of course, but there is a difference, and it comes out perhaps most clearly in the story of Kitty Genovese, who, as you will remember, was murdered while thirty-eight people watched or listened, and did nothing at all to help her. A Good Samaritan would have rushed out to give direct assistance against the murderer. Or perhaps we had better allow that it would have been a Splendid Samaritan who did this, on the ground that it would have involved a risk of death for himself. But the thirty-eight not only did not do this, they did not even trouble to pick up a phone to call the police. Minimally Decent Samaritanism would call for doing at least that, and their not having done it was monstrous.

After telling the story of the Good Samaritan, Jesus said, "Go, and do thou likewise." Perhaps he meant that we are morally required to act as the Good Samaritan did. Perhaps he was urging people to do more than is morally required of them. At all events it seems plain that it was not morally required of any of the thirty-eight that he rush out to give direct assistance at the risk of his own life, and that it is not morally required of anyone that he give long stretches of his life—nine years or nine months—to sustaining the life of a person who has no special right (we were leaving open the possibility of this) to demand it.

Indeed, with one rather striking class of exceptions, no one in any country in the world is *legally* required to do anywhere near as much as this for anyone else. The class of exceptions is obvious. My main concern here is not the state of the law in respect to abortion, but it is worth drawing attention to the fact that in no state in this country is any man compelled by law to be even a Minimally Decent Samaritan to any person; there is no law under which charges could be brought against the thirty-eight who stood by while Kitty Genovese died. By contrast, in most states in this country women are compelled by law to be not merely Minimally Decent Samaritans, but Good Samaritans to unborn persons inside them. This doesn't by itself settle anything one way or the other, because it may well be argued that there should be laws in this country—as there are in many European countries—compelling at least Minimally Decent Samaritanism. But it does show that there is a gross injustice in the existing state of the law. And it shows also that the groups currently working against liberalization of abortion laws, in fact working toward having it declared unconstitutional for a state to permit abortion, had better start working for the adoption of Good Samaritan laws generally, or earn the charge that they are acting in bad faith.

I should think, myself, that Minimally Decent Samaritan laws would be one thing, Good Samaritan laws quite another, and in fact highly improper. But we are not here concerned with the law. What we should ask is not whether anybody should be compelled by law to be a Good Samaritan, but whether we must accede to a situation in which somebody is being compelled—by nature, perhaps—to be a Good Samaritan. We have, in other words, to look now at third-party interventions. I have been arguing that no person is morally required to make large sacrifices to sustain the life of another who has no right to demand them, and this even where the sacrifices do not include life itself; we are not morally required to be Good Samaritans or anyway Very Good Samaritans to one another. But what if a man cannot extricate himself from such a situation? What if he appeals to us to extricate him? It seems to me plain that there are cases in which we can, cases in which a Good Samaritan would extricate him. There you are, you were kidnapped, and nine years in bed with that violinist lie ahead of you. You have your own life to lead. You are sorry, but you simply cannot see giving up so much of your life to the sustaining of his. You cannot extricate yourself, and ask us to do so. I should have thought that—in light of his having no right to the use of your body—it was obvious that we do not have to accede to your being forced to give up so much. We can do what you ask. There is no injustice to the violinist in our doing so.

7. Following the lead of the opponents of abortion, I have throughout been speaking of the fetus merely as a person, and what I have been asking is whether or not the argument we began with, which proceeds only from the fetus's being a person, really does establish its conclusion. I have argued that it does not.

But of course there are arguments and arguments, and it may be said that I have simply fastened on the wrong one. It may be said that what is important is not merely the fact that the fetus is a person, but that it is a person for whom the woman has a special kind of responsibility issuing from the fact that she is its mother. And it might be argued that all my analogies are therefore irrelevant—for you do not have that special kind of responsibility for that violinist, Henry Fonda does not have that special kind of responsibility for me. And our attention might be drawn to the fact that men and women both *are* compelled by law to provide support for their children.

I have in effect dealt (briefly) with this argument in section 4 above; but a (still briefer) recapitulation now may be in order. Surely we do not have any such "special responsibility" for a person unless we have assumed it, explicitly or implicitly. If a set of parents do not try to prevent pregnancy, do not obtain an abortion, and then at the time of birth of the child do not put it out for adoption, but rather take it home with them, then they have assumed responsibility for it, they have given it rights, and they cannot *now* withdraw support from it at the cost of its life because they now find it difficult to go on providing for it. But if they have taken all reasonable precautions against having a child, they do not simply by virtue of their biological relationship to the child who comes into existence have a special responsibility for it. They may wish to assume responsibility for it, or they may not wish to. And I am suggesting that if assuming responsibility for it would require large sacrifices, then these parents may refuse. A Good Samaritan would not refuse—or anyway, a Splendid Samaritan, if the sacrifices that had to be made were enormous. But then so would a Good Samaritan assume responsibility for that violinist; so would Henry Fonda, if he is a Good Samaritan, fly in from the West Coast and assume responsibility for me.

8. My argument will be found unsatisfactory on two counts by many of those who want to regard abortion as morally permissible. First, while I do argue that abortion is not impermissible, I do not argue that it is always permissible. There may well be cases in which carrying the child to term requires only Minimally Decent Samaritanism of the mother, and this is a standard we must not fall below. I am inclined to think it a merit of my account precisely that it does *not* give a general yes or a general no. It allows for and supports our sense that, for example, a sick and desperately frightened fourteen-year-old schoolgirl, pregnant due to rape, may *of course* choose abortion, and that any law which rules this out is an insane law. And it also allows for and supports our sense that in other cases resort to abortion is even positively indecent. It would be indecent in the woman to request an abortion, and indecent in a doctor to perform it, if she is in her seventh month, and wants the abortion just to avoid the nuisance of postponing a trip abroad. The very fact that the arguments I have been drawing attention to treat all cases of abortion, or even all cases of abortion in which the mother's life is not at stake, as morally on a par ought to have made them suspect at the outset.

Secondly, while I am arguing for the permissibility of abortion in some cases, I am not arguing for the right to secure the death of the unborn child. It is easy to confuse these two things in that up to a certain point in the life of the fetus it is not able to survive outside the mother's body; hence removing it from her body guarantees its death. But they are importantly different. I have argued that you are not morally required to spend nine months in bed, sustaining the life of that violinist; but to say this is by no means to say that if, when you unplug yourself, there is a miracle and he survives, you then have a right to turn round and slit his throat. You may detach yourself even if this costs him his life; you have no right to be guaranteed his death, by some other means, if unplugging yourself does not kill him. There are some people who will feel dissatisfied by this feature of my argument. A woman may be utterly devastated by the thought of a child, a bit of herself, put out for adoption and never seen or heard of again. She may therefore want not merely that the child be detached from her, but more, that it die. Some opponents of abortion are inclined to regard this as beneath contempt—thereby showing insensitivity to what is surely a powerful source of despair. All the same, I agree that the desire for the child's death is not one which anybody may gratify, should it turn out to be possible to detach the child alive.

At this place, however, it should be remembered that we have only been pretending throughout that the fetus is a human being from the moment of conception. A very early abortion is surely not the killing of a person, and so is not dealt with by anything I have said here.

QUESTIONS FOR ANALYSIS AND DISCUSSION

1. Since the time of Plato, analogies have been a valued device in argument. It was by analogy—the state is to the citizen as a parent is to the child—that Socrates refuted his friend Crito's pleas to escape prison rather than die tomorrow. Throughout her essay, from famous violinists to boys squabbling over chocolates, Thomson uses analogies to make her points. However, as logic teachers remind us, even the best analogies have a potential problem or two. Is there an important difference between the woman-with-child and the patient-with-violinist? If so, what are the moral implications? If not, can you continue the analogy by arguing that anyone who is immediately and vitally dependent on someone else does not have a right to life? Clarify your thoughts.

2. Throughout her essay Thomson uses the concepts just and unjust to help us decide the morality of abortion. For example, in talking about the brothers fighting over chocolates, Thomson writes, "If the boy refuses to give his brother any, he is greedy, stingy, callous—but not unjust." Virtue theorists would likely conclude that this boy has some real moral problems and that not being unjust is hardly a redeeming factor. How do you think Thomson understands justice? Does that help you agree or disagree with her general defense of abortion?

3. Recent surveys suggest that many Americans are ambivalent about abortion. In a recent interview one popular feminist, Gloria Steinem, admitted with dismay that she had no intention that legalizing abortion would make the deed so ordinary—roughly two million annually in this country alone. Some of this ambivalence may be indifference, but some is the result of thoughtful but uncertain reflection about the issue of abortion. Thomson's essay has the second audience in mind. Has she helped you resolve your ambivalence or rethink your beliefs? Specify your position.

4. As with Noonan, Thomson makes an exception or two. The idea of a woman undergoing an abortion so a trip abroad won't be postponed, she calls indecent. She does not say unjust. What is the difference between indecent and

unjust? If you heard of such a woman, would you call her indecent, unjust, immoral, or vicious? Or is she an honest moral egoist? Support your answer.

73.

SUSAN SHERWIN

Abortion: A Feminist Perspective

For many disputants in the abortion controversy, the primary factor has to do with women's bodies and lives, and who should have control over them. Feminists often hold that abortion is first a woman's issue, and then a general issue. Philosopher Susan Sherwin (b. 1947) reviews the central themes of the abortion controversy and clarifies how a feminist approach reshapes the importance of issues such as the status of the fetus, the difference between adoption and abortion, and the unique relation a woman has with the fetus that is barely comprehensible by a man. Sherwin concludes that the abortion debate should not be confined to ethics but must address the political dimension as well.

CRITICAL READING QUESTIONS

1. What are the key differences between feminists and nonfeminists in their approach to the morality of abortion?

2. According to Sherwin, what is a patriarchal society, and how does it affect the abortion controversy?

3. What is meant by a gender-neutral account of abortion? Does Sherwin think such an account is plausible?

4. How does Sherwin understand the nature of a person? To what extent does a fetus satisfy or fail the test for being a person?

5. How has contemporary medical research contributed to the idea that the fetus is a separate human being?

"Abortion: A Feminist Perspective," from *No Longer Patient: Feminist Ethics and Health Care* (Philadelphia, PA: Temple University Press, 1992), pp. 99–116. Notes have been omitted.

Feminist reasoning in support of women's right to choose abortion is significantly different from the reasoning used by nonfeminist supporters of similar positions. For instance, most feminist accounts evaluate abortion policy within a broader framework, according to its place among the social institutions that support the subordination of women. In contrast, most nonfeminist discussions of abortion consider the moral or legal permissibility of abortion in isolation; they ignore (and thereby obscure) relevant connections with other social practices, including the ongoing power struggle within sexist societies over the control of women and their reproduction. Feminist arguments take into account the actual concerns that particular women attend to in their decision-making on abortion, such as the nature of a woman's feelings about her fetus, her relationships with her partner, other children she may have, and her various obligations to herself and others. In contrast, most nonfeminist discussions evaluate abortion decisions in their most abstract form (for example, questioning what sort of being a fetus is); from this perspective, specific questions of context are deemed irrelevant. In addition, nonfeminist arguments in support of choice about abortion are generally grounded in masculinist conceptions of freedom (such as privacy, individual choice, and individuals' property rights with respect to their own bodies), which do not meet the needs, interests, and intuitions of many of the women concerned.

Feminists also differ from nonfeminists in their conception of what is morally at issue with abortion. Nonfeminists focus exclusively on the morality and legality of performing abortions, whereas feminists insist that other issues, including the accessibility and delivery of abortion services, must also be addressed. . . .

Women and Abortion

The most obvious difference between feminist and nonfeminist approaches to abortion lies in the relative attention each gives in its analysis to the interests and experiences of women. Feminist analysis regards the effects of unwanted pregnancies on the lives of women individually and collectively as the central element in the moral examination of abortion; it is considered self-evident that the pregnant woman is the subject of principal concern in abortion decisions. In many nonfeminist accounts, however, not only is the pregnant woman not perceived as central, she is often rendered virtually invisible. Nonfeminist theorists, whether they support or oppose women's right to choose abortion, generally focus almost all their attention on the moral status of the fetus.

In pursuing a distinctively feminist ethics, it is appropriate to begin with a look at the role of abortion in women's lives. The need for abortion can be very intense; no matter how appalling and dangerous the conditions, women from widely diverse cultures and historical periods have pursued abortions. No one denies that if abortion is not made legal, safe, and accessible in our society, women will seek out illegal and life-threatening abortions to terminate pregnancies they cannot accept. Antiabortion activists seem willing to accept this cost, although liberals definitely are not; feminists, who explicitly value women, judge the inevitable loss of women's lives that results from restrictive abortion policies to be a matter of fundamental concern.

Antiabortion campaigners imagine that women often make frivolous and irresponsible decisions about abortion, but feminists recognize that women have abortions for a wide variety of compelling reasons. Some women, for instance, find themselves seriously ill and incapacitated throughout pregnancy; they cannot continue in their jobs and may face insurmountable difficulties in fulfilling their responsibilities at home. Many employers and schools will not tolerate pregnancy in their employees or students, and not every woman is able to put her job, career, or studies on hold. Women of limited means may be unable to take adequate care of children they have already borne, and they may know that another mouth to feed will reduce their ability to provide for their existing children. Women who suffer from chronic disease, who believe themselves too young or too old to have children, or who are unable to maintain lasting relationships may recognize that they will not be able to care properly for a child when they face the decision. Some who are homeless, addicted to drugs, or diagnosed as carrying the AIDS virus may be unwilling to allow a child to enter the world with the handicaps that would result from the mother's condition. If the fetus is a result of rape or incest, then the psychological pain of carrying it may be unbearable, and the woman may recognize that her attitude to the child after birth will be tinged with bitterness. Some women learn that the fetuses that they carry have serious chromosomal anomalies and consider it best to prevent them from being born with a condition that is bound to cause them to suffer. Others, knowing the fathers to be brutal and violent, may be unwilling to subject a child to the beatings or incestuous attacks they anticipate; some may have no other realistic way to remove the child (or themselves) from the relationship.

Finally, a woman may simply believe that bearing a child is incompatible with her life plans at the time. Continuing a pregnancy may have devastating repercussions throughout a woman's life. If the woman is young, then a pregnancy will likely reduce her chances of pursuing an education and hence limit her career and life opportunities: "The earlier a woman has a baby, it seems, the more likely she is to drop out of school; the less education she gets, the more likely she is to remain poorly paid, peripheral to the labor market, or unemployed, and the more children she will have." In many circumstances, having a child will exacerbate the social and economic forces already stacked against a woman by virtue of her sex (and her race, class, age, sexual orientation, disabilities, and so forth). Access to abortion is necessary for many women if they are to escape the oppressive conditions of poverty.

Whatever the specific reasons are for abortion, most feminists believe that the women concerned are in the best position to judge whether abortion is the appropriate response to a pregnancy. Because usually only the woman choosing abortion is properly situated to weigh all the relevant factors, most feminists resist attempts to offer general, abstract rules for determining when abortion is morally justified. Women's personal deliberations about abortion involve contextually defined considerations that reflect their commitments to the needs and interests of everyone concerned, including themselves, the fetuses they carry, other members of their household, and so forth. Because no single formula is available for balancing these complex factors through all possible cases, it is vital that feminists insist on protecting each woman's right to come to her own conclusions and resist the attempts of other philosophers and moralists to set the agenda for these considerations. Feminists stress that women must be acknowledged as full moral agents, responsible for making moral decisions about their own pregnancies. Women may sometimes make mistakes in their moral judgments, but no one else can be assumed to have the authority to evaluate and overrule their judgments.

. . . Because we live in a patriarchal society, it is especially important to ensure that women have the authority to control their own reproduction. Despite the diversity of opinion found among feminists on most other matters, most feminists agree that women must gain full control over their own reproductive lives if they are to free themselves from male dominance.

Moreover, women's freedom to choose abortion is linked to their ability to control their own sexuality. Women's subordinate status often prevents them from refusing men sexual access to their bodies. If women cannot end the unwanted pregnancies that result from male sexual dominance, then their sexual vulnerability to particular men may increase, because caring for an(other) infant involves greater financial needs and reduced economic opportunities for women. As a result, pregnancy often forces women to become dependent on particular men. Because a woman's dependence on a man is assumed to entail her continued sexual loyalty to him, restriction of abortion serves to commit women to remaining sexually accessible to particular men and thus helps to perpetuate the cycle of oppression.

In contrast to most nonfeminist accounts, feminist analyses of abortion direct attention to how women get pregnant. Those who reject abortion seem to believe that women can avoid unwanted pregnancies "simply" by avoiding sexual intercourse. These views show little appreciation for the power of sexual politics in a culture that oppresses women. Existing patterns of sexual dominance mean that women often have little control over their sexual lives. They may be subject to rape by their husbands, boyfriends, colleagues, employers, customers, fathers, brothers, uncles, and dates, as well as by strangers. Often the sexual coercion is not even recognized as such by the participants but is the price of continued "good will"— popularity, economic survival, peace, or simple acceptance. Many women have found themselves in circumstances where they do not feel free to refuse a man's demands for intercourse, either because he is holding a gun to her head or because he threatens to be emotionally hurt if she refuses (or both). Women are socialized to be compliant and accommodating, sensitive to the feelings of others, and frightened of physical power; men are socialized to take advantage of every opportunity to engage in sexual intercourse and to use sex to express dominance and power. Under such circumstances, it is difficult to argue that women could simply "choose" to avoid heterosexual activity if they wish to avoid pregnancy. Catharine MacKinnon neatly sums it up: "The logic by which women are supposed to consent to sex [is]: preclude the alternatives, then call the remaining option 'her choice.'"

Furthermore, women cannot reply on birth control to avoid pregnancy. No form of contraception that is fully safe and reliable is available, other than sterilization; because women may wish only to avoid pregnancy temporarily, not permanently, sterilization is not always an acceptable choice. The pill and the IUD are the most effective contraceptive means offered, but both involve significant health hazards to women and are quite dangerous for some. No woman should spend the thirty to forty years of her reproductive life on either form of birth control. Further, both have been associated with subsequent problems of involuntary infertility, so they are far from optimal for women who seek to control the timing of their pregnancies.

The safest form of birth control involves the use of barrier methods (condoms or diaphragms) in combination with spermicidal foams or jelly. But these methods also pose difficulties for women. They are sometimes socially awkward to use. Young women are discouraged from preparing for sexual activity that might never happen and are offered instead romantic models of spontaneous passion; few films or novels interrupt scenes of seduction for a partner to fetch contraceptives. Many women find their male partners unwilling to use barrier methods of contraception, and they often find themselves in no position to insist. Further, cost is a limiting factor for many women. Condoms and spermicides are expensive and are not covered under most health care plans. Only one contraceptive option offers women safe and fully effective birth control: barrier methods with the backup option of abortion.

From a feminist perspective, the central moral feature of pregnancy is that it takes place in women's bodies and has profound effects on women's lives. Gender-neutral accounts of pregnancy are not available; pregnancy is explicitly a condition associated with the female body. Because only women experience a need for abortion, policies about abortion affect women uniquely. Therefore, it is important to consider how proposed policies on abortion fit into general patterns of oppression for women. Unlike nonfeminist accounts, feminist ethics demands that the effects of abortion policies on the oppression of women be of principal consideration in our ethical evaluations.

The Fetus

In contrast to feminist ethics, most nonfeminist analysts believe that the moral acceptability of abortion turns entirely on the question of the moral status of the fetus. Even those who support women's right to choose abortion tend to accept the premise of the antiabortion proponents that abortion can be tolerated only if we can first prove that the fetus lacks full personhood. Opponents of abortion demand that we define the status of the fetus either as a being that is valued in the same way as other humans, and hence is entitled not to be killed, or as a being that lacks in all value. Rather than challenging the logic of this formulation, many defenders of abortion have concentrated on showing that the fetus is indeed without significant value; others, such as L. W. Sumner, offer a more subtle account that reflects the gradual development of fetuses and distinguishes between early fetal stages, where the relevant criterion for personhood is absent, and later stages, where it is present. Thus the debate often rages between abortion opponents, who describe the fetus as an "innocent," vulnerable, morally important, separate being whose life is threatened and who must be protected at all costs, and abortion sup- porters, who try to establish that fetuses are deficient in some critical respect and hence are outside the scope of the moral community. In both cases, however, the nature of the fetus as an independent being is said to determine the moral status of abortion.

The woman on whom the fetus depends for survival is considered as secondary (if she is considered at all) in these debates. The actual experiences and responsi- bilities of real women are not perceived as morally relevant to the debate, unless these women too, can be proved innocent by establishing that their pregnancies are a result of rape or incest. In some contexts, women's role in gestation is literally reduced to that of "fetal containers"; the individual women disappear or are per- ceived simply as mechanical life-support systems.

The current rhetoric against abortion stresses that the genetic makeup of the fetus is determined at conception and the genetic code is incontestably human. Lest there be any doubt about the humanity of the fetus, we are assailed with photo- graphs of fetuses at various stages of development that demonstrate the early ap- pearance of recognizably human characteristics, such as eyes, fingers, and toes. Modern ultrasound technology is used to obtain "baby's first picture" and stimu- late bonding between pregnant women and their fetuses. That the fetus in its early stages is microscopic, virtually indistinguishable to the untrained eye from fetuses of other species, and lacking in the capacities that make human life meaningful and valuable is not deemed relevant by the self-appointed defenders of the fetus. The antiabortion campaign is directed at evoking sympathetic attitudes toward a tiny, helpless being whose life is threatened by its own mother; the fetus is charac- terized as a being entangled in an adversarial relationship with the (presumably irresponsible) woman who carries it. People are encouraged to identify with the "unborn child," not with the woman whose life is also at issue.

In the nonfeminist literature, both defenders and opponents of women's right to choose abortion agree that the difference between a late-term fetus and a newborn infant is "merely geographical" and cannot be considered morally significant. Daniel Callahan, for instance, maintains a pro-choice stand but professes increas- ing uneasiness about this position in light of new medical and scientific develop- ments that increase our knowledge of embryology and hasten the date of potential viability for fetuses; he insists that defenders of women's right to choose must come to terms with the question of the fetus and the effects of science on the fetus's prospects apart from the woman who carries it. Arguments that focus on the simi- larities between infants and fetuses, however, generally fail to acknowledge that a fetus inhabits a woman's body and is wholly dependent on her unique contribution to its maintenance, whereas a newborn is physically independent, although still in need of a lot of care. One can only view the distinction between being in or out of a woman's womb as morally irrelevant if one discounts the perspective of the preg- nant woman; feminists seem to be alone in recognizing the woman's perspective as morally important to the distinction.

In antiabortion arguments, fetuses are identified as individuals; in our culture, which views the (abstract) individual as sacred, fetuses qua individuals are to be honored and preserved. Extraordinary claims are made to establish the individuality and moral agency of fetuses. At the same time, the women who carry these fetal individuals are viewed as passive hosts whose only significant role is to refrain from aborting or harming their fetuses. Because it is widely believed that a woman does not actually have to do anything to protect the life of her fetus, pregnancy is often considered (abstractly) to be a tolerable burden to protect the life of an individual so like us.

Medicine has played its part in supporting these attitudes. Fetal medicine is a rapidly expanding specialty, and it is commonplace in professional medical journals to find references to pregnant women as "the maternal environment." Fetal surgeons now have at their disposal a repertoire of sophisticated technology that can save the lives of dangerously ill fetuses; in light of the excitement of such heroic successes, it is perhaps understandable that women have disappeared from their view. These specialists see the fetuses as their patients, not the women who nurture the fetuses. As the "active" agents in saving fetal lives (unlike the pregnant women, whose role is seen as purely passive), doctors perceive themselves as developing independent relationships with the fetuses they treat. Barbara Katz Rothman observes: "The medical model of pregnancy, as an essentially parasitic and vaguely pathological relationship, encourages the physician to view the fetus and mother as two separate patients, and to see pregnancy as inherently a conflict of interests between the two". . . .

In other words, some physicians have joined antiabortion campaigners in fostering a cultural acceptance of the view that fetuses are distinct individuals who are physically, ontologically, and socially separate from the women whose bodies they inhabit and that they have their own distinct interests. In this picture, pregnant women are either ignored altogether or are viewed as deficient in some crucial respect, and hence they can be subject to coercion for the sake of their fetuses. In the former case, the interests of the women concerned are assumed to be identical with those of the fetus; in the latter, the women's interests are irrelevant, because they are perceived as immoral, unimportant, or unnatural. Focus on the fetus as an independent entity has led to presumptions that deny pregnant women their roles as active, independent, moral agents with a primary interest in what becomes of the fetuses they carry. The moral question of the fetus's status is quickly translated into a license to interfere with women's reproductive freedom.

On a feminist account fetal development is examined in the context in which it occurs, within women's bodies, rather than in the isolation of imagined abstraction. Fetuses develop in specific pregnancies that occur in the lives of particular women. They are not individuals housed in generic female wombs or full persons at risk only because they are small and subject to the whims of women. Their very existence is relationally defined, reflecting their development within particular women's bodies; that relationship gives those women reason to be concerned about them. Many feminists argue against a perspective that regards the fetus as an independent being and suggest that a more accurate and valuable understanding of pregnancy would involve regarding the pregnant woman "as a biological and social unit." . . .

Most feminist views of what is valuable about persons reflect the social nature of individual existence. No human, especially no fetus, can exist apart from relationships; efforts to speak of the fetus itself, as if it were not inseparable from the woman in whom it develops, are distorting and dishonest. Fetuses have a unique physical status—within and dependent on particular women. That gives them also a unique social status. However much some might prefer it to be otherwise, no one other than the pregnant woman in question can do anything to support or harm a fetus without doing something to the woman who nurtures it. Because of this inexorable biological reality, the responsibility and privilege of determining a fetus's specific social status and value must rest with the woman carrying it. . . .

No absolute value attaches to fetuses apart from their relational status, which is determined in the context of their particular development. This is not the same, however, as saying that they have no value at all or that they have merely instrumental value, as some liberals suggest. The value that women place on their own fetuses is the sort of value that attaches to an emerging human relationship.

Nevertheless, fetuses are not persons, because they have not developed sufficiently in their capacity for social relationships to be persons in any morally significant sense (that is, they are not yet second persons). In this way they differ from newborns, who immediately begin to develop into persons by virtue of their place as subjects in human relationships; newborns are capable of some forms of communication and response. The moral status of fetuses is determined by the nature of their primary relationship and the value that is created there. Therefore, feminist accounts of abortion emphasize the importance of protecting women's rights to continue or to terminate pregnancies as each sees fit.

The Politics of Abortion

Feminist accounts explore the connections between particular social policies and the general patterns of power relationships in our society. . . . When we place abortion in the larger political context, we see that most of the groups active in the struggle to prohibit abortion also support other conservative measures to maintain the forms of dominance that characterize patriarchy (and often class and racial oppression as well). The movement against abortion is led by the Catholic church and other conservative religious institutions, which explicitly endorse not only fetal rights but also male dominance in the home and the church. Most opponents of abortion also oppose virtually all forms of birth control and all forms of sexuality other than monogamous, reproductive sex; usually, they also resist having women assume positions of authority in dominant public institutions. Typically, antiabortion activists support conservative economic measures that protect the interests of the privileged classes of society and ignore the needs of the oppressed and disadvantaged. Although they stress their commitment to preserving life, many systematically work to dismantle key social programs that provide life necessities to the underclass. Moreover, some current campaigns against abortion retain elements of the racism that dominated the North American abortion literature in the early years of the twentieth century, wherein abortion was opposed on the grounds that it amounted to racial suicide on the part of whites.

In the eyes of its principal opponents, then, abortion is not an isolated practice; their opposition to abortion is central to a set of social values that runs counter to feminism's objectives. Hence antiabortion activists generally do not offer alternatives to abortion that support feminist interests in overturning the patterns of oppression that confront women. Most deny that there are any legitimate grounds for abortion, short of the need to save a woman's life—and some are not even persuaded by this criterion. They believe that any pregnancy can and should be endured. If the mother is unable or unwilling to care for the child after birth, then they assume that adoption can be easily arranged.

It is doubtful, however, that adoptions are possible for every child whose mother cannot care for it. The world abounds with homeless orphans; even in the industrialized West, where there is a waiting list for adoption of healthy (white) babies, suitable homes cannot always be found for troubled adolescents; inner-city, AIDS babies; or many of the multiply handicapped children whose parents may have tried to care for them but whose marriages broke under the strain.

Furthermore, even if an infant were born healthy and could be readily adopted, we must recognize that surrendering one's child for adoption is an extremely difficult act for most women. The bond that commonly forms between women and their fetuses over the full term of pregnancy is intimate and often intense; many women find that it is not easily broken after birth. Psychologically, for many women adoption is a far more difficult response to unwanted pregnancies than abortion. Therefore, it is misleading to describe pregnancy as merely a nine-month commitment; for most women, seeing a pregnancy through to term involves a lifetime of responsibility and involvement with the resulting child and, in the overwhelming majority of cases, disproportionate burden on the woman through the child-rearing years. An ethics that cares about women would recognize that abortion is often the only acceptable recourse for them.

QUESTIONS FOR ANALYSIS AND DISCUSSION

1. Part of Sherwin's argument relies on the contrast between feminist and nonfeminist ethics. How do you understand this contrast? Does her contrast imply that feminist thinkers all agree on moral issues and that nonfeminist thinkers all agree on moral issues? If so, is the abortion debate primarily a matter of feminists and nonfeminists reaching some sort of consensus? If feminists (and nonfeminists too) disagree among themselves, does this affect her general argument?

2. Sherwin asserts that "most feminist views of what is valuable about persons reflect the social nature of the individual existence." She also claims that abortion is not a gender-neutral issue for it is fundamentally about women. Do you think these two views are compatible? If the United States is contemplating war and the Pentagon says only male soldiers will be on the front line risking their lives, does that mean only men can debate the merits of engaging in war? Address the merits or weaknesses of this analogy in terms of Sherwin's

point about the social nature of individuals and the woman-only nature of the abortion debate.

3. Responding to "there's always the adoption option," Sherwin says that for many women it is psychologically "far more difficult" to give up a baby through adoption than through abortion. Do you agree or disagree with this view? If you are a teenager looking forward to college, would giving up a baby by adoption rather than undergoing an abortion in the first trimester be an easier or harder deed? Clarify your reasons.

4. Sherwin observes that most opponents of the legalization of abortion are political and religious conservatives in most other areas of life too. They support a patriarchal society in which sexual, racial, and class oppression are legitimate. Do you find any evidence in Noonan's essay to support Sherwin's charges? Do you find contrary evidence? Be specific.

74.

ROSALIND HURSTHOUSE

Virtue Theory and Abortion

Many of the debates on abortion are so caustic that the sides become more polarized after any kind of exchange. Men versus women, feminists versus nonfeminists, baby-killers versus freedom fighters, conservatives versus liberals — all are among the divisive labels adorning the abortion landscape. British philosopher Rosalind Hursthouse thinks this direction is unfortunate and avoidable, adding that the rancor created contributes to moral confusion rather than to education on an important issue. One way to circumvent this is by examining how a virtue-based ethics approach can help clarify and enrich the options of those confronted with a possible abortion. In developing this approach Hursthouse undercuts the efforts of most disputants on abortion who insist that the only solution is a universal principle or law either forbidding or allowing abortion.

"Virtue Theory and Abortion," *Philosophy and Public Affairs*, Summer 1991, 20(3): 223, 233–246. Notes have been omitted.

CRITICAL READING QUESTIONS

1. For Hursthouse what are the two main considerations dominating the abortion argument? How are they limiting?
2. What is the difference between the morality and legality of abortion?
3. What is meant by "callousness"? How does Hursthouse use it to illustrate some perspectives on abortion?
4. How does Hursthouse view the argument that justifies an abortion because a couple wants to have more good times together or more chances for self-realization?
5. In what sense is the biological status of the fetus irrelevant to the virtue ethics approach to abortion?

The sort of ethical theory derived from Aristotle, variously described as virtue ethics, virtue-based ethics, or neo-Aristotelianism, is becoming better known, and is now quite widely recognized as at least a possible rival to deontological and utilitarian theories. With recognition has come criticism, of varying quality. In this article I shall discuss [several] criticisms that I have frequently encountered, most of which seem to me to betray an inadequate grasp either of the structure of virtue theory or of what would be involved in thinking about a real moral issue in its terms. In the first half I aim particularly to secure an understanding that will reveal that many of these criticisms are simply misplaced, and to articulate what I take to be the major criticism of virtue theory. I reject this criticism, but do not claim that it is necessarily misplaced. In the second half I aim to deepen that understanding and highlight the issues raised by the criticisms by illustrating what the theory looks like when it is applied to a particular issue, in this case, abortion.

I do not assume, or expect, that all of my readers will agree with everything I am about to say. On the contrary, given the plausible assumption that some are morally wiser than I am, and some less so, the theory has built into it that we are bound to disagree on some points. For instance, we may well disagree about the particular application of some of the virtue and vice terms; and we may disagree about what is worthwhile or serious, worthless or trivial. But my aim is to make clear how these concepts figure in a discussion conducted in terms of virtue theory. What is at issue is whether these concepts are indeed the ones that should come in, that is, whether virtue theory should be criticized for employing them. The problem of abortion highlights this issue dramatically since virtue theory quite transforms the discussion of it.

Abortion

As everyone knows, the morality of abortion is commonly discussed in relation to just two considerations: first, and predominantly, the status of the fetus and whether or not it is the sort of thing that may or may not be innocuously or justifiably killed; and second, and less predominantly (when, that is, the discussion concerns the *morality* of abortion rather than the question of permissible legislation in a just society), women's rights. If one thinks within this familiar framework, one may well be puzzled about what virtue theory, as such, could contribute. Some people assume the discussion will be conducted solely in terms of what the virtuous agent would or would not do. Others assume that only justice, or at most justice and charity, will be applied to the issue, generating a discussion very similar to Judith Jarvis Thomson's.

Now if this is the way the virtue theorist's discussion of abortion is imagined to be, no wonder people think little of it. It seems obvious in advance that in any such discussion there must be either a great deal of extremely tendentious application of the virtue terms *just, charitable,* and so on or a lot of rhetorical appeal to "this is what only the virtuous agent knows." But these are caricatures; they fail to appreciate the way in which virtue theory quite transforms the discussion of abortion by dismissing the two familiar dominating considerations as, in a way, fundamentally irrelevant. In what way or ways, I hope to make both clear and plausible.

Let us first consider women's rights. Let me emphasize again that we are discussing the *morality* of abortion, not the rights and wrongs of laws prohibiting or permitting it. If we suppose that women do have a moral right to do as they choose with their own bodies, or, more particularly, to terminate their pregnancies, then it may well follow that a *law* forbidding abortion would be unjust. Indeed, even if they have no such right, such a law might be, as things stand at the moment, unjust, or impractical, or inhumane: on this issue I have nothing to say in this article. But, putting all questions about the justice or injustice of laws to one side, and supposing only that women have such a moral right, *nothing* follows from this supposition about the morality of abortion, according to virtue theory, once it is noted (quite generally, not with particular reference to abortion) that in exercising a moral right I can do something cruel, or callous, or selfish, light-minded, self-righteous, stupid, inconsiderate, disloyal, dishonest—that is, act viciously. Love and friendship do not survive their parties' constantly insisting on their rights, nor do people live well when they think that getting what they have a right to is of preeminent importance; they harm others, and they harm themselves. So whether women have a moral right to terminate their pregnancies is irrelevant within virtue theory, for it is irrelevant to the question "In having an abortion in these circumstances, would the agent be acting virtuously or viciously or neither?"

What about the consideration of the status of the fetus—what can virtue theory say about that? One might say that this issue is not in the province of *any* moral theory; it is a metaphysical question, and an extremely difficult one at that. Must virtue theory then wait upon metaphysics to come up with the answer?

At first sight it might seem so. For virtue is said to involve knowledge, and part of this knowledge consists in having the *right* attitude to things. "Right" here does not just mean "morally right" or "proper" or "nice" in the modern sense; it means "accurate, true." One cannot have the right or correct attitude to something if the attitude is based on or involves false beliefs. And this suggests that if the status of the fetus is relevant to the rightness or wrongness of abortion, its status must be known, as a truth, to the fully wise and virtuous person.

But the sort of wisdom that the fully virtuous person has is not supposed to be recondite; it does not call for fancy philosophical sophistication, and it does not depend upon, let alone wait upon, the discoveries of academic philosophers. And this entails the following, rather startling, conclusion: that the status of the fetus—that issue over which so much ink has been spilt—is, according to virtue theory, simply not relevant to the rightness or wrongness of abortion (within, that is, a secular morality).

Or rather, since that is clearly too radical a conclusion, it is in a sense relevant, but only in the sense that the familiar biological facts are relevant. By "the familiar biological facts" I mean the facts that most human societies are and have been familiar with—that, standardly (but not invariably), pregnancy occurs as the result of sexual intercourse, that it lasts about nine months, during which time the fetus grows and develops, that standardly it terminates in the birth of a living baby, and that this is how we all come to be.

It might be thought that this distinction—between the familiar biological facts and the status of the fetus—is a distinction without a difference. But this is not so. To attach relevance to the status of the fetus, in the sense in which virtue theory claims it is not relevant, is to be gripped by the conviction that we must go beyond the familiar biological facts, deriving some sort of conclusion from them, such as that the fetus has rights, or is not a person, or something similar. It is also to believe that this exhausts the relevance of the familiar biological facts, that all they are relevant to is the status of the fetus and whether or not it is the sort of thing that may or may not be killed.

These convictions, I suspect, are rooted in the desire to solve the problem of abortion by getting it to fall under some general rule such as "You ought not to kill anything with the right to life but may kill anything else." But they have resulted in what should surely strike any nonphilosopher as a most bizarre aspect of nearly all the current philosophical literature on abortion, namely, that, far from treating abortion as a unique moral problem, markedly unlike any other, nearly everything written on the status of the fetus and its bearing on the abortion issue would be consistent with the human reproductive facts' (to say nothing of family life) being totally different from what they are. Imagine that you are an alien extraterrestrial anthropologist who does not know that the human race is roughly 50 percent female and 50 percent male, or that our only (natural) form of reproduction involves heterosexual intercourse, viviparous birth, and the female's (and only the female's) being pregnant for nine months, or that females are capable of childbearing from late childhood to late middle age, or that childbearing is painful, dangerous, and emotionally charged—do you think you would pick up these facts from the hundreds of articles written on the status of the fetus? I am quite sure you would not. And that, I think, shows that the current philosophical literature on abortion has got badly out of touch with reality.

Now if we are using virtue theory, our first question is not "What do the familiar biological facts show—what can be derived from them about the status of the fetus?" but "How do these facts figure in the practical reasoning, actions and passions, thoughts and reactions, of the virtuous and the nonvirtuous? What is the mark of having the right attitude to these facts and what manifests having the wrong attitude to them?" This immediately makes essentially relevant not only all the facts about human reproduction I mentioned above, but a whole range of facts about our emotions in relation to them as well. I mean such facts as that human parents, both male and female, tend to care passionately about their offspring, and that family relationships are among the deepest and strongest in our lives—and, significantly, among the longest-lasting.

These facts make it obvious that pregnancy is not just one among many other physical conditions; and hence that anyone who genuinely believes that an abortion is comparable to a haircut or an appendectomy is mistaken. The fact that the premature termination of a pregnancy is, in some sense, the cutting off of a new human life, and thereby, like the procreation of a new human life, connects with all our thoughts about human life and death, parenthood, and family relationships, must make it a serious matter. To disregard this fact about it, to think of abortion as nothing but the killing of something that does not matter, or as nothing but the exercise of some right or rights one has, or as the incidental means to some desirable state of affairs, is to do something callous and light-minded, the sort of thing that no virtuous and wise person would do. It is to have the wrong attitude not only to fetuses, but more generally to human life and death, parenthood, and family relationships.

Although I say that the facts make this obvious, I know that this is one of my tendentious points. In partial support of it I note that even the most dedicated proponents of the view that deliberate abortion is just like an appendectomy or haircut rarely hold the same view of spontaneous abortion, that is, miscarriage. It is not so tendentious of me to claim that to react to people's grief over miscarriage by saying, or even thinking, "What a fuss about nothing!" would be callous and light-minded, whereas to try to laugh someone out of grief over an appendectomy scar or a botched haircut would not be. It is hard to give this point due prominence within act-centered theories, for the inconsistency is an inconsistency in attitude about the seriousness of loss of life, not in beliefs about which acts are right or wrong. Moreover, an act-centered theorist may say, "Well, there is nothing wrong with *thinking* 'What a fuss about nothing!' as long as you do not say it and hurt the person who is grieving. And besides, we cannot be held responsible for our thoughts, only for the intentional actions they give rise to." But the character traits that virtue theory emphasizes are not simply dispositions to intentional actions, but a seamless disposition to certain actions and passions, thoughts and reactions.

To say that the cutting off of a human life is always a matter of some seriousness, at any stage, is not to deny the relevance of gradual fetal development. Notwithstanding the well-worn point that clear boundary lines cannot be drawn, our emotions and attitudes regarding the fetus do change as it develops, and again when it is born, and indeed further as the baby grows. Abortion for shallow reasons in the later stages is much more shocking than abortion for the same reasons in the early stages in a way that matches the fact that deep grief over miscarriage in the later stages is more appropriate than it is over miscarriage in the earlier stages (when, that is, the grief is solely about the loss of *this* child, not about, as might be the case, the loss of one's only hope of having a child or of having one's husband's child). Imagine (or recall) a woman who already has children; she had not intended to have more, but finds herself unexpectedly pregnant. Though contrary to her plans, the pregnancy, once established as a fact, is welcomed—and then she loses the embryo almost immediately. If this were bemoaned as a tragedy, it would, I think, be a misapplication of the concept of what is tragic. But it may still properly be mourned as a loss. The grief is expressed in such terms as "I shall always wonder how she or he would have turned out" or "When I look at the others, I shall think, 'How different their lives would have been if this other one had been part of them.'" It would, I take it, be callous and light-minded to say, or think, "Well, she has already *got* four children; what's the problem?"; it would be neither, nor arrogantly intrusive in the case of a close friend, to try to correct prolonged mourning by saying, "I know it's sad, but it's not a tragedy; rejoice in the ones you have." The application of *tragic* becomes more appropriate as the fetus grows, for the mere fact that one has lived with it for longer, conscious of its existence, makes a difference. To shrug off an early abortion is understandable just because it is very hard to be fully conscious of the fetus's existence in the early stages and hence hard to appreciate that an early abortion is the destruction of life. It is particularly hard for the young and inexperienced to appreciate this, because appreciation of it usually comes only with experience.

I do not mean "with the experience of having an abortion" (though that may be part of it) but, quite generally, "with the experience of life." Many women who have borne children contrast their later pregnancies with their first successful one, saying that in the later ones they were conscious of a new life growing in them from very early on. And, more generally, as one reaches the age at which the next generation is coming up close behind one, the counterfactuals "If I, or she, had had an abortion, Alice, or Bob, would not have been born" acquire a significant application, which casts a new light on the conditionals "If I or Alice have an abortion then some Caroline or Bill will not be born."

The fact that pregnancy is not just one among many physical conditions does not mean that one can never regard it in that light without manifesting a vice. When women are in very poor physical health, or worn out from childbearing, or forced to do very physically demanding jobs, then they cannot be described as self-indulgent, callous, irresponsible, or light-minded if they seek abortions mainly with a view to avoiding pregnancy as the physical condition that it is. To go through with a pregnancy when one is utterly exhausted, or when one's job consists of crawling along tunnels hauling coal, as many women in the nineteenth century were obliged to do, is perhaps heroic, but people who do not achieve heroism are not necessarily vicious. That they can view the pregnancy only as eight months of misery, followed by hours if not days of agony and exhaustion, and abortion only as the blessed escape from this prospect, is entirely understandable and does not manifest any lack of serious respect for human life or a shallow attitude to motherhood. What it does show is that something is terribly amiss in the conditions of their lives, which make it so hard to recognize pregnancy and childbearing as the good that they can be.

In relation to this last point I should draw attention to the way in which virtue theory has a sort of built-in indexicality. Philosophers arguing against anything remotely resembling a belief in the sanctity of life (which the above claims clearly embody) frequently appeal to the existence of other communities in which abortion and infanticide are practiced. We should not automatically assume that it is impossible that some other communities could be morally inferior to our own; maybe some are, or have been, precisely insofar as their members are, typically, callous or light-minded or unjust. But in communities in which life is a great deal tougher for everyone than it is in ours, having the right attitude to human life and death, parenthood, and family relationships might well manifest itself in ways that are unlike ours. When it is essential to survival that most members of the community fend for themselves at a very young age or work during most of their waking hours, selective abortion or infanticide might be practiced either as a form of genuine euthanasia or for the sake of the community and not, I think, be thought callous or light-minded. But this does not make everything all right; as before, it shows that there is something amiss with the conditions of their lives, which are making it impossible for them to live really well.

The foregoing discussion, insofar as it emphasizes the right attitude to human life and death, parallels to a certain extent those standard discussions of abortion that concentrate on it solely as an issue of killing. But it does not, as those discussions do, gloss over the fact, emphasized by those who discuss the morality of abortion in terms of women's rights, that abortion, wildly unlike any other form of killing, is the termination of a pregnancy, which is a condition of a woman's body and results in *her* having a child if it is not aborted. This fact is given due recognition not by appeal to women's rights but by emphasizing the relevance of the familiar biological and psychological facts and their connection with having the right attitude to parenthood and family relationships. But it may well be thought that failing to bring in women's rights still leaves some important aspects of the problem of abortion untouched.

Speaking in terms of women's rights, people sometimes say things like, "Well, it's her life you're talking about too, you know; she's got a right to her own life, her own happiness." And the discussion stops there. But in the context of virtue theory, given that we are particularly concerned with what constitutes a good human life, with what true happiness or *eudaimonia* is, this is no place to stop. We go on to ask, "And is this life of hers a good one? Is she living well?"

If we are to go on to talk about good human lives, in the context of abortion, we have to bring in our thoughts about the value of love and family life, and our proper emotional development through a natural life cycle. The familiar facts support the view that parenthood in general, and motherhood and childbearing in particular, are intrinsically worthwhile, are among the things that can be correctly thought to be partially constitutive of a flourishing human life. If this is right, then a woman who opts for not being a mother (at all, or again, or now) by opting for abortion may thereby be manifesting a flawed grasp of what her life should be, and be about—a grasp that is childish, or grossly materialistic, or shortsighted, or shallow.

I said "*may* thereby": this *need* not be so. Consider, for instance, a woman who has already had several children and fears that to have another will seriously affect her capacity to be a good mother to the ones she has—she does not show a lack of appreciation of the intrinsic value of being a parent by opting for abortion.

Nor does a woman who has been a good mother and is approaching the age at which she may be looking forward to being a good grandmother. Nor does a woman who discovers that her pregnancy may well kill her, and opts for abortion and adoption. Nor, necessarily, does a woman who has decided to lead a life centered around some other worthwhile activity or activities with which motherhood would compete.

People who are childless by choice are sometimes described as "irresponsible," or "selfish," or "refusing to grow up," or "not knowing what life is about." But one can hold that having children is intrinsically worthwhile without endorsing this, for we are, after all, in the happy position of there being more worthwhile things to do than can be fitted into one lifetime. Parenthood, and motherhood in particular, even if granted to be intrinsically worthwhile, undoubtedly take up a lot of one's adult life, leaving no room for some other worthwhile pursuits. But some women who choose abortion rather than have their first child, and some men who encourage their partners to choose abortion, are not avoiding parenthood for the sake of other worthwhile pursuits, but for the worthless one of "having a good time," or for the pursuit of some false vision of the ideals of freedom or self-realization. And some others who say "I am not ready for parenthood yet" are making some sort of mistake about the extent to which one can manipulate the circumstances of one's life so as to make it fulfill some dream that one has. Perhaps one's dream is to have two perfect children, a girl and a boy, within a perfect marriage, in financially secure circumstances, with an interesting job of one's own. But to care too much about that dream, to demand of life that it give it to one and act accordingly, may be both greedy and foolish, and is to run the risk of missing out on happiness entirely. Not only may fate make the dream impossible, or destroy it, but one's own attachment to it may make it impossible. Good marriages, and the most promising children, can be destroyed by just one adult's excessive demand for perfection.

Once again, this is not to deny that girls may quite properly say "I am not ready for motherhood yet," especially in our society, and, far from manifesting irresponsibility or light-mindedness, show an appropriate modesty or humility, or a fearfulness that does not amount to cowardice. However, even when the decision to have an abortion is the right decision—one that does not itself fall under a vice-related term and thereby one that the perfectly virtuous could recommend—it does not follow that there is no sense in which having the abortion is wrong, or guilt inappropriate. For, by virtue of the fact that a human life has been cut short, some evil has probably been brought about, and that circumstances make the decision to bring about some evil the right decision will be a ground for guilt if getting into those circumstances in the first place itself manifested a flaw in character.

What "gets one into those circumstances" in the case of abortion is, except in the case of rape, one's sexual activity and one's choices, or the lack of them, about one's sexual partner and about contraception. The virtuous woman (which here of course does not mean simply "chaste woman" but "woman with the virtues") has such character traits as strength, independence, resoluteness, decisiveness, self-confidence, responsibility, serious-mindedness, and self-determination—and no one, I think, could deny that many women become pregnant in circumstances in which they cannot welcome or cannot face the thought of having *this* child precisely because they lack one or some of these character traits. So even in the cases where the decision to have an abortion is the right one, it can still be the reflection of a moral failing—not because the decision itself is weak or cowardly or irresolute or irresponsible or light-minded, but because lack of the requisite opposite of these failings landed one in the circumstances in the first place. Hence the common universalized claim that guilt and remorse are never appropriate emotions about an abortion is denied. They may be appropriate, and appropriately inculcated, even when the decision was the right one.

Another motivation for bringing women's rights into the discussion may be to attempt to correct the implication, carried by the killing-centered approach, that insofar as abortion is wrong, it is a wrong that only women do, or at least (given the preponderance of male doctors) that only women instigate. I do not myself believe that we can thus escape the fact that nature bears harder on women than it does on men, but virtue theory can certainly correct many of the injustices that the emphasis on women's rights is rightly concerned about. With very little amendment, everything that has been said above applies to boys and men too. Although the abortion decision is, in a natural sense, the woman's decision, proper to her, boys and men are often party to it, for well or ill, and even when they are not, they are bound to have been party to the circumstances that brought it up. No less than girls and women, boys and men can, in their actions, manifest self-centeredness, callousness, and light-mindedness about life and parenthood in relation to abortion. They can be self-centered or courageous about the possibility of disability in their offspring; they need to reflect on their sexual activity and their choices, or the lack of them, about their sexual partner and contraception; they need to grow up and take responsibility for their own actions and life in relation to fatherhood. If it is true, as I maintain, that insofar as motherhood is intrinsically worthwhile, being a mother is an important purpose in women's lives, being a father (rather than a mere generator) is an important purpose in men's lives as well, and it is adolescent of men to turn a blind eye to this and pretend that they have many more important things to do.

Conclusion

Much more might be said, but I shall end the actual discussion of the problem of abortion here, and conclude by highlighting what I take to be its significant features. These hark back to many of the criticisms of virtue theory discussed earlier.

The discussion does not proceed simply by our trying to answer the question "Would a perfectly virtuous agent ever have an abortion and, if so, when?"; virtue theory is not limited to considering "Would Socrates have had an abortion if he were a raped, pregnant fifteen-year-old?" nor automatically stumped when we are considering circumstances into which no virtuous agent would have got herself. Instead, much of the discussion proceeds in the virtue- and vice-related terms whose application, in several cases, yields practical conclusions (cf. the third and fourth criticisms above). These terms are difficult to apply correctly, and anyone might challenge my application of any one of them. So, for example, I have claimed that some abortions, done for certain reasons, would be callous or light-minded; that others might indicate an appropriate modesty or humility; that others would reflect a greedy and foolish attitude to what one could expect out of life. Any of these examples may be disputed, but what is at issue is, should these difficult terms be there, or should the discussion be couched in terms that all clever adolescents can apply correctly?

Proceeding as it does in the virtue- and vice-related terms, the discussion thereby, inevitably, also contains claims about what is worthwhile, serious and important, good and evil, in our lives. So, for example, I claimed that parenthood is intrinsically worthwhile, and that having a good time was a worthless end (in life, not on individual occasions); that losing a fetus is always a serious matter (albeit not a tragedy in itself in the first trimester) whereas acquiring an appendectomy scar is a trivial one; that (human) death is an evil. Once again, these are difficult matters, and anyone might challenge any one of my claims. But what is at issue is, as before, should those difficult claims be there or can one reach practical conclusions about real moral issues that are in no way determined by premises about such matters?

The discussion also thereby, inevitably, contains claims about what life is like (e.g., my claim that love and friendship do not survive their parties' constantly insisting on their rights; or the claim that to demand perfection of life is to run the risk of missing out on happiness entirely). What is at issue is, should those disputable claims be there, or is our knowledge (or are our false opinions) about what life is like irrelevant to our understanding of real moral issues?

Naturally, my own view is that all these concepts should be there in any discussion of real moral issues and that virtue theory, which uses all of them, is the right theory to apply to them. I do not pretend to have shown this. I realize that proponents of rival theories may say that, now that they have understood how virtue theory uses the range of concepts it draws on, they are more convinced than ever that such concepts should not figure in an adequate normative theory, because they are sectarian, or vague, or too particular, or improperly anthropocentric, and reinstate what I called the "major criticism." Or, finding many of the details of the discussion appropriate, they may agree that many, perhaps even all, of the concepts should figure, but argue that virtue theory gives an inaccurate account of the way the concepts fit together (and indeed of the concepts themselves) and that another theory provides a better account; that would be interesting to see. Moreover, I admitted that there were at least two problems for virtue theory: that it has to argue against moral skepticism, "pluralism," and cultural relativism, and that it has to find something to say about conflicting requirements of different virtues. Proponents of rival theories might argue that their favored theory provides better solutions to these problems than virtue theory can. Indeed, they might criticize virtue theory for finding problems here at all. Anyone who argued for at least one of moral skepticism, "pluralism," or cultural relativism could presumably do so (provided their favored theory does not find a similar problem); and a utilitarian might say that benevolence is the only virtue and hence that virtue theory errs when it discusses even apparent conflicts between the requirements of benevolence and some other character trait such as honesty.

Defending virtue theory against all possible, or even likely, criticisms of it would be a lifelong task. As I said at the outset, in this article I aimed to defend the theory against some criticisms which I thought arose from an inadequate understanding of it, and to improve that understanding. If I have succeeded, we may hope for more comprehending criticisms of virtue theory than have appeared hitherto.

QUESTIONS FOR ANALYSIS AND DISCUSSION

1. What does Hursthouse mean by saying that a right to an abortion is irrelevant to virtue ethics? Is she implying that a moral person ignores rights, that there are some situations that call for rights and other situations that do not, or that rights do not exhaust the moral considerations a virtuous persons needs to weigh? If you agree with Hursthouse, does that mean laws on abortion are also irrelevant?

2. Why are the biological facts about the fetus largely immaterial in the moral issues of abortion, according to Hursthouse's version of virtue ethics? When she observes that "the current philosophical literature on abortion has got badly out of touch with reality," do you think this could apply to Noonan, Thomson, or Sherwin? Clarify your response in light of any of these essays on abortion. Or do you find Hursthouse's essay as bearing little resemblance to the concerns of those actually weighing the decision on abortion?

3. Contrary to many disputants, Hursthouse claims that the moral issues regarding abortion involve both women and men. Her reasoning seems to be that the virtues and vices that shape the character and attitudes of those considering an abortion apply to everyone, hence to the man and woman most directly responsible for the fetus's future. A virtuous woman may unwittingly choose an abortion by yielding to the vicious attitudes of her husband or boyfriend. Which specific virtues or vices do you see as central in Hursthouse's moral deliberations? Could you add others?

4. A moral theory should help anyone contemplating a moral dilemma. Does Hursthouse's virtue ethics approach offer more or less help than the other approaches you are familiar with? Explain your answer.

75.

DANIEL CALLAHAN

The Value and the Limits of Aging

A different side of burdensome lives is something women and men face equally: getting old. Everyone has parents, grandparents, and friends whose physical and mental powers are weakening simply by natural course. Most of us desire a long life, although we are not always alert to the surprising and painful reminders life offers us as we reach old age. Before the advent of Social Security, Medicare, and pension funds, the golden age of retirement was a luxury for the rich. Now ordinary folks can also look forward to an enjoyable retirement. However, with the rapid sophistication of medical technologies and the fear of multimillion dollar lawsuits, images of old age now include the dread that the last days or years of life will be strung out with painful, expensive, and unrewarding operations and hospital stays. Does it have to be this way?

According to Daniel Callahan (b. 1930), a widely read ethics scholar and cofounder of the Hastings Center, society needs to make several careful decisions about what it can and should do for the elderly. Callahan is perhaps best known for his proposal that society set limits on the kind of medical care offered to the elderly. Though at first glance this sounds harsh, inviting the slippery slope argument that Callahan may be calling for widespread euthanasia of the aged, he is in fact inviting candid discussion about which sorts of limits need to be spelled out. To give some balance to this position, consider how Callahan encourages a reevaluation of how the elderly can live meaningful lives. This involves more than being taken care of—it calls for the elderly to remain a part of social life.

"The Value and the Limits of Aging," from *Setting Limits* (New York: Touchstone, 1987), pp. 41–51, 133–138. Notes have been omitted.

┤ **CRITICAL READING QUESTIONS** ├

1. Which senses of time—past, present, future—can the elderly help us appreciate?

2. What can the elderly contribute to the youth of society? Why only the elderly?

3. Which virtues does Callahan (with William May) see best represented by a moral person who is getting old?

4. What criteria does Callahan think should be used to decide whether someone deserves further medical attention?

5. What three guidelines does Callahan endorse regarding government policy toward the elderly?

The Construction of Meaning

Out of what cloth can the old cut integrity, wisdom, and meaning? Erikson hints at an answer by affirming that old age ought not to represent a repudiation of the earlier adult stage of generativity, encompassing as it did procreativity, productivity, and creativity. It must now take a different, more capacious, form—what he calls a *"grand*-generative function." Erikson provides few details about what that might consist of other than to say, all too vaguely, that it will require a kind of "vital involvement." The problem is that in the face of modernization, the involvement must be much different from and richer than the kind of vigorous and vital carrying-on, more-of-the-same, open-ended, meaning-evasive philosophy which is by now its standard version. As a general specification, it must fully acknowledge the vitality built on better health and more years that are now part of ordinary old age and open to still more modification in the future. It must no less acknowledge that life is still finite and time-limited, bounded as ever by death and usually still preceded by a decline of many vital capacities. It is still a stage of life shot through with loss and desperately requiring that sense be made of it, that its mysteries and terrors be confronted.

Various sources of meaning and significance are available for the aged, each still possible and each still needed. Time will provide me with a metaphor as I try to suggest what they might be. The elderly are in the best position to keep alive the *past,* to integrate the history of which they are a living link with that present which they share with younger generations. This could be as valuable in our society as it was in preliterate societies. The integration of what was and what is, and how they cohere with each other, is something that only the elderly can provide within the confines of family and local community life. Only they are in a position to have experienced some patterns and cycles; the young tend to think they saw the dawn of history. The various movements to encourage the elderly to recapture their own pasts, and to make them available to the young, is a healthy recognition of the value of that role. It is both their unique privilege and their unique obligation.

The aged are exceedingly well placed to appreciate what it means to live in the *present*. Their future is foreshortened, and unlike the young, they are not as a rule preparing themselves to be something other than they already are. What they have today is all they have. Even if there is a tomorrow, and a day after that, it will pass all too quickly. Making the most of today is an art which a person of any age can cultivate, and an old person is compelled to cultivate. That much old age is now accompanied by some degree of chronic illness makes the task both more necessary and more complicated: the mind must be distanced, the limitations framed and domesticated, and the present—in whatever form it presents itself—enjoyed or at least made the most of.

The aged bear a particular obligation to the *future*, and it is that aspect I most want to dwell on here. Not only is it the most neglected perspective on the elderly, but it is the most pertinent as we try to understand the problem of their health care. The young—children and young adults—most justly and appropriately spend their time preparing for future roles and developing a self pertinent to them. The mature adult has the responsibility to procreate and rear the next generation and to manage the present society. What can the elderly most appropriately do? It should be the special role of the elderly to be the moral conservators of that which has been and the most active proponents of that which will be after they are no longer here. Their indispensable role as conservators is what generates what I believe ought to be the *primary* aspiration of the old, which is to serve the young and the future. Just as they were once the heirs of a society built by others, who passed on to them what they needed to know to keep it going, so are they likewise obliged to do the same for those who will follow them.

Only the old—who alone have seen in their long lives first a future on the horizon and then its actual arrival—can know what it means to go from past through present to future. That is valuable and unique knowledge. If the young are to flourish, then the old should step aside in an active way, working until the very end to do what they can to leave behind them a world hopeful for the young and worthy of bequest. The acceptance of their aging and death will be the principal stimulus to doing this. It is this seemingly paradoxical combination of withdrawal to prepare for death and an active, helpful leave-taking oriented toward the young which provides the possibility for meaning and significance in a contemporary context. Meaning is provided because there is a purpose in that kind of aging, combining an identity for the self with the serving of a critical function in the lives of others— that of linking the past, present, and future—something which, even if they are unaware of it, they cannot do without. Significance is provided because society, in recognizing and encouraging the aged in their duties toward the young, gives them a clear and important role, one that both is necessary for the common good and that *only* they can play.

Aspirations to Serve the Young

Is it even necessary to stress service to the young as an aspiration of the old? Is it not true that even now, the elderly are a prime resource, through the family, to the young? That is perfectly true and should not be forgotten. The elderly already provide everything from child care (some 17 percent of the care of children of working mothers is provided by grandparents), to living space, to supplementary and emergency income, to advice for younger family members. In fragmented families they are often the only source of unity and stability. The family remains the most important mechanism for income redistribution, and there is evidence to suggest that within the family, the elderly may give more assistance than they receive. The importance of the elderly in the lives of families is, then, as vital as it is undeniable. Family life would be immeasurably poorer without their contributions.

Yet it would be a serious mistake to think that, as important as they are, service and sacrifice within the context of the family can suffice to provide either full meaning or significance for the aged. Meaning is enhanced by a sense of obligation to other age groups and a linkage to other generations. The elderly, if they want to find a larger meaning, need to serve the young in the larger, public society as well. Not all will be able physically to do this, but many will. A contribution in the private sphere of the family is not tantamount to service to the public welfare, even if the latter requires such service for its own flourishing. The money that family members may give each other is not the same as the payment of taxes or voluntary activities to help other people's children; each serves important, but different, ends. (A similar point should be made about younger people. They need to develop, early in life, their own feelings of obligation to those still younger—not only their siblings, but others as well.)

There is another important distinction to be made. Many services and benefits provided within families by the old are not of a kind that only an older person could provide; again, it is usually a case of the older person's having available time or disposable income, something that others could in principle provide. In saying this, I do not mean to minimize or belittle that kind of assistance. It counts for much and bespeaks a considerable reservoir of affection and devotion between young and old within families. It does not, however, wholly meet the criteria I believe central—the discovery of a place for the old in their own minds and in that of society which they, and only they, can take precisely because they are aged. The provision of advice and counsel to younger friends and family members comes closest to what I have in mind; that is where the age and experience do count. There is, then, a painful irony here. If we had a better system of social services— income maintenance, home care for chronically ill or injured children and young adults, child-care facilities—then there would be much less need for the many things that older family members now of necessity do for younger ones. Their role would diminish and might be adequately performed by others. In that respect, some of the present roles of the elderly within families are valuable but not irre-placeable. The elderly need a more solid footing in the life of the community than that.

What is it that *only* the old can provide the young, that which is irreplaceable in their contribution? *Only* the aged can provide a perspective the young need if they are properly to envision their own lives: that of the cycle of the generations and its import for the living of a life. The young may be indifferent to that perspec-tive; the elderly may have to struggle to make it known. What the old know, though too poignantly at times perhaps, is that the generations come and go and that time unceasingly marches on, and on, and on, all too soon passing us all by. For the very young, the sole world they know or can well imagine is the present world in which they exist. Time for them usually moves too slowly, withholding the freedoms and self-realizations they long for. The past is little more than an illusion, something to be found in history books, not in their memories. In one sense, time will cure their problem; it will march on for them also. In another sense, they need the old to give them a perspective they desperately, if unknowingly, re-quire while still young, that of the need to visualize their life as a whole, to see where they are going, to be helped to know where they ought to be going, to be given a prod toward asking early on what they would like, when the end has come, to have made of themselves and to be remembered for.

As Alasdair MacIntyre has written of the moral life: ". . . both childhood and old age have [mistakenly] been wrenched from the rest of human life and made over into distinct realms. . . . it is the distinctiveness of each and not the unity of the life of the individual . . . of which we are taught to think and to feel. . . . The unity of a human life [should instead be] the unity of a narrative quest." The notion of a "narrative quest," MacIntyre reminds us, requires that we have some concep-tion of a goal, a *telos*, toward which the quest works; it requires both self-knowl-edge and a sense of the nature of the good that is sought. The good in this case, I propose, is that of providing the young with an image of the pursuit of a life of meaning.

Both the old and the young turn out to need the same thing: a way of imagina-tively and reflectively integrating their individual life stages into the larger cycle of the generations. The young are not in a position to do this well for themselves. They ordinarily have neither the experience nor the seasoned sensibilities necessary to do so. Only the old can bring them to it. The young, in that respect, need the old to help them discover their own sense of meaning (just as the young, for their part, need to do it for those still younger than they). At the same time, it is the provision of that kind of meaning to the young which ought to be the greatest source of meaning for the old themselves. None but they in a society can do that. There is no substitute for age in that kind of quest, as there can be if only money is needed, or help with child care. By this kind of service to the young, by this con-struction of a world of meaning, the old turn out to be benefiting not only the present welfare of the young, but also, and simultaneously, their future welfare— and, even more, the welfare of still another generation after that, for they are tacitly instructing the young and middle-aged in what they should begin doing with the generation that is to succeed them.

What I am saying requires two assumptions. The young must be prepared to look among the old for models, and the old should be willing to see themselves in the service of future generations in general, not only the welfare of their own children and grandchildren in particular. There is no way to ensure that the young will look to the old; but there are some grounds for thinking that the chances are greater now than in the past: the increasing proportion of the aged, making them more visible and more present as a daily reality and as people the young will personally know; the better health of the aged, enhancing the likelihood they will be more active in the community; and the possibility that, as the aged increasingly contemplate their own role, they will see the value of working toward the future of the young and of providing a model for them as an attractive one. As for the possibility that the old will come to that last perception, I can only try to sketch here some reasons why they should, hoping that their own need to find meaning for themselves, and the need of society to reconstitute and find significance for their social status, will provide a helpful prod.

The unique capacity of the elderly to see the way past, present, and future interact provides the foundation for the contribution they can make to the young and to future generations. "Society," Edmund Burke wrote in *Reflections on the Revolution in France,* is a "partnership not only between those who are living, but between those who are living, those who are dead and those who are to be born." That may be perfectly true; but why should the old, who will be passing from the scene, have any motivation to continue that partnership or feel they have any special contribution to make to it? They should know that they have their own debt to the past and that from that debt springs their own obligation to the future. The best retort to the old and cynical query "What has posterity ever done for me?" is that it can and will judge us for what we left it. If we value our own life at all, then we should value and feel some obligation toward those who made that life possible, our own families and the past societies which supported them. We owe to those coming after us at least what we were given by those who came before us, the possibility of life and survival. We also owe to the future an amelioration of those conditions which, in our own life, lessened our possibilities of living a decent life and which, if they persist, will do the same for coming generations. If the aged, moreover, want to find meaning in their lives, and a significant place in society, then this is their most promising direction, drawing on that which only they can give.

There is a necessary biological and social link between the generations; later generations exist because of burdens assumed by earlier generations. This is most evident in the case of close successor generations. The later requires the earlier. It is no less present even when the generations are separated over time. To live at all is to be linked in an inextricable way to the past, and to be no less a powerful determinant of the fate of future generations. That is what the aged can see, and that is what they can pass on to the young.

Even more can be said, a still more powerful motivation invoked. It may be only through passing life and culture along to the next generation—in an active and responsible and yet gradually self-emptying way—that any kind of transcendence can be found. Leon Kass has written suggestively that ". . . biology has its own view of our nature and its inclinations. Biology also teaches about transcendence, though it eschews talk about the soul. For self-preservation is one thing, reproduction quite another; in bearing and caring for their young, many animals risk and even sacrifice their own lives. Indeed, in all higher animals, to reproduce *as such* implies both acceptance of the death of self and participation in its transcendence. . . . human biology, too, teaches us how our life points beyond itself—to our offspring, to our community, to our species. Man, like the other animals, is built for reproduction. Man, more than the other animals, is also built for sociality. And man, alone among the animals, is built for culture—not only through capacities to transmit and receive skills and techniques, but also through capacities for shared beliefs, opinions, rituals, traditions."

Obligations and Virtues

The modernizers of aging, I suppose, might have a retort to my particular projection of a role for the elderly. They might say that, to the extent the old (say, the "young-old") are still in good health and vigorous in their outlook, they should be allowed to relinquish the burdens of responsibility to the young; they do not need "transcendence" so much as an opportunity to cultivate their own fulfillment during their last years. Have they not done enough already? Can they not be allowed at last to live for themselves? If they are in addition already ill or disabled is it not naive to expect of them much more than survival? How can they be expected to serve younger generations, and why should that weight be added to the weights imposed by their years?

That viewpoint deserves some sympathy, but it also presents a dilemma. If the old are to have meaning in their own lives and significance in the larger social world, they cannot claim a right to self-absorption or an exemption from civic duties. Those same forces of modernization which would have them pretend that aging does not occur, or can with sufficient energy be brought to heel, work against giving the aged their own unique and valued role. This can be achieved only through recognition that old age is the last phase of life, that it cannot go on for long, and that death is on its way. But aging as a stage of life can be given a meaning equal in value to earlier stages only if it is understood as requiring every bit as much vigor, dedication, and imagination as those earlier stages. Gruman has argued that only *more* modernization will suffice to bring to completion the modernization project now under way; we cannot, in his view, stop now without risking the loss of what we already have. I want to argue, by way of repudiating this project, that it is only through toughly and energetically embracing old age as a time of both service to the future and decline and withdrawal that its value as a stage in life can ultimately be redeemed.

It is grace under adversity that can impress the young, not the ability of the old to pretend they are still young. It will be the political skills and voting-participation rates turned to the service of the young that will commend the old to the young and to future generations, not the search for their own security. It will be the wisdom of the old—that old-fashioned, supposedly anachronistic virtue—which will, if the old work to cultivate their perceptions, catch the ear of the young—not the street smarts of the old in knowing how to survive in a world of young people. The dilemma of the old, in sum, cannot be resolved except by their taking the harder, more demanding role, one that will not allow them to let up, or be excused, because of their age; or allow them, through the modernizing impulse, to reject aging altogether.

How are we to strike the right balance here? To age with grace is to accept decline and loss, to accept the reality that one's life is coming to an end, to understand that a final attempt must be made to make sense of oneself and one's place in relation to those who went before and those who will come after. This need not be a wholly passive self-examination, or preclude an active engagement in the life around one; "disengagement" can be understood in an active sense. The great danger is self-absorption, the embracing of service to self or the "rewarding" of oneself as a way of warding off, or attempting to compensate for, the death that is to come. The common phrase that "it is my turn" manifests this tendency. Two writers, at a great historical remove from each other, have addressed that danger, but in different ways.

Simone de Beauvoir wrote in *The Coming of Age:* "The greatest good fortune, even greater than health, for the old person is to have his world inhabited by projects; then, busy and useful, he escapes both from boredom and from decay. . . . There is only one solution if old age is not to be an absurd parody of our former life, and that is to go on pursuing ends that give our existence a meaning—devotion to individuals, to groups or to causes, social, political, intellectual or creative work. In spite of the moralists' opinion to the contrary, in old age we should still wish to have passions strong enough to prevent us turning in upon ourselves." Harry R. Moody has characterized this passage as one displaying "an activist style of growing old. . . . Old age, in this view, is not a time for wisdom or summing up. It is a time for continual engagement." I am less certain about how this passage should be understood. Nothing that Mme. de Beauvoir says need be rejected by one who believes that the most important aspect of growing old should be a focus on larger questions of meaning; this does not preclude an active concern about the world one is soon to leave. But if the "turning in" that de Beauvoir would have us avoid is meant to evade these questions, then it will be a mistake.

Cicero, writing in 44 B.C., strikes a different note. While the old should see their physical labors reduced, their mental and social activities should actually increase. "Old men . . . as they become less capable of physical exertion, should redouble their intellectual activity, and their principal occupation should be to assist the young, their friends, and above all their country with their wisdom and sagacity. There is nothing they should guard against so much as languor and sloth. Luxury, which is shameful at every period of life, makes old age hideous. If it is united with sensuality, the evil is two-fold. Age thus brings disgrace on itself and aggravates the shameless license of the young." The combination of a rejection of old age as a time for self-indulgence, the astute observation that the old can provide poor models of morality for the young if they are not careful, and the idea of service to the larger community suggests dimensions in the understanding of old age of a kind wider than those of de Beauvoir.

For our own time, we need just those virtues which Cicero stressed. To complement an ethos that for well over two decades now has stressed the rights and entitlements of the elderly, there would be one which held them up to high standards of service and stewardship, and did so because of their important and indispensable contributions which could not otherwise be realized. William F. May has written that "Any serious reflection on the moral status of the aged requires reflection on the specific virtues that age calls for." "Such discussion," he cautions, "will deteriorate into the sentimental if we do not remind ourselves that virtues hardly come automatically with age; rather, they are structures of character that come with resolution, prayer, suffering, and persevering." Among the virtues he lists are *courage* in the face of certain decline and death; *humility* in response to progressive loss and the humiliation of body and dignity that it can bring; *patience* out of a need to take control of oneself when the loss of control begins to gain sway; *simplicity* as a way of traveling light; *benignity* (a kind of "purified benevolence") to offset tendencies to avarice, possessiveness, and manipulation; and (most surprisingly) *hilarity* ". . . a celestial gaiety in those who have seen a lot, done a lot, grieved a lot, but now acquire that detachment of the fly on the ceiling looking down on the human scene." To this list I would add *vigor of spirit,* by which I mean the drive to keep going to carry out one's hope to serve the young, an impulse of dogged determination to work to the very end for a future one will not see. None of this is to deny that the elderly can become tired, can feel a strong need to pull away from the fray of life. That should be their right if they can bear no more. Yet one may be allowed to hope that however diminished the body, the mind and spirit will struggle on.

Setting Limits

I have considered five responses pertinent to the contention that there is a need to ration health care for the elderly; while each of them has a certain plausibility, none is wholly convincing: It is possible and necessary to generalize about the elderly. It is possible that benefits to the aged will not automatically benefit other age groups. It is not premature to take the idea of rationing seriously. It is not a mistake to consider limitations on health care for the elderly even if there continue to be other social expenditures that we individually think wasteful. And it is more wishful thinking than anything else to believe that more efficient care of the elderly dying could save vast amounts of money. All those objections reflect a laudable desire to avoid any future policies that would require limiting benefits to the aging and that would use age as a standard for that limitation. They also betray a wish that economic realities would be happily coincidental with a commitment to the unrestricted good of the elderly. That may no longer be possible. A carefully drawn, widely discussed allocation policy is likely to be one safer in the long run for the elderly than the kind of ad hoc rationing (such as increased cost-sharing under Medicare) now present and increasing.

How might we devise a plan to limit health care for the aged that is fair, humane, and sensitive to the special requirements and dignity of the aged? . . . [N]either in moral theory nor in the various recent traditions of the welfare state is there any single and consistent basis for health care for the elderly. The ideas of veteranship, of earned merit, of need, of respect for age as such, and various pragmatic motives have all played a part in different societies and in our own as well. The earlier presumption of a basic obligation on the part of families to take care of their elderly, rooted in filial obligation, has gradually given way to the acceptance of a state obligation for basic welfare and medical needs. While the need and dependency of the elderly would appear to be the strongest basis of the obligation, it has never been clear just how medical "need" is to be understood or the extent of the claim that can be drawn from it. Minimal requirements for food, clothing, shelter, and income for the aged can be calculated with some degree of accuracy and, if inflation is taken into account, can remain reasonably stable and predictable. Medical "needs," by contrast, admit of no such stable calculation. Forecasts about life expectancy and about health needs have, as noted, consistently been mistaken underestimates in the past. Constant technological innovation and refinement means not only that new ways are always being found to extend life or improve therapy, but also that "need" itself becomes redefined in the process. New horizons for research are created, new desires for cures encouraged, and new hopes for relief of disability engendered. Together they induce and shape changing and, ordinarily, escalating perceptions of need. Medical need is not a fixed concept but a function of technological possibility and regnant social expectations.

If this is true of medical care in general, it seems all the more true of health care for the aged: it is a new medical frontier, and the possibilities for improvement are open, beckoning, and flexible. Medical need on that frontier in principle knows no boundaries; death and illness will always be waiting no matter how far we go. The young can already for the most part be given an adequate level of health care to ensure their likely survival to old age (even if there also remain struggles about what their needs are). For the aged, however, the forestalling of bodily deterioration and an eventually inevitable death provide the motivation for a constant, never-ending struggle. That struggle will turn on the meaning of medical need, an always malleable concept, and will move on from there to a struggle about the claims of the elderly relative to other age groups and other social needs. That these struggles are carried on in a society wary about the propriety of even trying to achieve a consensus on appropriate individual needs does not help matters.

For all of its difficulties, nonetheless, only some acceptable and reasonably stable notion of need is likely to provide a foundation for resource allocation. The use of merit, or wealth, or social worth as a standard for distributing lifesaving benefits through governmental mechanisms would seem both unfair at best and morally outrageous at worst. We must try, then, to establish a consensus on the health needs of different age groups, especially the elderly, and establish priorities to meet them. At the same time, those standards of need must have the capacity to resist the redefining, escalating power of technological change; otherwise they will lack all solidity. The nexus between need and technological possibility has to be broken, not only that some stability can be brought to a definition of adequate health care, but also that the dominance of technology as a determinant of values can be overcome.

Need will not be a manageable idea, however, unless we forthrightly recognize that it is only in part an empirical concept. It can make use of physical indicators, but it will also be a reflection of our values, what we think people require for an acceptable life. In the case of the aged, I have proposed that our ideal of old age should be achieving a life span that enables each of us to accomplish the ordinary scope of possibilities that life affords, recognizing that this may encompass a range of time rather than pointing to a precise age. On the basis of that ideal, the aged would need only those resources which would allow them a solid chance to live that long and, once they had passed that stage, to finish out their years free of pain and avoidable suffering. I will, therefore, define need in the old as primarily to achieve a natural life span and thereafter to have their suffering relieved.

The needs of the aged, as so defined, would therefore be based on a general and socially established ideal of old age and not exclusively, as at present, on individual desires—even the widespread desire to live a longer life. That standard would make possible an allocation of resources to the aged which rested upon criteria that were at once age-based (aiming to achieve a natural life span) and need-based (sensitive to the differing health needs of individuals in achieving that goal). A fair basis for limits to health care for the aged would be established, making a clear use of age as a standard, but also recognizing the heterogeneity of the needs of the old within those limits.

Norman Daniels has helpfully formulated a key principle for my purposes: the concept of a "normal opportunity range" for the allocation of resources to different individuals and age groups. The foundation of his idea is that "meeting health-care needs is of special importance because it promotes fair equality of opportunity. It helps guarantee individuals a fair chance to enjoy the normal opportunity range for their society." A "fair chance," however, is one that recognizes different needs and different opportunities for each stage of life; it is an "age-relative opportunity range." Even though fairness in this conception is based upon age distinctions, it is not unfairly discriminatory: it aims to provide people with that level of medical care necessary to allow them to pursue the opportunities ordinarily available to those of their age. Everyone needs to walk, for example, but some require an artificial hip to do so. It also recognizes that different ages entail different needs and opportunities. A principle of limitation is also implicit: "Only where differences in talents and skills are the results of disease and disability, not merely normal variation, is some effort required to correct for the effects of the 'natural lottery.'"

Yet there are two emendations to this approach that would help it better serve my purposes. For one thing, moral and normative possibilities of what *ought* to count as "normal opportunity range" are left unaddressed. For another, the concept should be extended to encompass what I will call a normal "life-span opportunity range"—what opportunities is it reasonable for people to hope for over their lifetimes?—and we will need to know what *ought* to count as "normal" within that range also. For those purposes we will have to resist the implications of the modernizing view of old age, which would deliberately make it an unending frontier, constantly to be pushed back, subject to no fixed standards of "normal" at all. Otherwise the combination of that ideology and technological progress could make Daniels' idea of a normal opportunity range for the elderly as an age group and my concept of a life-span opportunity range for individuals intractable and useless as a standard for fair allocation among the generations. The aged, always at the edge of death, would inevitably have medical needs—if defined as the avoidance of decline and death—greater than other age groups. No other claims could ever trump theirs.

Those considerations underscore the urgency of devising an ideal of old age that offers serious resistance to an unlimited claim on resources in the name of medical need, and yet also aims to help everyone achieve a minimally adequate standard. For that purpose we require an understanding of a "normal opportunity range" that is not determined by the state-of-the-art of medicine and consequently by fluctuating values of what counts as a need. "Need" will have no fixed reference point at all apart from a technology-free (or nearly so) definition. Where Daniels uses the term "normal" in a statistical sense, it should instead be given a normative meaning; that is, what counts as morally and socially adequate and generally acceptable. That is the aim of my standard of a natural life span, one that I believe is morally defensible for policy purposes. Such a life can be achieved within a certain, roughly specifiable, number of years and can be relatively impervious to technological advances. The minimal purpose is to try to bring everyone up to this standard, leaving any decision to extend life beyond that point as a separate social choice (though one I think we should reject, available resources or not). Daniels recognizes that his strategy has the implication that it "would dictate giving greater emphasis to enhancing individual chances of reaching a normal lifespan than to extending the normal lifespan." But I think that that implication, to me highly desirable, really follows only if taken in conjunction with some theory of what *ought* to count as a "normal opportunity range" and not simply what happens to so count at any given historical and technological moment. The notion of a natural life span fills that gap.

With those general points as background, I offer these principles:

1. Government has a duty, based on our collective social obligations, to help people live out a natural life span, but not actively to help extend life medically beyond that point. By life-extending treatment, I will mean any medical intervention, technology, procedure, or medication whose ordinary effect is to forestall the moment of death, whether or not the treatment affects the underlying life-threatening disease or biological process.

2. Government is obliged to develop, employ, and pay for only that kind and degree of life-extending technology necessary for medicine to achieve and serve the

end of a natural life span; the question is not whether a technology is available that can save a life, but whether there is an obligation to use the technology.

3. Beyond the point of a natural life span, government should provide only the means necessary for the relief of suffering, not life-extending technology.

These principles both establish an upper age limit on life-extending care and yet recognize that great diversity can mark the needs of individuals to attain that limit or, beyond it, to attain relief of suffering.

QUESTIONS FOR ANALYSIS AND DISCUSSION

1. Callahan admits (in the preface of his book) that he is not sure how he will react when facing the conditions he describes. Do you think there is an inherent difficulty in some moral issues, such as treating the elderly, that make sense from a distance but not when you are directly involved? For example, it seems reasonable for governments to formulate guidelines about when to offer extreme medical care. But when it comes to our own grandparent or parent, the rationality of the guidelines no longer seems to matter. Is there any way to overcome this difficulty? Clarify your response.

2. Callahan is careful to highlight the value of the elderly insofar as they can and should contribute to the worth of everyday life. Indeed, he says there are some goods that only the elderly can contribute. What do you think these goods include? Consider the contributions elderly persons make in your everyday life. Are they substantive or trivial? Do they reflect some of the goods Callahan praises? If elderly persons are largely absent from your life now, how does it compare to a time when elderly persons were a significant part of your everyday life?

3. Look over the list of virtues that the elderly can embrace. Could you rank them in terms of importance? Can you develop a list of corresponding vices most tempting to the elderly? Briefly explain two or three.

4. Callahan reminds us that he is introducing his proposals for further discussion rather than as definite answers. Do you think his three guidelines for government are an adequate starting point? Callahan notes our duty to help people live out a "natural life span." Is that a useful notion? At a certain point in the elderly's decline, only the relief of suffering should be offered, suggests Callahan. Who, in your opinion, should tell the patient of this decision: (a) the family physician, (b) a spouse, (c) the first-mentioned heir in the patient's will, (d) an adult child or friend, (e) the patient's insurance representative, (f) the patient should know this intuitively and not need to be told, or (g) someone else. Briefly justify your answer.

76.

SUSAN M. PURVIANCE

Age Rationing, the Virtues, and Wanting More Life

Callahan addresses the virtues and old age but relies more on the idea of justice. According to Susan M. Purviance, a philosophy professor at the University of Toledo, Callahan's overall argument is unsuccessful in deciding how to set the limits for the elderly. As Purviance sees it, Callahan doesn't pay sufficient attention to who decides what is just in treating the elderly. It is this "who" that is the source of tension between the viewpoints of Callahan and Purviance. What counts as a virtuous person or a vicious deed changes as one gets older. In Purviance's view, the moral significance in old age has much to do with the virtues and the vices, but this significance has little to do with Callahan's proposals concerning social justice.

CRITICAL READING QUESTIONS
---

1. What does Purviance mean by calling Callahan's approach the "fair share argument"?
2. How does she distinguish inner justice from outer justice?
3. What is the difference between greed and gluttony in the context of Purviance's response to Callahan?
4. What age does Callahan suggest as a limit? What is Purviance's criticism?

Daniel Callahan offers an age-based criterion for the denial of life-extending health care to the elderly. Arguing that the attainment of a normal life span is a regulative principle of medical decision making, he holds that once the elderly have received this benefit, care aimed principally at extending life ought not to be afforded them. He offers what is in part an instrumental argument. Withholding life-extending procedures would conserve health resources and would allow more health care

---

"Age Rationing, the Virtues, and Wanting More Life," *Journal of Medical Humanities*, 1993, 14(3): 149–152, 156–163. Notes have been omitted.

resources to be made available to others who are at risk of not attaining their normal life span.

However, Callahan does not rely exclusively upon the instrumental value of age rationing. In his view, age rationing is a desirable principle of social order, to be applied regardless of the relative scarcity of health care resources. He believes that even if health resources were not at a premium we would have good reasons to reject a social policy of unqualified pursuit of life extension for the old.

> Although economic pressures have put the question of health care before the public eye, and constitute a serious issue, it is also part of my purpose to argue that, no less importantly, the meaning and significance of life for the elderly themselves is best founded on a sense of limits to health care. Even if we had unlimited resources, we would still be wise to establish boundaries.*

Setting Limits attempts to discover an ethical foundation for limits to life-extending medicine in a particular conception of social life. This paper is about the philosophical and ethical assumptions which underlie alternative views about the pursuit of social goods. In particular, it is designed to show that Callahan's reasons for withholding life-extending care cannot be made out exclusively in terms of contemporary notions of distributive justice and fair allocation. In fact, he relies upon a conception of justice which links the merit of the individual with the fairness of a social pattern of shares, and this means that the moral character of the age groups under consideration is taken to have relevance to the discussion of what society owes them. As a result, Callahan imputes vice to the elderly as he denies them eligibility for life-prolonging care. All this leads to the strange conclusion that, not only that it is bad for some professionals to attempt to extend the life span of older persons, but it is bad for those older persons to want more life.

Since the link between moral character and social desert is forged by the use of virtue—theoretic concepts to characterize age groups, analyzing the arguments in light of a generally Aristotelian framework of moral excellence, or virtue, and moral desert, or justice, will provide the most insight into his age-contextualized theory of the virtues. Specifically, Aristotelian reasoning links external justice, justice in social relations, and internal justice, justice in the soul. Out of this Aristotelian interpretation of Callahan's claims about the duties of the young and the old, and his consequent support of age rationing, emerges a new critical standpoint from which to assess his work on this issue. For what is at the heart of the matter is a claim about the proper disposition of elderly persons toward the good of continued life.

Understanding the virtue—theoretic underpinning of the work allows one to see that much of the attempt to link it to contemporary discussions of distributive justice serves only to obscure his paramount concern with the rehabilitation of virtue. Making that aspect of his project salient requires some careful work. In my

---

*Daniel Callahan, *Setting Limits*, Simon and Schuster, 1987 p. 116, hereafter abbreviated as SL. See also p. 137.

view *Setting Limits* brings virtue ethics into the discussion of age rationing, but in the wrong way. This paper offers an alternative analysis of the disposition to seek continued life, one which I believe is consistent with widely held views about individual autonomy and distributive justice. By contrast, one of the most crucial arguments in *Setting Limits,* the Fair Share Argument, is interwoven with the Aristotelian virtue concept of injustice as graspingness or overreaching (*pleonexia*). This concept, which naturally resides in a theory of good character and not in theory of distributive justice for contemporary societies, cannot be properly applied to the shares in question. The alternative ethics of good character which I offer employs Aristotelian insights about the virtues, but greatly restricts their applicability to the issue of rationing health care resources.

Just Order and Just Person: The Fair and the Equal

Setting Limits presupposes a connection between the virtue-theoretic concept of justice, or the just person, and the principle-theoretic concept of distributive justice, or justice in distribution, in the following way. It says that the institutions of social and political order in a community should be arranged so as to cultivate dispositions to just behavior in individuals, and, no less importantly, that those social institutions should ensure fairness when conferring benefits and imposing burdens. In a similar manner, Aristotle takes justice to be both a principle of order in the soul and a principle of social order. The principle of just order in the soul is the rational principle, *logos.* The principle of just order in the community is *dike,* justice proper.

It is essential to Callahan's project to establish that there is such a thing as proper disposition or attitude toward one's own continued existence, for among the benefits that health care confers is life extension. Arguments to this effect are absent from the text, yet he cites many customary Classical virtues of proper disposition with respect to one's physical and social condition: grace under adversity, moral courage, simplicity, benignity, hilarity or good humor, and vigor of spirit (SL 48-51). Not since Adam Smith's *The Theory of Moral Sentiments* has the thesis of virtue as propriety been so clearly advocated. But what makes these dispositions proper to the condition of the very old? In support of them he invokes neither the rational principle of the mean, nor the common moral sentiments of mankind. However, he does claim that the social structure should foster the conditions necessary for the attainment and exercise of moral virtue. Moral virtue is to be exercised throughout the life span, and by persons of each age group in relations with persons of other age groups.

Although Callahan neglects to include it on his list, the proper disposition toward the good of extended life must itself be identified as virtue, if his goal of reforming the culture of aging is to succeed. This virtue emerges out of the other virtues, and its possession facilitates just behavior towards others. The best way to see this is to examine the Aristotelian account of moral virtue.

. . .

Justice and Practical Wisdom in Health Care

There is not much point in calling for a reconstruction of the ends of aging, if the ends have already been chosen for us. From these ends, as much as from principles of justice, specific policy decisions have been derived. If it could be agreed upon that these are the distinctively human goods, and that this dual aspect view of justice is the correct view, then perhaps we would have to accept these constraints on an ethic of the ages of life, and the goods pertaining to each age. More reasons for rejecting each of these assumptions will be provided shortly, but first I would like to present some reservations about the interpretation of Aristotle on which it rests.

Even Aristotelian moral philosophy does not offer unequivocal support for Callahan's conclusions regarding life limitation. If an alternative conception of the social implications of Aristotelian virtues and practical wisdom for the question of forgoing life-extending care can be provided, Callahan's argument loses some of its theoretical coherence and much of its communitarian appeal. But even for those communitarian theories which seek a return to the synthesis of virtue and justice, there is evidence sufficient to raise serious doubts about Callahan's understanding of the condition of complete virtue known as practical wisdom.

. . .

By shifting the focus of the concept of function to that of the distinct activity of each age of life, he undermines the moral status of individuals as rational agents. As a result, even though each member of each age group is similarly undermined in her rational agency by being assigned an age of life function, the elderly are most disadvantaged. They have the most to lose, because it is their supposed unwillingness to live in accordance with their assigned task of forgoing treatment which is especially disruptive of the social order.

Where Aristotle distinguishes the characteristic, species function of the human being from the social function of groups of persons, Callahan reduces the function of the elderly to their social function. Although *ergon* may be used to refer to the work of any animate creature or artifact, Aristotle explicitly distinguishes the human function from the specific functions persons may serve in the social order:

> Have the carpenter, then, and the tanner certain functions or activities, and has man none? Is he born without a function?

Carpenters and tanners perform their function by means of the characteristically human function. Without that most fundamental functioning of the human being, reasoning, no other specific social or occupational role could be performed in any complex society. Human beings have "an active life of the element that has a rational principle (*logos*)," and it is in virtue of this capacity that they achieve distinctively human goods. Even inferior persons—children, slaves, women—are capable of voluntary actions in pursuit of some goods. Aristotle does not make the fulfillment of role-related duties the whole end of life and measure of desert in an unqualified way. The end of life is *eudaimonia*.

Callahan has gone wrong, but where? The error consists in making the virtues depend *entirely* upon the ages of life. The argument for health care rationing builds rather alarmingly from this point. Once fulfillment of life cycle functions is taken to be the whole end of those lives, then those lives are accorded value only in relation to that less than distinctively human end. Hence the prolongation of those lives can be given differential weight according to that group's need for continued life to complete their social work.

> Those in the process of aging, or already aged, should ask of medicine not a longer life, but help in maintaining a life that can complete its work as close to the time of death as possible (SL, 77).

A priority is placed upon completing a normal life span *as a social good*. Aristotle's notion of the human function need not make social work basic, even if Aristotle himself assigns certain age and gender groups an inferior status.

Setting Limits has failed to keep the distinction between what pertains to us as humans and what pertains to us as social beings. As social beings, and as members of distinct age groups, individuals must harmonize the pursuit of their ends. But human rational nature is the capacity to choose and pursue ends. Since having a life with a certain meaning, shape, and length is part of what we want for ourselves, whatever else we might want, we ought to consider how different sorts of character ethics can lead to different assessments of the moral worth of choosing continued life in old age.

Greed, Fair Shares, and Gluttony: Wanting More Life

It was claimed that if the elderly can fulfill their social function without a guarantee of access to life-extending care, it is permissible to deny that care. Life span opportunities can be enhanced or diminished by the distribution of health care, and policies can be devised to maximally ensure equal life span opportunity. The elderly have achieved normal life span, while other groups have yet to achieve it. Given the previous assumptions and these premises it appears that the elderly would have received a fair share of life under such policies, and so are not entitled to the benefit of life extension. In this way the principle of equal desert was used to determine that some care, however personally beneficial, may be withheld from the elderly.

But what of those elderly who continue to claim a greater share of life for themselves, demanding life prolongation? What can be said of their character, as well as of their claim? Callahan evaluates both, and he avails himself of virtue-based reasoning again. As was said earlier, he cannot help but impute vice to the elderly once his argument makes them ineligible for life-extending care, for it is a vice to seek more than one's fair share.

The fair share argument depends upon understanding which vice is in question, as well as upon a coherent notion of fair shares of life-extending care (SL, 140). Wanting more than one's fair share is greed. Persons displaying the character defect are called greedy or grasping. Aristotle's term for this is *pleonexia*, and the trait connects with injustice in the special sense. As he notes in the *Nicomachean*

Ethics, almost any vicious disposition may lead one to unlawful acts, causing injustice in the general sense; only *pleonexia* necessarily leads one to violate the principle of equity.

The vice of greed brings together arguments about principles of just social choice and principles of moral virtue. It links lack of virtue in the citizenry with injustice in the State. Greed, the passion which disposes one to deal unfairly with others and to grasp for more than one's rightful share, is necessarily related to acts of injustice. In order to see why one should not endorse the link, one must first question the nature of greed, and then its application to the dispositions of the elderly with respect to the good of continued life. Just exactly what is the relationship between justice and greed in the health care context? Is it greedy to claim for oneself, for one's own sake, more than one's fair share of anything? Yes, by definition. But definitions are uninteresting. Is it greedy to desire to attain more than a normal life span?

The argument in favor of that claim might proceed in this way. Since the elderly attained that life span partly at least by means of health care, and since others younger than they also have a need to attain a normal life span, they are being greedy when they insist upon life-extending care, because they have already received their fair share of life-extending care. For the good of all, this passion must be held in check, at least under conditions of scarcity of health care resources.

Unfortunately, all the interesting reasoning in the fair share argument for age rationing turns upon the definition of greed itself: claiming more than one's fair share. But the meaning of "greed," a concept of character ethics, cannot establish a criterion for determining one's fair share, the work of principles of social justice. Greed is simply the disposition to take more than one's fair share. Fair share must be established independently, perhaps through the examination of effects on others of claims on scarce resources, and Callahan's normative life span opportunity principle does this. The appeal to the notion of culturally sanctioned greed on the part of the elderly is thus superfluous.

Virtue Ethics and the Elderly: An Alternative View

Another understanding of the desire for continued life is possible. Vices are character traits, dispositions to respond in certain ways. The desire for more life disposes one to act in certain ways under certain conditions, and those dispositions are the states of character at issue. The definition of the vice greed can make reference to fair share. Yet the desire for more life cannot be morally evaluated in the abstract. It is not inherently greedy to desire to continue to live. Nor can the mere fact that the desire for more life is the desire for more help us to decide that the act it leads to is one of greed. Having a desire to live longer, one does possess a motive for seeking life-extending care. But the mere possession of a motive does not make one vicious. Instead, following Aristotle, I would say that the strength of the desire may make acting on the desire a vice, and the disposition of the desire toward inappropriate objects may make acting on it vicious.

One cannot determine whether to impute vice to a person until we know what they desire, and whether the desire is misdirected or excessive or deficient. The desire for life extension is not comparative in nature. It is not a desire for a quantity or length of life greater than others. Taking action to obtain what is desired, life-extending care, may have as a consequence a shorter life for others. However, a variety of defeating conditions must be employed when determining whether virtues or vices can be imputed to agents. The consequences for others may not be foreseeable; nor would their being foreseen make them intended. There is no reason to think that the agent's acting on the desire or insisting that others act on it allows one to infer that he intends a shorter life for another.

Perhaps then the desire of the elderly for life-extending care is misdirected or out of proportion. As regards temperance, Aristotle says ". . . the temperate man craves for the things he ought, as he ought, and when he ought. . . ." One might argue that it is misdirected when the anticipated quality of life is so poor as to not be worth having. Either a subjective standard or an objective standard of the quality of life might be used to determine this.

Certainly the desire to live longer at all costs might move us to make bad choices, leading us to degrade and dishonor ourselves and our families. Seeking continued life under conditions of dishonor—moral degradation, enslavement—would appear vicious, shameful, to Aristotle's audience, perhaps to us as well. If a human enemy can offer [any] temptation to degrade oneself in exchange for life, then medicine in a society which offers life-prolonging treatments to the ill elderly might offer similar opportunities.

Even if this reasoning persuades, the vice displayed is not greed, but servility. The person caves in to the power of others, rather than arrogating excessive power and goods to herself. Her wanting more life is inappropriate because intemperate and excessive. But this is not the excess of *pleonexia*.

A dishonorable *intemperance* with respect to the good of continued life could be made out. But this would not apply to all situations where life-extending care is to be withheld. Honorable and comfortable old age, lived out in a loving and respectful family circle is an inherently good condition, the very description of *eudaimonia*. Priam's life is ruined, not by living long, but by living long enough to suffer the ruin of his family and his people.

It is time to give character ethics its due. Character ethics can offer subtle and complex account of how many important virtues and vices pertain to the phenomenon of aging and dying. In my view, Aristotle's doctrine of the mean has a role to play in the account of dispositions to feel and act as one should. Let a desire for something which is in excess of or falls short of the mean be called a vice. The mean with respect to the desire would be determined by a rational principle by which a person of practical wisdom would govern her choices. Now consider the desire for life-prolonging care on the part of a very old person, a person who in Western industrialized nations would be over the age of 85. Callahan suggests that renewing the thirst for life in such a person is inherently bad, because it is desire without a terminus:

> The possibility of and the desire for the unfolding of new experiences in old age logically mean that death at no point could ever be acceptable; there would *always* be further possibilities.

This is a strange argument. It tries to derive a social policy of not renewing the desire for continued life in old people from an examination of the nature of the desire itself. The previous arguments should show why this abuses character ethics. Social policy should not be derived from the virtues in this way. That does not mean that the virtues have no role to play in evaluating the moral worth of an individual's conduct. If the vice one has in mind is self-indulgence, one could say that there is, or should be, a mean for the disposition to seek new experiences. In that respect, judged according to their character, some old people might be gluttons for life, lacking in self-control.

Who is to say, after all, that my desire to have new experiences, to continue to form relationships with others, and to continue to work and think new thoughts is inappropriate? Aristotle himself holds that sensation and perception is in itself normal and a pleasure to any sentient, percipient being. Many have found this argument objectionable, but it is not in itself an abuse of character ethics.

Theories of the psyche aside, if there is to be such discerning of the mean, who will discern it? This much is clear. Discernment cannot be restricted to the members of any one age group, and younger adults should not make it their business to discern the mean for the elderly. The standard of virtue resides in those qualified to judge, and not in those who have an interest in rigging the mean to their own advantage. Some might say that the elderly themselves would rig the mean to their own advantage, but I believe that the vast majority of elderly people have clearly demonstrated their practical wisdom. Rather than fighting for medical assistance in staving off death, many are striving to obtain a right to refuse life-extending care. Having a right does not settle the question of whether a particular person's decision to seek care or refuse care is a good one, or settle the question of her character. But the effort to obtain this right does not simply suggest an abstract concern with liberty at the expense of social obligations. Rather, as seen from their own life span perspective many elderly judge some forms of life-extending care to offer at best marginal benefit.

Aristotle's doctrine of the mean is a useful tool for character evaluation. One can speak meaningfully of a proper disposition of a person of a certain type (an elderly person) with respect to the good of continued life. I would say that the mean of one's disposition with respect to the good of continued life would be relative to one's age, and would be determined by that principle by which an elderly person of practical wisdom would determine it.

Finally, what needs to be contextualized is the determination of the person of practical wisdom with respect to that good—in this case, the elderly person. Not all elderly people have practical wisdom about the goods that pertain especially to them, but for the most part elderly people are in the best position to exercise practical wisdom with respect to the good of continued life.

This does not mean that there do not exist situations which justify rationing. No one has the right to have their lives continued at the expense of others without regard to the burden it places on others in the community. But in such situations the ethics of good character principally concerns the way in which a person acquiesces and bears his fate. Social roles have little to do with excellence in this. Greed or being grasping, Aristotle's *pleonexia,* deprives others of what is rightfully theirs. It is no part of gluttony that it so deprive others. One cannot be grasping, and therefore unjust, unless those things which one would take from others are their rightful share. Unfortunately, with health care as with other goods, it is difficult to tell gluttony from greed solely on the basis of their consequences. One's rightful share is just what is at issue in distributive justice.

The virtue with respect to the good of continued life is a complex one, involving temperance and honor. It is part of the complete virtue of the person, but it is not in itself the virtue of justice. Like justice, however, and in restricted context of the last stage of life, it may seem to yield a dominant principle for regulating one's conduct.

This analysis throughout has resisted the tendency to collapse virtue theoretic structures (virtue and vice as dispositions of the soul) into principle theoretic structures (principles of just social order). Callahan's attempt to develop a critique of health care demands from the point of view of the age-related virtues falters on this point. A standard of virtue cannot be used, either alone or in combination with standard principles of distributive justice, to identify demands for care which need not be met. The moral desert of persons cannot be indexed to the social value of the age groups. In contemporary life justice and injustice have become virtues of societies, not of persons. Health care policy should not corrupt people's virtue, but it should not make virtue the standard of merit.

QUESTIONS FOR ANALYSIS AND DISCUSSION

1. Why does Purviance think that as we age the moral emphasis shifts from outer to inner justice? Observing the elderly in your life, do you agree or disagree with this view? Why?

2. Aristotle's notion of *pleonexia* is central to the latter part of the essay. As you understand Purviance's discussion, do you think it is wrong to be too greedy or too gluttonous about wanting to live as long as possible, no matter the consequences or unfairness of it relative to anyone else?

3. Part of the criticism of Callahan's proposal lies in his shift from virtues of persons to justice in society. As Purviance concludes, "Health care policy should not corrupt people's virtue, but it should not make virtue the standard of merit." Does Purviance offer a preferable alternative to Callahan in developing a moral perspective on our relation with the elderly? Does she clarify a more plausible framework for dealing with the moral dilemmas that pertain to old age? Explain your response.

77.

TIMOTHY QUILL

A Case for Assisted Suicide

Some of the most sensational media news stories during the last decade have involved assisted suicide. To some extent, these news stories have become media spectaculars. This kind of attention has had the inadvertent effect of allowing us to overlook the real-life drama and emotional experience that arises for a doctor when helping someone with suicide. Timothy Quill, a medical doctor in Rochester, New York, discusses his role as physician of a patient named Diane. Quill reflects on the drama and moral intensity pervading the experience of contributing to another's suicide.

┤ CRITICAL READING QUESTIONS ├

1. What were Diane's chances for survival? What were the risks?
2. Which society did Quill recommend for Diane? Why?
3. What is the importance of Lake Geneva in Quill's reflections?
4. What is written as the cause of death on Diane's death certificate? Why?

A Case of Individualized Decision Making

Diane was feeling tired and had a rash. A common scenario, though there was something subliminally worrisome that prompted me to check her blood count. Her hematocrit was 22, and the white-cell count was 4.3 with some metamyelocytes and unusual white cells. I wanted it to be viral, trying to deny what was staring me in the face. Perhaps in a repeated count it would disappear. I called Diane and told her it might be more serious than I had initially thought—that the test needed to be repeated and that if she felt worse, we might have to move quickly. When she pressed for the possibilities, I reluctantly opened the door to leukemia. Hearing the word seemed to make it exist. "Oh, shit!" she said. "Don't tell me that." Oh, shit! I thought, I wish I didn't have to.

Diane was no ordinary person (although no one I have ever come to know has been really ordinary). She was raised in an alcoholic family and had felt alone for

---

"A Case for Assisted Suicide," *New England Journal of Medicine*, March 7, 1991, 324(10): 691–694.

much of her life. She had vaginal cancer as a young woman. Through much of her adult life, she had struggled with depression and her own alcoholism. I had come to know, respect, and admire her over the previous eight years as she confronted these problems and gradually overcame them. She was an incredibly clear, at times brutally honest, thinker and communicator. As she took control of her life, she developed a strong sense of independence and confidence. In the previous 3½ years, her hard work had paid off. She was completely abstinent from alcohol, she had established much deeper connections with her husband, college-age son, and several friends, and her business and her artistic work were blossoming. She felt she was really living fully for the first time.

Not surprisingly, the repeated blood count was abnormal, and detailed examination of the peripheral-blood smear showed myelocytes. I advised her to come into the hospital, explaining that we needed to do a bone marrow biopsy and make some decisions relatively rapidly. She came to the hospital knowing what we would find. She was terrified, angry, and sad. Although we knew the odds, we both clung to the thread of possibility that it might be something else.

The bone marrow confirmed the worst: acute myelomonocytic leukemia. In the face of this tragedy, we looked for signs of hope. This is an area of medicine in which technological intervention has been successful, with cures 25 percent of the time—long-term cures. As I probed the costs of these cures, I heard about induction chemotherapy (three weeks in the hospital, prolonged neutropenia, probable infectious complications, and hair loss; 75 percent of patients respond, 25 percent do not). For the survivors, this is followed by consolidation chemotherapy (with similar side effects; another 25 percent die, for a net survival of 50 percent). Those still alive, to have a reasonable chance of long-term survival, then need bone marrow transplantation (hospitalization for two months and whole-body irradiation, with complete killing of the bone marrow, infectious complications, and the possibility for graft-versus-host disease—with a survival of approximately 50 percent, or 25 percent of the original group). Though hematologists may argue over the exact percentages, they don't argue about the outcome of no treatment—certain death in days, weeks, or at most a few months.

Believing that delay was dangerous, our oncologist broke the news to Diane and began making plans to insert a Hickman catheter and begin induction chemotherapy that afternoon. When I saw her shortly thereafter, she was enraged at his presumption that she would want treatment, and devastated by the finality of the diagnosis. All she wanted to do was go home and be with her family. She had no further questions about treatment and in fact had decided that she wanted none. Together we lamented her tragedy and the unfairness of life. Before she left, I felt the need to be sure that she and her husband understood that there was some risk in delay, that the problem was not going to go away, and that we needed to keep considering the options over the next several days. We agreed to meet in two days.

She returned in two days with her husband and son. They had talked extensively about the problem and the options. She remained very clear about her wish not to undergo chemotherapy and to live whatever time she had left outside the hospital. As we explored her thinking further, it became clear that she was convinced she would die during the period of treatment and would suffer unspeakably in the process (from hospitalization, from lack of control over her body, from the side effects of chemotherapy, and from pain and anguish). Although I could offer support and my best effort to minimize her suffering if she chose treatment, there was no way I could say any of this would not occur. In fact, the last four patients with acute leukemia at our hospital had died very painful deaths in the hospital during various stages of treatment (a fact I did not share with her). Her family wished she would choose treatment but sadly accepted her decision. She articulated very clearly that it was she who would be experiencing all the side effects of treatment and that odds of 25 percent were not good enough for her to undergo so toxic a course of therapy, given her expectations of chemotherapy and hospitalization and the absence of a closely matched bone marrow donor. I had her repeat her understanding of the treatment, the odds, and what to expect if there were no treatment. I clarified a few misunderstandings, but she had a remarkable grasp of the options and implications.

I have been a longtime advocate of active, informed patient choice of treatment or nontreatment, and of a patient's right to die with as much control and dignity as possible. Yet there was something about her giving up a 25 percent chance of long-term survival in favor of almost certain death that disturbed me. I had seen Diane fight and use her considerable inner resources to overcome alcoholism and depression, and I half expected her to change her mind over the next week. Since the window of time in which effective treatment can be initiated is rather narrow, we met several times that week. We obtained a second hematology consultation and talked at length about the meaning and implications of treatment and nontreatment. She talked to a psychologist she had seen in the past. I gradually understood the decision from her perspective and became convinced that it was the right decision for her. We arranged for home hospice care (although at that time Diane felt reasonably well, was active, and looked healthy), left the door open for her to change her mind, and tried to anticipate how to keep her comfortable in the time she had left.

Just as I was adjusting to her decision, she opened up another area that would stretch me profoundly. It was extraordinarily important to Diane to maintain control of herself and her own dignity during the time remaining to her. When this was no longer possible, she clearly wanted to die. As a former director of a hospice program, I know how to use pain medicines to keep patients comfortable and lessen suffering. I explained the philosophy of comfort care, which I strongly believe in. Although Diane understood and appreciated this, she had known of people lingering in what was called relative comfort, and she wanted no part of it. When the time came, she wanted to take her life in the least painful way possible. Knowing of her desire for independence and her decision to stay in control, I thought this request made perfect sense. I acknowledged and explored this wish but also thought that it was out of the realm of currently accepted medical practice and that it was more than I could offer or promise. In our discussion, it became clear that preoccupation with her fear of a lingering death would interfere with Diane's getting the most out of the time she had left until she found a safe way to ensure her death. I feared the effects of a violent death on her family, the consequences of an ineffective suicide that would leave her lingering in precisely the state she dreaded so much, and the possibility that a family member would be forced to assist her, with all the legal and personal repercussions that would follow. She discussed this at length with her family. They believed that they should respect her choice. With this in mind, I told Diane that information was available from the Hemlock Society that might be helpful to her.

A week later she phoned me with a request for barbiturates for sleep. Since I knew that this was an essential ingredient in a Hemlock Society suicide, I asked her to come to the office to talk things over. She was more than willing to protect me by participating in a superficial conversation about her insomnia, but it was important to me to know how she planned to use the drugs and to be sure that she was not in despair or overwhelmed in a way that might color her judgment. In our discussion, it was apparent that she was having trouble sleeping, but it was also evident that the security of having enough barbiturates available to commit suicide when and if the time came would leave her secure enough to live fully and concentrate on the present. It was clear that she was not despondent and that in fact she was making deep, personal connections with her family and close friends. I made sure that she knew how to use the barbiturates for sleep, and also that she knew the amount needed to commit suicide. We agreed to meet regularly, and she promised to meet with me before taking her life, to ensure that all other avenues had been exhausted. I wrote the prescription with an uneasy feeling about the boundaries I was exploring—spiritual, legal, professional, and personal. Yet I also felt strongly that I was setting her free to get the most out of the time she had left, and to maintain dignity and control on her own terms until her death.

The next several months were very intense and important for Diane. Her son stayed home from college, and they were able to be with one another and say much that had not been said earlier. Her husband did his work at home so that he and Diane could spend more time together. She spent time with her closest friends. I had her come into the hospital for a conference with our residents, at which she illustrated in a most profound and personal way the importance of informed decision making, the right to refuse treatment, and the extraordinarily personal effects of illness and interaction with the medical system. There were emotional and physical hardships as well. She had periods of intense sadness and anger. Several times she became very weak, but she received transfusions as an outpatient and responded with marked improvement of symptoms. She had two serious infections that responded surprisingly well to empirical courses of oral antibiotics. After three tumultuous months, there were two weeks of relative calm and well-being, and fantasies of a miracle began to surface.

Unfortunately, we had no miracle. Bone pain, weakness, fatigue, and fevers began to dominate her life. Although the hospice workers, family members, and I tried our best to minimize the suffering and promote comfort, it was clear that the end was approaching. Diane's immediate future held what she feared the most—increasing discomfort, dependence, and hard choices between pain and sedation. She called up her closest friends and asked them to come over to say goodbye, telling them that she would be leaving soon. As we had agreed, she let me know as well. When we met, it was clear that she knew what she was doing, that she was sad and frightened to be leaving, but that she would be even more terrified to stay and suffer. In our tearful goodbye, she promised a reunion in the future at her favorite spot on the edge of Lake Geneva, with dragons swimming in the sunset.

Two days later her husband called to say that Diane had died. She had said her final goodbyes to her husband and son that morning, and asked them to leave her alone for an hour. After an hour, which must have seemed an eternity, they found her on the couch, lying very still and covered by her favorite shawl. There was no sign of struggle. She seemed to be at peace. They called me for advice about how to proceed. When I arrived at their house, Diane indeed seemed peaceful. Her husband and son were quiet. We talked about what a remarkable person she had been. They seemed to have no doubts about the course she had chosen or about their cooperation, although the unfairness of her illness and the finality of her death were overwhelming to us all.

I called the medical examiner to inform him that a hospice patient had died. When asked about the cause of death, I said, "acute leukemia." He said that was fine and that we should call a funeral director. Although acute leukemia was the truth, it was not the whole story. Yet any mention of suicide would have given rise to a police investigation and probably brought the arrival of an ambulance crew for resuscitation. Diane would have become a "coroner's case," and the decision to perform an autopsy would have been made at the discretion of the medical examiner. The family or I could have been subject to criminal prosecution, and I to professional review, for our roles in support of Diane's choices. Although I truly believe that the family and I gave her the best care possible, allowing her to define her limits and directions as much as possible, I am not sure the law, society, or the medical profession would agree. So I said "acute leukemia" to protect all of us, to protect Diane from an invasion into her past and her body, and to continue to shield society from the knowledge of the degree of suffering that people often undergo in the process of dying. Suffering can be lessened to some extent, but in no way eliminated or made benign, by the careful intervention of a competent, caring physician, given current social constraints.

Diane taught me about the range of help I can provide if I know people well and if I allow them to say what they really want. She taught me about life, death, and honesty and about taking charge and facing tragedy squarely when it strikes. She taught me that I can take small risks for people that I really know and care about. Although I did not assist in her suicide directly, I helped indirectly to make it possible, successful, and relatively painless. Although I know we have measures to help control pain and lessen suffering, to think that people do not suffer in the process of dying is an illusion. Prolonged dying can occasionally be peaceful, but more often the role of the physician and family is limited to lessening but not eliminating severe suffering.

I wonder how many families and physicians secretly help patients over the edge into death in the face of such severe suffering. I wonder how many severely ill or dying patients secretly take their lives, dying alone in despair. I wonder whether the image of Diane's final aloneness will persist in the minds of her family, or if they will remember more the intense, meaningful months they had together before she died. I wonder whether Diane struggled in that last hour, and whether the Hemlock Society's way of death by suicide is the most benign. I wonder why Diane, who gave so much to so many of us, had to be alone for the last hour of her life. I wonder whether I will see Diane again, on the shore of Lake Geneva at sunset, with dragons swimming on the horizon.

QUESTIONS FOR ANALYSIS AND DISCUSSION

1. From Quill's brief account we learn that Diane had troubles with alcoholism, vaginal cancer, and depression. At which point do you think Diane, or Quill, felt Diane's life had become too burdensome? Do you think this point primarily involves a physiological, medical, emotional, mental, spiritual, or some other perspective? At what point do you think life is too burdensome?

2. Quill often mentions dignity. What do you think this term means? Do you think it is too vague or subjective to be useful in deciding dilemmas such as assisted suicide? Given that dying nearly always involves some suffering, is dying with dignity the least negative way to die? Clarify your thoughts.

3. When the *New England Journal of Medicine* printed some of the responses to Dr. Quill's essay, several letters to the editor took opposing views. One professor called Quill courageous, wishing he would have been available when his own mother died. Another doctor accused Quill of withholding sufficient care by allowing a woman with one in four odds to die. Some letters praised Quill for his professional caring and un-Kevorkian-like conscientiousness; others questioned Quill's deception in omitting assisted suicide as a cause of death and his tolerance of doctors who break the law by assisting a suicide. Which point of view best reflects your thoughts on assisted suicide? If you think it is morally permissible, should anyone be allowed to practice it or only physicians? On what basis do you justify your decision? If you think it is wrong, is your reasoning based on the evil of suicide or the immorality of helping someone commit suicide? Clarify your reasons.

78.

JAMES BOGEN

Suicide and Virtue

For many people, whether assisted or unassisted, suicide is largely a matter of individual rights. Who are we to say whether someone should continue to live? Indeed, those who defend abortion on the basis of controlling one's body are probably consistent in morally permitting suicide for similar control. In any case, it seems pointless to formulate moral

---

"Suicide and Virtue," from *Suicide: The Philosophical Issues*, edited by Margaret Battin and David Mayo (New York: St. Martin's Press, 1980). Some notes have been omitted.

prohibitions against suicide. Unlike every other deed of illegal or sinful proportions, sui-cide cannot be punished, at least not by contemporary standards. (In earlier times a sui-cide could be subject to shameful disposal of the body, survivors could be denied insurance claims, or a suicide victim could be sent to Hell.)

Is suicide essentially an individual matter? According to James Bogen, if we consider the morality of suicide from the perspective of virtue ethics, it is difficult to conclude that the answer is yes. Ethical perspectives that rely on rights, social utility, or duties tend to simplify the nature of suicide. As Bogen puts it, though, the right to commit suicide does not translate into it being morally good. To develop his case Bogen outlines three scenarios in which one is confronted with the possibility of suicide.

CRITICAL READING QUESTIONS

1. Why can suicide be interpreted as a cowardly deed?
2. How could suicide be viewed as an altruistic act of charity?
3. For Bogen, which theory is preferable to a moral theory of rights or duties? Which philosophers are the best models for this theory?

Most contemporary philosophical discussion of the moral issues involved in sui-cide and suicide intervention presume that the crucial questions boil down to ques-tions of rights and obligation: does one have the right to end one's own life, or does one have an obligation to refrain from doing so, and what ought third parties do to honor these rights and obligations? However, it is generally acknowledged among philosophers that no one has given a convincing argument to show that there is an obligation against suicide, at least when the suicide has no obligations to others whose fulfillment would be ruled out.

This makes it appear that if someone has a right to take his own life (because he has neither an obligation nor a duty not to), there should be no serious moral reasons not to do so, and this, I think, has been the prevalent view among philos-ophers at least since Kant.[1] I want to argue in this paper that this is incorrect, and that an adequate treatment of the morality of suicide must deal with questions which cannot be illuminated by a consideration of rights, obligations, and duties. I shall not attempt any answer to these questions, but if I am right to think they are both important and neglected, it should be worthwhile just to draw atten-tion to them and show how they differ from the questions about obligations, du-

---

[1] Kant is an excellent example of the view I oppose: that all moral issues concerning suicide (and ev-erything else, as a matter of fact) are questions of duty. His famous attempt to show for a special and limited class of cases that suicide violates duty can be found in Immanuel Kant, *Groundwork of the Metaphysics of Morals*, ed. and trans. H. J. Paton (New York: Harper Torchbooks, 1956), p. 89.

ties, and responsibilities, which are (wrongly, I think) so heavily emphasized by philosophers.

I will assume in what follows that there are no such duties or obligations against suicide *per se,* and therefore that a man does have a right to commit suicide in cases where this would not lead to the violation of other duties and obligations (e.g., to friends and family) which he has no excuse for violating. Perhaps this assumption is more controversial than I take it to be, but that will not affect the argument of this paper. What I want to show is that *if* (as I take to be the case) a man does have a right to take his own life, grave moral questions which typically confront potential suicides and interventionists remain. Here are some hypothetical cases intended to show how little is settled by the view that a man has a right to, and no duty or obligation not to, take his own life.

Case 1: Jones suffers from Huntington's chorea and is convinced that in its progression the disease will become intolerable to him, that it is incurable, and that eventually it will make him a burden to everyone he knows, incapable of discharging any duties or obligations he might have. But he also believes that one ought not to be a coward and fears that his suicide would be a cowardly act.[2] To tell Jones he has a right (has no duty or obligation not) to commit suicide will do nothing to settle the moral issue of cowardice. That is because in cases in which a cowardly act does not violate a duty or obligation, we have a right to do what is cowardly even though cowardice is morally reprehensible. Thus a policeman has no right to refuse out of cowardice to pursue criminals, but that is because he has a duty to pursue criminals, not because he has no right to be a coward. Where a cowardly act does not involve the neglect of such duties, one has a right to do it, but all this means is that no one can justify moral criticism of the agent, punishment, or intervention intended to prevent or discourage the cowardly behavior *on the grounds that he has no right to it.* Nor can one justify the kind of coercive interference which may be appropriately directed against someone who is about to do what he has no right to do. It does not follow from a man's right to cowardice that there should be no intervention of any kind or that the coward's behavior is morally acceptable and not to be criticized, or that a man *should* do what is cowardly. The point is that what is wrong with cowardice is not that it violates duty or obligation,

---

[2] At this point I face a serious vocabulary problem of a kind which is endemic and, for all I know, peculiar, to philosophy. In ordinary, nonphilosophical talk, we say we ought to do some things because they are required by duty and others because they would be good things to do, because they are means toward good ends, and for many other reasons. "Ought" is also used in nonmoral contexts, as in the advice, "Try this crowbar; it ought to be strong enough to move that rock." Part of the business of philosophers is to give accounts of ordinary concepts like these. Had I written this paper a long time ago, readers would have assumed (wrongly) that *all* moral "shoulds" and "oughts" have to do with what is good or conducive to the good. Today most moral and political philosophers assume (wrongly) that one ought to or should do something only if it is obligatory or required by duty. Thus many readers may object that I cannot say both that Jones (either one) ought (not) or should (not) take his life and also that this is not a question of duties and obligations. This objection begs the question. What I am trying to show in these examples is that there are cases in which it is quite natural for nonphilosophers to ask what they should or ought to do, but where their questions are not questions about duty, obligation, or rights.

or that one has no right to it. Jones and those affected by his decision must decide whether his suicide would be inexcusably cowardly; but no amount of knowledge about his rights, duties, and obligations will shed any light on this question.

Case 2:   Another Jones has good reason to think that taking his own life would harm no one and would be of great benefit to a number of people. If he believes he has a right to commit suicide, it would be perfectly consistent for him to ask if he (morally) *should* take his own life. He might so decide on the grounds that suicide would be a generous, charitable, or kindly act. But having a right to commit suicide (as Jones II believes he does) neither entails nor implies that he should do it. Jones II must ask whether in fact his suicide would be an act of sufficient kindness or charity to merit the sacrifice. It might be misguided (as when one donates money to an unworthy cause). In the long run the benefits to others might not merit the sacrifice. Alternatively, even if the act would be the sort of thing a genuinely charitable person would do, Jones II's real motive might not be the good his suicide would do for others, but, for example, an unworthy desire for posthumous gratitude. Such questions are by no means settled by the assumption that Jones II has a right to take his own life.

Case 3:   A third Jones who is a friend of Jones I and Jones II must decide what to do about their contemplation of suicide. Should he try to talk them out of it? If so, how much can he do without becoming a meddler, and how little without falling short of being a true friend? Should he approach them or wait for them to come to him? Would any kind of restraint be justifiable? Should he help them in any way if he finds their decisions are irrevocable? And so on and so on. It seems to me that these are the sorts of questions which face people who find themselves in the role of potential suicide interventionists. And all of them can be asked by someone who believes Jones I and Jones II have a right to take their own lives. Once again, I think these are serious moral issues which are quite distinct from the question of rights, obligations, and the like.

Let us see, then, how the questions raised in the hypothetical cases differ from questions about rights, duties, and obligations.

The crucial distinction between them has to do with the fact that the various Joneses are concerned over whether certain conduct would be worthwhile and good, and whether alternative courses of action would be bad or unworthy. In contrast, rights, obligations, and duties tend in general to preclude such questions. If I violate a duty or obligation (e.g., I do not perform the services I am under contract to perform, I fail to do what I promised, I do not pay my debts, etc.) it is no excuse that what I did was good or for the good. This is seen clearly in the case of promises and the obligations they generate. In asking you to promise to do a certain thing, I want you to commit yourself to do it. A reason for extracting a promise is that I do *not* want you to decide later what to do on the basis of what is best or most worthwhile. It is to be expected that you will settle such questions before promising, and that once you have promised, all things being equal, you will not raise them in deciding whether to perform. This is one of the senses in which promises are said to be binding: they preclude certain considerations on the basis of which your decisions would otherwise be made. But the same sort of point

holds in general for obligations and duties. The performance of a duty or obligation is not morally required as a means toward some good end. If it were, nonper-
formance would be excusable on the grounds that it accomplishes more good than
performance. Instead, it is simply required; *ceteris paribus,* considerations of what
is best are not relevant to the question whether the obligation or duty should be
performed. A related point holds for rights. If someone has a right to do something, it does not follow either that it is a good or worthwhile thing to do, or that
its being good is a reason for honoring his right. Thus the right to free speech is,
subject to certain very special limitations (e.g., the familiar limitation which precludes yelling "fire" in a crowded room), the right to say things even if they are so
vicious and stupid that the saying of them will be bad for the speaker and those
who hear him. Similarly, to say that Jones has a right to take his own life is to say
nothing about whether he should (whether it would be good or bad for him to do
so) or whether noncoercive intervention (e.g., trying to talk him out of it) would
be morally commendable or not.

But now consider the questions faced by the potential suicide and the potential
interventionist. Jones I's question is whether it is better to face (and whether he
would be a better person if he faced) the dismal life that lies ahead for him as
courageously as possible than to avoid it. Jones II asks whether it is better (and
whether he would be a better person for doing it) to live on without making a
sacrifice of great generosity than to make that sacrifice. Their friend asks whether
a virtuous man would intervene (and if so, how) and, perhaps, whether it would
be an act of friendship or kindness to help Jones take his life or settle his affairs if
the intervention fails. These are not questions about what is obligatory or what is
called for by duty.[3] They are questions about what is the best way to live and to
end one's life, about what it is to be a good person, and about which sorts of
circumstances and happenings should be welcomed, which should be tolerated and
not avoided, and which should be feared as so genuinely bad that they should be
avoided. And they are questions about what sorts of conduct are constitutive of or
conducive to a good life and/or death. That is to say that they are precisely the
kinds of questions which do not arise in connection with a theory of duty, rights,
and obligations. They are the questions raised by Plato, Aristotle, the Stoics, and
other ancient Greek philosophers, who had what is to us surprisingly little to say
about obligations and rights.

Ronald Rubin has suggested to me in conversation that there is a good historical
reason for this. In a society whose members agree pretty much about the good,
little consideration need be given to the notion of rights. The concept develops into
full use where the consensus is lost, and the members of a society find it intolerable
to live according to each others' notions of what is good. To avoid this there develops the idea that certain conduct should not be interfered with by the state even

---

[3] In support of this, consider the plausible and familiar claim that what is done *merely* out of duty or
obligation, though it may be morally correct and praiseworthy, is not praiseworthy as an act of friendship, kindness, bravery, or charity.

though its ruling party, or other factions, believes it to be bad. This secures freedom of action without general agreement on what is good. If this is historically correct and the concept of rights developed to solve the problem of how to insure the freedom of those with whose conceptions of the good we disagree, it is not surprising that to decide what is within your or my rights is by no means to decide whether it is good or bad.

It will now be obvious why I cannot answer what I consider to be fundamental questions about the morality of suicide; their answer requires nothing less than a theory of the good and of the virtues (like courage and charity) which promote it and the vices (like cowardice and meanness) which oppose it. But I hope that the questions raised in the examples will strike the reader as genuine questions which do actually arise in real cases involving suicide, and that what I have said is enough to show that they are not questions of duty, obligation, and rights.

QUESTIONS FOR ANALYSIS AND DISCUSSION

1. Bogen concludes on an ambiguous note. He does not specify how or whether one should consider suicide, but he does hold that virtue ethics offers a deeper and more considered approach. Does this ambiguity challenge you to continue his line of thought about the importance of the virtues and vices? Or is the ambiguity a sign of weakness in virtue ethics as formulated by Bogen? Explain your response.

2. How do you think Bogen would judge Dr. Quill's role in assisted suicide? Would Bogen construe the death of Diane as an exercise of one's rights? Or is this assisted suicide a worthy example of how virtue ethics helps moral persons to do good (or help identify viciousness).

3. As final exam week nears, you take a break from your studies to stop by a friend's apartment. His condition stuns you. Sloppy drunk, he grumbles about how lousy his grades are this semester and how he's not even looking forward to semester break because his girlfriend just dumped him. You try to cheer him up, then sober him up, going to the kitchen to make some coffee. Returning to the living room you see him fiddling with a revolver. You decide to: (a) call 911, (b) call the Hemlock Society to rush over its how-to-commit suicide manual so your friend doesn't botch the job, (c) jump for the gun and take it out of his shaking hands, (d) reassure him that he's acting within his rights, (e) do everything you can to intervene and prevent a suicide that would be a loss not just of your friend but for all those who care about him, or (f) other options. Which would Bogen or other moral theorists choose? Briefly state their reasoning.

CHAPTER TEN

Philosophy and the Good Life

This would surely have to result in a happiness that humanity has not known so far: the happiness of a god full of power and love, full of tears and laughter, a happiness that, like the sun in the evening, continually bestows its inexhaustible riches, pouring them into the sea, feeling richest, as the sun does, only when even the poorest fisherman is still rowing with golden oars! This godlike feeling would then be called—humaneness.

—Nietzsche, *"The Humaneness of the Future"*

You put in my hand a tiny silver statue, very old, votive offering cast into the river by a pilgrim perhaps hundreds of years ago. . . . I looked at you with wet eyes and realized that's all there was. Orphan boy you had given me everything you had. And then you told me that the small silver figure represented the reincarnation of Krishna named Gopal. Gopal. Gopal is you.

—Alphonso Lingis, *Excesses*

We have covered quite a bit of material on morality, virtues and vices, and contrary views of the good. Each assignment adds to the dulling sensation of yet another piece of labor. You count the meetings until the course is over. You look forward to the free time awaiting you—the time when life can be enjoyed again.

This existential despair in college life has an element of irony. The word *school* comes from the Latin *schola* and Greek *schole*, meaning leisure. Leisure, as Plato and Aristotle observe, is the result of a good and just society. Leisure is one of the goals of toil, business—even war. In leisure we have the fullest opportunity to experience happiness. For the ancient moralists the opposite of leisure is not work but slavery. Life in school, then, should be a free and happy experience.

Why is there such a discrepancy between the original meaning of school and contemporary attitudes toward it? Is this discrepancy reinforced by employers who insist that employees take more classes before they are considered for promotion? Is it instilled by professors who introduce their courses with syllabuses that read like war manifestos? Is school viewed like unfree time due to the pressures of grades and competition?

One way of addressing these questions is by considering two related points. First, we are often confused about the meaning of leisure. Does leisure refer to free time or dead time? Is leisure something left over from a busy day or something any decent person deserves? Does leisure provide an opportunity to realize our true selves or the chance to be slothful? Second, what is the value of leisure? Idle hands may be tools of the Devil's workshop, but one way we measure the progress of a society is by how much free time the average citizen enjoys. The goodness of leisure may lie not so much in its inherent value but rather in what we do with our leisure—or what we do not do.

The selections in this chapter use the ideas of leisure and happiness as departure points for examining the good life. The case study by architect and cultural observer Witold Rybczynski discusses an emerging confusion about the use and perception of leisure time. Surveys show that the average work week has not changed noticeably in the last couple of decades, but people believe they have much less free time than they did ten years ago, or less than the previous generation. Part of the problem, suggests Rybczynski, lies in how we use free time.

One of the gloomiest visions of leisure time comes from French essayist Blaise Pascal. Rather than devote ourselves to worthy endeavors, humans fill their free time with amusing diversions. Benjamin Franklin (see Chapter 3) offers the moral advice that free time should not be wasted in idleness. His famous reminder that time is money underlies the proper use of leisure and directs one to the good life. Novelist Thomas Pynchon examines the vice most associated with idleness— sloth. He outlines the range of those who enjoy sloth, from the writer to the couch potato, and clarifies its relation to the deadliest sin, acedia. A different take on the role of television in modern life is formulated by communications researcher George Gerbner. He thinks television occupies the contemporary mind so extensively that it has replaced religion as the common focal point of our culture.

The selections by Aristotle and Plato emphasize leisure as a social and philosophical good. In the dialogue *Theaetetus* Socrates debates the merits of the view that man is the measure of all things. In the middle of the discussion Socrates praises leisure as essential to philosophical life. In *Politics* Aristotle emphasizes the social value of leisure, stating that the extent of free time is an indicator of the productive and just society, contrary to a society devoted to war, conquest, or internal strife.

Recent essays by philosophers David Hollenbach and Chandra Saeng offer two different perspectives but agree on one major point: The luxuries of modern life and the freedoms it has brought have too often been used for material and individual purposes rather than for the common good. Hollenbach believes that a vibrant democracy is at stake if people continue to act as if free time means escaping rather than participating in community life. Saeng emphasizes the dangers of capitalism. Although capitalism has spawned industrialization and all the material gains many of us enjoy, it also is a breeding ground for the most dangerous social vices. Saeng concludes that the lessons of Buddhism on the simple life offer an antidote.

Finally, philosopher Alphonso Lingis (see Chapter 2) uses his leisure to travel to remote places of the world. There he finds forms and expressions of thought that contrast with the more familiar ideas taught by Western philosophers. These contrasts are illuminated not by well-known writers and thinkers but by anonymous figures who teach Lingis new lessons about the good.

79.

WITOLD RYBCZYNSKI

Case Study: The Problem of Leisure

One way of comprehending our confusion about the meaning of leisure is by seeing the conflicting moral resources that shape our beliefs and habits. Our Puritanical tradition leaves us wary of any frivolous use of free time, but a hedonistic bent encourages us to live it up because we have only one trip in this world. A large part of everyday life is full of advertisements enticing us to buy this or that. These points are elucidated by cultural historian and architect Witold Rybczynski (b. 1943). He supports leisure time but recommends a careful rethinking of its importance in everyday life.

⊢ CRITICAL READING QUESTIONS ⊣

1. What is the point of the line by G. K. Chesterton about doing nothing?
2. Are hobbies a good or poor use of leisure time? Why?
3. If people are working less, why do they feel they have less free time?
4. What is one recommendation proposed by Rybczynski?

In 1919 the Hungarian psychiatrist Sándor Ferenczi published a short paper entitled "Sunday Neuroses." He recounted that in his medical practice he had encountered several neurotics whose symptoms recurred on a regular basis. Although it's common for a repressed memory to return at the same time of year as the original experience, the symptoms he described appeared every week. Even more novel,

---

"The Problem of Leisure," from *Waiting for the Weekend* (New York: Penguin, 1991), pp. 210–212, 216–225, 232–234. Some notes have been omitted.

they appeared most frequently on one day: Sunday. Having eliminated possible physical factors associated with Sunday, such as sleeping in, special holiday foods, and overeating, he decided that his patients' hysterical symptoms were caused by the holiday character of the day. This hypothesis seemed to be borne out by one particular case, that of a Jewish boy whose symptoms appeared on Friday evening, the commencement of the Sabbath. Ferenczi speculated that the headaches and vomiting of these holiday neurotics were a reaction to the freedom that the weekly day of rest offered. Since Sunday allowed all sorts of relaxed behavior (noisy family games, playful picnics, casual dress), Ferenczi reasoned that people who were neurotically disposed might feel uncomfortable "venting their holiday wantonness," either because they had dangerous impulses to control or because they felt guilty about letting go their inhibitions.

Ferenczi described the Sunday holiday as a day when "we are our own masters and feel ourselves free from all the fetters that the duties and compulsions of circumstances impose on us; there occurs in us—parallel with this—a kind of inner liberation also." Although "Sunday neurosis" was a clinical term, the concept of a liberation of repressed instincts coupled with a greater availability of free time raised the menacing image of a whole society running amok. Throughout the 1920s there were dozens of articles and books of a more general nature, published by psychiatrists, psychologists, and social scientists in both Europe and America, on the perils of what was often called the New Leisure. There was a widespread feeling that the working class would not really know what to do with all this extra free time.

The underlying theme was an old one: less work meant more leisure, more leisure led to idleness, and idle hands, as everyone knew, were ripe for Satan's mischief. This was precisely the argument advanced by the supporters of Prohibition, who maintained that shorter hours provided workers with more free time which they would only squander on drink. Whatever the merits of this argument—and undoubtedly drinking was popular—one senses that this and other such "concerns" really masked an unwillingness to accept the personal freedom that was implicit in leisure. The pessimism of social reformers—and many intellectuals—about the abilities of ordinary people to amuse themselves has always been profound, and never more so than when popular amusements do not accord with established notions of what constitutes a good time.

. . .

Ask anyone how long they spend at work and they can tell you exactly; it is more difficult to keep track of leisure. For one thing, it is irregular; for another, it varies from person to person. For some, cutting the lawn is a burden; for others it is a pleasurable pastime. Going to the mall can be a casual Saturday outing, or it can be a chore. Most would count watching television as leisure, but what about Sunday brunch? Sometimes the same activity—walking the dog—can be a pleasure, sometimes not, depending on the weather. Finally, whether an activity is part of our leisure depends as much on our frame of mind as anything else.

Surveys of leisure habits often show diverging results. Two recent surveys, by the University of Maryland and by Michigan's Survey Research Center, both suggest that most Americans enjoy about thirty-nine hours of leisure time weekly. On the other hand, a 1988 survey conducted by the National Research Center of the Arts came to a very different conclusion and found that "Americans report a median 16.6 hours of leisure time each week." The truth is probably somewhere in between.

Less surprising, given the number of people working more than forty-nine hours a week, was the National Research Center's conclusion that most Americans have suffered a decline in weekly leisure time of 9.6 hours over the last fifteen years. The nineteenth-century activists who struggled so hard for a shorter workweek and more free time would have been taken aback by this statistic—what had happened to the "Eight Hours for What We Will"?

There are undoubtedly people who work longer hours out of personal ambition, to escape problems at home, or from compulsion. The term "workaholic" (a postwar Americanism) is recent, but addiction to work is not—Thomas Jefferson, for example, was a compulsive worker, as was G. K. Chesterton—and there is no evidence that there are more such people today than in the past. Of course, for many, longer hours are not voluntary—they are obliged to work more merely to make ends meet. This has been particularly true since the 1970s, when poverty in America began to increase, but since the shrinking of leisure time began during the prosperous 1960s, economic need isn't the only explanation.

Twenty years ago Staffan Linder, a Swedish sociologist, wrote a book about the paradox of increasing affluence and decreasing leisure time in the United States. Following in Lippmann's steps, Linder observed that in a prosperous consumer society there was a conflict between the market's promotion of luxury goods and the individual's leisure time. When work hours were first shortened, there were few luxury items available to the general public, and the extra free time was generally devoted to leisure. With the growth of the so-called "leisure industry," people were offered a choice: more free time or more spending? Only the wealthy could have both. If the average person wanted to indulge in expensive recreations such as skiing or sailing, or to buy expensive entertainment devices, it would be necessary to work more—to trade his or her free time for overtime or a second job. Whether because of the effectiveness of advertising or from simple acquisitiveness, most people chose spending over more free time.

Linder's thesis was that economic growth caused an increasing scarcity of time, and that statistics showing an increase in personal incomes were not necessarily a sign of growing prosperity. People were earning more because they were working more. A large percentage of free time was being converted into what he called "consumption time," and mirrored a shift from "time-intensive" to "goods-intensive" leisure. According to *U.S. News & World Report*, Americans now spend more than $13 billion annually on sports clothing; put another way, about 1.3 billion hours of potential leisure time are exchanged for leisure wear—for increasingly elaborate running shoes, certified hiking shorts, and monogrammed warm-up suits. In 1989, to pay for these indulgences, more workers than ever before—6.2 percent—held a second, part-time job; in factories, overtime work increased to an average of four hours a week, the highest number in nearly twenty years.

Probably the most dramatic change is the large-scale entry of women into the labor force. In 1950 only thirty percent of American women worked outside the home, and this primarily out of economic necessity. Beginning in the 1960s middle-class women, dissatisfied with their suburban isolation and willing to trade at least some of their leisure time for purchasing power, started to look for paid employment. By 1986 more than half of all adult women—including married women with children—worked outside the home. Nor are these trends slowing down; between 1980 and 1988, the number of families with two or more wage earners rose from 19 to 21 million.

"Working outside the home" is the correct way to describe the situation, for housework (three or four hours a day) still needs to be done. Whether it is shared, or, more commonly, falls on the shoulders of women as part of their "second shift," leisure time for one or both partners is drastically reduced. Moreover, homes are larger than at any time in the postwar period, and bigger houses also mean more time spent in cleaning, upkeep, and repairs.*

Even if one chooses to consume less and stay at home, there are other things that cut into free time. Commuting to and from work takes longer than it used to. So does shopping—the weekly trip to the mall consumes more time than a stroll to the neighborhood corner store. Decentralized suburban life, which is to say American life, is based on the automobile. Parents become chauffeurs, ferrying their children back and forth to dance classes, hockey games, and the community pool. At home, telephone answering machines have to be played back, the household budget entered into the personal computer, the lawn mower dropped off at the repair shop, the car—or cars—serviced. All these convenient labor-saving devices relentlessly eat into our discretionary time. For many executives, administrators, and managers, the reduction of leisure time is also the result of office technology that brings work to the home. Fax machines, paging devices, and portable computers mean that taking work home at night is no longer difficult or voluntary. Even the contemplative quiet of the morning automobile commute is now disrupted by the presence of the cellular telephone.

There is no contradiction between the surveys that indicate a reversing trend, resulting in less free time, and the claim that the weekend dominates our leisure. Longer work hours and more overtime cut mainly into weekday leisure. So do longer commuting, driving the kids, and Friday-night shopping. The weekend—or what's left of it, after Saturday household chores—is when we have time to relax.

But the weekend has imposed a rigid schedule on our free time, which can result in a sense of urgency ("soon it will be Monday") that is at odds with relaxation. The weekly rush to the cottage is hardly leisurely, nor is the compression of various recreational activities into the two-day break. The freedom to do something has become the obligation to do something, just as Chesterton foretold, and the list of dutiful recreations includes strenuous disciplines intended for self-improvement (fitness exercises, jogging, bicycling), competitive sports (tennis, golf), and skill-testing pastimes (sailing, skiing).

Recreations such as tennis or sailing are hardly new, but before the arrival of

---

* The average size of a new American home in the 1950s was less than 1,000 square feet; by 1983 it had increased to 1,710 square feet, and in 1986 had expanded another 115 square feet.

the weekend, for most people, they were chiefly seasonal activities. Once a year, when vacation time came around, tennis racquets were removed from the back of the cupboard, swimwear was taken out of mothballs, skis were dusted off. The accent was less on technique than on having a good time. It was like playing Scrabble at the summer cottage: no one remembers all the rules, but everyone can still enjoy the game. Now the availability of free time every weekend has changed this casual attitude. The very frequency of weekend recreations allows continual participation and continual improvement, which encourage the development of proficiency and skill.

Skill is necessary since difficulty characterizes modern recreations. Many nineteenth-century amusements, such as rowing, were not particularly involved and required little instruction; mastering windsurfing, on the other hand, takes considerable practice and dexterity—which is part of the attraction. Even relatively simple games are complicated by the need to excel. Hence the emphasis on professionalism, which is expressed by the need to have the proper equipment and the correct costume (especially the right shoes). The desire for mastery isn't limited to outdoor recreations; it also includes complicated hobbies such as woodworking, electronics, and automobile restoration. All this suggests that the modern weekend is characterized by not only the sense of obligation to do something but the obligation to do it *well*.

The desire to do something well, whether it is sailing a boat—or building a boat—reflects a need that was previously met in the workplace. Competence was shown on the job—holidays were for messing around. Nowadays the situation is reversed. Technology has removed craft from most occupations. This is true in assembly-line jobs, where almost no training or experience, hence no skill, is required, as well as in most service positions (store clerks, fast-food attendants) where the only talent required is to learn how to smile and say "have a good day." But it's also increasingly true in such skill-dependent work as house construction, where the majority of parts come ready-made from the factory and the carpenter merely assembles them, or automobile repair, which consists largely in replacing one throwaway part with another. Nor is the reduction of skills limited to manual work. Memory, once the prerequisite skill of the white-collar worker, has been rendered superfluous by computers; teachers, who once needed dramatic skills, now depend on mechanical aids such as slide projectors and video machines; in politics, oratory has been killed by the thirty-second sound bite.

Hence an unexpected development in the history of leisure. For many, weekend free time has become not a chance to escape work but a chance to create work that is more meaningful—to work at recreation—in order to realize the personal satisfactions that the workplace no longer offers.

"Leisure" is the most misunderstood word in our vocabulary. We often use the words "recreation" and "leisure" interchangeably—recreation room, rest and recreation, leisure suit, leisure industry—but they really embody two different ideas. Recreation carries with it a sense of necessity and purpose. However pleasurable this antidote to work may be, it's a form of active employment, engaged in with a specific end in mind—a refreshment of the spirit, or the body, or both. Implicit in this idea of renewal—usually organized renewal—is the notion that recreation is both a consequence of work and a preparation for more of it.

Leisure is different. That was what Lippmann was getting at when he contrasted commercial recreation with individual leisure. Leisure is not tied to work the way that recreation is—leisure is self-contained. The root of the word is the Latin *licere* which means "to be permitted," suggesting that leisure is about freedom. But freedom for what? According to Chesterton's cheerful view, leisure was above all an opportunity to do nothing. When he said "doing nothing," however, he was describing not emptiness but an occasion for reflection and contemplation, a chance to look inward rather than outward. A chance to tend one's garden, as Voltaire put it. That is why Chesterton called this kind of leisure "the most precious, the most consoling, the most pure and holy."

. . .

The differences in national attitudes toward leisure are arresting because we live in a world where the character of work is increasingly international. Around the world, in different countries, what happens between nine and five during the week is becoming standardized. Because of international competition and transnational ownership of companies, the transfer of technology from one country to another is almost instantaneous. All offices contain the same telephones, photocopiers, word processors, computers, and fax machines. The Japanese build automobile plants in the United States and Canada, the Americans build factories in Eastern Europe, the Europeans in South America. Industries are increasingly dominated by a diminishing number of extremely large and similar corporations. The reorganization of the workplace in Communist and formerly Communist countries, along more capitalist lines, is one more step in the standardization of work. And as work becomes more standardized, and international, one can expect that leisure, by contrast, will be even more national, more regional, more different.

Leisure has always been partly a refuge from labor. The weekend, too, is a retreat from work, but in a different way: a retreat from the abstract and the universal to the local and the particular. In that sense, leisure is likely to continue to be, as Pieper claimed, the basis of culture. Every culture chooses a different structure for its work and leisure, and in doing so it makes a profound statement about itself. It invents, adapts, and recombines old models, hence the long list of leisure days: public festivals, family celebrations, market days, taboo days, evil days, holy days, feasts, Saint Mondays and Saint Tuesdays, commemorative holidays, summer vacations—and weekends.

The weekend is our own contribution, another way of dealing with the ancient duality. The institution of the weekend reflects the many unresolved contradictions in modern attitudes toward leisure. We want to have our cake, and eat it too. We want the freedom to be leisurely, but we want it regularly, every week, like clockwork. The attraction of Saint Monday was that one could "go fishing" when one willed; the regularity of the weekend—every five days—is at odds with the ideas of personal freedom and spontaneity. There is something mechanical about this oscillation, which creates a sense of obligation that interferes with leisure. Like sacred time, the weekend is comfortingly repetitive, but the conventionality of weekend free time, which must exist side by side with private pastimes and idiosyncratic hobbies, often appears restrictive. "What did you do on the weekend?" "The usual," we answer, mixing dismay with relief.

We have invented the weekend, but the dark cloud of old taboos still hangs over the holiday, and the combination of the secular with the holy leaves us uneasy. This tension only compounds the guilt that many of us continue to feel about not working, and leads to the nagging feeling that our free time should be used for some purpose higher than having fun. We want leisure, but we are afraid of it too.

Do we work to have leisure, or the other way around? Unsure of the answer, we have decided to keep the two separate. If C. P. Snow had not already used the term in another context, it would be tempting to speak of Two Cultures. We pass weekly from one to the other—from the mundane, communal, increasingly impersonal, increasingly demanding, increasingly bureaucratic world of work to the reflective, private, controllable, consoling world of leisure. The weekend; our own, and not our own, it is what we wait for all week long.

QUESTIONS FOR ANALYSIS AND DISCUSSION

1. Rybczynski is adept in interweaving a variety of sources, from historians to painters and literary figures. From which sources do you learn about the good or poor use of leisure time?

2. The individualistic tendencies of Americans suggest that social institutions and political life do not or should not have much say about what we do with our free time. How does Rybczynski address this issue? Do you agree or disagree?

3. Consider how many hours a week you spend in the car going to work or school. Add the number of hours you work to pay for the gas, car insurance, and installments. Do these hours register as a positive on the cost-benefit scale? That is, are the hours a worthy investment because they actually produce more hours of free time? Or do they register as a negative because they eat up hours of your free time that cannot be redeemed? What is Rybczynski's view on this issue?

80.

BLAISE PASCAL

On Diversions

Much of our free time is obviously misused, says Pascal (1623–1662). A remarkable mind, well-known for his writings on geometry, mathematics, human nature, and religion (and later famous when his name was attached to computer programs), Pascal became

---

"On Diversions," from *Pensées*, translated by W. F. Trotter (London: J. M. Dent, 1908, 1931), pp. 196–203. Notes have been omitted.

quite cynical about human endeavors as he became more devoted to Christian faith. This cynicism is reflected in his essays and aphorisms on diversions, which have universal appeal. From the noblest kings to the lowliest peasants, Pascal shows that humans much prefer indulging in superficial amusements to addressing more fundamental issues such as their relation to God, their mortality, or their moral direction.

┤ **CRITICAL READING QUESTIONS** ├

1. What does Pascal claim is the relation between solitude and happiness for most people?
2. What does Pascal see as two secret instincts?
3. How are self-knowledge and the pursuit of diversions related?
4. For Pascal, where lies the chief dignity of humans?
5. How does vanity contribute to our delight in diversions?

---

139. *Diversion.*—When I have occasionally set myself to consider the different distractions of men, the pains and perils to which they expose themselves at court or in war, whence arise so many quarrels, passions, bold and often bad ventures, etc., I have discovered that all the unhappiness of men arises from one single fact, that they cannot stay quietly in their own chamber. A man who has enough to live on, if he knew how to stay with pleasure at home, would not leave it go to sea or to besiege a town. A commission in the army would not be bought so dearly, but that it is found insufferable not to budge from the town; and men only seek conversation and entering games, because they cannot remain with pleasure at home.

But, on further consideration, when, after finding the cause of all our ills, I have sought to discover the reason of it, I have found that there is one very real reason, namely, the natural poverty of our feeble and mortal condition, so miserable that nothing can comfort us when we think of it closely.

Whatever condition we picture to ourselves, if we muster all the good things which it is possible to possess, royalty is the finest position in the world. Yet, when we imagine a king attended with every pleasure he can feel, if he be without diversion and be left to consider and reflect on what he is, this feeble happiness will not sustain him; he will necessarily fall into forebodings of dangers, of revolutions which may happen, and, finally, of death and inevitable disease; so that, if he be without what is called diversion, he is unhappy and more unhappy than the least of his subjects who plays and diverts himself.

Hence it comes that play and the society of women, war and high posts, are so sought after. Not that there is in fact any happiness in them, or that men imagine true bliss to consist in money won at play, or in the hare which they hunt; we would not take these as a gift. We do not seek that easy and peaceful lot which permits us to think of our unhappy condition, nor the dangers of war, nor the labour of office, but the bustle which averts these thoughts of ours and amuses us.

Reasons why we like the chase better than the quarry.

Hence it comes that men so much love noise and stir; hence it comes that the prison is so horrible a punishment; hence it comes that the pleasure of solitude is a thing incomprehensible. And it is, in fact, the greatest source of happiness in the condition of kings that men try incessantly to divert them and to procure for them all kinds of pleasures.

The king is surrounded by persons whose only thought is to divert the king and to prevent his thinking of self. For he is unhappy, king though he be, if he think of himself.

This is all that men have been able to discover to make themselves happy. And those who philosophise on the matter, and who think men unreasonable for spending a whole day in chasing a hare which they would not have bought, scarce know our nature. The hare in itself would not screen us from the sight of death and calamities; but the chase, which turns away our attention from these, does screen us.

The advice given to Pyrrhus, to take the rest which he was about to seek with so much labour, was full of difficulties.

[To bid a man live quietly is to bid him live happily. It is to advise him to be in a state perfectly happy, in which he can think at leisure without finding therein a cause of distress. This is to misunderstand nature.]

As men who naturally understand their own condition avoid nothing so much as rest, so there is nothing they leave undone in seeking turmoil. Not that they have an instinctive knowledge of true happiness. . .

So we are wrong in blaming them. Their error does not lie in seeking excitement, if they seek it only as a diversion; the evil is that they seek it as if the possession of the objects of their quest would make them really happy. In this respect it is right to call their quest a vain one. Hence in all this both the censurers and the censured do not understand man's true nature.

And thus, when we take the exception against them, that what they seek with such fervour cannot satisfy them, if they replied—as they should do if they considered the matter thoroughly—that they sought in it only a violent and impetuous occupation which turned their thoughts from self, and that they therefore chose an attractive object to charm and ardently attract them, they would leave their opponents without a reply. But they do not make this reply, because they do not know themselves. They do not know that it is the chase, and not the quarry, which they seek.

Dancing: We must consider rightly where to place our feet.—A gentleman sincerely believes that hunting is great and royal sport; but a beater is not of this opinion.

They imagine that, if they obtained such a post, they would then rest with pleasure and are insensible of the insatiable nature of their desire. They think they are truly seeking quiet, and they are only seeking excitement.

They have a secret instinct which impels them to seek amusement and occupation abroad, and which arises from the sense of their constant unhappiness. They have another secret instinct, a remnant of the greatness of our original nature, which teaches them that happiness in reality consists only in rest and not in stir. And of these two contrary instincts they form within themselves a confused idea, which hides itself from their view in the depths of their soul, inciting them to aim at rest through excitement, and always to fancy that the satisfaction which they have not will come to them, if, by surmounting whatever difficulties confront them, they can thereby open the door to rest.

Thus passes away all man's life. Men seek rest in a struggle against difficulties; and when they have conquered these, rest becomes insufferable. For we think either of the misfortunes we have or of those which threaten us. And even if we should see ourselves sufficiently sheltered on all sides, weariness of its own accord would not fail to arise from the depths of the heart wherein it has its natural roots and to fill the mind with its poison.

Thus so wretched is man that he would weary even without any cause for weariness from the peculiar state of his disposition; and so frivolous is he that, though full of a thousand reasons for weariness, the least thing, such as playing billiards or hitting a ball, is sufficient to amuse him.

But will you say what object has he in all this? The pleasure of bragging tomorrow among his friends that he has played better than another. So others sweat in their own rooms to show to the learned that they have solved a problem in algebra, which no one had hitherto been able to solve. Many more expose themselves to extreme perils, in my opinion as foolishly, in order to boast afterwards that they have captured a town. Lastly, others wear themselves out in studying all these things, not in order to become wiser, but only in order to prove that they know them; and these are the most senseless of the band, since they are so knowingly, whereas one may suppose of the others that, if they knew it, they would no longer be foolish.

This man spends his life without weariness in playing every day for a small stake. Give him each morning the money he can win each day, on condition he does not play; you make him miserable. It will perhaps be said that he seeks the amusement of play and not the winnings. Make him, then, play for nothing; he will not become excited over it and will feel bored. It is, then, not the amusement alone that he seeks; a languid and passionless amusement will weary him. He must get excited over it and deceive himself by the fancy that he will be happy to win what he would not have as a gift on condition of not playing; and he must make for himself an object of passion, and excite over it his desire, his anger, his fear, to obtain his imagined end, as children are frightened at the face they have blackened.

Whence comes it that this man, who lost his only son a few months ago, or who this morning was in such trouble through being distressed by lawsuits and quarrels, now no longer thinks of them? Do not wonder; he is quite taken up in looking out for the boar which his dogs have been hunting so hotly for the last six hours. He requires nothing more. However full of sadness a man may be, he is happy for the time, if you can prevail upon him to enter into some amusement; and however happy a man may be, he will soon be discontented and wretched, if he be not diverted and occupied by some passion or pursuit which prevents weariness from overcoming him. Without amusement there is no joy; with amusement there is no sadness. And this also constitutes the happiness of persons in high position, that they have a number of people to amuse them and have the power to keep themselves in this state.

Consider this. What is it to be superintendent, chancellor, first president, but to be in a condition wherein from early morning a large number of people come from all quarters to see them, so as not to leave them an hour in the day in which they can think of themselves? And when they are in disgrace and sent back to their country houses, where they lack neither wealth nor servants to help them on occasion, they do not fail to be wretched and desolate, because no one prevents them from thinking of themselves.

. . .

143. *Diversion.*—Men are entrusted from infancy with the care of their honour, their property, their friends, and even with the property and the honour of their friends. They are overwhelmed with business, with the study of languages, and with physical exercise; and they are made to understand that they cannot be happy unless their health, their honour, their fortune and that of their friends be in good condition, and that a single thing wanting will make them unhappy. Thus they are given cares and business which make them bustle about from break of day.—It is, you will exclaim, a strange way to make them happy! What more could be done to make them miserable?—Indeed! what could be done? We should only have to relieve them from all these cares; for then they would see themselves: they would reflect on what they are, whence they came, whither they go, and thus we cannot employ and divert them too much. And this is why, after having given them so much business, we advise them, if they have some time for relaxation, to employ it in amusement, in play, and to be always fully occupied.

How hollow and full of ribaldry is the heart of man!

144. I spent a long time in the study of the abstract sciences, and was disheartened by the small number of fellow-students in them. When I commenced the study of man, I saw that these abstract sciences are not suited to man and that I was wandering farther from my own state in examining them than others in not knowing them. I pardoned their little knowledge; but I thought at least to find many companions in the study of man and that it was the true study which is suited to him. I have been deceived; still fewer study it than geometry. It is only from the want of knowing how to study this that we seek the other studies. But is it not that even here is not the knowledge which man should have and that for the purpose of happiness it is better for him not to know himself?

. . .

146. Man is obviously made to think. It is his whole dignity and his whole merit; and his whole duty is to think as he ought. Now, the order of thought is to begin with self, and with its Author and its end.

Now, of what does the world think? Never of this, but of dancing, playing the lute, singing, making verses, running at the ring, etc., fighting, making oneself king, without thinking what it is to be a king and what to be a man.

147. We do not content ourselves with the life we have in ourselves and in our

own being; we desire to live an imaginary life in the mind of others, and for this purpose we endeavor to shine. We labour unceasingly to adorn and preserve this imaginary existence and neglect the real. And if we possess calmness, or generosity, or truthfulness, we are eager to make it known, so as to attach these virtues to that imaginary existence. We would rather separate them from ourselves to join them to it; and we would willingly be cowards in order to acquire the reputation of being brave. A great proof of the nothingness of our being, not to be satisfied with the one without the other, and to renounce the one for the other! For he would be infamous who would not die to preserve his honour.

148. We are so presumptuous that we would wish to be known by all the world, even by people who shall come after, when we shall be no more; and we are so vain that the esteem of five or six neighbours delights and contents us.

149. We do not trouble ourselves about being esteemed in the towns through which we pass. But if we are to remain a little while there, we are so concerned. How long is necessary? A time commensurate with our vain and paltry life.

150. Vanity is so anchored in the heart of man that a soldier, a soldier's servant, a cook, a porter brags and wishes to have his admirers. Even philosophers wish for them. Those who write against it want to have the glory of having written well; and those who read it desire the glory of having read it. I who write this have perhaps this desire, and perhaps those who will read it. . .

. . .

165. *Thoughts.*—*In omnibus requiem quæsivi.* If our condition were truly happy, we would not need diversion from thinking of it in order to make ourselves happy.

166. *Diversion.*—Death is easier to bear without thinking of it than is the thought of death without peril.

167. The miseries of human life has established all this: as men have seen this, they have taken up diversion.

168. *Diversion.*—As men are not able to fight against death, misery, ignorance, they have taken it into their heads, in order to be happy, not to think of them at all.

169. Despite these miseries, man wishes to be happy, and only wishes to be happy, and cannot wish not to be so. But how will he set about it? To be happy he would have to make himself immortal; but, not being able to do so, it has occurred to him to prevent himself from thinking of death.

170. *Diversion.*—If man were happy, he would be the more so, the less he was diverted, like the Saints and God. Yes; but is it not to be happy to have a faculty of being amused by diversion? No; for that comes from elsewhere and from without, and thus is dependent, and therefore subject to be disturbed by a thousand accidents, which bring inevitable griefs.

171. *Misery.*—The only thing which consoles us for our miseries is diversion, and yet this is the greatest of our miseries. For it is this which principally hinders us from reflecting upon ourselves and which makes us insensibly ruin ourselves. Without this we should be in a state of weariness, and this weariness would spur us to seek a more solid means of escaping from it. But diversion amuses us, and leads us unconsciously to death.

QUESTIONS FOR ANALYSIS AND DISCUSSION

1. Pascal accuses most men of seeking happiness through diversions, but without success. How can Pascal, or anyone, detect that humans who seem to be having a good time are not happy? Does this detection require some sense of falseness of others, or does it rely on a specific notion of happiness? Do you think we are incapable of determining whether others are happy?

2. In his argument about the motives behind the search for diversions, Pascal observes, "Hence in all this both the censurers and the censured do not understand man's true nature." What do you think Pascal means? Do you get a sense of Pascal's idea of man's true nature? Clarify the key features, and consider your own thoughts about Pascal's attempt to understand human nature.

3. How many diversions does Pascal cite that are still enjoyed today? Consider some of the examples you participate in or observe, such as billiards or gambling (or studying philosophy). Would you conclude that these diversions are symptoms of escape from oneself? Develop your agreement or disagreement with Pascal's conclusions.

4. One of the driving forces to games, hunting, even writing, is the chance to brag. What are Pascal's main points about bragging? Now consider your own thoughts about the power of bragging. In your view, has Pascal anticipated a driving force in human behavior, or is he exaggerating the value of bragging?

5. For Pascal the main task of humans lies in addressing their mortality, which includes understanding their relation to God. Do you agree with this view? If not, is there a more important task? How does your response affect your assessment of Pascal's observations on diversions?

81.

BENJAMIN FRANKLIN

Advice to a Young Tradesman

How best to assess the value of free time? In the eyes of Franklin the most precise way is by treating time as a financial value. Time wasted is money lost. Time properly used is money either earned or saved. With these basic precepts in mind, Franklin describes how one can lead the good life.

"Advice to a Young Tradesman," from *The Political Thought of Benjamin Franklin*, edited by Ralph Ketcham (Indianapolis, IN: Bobbs-Merrill, 1965), pp. 51–54.

┤ **CRITICAL READING QUESTIONS** ├

1. If you earn fifty dollars a day at work and take Saturday off to go to the movies on a date that costs about twenty dollars, according to Franklin, how much money have you lost?
2. What is meant by money being of a "prolific generating Nature"?
3. Is it better to borrow or to lend money?
4. What are the two main virtues needed for achieving wealth?

Remember that Time is Money. He that can earn Ten Shillings a Day by his Labour, and goes abroad, or sits idle one half of that Day, tho' he spends but Sixpence during his Diversion or Idleness, ought not to reckon That the only Expence; he has really spent or rather thrown away Five Shillings besides.

Remember that Credit is Money. If a Man lets his Money lie in my Hands after it is due, he gives me the Interest, or so much as I can make of it during that Time. This amounts to a considerable Sum where a Man has good and large Credit, and makes good Use of it.

Remember that Money is of a prolific generating Nature. Money can beget Money, and its Offspring can beget more, and so on. Five Shillings turn'd, is *Six:* Turn'd again, 'tis Seven and Three Pence; and so on 'til it becomes an Hundred Pound. The more there is of it, the more it produces every Turning, so that the Profits rise quicker and quicker. He that kills a breeding Sow, destroys all her Offspring to the thousandth Generation. He that murders a Crown, destroys all it might have produc'd, even Scores of Pounds.

Remember that Six Pounds a Year is but a Groat a Day. For this little Sum (which may be daily wasted either in Time or Expence unperciev'd) a Man of Credit may on his own Security have the constant Possession and Use of an Hundred Pounds. So much in Stock briskly turn'd by an industrious Man, produces great Advantage.

Remember this Saying, *That the good Paymaster is Lord of another Man's Purse.* He that is known to pay punctually and exactly to the Time he promises, may at any Time, and on any Occasion, raise all the Money his Friends can spare. This is sometimes of great Use: Therefore never keep borrow'd Money an Hour beyond the Time you promis'd, lest a Disappointment shuts up your Friends Purse forever.

The most trifling Actions that affect a Man's Credit, are to be regarded. The Sound of your Hammer at Five in the Morning or Nine at Night, heard by a Creditor, makes him easy Six Months longer. But if he sees you at a Billiard Table, or hears your Voice in a Tavern, when you should be at Work, he sends for his Money the next Day. Finer Cloaths than he or his Wife wears, or greater Expence in any particular than he affords himself, shocks his Pride, and he duns you to humble you. Creditors are a kind of People, that have the sharpest Eyes and Ears, as well as the best Memories of any in the World.

Good-natur'd Creditors (and such one would always chuse to deal with if one could) feel Pain when they are oblig'd to ask for Money. Spare 'em that Pain, and they will love you. When you receive a Sum of Money, divide it among 'em in 'Proportion to your Debts. Don't be asham'd of paying a small Sum because you owe a greater. Money, more or less, is always welcome; and your Creditor had rather be at the Trouble of receiving Ten Pounds voluntarily brought him, tho' at ten different Times or Payments, than be oblig'd to go ten Times to demand it before he can receive it in a Lump. It shews, besides, that you are mindful of what you owe; it makes you appear a careful as well as an honest Man; and that still encreases your Credit.

Beware of thinking all your own that you possess, and of living accordingly. 'Tis a Mistake that many People who have Credit fall into. To prevent this, keep an exact Account for some Time of both your Expences and your Incomes. If you take the Pains at first to mention Particulars, it will have this good Effect; you will discover how wonderfully small trifling Expences mount up to large Sums, and will discern what might have been, and may for the future be saved, without occasioning any great Inconvenience.

In short, the Way to Wealth, if you desire it, is as plain as the Way to Market. It depends chiefly on two Words, Industry and Frugality; i.e. Waste neither Time nor Money, but make the best Use of both. He that gets all he can honestly, and saves all he gets (necessary Expences excepted) will certainly become Rich, If that Being who governs the World, to whom all should look for a Blessing on their honest Endeavours, doth not in his wide Providence otherwise determine.

QUESTIONS FOR ANALYSIS AND DISCUSSION

1. Do you think Franklin's famous axiom that "time is money" should be taken literally? If so, how far can this axiom be applied? For example, can you apply it to love and courtship? Has a reluctant lover ever cost you too much time (too much money in Franklin's view)? Clarify your answer. Is this a moral response? How much would you be willing to "spend" on love? Is time a necessary expenditure for courtship?

2. Why does Franklin describe money as begetting more money? Does he ever clarify what one will do with the money accumulated? Is money an inherent good? Does having it bring happiness? Consider to what extent Franklin has or has not characterized much of contemporary American life. Use evidence from current life to support your answer.

3. How does Franklin portray the creditor? Is the creditor a reliable person? Would you want the creditor as a friend? How do you think Franklin would answer these questions? Consider who are the creditors today. Are they reliable or friendly (commercials notwithstanding)?

4. Can you imagine living life worrying about how much your time is worth in monetary numbers? Imagine that you didn't return a phone call to one friend who is only worth four dollars of your presence but that you did return the call of a friend who is worth eleven dollars of your presence, the second

highest among your friends. Is this approach plausible? Is it moral? Develop your thoughts on the practical aspects of Franklin's advice.

5. Would you add industry and frugality to the major virtues (courage, love, truthfulness, and care)? Do either industry or frugality directly help in battling the vices? Clarify your thoughts, using current examples to make your points.

82.

THOMAS PYNCHON

Sloth

One possible vice that industry and frugality can help oppose is sloth, writes novelist Thomas Pynchon (b. 1937). In a witty and informative account of diverse writers, Pynchon proposes that we see the virtues supported in Franklin's time as replacing virtues that lost their influence in a less Christian world. The viciousness of sloth did not change, but its virtuous enemies did. Lately, however, as Pynchon insightfully reminds us, the meaning of sloth itself is not clear.

┤ **CRITICAL READING QUESTIONS** ├

1. Why are writers the "mavens of sloth"?
2. Which virtue might be an offspring of sloth? Why?
3. When in the twentieth century was sloth's finest hour?
4. How is watching television related to sloth?
5. What is the best candidate to replace television as the central image of the slothful person?

In his classical discussion of the subject in the *Summa Theologica*, Aquinas termed Sloth, or *acedia*, one of the seven capital sins. He said he was using "capital" to mean "primary" or "at the head of" because such sins gave rise to others, but

---

"Sloth," from *Deadly Sins* (New York: Morrow, 1993), pp. 13–23.

there was an additional and darker sense resonating luridly just beneath and not hurting the power of his argument, for the word also meant "deserving of capital punishment." Hence the equivalent term "mortal," as well as the punchier English "deadly."

But come on, isn't that kind of extreme, death for something as lightweight as Sloth? Sitting there on some medieval death row, going, "So, look, no offense, but what'd they pop you for anyway?"

"Ah, usual story, they came around at the wrong time of day, I end up taking out half of some sheriff's unit with my two-cubit crossbow, firing three-quarter-inch bolts on auto feed. Anger, I guess. . . . How about you?"

"Um, well . . . it wasn't anger. . . ."

"Ha! Another one of these Sloth cases, right?"

". . . fact, it wasn't even me."

"Never is, slugger—say, look, it's almost time for lunch. You wouldn't happen to be a writer, by any chance?"

Writers of course are considered the mavens of Sloth. They are approached all the time on the subject, not only for free advice, but also to speak at Sloth Symposia, head up Sloth Task Forces, testify as expert witnesses at Sloth Hearings. The stereotype arises in part from our conspicuous presence in jobs where pay is by the word, and deadlines are tight and final—we are presumed to know from piecework and the convertibility of time and money. In addition, there is all the glamorous folklore surrounding writer's block, an affliction known sometimes to resolve itself dramatically and without warning, much like constipation, and (hence?) finding wide sympathy among readers.

Writer's block, however, is a trip to the theme park of your choice alongside the mortal sin that produces it. Like each of the other six, Sloth was supposed to be the progenitor of a whole family of lesser, or venial, sins, among them Idleness, Drowsiness, Restlessness of the Body, Instability, and Loquacity. "Acedia" in Latin means sorrow, deliberately self-directed, turned away from God, a loss of spiritual determination that then feeds back on in to the process, soon enough producing what are currently known as guilt and depression, eventually pushing us to where we will do anything, in the way of venial sin and bad judgment, to avoid the discomfort.

But Sloth's offspring, though bad—to paraphrase the Shangri-Las—are not always evil, for example what Aquinas terms Uneasiness of the Mind, or "rushing after various things without rhyme or reason," which, "if it pertains to the imaginative power . . . is called curiosity." It is of course precisely in such episodes of mental traveling that writers are known to do good work, sometimes even their best, solving formal problems, getting advice from Beyond, having hypnagogic adventures that with luck can be recovered later on. Idle dreaming is often of the essence of what we do. We sell our dreams. So real money actually proceeds from Sloth, although this transformation is said to be even more amazing elsewhere in the entertainment sector, where idle exercises in poolside loquacity have not infrequently generated tens of millions of dollars in revenue.

As a topic for fiction, Sloth over the next few centuries after Aquinas had a few big successes, notably *Hamlet,* but not until arriving on the shores of America did it take the next important step in its evolution. Between Franklin's hectic aphorist, Poor Richard, and Melville's doomed scrivener, Bartleby, lies about a century of early America, consolidating itself as a Christian capitalist state, even as acedia was in the last stages of its shift over from a spiritual to a secular condition.

Philadelphia, by Franklin's time, answered less and less to the religious vision that William Penn had started off with. The city was becoming a kind of high-output machine, materials and labor going in, goods and services coming out, traffic inside flowing briskly about a grid of regular city blocks. The urban mazework of London, leading into ambiguities and indeed evils, was here all rectified, orthogonal. (Dickens, visiting in 1842, remarked, "After walking about in it for an hour or two, I felt that I would have given the world for a crooked street.") Spiritual matters were not quite as immediate as material ones, like productivity. Sloth was no longer so much a sin against God or spiritual good as against a particular sort of time, uniform, one-way, in general nor reversible—that is, against clock time, which got everybody early to bed and early to rise.

Poor Richard was not shy in expressing his distaste for Sloth. When he was not merely repeating well-known British proverbs on the subject, he was contributing Great Awakening–style outbursts of his own—"O Lazy-bones! Dost think God would have given thee arms and legs if he had not designed thou shouldst use them?" Beneath the rubato of the day abided a stern pulse beating on, ineluctable, unforgiving, whereby whatever was evaded or put off now had to be made up for later, and at a higher level of intensity. "You may delay, but time will not." And Sloth, being continual evasion, just kept piling up like a budget deficit, while the dimensions of the inevitable payback grew ever less merciful.

In the idea of time that had begun to rule city life in Poor Richard's day, where every second was of equal length and irrevocable, not much in the course of its flow could have been called nonlinear, unless you counted the ungovernable warp of dreams, for which Poor Richard had scant use. In Frances M. Barbour's 1974 concordance of the sayings, there is nothing to be found under "Dreams," dreams being as unwelcome in Philly back then as their frequent companion, sleep, which was considered time away from accumulating wealth, time that had to be tithed back into the order of things to purchase twenty hours of productive waking. During the Poor Richard years, Franklin, according to the "Autobiography," was allowing himself from 1 A.M. to 5 A.M. for sleep. The other major nonwork block of time was four hours, 9 P.M. to 1 A.M. devoted to the Evening Question, "What good have I done this day?" This must have been the schedule's only occasion for drifting into reverie—there would seem to have been no other room for speculations, dreams, fantasies, fiction. Life in that orthogonal machine was supposed to be nonfiction.

By the time of *Bartleby the Scrivener: A Story of Wall-Street* (1853), acedia had lost the last of its religious reverberations and was now an offense against the economy. Right in the heart of robber-baron capitalism, the title character develops what proves to be terminal acedia. It is like one of those western tales where the desperado keeps making choices that only herd him closer to the one disagreeable finale. Bartleby just sits there in an office on Wall Street repeating, "I would prefer not to." While his options go rapidly narrowing, his employer, a man of affairs and substance, is actually brought to question the assumptions of his own life by this miserable scrivener—this writer!—who, though among the lowest of the low in the bilges of capitalism, nevertheless refuses to go on interacting any-more with the daily order, thus bringing up the interesting question: who is more guilty of Sloth, a person who collaborates with the root of all evil, accepting things-as-they-are in return for a paycheck and a hassle-free life, or one who does nothing, finally, but persist in sorrow? *Bartleby* is the first great epic of modern Sloth, pres-ently to be followed by work from the likes of Kafka, Hemingway, Proust, Sartre, Musil, and others—take your own favorite list of writers after Melville and you're bound sooner or later to run into a character bearing a sorrow recognizable as peculiarly of our own time.

In this century we have come to think of Sloth as primarily political, a failure of public will allowing the introduction of evil policies and the rise of evil regimes, the worldwide fascist ascendency of the 1920's and 30's being perhaps Sloth's fin-est hour, though the Vietnam era and the Reagan–Bush years are not far behind. Fiction and nonfiction alike are full of characters who fail to do what they should because of the effort involved. How can we not recognize our world? Occasions for choosing good present themselves in public and private for us every day, and we pass them by. Acedia is the vernacular of everyday moral life. Though it has never lost its deepest notes of mortal anxiety, it never gets as painful as outright despair, or as real, for it is despair bought at a discount price, a deliberate turning against faith in anything because of the inconvenience faith presents to the pursuit of quotidian lusts, angers, and the rest. The compulsive pessimist's last defense—stay still enough and the blade of the scythe, somehow, will pass by—Sloth is our background radiation, our easy-listening station—it is everywhere, and no longer noticed.

Any discussion of Sloth in the present day is of course incomplete without con-sidering television, with its gifts of paralysis, along with its creature and symbiont, the notorious Couch Potato. Tales spun in idleness find us Tubeside, supine, chi-ropractic fodder, sucking it all in, reenacting in reverse the transaction between dream and revenue that brought these colored shadows here to begin with so that we might feed, uncritically, committing the six other deadly sins in parallel, eating too much, envying the celebrated, coveting merchandise, lusting after images, an-gry at the news, perversely proud of whatever distance we may enjoy between our couches and what appears on the screen.

Sad but true. Yet, chiefly owing to the timely invention—not a minute too soon!—of the remote control and the VCR, maybe there is hope after all. Televi-sion time is no longer the linear and uniform commodity it once was. Not when you have instant channel selection, fast-forward, rewind, and so forth. Video time can be reshaped at will. What may have seemed under the old dispensation like time wasted and unrecoverable is now perhaps not quite as simply structured. If Sloth can be defined as the pretense, in the tradition of American settlement and spoliation, that time is one more nonfinite resource, there to be exploited forever, then we may for now at least have found the illusion, the effect, of controlling, reversing, slowing, speeding, and repeating time—even imagining that we can es-cape it. Sins against video time will have to be radically redefined.

Is some kind of change already in the offing? A recent issue of *The National Enquirer* announced the winner of their contest for the King of Spuds, or top Couch Potato in the United States, culled from about a thousand entries. "'All I do is watch television and work,' admits the 35-year-old bachelor, who keeps three TV sets blaring 24 hours a day at his Fridley, Minn., home and watches a fourth set on the job.

"'There's nothing I like more than sitting around with a six-pack of beer, some chips and a remote control. . . . The TV station even featured me in a town parade. They went into my house, got my couch and put it on a float. I sat on the couch in my bathrobe and rode in the parade!'"

Sure, but is it Sloth? The fourth television set at work, the fact that twice, the Tuber in question mentions sitting and not reclining, suggest something different here. Channel-surfing and VCR-jockeying may require a more nonlinear awareness than may be entirely compatible with the venerable sin of Sloth—some inner alertness or tension, as of someone sitting in a yoga posture, or in Zen meditation. Is Sloth once more about to be, somehow, transcended? Another possibility of course is that we have not passed beyond acedia at all, but that it has only retreated from its long-familiar venue, television, and is seeking other, more shadowy environments—who knows? computer games, cult religions, obscure trading floors in faraway cities—ready to pop up again in some new form to offer us cosmic despair on the cheap.

Unless the state of our souls becomes once more a subject of serious concern, there is little question that Sloth will continue to evolve away from its origins in the long-ago age of faith and miracle, when daily life really was the Holy Ghost visibly at work and time was a story, with a beginning, middle, and end. Belief was intense, engagement deep and fatal. The Christian God was near. Felt. Sloth—defiant sorrow in the face of God's good intentions—was a deadly sin.

Perhaps the future of Sloth will lie in sinning against what now seems increasingly to define us—technology. Persisting in Luddite sorrow, despite technology's good intentions, there we'll sit with our heads in virtual reality, glumly refusing to be absorbed in its idle, disposable fantasies, even those about superheroes of Sloth back in Sloth's good old days, full of leisurely but lethal misadventures with the ruthless villains of the Acedia Squad.

QUESTIONS FOR ANALYSIS AND DISCUSSION

1. What is your response to Pynchon's comparison of television to computers or virtual reality?

2. Acknowledging the decline of religion's centrality to ethics, Pynchon's wit often focuses on the strange ways sloth expresses itself. It plays on our self-deceit. It promises us that we can get something without doing anything. In that sense, religious ethics may have been correct in identifying sloth as the worst vice even though it had trouble overcoming sloth. How does Pynchon see the current danger of sloth or acedia? Do you agree or disagree with his observations?

3. The remote control and the VCR have altered our reality, at least the reality for those of the television generation. Do Pynchon's humorous descriptions also, in your view, capture some of the truths about the virtual world? How do your observations of human conduct around the remote control, VCR, and computer stations compare with Pynchon's descriptions? Do you draw similar moral conclusions? Explain your answer.

83.

GEORGE GERBNER

Television: The New State Religion?

We should be careful not to underestimate the enduring power of television. From the perspective of George Gerbner (b. 1919), communications professor at Temple University, television has reached a level of importance in our culture comparable to the centrality of religion in other cultures. What makes an institution central to everyday life? Gerbner outlines several features that characterize a religious culture. These features have the effect of being a common basis for people's lives, from the information they obtain about the world to the way they interpret and value the events affecting them. He then applies these features to television and concludes that in contemporary life television now rivals, if not displaces, the central role long held by religion.

⊢ CRITICAL READING QUESTIONS ⊢

1. What are the main features of an institution when it is the basis of cultural life?
2. In Gerbner's view, how does television occupy our free time?
3. Does Gerbner think the gradual replacement of religion by television is a positive or negative event? Does he prefer a return to a religious culture?

"Television: The New State Religion?" from *Technology As a Human Affair*, edited by Larry A. Hickman (New York: McGraw-Hill, 1990), pp. 192–196.

Both classical electoral and classical Marxist theories of government are based on assumptions rooted in cultural developments of the eighteenth and nineteenth centuries. These developments also gave rise to mass communications and eventually to research on mass communications. In the past few decades, however, rapidly accumulating changes brought about a profound transformation of the cultural conditions on which modern theories of government and of mass communications rest. That change presents an historic challenge to these theories and to scientific workers concerned with these theories. I would like to sketch the nature of that challenge and to make a few tentative suggestions about the tasks ahead.

Human consciousness seems to differ from that of other animals chiefly in that humans experience reality in a symbolic context. Human consciousness is a fabric of images and messages drawn from those towering symbolic structures of a culture that express and regulate the relationships of a social system. When those relationships change, sooner or later the cultural patterns also change to express and maintain the new social order.

For most of humankind's existence, these systems of society and culture changed very slowly and usually under the impact of a collapse or invasion. The long-enduring, face-to-face, preindustrial, preliterate cultural patterns, relatively isolated from each other, encompassed most of the storytelling, and the rituals, art, science, statecraft, and celebrations of the tribe or larger community. They explained over and over again the nature of the universe and the meaning of life. Their repetitive patterns, memorized incantations, popular sayings, and stories demonstrated the values, roles, productive tasks, and power relationships of society. Children were born into them, old men and women died to their ministrations, and both rulers and the ruled acted out their respective roles according to their tenets. These organically integrated symbolic patterns permeated the life space of every member of the community. Nonselective participation of all in the same symbolic world generated mistrust of strangers, the quest for security through protection by the powerful, and a sense of apprehension of and resistance to change. Conflicts of interest were submerged and dissent suppressed in the interests of what to most people seemed to be the only possible design for life.

All of this changed when the industrial revolution altered the contours of power and the structure of society. The extension of mass production into symbol-making correspondingly altered the symbolic context of consciousness and created cultural conditions necessary for the rise of modern theories of government.

One of the first industrial products was the printed book. Printing made it possible to relieve memory of its formula-bound burdens and opened the way to the endless accumulation of information and innovation. "Packaged knowledge" (the Book) could be given directly to individuals, bypassing its previously all-powerful dispensers, and could cross the old boundaries of status and community. Images and messages could now be used *selectively*. They could be chosen to express and advance individual and group interests. Printed stories—broadsides, crime and news, mercantile intelligence, romantic novels—could now speak selectively to different groups in the population and explain the newly differentiated social relationships which emerged from the industrial revolution. Print made it possible for the newly differentiated consciousness to spread beyond the limiting confines of face-to-face communication. Selectivity of symbolic participation was the prerequisite to the differentiation of consciousness among class and other interest groups within large and heterogeneous societies.

Publics are created and maintained through *publication*. Electoral theories of government are predicated upon the assumption of cultural conditions in which each public can produce and select information suited to the advancement of its own interests. Representatives of those interests are then supposed to formulate laws and administer policies that orchestrate different group interests on behalf of society as a whole.

Marxist-Leninist theories of government similarly (albeit more implicitly) assume cultural conditions that permit selectivity of symbolic production and participation, and thus differentiation of consciousness along class lines. Lenin's characterization of the press as collective organizer and mobilizer assumes (not unlike advertisers do in capitalist countries) that the major mass media are the cultural organs of the groups that own and operate (or sponsor) them. Only in that way could working class organizations (or business corporations) produce ideologically coherent and autonomous symbol systems for their publics.

Before these theories of government came to full fruition, the cultural conditions upon which they were explicitly or implicitly based began to change. Private corporate organizations grew to the size and power of many governments. The increasingly massive mass media became their cultural arms and the First Amendment their shield. Commercial pressures made the service of many small, poor, or dissenting publics impractical. Public relations replaced the autonomous aggregation of many publics. Public opinion became the published opinions of cross-sections of atomized individuals rather than a differentiated mosaic reflecting the composite of organized publics, each conscious of its own interest.

In the young socialist countries and People's Democracies, mass media became centralized organs of revolutionary establishments. Their governing responsibilities made it difficult to cultivate a distinctly working class consciousness and to institutionalize the critical functions of the press.

These problems and difficulties arose under essentially print-based cultural conditions. But in the past few decades even those conditions began to change.

The harbinger of that change is television. The special characteristics of television set it apart from other mass media to such an extent that it is misleading to think of it in the same terms or to research it in the same terms. Furthermore, these special characteristics are only the forerunners of the prospect of an all-electronic organically composed and orchestrated total symbolic environment.

What are these special characteristics of television? My observations are based primarily on our research and experience in the United States. We do not yet know to what extent they are applicable to other countries. (That, I think, should be an early task for communications research to discover.)

1. Television consumes more time and attention of more people than all other media and leisure time activities combined. The television set is on for six hours and fifteen minutes a day in the average American home, and its sounds and images now fill the living space and symbolic world of most Americans.

2. Unlike the other media, you do not have to wait for, plan for, go out to, or seek out television. It comes to you directly at home and is there all the time. It has become a member of the family, telling its stories patiently, compellingly, untiringly. Few parents, teachers, or priests can compete with its vivid demonstrations of what people of all kinds are like and how society works.

3. Just as television requires no mobility, it requires no literacy. In fact, it shows and tells about the world to the less educated and the nonreader—those who have never before shared the culture of the literate—with special authority and force. Television now informs most people in the United States—many of its viewers simply do not read—and much of its information comes from what is called entertainment. As in ancient times of great rituals, festivals, and circuses, the information-poor are again royally entertained by the organic symbolic patterns informing those who do not seek information.

4. These organic patterns have to be seen—and analyzed—as total systems. The content differentiations of the print era, where there were sharp distinctions between information (news) and entertainment (drama, etc.) or fiction and documentary or other genres, no longer apply. Besides, viewers typically select not programs but hours of the day and watch whatever is on during those hours. Unlike books, newspapers, magazines, or movies, television's content and effects do not depend on individually crafted and selected works, stories, etc. Assembly line production fills total programming formulas whose structure encompasses all groups but serves one overall perspective. Storytelling (drama and legendary) is at the heart of this—as of any other—symbol system. "Real-life" demonstrations of the same value structure, as in television news, provide verisimilitude and "documentary" confirmation to the mythological world of television. All types of programming within the program structure complement and reinforce one another. It makes no sense to study the content or impact of one type of program in isolation from the others. The same viewers watch them all: the total system as a whole is absorbed into the mainstream of common consciousness.

5. For the first time since the preindustrial age, or perhaps in all of history, there is little age-grading or separation of the symbolic materials that socialize members into the community. Television is truly a cradle-to-grave experience. Infants are born into a television home and learn from its sounds and images before they can speak, let alone read. By the time they reach school age they will have spent more hours with television than they would spend in a college classroom. At the far end of the life cycle, old people, and most institutionalized populations, are almost totally dependent on television for regular "human" contact and engagement in the larger world. Only a minority of children and older age groups watch the few programs (none in "prime time") especially designed for them. Unlike other media, television tells its stories to children, parents, and grandparents, all at the same time.

6. Television is essentially in the business of assembling heterogeneous audiences and selling their time to advertisers or other institutional sponsors. The audiences include all age, sex, ethnic, racial, and other interest groups. They are all exposed to the same repetitive messages conveying the largest common denominator of values and conduct in society. Minority groups see their own image shaped by the dominant interests of the larger culture. This means the dissolution

of the concept of autonomous publics and of any authentic group or class consciousness. Television provides an organically related synthetic symbolic structure which once again presents a total world of meanings for all. It is related to the State as only the church was in ancient times.

All this adds up to a non-selectively used cultural pattern which can no longer serve the tasks of cultivating selective and differentiated group, class, or other public consciousness. The pattern is formula-bound, ritualistic, repetitive. It thrives on novelty but is resistant to change, and it cultivates resistance to change. In that, too, television's social symbolic functions resemble preindustrial religions more than they do the media that preceded it. The process has tremendous popular mobilizing power which holds the least informed and least educated most in its spell. Results of our research (reported under the title "Living with Television: The Violence Profile" in the Spring 1976 issue of the *Journal of Communication*) indicate that television viewing tends to cultivate its own particular outlook on social reality even among the well-educated and traditionally "elite" groups.

Heavy viewers of television are more apprehensive, anxious, and mistrustful of others than light viewers in the same age, sex, and educational groups. The fear that viewing American television seems to generate, the consequent quest for security and protection by the authorities, the effective dissolution of autonomous publics, and the ease with which credible threats and scares can be used (or provoked) to justify almost any policy create a fundamentally new cultural situation. The new conditions of synthetic consciousness-making pose new problems, difficulties, and challenges for those who wish to realistically analyze or guide public understanding of society.

Researchers and scholars of communication and culture should now devote major attention to long-range cross-cultural comparative media studies that investigate the policies, processes, and consequences of the mass-production of major symbol systems in light of the respective structures and aims of different social systems. Do media really do what they are designed to do according to the theories governing (or used to explain) the societies in which they exist? What are the differences and similarities among them? What are the cultural and human consequences of the international exchange of media materials? What are the effects of changing cultural, technological, and institutional conditions upon the social functions of media, particularly television? What are the new organizational, professional, artistic, and educational requirements for the effective fulfillment of societal goals in different cultural and social systems? And, finally, how can liberation from the age-old bonds of humankind lead to cultural conditions that enrich rather than limit visions of further options and possibilities?

These are broad and difficult tasks but we can at least begin to tackle them. Much depends on the success of the effort.

QUESTIONS FOR ANALYSIS AND DISCUSSION

1. For many people, particularly those with faith, Gerbner's view of religion is inadequate because it does not emphasize the belief in God. Do you think this is relevant to Gerbner's argument? Why, or why not?

2. If leisure is part of the good life and people should be able to enjoy their leisure as they choose, on what basis can Gerbner support his social or moral objections to the role of television? Outline what you see as Gerbner's basic objection, then clarify your own response to it.

3. In pagan times people enjoyed their leisure in stretches at a time. According to historian Paul Veyne, in ancient Rome political and social leaders competed to sponsor the most exciting spectacles for their citizens. These spectacles included circuses, chariot races, gladiator battles, and public tortures of criminals or religious heretics. Moreover, during the week or two that these spectacles were offered, citizens from all levels of society were brought together. Do you think television offers similar spectacles? Is it fair to say that advertisers are the patrons, celebrities are the gods, and sound bites are the new gospel? Or is television little more than it claims to be—a box of images that you can turn on or off?

4. In the previous essay Thomas Pynchon speculates that virtual communications may be displacing television. Gerbner's essay was written in the late 1970s. Have the last two decades shown the limitations of Gerbner's analysis? To what extent do Pynchon and Gerbner agree that both television and cyberspace contribute to the moral decline of Americans because they insidiously condone sloth? Do you agree with their speculations?

84.

ARISTOTLE

Politics, Leisure, and Happiness

Happiness is the realization and exercise of virtue, maintains Aristotle. This results not only from the personal development of character but also through social efforts to encourage a good life for all citizens. Hence, a virtuous citizen and a virtuous society reflect one another. One manifestation of the virtuous society is the amount and value of leisure. In this selection from Politics, *Aristotle explains how a good society directs itself toward peace and leisure, for this allows its citizens to pursue happiness. In contrast, a society driven toward conquest and greed rarely allows its citizens free time to develop their talents.*

"Politics, Leisure, and Happiness," from *Politics*, book VII, Chapters 13–15, edited by Richard McKeon (New York: Random House, 1941), pp. 1294–1301. Notes have been omitted.

⊣ CRITICAL READING QUESTIONS ⊢

1. What is the difference between the goods from fortune and the goods from knowledge and purpose?

2. Which three things contribute to the virtuous life? Which do only humans have?

3. Aristotle believes life is divided into two parts. If peace is the part that contrasts with war, what contrasts with leisure?

4. Before the virtue of leisure is enjoyed, which other virtues must citizens and society encourage?

5. How does Aristotle distinguish between conditional and absolute goods?

---

13. Returning to the constitution itself, let us seek to determine out of what and what sort of elements the state which is to be happy and well-governed should be composed. There are two things in which all well-being consists: one of them is the choice of a right end and aim of action, and the other the discovery of the actions which are means towards it; for the means and the end may agree or disagree. Sometimes the right end is set before men, but in practice they fail to attain it; in other cases they are successful in all the means, but they propose to themselves a bad end; and sometimes they fail in both. Take, for example, the art of medicine; physicians do not always understand the nature of health, and also the means which they use may not effect the desired end. In all arts and sciences both the end and the means should be equally within our control.

The happiness and well-being which all men manifestly desire, some have the power of attaining, but to others, from some accident or defect of nature, the attainment of them is not granted; for a good life requires a supply of external goods, in a less degree when men are in a good state, in a greater degree when they are in a lower state. Others again, who possess the conditions of happiness, go utterly wrong from the first in the pursuit of it. But since our object is to discover the best form of government, that, namely, under which a city will be best governed, and since the city is best governed which has the greatest opportunity of obtaining happiness, it is evident that we must clearly ascertain the nature of happiness.

We maintain, and have said in the *Ethics,* if the arguments there adduced are of any value, that happiness is the realization and perfect exercise of virtue, and this not conditional, but absolute. And I used the term "conditional" to express that which is indispensable, and "absolute" to express that which is good in itself. Take the case of just actions; just punishments and chastisements do indeed spring from a good principle, but they are good only because we cannot do without them—it would be better that neither individuals nor states should need anything of the sort—but actions which aim at honour and advantage are absolutely the best. The conditional action is only the choice of a lesser evil; whereas these are the foundation and creation of good. A good man may make the best even of poverty and disease, and the other ills of life; but he can only attain happiness under the opposite conditions (for this also has been determined in accordance with ethical arguments, that the good man is he for whom, because he is virtuous, the things that are absolutely good are good; it is also plain that his use of these goods must be virtuous and in the absolute sense good). This makes men fancy that external goods are the cause of happiness, yet we might as well say that a brilliant performance on the lyre was to be attributed to the instrument and not to the skill of the performer.

It follows then from what has been said that some things the legislator must find ready to his hand in a state, others he must provide. And therefore we can only say: May our state be constituted in such a manner as to be blessed with the goods of which fortune disposes (for we acknowledge her power): whereas virtue and goodness in the state are not a matter of chance but the result of knowledge and purpose. A city can be virtuous only when the citizens who have a share in the government are virtuous, and in our state all the citizens share in the government; let us then inquire how a man becomes virtuous. For even if we could suppose the citizen body to be virtuous, without each of them being so, yet the latter would be better, for in the virtue of each the virtue of all is involved.

There are three things which make men good and virtuous; these are nature, habit, rational principle. In the first place, every one must be born a man and not some other animal; so, too, he must have a certain character, both of body and soul. But some qualities there is no use in having at birth, for they are altered by habit, and there are some gifts which by nature are made to be turned by habit to good or bad. Animals lead for the most part a life of nature, although in lesser particulars some are influenced by habit as well. Man has rational principle, in addition, and man only. Wherefore nature, habit, rational principle must be in harmony with one another; for they do not always agree; men do many things against habit and nature, if rational principle persuades them that they ought. We have already determined what natures are likely to be most easily moulded by the hands of the legislator. All else is the work of education; we learn some things by habit and some by instruction.

14. . . . Now the soul of man is divided into two parts, one of which has a rational principle in itself, and the other, not having a rational principle in itself, is able to obey such a principle. And we call a man in any way good because he has the virtues of these two parts. In which of them the end is more likely to be found is no matter of doubt to those who adopt our division; for in the world both of nature and of art the inferior always exists for the sake of the better or superior, and the better or superior is that which has a rational principle. This principle, too, in our ordinary way of speaking, is divided into two kinds, for there is a practical and a speculative principle. This part, then, must evidently be similarly divided. And there must be a corresponding division of actions; the actions of the naturally better part are to be preferred by those who have it in their power to attain to two out of the three or to all, for that is always to every one the most eligible which is the highest attainable by him. The whole of life is further divided into two parts, business and leisure, war and peace, and of actions some aim at what is necessary and useful, and some at what is honourable. And the preference given to one or

the other class of actions must necessarily be like the preference given to one or other part of the soul and its actions over the other; there must be war for the sake of peace, business for the sake of leisure, things useful and necessary for the sake of things honourable. All these points the statesman should keep in view when he frames his laws; he should consider the parts of the soul and their functions, and above all the better and the end; he should also remember the diversities of human lives and actions. For men must be able to engage in business and go to war, but leisure and peace are better; they must do what is necessary and indeed what is useful, but what is honourable is better. On such principles children and persons of every age which requires education should be trained. Whereas even the Hellenes of the present day who are reputed to be best governed, and the legislators who gave them their constitutions, do not appear to have framed their governments with a regard to the best end, or to have given them laws and education with a view to all the virtues, but in a vulgar spirit have fallen back on those which promised to be more useful and profitable. Many modern writers have taken a similar view: they commend the Lacedaemonian constitution, and praise the legislator for making conquest and war his sole aim, a doctrine which may be refuted by argument and has long ago been refuted by facts. For most men desire empire in the hope of accumulating the goods of fortune; and on this ground Thibron and all those who have written about the Lacedaemonian constitution have praised their legislator, because the Lacedaemonians, by being trained to meet dangers, gained great power. But surely they are not a happy people now that their empire has passed away, nor was their legislator right. How ridiculous is the result, if, while they are continuing in the observance of his laws and no one interferes with them, they have lost the better part of life! These writers further err about the sort of government which the legislator should approve, for the government of freemen is nobler and implies more virtue than despotic government. Neither is a city to be deemed happy or a legislator to be praised because he trains his citizens to conquer and obtain dominion over their neighbours, for there is great evil in this. On a similar principle any citizen who could, should obviously try to obtain the power in his own state—the crime which the Lacedaemonians accuse king Pausanias of attempting, although he had so great honour already. No such principle and no law having this object is either statesmanlike or useful or right. For the same things are best both for individuals and for states, and these are the things which the legislator ought to implant in the minds of his citizens. Neither should men study war with a view to the enslavement of those who do not deserve to be enslaved; but first of all they should provide against their own enslavement, and in the second place obtain empire for the good of the governed, and not for the sake of exercising a general despotism, and in the third place they should seek to be masters only over those who deserve to be slaves. Facts, as well as arguments, prove that the legislator should direct all his military and other measures to the provision of leisure and the establishment of peace. For most of these military states are safe only while they are at war, but fall when they have acquired their empire; like unused iron they lose their temper in time of peace. And for this the legislator is to blame, he never having taught them how to lead the life of peace.

15. Since the end of individuals and of states is the same, the end of the best

man and of the best constitution must also be the same; it is therefore evident that there ought to exist in both of them the virtues of leisure; for peace, as has been often repeated, is the end of war, and leisure of toil. But leisure and cultivation may be promoted, not only by those virtues which are practised in leisure, but also by some of those which are useful to business. For many necessaries of life have to be supplied before we can have leisure. Therefore a city must be temperate and brave, and able to endure: for truly, as the proverb says, "There is no leisure for slaves," and those who cannot face danger like men are the slaves of any invader. Courage and endurance are required for business and philosophy for leisure, temperance and justice for both, and more especially in times of peace and leisure, for war compels men to be just and temperate, whereas the enjoyment of good fortune and the leisure which comes with peace tend to make them insolent. Those then who seem to be the best-off and to be in the possession of every good, have special need of justice and temperance—for example, those (if such there be, as the poets say) who dwell in the Islands of the Blest; they above all will need philosophy and temperance and justice, and all the more the more leisure they have, living in the midst of abundance. There is no difficulty in seeing why the state that would be happy and good ought to have these virtues. If it be disgraceful in men not to be able to use the goods of life, it is peculiarly disgraceful not to be able to use them in time of leisure—to show excellent qualities in action and war, and when they have peace and leisure to be no better than slaves. Wherefore we should not practise virtue after the manner of the Lacedaemonians. For they, while agreeing with other men in their conception of the highest goods, differ from the rest of mankind in thinking that they are to be obtained by the practice of a single virtue. And since [they think] these goods and the enjoyment of them greater than the enjoyment derived from the virtues . . . and that [it should be practised] for its own sake, is evident from what has been said; we must now consider how and by what means it is to be attained.

We have already determined that nature and habit and rational principle are required, and, of these, the proper *nature* of the citizens has also been defined by us. But we have still to consider whether the training of early life is to be that of rational principle or habit, for these two must accord, and when in accord they will then form the best of harmonies. The rational principle may be mistaken and fail in attaining the highest ideal of life, and there may be a like evil influence of habit. Thus much is clear in the first place, that, as in all other things, birth implies an antecedent beginning, and that there are beginnings whose end is relative to a further end. Now, in men rational principle and mind are the end towards which nature strives, so that the birth and moral discipline of the citizens ought to be ordered with a view to them. In the second place, as the soul and body are two, we see also that there are two parts of the soul, the rational and the irrational, and two corresponding states—reason and appetite. And as the body is prior in order of generation to the soul, so the irrational is prior to the rational. The proof is that anger and wishing and desire are implanted in children from their very birth, but reason and understanding are developed as they grow older. Wherefore, the care of the body ought to precede that of the soul, and the training of the appetitive part should follow: none the less our care of it must be for the sake of the reason, and our care of the body for the sake of the soul.

QUESTIONS FOR ANALYSIS AND DISCUSSION

1. Aristotle says that a good man can make the best of difficult conditions but will not be happy in them. What does he mean by this? How do you distinguish between difficult conditions and their opposite? Do you accept this distinction between surviving and being happy?

2. The combination of nature, habit, and reason makes a person virtuous. How do you think they are related in moral development? Aristotle indicates that animals have nature and habit, but not reason. Yet he adds that humans will use reason to go against nature and habit. Can you illustrate what you think he has in mind? Does reason correct the flaws nature and habit give us, or can reason corrupt the good things nature and habit give us?

3. A virtuous government and a virtuous citizenry go hand in hand. Imagine Aristotle living today. How do you think his axiom would make sense of current politics? When Aristotle emphasizes the task of legislators to shape virtuous citizens, does this mean the legislators should have the same virtues as the citizens? Are the virtues that make good leaders different from the virtues that make good citizens? In your response address a current political controversy.

4. What do you think is meant by the proverb, "There is no leisure for slaves"? In clarifying your understanding, pay special attention to what is meant by "slaves."

85.

PLATO

On Free Time and Truth

Leisure affords another good—the chance to think and discuss matters of truth. In the dialogue Theaetetus, *Plato has Socrates engaging his friend Theodorus about the merits of Protagoras's famous principle that "man is the measure of all things." The excerpt picks up with Socrates arguing that if we accept this principle, then what everyone says is true. Hence, the principle itself is true if someone believes it and false if someone else says it. In other words, Socrates observes, Protagoras's principle does not help us to decide*

"On Free Time and Truth," from *Theaetetus*, translated by F. M. Cornford, (Princeton NJ: Princeton University Press, 1935), pp. 877–881.

*matters of truth and falsehood. Then Socrates shifts focus by asking who is best able
to discuss these matters. He points to the free man. The antithesis of the free man—the
slave—is too wrapped up in worldly concerns. At stake in this antagonism, notes Socrates, is the "true life of happiness for gods and men."*

CRITICAL READING QUESTIONS

1. If man is the measure of all things, does that imply that everyone is
   equal or that the best measurers are the best humans?
2. How is the philosophical person distinguished from the speaker in a
   court of law?
3. How does the anecdote about Thales exemplify the popular attitude
   toward philosophy?
4. What happens to the legal mind when it tries to reflect on the nature
   of human happiness and misery?

SOCRATES: On all hands, then, Protagoras included, his opinion will be disputed,
   or rather Protagoras will join in the general consent—when he admits to an
   opponent the truth of his contrary opinion, from that moment Protagoras
   himself will be admitting that a dog or the man in the street is not a measure of
   anything whatever that he does not understand. Isn't that so?

THEODORUS: Yes.

SOCRATES: Then, since it is disputed by everyone, the *Truth* of Protagoras is true
   to nobody—to himself no more than to anyone else.

THEODORUS: We are running my old friend too hard, Socrates.

SOCRATES: But it is not clear that we are outrunning the truth, my friend. Of
   course it is likely that, as an older man, he was wiser than we are, and if at this
   moment he could pop his head up through the ground there as far as to the
   neck, very probably he would expose me thoroughly for talking such nonsense
   and you for agreeing to it, before he sank out of sight and took to his heels.
   However, we must do our best with such lights as we have and continue to say
   what we think. Now, for instance, must we not say that everyone would agree
   at least to this, that one man can be wiser or more ignorant than another?

THEODORUS: I certainly think so.

SOCRATES: And further, shall we say that the doctrine would find its firmest footing in the position we traced out in our defense of Protagoras, that most
   things—hot, dry, sweet, everything of that sort—are to each person as they
   appear to him? Whereas, if there is any case in which the theory would con-

cede that one man is superior to another, it might consent to admit that, in the matter of good or bad health, not any woman or child—or animal, for that matter—knows what is wholesome for it and is capable of curing itself, but that here, if anywhere, one person is superior to another.

THEODORUS: I should certainly say so.

SOCRATES: And again in social matters, the theory will say that, so far as good and bad customs or rights and wrongs or matters of religion are concerned, whatever any state makes up its mind to enact as lawful for itself, really is lawful for it, and in this field no individual or state is wiser than another. But where it is a question of laying down what is for its advantage or disadvantage, once more there, if anywhere, the theory will admit a difference between two advisers or between the decisions of two different states in respect of truth, and would hardly venture to assert that any enactment which a state supposes to be for its advantage will quite certainly be so.

But, in that field I am speaking of—in right and wrong and matters of religion—people are ready to affirm that none of these things is natural, with a reality of its own, but rather that the public decision becomes true at the moment when it is made and remains true so long as the decision stands, and those who do not argue altogether as Protagoras does carry on their philosophy on these lines.

But one theory after another is coming upon us, Theodorus, and the last is more important than the one before.

THEODORUS: Well, Socrates, we have time at our disposal.

SOCRATES: Evidently. And it strikes me now, as often before, how natural it is that men who have spent much time in philosophical studies should look ridiculous when they appear as speakers in a court of law.

THEODORUS: How do you mean?

SOCRATES: When you compare men who have knocked about from their youth up in law courts and such places with others bred in philosophical pursuits, the one set seems to have been trained as slaves, the others as free men.

THEODORUS: In what way?

SOCRATES: In the way you spoke of. The free man always has time at his disposal to converse in peace at his leisure. He will pass, as we are doing now, from one argument to another—we have just reached the third. Like us, he will leave the old for a fresh one which takes his fancy more, and he does not care how long or short the discussion may be, if only it attains the truth. The orator is always talking against time, hurried on by the clock; there is no space to enlarge upon any subject he chooses, but the adversary stands over him ready to recite a schedule of the points to which he must confine himself. He is a slave disputing about a fellow slave before a master sitting in judgment with some definite plea in his hand, and the issue is never indifferent, but his personal concerns are always at stake, sometimes even his life. Hence he acquires a tense and bitter shrewdness; he knows how to flatter his master and earn his good graces, but his mind is narrow and crooked. An apprenticeship in slavery has dwarfed and twisted his growth and robbed him of his free spirit, driving him into devious ways, threatening him with fears and dangers which the tenderness of youth could not face with truth and honesty; so, turning from the first to lies and the requital of wrong with wrong, warped and stunted, he passes from youth to manhood with no soundness in him and turns out, in the end, a man of formidable intellect—as he imagines.

So much for the orator, Theodorus. Shall I now describe the philosophical choir to which we belong, or would you rather leave that and go back to our discussion? We must not abuse that freedom we claimed of ranging from one subject to another.

THEODORUS: No, Socrates, let us have your description first. As you said quite rightly, we are not the servants of the argument, which must stand and wait for the moment when we choose to pursue this or that topic to a conclusion. We are not in a court under the judge's eye, nor in the theater with an audience to criticize our philosophical evolutions.

SOCRATES: Then, if that is your wish, let us speak of the leaders in philosophy, for the weaker members may be neglected. From their youth up they have never known the way to market place or law court or Council Chamber or any other place of public assembly; they never hear a decree read out or look at the text of a law. To take any interest in the rivalries of political cliques, in meetings, dinners, and merrymakings with flute girls, never occurs to them even in dreams. Whether any fellow citizen is well- or ill-born or has inherited some defect from his ancestors on either side, the philosopher knows no more than how many pints of water there are in the sea. He is not even aware that he knows nothing of all this, for if he holds aloof, it is not for reputation's sake, but because it is really only his body that sojourns in his city, while his thought, disdaining all such things as worthless, takes wings, as Pindar says, "beyond the sky, beneath the earth," searching the heavens and measuring the plains, everywhere seeking the true nature of everything as a whole, never sinking to what lies close at hand.

THEODORUS: What do you mean, Socrates?

SOCRATES: The same thing as the story about the Thracian maidservant who exercised her wit at the expense of Thales, when he was looking up to study the stars and tumbled down a well. She scoffed at him for being so eager to know what was happening in the sky that he could not see what lay at his feet. Anyone who gives his life to philosophy is open to such mockery. It is true that he is unaware what his next-door neighbor is doing, hardly knows, indeed, whether the creature is a man at all; he spends all his pains on the question, what man is, and what powers and properties distinguish such a nature from any other. You see what I mean, Theodorus?

THEODORUS: Yes, and it is true.

SOCRATES: And so, my friend, as I said at first, on a public occasion or in private company, in a law court or anywhere else, when he is forced to talk about what lies at his feet or is before his eyes, the whole rabble will join the maidservants in laughing at him, as from inexperience he walks blindly and stumbles into every pitfall. His terrible clumsiness makes him seem so stupid. He cannot engage in an exchange of abuse, for, never having made a study of anyone's peculiar weaknesses, he has no personal scandals to bring up; so in his helplessness he looks a fool. When people vaunt their own or other men's merits, his unaffected laughter makes him conspicuous and they think he is frivolous. When a despot or king is eulogized, he fancies he is hearing some keeper of swine or sheep or cows being congratulated on the quantity of milk he has squeezed out of his flock; only he reflects that the animal that princes tend and milk is more given than sheep or cows to nurse a sullen grievance, and that a herdsman of this sort, penned up in his castle, is doomed by sheer press of work to be as rude and uncultivated as the shepherd in his mountain fold. He hears of the marvelous wealth of some landlord who owns ten thousand acres or more, but that seems a small matter to one accustomed to think of the earth as a whole. When they harp upon birth—some gentleman who can point to seven generations of wealthy ancestors—he thinks that such commendation must come from men of purblind vision, too uneducated to keep their eyes fixed on the whole or to reflect that any man has had countless myriads of ancestors and among them any number of rich men and beggars, kings and slaves, Greeks and barbarians. To pride oneself on a catalogue of twenty-five progenitors going back to Heracles, son of Amphitryon, strikes him as showing a strange pettiness of outlook. He laughs at a man who cannot rid his mind of foolish vanity by reckoning that before Amphityron there was a twenty-fifth ancestor, and before him a fiftieth, whose fortunes were as luck would have it. But in all these matters the world has the laugh of the philosopher, partly because he seems arrogant, partly because of his helpless ignorance in matters of daily life.

THEODORUS: Yes, Socrates, that is exactly what happens.

SOCRATES: On the other hand, my friend, when the philosopher drags the other upward to a height at which he may consent to drop the question, "What injustice have I done to you or you to me?" and to think about justice and injustice in themselves, what each is, and how they differ from one another and from anything else, or to stop quoting poetry about the happiness of kings or of men with gold in store and think about the meaning of kingship and the whole question of human happiness and misery, what their nature is, and how humanity can gain the one and escape the other—in all this field, when that small, shrewd, legal mind has to render an account, then the situation is reversed. Now it is he who is dizzy from hanging at such an unaccustomed height and looking down from mid-air. Lost and dismayed and stammering, he will be laughed at, not by maidservants or the uneducated—they will not see what is happening—but by everyone whose breeding has been the antithesis of a slave's.

Such are the two characters, Theodorus. The one is nursed in freedom and leisure, the philosopher, as you call him. He may be excused if he looks foolish or useless when faced with some menial task, if he cannot tie up bedclothes into a neat bundle or flavor a dish with spices and a speech with flattery. The other is smart in the dispatch of all such services, but has not learned to wear his cloak like a gentleman, or caught the accent of discourse that will rightly celebrate the true life of happiness for gods and men.

THEODORUS: If you could convince everyone, Socrates, as you convince me, there would be more peace and fewer evils in the world.

SOCRATES: Evils, Theodorus, can never be done away with, for the good must always have its contrary; nor have they any place in the divine world, but they must needs haunt this region of our mortal nature. That is why we should make all speed to take flight from this world to the other, and that means becoming like the divine so far as we can, and that again is to become righteous with the help of wisdom. But it is no such easy matter to convince men that the reasons for avoiding wickedness and seeking after goodness are not those which the world gives. The right motive is not that one should seem innocent and good—that is no better, to my thinking, than an old wives' tale—but let us state the truth in this way. In the divine there is no shadow of unrighteousness, only the perfection of righteousness, and nothing is more like the divine than any one of us who becomes as righteous as possible. It is here that a man shows his true spirit and power or lack of spirit and nothingness. For to know this is wisdom and excellence of the genuine sort; not to know it is to be manifestly blind and base. All other forms of seeming power and intelligence in the rulers of society are as mean and vulgar as the mechanic's skill in handicraft. If a man's words and deeds are unrighteous and profane, he had best not persuade himself that he is a great man because he sticks at nothing, glorying in his shame as such men do when they fancy that others say of them. They are no fools, no useless burdens to the earth, but men of the right sort to weather the storms of public life.

Let the truth be told. They are what they fancy they are not, all the more for deceiving themselves, for they are ignorant of the very thing it most concerns them to know—the penalty of injustice. This is not as they imagine, stripes and death, which do not always fall on the wrongdoer, but a penalty that cannot be escaped.

THEODORUS: What penalty is that?

SOCRATES: There are two patterns, my friend, in the unchangeable nature of things, one of divine happiness, the other of godless misery—a truth to which their folly makes them utterly blind, unaware that in doing injustice they are growing less like one of these patterns and more like the other. The penalty they pay is the life they lead, answering to the pattern they resemble. But if we tell them that, unless they rid themselves of their superior cunning, that other region which is free from all evil will not receive them after death, but here on earth they will dwell for all time in some form of life resembling their own and in the society of things as evil as themselves, all this will sound like foolishness to such strong and unscrupulous minds.

THEODORUS: So it will, Socrates.

QUESTIONS FOR ANALYSIS AND DISCUSSION

1. Speakers in the court of law talk about justice; philosophers talk about justice. Why does Socrates insist that the former are so rushed by the clock that they are incapable of true reflection? The orator, says Socrates, "acquires a tense and bitter shrewdness; he knows how to flatter his master and earn his good graces, but his mind is narrow and crooked." How does this portrayal contrast with one able to engage freely in matters of truth?

2. Philosophical reflection requires leisure. Leisure is partly the result of society's work. This work is good, for without it we could not engage in philosophical reflection. Plato is not the only philosopher to look at leisure this way. Still, is it a self-serving argument? That is, philosophers like leisure because without it there would be no philosophers. Is this analogous to a warrior saying war is needed because without it there would be no need for warriors? One rejoinder has Socrates saying that the philosophical part of anyone's life is best realized in freedom, when one can think, read, and talk about things without the pressure of performing or pleasing. Without engaging in philosophical wonderment and reflection from time to time, one loses sense of what is the good in life. That is, one's life is reduced to routine. One becomes a slave to time. What are your thoughts about the role of the philosophical activity in terms of the good life?

3. Socrates admits philosophical endeavors risk the mockery of the rabble. Yet Socrates concludes this excerpt by noting how ordinary events and people incite philosophical laughter. But this laughter is not exclusive to those who read and study books about philosophical problems and issues. When hearing of someone who falls from vanity or greed, when hearing that someone's pretense or envy is exposed, Socrates remarks, "in all these matters the world has the laugh of the philosopher." How can you explain this laughter? How is it distinguished from other kinds of laughter?

4. Cartoons often portray the sage sitting alone on the hilltop. Seen from a distance, the activities of philosophers seem eccentric, superfluous, or foolish. On a closer look, according to Plato, who is the real fool on the hill? Why?

86.

DAVID HOLLENBACH, S.J.

Virtue, the Common Good, and Democracy

Some critics of virtue ethics contend that ancient moralists could talk seriously about virtues and vices because their sense of sociability was framed by a sense of political community, and people knew one another directly or indirectly. In modern times when most people live in urban or suburban areas with over a million residents, talk about virtues and vices seems quaint but unrealistic. In this setting, should government keep the peace, promote prosperity, and leave people alone? Critics claim that legislators neither can nor should try to make its citizens moral. Social philosopher David Hollenbach does not believe it has to be this way. Indeed, he argues that much of the demise of cultural life in the United States can be attributed to the neglect of virtues and vices by political theorists. Their focus on issues such as individual rights, just distribution of goods, and separation of private and public life have undercut the potential contributions from virtue theorists. To fill this absence, Hollenbach reviews the importance of familiar virtues and introduces two that can reinvigorate modern democracy.

⊢ CRITICAL READING QUESTIONS ⊢

1. What is pluralism? What does pluralism say about the common good?
2. Why does Hollenbach think we are going through an "eclipse of citizenship"?
3. How is fragmentation of the social world evident today?
4. Which two virtues does Hollenbach propose to rejuvenate democratic life?
5. Who does Hollenbach expect to be the leaders in discussing the common good? Where does he think these discussions should take place?

"Virtue, the Common Good, and Democracy," from *New Communitarian Thinking: Persons, Virtues, Institutions, and Communities,* edited by Amitai Etzioni (Charlottesville: University Press of Virginia, 1996), pp. 143–153. Notes have been omitted.

This essay argues that a recovery of the idea of the common good and a strong sense of the virtues of citizenship are vitally important in the present moment of American history. It claims that sustaining a democratic form of life depends on the presence of citizens who understand themselves as responsible to and for the quality for their common life together. Thus, individualistic understandings of the human person common in American culture today need to be transformed by more communal and solidaristic sensibilities.

In order to make a plausible case for virtue and the common good, however, it is necessary to address legitimate fears that revival of these notions in practice will lead to a stifling of freedom. It is a historical fact that individualistic concepts of self-realization emerged out of the struggle against arbitrary power, both the political power of the monarchies of the ancien régime and the economic power of the aristocracy. The defense of individual rights and freedoms was without doubt a kind of liberation movement. Contemporary liberal theorists are rightly wary of forms of communal solidarity that threaten freedom through paternalistic or authoritarian political programs. They are also suspicious of the potential for conflict and even violence that strong religious, ethnic, and national solidarities have exhibited in the past and continue to show today in some settings.

These fears are founded on what John Rawls calls "the fact of pluralism." The stress on freedom and autonomy characteristic of modern liberal democracies developed historically as a way of responding to the diversity of conceptions of the meaning and purpose of life. This pluralism is most evident in the religious domain. But there is also a deep pluralism in philosophical conceptions of how to live a good life. Rawls says that this religious and philosophical pluralism "is not a mere historical condition that will soon pass away; it is, I believe, a permanent feature of the public culture of modern democracies. Under the political and social conditions secured by the basic rights and liberties historically associated with these regimes, the diversity of views will persist and may increase." Thus, the "common sense political sociology of democratic societies" tells us that agreement on a single conception of the good life among all citizens is unattainable. Such agreement could be maintained "only by the oppressive use of state power."

There is no doubt that Rawls is right about the deep disputes about the meaning of the good life that are present in our society. But for him there is no way to resolve these disputes. Therefore, he argues that in politics we must deal with disagreements about the comprehensive good of human life by what he calls "the method of avoidance." By this he means that in political life "we try, so far as we can, neither to assert nor to deny any religious, philosophical or moral views, or their associated philosophical accounts of truth and the status of values." Only in this way will we have a chance of achieving that level of consensus that is necessary for social harmony to exist at all. His prescription, therefore, is that "we apply the principle of toleration to philosophy itself" when debating the basic political and economic institutions that will structure social life. Each man or woman must be free to hold his or her view of what the full good really is. But these comprehensive views of the good life must remain the private convictions of individuals. "In applying the principle of toleration to philosophy itself it is left to citizens individually to resolve the questions of religion, philosophy and morals in accordance with the views they freely affirm." Or as Richard Rorty puts it, religious and philosophical convictions should be exempt from coercion in a liberal society under one condition: that such convictions "be reserved for private life." Argument about the common good is also to be avoided in debates about more specific public policies. Liberal democracy aims at "disengaging discussions of such questions from discussions of public policy." This privatization of "thick" visions of the good is not only a sociologically given fact; it is a moral constraint on political activity.

As one contemplates the sad state of the former Yugoslavia and other places where communal conflict is rife, the dangers of exclusivist forms of solidarity and the virtues of liberal tolerance are evident. One can ask, however, whether the prescription that comprehensive visions of the good life should be reserved for the private sphere and that public life should be built solely around the value of tolerance is in fact the medicine needed to heal what ails the United States today. For example, in the United States citizenship has itself become a problematic concept in our time, and we are experiencing an "eclipse of citizenship." The low percentage of Americans who exercise their right to vote is the most visible evidence for this. This is caused in part by a lack of confidence that individual people can have any meaningful influence in a political society as vast as ours. Many people, including many in the middle class, feel politically powerless.

In an insightful book titled *Why Americans Hate Politics,* E. J. Dionne argues that this alienation can be attributed to the fact that current political discourse fails to address the real needs of communities. This failure is itself partly the result of the fact that interest-group politics is frequently incapable of even naming the social bonds that increasingly destine us to sharing either a common good or a "common bad." Politics is perceived as a contest among groups with little or no concern for the wider society and its problems. Rawls's recommendation that we avoid introducing conceptions of the full human good into political discourse is designed to neutralize potential conflicts and to promote democratic social harmony. But it may ironically have the effect of threatening democracy through alienation and anomie rather than conflict or violence. A principled commitment to avoiding sustained discourse about the common good can produce a downward spiral in which shared meaning, understanding, and community become even harder to achieve in practice.

This was the fear implicit in the United States Catholic bishops' 1986 pastoral letter, *Economic Justice for All.* Echoing numerous sociologists, the bishops noted that there are deep structural causes for the contemporary devaluation of citizenship. Modern societies are characterized by a division of labor into highly specialized jobs and professions. Individual lives are further fragmented by the way family life, the world of work, networks of friendship, and religious community are so often lived out in separate compartments. In the words of Robert Bellah and his coauthors in the book *Habits of the Heart,* contemporary American culture is a "culture of separation." It is increasingly difficult to see how our chopped-up segments of experience fit together in anything like a meaningful whole. "The world comes to us in pieces, in fragments, lacking any overall pattern." This fragmentation can undermine the sense of overall purpose in the lives of individual persons, leading to a seemingly endless quest for one's own identity. Because of the complexity and high degree of differentiation characteristic of modern social existence, individuals lack a readily intelligible map by which they can locate themselves and chart their course through life.

Thus, when modern society and culture are contrasted with the more organic and integrated world of the premodern era, a characteristic of great moral significance stands out. In Peter Berger's analysis this fragmentation of the social world means that "the individual's experience of himself becomes more real to him than his experience of the objective social world. Therefore, the individual seeks to find his 'foothold' in reality in himself rather than outside himself. One of the consequences of this is that the individual's subjective reality . . . becomes increasingly differentiated, complex—and 'interesting' to himself. Subjectivity acquires previously unconceived depths." Such preoccupation with personal identity makes it very difficult to see how the kinds of lives we lead make a difference for the common good of the whole community. And lack of public discussion of the common good in turn generates a heightened sense that individuals are powerless over the larger social forces that shape their lives. It also helps explain the prevalence of single-issue styles of political action among many who do continue to see politics as a sphere open to at least some influence.

There is great irony here. For the same social conditions that encourage individualism and preoccupation with the private world of subjectivity on the level of consciousness are also the sources of a qualitatively new form of objective, structured interdependence among persons. Technology, bureaucracy, mobility, and mass communication make the public world seem alien and impersonal. At the same time these factors heighten the impact that the structures of the public world actually have on the dignity and meaning of individual lives. In such circumstances narrow focus on private goods and individual interests threatens to allow large domains of social existence to slip from the control of human freedom or to fall under the direction of powerful elites. Thus at the very time that it has become increasingly difficult to sustain a vision of the common good, it is also more urgently important to do so if we are to sustain democratic practices.

I would propose that achieving this desideratum depends on rethinking the sharp division between the private and public spheres of social existence. Thinkers like Rawls and Rorty fear the presence of comprehensive understandings of the good life in public because they identify public life with the domain governed by the coercive power of the state. Others with a more libertarian bent are worried that too much public presence of visions of the common good will restrict economic freedom by setting political constraints on the market. In both cases the discussion of the role of comprehensive understandings of the good in public life presupposes that the public sphere is identified with the state and/or the market. The relation of private and public spheres is one of isolated individuals confronting anonymous and impersonal "megastructures." The defense of freedom thus becomes identified with the defense of a zone of privacy.

One can raise serious questions, however, about the adequacy of this bipolar disjunction of human activity into public and private spheres. For example, Alan Wolfe has argued that the increasingly dense and complex spheres of government and the marketplace threaten to overwhelm whatever remnants of private freedom still exist in advanced modern societies. The sphere of freedom is "increasingly squeezed from two directions": from the one side by the bureaucracy of the administrative state and from the other by powerful determinisms of markets linked together in a vast global network. Wolfe argues that if the freedom promised by modernity is to survive under the conditions that prevail in advanced societies in the late twentieth century, we need a counterweight to this pressure from the state and the market. Solitary, private individuals cannot provide this counterweight. In his words, "We need civil society—families, communities, friendship networks, solidaristic workplace ties, voluntarism, spontaneous groups and movements—not to reject, but to complete the project of modernity." The strong communal links found in the diverse groups of civil society must have greater public presence.

Wolfe's argument strikes a sympathetic chord in one like myself who has been shaped by the tradition of Roman Catholic social thought. For a variety of reasons, Catholicism had an adversarial relationship with the rising liberal democracies of western Europe through the modern period up to the middle of this century. Through the influence of thinkers such as Jacques Maritain and John Courtney Murray, however, in recent decades this relationship has been transformed into a strong Catholic alliance with democratic principles. This alliance has been evident in the highly visible role played by the Catholic community in numerous recent democratic movements from Poland to the Philippines, from Chile to South Korea. One of the central conceptual sources of this dramatic shift was Maritain and Murray's retrieval of the distinction between civil society and the state. Civil society is the more encompassing reality, composed of numerous communities of small or intermediate size such as families, neighborhoods, churches, labor unions, corporations, professional associations, credit unions, cooperatives, universities, and a host of other associations. Note that though these communities are not political in the sense of being part of the government, they are not private either. They are social realities and form the rich fabric of the body politic.

In a democratic society government does not rule but rather serves the social "body" animated by the activity of these intermediate communities. The bonds of communal solidarity formed in them enable persons to act together, empowering them to influence larger social institutions such as the state and the economy. Pope Pius XI formulated the matter in what came to be known as the principle of subsidiarity: government "should, by its very nature, provide help [subsidium] to members of the body social, it should never destroy or absorb them.

According to this way of thinking, the basis of democracy is not atomistic individual autonomy. Participation in democratic life and the exercise of real freedom in society depend on the strength of the communal relationships that give persons a measure of real power to shape their environment, including their political environment. As John Coleman has argued, the Catholic commitment to democracy rests on "a presumptive rule about where real vitality exists in society." The presumption here is that solitary individuals, especially solitary individuals motivated solely by self-interest and the protection of their rights to privacy, will be incapable of democratic self-government. Democracy requires more than this. It requires the virtues of mutual cooperation, mutual responsibility, and what Aristotle called friendship, concord, and amity.

Of course Aristotle knew well that there were limits to how wide a circle of friends one might have, as he knew there were limits to the size of a city-state. Today we are acutely aware that a nation as vast and diverse as the United States cannot hope to achieve the kind of social unity that might have been possible in the Athenian polis. While it might be true that the virtues of mutual cooperation, responsibility, and friendship can exert positive influence in small communities governed by town meetings, in clubs, and in churches that share a common vision of the final good and meaning of life, we hardly expect this to occur on a national, much less the international, level.

But here the irony of modernity once again becomes vividly visible. As the scale and diversity of the world tempt us to conclude that community is achievable only in private enclaves of the like-minded, de facto technological, political, and economic interdependence calls out for a conscious acknowledgment of and commitment to our moral interdependence. The principle of subsidiarity, with its stress on the importance of the local, the small-scale, and the particular, must be complemented by a kind of solidarity that is more universal in scope. This wider solidarity is essential if communitarian values are to avoid becoming a source of increased conflict in a world already riven by narrowness of vision. Commitment to small-scale communities with particular traditions must be complemented by a sense of the national and the global common good and the need for a vision shaped not only by particularist traditions but by hospitable encounters with traditions and peoples that are different.

The tradition of Western liberalism deals with the problem of diversity of communities, traditions, and peoples by invoking the idea of toleration. In public at least, it proposes that these differences be dealt with by finding a way to avoid discussing them. In my view, however, what Rawls calls "the method of avoidance" is inadequate to the challenge we face today. The problems of a deeply interdependent world in which diverse communities not only rub shoulders but must rely on each other for their very survival demand more. They demand positive engagement with those who are other or different. Such positive engagement cannot be mandated by an administrative state, much less an authoritarian one. It can be dealt with only on the cultural level, the domain where people's values and imaginative vision of the good are operative in uncoerced, free interaction with each other. This larger solidarity, therefore, is a matter of the kind of virtue that members of the body politic or civil society are capable of attaining.

Solidarity does not appear among the cardinal virtues of prudence, justice, temperance, and fortitude that were central for the Greeks and Romans, nor among the theological virtues of faith, hope, and love enumerated by Christian thinkers like Augustine and Aquinas. Pope John Paul II, however, has recently proposed to add solidarity to these classic lists by calling solidarity a key virtue needed to address the problems of our world. He defined this virtue as "a firm and persevering determination to commit oneself to the common good." It is a moral attitude and social awareness which transforms the de facto interdependence of persons and groups into a conscious bond of mutual responsibility.

Such solidarity has both intellectual and social dimensions. What I propose to call *intellectual solidarity* is a spirit of willingness to take other persons and groups seriously enough to engage them in conversation and debate about how the inter-dependent world we share should be shaped and structured. Thus, it calls for pub-lic discourse about diverse visions of the good life. Such discourse is quite different from the tolerance recommended by Rawls as the best we can do in responding to pluralism. Tolerance is a strategy of disengagement and avoidance of fundamental questions of value in public life. This disengagement is precisely what we cannot afford if we wish to shape our interdependent existence in humanly worthy ways. In contrast with this, intellectual solidarity calls for engagement with the other through both listening and speaking, in the hope that understanding might replace incomprehension and that perhaps even agreement could result.

The principal venues in which such intellectual solidarity can develop are the domains of civil society and culture. Though the achievement of such solidarity will ultimately have important political and economic implications, it is more a matter of imagination and the larger vision of what makes for good human lives than debate about specific public policies. And since intellectual solidarity de-mands mutual listening and speaking, it can only occur in an environment where all are genuinely free to set forward their vision of the common good and the rea-sons why they hold it. Aristotle maintained that the very existence of the polis is dependent on the human power of speech, the ability of citizens to set forth their understanding of "the expedient and the inexpedient, and therefore likewise the just and the unjust." And these understandings are rooted in a "sense of good and evil" which only human beings possess. Thus, to avoid serious public speech about the good life and the good society is itself already to surrender a major dimension of the human good. It will also have the further effect of undermining the concrete conditions necessary for a life of freedom. As Benjamin Barber has warned, "Citi-zens so tame as to shrink from the consequences of what they take to be public justice and common interest are scarcely citizens at all and are unlikely to be ca-pable of defending freedom in any form." Put positively, because intellectual soli-darity is mutual, the freedom it both presupposes and generates will not be the freedom of an atomistic self. Where conversation about the good life begins and develops in intellectual solidarity, a community of freedom begins to exist. And this is itself a major part of the common good. Indeed, it is this freedom in recip-rocal dialogue that is one of the characteristics that distinguishes a community of solidarity from one marked by domination and repression.

Such conversation and argument about the common good will not occur, in the first instance, in the legislature or in the political sphere narrowly conceived as the domain in which conflict of interest and power are adjudicated. Rather, it will develop a genuine freedom in those components of civil society that are the pri-mary bearers of cultural meaning and value. These include universities, religious communities, the world of the arts, the sphere of serious journalism. It can occur wherever thoughtful men and women bring their received historical traditions on the meaning of the good life into intelligent and critical encounter with under-standings of this good held by other peoples with other traditions. It occurs, in short, wherever education about and serious inquiry into the meaning of the good life takes place.

Despite its seeming abstractness, this virtue of intellectual solidarity has significant concrete implications. For example, it means that universities should be places where real argument about the adequacy and, yes, the truth of diverse visions of the common good should be occurring. Rawls's effort to construct a political philosophy based on the conviction that such argument will almost certainly be fruitless unfortunately seems to me a counsel of despair which not only encourages political alienation but threatens the intellectual mission of the university as well. Religious communities are similarly challenged to real encounter and dialogue with those of other faiths as they seek some degree of common understanding of our life together on this planet. Much of discussion of the public role of religion in recent political thought presupposes that religion is more likely to fan the flames of discord than to contribute to social concord. This is certainly true of some forms of religious belief, but hardly of all. Many religious communities recognize that their traditions are dynamic and that their understandings of God are not identical with the reality of God. Such communities have in the past and can in the future engage in the religious equivalent of intellectual solidarity called ecumenical or interreligious dialogue. And the "velvet revolution" in Czechoslovakia that began in Prague's Magic Lantern Theater provided vivid evidence of the role that the arts can play in encouraging both democracy and a vision of the social good.

In addition to these intellectual aspects, the virtue of solidarity also has a social dimension. A virtuous community of freedom must address not only heights to which human culture can rise but also the depths of suffering into which societies can descend. There are strong currents in American life today that insulate many of the privileged parts of civil society from experience of the suffering that exists in other parts of the body politic. Though it is obvious that individuals and groups can never share the experience of all others, nevertheless encouraging commitment to the common good calls for new ways of overcoming this insularity in at least incremental ways. Here again, universities, churches, the arts, and journalism can play important roles in opening up avenues to enhanced social solidarity.

The impact of the growth of these forms of solidarity in civil society and culture on the political sphere of government will be largely indirect. But its importance should not be underestimated. Rawls maintains that argument about both the basic structure of democratic societies and more specific policies that rely on the coercive power of government should be based on "public reason." This he defines as "the shared methods of, and the public knowledge available to, common sense, and the conclusions of science when these are not controversial." As noted above, he also maintains that the "common sense political sociology of democratic societies" indicates that full agreement on the meaning of the good life is unattainable in a pluralistic society. On this latter point, I am in agreement: unanimous consensus on the full meaning of the common good is not historically achievable. But this most definitely does not mean that no consensus is possible at all (a view that Rawls himself rejects) or that variations in the degree and scope of consensus are negligible. I would argue that the conversation and argument that can occur in civil society when citizens act on the basis of the virtues of intellectual and social solidarity can broaden and deepen the level of consensus they attain. Similarly, failure to act in accord with these virtues will shrink the common ground they share. This means that the "common sense" that regulates what counts as "public reason" in arguments about basic institutions and public policies can have different meanings at different historical moments. The interaction that takes place in the community of freedom that is civil society thus determines what sort of arguments can legitimately be made about the use of political power.

For example, the abolition of slavery, the expansion of suffrage to include women, the development of legal protections for labor, the civil rights movements, and the growing efforts to secure adequate health care and environmental standards all occurred through challenging previously reigning standards of common sense. Churches, universities, and numerous voluntary associations mounted these challenges by raising arguments that were not at the time taken for granted in the culture but that subsequently became so. In so doing they helped form new standards of political rationality in the United States.

This process of expanding and deepening the consensus so far achieved must continue if we are to deal with the new forms of social interdependence that mark the late twentieth century. The virtues of solidarity and mutual responsibility among citizens are prerequisites for addressing this interdependence in a way which is both oriented to the common good and at the same time democratic.

QUESTIONS FOR ANALYSIS AND DISCUSSION

1. Hollenbach doubts that self-realization should be the cornerstone of democratic ideals, but he recognizes its historical importance in liberating people from oppressive political and economic conditions. Oddly, it was often under these conditions that virtue ethics dominated moral discourse. How much importance do you attribute to self-realization? Should the self-realization of as many citizens as possible be the goal of a good democracy?

2. Tolerance, in Hollenbach's view, is probably the strongest intellectual opponent to a coherent view of virtues and the common good. How do you understand the main points of this conflict? To what extent do you believe tolerance and the common good could be mutually supportive? Use your neighborhood, workplace, or college as a small-scale model of a democratic society to illustrate your answer.

3. If solidarity and mutual responsibility are the two virtues that will lead to a richer sense of participant democracy, what vices might oppose these virtues? Describe the tension between these virtues and vices.

4. After reading Gerbner on television as a religion, Pynchon on technology and sloth, and Rybczynski on the modern fears of wasting leisure time, do you think Hollenbach's call for solidarity is out of touch with ordinary lives? Or do you think his call for solidarity and mutual responsibility through local groups is a direct response to the impersonal and shallow sense of everyday life fostered by fancy technologies, greedy corporations, and lethargic bureaucracies? In developing your answer, consider how your own life reflects the observations made by Hollenbach about contemporary life in a democracy.

87.

CHANDRA N. SAENG

Insight—Virtue—Morality

*Is modern life that vacuous? Are we too involved with our own lives? In the eyes of
Chandra Saeng, a philosopher from Thailand, things are actually much worse. Much
of the world is in moral decline; those who are well off prefer not to address the increasing misery and injustice rampant outside their small fields of vision. Saeng attributes part
of this growing inequality in the world to the continuing expansion of capitalist enterprises and mentalities. Another cause is the neglect of traditional wisdoms about human
nature. For Saeng, the lessons of Buddhism are most adept in helping us restore a sense
of the good for human beings. Outlining the basic truths and principles of Buddhism,
Saeng encourages virtuous people to challenge capitalism by rethinking the value of the
simple life.*

CRITICAL READING QUESTIONS

1. What are four indicators that the world is going through moral decline?
2. Why does Saeng describe society as a volcano?
3. Which vice is encouraged by capitalism and industrialism but poses the greatest threat to social morality?
4. What is meant by "dependent origination," and what are the three main factors that contribute to it?
5. What will result from realizing the three basic truths?

Introduction

The world today is in a state of moral decline, the symptoms of which can be
detected in the ever increasing rates of crime, conflict, violence, and war. Despite
our scientific, technological, and social progress, humanity continues to live in
fear, restlessness, and suffering. People in developing countries especially suffer

---

"Insight—Virtue—Morality," from *Buddhist Ethics and Modern Society*, edited by Charles Wei-hsun
Fu and Sandra Wawrytko (Westport, CT: Greenwood Press, 1991), pp. 167–172.

from this moral decadence. Industrialization and modernization entail mindless exploitation of natural resources. Large trees have been felled to feed the saw-mills; small trees have been wiped out in recent years to be replaced by cash crops for export.

The denuded landscape has ushered in drought, soil erosion, and declining soil quality. Poor farmers are forced to sell their land at low prices and move into new territories in search of new lands to cultivate. Thus, the deforestation process continues in many countries. Some peasants leave their poor lands and head for big cities, looking for menial employment; most wind up in urban slums. Capitalism and free enterprise have caused keen competition, selfishness, conflict and mutual destruction. Mafia overlords rule secret kingdoms with hired guns. Corruption prevails at all levels of government administration. The gap between the rich and the poor widens daily. To survive, the poor sell all they have, including their labor, their daughters, and their right to vote in general elections. Those in hopeless situations turn to drugs for illusory relief. Religion and morality are exploited for material gain.

Under these circumstances people live in anxiety and fear, with no guarantee for safety and security of life, property, or loved ones. There is no real happiness and peace in life. The whole society can be compared to a defunct volcano that seems peaceful from the outside, but inside is turbulent and ready to erupt at any moment.

The Root of Current Moral Problems

Scholars have studied and discovered various causes for the present moral degeneration, which we need not present here. I will simply offer my opinion of the root cause of today's moral problems, which seems to be greed (*lobha*) or desire (*taṇhā*).

During the Greek period, the desire for knowledge came to the fore. The Greek thinkers began to search for answers to the four basic concerns of humankind:

1. Where am I?
2. What am I?
3. Where am I going?
4. How will I get there?

Responses to these questions became the foundation of Greek philosophical, scientific, and political thought. The Western world has inherited from the Greeks the desire for knowledge, that has been strengthened in this age of information.

During the Roman period, the desire for power came to the fore. This led to the conquest of the world and, consequently, the mighty Roman Empire. As the Greeks desired knowledge, the Romans desired power, both of which desires have been transmitted to the Western world. During the Middle Ages, the desire for salvation was emphasized, while the other two desires slipped into the background. The papacy and the church were at times more powerful than the emperors, kings, and princes. The desire for salvation led to religious or spiritual imperialism in later ages.

In the modern period, the desire for knowledge has given birth to modern science. Scientific knowledge in the fields of chemistry, physics, biology, and mathematics gave birth to technology and invention, which in turn brought about industrialization. This is the real cause of our present troubles.

The Consequences of Industrialization

Industrialization means the mass production of consumer goods, creating a need for raw materials and leading to the exploitation of natural resources. When local supplies became exhausted, capitalists began to look for other sources of raw materials. This greed for raw materials was the cause of the Western conquest of the world, or colonialism. It aimed not only at providing domestic factories with raw materials, but also at procuring new markets for their surplus products. Spiritual imperialism also played a significant role in the colonization of underdeveloped lands and peoples. In most cases political imperialism and spiritual imperialism worked hand in hand to conquer and exploit the world.

Industrialization leads to commercialism, marketing, and consumption. The world today is a world of consumption: of raw materials, industrial products, information, and sensual pleasure. The other by-products of industrialization and colonialism are competition and conflict. Some conflicts are very violent and disastrous, which is why the two world wars began in industrialized nations. We can conclude that greed has been the root of all troubles in the world from ancient times up to the present.

The West's Impact on the East

When the West conquered the East, the conquerors began to flood their colonies with industrial products, rather than with scientific knowledge and know-how. The poor and ignorant natives, encountering the West's wonderful gadgets for the first time, could not help marveling at them. Their desire to own and use the Western novelties was stimulated to such an extent that they sacrificed their limited resources to obtain the wonders of the West. Today, the poor peasants in Thailand have to work many times harder than previously to own motorcycles and refrigerators that they do not really need. These technological products satisfy their desires and allow them to show off to their neighbors. Their lifestyles and value systems are those of urban dwellers, while their knowledge, skills, and resources are those of poor villagers. Imagine how difficult it is for poor farmers to maintain their high standard of living and keep pace with daily progress. The cost of maintaining this standard is so high that desperate peasants have to resort to robbery, fraud, larceny, and prostitution to procure money.

After being consumer-customers of industrialized countries for almost a century, some people began to feel the need to become producers themselves. They wanted to liberate themselves from the yoke of economic imperialism imposed by industrialized nations. They started their own industrial revolution, following in the steps of the West. Thus the process of industrialization, commercialism, marketing, and consumption is repeating itself in the East with remarkable success. Unfortunately, the East has inherited from the West not only industrialization but also its undesirable by-products, such as the depletion of natural resources, the exploitation of labor, and ecological pollution. Above all, Western greed also has been transmitted to the Eastern mind.

After centuries of competition, conflict, and violence, Western nations seem to have learned some lessons from their own follies. They have learned that violence comes from conflict and conflict from competition. To get rid of violence and conflict, competition must be stopped and replaced by cooperation. As a result, industrialized nations of the West have banded together to form a community of nations that produce, trade, and consume together. The scheme has proven successful so far, but its future is uncertain as long as greed, the cause of all troubles, remains untouched.

Another segment of the West seems to have discovered the root of the problem—greed—realizing that greed has to be removed by abolishing private ownership of the means of production. This philosophy has been applied in socialist countries and has been successful to some extent, but not entirely. Even without private ownership, greed has not been abolished. Being suppressed by circumstances, it only lurks in the human mind, ready to ooze out at any time. Although great efforts have been made to eliminate greed, the greed of the state has been nurtured. Citizens are encouraged to satisfy the greed of the state at the expense of their own greed. Recent developments in Eastern Europe have proven that the socialist method of abolishing greed has failed.

The Buddhist Way of Solving Problems

More than any other religion, Buddhism has paid special attention to the analysis of human nature. The truths it discovered thousands of years ago remain relevant and applicable today. The Buddhist way of solving problems, whether personal or social, is based on the law of causality or Dependent Origination (*paticca-samuppāda*). According to this law, every phenomenon is due to some cause or causes. The cause itself is the effect of a prior cause, and its effect serves as the cause of another, future effect. This being the case, the law of causality works in a sequence, not as a unit consisting of an ultimate cause and a final effect. In Buddhism there is no ultimate cause.

The movement of causality is not straight but circular. It proceeds to a certain point and then turns around to repeat the same process, over and over. According to the law of Dependent Origination, the human life process consists of twelve links, with ignorance being the starting point and suffering the final link. However, since suffering nurtures ignorance, the whole process is self-perpetuating.

The twelve links of the Dependent Origination are usually summarized in terms of three main factors:

1. Impurities (*kleśa*—ignorance, desire and clinging)
2. Act (*kamma*—thought formation)

3. Result (*vipāka*—consciousness, name and form, the six senses, contact, feel-
    ings, becoming, birth, old age and death).

In other words, mental impurities motivate a person to act, and these actions produce results, which in turn nurture mental impurities. Ultimately, all social problems are the result of human acts and all acts are inspired by mental drives or
impulses.

Where to Start

Social problems are similar to a tree, with its three main component parts: the
branches, the trunk, and the roots. Social problems are the branches, human actions the trunk, and mental drives the roots. Although the branches may be cut off,
as long as the trunk remains, they will grow again. The trunk can be cut down, but
as long as the roots remain, it too will grow again. Only when the roots are dug
up and dried will the trunk and the branches cease to grow. In the same way, when
we attempt to solve personal or social problems, we should deal with the roots—
mental drives—first.

The most important mental impurity is ignorance of *avijja*, the absence of intuitive insight into the fundamental truths of life and the world around us. From
ignorance arises delusion (*moha*), and because of delusion people create a dualistic
conception of the world, dividing things into what is desirable and undesirable.
They seek to acquire things and to maintain what is desired (*kāmataṇhā* and *bhav-
ataṇhā*), as well as to eliminate what is undesirable (*vibhavataṇhā*). Desire for gain
stimulates people to search for, create, and grasp things; desire to be rid of things
drives us to destroy, initiating the endless cycle of creation and destruction. Success
in creating, maintaining, and destroying things brings temporary satisfaction. Failure brings disappointment and grief. It is therefore necessary to strike at the very
roots of the problem, that is, to subdue negative mental drives.

Removing Mental Impurities

Since ignorance is the root of all troubles, we must get rid of it first. Ignorance is
something like darkness in a room: to expel darkness from the room, the light must
be turned on. In the same manner, we must stimulate insight in our mind to expel
ignorance, insight into the three basic truths of life:

1. imperfection (*dukkha*) of life, pain and the struggle to relieve it;

2. impermanence (*anicca*) of life; and

3. impersonality (*anattā*) of life—life is but a psycho-physical process that flows
    on and on in time and space, depending on the law of cause and effect, with-
    out any permanent entity being involved.

It is not difficult to realize these three basic truths, since they manifest themselves
everywhere and at all times. The problem is that worldlings are so afraid that they

close their eyes to them. They behave like the ostrich that buries its head in the sand and thinks that it is thus safe from imminent danger.

Once a person has realized these three truths, change occurs. The realization of imperfection (or suffering, as it is usually known) gives birth to compassion (*karuṇā*), and compassion in turn motivates one to refrain from harming other living beings (what is called *śīla* in Buddhism). Instead of inflicting harm, one will try to help others with whatever resources are in one's possession; this is called generosity (*dāna*) in Buddhism.

The realization of the second truth, impermanence, automatically gives rise to detachment. Since everything flows on and on, it is not worth clinging to. Clinging to things that are in constant flux will only result in disappointment and sorrow. Detachment will automatically weaken greed. People without greed will not hoard wealth at the expense of others. Exploitation of natural resources and our fellow human beings will not occur.

The realization of the third truth, impersonality, will rid one of self-delusion and egotism. One will look at life as a natural stream that flows on and on according to the law of cause and effect. One will live with oneself in peace and harmony.

The scientific knowledge and technology of the West have provided humankind with convenience, comfort, and pleasure, but no true happiness and peace. That is why the West, in spite of its great progress and wealth, still lives in frustration, anxiety, fear, and suffering. The Buddhist knowledge of the three basic truths has enabled human beings to live peacefully with Nature, with fellow human beings, and with themselves. So much emphasis has been given to detachment and renunciation that physical comfort has been neglected and ignored. Consequently, the masses of the East have had to live with hunger, disease, and ignorance. The best way to proceed, then, is a middle way that lies between the extreme materialism of the West and the extreme idealism of the East.

QUESTIONS FOR ANALYSIS AND DISCUSSION

1. Do you accept the analogy of modern society being like a volcano? Consider Saeng's reasons. Can you offer a counterargument that addresses her evidence or points she may have overlooked?

2. What is the relation between desire and greed? Can one have desire without getting greedy? If desire is natural to all sentient creatures, how is it that not everyone is greedy? Is greed learned, imitated, or innate among different humans? In answering this, address Saeng's suggestion that greed was transported from Western industrial society to non-Western cultures.

3. How do you understand the importance of the three main factors of the law of dependent origination in solving problems? Can you illustrate Saeng's point with a mental impurity you recognize in yourself or others? Briefly explain whether this impurity presents a moral problem and whether it can be resolved through Saeng's diagnosis.

4. Reread the three basic truths and their effects. Are ideas such as detachment or compassion universal or relevant only to a particular culture? Ethical relativists (see Chapter 1) contend that moral truths have value only within the

culture that espouses them. They are true because they are functional for that culture. Does the relativist argument work against Saeng's proposal for the good life that is found in peace and harmony? Of the essays in this chapter, which support, question, or are neutral to Saeng's perspective?

88.

ALPHONSO LINGIS

Cargo Cult

Another way of questioning the boundaries of more familiar traditions, beliefs, or values is presented by philosopher Alphonso Lingis (see Chapter 2). For Lingis, questioning these boundaries often relies on what we can learn from relatively obscure figures. Lingis describes the moral truths these figures have to offer us. Although these truths are not easily accessible, Lingis helps us and challenges us by turns. The help comes in the spirit of true journalism—a daily, detailed account of how other people live and think. The challenge appears as the philosopher asks us about truth. Do the truths of obscure figures remain inaccessible because we do not want to hear them? Do we lack the moral strength—what traditionalists call virtue—of those who show their virtues even to strangers? Which of our vicious deeds do we tolerate or excuse ourselves from? This last selection revives the question of the moral self. It presents one answer, an answer that emphasizes deeds in which the virtuous person delights not in consuming but in giving—like the sun.

CRITICAL READING QUESTIONS

1. Who is Devika? What does he think Lingis does for a living?
2. How does Arun trick Lingis, and where in Calcutta does he take him?
3. Why does Mohan annoy Lingis? Why can't Lingis look at him?
4. What are the three stages of colonialization? As emissaries, where do they lead?
5. On which river will Gopal Hartilay be burned? What kind of coins does he give Lingis?

"Cargo Cult," from *Excesses* (Albany, NY: State University of New York Press, 1983), pp. 135–138, 141–144, 146–153, 159–162. Notes have been omitted.

Will I speak the truth to you? To you, Devika?

Through speech one comes into the presence of the other, in his alterity. Perception, feeling, even sympathetic or empathetic feeling, and action, even collaboration, may remain on the phenomenal surfaces, where the other is but appearance and relative being. But genuine speech, which answers to a demand and answers a contestation, is responsibility before an appeal and initiative of justification, reveals the veritably other. This speech has to be itself veridical. Mendacious speech not only distorts the forms and effaces the significance of things, it obscures the visage of the other, even if it can be motivated only by the continual evidence of his presence. That is why, for Hegel, truth, and not only subjective certainty, is at stake when the other is encountered, and the struggle for recognition begins. It is not simply that truth would be defined, arbitrarily, as what exists actually for at least two and potentially for all. It is that the very perception of another is an acknowledgement made in speech and only in veridical speech.

That is also why, even though the other, to be veritably and irreducibly other, is outside all that is set forth and included in speech, still the very discovery and acknowledgement of this alterity requires that the world be set forth, and set forth in a true and total representation (true, that is, total, Hegel would say). For speech recognizes the other not by representing him to oneself, but by representing the world for him, by responding to his interrogation and putting before his judgment. The veritable approach to the other requires veridical speech, and ultimately requires the totally veridical, total speech. Crossing the whole world one comes into the proximity of the other. One advances, reducing distances, a quantitative problem, of miles, of years, of sex, of money. Not all of these movements into proximity are equally easy or difficult.

The power to lie, however, seems to be a faculty intrinsic to sovereignty, which is the power to conform oneself, and not the fatality of being conformed, to the course of the world. Mendacity does not preclude a veritable relationship with the veritable layout of the world, since it presupposes it and goes beyond it. But it does nullify the relationship with the other. One cannot retreat behind one's opaqueness and travesties, and still retain intact one's perception of the other. For the other, in his alterity, is not a datum of perception, but is present only as an appeal answered, a contestation recognized, in an *apologia pro vita sua*.

Naturally I did not say I wanted to get close to you, Devika. I said I was looking for the Amri Yahyah, the best, batik workshop. Words that say that I want to spend surplus money, and that I know how to get there by myself, knowing the name of the shop and being on the right street, and know also you will get a five-percent commission if you turn up at the door with me in hand. To say all that in one word, I could have said to you I was American. But, to be understood, I said I was Belgian, Latvian, Etruscan. You told me you were a dancer in the *wayang wong*. Is that an occupation? And aren't you at least twenty-two years old? Is that sleek face and adolescent breast due to malnutrition? When you pointed to things and gestured as we talked, your fingers fluttered like a Balinese *legong*, sometimes moving only the first joints of the finger, or bending them back into such an unlikely arc.

The Swedish girl had not been able to do that after three years in Suryabrata's class. I said I was a journalist, so as to say I had time to just travel in Java without being rich. I did not say I was a professor, wanting to discover Yogyakarta by night as well as by day with you, not closing the possibility of love with you. Three days later when I suggested photographing you with my journalist's camera, you said the guru had gone to Solo and had locked up all the dance costumes. Did you believe me when I said I was paying 5,000 rupiahs a night at this boarding house—didn't you know, from the room-boy, that it cost 10,000, what university professors in the Gajah Mada earn a month? You told me what it was like in the monkey cages of Sumatra, where women political subversives are locked up with their children. Was it youthful grace, the artist soul of a pretechnological Eastern people, the political passions of oppressed Java, the Oriental wizard intelligence that was so skilled in alluring me, that I loved in you, Devika? Did I believe any of these things? Were you real to me only in the continually rearising suspicion that you are not a dancer at all, not sixteen years old, not a Hindu, not a revolutionary militant? Did I want an answer to any of these doubts, since I compulsively told you I was older or younger, poorer, less educated, less knowledgeable about your country, more, or less, religious, political, libertine than I wanted you to be? What would we have talked about over a meal like I eat when I am alone, costing what you have to live on maybe for a month?

In Books Theta and Iota of Aristotle's *Nichomachean Ethics* the criteria and principles regulating friendship are determined out of a general theory of the nature of social bonding.

Association is not produced by simple juxtaposition; it is actual in exchange. The three species of *philia* are characterized by the exchange of goods—association based on utility; the exchange of pleasures; and the exchange of virtue—the association of those who, having functional excellence in themselves, are good for one another, and do good to one another. The telos of the association is not the constantly augmenting production of goods; rather the circulation of goods, pleasures, and virtues is the means by which association actively maintains itself. In the economy of friendship there is no capitalizing of wealth, no usury or profiteering.

Duration—abiding presence, constancy—is the criterion for the evaluation of the kinds of association in this metaphysics of presence. An ephemeral friendship, however intense—what Nietzsche called star friendship, that of those whose orbits make contact, but whom the eternal necessity of each having his own orbit will take apart again—will for that reason be inferior. It is also why Aristotle can write that the friendship of witty people is superior to the relationship between lover and beloved. When the bloom of youth passes, the pleasure the sight of the beloved gave passes too; but two loquacious friends can exchange wit indefinitely. Duration is also the argument for the superiority of friendship among the virtuous over that among adventurers or rascals. "Only the friendship of good men is proof against slander. For a man does not easily trust anyone's word about a person whom he has himself tried and tested over a long period of time. . . . In other kinds of friendship, however, there is no safeguard against slander and lack of trust."

An association endures through its inner activity, which is the circulation of goods, pleasures, or virtues. The circulation can continue inasmuch as each movement of goods, pleasures, or virtues is compensated for; whence the principle of equality. The exchange is rational, is reckoned. "Both partners receive and wish the same things from and for one another, or they exchange one thing for another, for instance, pleasure for material advantage."

. . .

🌿 🌿 🌿

How could I sleep in a bed in Calcutta?

It was dark, Arun, when I arrived at Dumdum airport, and raining. A white man invited me to share a cab into the city with him, a British bookie, last clerk of the Raj, capitalizing the surplus value produced each Saturday by the industrial transformation of the raw material of chance. He supplied the name of a hotel cheap and centrally located when I asked; a scorpion crawled out of the cot when I put my suitcase on it. Then I went out to get a look at Calcutta before it all shut up; the hotel proprietor told me that Chowringhee Circus, the central square of the imperial city, was but five minutes' walk away. There were thin crowds in the drizzle; but after a few steps I realized that all along the walls there were squatting or sprawled out human beings, some under little shelters of cardboard or banana leaves. With a few more steps my white skin had attracted a circle of black marketeers offering to change money, skeletal women showing me their dried dugs at which bloated babies chewed, lepers poking scabby stumps at me with tin cans tied to them, pimps offering me English girls or Eurasians convent-educated, or young boys. I recognized the feeling in me was turning into fear—not of these wretches whining their hopeless prayers—but of something evil and immense in these dark streets, in this night. The pain. I used to think that there was a proportion, that the pain was human, that if there was pain there was also a capacity to the measure of the pain. Like Nietzsche, who said that man is the animal that suffers most, but because he is the bravest animal, even seeking out suffering to his own measure, out of strength. In a half hour I was back, trembling, in my room. How could one look at, how could one comprehend the pain of that dreadful night? It was beyond all proportion, an abyss; now, here, five thousand miles away, Arun, I find I cannot even imagine what I felt and saw that night; in fact a week after I left Calcutta I could no longer remember or imagine. It was beyond the capacity of the mind to apprehend or the memory to retain. You, Arun, I remember, you softly said in my ear, "I give you body massage," and I looked at you, and wondered what you were insinuating with your hushed voice and big eyes. I looked at you and found you unappealing, boney and dirty and vacant. Every night you were there when I passed. Three weeks later I was already getting the sickness that was to end in those hospitals in Madras, but I did not know it at the time; I supposed that it was just another bout of dysentery that made me so weak and nauseous. That evening when I passed you I thought you had or could get dope and I wanted dope to get through the night. We went through the arguing over the price, I was bored and irritable and was only going through the motions, arguing over a rupee, which in my country is seven cents, but one has to keep to discipline, make the effort to frame arguments to your understanding, a rhetoric of persuasion to bend your will. One has to discipline oneself to keep within discourse and in contractual bonds. And so we haggled, and I refused you the seven cents, and then went off to spend a buck for *Time* magazine and go to my hotel room where I got fucking sick smoking your dope and puked half the night. That is why when I saw you the next night you had gone up in my eyes, having outwitted me, and I lingered with you as you insinuated slyly other ways you could be of service to me, wondering if it was opium or virgin girls or yourself that might be my vice. I strung you on, so that I could find the natural moment to invite you to sit down to a meal on me, and that is when I learned you were from Lucknow, where my car had been demolished by a truck my second trip to India, and we remembered the dikes and the imambaras of Lucknow, and you showed me your cobra tattoos, and told me of the Naga shrine where your mother had put our milk for the cobras every morning since the day you were born. You astonished me by telling me you were twenty-two not fifteen, had a wife and two kids, sleeping in a doorway somewhere. I ordered the biggest meal they had to encourage you, but you only wanted some plain rice you said.

When, a month of sickness and two operations later, I got back to Calcutta, just for overnight, on the way out of India, how moved I was, you appearing there in the alley, greeting me with such a look of surprise and pleasure. You asked where I had been and what I had done, you wanted to know about the sickness, and said we could smoke a chilum, but I knew that your buddy slipped off to beg or borrow a crumb of dope, you didn't have any. And we sat there, against the wall in the alley, and you told me how, by night, to get into the Towers of Silence for the food which the Parsees leave with the corpses of their dead they put out for the vultures, how one rolls the tourists who are out for skin, where in the Maidan the addicts get their fix by having their forearms bitten by young cobras, there was not enough time in your breaths to cram in all the life you had to tell me. And I remembered, too, a time years back when, your age, I slept each night in a different flop-house on Chicago's skid row, the down-and-out-in-Paris-and-London trip, but, unlike you, me knowing there would be another trip after that one. And then you took me under the Howrah Bridge where the lepers were huddled to keep out of the rain, and you pulled out a blanket from the derelict boy you share your rice with when you have some, and you laid me on it and gave me the massage a thousand years of Lucknow caste skill can give, and sang me the song of the prayer of the blind man asking Lord Shiva to give him eyes so he can see that lord of destruction. And then my mind got all tangled up calculating how much I could pay you for this massage, what would be the strict professional price, which I could pass on to you without fucking up everything between us. I had lied to you which hotel I was really staying at, and you accompanied me back to the hovel I said instead, and after you left I went out again to the one I had really booked into. You left to sleep somewhere with your wife and babies in the street. I never saw you again, that night I slept in a bed, and the next night in New York.

Where I could not remember, and could not imagine the pain. I tried to talk about it sometimes. And sometimes they say to me, how could you stay there? They would usually put it that way, not saying, how could you sleep in a bed in Calcutta?

I did; and on the other side of the wall, in the street, you were lying on the ground. All I ever found to say, to those sitting in couches in living rooms, was that, once you have seen that, once I know you are there, Arun, is anything changed if I move to a bed a hundred miles, or five thousand miles, away?

. . .

In 1819, a British officer of the Madras regiment was tracking a panther in a stretch of uninhabited jungle in the Indhyadri Hills, in Hyderabad. About midday he came to the brink of a gorge, some thousand meters deep, cut by the circling arc of the Waghora river. One of the bearers caught sight of the panther on the face of the cliff, disappearing half-way down into the tangles of vegetation. The officer dismounted and began to descend the cliff wall on foot. He found the hole into which the panther had disappeared—but one side was rock cut vertical. He thus came upon the cave temples of Ajanta, a complex of thirty temples and monasteries carved out of solid rock in the cliff face of the Ajanta gorge, 500 meters above the river, by Buddhist monks 2,200 years ago; the falling mud and rocks and a dense tangle of vines and lianas had sealed the entrances for the last twelve hundred years. The excavators subsequently were to find frescos inside that rank with those of Fra Angelico and Masaccio in the spiritual treasury of humanity. There didn't seem to be any reason to suffer the rude four days' bus ride from Bombay; I took the plane to Aurangabad and a bus the 109 kilometers from there. It was the middle of the July monsoon, mud and water dripping over the cliff walls made the descent difficult, and down in the gorge no breeze stirred; by ten o'clock when the sun's rays descended into it, the heat made my head fevered and my heart pound. Then, across the river and on the far wall, I saw the path. A footpath climbing up to the rim of the gorge, where a small roofed shelter could be seen, no doubt for pilgrims to rest in the breezes of the surface. I at once decided to wait out the heat of the day up there, reading a book I had purchased on the history, architecture and iconography of the Ajanta cave temples and frescos. I crossed the river on a vine bridge and headed up the steep path; the climb took two hours. At the top the breezes greeted me, and there was the little pavilion, with wooden seats.

There you were also, Mohan. When I saw you you looked up and said your name was Mohan. Crouched on the ground, your head wrinkled, covered thinly with strands of yellow-white hair, your deformed legs lying in the dust, how long had you been there. I sat down on the far side from you. But after a moment using your stick you pulled yourself over before me, and with an obsequious murmur of "Sahib!" stretched out your hand in supplication.

The sun was now high in the sky; no one further would pass this path before late afternoon. I could not descend into the fetid gorge again; and all round there was only dense scrub buzzing with gnats and, no doubt, malarial mosquitos. The afternoon gaped open. I had my book and my task, to understand the cliff temples. You were also there, Mohan.

I could give you a coin at once. But, be it large or small, what else have you to do, the length of the afternoon neither you nor I could leave and no one else was to be hoped for, but ask piteously for another coin? Were I rich as Rockefeller, would a certain quantum of coins finally slake your want, stanch the waste of your substance? Would each coin, held back and finally dropped, buy me a quantum of time to read five or ten pages, before your supplication moaned again under me? Am I to become an obstinacy, working in resistance of that cloying entreaty— absurd and hateful contest?

I decide to give you an alms—when I leave. Not a quantity commensurate with your need or the degree of your misery, but only commensurate with what my state as a rich and physically sound sahib requires. I am not going to dribble it out, coin by coin, at ten minute intervals. That is all I am going to be able to do for you. Why should it not be compatible with what I can do for myself—recover my breath, rest in the shade, read this book to learn what drove Buddhists to carve out the sanctuaries below 2,200 years ago? I will impose my own assignment here, there will be no exchange between us until I depart.

This plan requires that I command silence from the start. I can only refuse to acknowledge your presence and your supplication. I open my book. You are now beneath me. It is going to require attention not to let my eyes meet yours. You begin your "Alms, Sahib!" out of your ravaged throat.

You are not going to stop or go away. I take my book and move to the far side of the pavilion. After five minutes you have dragged yourself once more under my feet.

The afternoon creeps viscuously along. Never has it been more laborious to pick off the message from the marks on the page for hour on end. In this tedium I feel hatred for you, Mohan, over the pointlessness of the imposition of your despoiled existence on me. A scab-covered dog lopes up out of the scrub, and cringes at the pavilion, panting from the heat. You stir, you slowly extract out of your rags a tin can, and out of it dump some crusts of dirty bread.

And then my eyes know without daring to look that you are breaking off some of your bread and stretching it out to the dog.

The reduction of all social existence to an exchange of complementary values does not split the social order from nature; it is a naturalization of the social order. According to Aristotle, society as a field of circulation of equivalents does not only fit harmoniously, microcosm into macrocosm, into nature as a whole; it is itself a nature. That is, an individual that maintains its identity through its self-regulated intrinsic *energeia*. We can see in human commerce the national essence of nature, a system maintaining its identity through an internal economy of reckoned compensations.

Aristotle's poetics assigns a psychological-cathartic function to tragic theater, and his physics replaces a tragic concept of nature, that which sees the force of nature regulated according to a solar economy, an economy of expenditure without recompense, economy of horror, that of the sun, hub of nature, which produces a surplus energy which it squanders in the void, receiving no return from the minute quantity which, far from itself, engenders satellites, wandering planets, their Apollonian-Dionysian life, dreaming and dancing life—which is only burning itself out as fast as it can. This expenditure without recompense would be the very radiance, the glory of the sun. And its happiness—"a divine happiness," Nietzsche wrote, "which like the sun in the evening, continually gives of its inexhaustible riches and empties into the sea—and like the sun, too, feels itself richest when even the poorest fisherman rows with golden oars!"

. . .

Irian—"New Guinea"—how long the way, through its venomous swamps and jungles, high into its mountain retreats, to the Stone Age, headhunters and cannibals. The Dutch touched the shore to claim the west side for the Dutch East Indies in 1828; in 1884 the English came to lay claim to the south side facing Australia, the same year the Germans claimed the north coast. There were three stages to their coming; the traders, the troops, and the missionaries. Traders came first, to make contact with the tribes, bringing a glut of beads and shells, but also bringing steel axes. The Stone Age was finally over. On their heels came the troops, imposing an end to the ceaseless tribal warfare, or, more exactly, in very many areas, headhunting between one compound and the next. A few lessons showing what firearms could do did the trick in most places, and the patrols could move on, the populations apparently only too happy that the millennia of fear were over, and the isolation so extreme that on this island, in a population of a million or so, over 700 mutually incomprehensible languages had congealed, fully one third of the tongues of humanity! Then came the missionaries, and the single, limpid, all-benevolent divinity, the Gospel of Salvation.

The steel axe cut down the trees for the gardens and the huts in about one fourth the time it takes with the stone axe. But that is the main work that had to be done; once the trees are cut the planting of the garden, in this luxuriating tropics, is nothing. In socioeconomic terms, step one produced an instant leisure population in the jungle. The pacification also freed an enormous quantity of energy; one can think not only of the quantity of energy spent in the actual battles and raids, but also of that expended on the manufacture of weapons, decorations, the joustings, boastings, on purification rituals, shamanist trance consultations, victory orgies and funerals and self-mutilations of defeat. Thirdly, the redemption brought by the missionaries wiped out at a single stroke a dense population of totemic, ancestral and cannibalized spirits, all the juju demonology. Suddenly each mind was liberated of the occupation of being on the lookout for portents and omens, learning the ways of dealing with an unendingly complicated and capricious underworld, each mind having to decide on its own what fragmentary information is to be trusted, which comes from the white shaman and which from the black, each night's shadows, owl cries, serpent movements, dreams, fevers, having to be deciphered—suddenly this vast and meticulous ingenuity is disconnected and vaporized before a high noon deity which, if invisible and unimaginable, is nonetheless known with the simple certainties of the logic of benevolence, and requires after all very little of your time or mental energies, it being enough to assemble weekly about his white priest mumbling the Dutch, English, German, or Latin.

The three steps, these three emissaries to savagery, are of course not civilization, but only the preparation for it. What did the white man have in mind to do with the Papuans once brought out of the Stone Age, pacified, and saved? The very swamps and jungle had now to be civilized. The white superiority that brought the steel axes, the peace, and the salvation rests on an economic base; the pacified and monotheized savages were set to work copra, rubber, cocoa, clove plantations. Recruiters were sent to the bush, to explain to the big men that it is labor white man's way that produced all the beads, steel axes, rifles, cargo birds, all the excitement; the usual contract under German rule was seven years at ninety cents a month, paid when the term was over; under Australian rule until 1951 it was three years for ten shillings a month, paid also when the term was up and the debts, damage caused to plantation property, and medications issued, deducted.

One should not conclude that somebody was getting rich out of that—the Germans who were just as happy to get out when the motherland went to war, the Dutch who were making their fortunes in Java, or the Australians who pushed and shoved their ward into independence with, in the end, unseemly haste. What wealth there was to circulate came from across the seas, in cargo ships, across the skies, in cargo planes. Everyone ran up against the irreducible indolence of the Papuan. Some theorized that they were in reality debilitated by the malaria, biharzia, scrub typhus from all time, and, now, from the gonorrhea and the syphilis, but the medical evidence was inconclusive and most spoke simply of some Stone Age absence of motivation. Certainly the Papuans are broad and robust physically, compared with the Javanese and Chinese coolies the Germans and Australians resorted to in the end.

Fevers and delirium circulated among the rubber and clove trees. It was not to the plantations but to the bird-of-paradise plume dealers that the cargo ships came. Today it is to the preachers of paradise that the cargo planes come, their bellies full of tinned food, frozen meats, whiskey, CB radios, guns, live cows and horses, jeeps, film projectors, altars.

How long it has been since I celebrated Christmas, Father Coenan! I did not dare tell you. How beautiful your Delft chinaware, how delicious your roast goose, how mellow your burgundy! Frankly, I did not expect, on the walls of a mission house in Moanemani, a signed Appel print, nor novels by Kawabata and Genet, theological writings by Hans Küng and some of the philosophical books of Foucault and Derrida. How gracious you were to me, how much information you gave me out of your twenty-six years in Irian Jaya! Finally I ventured to ask you about the Cargo cults so much talked about—whether here, in your parish too, there were Papuans who gather on top of some hill sacred to ancestors or totemic birds, clear the ground for the cargo plane, gather around an altar with the effigy not of Jesus on his cross but of the cargo plane, manufactured with flint blades out of coconut wood, jabber meaninglessly over the open pages of Dutch or English Bibles pilvered from the mission, and wait. You smiled. At my journalistic tastes. You turned to Obeth Badii. Seminarian, one of seven in Irian Jaya, home for the holidays from the Franciscan Studies House in Djayapura, one more year to go before ordination into the Roman Catholic priesthood.

The next day you took off your mission clothes, Obeth Badii, greased your body with pig fat, put the *kotecka* on your penis, and took me over the mountain wall. For a week we slept in your village; I tried to make myself useful, chopping away at the brush with a stone adz for a new garden. You did not answer me, Obeth

Badii, when on New Year's Day I finally asked you if I could see the shrine of the Cargo cult. When we parted your brother Adof presented me with a magnificent set of Kapauku bow and arrows. Some for the hunt, barbed in different ways for wild pigs, tree kangaroos, large birds. Some for war, smooth, not poisoned, but with coils of orchid fibers wound on the tips, which will come off when the arrow is pulled out of the wound, will stay in the wound, to infect. I understood, Obeth Badii. I understood this was not a gift; it was an exchange. I understood I am to return to you, with guns.

The phenomenology of the Cargo cult is an investigation of the way the rational economy of the white man is refracted on the dark soul of the Stone Age. Its obverse, less studied academically, is an inquiry into the ethical impact of the destitution of . . . millions . . . upon the soul of a lonely traveler. . . .

I came to the Ganges at Varanasi, like everyone else, to die. Not knowing how old I was nor how young I was yet to be. There I knew you, Gopal Hartilay. You came to me at sunset, frail boy out of so many thousands of Hindus, each silent and alone, descending into the holy river to consign to it the sweat and dirt and fatigue of the day, as, one day, to consign to it the sweat and dirt and fatigue of life. You took me by the hand to the Manikarnika ghat, where among the garlanded cows we watched the fires whisper over the bodies of the dead, and the kites and nightjars circling overhead. One day you will be burned there, and your ashes swept into the strong arms of the river. You took me by the hand to your boat, which you tie at the Dashashwamedha ghat in the unlikely hope of enticing a party of pilgrims to choose yours from among so many dozens of larger, sounder, safer boats. As we rocked on the waters of the river you explained to me in tangled complication the epic drama that was being ceremonially reenacted by priests with foreheads marked with the mark of Shiva the Destroyer on the far bank of the Ganga. How little I understood of it; it was enough for me to watch your black eyes catch the last rays of the sun. When it got completely dark they shone still as you rowed back to the city, where we went to eat a banana leaf of rice under an aswatha tree full of sleeping monkeys. The clanging of cymbals announced a bride heading for her bridegroom under the full moon in a procession of four elephants, a white horse, a strident band, fireworks, and half the gods of the Mahabharata in effigy being carried along, and we went too. But we stopped at the Durga temple, where you wanted me to contribute something for a blood sacrifice to Kali, who took your mother and father with cholera the year you were born, but who wants you here still. How did I come so far, through so many dense crowds, to find you? What law dictated that you chose to be my friend? You clanged the bells loudly to alert the attention of the goddess, but alerted also the monkeys who stole the sacrifice and hissed at you from the temple roofs. We walked back to the Dashashwamedha ghat where you will sleep, having no room in a house and having to guard your boat. There were still fires on the ghats, and, here and there, solitary pilgrims chanting mantras like the names of the stars. I desperately wanted to give you a gift, and the gift I had in mind I would make with my camera, because it would be just you—images of you, images that duplicate not the frail and wild bliss that plays in your heart, but only a momentary look of your eyes, a breath, a shudder. I wanted to manufacture these shadows of you, I would have liked an infinite number of them. Not for myself; to give to you, because I could not imagine ever coming upon anything outside of you that could embellish you, my friend whom I found on the banks of the Ganges among the funeral pyres and whom perhaps I shall not meet again on this bank of life. Then I awkwardly explained to you that I had only a two-week visa for Nepal, and had to leave tomorrow early morning and could not drive through the thick of the city if I were to make the frontier in time, and that was why I wanted you to come to me, tomorrow, to my hotel, four miles out of the city, to come at dawn, so I could photograph you before I left. The next morning I got up in the dark, dressed, packed, had breakfast, waited; the sun rose, and there was no sign of you. I waited an hour, then finally got into the car and drove into the city. Half-way I saw you, in the crowds, on a borrowed bicycle, on your way. We went to the river, we went to your boat, to the Manikarnika ghat, it seemed to me that each wave of the river and each shadow of the city in which you glanced harbored an image of you; it was past noon when I got into the car to leave, and you accompanied me on your bicycle to the bridge over the river where we said farewell. Two days later, in Kathmandu, I took the films to be developed, and there was nothing on them. All blank. I met some travelers who would later go to Varanasi, and I made them promise to go to the Dashashwamedha ghat and find you, and tell you about the dead films. After Nepal I went to Calcutta, and three months later was driving back across northern India on my way back to Europe, and once out of Calcutta I decided to take the long detour to go back to Varanasi, to you, in order to see you, in order to photograph you. I arrived late in the night, parked the car at the first lodging on the edge of the city, and the next morning took a ricksha to the river to find you. But at the Dashashwamedha ghat you were nowhere to be seen, nor your boat. I asked the priests, bystanders, I sent off boys to look for Gopal Hartilay, I climbed up the Manmandir observatory where I could see far down the river, and at length I saw a cloud of dust and someone running and I rushed down again, knowing it was you. We fell into one another's arms, and had nothing to say to one another; to break the spell I said I was hungry for rice and asked if we could go again where we had eaten under the tree of the sleeping monkeys. We climbed up the ghats and suddenly you stopped and told me to go on, and after a few moments you reappeared, and you put in my hand a tiny silver statue, very old, votive offering cast into the river by a pilgrim perhaps hundreds of years ago, which you told me you found one day in the river, and which I recognized at once, and verified later by a jeweler, to be of great value. You could eat rice for many months, perhaps years, with the value of this. I looked at you, dazed, you folded my fingers about it, and your hand about mine. My head was dizzy; if I gave you all the possessions I had it would not be the equivalent, since I have a job, and more salary comes in, automatically, each month, with pension till I die. And then you vanished again, and when you returned you put in my hand some old Tibetan coins, currency of a kingdom that no longer exists, which you also found in the river. I looked at you with wet eyes and realized that's all there was. Orphan boy you had given me everything you had. And then you told me that the small silver figure represented the reincarnation of Krishna named Gopal. Gopal. Gopal is you.

QUESTIONS FOR ANALYSIS AND DISCUSSION

1. If you were to transform the deeds of one of the persons Lingis encounters into a moral argument, how would you set up your major premises? How would they support your conclusion? If you do not see a moral argument possible, then how do you respond to the reality lived by Arun or Mohan? Can you explain your ordinary life, and theirs?

2. Which of the virtues or vices are best portrayed in the encounters described? Most of us occasionally come across someone who clearly could use a bit of our help, but we decline. If we do not always give, are we never moral? At what point do we know we could easily give yet still refuse? Is there a vice for not always giving? Lingis's careful attention to the lives of these obscure figures suggests that they did not think of any rational balance. They experience happiness in a divine way. Consider your own experiences of receiving and expending. What and why do you give? What happens when you receive?

3. Why is this reading titled "Cargo Cult"?

4. What does Lingis see in Calcutta that leaves him trembling? Do you agree with his conclusions of the meaning of this experience? Why, or why not? What might this experience tell us about the scope of justice and the nature of the good life?

Credits

Chapter One: p. 3 Robert Coles, "The Disparity Between Intellect and Character," *The Chronicle of Higher Education,* September 22, 1995. Reprinted with permission from the author. p. 16 Richard Garrett, "Dilemma's Case for Ethical Relativism," from *Dialogues Concerning the Foundations of Ethics,* Rowman & Littlefield, 1990. Used with permission from the publisher. p. 26 Reprinted by permission of the publisher from *Sociobiology* by E. O. Wilson, Cambridge, MA: Harvard University Press. Copyright © 1975 by the President and Fellows of Harvard College. p. 31 J. L. Mackie, "The Law of the Jungle: Moral Alternatives and Principles of Evolution," *Philosophy, 53,* 1978:455–464, Cambridge University Press. Reprinted with permission of the publisher. p. 40 From the *New Revised Standard Version of The Bible.* Copyright © 1989 by the Division of Christian Education of the National Council of the Churches of Christ in the USA. Used by permission. p. 48 Chuang Tzu, "Let It Be: Meditations on Tao and Freedom," from *Chuang Tzu: Basic Writings,* translated by Burton Watson, Columbia University Press, 1964. Copyright © 1964 Columbia University Press. Reprinted with the permission of the publisher. p. 55 Reprinted from *How I Found Freedom in an Unfree World* by Harry Browne, Macmillan, 1973. Copyright © 1993 Harry Browne. By permission of Collier Associates, P. O. Box 21361, West Palm Beach, FL 33416, USA. p. 60 Nel Noddings, *Women and Evil,* University of California Press, 1989. Copyright © 1989 The Regents of the University of California. Used with permission of the publisher.

Chapter Two: p. 68 Alphonso Lingis, *Abuses,* University of California Press, 1994. Copyright © 1994 The Regents of the University of California. Used with permission from the publisher. p. 73 From *What Does It All Mean?: A Very Short Introduction to Philosophy* by Thomas Nagel. Copyright © 1987 by Thomas Nagel. Used by permission of Oxford University Press, Inc. p. 84 James Rachels, "The Debate over Utilitarianism," in *The Elements of Moral Philosophy* by James Rachels, McGraw-Hill, 1986. Reprinted with permission from the publisher. p. 106 Bonnie Stelmach, "A Dialogue between Generations for the 'Soul' Purpose of Understanding Immanuel Kant's Categorical Imperative," *Cogito,* Vol. 10, July 1996, pp. 142–151. Used with permission from Carfax Publishing Limited, P. O. Box 25, Abingdon, Oxfordshire OX14 3UE, UK. p. 118 Simone De Beauvoir, "Ambiguity," from *Ethics of Ambiguity,* translated by Bernard Frechtman, Citadel Press, 1976. Copyright © 1948, 1976 by Philosophical Library. Published by arrangement with Carol Publishing Group. A Citadel Press Book. Used with permission from the publisher. p. 124 Lao Tzu, "Wisdom and Artificial Codes," from *Tao Teh King,* interpreted by Archie J. Bahm, Frederick Unger, 1958. Used with permission from Raymond Bahm and World Books.

Chapter Three: p. 135 Lore Segal, "My Grandfather's Walking Stick, or the Pink Lie," *Social Research,* Vol. 63, No. 3, Fall 1996. Reprinted with permission. p. 143 M. Hiriyanna, "Philosophy of Values," from *The Cultural Heritage of India,* 1953. Used with permission from The Ramakrishna Mission Institute of Culture, Calcutta. p. 151 Reprinted from Paul Jordan-Smith, "Seven Deadly Sins," *Parabola, The Magazine of Myth and Tradition,* Vol. X, No. 4, Winter, 1985. permission from the author. p. 169 Aristotle, "Virtue and Moral Character," from *Nicomachean Ethics,* translated by W. D. Ross, 1925, Oxford University Press. Reprinted by permission University Press. p. 179 David Carr, "The Primacy of Virtues in Ethical Theory: Part 10, Spring 1996:34–40. Used with permission from Carfax Publishing Limited, P don, Oxfordshire OX14 3UE, UK.

Chapter Four: p. 188 Wendy Doniger, "Sex, Lies, and Tall Tales," *Social Resear* Fall 1996. Reprinted with permission. p. 197 From *Lying: Moral Choice in Pu*